Advertising

Advertising

Second Edition

Kenneth E. Runyon
Northern Arizona University

Charles E. Merrill Publishing Company
A Bell & Howell Company
Columbus □ Toronto □ London □ Sydney

Published by
Charles E. Merrill Publishing Company
A Bell & Howell Company
Columbus, Ohio 43216

This book was set in Bookman.
Production Editor: Constantina Geldis
Text Designer: Cynthia Brunk
Cover Designer: Tony Faiola

The first edition of this book was published under the title *Advertising and the Practice of Marketing*.

Library of Congress Catalog Card Number: 83-61930
International Standard Book Number: 0-675-20088-1
Printed in the United States of America
1 2 3 4 5 6 7 8 9 10—88 87 86 85 84

Cover image courtesy of Amoco Chemicals Corporation

This book is dedicated to the men and women in advertising with whom I have worked and from whom I learned that advertising just doesn't happen; it is the result of systematic analysis, hard work, disciplined creativity, and dedication.

PREFACE

I am deeply indebted to the instructors and students who, having used the first edition of *Advertising,* offered suggestions for modifying the text so that it better fits their needs. Their counsel has guided the preparation of this second edition.

Because a number of users thought that the amount of material devoted to marketing duplicated content presented in introductory marketing texts, the material on this topic has been abbreviated. At the same time, material dealing directly with advertising's organizations and practices has been expanded. The net result of these changes has been to shift the focus of the text more clearly to advertising, while retaining its marketing orientation.

Several parts of the book have been rewritten to elaborate and clarify specific topics. Numerous advertisements have been added as well as a number of classic ads that demonstrate outstanding creative work. Some new examples have been inserted at the beginning of most chapters; others have been sprinkled liberally throughout the text. Statistics have been updated, and several references have been added. To keep abreast of changes in the profession, new material on motivation, the nature of advertising, verbal and nonverbal communications, and theories of advertising have also been included. In addition, there is now a chapter on industrial and international advertising.

Each chapter ends with: (a) review questions designed to serve as a study guide for chapter content; (b) discussion questions relevant to chapter material; and (c) a problem that permits students to apply, and gain experience with, key concepts covered in the chapter.

The basic content of the text is still structured around the marketing plan, the vehicle that gives direction and coherence to marketing activities and advertising campaigns. Following Part 1's introductory chapters on the marketing process, advertisers, advertising agencies, and the marketing plan itself, Part 2 examines the role of analysis and marketing research, consumer behavior, the product, brand, package, pricing, and distribution. All of these variables have an impact on advertising and the ways that it is used.

Part 3 deals with the nature of marketing communications, theories and kinds of advertising, design, layout, mechanical production, and broadcast advertising, while Part 4 addresses media and media strategy, newspapers, magazines, television, radio, and other media. Sales promotion and its relation to advertising and the marketing process are explained in Part 5. Part 6 deals with publicity, market testing, marketing research, and corporate advertising when these areas are the objects of marketing strategies. The final section turns the spotlight on industrial and multinational advertising, measuring advertising effectiveness, and the legal restrictions placed on advertising. Together with the introductory chapters, these sections provide a comprehensive picture of advertising as it is practiced in the real world of marketing.

The instructor's manual contains raw data on several product groups that students can use in developing their own marketing plans as a course project. In addition, the manual provides cost data for major media, production, and sales promotion that can be used for planning purposes.

This text is the result of twenty years of experience in a major advertising agency and fourteen years of teaching in a university setting. It brings together the pragmatic considerations of the real world of advertising and the contribution of academic disciplines.

In preparing this book, I am indebted to many people, particularly four former presidents of the Gardner Advertising Company with whom I worked over twenty years: Elmer Marshutz, who brought a sense of humanity and compassion to the practice of advertising; Charlie Claggett, whose tolerance of my idiosyncrasies taught me the importance of patience and forbearance; Champ Humphrey, who helped me understand the meaning of personal integrity; and Warren Kratky, from whom I learned the value of analysis and systematic thinking.

There are others from Gardner who made significant contributions to my education: Bea Adams, a great copywriter; Rudy Czufin, executive art director; John Davidson and Earl Hotze, account supervisors; Bill Spencer, executive director of the creative department; and many others. On the client side, I am indebted to Bob Piggott, director of advertising for Pet, Inc., who helped me understand that good clients are a necessary ingredient for great advertising.

I am particularly grateful to Glenn Tinterra, executive vice-president of the St. Louis office of D'Arcy-MacManus & Masius, Inc., who was instrumental in developing the sketches of the daily activities of the advertising people that appear in this edition, and for providing insights into recent developments in advertising agencies.

I would also like to thank the following reviewers for providing beneficial comments and suggestions: Sharon Brock, The Ohio State University; Joyce L. Grahn, University of Wisconsin-Eau Claire; Thomas W. Leigh, Pennsylvania State University; Peter Lynagh, University of Baltimore; Charles H. Patti, University of Denver; and Nancy Stephens, Arizona State University.

These debts can only be acknowledged; they can never be repaid.

Kenneth E. Runyon

CONTENTS

ix

CONTENTS

CONTENTS

Advertising

I

The Setting

Advertising is a fundamental part of the marketing process; but it is only a part. In order to understand advertising's role and importance, one must understand its organizational setting and place in the marketing plans of products.

Chapter 1 examines advertising as a part of the marketing mix; it provides a formal definition and examines advertising's essential nature. Key marketing terms, the role of marketing communications, and participants in the advertising industry are described.

Chapter 2 deals with the advertiser, or client—the segment of the marketing industry that uses advertising to sell its products and services. A discussion of the client organization, relationship between the client and its advertising agency or agencies, and role of the client advertising department is included, as well as methods for determining an advertising budget and its allocation.

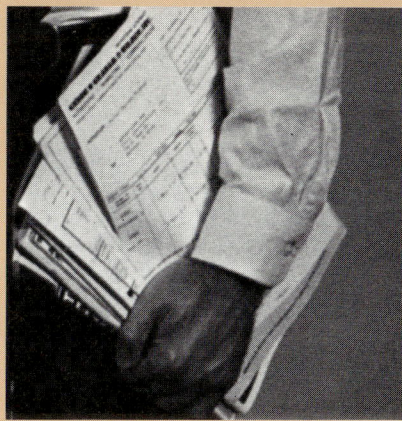

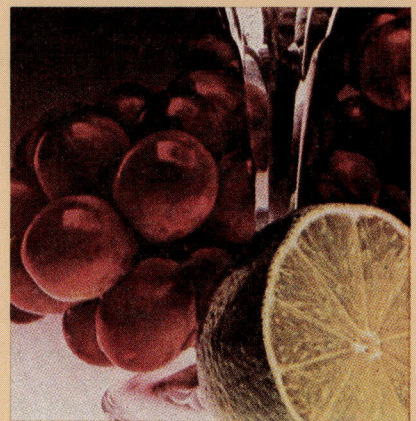

The inner workings of an advertising agency are explained in Chapter 3. Focus is placed on the types of advertising agencies, their organizational structure, methods of compensation, conflicts that exist both within the agency and between agencies and their clients, and changes that are taking place in advertising agencies.

Finally, Chapter 4 is concerned with the marketing plan, the control document that gives coherence to the marketing and advertising effort. This chapter not only describes the functions and content of the marketing plan, it also provides a practical guide on how to write one. The sections are

outlined, content explained, and examples of typical statements given.

Read this chapter for understanding.

Keep it as a reference.

Use it as a guide in writing your own marketing plans.

1

The Marketing Process

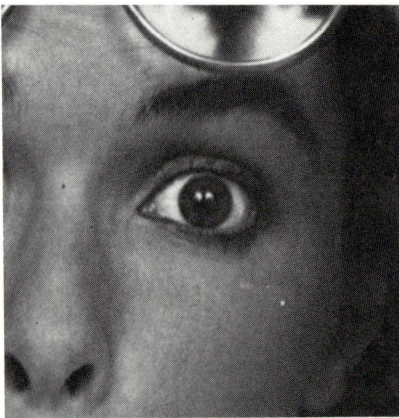

VOLKSWAGEN

Or the Magic Transformation of the Beetle: in which a Jewish Advertising Agency turns a Nazi automobile into the Sixth-Largest-Selling Car in the United States, as William Bernbach, Helmut Krone, and Julian Koenig take a Small, Cheap, Ugly, Slow, Imported German Car, and without laying Hand to Fender change it into a Popular, Desirable, Lovable, Attractive Staple of American Life; Or, THANK GOD FOR THE SECOND WORLD WAR: IT BROUGHT US ALL CLOSER TOGETHER.[1]

Thus, Robert Glatzer begins the story of Volkswagen, a marketing phenomenon of the 1960s. All of us have our favorite Volkswagen headlines: "Lemon," "Think small," "How does the man who drives the snow plow get to work?" or, the commercial storyboard shown in Figure 1–1: "Got a lot to carry? Get a box."

When we think of Volkswagen's success, we think of advertising. But, that's not where it started. Volkswagen had sold tens of thousands of automobiles in the United States before its national advertising began. It was a marketing success *before* it started advertising. Advertising only helped it to become a greater success. There is often a tendency to overemphasize the role of advertising in the success or failure of a product or service and to assume that increased sales are the inevitable result of sound advertising and faltering sales the dependable consequence of weak advertising. We sometimes forget that other factors in the marketing mix can sabotage an outstanding advertising campaign or camouflage the shortcomings of a weak one.

Rosser Reeves, an outstanding advertising practitioner, speaks to this point with the following observations:

---

[1]Robert Glatzer, *The New Advertising* (New York: The Citadel Press, 1970), 19. Copyright © 1970 by Robert Glatzer. Published by Citadel Press, a division of Lyle Stuart, Inc.

A famous razor-blade manufacturer had been running a brilliant campaign. Sales had been forging ahead. Then, by accident, millions of blades with defective steel were let loose on the market. Sales shot down, and the brand was almost crippled, but—the decline was not the fault of advertising.

A great laxative had been running a strong campaign. For years it had produced a steady increase in sales. Then, an accident of chemistry made thousands of bottles highly toxic. The brand almost disappeared from the market, but again—the decline was not the fault of advertising.

A food product, on the other hand, had been running a very poor campaign. Competitors were moving steadily ahead. Then, a change in product made the brand almost a household sensation, and sales shot up—with no change in advertising.

One of America's richest companies decided to enter the dentifrice field. Within a period of three years this company introduced not one, but two major brands—spending over $50,000,000 in powerful advertising, sampling, and promotion. The share of market of many of the older brands, naturally, dipped down. It would be folly, however, to equate this decline with their advertising campaigns. . . .

Recently a group of marketing men, almost idly, at a luncheon table, listed thirty-seven different factors, any or all of which could cause the total sales of a brand to move up or down.

Advertising was only one of these.

The product may be wrong. Price may be at fault. Distribution may be poor. The sales force may not be adequate. Budgets may be too low. A better product may be sweeping the market. A competitor may be outwitting you with strong deals. There are many variables.

And when a wheel has many spokes, who can say which spoke is supporting the wheel?[2]

A great advertising program does not stand alone. It is firmly rooted in sound marketing strategies and coordinated with other marketing activities. Volkswagen is a case in point. The indomitable

---

[2]From *Reality in Advertising* by Rosser Reeves, pp. 3–5. Copyright © 1960, 1961 by Rosser Reeves. Reprinted by permission of Alfred A. Knopf, Inc.

1. ANNCR: Suppose you had a lot to carry.

2. You get a box.

3. And suppose you wanted to carry lots of people too.

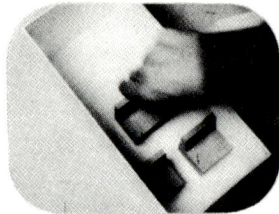

4. You need seats.

5. And maybe you'd work it so you can walk to the back . . .

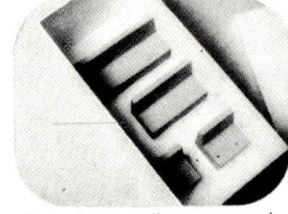

6. to change a diaper or squash a rebellion.

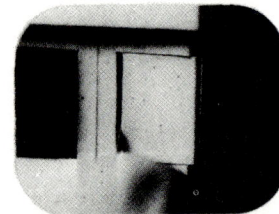

7. And windows ...

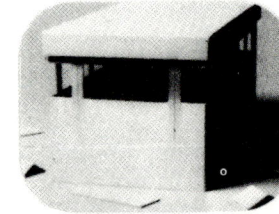

8. 23 at least.

9. And why not a hole in the roof . . .

10. to let the sun in.

11. Doors ... of course. Two in front.

12. Two big ones here ...

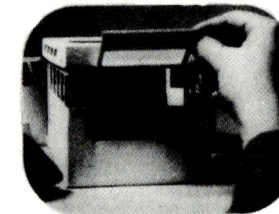

13. and one here. In the back.

14. Paint it up real pretty. Put it on wheels. (SFX)

15. And you've got the whole idea behind the Volkswagen station wagon.

FIGURE 1–1   (Courtesy Volkswagen of America, Inc.)

Beetle, or Bug, burst on the American scene at a propitious time. American cars were getting bigger, flashier, and more expensive—both to buy and operate. Planned obsolescence, a marketing strategy based on annual design changes, turned last year's dream into an antique. Americans were becoming more affluent, and a second car was becoming a psychological necessity in a society dominated by suburban living, widely dispersed shopping centers, and almost nonexistent public transportation. The American housewife was becoming a prisoner in her suburban castle. But even increased affluence was hard pressed to accommodate two or more standard sized American cars plus all of the other attractive consumer goods that were inundating the marketplace. Volkswagen was an answer to this problem. It was a small, inexpensive car that could be parked on a dime and turned on a nickel, a car designed for short trips and overcrowded parking lots—an ideal complement to the "monsters" that filled American garages.

Another time, another place, another competitive situation, another consumer psychology, and the Volkswagen advertising campaign might have been unheeded; the Bug would have been another also ran. After all, the 1930s' Baby Austin and the 1940s' Crosley were small cars that didn't really make a ripple on the marketing pond.

Nor did the Volkswagen era last forever. By the early 1970s, Volkswagen was in deep trouble. Its market was invaded by economy cars that were roomier and more attractive. As a result of this competition, the Beetle virtually disappeared from the world market. Today it is only manufactured in Brazil, Mexico, and Nigeria. In 1974 the Volkswagen company lost $313 million, and its liquid assets had dwindled to $183 million against $2.2 billion in short term debt.[3] A massive crash program to redesign and restyle the Volkswagen line was initiated and in the late 1970s the Volkswagen Rabbit enabled the company's advertising to trumpet "Volkswagen's done it—again."

ADVERTISING—THE TIP OF THE ICEBERG

In a sense, advertising is only the tip of the iceberg. True, with over $54 billion spent on advertising in 1980, it is an expensive tip. But even this number does not communicate the real dimensions of advertising. Its true magnitude is better expressed through the following excerpt from *Advertising Age*.

Every day 4.2 billion advertising messages pour forth from 1754 daily newspapers, millions of others from 8151 weeklies, and 1.4 billion more each day from 4147 magazines and periodicals. There are 3895 AM and 1136 FM radio stations broadcasting an average of 730,000 commercials a day, and 770 television stations broadcast 100,000 commercials a day. Every day millions of people are confronted with

---

[3]For a discussion of the recovery of Volkswagen, see Robert Ball, "Volkswagen Hops a Rabbit Back to Prosperity," *Fortune*, 3 August 1979, 120–28.

330,000 outdoor billboards, with 2,500,000 cards and posters in buses, subways, and commuter trains, with 51,300,000 direct mail pieces and leaflets, and with billions of display and promotion items.[4]

Advertising is the most visible portion of the entire marketing effort. Behind every radio or television commercial and every magazine or newspaper ad are thousands of hours spent in research and development, data analysis, strategic planning, plan preparation, creative conceptualization, and mechanical production, in addition to all of the clerical functions accompanying these activities. In order to understand advertising, we must understand its genesis—how it develops and the rationale behind it. First, we must define some key marketing concepts.

SOME KEY MARKETING CONCEPTS

Before we turn to the role of advertising and other forms of mass communications used to market products and services, we need to define a few marketing terms that are central to the entire process. In this section, marketing, market, marketing concept, product differentiation, market segmentation, product space, product positioning, and product concept are defined.

MARKETING

According to Peter Drucker, a leading management consultant, the only valid purpose of a business is to create a customer.

> Because its purpose is to create a customer, the business enterprise has two—and only these two—basic functions: marketing and innovation. Marketing and innovation produce results; all the rest are "costs."
>
> Marketing is the distinguishing, unique function of the business. A business is set apart from all other human organizations by the fact that it markets a product or a service. Neither church, nor army, nor school, nor state does that. Any organization that fulfills itself through marketing a product or a service is a business. Any organization in which marketing is either absent or incidental is not a business and should never be managed as if it were one.[5]

Drucker emphasizes marketing in terms of its relationship to a business or profit-making enterprise. Since the early 1970s, there has been a strong movement to extend the definition of marketing to include nonbusiness organizations, such as churches, charities, and government.[6] Supporters argue that many marketing activities can be used to bolster nonprofit organizations. They are quite right, of course. Many marketing tools—objective and systematic thinking, identification of target groups for persuasion, and paid communications (advertising)—can be applied to other areas of human activ-

---

[4]Leo Bogart, *Strategy in Advertising* (New York: Harcourt, Brace & Jovanovich, 1967), as reported in "The Ads Pour Forth," *Advertising Age*, 21 November 1973, 7.

[5]From p. 61–62 in *Management: Tasks, Responsibilities, Practices* by Peter F. Drucker. Copyright © 1973, 1974 by Peter F. Drucker. Reprinted by permission of Harper & Row Publishers Inc.

[6]Philip Kotler and Sidney J. Levy, "Broadening the Concept of Marketing," *Journal of Marketing* (January 1969): 10–15.

ity. However, advocates go beyond this point. They say, in effect, marketing involves the exchange of money for goods or services. Therefore, marketing is exchange. Furthermore, nonprofit organizations also involve exchange—a charitable contribution for a feeling of philanthropy, a vote for a political promise, church membership for personal salvation. Thus, since marketing is exchange, all exchange is marketing.

Critics of this point of view insist that saying "marketing is exchange, therefore all exchange is marketing" is like saying "a dog is an animal, therefore all animals are dogs"—an obvious fallacy. They agree that many marketing activities can be applied to nonprofit organizations and causes. However, they insist that marketing is more than a bundle of techniques; it involves a system of ethics and an economic philosophy that may not be applicable to charitable foundations, churches, politics, and similar nonprofit endeavors.

For the purposes of this text, marketing will be treated as it applies to business, always recognizing that some of the marketing tools we discuss may be useful in other situations.

In keeping with this approach, we will define **marketing** as the performance of business activities that directs the flow of goods and services from producer to consumer or user.[7] This definition may be referred to as *micromarketing* since it deals with the activities of individual firms. By contrast, the term *macromarketing* is used to refer to the aggregate activity of business, or the total economic activities of a society. Although our focus throughout this book will be on micromarketing, we must recognize that micromarketing is carried out within the philosophy and constraints of the macroeconomic system.

MARKETS

The term **market** is a somewhat ambiguous concept. Generically, the market is a group of people with purchasing power who are willing to spend money to satisfy their needs. Three aspects of this definition should be noted: people, purchasing power, and willingness to spend.

People.   All products and services are acquired by people, and these people are the object of all marketing activity. This is true whether we are speaking of a pet owner buying food for the family pet, an industrial buyer making a purchase for a company, a housewife buying for other members of her family, or an individual making a personal purchase.

Purchasing power.   Without purchasing power, there is no market in the business sense. Most people, for example, are not a part of the Rolls-Royce market simply because they do not have the $100,000 that is required to buy the economy model.

Willingness to spend.   People must be willing to spend their purchasing power before they can be considered a part of a product's

---

[7]R. I. Alexander and the Committee on Definitions of the American Marketing Association, *Marketing Definitions* (Chicago: American Marketing Association, 1960), 15.

market. People spend their money in satisfaction of their needs. As Peter Drucker has pointed out: "It is the customer alone whose willingness to pay for a good or for a service converts resources into wealth."[8]

These three elements—people, purchasing power, and willingness to spend—constitute our basic definition of a market. *Market* may be used in other ways also; we may speak of a city as a market, or we may speak of the automobile market (meaning all people who want and are able to purchase an automobile). In all cases, however, the use will imply or assume these three elements.

MARKETING CONCEPT

The **marketing concept** is the central theory in marketing. It has emerged over time as the response of business to changes in the economic environment. During its history as a nation, the United States has grown from an undeveloped economy to a highly developed one, from an agricultural society with few manufacturing facilities to an industrial society that produces an almost infinite variety of manufactured goods in a constant stream. The growth of its manufacturing capabilities, along with the development of an extensive system of distribution, became so great that consumers began demanding choice in the things they purchased. They were no longer willing to buy what business wanted to produce. It was no longer sufficient to produce a product, distribute it, and high-pressure consumers into buying it. Consumers became particular. They demanded products that were tailored to their specific needs.

Instead of manufacturing a product and then trying to sell it, a business enterprise operating under the marketing concept first finds out what the consumer wants and then produces that product. The approach sounds simple, but it is often difficult to implement. The sellers' preoccupation with what the consumer wants is referred to as **consumer orientation.**

Consumer orientation alone is not enough to operate a successful business. It is possible to give consumers what they want and still fail to make a profit. We would all be delighted to buy a new Volkswagen Rabbit for $1,200, but Volkswagen could not afford to charge this price and avoid bankruptcy. Therefore, the second element of the marketing concept is **profit.** Business must please the consumer, but it must also make a profit.

A business is a complex organization, and communication and coordination within the enterprise are difficult to bring about. Decisions at one level or in one division of a business operation may be cancelled out, unconsciously or intentionally, by the activities at another level or in another sector. The product designed with the consumer in mind may be sabotaged by a cost-conscious production department. The effort of a salesperson to build warm customer relations may be erased by the thoughtless decision of a credit manager. To avoid such errors, consumer orientation must permeate the

---

[8]Drucker, *Management: Tasks, Responsibilities, Practices,* 61.

entire enterprise, and the company must possess adequate **internal organization** for the service of the consumer. Lack of such coordination may lead to the situation depicted in the cartoon in Figure 1–2.

The marketing concept has certain clear implications for the manufacturer who adopts it as a business philosophy. First, a basic understanding of consumer needs and the psychological and social factors that influence consumer behavior must exist. Second, the manufacturer must keep in constant touch with consumers through marketing research so that the product will continue to reflect those attributes that are important to consumers.

PRODUCT DIFFERENTIATION AND MARKET SEGMENTATION

Product differentiation and market segmentation are the two basic strategies that a seller may use in approaching a given market. In **product differentiation,** the marketer goes after the whole market, but attempts to distinguish the company's brand from its competitors through the use of unique product features or advertising claims alone. In **market segmentation,** often referred to as *target marketing,* the marketer isolates a segment of the market and directs the marketing effort toward this segment alone.[9]

Product differentiation. In many markets, a number of similar products compete for consumer sales. For all practical purposes, the products are identical in function and may be used interchangeably.

FIGURE 1–2 Internal communication

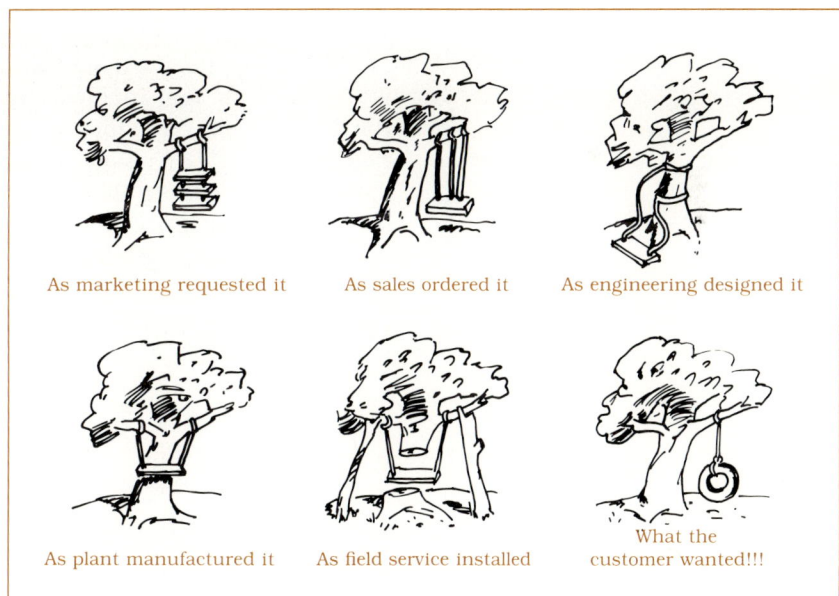

As marketing requested it   As sales ordered it   As engineering designed it

As plant manufactured it   As field service installed   What the customer wanted!!!

---

[9]W. R. Smith, "Product Differentiation and Market Segmentation as Alternative Marketing Strategies," *Journal of Marketing* (July 1956): 3–8.

A firm faced with this kind of competitive situation may attempt to create consumer preference by using unique advertising techniques or modifying the product so that it *appears* different and can be distinguished from competitive brands. Styling differences in the automotive industry are an example of product differentiation. Pall Mall's gold package is an attempt to impute quality and differentiate the brand from other cigarettes. In an effort to achieve the same end, one lawn and garden fertilizer reinforces its "green power" advertising claim by placing green crystals in the product. The headline "Helps build strong bodies 12 ways" is Wonder Bread's method of setting itself apart from the competition. Thus, applied effectively, product differentiation can be successful in creating sales and increasing market share. This is particularly true when the differentiated claim makes sense to consumers and is consistent with what they believe to be important in terms of product performance.

The Sunbeam electric blanket advertisement (Figure 1–3) is an excellent example of product differentiation; it addresses the entire market, but features product advantages that set Sunbeam apart from competitive products.

Market segmentation.   Few markets are entirely homogeneous. The market for a particular product type is often composed of several consumer submarkets, each with somewhat different product expectations and needs. Market segmentation is the development of a different marketing approach for each identifiable market sector. Philip Kotler has defined market segmentation in the following way:

> Market segmentation . . . is breaking the total market into logical market segments (also called submarkets) that differ in their requirements, buying habits, or other critical characteristics.[10]

Markets may be segmented in terms of demographic characteristics such as age, income, sex, occupation, and family size, or on the basis of psychological factors, sociological dimensions, quantities purchased, or usage patterns. A classic example of market segmentation is the strategy of economic segmentation recommended by a policy committee of General Motors in the early 1920s. This committee recommended that General Motors market six different automobiles, each one falling into one of the following price ranges:[11]

1   $ 450–$600
2   $ 600–$900
3   $ 900–$1,200
4   $1,200–$1,700
5   $1,700–$2,500
6   $2,500–$3,500

[10]Philip Kotler, *Marketing Management*, 4th ed., (Englewood Cliffs, New Jersey: Prentice-Hall, Inc., 1980), 82.
[11]Alfred P. Sloan, *My Years with General Motors* (New York: McFadden Books, 1965), 67.

The automobile industry has changed in the past sixty years. All prices have increased; in some cases, price distinctions have become blurred. Nonetheless, the segmentation strategy behind this initial pricing recommendation can be seen in the comparative price ranges of the Cadillac, Oldsmobile, and Chevrolet.

The cigarette market is segmented in terms of filter and nonfilter cigarettes—the presumed difference in consumers being their concern for a mild taste or fear of lung cancer or respiratory ailments. Within the filter market, cigarettes are segmented even further. Some cigarettes, such as Bensen & Hedges' Multi-Filter, are designed for the "sophisticated" individual; others, such as Marlboro, are for the "down to earth." Some advertisements emphasize fun; others emphasize independence, femininity, masculinity, or sex. An outstanding example of segmentation is represented by Virginia Slims and Eve. Both are directed at the women's segment of the cigarette market; but within this segment, they are clearly directed toward different kinds of women. The Virginia Slims package is almost masculine in its simplicity, enhanced only by the product name and edged on one side by a series of straight lines. The advertising is impudent and self-assertive. The model wears masculine clothes, exudes confidence, and is attractively audacious. The copy and illustration compare the traditional role of women with today's liberated woman and sum up the comparison with the slogan "You've come a long way, baby."

Then there is Eve—pretty Eve. The package is delicate and feminine, covered with frills and interwoven vines and leaves. The advertising carries out the feminine theme, characterizing femininity as soft, desirable, dependent, and unique. The choice is clear. Virginia Slims is for the liberated woman; Eve is for the woman who likes things the way they were. Virginia Slims and Eve represent two different kinds of women, dramatically different in personality.

Not all products can be segmented in the same way. The particular form of segmentation depends upon the needs and interests of the consumer groups involved. Furthermore, successful segmentation generally requires a market that is measurable, sizable, and reachable.

Measurable. A market segment should be subject to definition and measurement. If it cannot be defined, it cannot be measured; if it cannot be measured, its potential for sales cannot be estimated. Segmentation based on psychological or behavioral characteristics is more difficult to measure than segmentation made along standard demographic or geographic dimensions.

Sizable. The market segment must be large enough to support an independent marketing effort. Many market segments are too small either to justify the cost of developing a product or to produce sufficient revenue to permit the product to be advertised or promoted. The marketing system does not guarantee that all consumer needs will be served; it only serves those needs that can be served at a profit.

Reachable. A market segment also must be reachable with advertising and promotion. Often, special media exist, making it possible to reach particular markets. The baby market, a segment of the family market, may be accessible through magazines and gift packs distributed in the maternity wards of hospitals. Sports car buffs, a segment of the automotive market, may be reached through magazines edited with their specialized interests in mind. In some instances, a market segment may be large enough to justify the use of general media. The market for blond hair rinses, a segment of the cosmetic market, is an example.

Although market segmentation is a widely used marketing strategy, it is often difficult to identify viable market segments.

Thus, a survey of marketing executives found that "recognizing, defining, understanding, and segmenting markets" is one of their most worrisome problems.[12]

Every product type also has a variety of dimensions, or attributes, that make it distinguishable to consumers. Some attributes are characteristic of the physical product itself—for example, size, texture, taste, style, durability, and convenience or economy of use. Any of these characteristics may be used as a basis for market segmentation.

Other attributes are imputed or psychological. For example, status, masculinity, femininity, adventuresomeness, or any number of psychological consumer distinctions may not be based on actual physical differences in the product. Instead, these factors are often determined by what is said about the product and the symbols surrounding it. These imputed attributes can also be used in segmenting markets.

Consider the advertisements in Figures 1–4 and 1–5. The Dr Pepper advertisement is directed to that segment of the soft-drink market that is weight conscious. The basis for the market segmentation is inherent in the physical product itself; it has fewer calories. On the other hand, the Marlboro Lights advertisement is directed toward that segment of the cigarette market for which masculinity is important. Nothing in the physical makeup of this cigarette is more, or less, masculine than dozens of other brands. The masculinity of Marlboro Lights is imputed by its advertising and packaging—the words, colors, and symbols encompassing the brand. In fact, the advertiser has been so successful in imputing masculinity that the entire Marlboro advertising campaign has been referred to as the "campaign of the century."

One way to understand how product attributes can be used in segmenting markets is to think in terms of product space, position, and concept.

PRODUCT SPACE, PRODUCT POSITION, AND PRODUCT CONCEPT

Product space is an abstract space bounded by relevant product attributes. Relevant attributes may be inherent in the physical product, or they may be imputed. Thus, we can construct a product space on the basis of these real or imputed attributes. Figure 1–6 shows two examples of a linear product space based on a single attribute. The product space for automobiles is based on price—an attribute inherent in the cost of cars; the product space for cigarettes is based on a masculine versus feminine concept—an imputed product attribute.

Different automobile brands may be positioned on this line in terms of their price, such as the Chevette at one end and the Rolls-Royce at the other. Additional brands may be positioned in their appropriate places between these two extremes. A Dodge 400 costing $8,000 represents a possible **product position** on the price dimension, as does a $20,000 Cadillac. The position of a product in this

---

[12]C. N. Waldo, "What's Bothering Marketing Chiefs Most? Segmenting," *Advertising Age* (June 1973): 77.

FIGURE 1–4 (Courtesy Dr Pepper Company)

FIGURE 1–4 (Courtesy Dr Pepper Company)

product space governs the market segment in terms of product development, advertising, and promotion.

In the case of cigarettes, Virginia Slims is positioned at the feminine end of the product space, whereas Marlboro Lights is positioned at the masculine end.

Figure 1–7 shows a two-dimensional product space for a candy product whose product attributes are intensity of chocolate flavor and sweetness. Position A represents a product that has a slightly sweet and weak chocolate taste; B is slightly sweet with a strong chocolate flavor; C is very sweet with a weak chocolate flavor; and D is very sweet with a strong chocolate flavor. Other positions may be located at various intermediate points in the product space. Since consumers have different taste preferences for intensity of flavor and degree of sweetness, no one position in the product space equally satisfies all consumers.

FIGURE 1–5 (Courtesy Philip
Morris U.S.A.)

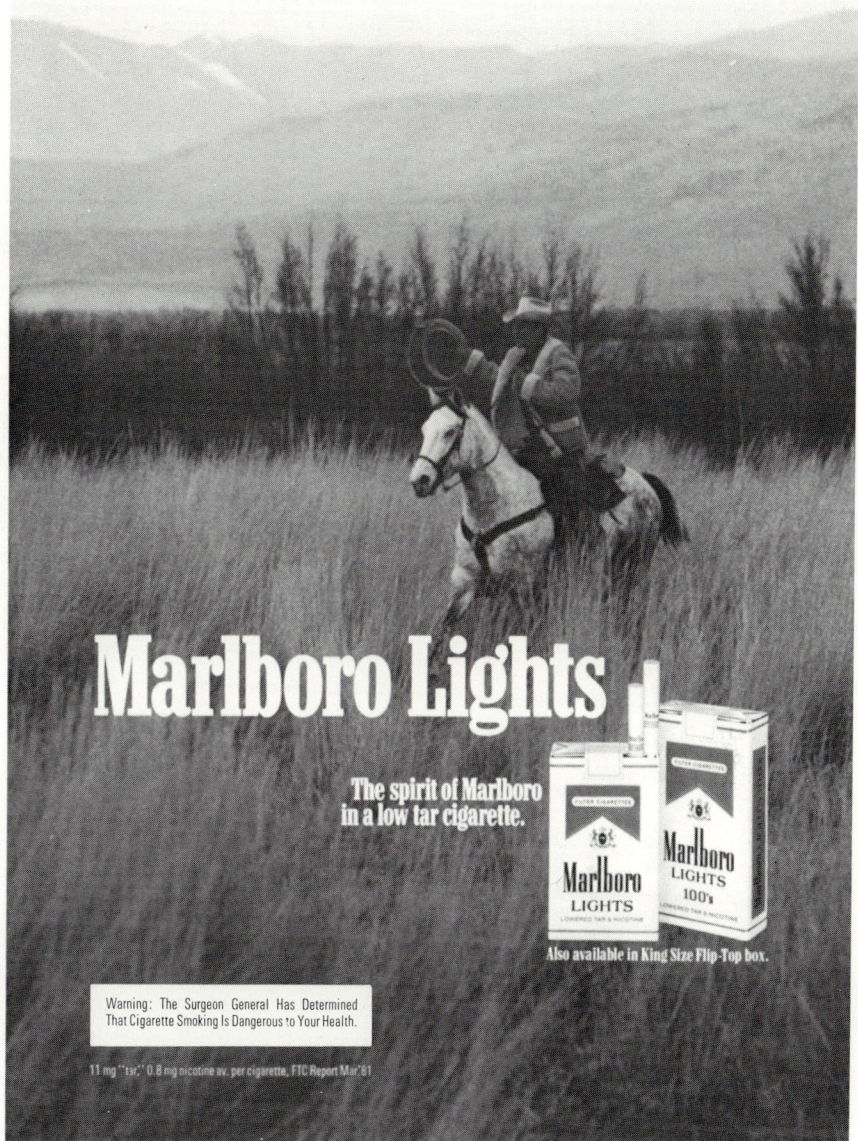

FIGURE 1–6 Examples of linear
product spaces

(a) Automobiles

Chevette	Rolls-Royce
$6,000	$100,000 +

(b) Cigarettes

Virginia Slims	Marlboro
Feminine	Masculine

CHAPTER 1 | THE MARKETING PROCESS

FIGURE 1–7 **FIGURE 1–7** Two-dimensional product space based on sweetness and flavor

Figure 1–8 shows a three-dimensional product space for a paper towel product based on three attributes: softness, absorbency, and general utility. Many positions can be located in this product space. Thus, the consumer market for paper towels can be segmented in a variety of ways, some viable as commercial enterprises and others not.

Depending upon the number of product attributes used in their construction, product spaces may be linear, two-dimensional, three-dimensional, or multidimensional. Not all product attributes are equally important to consumers; nor do all product positions appeal to enough consumers to justify an independent marketing effort. As a consequence, marketing research and imagination should be used to identify relevant product attributes and to measure the relative attractiveness of different positions in the product space. The goal of the marketer is to locate a position in the product space that appeals to a large number of consumers and is relatively free from competition.

The analysis of existing and potential product positions in a relevant product space enables the marketer to determine how the company's product should be positioned. The marketer then develops a **product** or **brand concept,** which defines the brand's characteristics according to the attributes of the selected product position. This, of course, requires a thorough knowledge of the product category and competition as well as an understanding of consumer needs. Assuming that an adequate product concept has been devel-

FIGURE 1–8 Three-dimensional product space based on softness, absorbency, and general utility

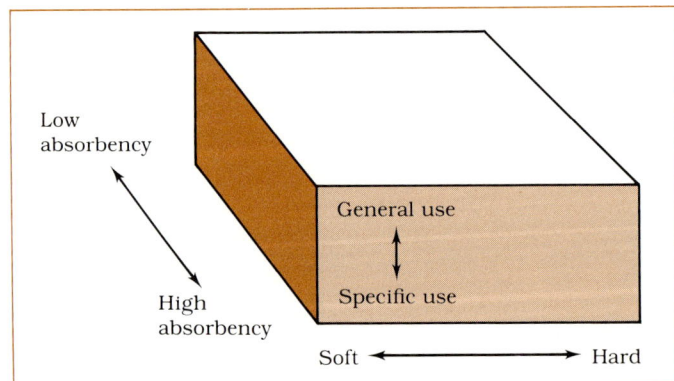

oped, the task of the marketer then becomes one of clearly communicating this concept to consumers.

MARKETING COMMUNICATIONS

Marketing communications is the process used to present the product concept to consumers. However, communications is more than the words we say and the symbols we use in an advertisement. Marketing communications encompasses *all* of the marketer's activities that are visible to the consumer.

Traditionally, the term **promotion** has been used to refer to the marketing communications process; **advertising, sales promotion, personal selling,** and **publicity** have been considered the tools of promotion. A thesis of this book proposes that the traditional view of promotion is inadequate and represents a *restricted* view of marketing communications. A more realistic approach takes an *extended* view of promotion, encompassing all of the activities undertaken by the marketer that are visible to consumers and may have an effect on their buying behavior. This point of view not only accepts the traditional promotional activities as a part of marketing communications, but also includes the product itself, the brand name, packaging, pricing, and the distribution method as communication variables. Surely, these activities are also important avenues for communicating with consumers.

BRAND IMAGE

The purpose of marketing communications is to translate the product concept into an appealing **brand image.** It is a fundamental marketing principle that consumers make their purchasing decisions on the basis of the images they form of the different brands offered to them on retail shelves.[13] Thus, brand image—the picture or likeness of the brand that exists in the consumer's mind—is the major motivating factor in determining brand preference. It is as real as any other psychological phenomenon. Created in response to certain stimuli to which the consumer is exposed, brand image constitutes the sum of the consumer's reactions to the brand.

The stimuli which give rise to the brand image are partly physical and partly psychological. They include purely physical stimuli (the product's physical nature) and purely psychological stimuli (the brand name). Between the two extremes, these stimuli embrace others (such as the product package) which are both physical and psychological in nature. Combined, the stimuli provoke in the consumer rational and emotional responses. The rational responses typically are judgments concerning the actual performance of the brand in relation to its price. The emotional responses also tend to be judgmental and related to product performance, but they are shaped primarily by the psychological overtones which have become attached to the brand in the consumer's mind. These two responses, rational and emotional, blend together in the consumer's mind to form an image of the brand. The brand is known and identified by

---

[13]Kenneth E. Runyon, "A Touch of Magic," in *New Directions in Marketing*, F. E. Webster, Jr., ed., (Chicago: American Marketing Association, 1965), 773–79.

this image. The degree to which the brand is accepted or rejected is governed by the strength and nature of the brand image.

Of course, the manufacturer can shape and manipulate the brand image by virtue of control over all major physical stimuli and most psychological stimuli that determine the product's ultimate image. Although the image itself exists in the consumer's mind, it is shaped by what the manufacturer does or fails to do. Properly shaped, image is an important marketing tool to create widespread consumer acceptance of a brand.

BUILDING THE BRAND IMAGE

Generally, there are six ways a manufacturer can shape the brand image that exists in the consumer's mind.

1   The *product* itself and the specific physical and performance characteristics it possesses.
2   The product *package*, which combines both physical attributes (size, shape, and convenience) and psychological overtones (conveyed primarily by label design and colors).
3   The brand *name* with its psychological significance.
4   The brand *price*, which also has psychological implications.
5   The *method of distribution*, since product outlets often carry connotations of quality, dependability, and value.
6   *Advertising and sales promotion*, which carry the burden of disseminating news of the brand and its features, as well as surrounding the brand with the psychological overtones and symbols that give its image consumer appeal.

By each of these means, a manufacturer can implement and reinforce the product's brand image. With careful and coordinated use of all six, the manufacturer will succeed in implanting the desired brand image in the consumer's mind.

However, if the manufacturer neglects to make use of these six means, or if the means are not carefully coordinated so they can reinforce one another, the opportunity to shape an appealing brand image will be lost. In this event, achievement of a strong, clear, and appealing image will be largely determined by chance. Prudent marketers do not rely on chance to insure their position in the marketplace.

THE VALUE OF THE BRAND IMAGE

The role of the brand image in marketing products is well recognized among marketing professionals. In the brewing industry, for example, consumers do not drink beer; they drink their *image* of a beer. This observation is supported by beer consumers' strong brand preferences, despite evidence from repeated tests that most beer drinkers cannot distinguish one beer from another on the basis of taste. W. A. Evans, lecturer in marketing at the Cranfield School of Management in England, has observed: "It is a product's . . . image which differentiates it from competing products in the market place, and once an image has been strongly established it is difficult, if not impossible, to change."[14] Irving White, in commenting on the brand image as a source of meaning, says

> The image of the brand appears to be a relatively stable organization of percepts about a product. Once established, a brand image lends the consistency and predictability in the consumer's relationship with the product which allow him to select and experience those aspects of the product he values. Schweppes quinine water must indeed be a different experience to those who have responded to its image than is that of several brands. The senses have become attuned differently, and the social value in the product-consumer interaction is different from brand to brand.[15]

Although repositioning a brand and changing its image is difficult, it can be done, particularly if the brand is poorly known among consumers. Sometimes the repositioning of a brand can have a dramatic effect on its sales. Take the case of Perrier.

Perrier, a naturally carbonated mineral water imported from France, was a minor specialty product sold through exclusive restaurants and specialty shops. Perrier's distribution was limited, its market select, and price high. In 1976 Perrier's sales volume in the United States was only 3.5 million bottles.

Bruce Nevin, president of Great Waters of France (the U.S. subsidiary of the Perrier Group), put two pieces of marketing information together and struck a bonanza. First, the U.S. market for mineral water was relatively small, whereas its market for soft drinks was over $6 billion. Second, in Europe the situation was reversed; mineral water outsold the leading cola drink by two to one. According to Nevin, "research showed the product itself had potential if only the company could improve its distribution system and lower the price. . . ."[16]

This potential was realized through two strategies: (a) The product was repositioned as a refreshing, healthful soft drink and promoted heavily to consumers, distributors, and retailers. (b) Distribution was switched from selected local outlets to centrally located soft drink bottlers and beer wholesalers. The distribution change, made in mid-1977, opened a mass market and reduced the retail price of a 23-ounce bottle from more than one dollar to about sixty-nine cents. By the end of 1978, Perrier's sales volume exceeded 90 million bottles, and a new mass market was born.[17]

The point to remember is that Perrier became a success story only after its new product position (or product concept) was communicated to consumers in the form of an appealing brand image.

MASS COMMUNICATIONS AND THE BRAND IMAGE

Not all marketing communications are mass communications. The activities of the sales force, essential ingredients in marketing suc-

[14]W. A. Evans, *Advertising Today and Tomorrow* (London: George Allen & Unwin Ltd., 1974), 47.

[15]I. S. White, "The Functions of Advertising in Our Culture," *Journal of Marketing* (July 1959): 12.

[16]*Sales and Marketing Management* (January 1979): 16–17.

[17]Ibid., 16–17.

cess, are personal communications. This is true whether we are talking about the contact of a salesperson with a chain store or an industrial buyer, a retail sales clerk in a department store, or the in-home calls of a Tupperware, Avon, or Fuller Brush representative.

This book is primarily concerned with mass communications—the nonpersonal communications of advertising, the package, brand name, price, and other mass communications variables. In a mass consumption society, these variables are crucial in the formation of the brand image and its success. Warren Kratky, former president of the Gardner Advertising Company, has observed:

> Modern marketing has become *primarily a matter of mass communications.*
>
> Once marketing was primarily a matter of mass production. Later it was primarily a matter of mass distribution. Then primarily a matter of mass selling. Now I maintain, marketing has become primarily a matter of mass communications.
>
> Today in most major businesses, it is mass communications that exert the major, decisive influence upon *how* the business is viewed by its customers.[18]

Further, the marketing plan is primarily a mass communications document. In most companies, the sales plan is separate from the marketing plan and is devised to detail the personal contact activities of the sales force. To do justice to the work of the company sales force would require a book in itself. As a consequence, while the importance of the sales force in marketing success is explicitly recognized, these activities will not be dealt with in this text.

THE ROLE OF ADVERTISING

Advertising is a major form of mass communications. Yet, even at the work-a-day level of marketing, advertising professionals cannot agree what advertising is or how it works. Hardheaded, cost-conscious business executives, who wouldn't approve a $10,000 expenditure for a new piece of equipment without a complete study of its proposed value, cost, and documented performance, will blithely approve $20 million for an advertising campaign based on a slick presentation and confidence in the presenter. Rosser Reeves quotes a company president as saying

> Advertising, to me, is really one of the mysteries of American business. I can inventory my stock. I can calculate the cost of my factories. I can figure my taxes, estimate my depreciation, determine my sales cost, derive my earnings per share. Yet, there are times when I spend as much as $18 million a year on advertising—and have no idea of what I am really getting for my money.[19]

Advertising has been defined by the American Marketing Association's Committee on Definitions as any paid form of nonpersonal presentation and promotion of ideas, goods, or services by an iden-

---

[18]Warren J. Kratky, remarks before a marketing conference in St. Louis, April, 1967.

[19]Rosser Reeves, *Reality in Advertising*, p. 1. Copyright © 1960, 1961 by Rosser Reeves. Reprinted by permission of Alfred A. Knopf, Inc.

tified sponsor.[20] The International Chamber of Commerce provides a similar definition in its *Dictionary of Marketing Terms.*

Although these definitions are useful in helping us distinguish what is and what is not advertising, they fail to capture its spirit. Four attempts at defining this spirit are examined briefly in the following material.

ADVERTISING AS INFORMATION

Advertising as information is a point of view widely held by economists and by critics of advertising. According to this definition, advertising's only purpose is to provide consumers with information that will reduce the time they spend searching for commercial products and enable them to make more intelligent buying decisions. Information is generally limited to objective data—product performance, price, and product quality. Persuasion is undesirable because it tends to obfuscate consumers' judgments, causing them to make non-objective decisions.

Generally, this is the perception of advertising held by the staff of the Federal Trade Commission (FTC). The FTC files suits against advertising that goes beyond this basic concept of "objective information."

The value of this point of view is its emphasis on truth in advertising, a proposition subscribed to by most advertisers who seek a long-term relationship with customers. This concept is limited, however, by its narrow definition of what constitutes information and the restrictions it imposes on the use of persuasion.

For most consumers, information is more than objective data on price, performance, and quality; it involves such product dimensions as style, prestige, and status. For most producers, effective advertising involves persuasion, or showing the product in its most favorable light. Since persuasion is an acceptable practice in most areas of human endeavor, it is probable that the objective information definition of advertising is unduly restrictive.

ADVERTISING AS A SUBSTITUTE FOR PERSONAL SELLING

In a conversation with Alfred Lasker in 1905, John E. Kennedy proposed a definition of advertising. A portion of the conversation is recorded below.

> So Kennedy said to me, "Do you know what advertising is?" I said, "I think I do," and I told him a story, just as I told it to you. I said, "It is news." I said I thought that I knew what advertising was—news—just exactly as the old sailors and astronomers thought the world was flat, and thinking the world was flat, they had worked up a system whereby they had quite a world. But Columbus came along and showed them the world was round. And that is what Kennedy showed me.
> He said, "No, news is a technique of presentation, but advertising is a very simple thing. I can give it to you in three words."
> "Well," I said, "I am hungry. What are those three words?"

---

[20]Alexander, *Marketing Definitions*, 9.

He said, "Salesmanship in print."

It had never before been defined in any dictionary or anything else, "salesmanship in print!" It was that in 1905 when Kennedy told it; it was that before anyone had ever told me, and it will always be that, and nothing else.[21]

Times have changed since 1905. Radio and television have appeared as alternative channels of communications, but the essential definition proposed by John E. Kennedy still prevails. In 1980 Sidney R. Bernstein, former editor and publisher of *Advertising Age*, wrote:

> . . . in essence, advertising is a substitute for the human salesman talking personally to an individual prospect or customer across a store counter or a desk or an open door. And as a substitute for the human salesman, advertising has pretty much the same functions, abilities, and attributes as the human salesman.
>
> It is less effective than personal selling, however, principally because it must be designed to appeal to a mass audience, in contrast with the personal salesman's ability to tailor his sales message to each individual prospect, and because, again, unlike the personal salesman, it has no opportunity to "talk back," explain or refute objections.
>
> This is advertising, no more and no less—a mechanical substitute for the personal salesman.[22]

This point of view makes a clear distinction between advertising and the techniques of advertising. This is an important distinction because copywriters and art directors often become so enamored by a particular technique that they lose sight of an advertisement's basic purpose.

This definition's weakness is precisely the one Sidney Bernstein identified—advertising, unlike the personal salesperson, has no opportunity to explain or refute objections. Advertising must present its message more clearly, succinctly, and tightly structured than that of a sales pitch.

ADVERTISING AS VALUE ADDED

Value-added theory, proposed by Martin Mayer in *Madison Avenue, U.S.A.*, is based on the proposition that advertising's suggestion power creates a value not inherent in the product itself. In short, advertising adds a new value to the one that exists. According to Mayer, this added value is relatively slight because advertising is highly effective in times of economic affluence, but relatively ineffective during a recession. Thus, when money is plentiful, a slightly more attractive product may seem worth the cost, but

---

[21]Albert Davis Lasker, *The Lasker Story: As He Told It* (Chicago, Illinois: Advertising Publications, Inc., 1963), 21.

[22]Sidney R. Bernstein, "What Is Advertising?" Reprinted with permission from the April 30, 1980 issue of *Advertising Age*. Copyright © 1980 by Crain Communications, Inc.

. . . when money is precious for the security that it alone can offer, the incremental value of advertising will seem slight indeed if a similar, less advertised or even unadvertised product can be bought for less . . . .

As a matter of strict logic, advertising *must* somehow change the product to which it is applied. In recent years, some advertising research psychologists have gingerly approached this question via Burleigh Gardner's concept of the "brand image." But the psychologist's habits of work lead him to assume that the image is something present in the consumer's mind, rather than something pervasive in the product itself. It is remarkable how many people who readily see that a new package or a new brand name will change a product fail to see that advertising inevitably has a very similar effect.[23]

Advertising does not change the product, as Mayer suggests. However, it may change the perception of the product and, thereby, add value to it.

The contribution of value-added theory is the recognition that advertising, in addition to providing information about a product, transforms a product into something more appealing to consumers than the physical object produced in the factory. However, one weakness of this theory is its inability to explain *how* this transformation takes place.

ADVERTISING AS A TRANSLATION OF PRODUCT CONCEPT INTO CONSUMER BENEFIT

A final definition of advertising suggests it is a form of communication that changes the consumer's perception of a product by endowing a benefit that relates to consumer needs. Thus, the basic task is to translate the product concept into a consumer benefit. The basic assumption is that consumers do not buy products; they buy satisfactions or benefits. Products become desirable to consumers only when they are perceived in terms of the benefits they provide.

Regarding product advertising in this manner has three values: (a) It shifts the attention of advertising from the product to the product benefit—a shift wholly compatible with the marketing concept. (b) It is consistent with the other definitions of product advertising that have been reviewed, recognizing the importance of relevant consumer information and the concept of advertising as a substitute for the personal salesperson. (c) It is an extension of value-added theory because it identifies the nature of the value that is added.

In the foregoing discussion, we have referred to *product* advertising. However, in a marketing sense, the concept of a product includes services as well as physical objects. Life insurance and the services of a mechanic, dentist, or lawyer are products insofar as marketing is concerned. Therefore, in this case, advertising must translate the concept of the service into a consumer benefit.

---

[23]Martin Mayer, *Madison Avenue, U.S.A.* (New York: Harper Brothers, Publishers, 1958), 308–15. Reprinted by permission of Curtis Brown, Ltd. Copyright © 1958 by Martin Praeger Mayer. Also see Vincent Norris, "Advertising and Value Added," in *The Role of Advertising*, C. H. Sandage and Vernon Fryburger, eds. (Homewood, Illinois: Richard D. Irwin, 1960), 145–56.

PARTICIPANTS IN THE ADVERTISING INDUSTRY

No discussion of the setting in which advertising is created would be complete without a brief mention of the industry's structure. The advertising industry is composed of four groups of participants: **advertisers** (often referred to as **clients**), **advertising agencies, media organizations,** and **collateral services.** In various combinations, these participants carry out the numerous tasks involved in marketing and advertising—identifying potential customers, developing products to meet customers' needs, pricing, promotion, physical distribution, and personal selling.

The advertiser is intimately involved in all of these activities. The agency, to a greater or lesser extent, is involved in the first four. Chapters 2 and 3 will deal specifically with the advertiser and the advertising agency.

Media organizations supply television, radio, newspapers, magazines, outdoor posters, and other specialized media. As a consequence, their participation is primarily concerned with advertising.

Collateral services include a wide range of specialized and limited functions used by advertisers, advertising agencies, and media. These organizations include package design houses, sales promotion firms, premium shops, media buying services, research organizations, printing companies, production studios, program producers, consulting firms, free-lance artists and copywriters, photographers, recording studios, mailing list houses, coupon redemption centers, and dozens of others. As the need for a particular service arises, companies emerge to meet the need. As needs are eclipsed, so are the companies that provide them.

THE TASKS OF ADVERTISING

Earlier, it was pointed out that advertising is the tip of the iceberg. Behind the commercial that is broadcast and the advertisement that appears in print media are thousands of hours of work requiring analytical skill, business judgment, organizational talent, executional ability, and creative inspiration. Markets must be analyzed, product concepts defined, products developed, packages designed, brand names selected, copy written, illustrations conceived and rendered, material produced, sales forecast, budgets set, media selected, and the entire program executed.

Throughout, innovation and creativity are essential to the marketing process and marketing communications. Not only is the idea behind the communication essential, but the form of expression is often critical. The right idea and the right words or symbols are the essence of creative expression. However, the creativity required by marketing communications is not the creativity of the artist or poet. "Art for the sake of art" is not the theme of marketing. Marketing creativity has a problem-solving character; it is a controlled creativity designed to persuade and convince. Charlie Brower, an outstanding advertising practitioner of recent years, has written:

> Creativity is the ability to have worthwhile ideas. Ideas alone are a dime a dozen. But the ability to have selling ideas within the restrictions of the market—and good selling ideas at that—is not

easy. Writing is not enough. Art is not enough. Production is not enough. The ideas are the thing, and the people who have them seem to be more scarce every year.[24]

The history of marketing is the history of ideas. "The Kodak Camera. You push the button, we do the rest" is a selling idea that first appeared in 1890 as the headline in an advertisement and helped Eastman Kodak to become a $6 billion company. "Always a bridesmaid but never a bride" is a marketing classic that introduced Listerine and launched a multimillion dollar product field. AT&T's "Let your fingers do the walking through the yellow pages"; Clairol's "Does she . . . or doesn't she"; Alka-Seltzer's "I can't believe I ate the whole thing"; Avis's "We're number two, so we try harder"; Purina Dog Chow's "So complete all you add is love"; Crest's "Look Mom! No cavities"; Virginia Slims' "You've come a long way, baby" are all expressions of selling ideas that have lifted products from obscurity to success. To produce and present these ideas to the public requires an enormous amount of planning and coordination.

COORDINATION

Truly complex tasks can only be accomplished by breaking them into their component parts and working on each part separately. This is the key to mass production and the success of the modern business organization. When the parts are reassembled, however, they will not fit together properly unless they have been constructed according to a single, overall design. In the manufacture of a physical object, such as an automobile, engineering plans specify how each component is to be constructed and the magnitude of allowable tolerances.

Marketing is a complex task. The instrument that provides the unity of design for the marketing effort is the marketing plan. The marketing plan will be discussed in detail in Chapter 4, and the rest of the book will be organized around the component parts of the marketing plan.

CONFLICTS

In a process as complex as that of marketing, interpersonal conflicts and disagreements inevitably arise. Some take place because participants differ about how a product should be positioned, a package designed, or a particular product or service advertised. These conflicts are desirable and necessary because they stimulate thinking, spark new ideas, and encourage creativity. The person who is uncomfortable in the face of conflict, and unable to deal with it, will probably not be happy in the marketing profession.

A less desirable conflict, however, arises from a lack of appreciation and understanding on the part of some participants for the problems and contributions of others. For example, the marketing analyst and planner, who is often business trained and profit ori-

---

[24]Charlie Brower, *Me and Other Advertising Geniuses* (Garden City, New York: Doubleday & Co., 1974), 196.

ented, may neither appreciate nor sympathize with the problems faced by the creative people who write advertisements, design packages, and produce commercials. The analyst and planner may see them as undisciplined, irresponsible, and unconcerned about the business requirements of the enterprise.

Creative people, on the other hand, often exhibit a similar disregard for the contributions of the business-oriented analyst and planner. To them, such people often appear unimaginative, unreasonable, unduly restrictive, unappreciative, and unconcerned about the marketing segment that is truly important—the advertising.

Such conflicts are unfortunate because these two groups of people need each other. Neither can devise an effective marketing program alone. Yet, their differences are often difficult to resolve because they appear to be rooted in different temperaments, value structures, and ways of thinking or approaching problems. They represent, in short, two different ways of looking at the world. These two world views have been characterized in a variety of ways: Dionysian versus Apollinian; cosmic versus rational; or intuitive versus logical. Manifestations of these two ways of thinking have been reflected in literature (Pirsig's *Zen and the Art of Motorcycle Maintenance* is one of the more recent examples),[25] in marketing (a series of articles by Jack Trout and Al Ries appeared in *Advertising Age*),[26] and in psychological literature (which suggests that these differences in thinking are rooted in neural physiology, and related to dominance by the left versus the right cerebral hemisphere).

Regardless of the cause, lack of understanding and failure to appreciate the point of view of co-workers is the result. One purpose of this book is to relate the planning and creative portions of marketing in such a way that their interdependence will become apparent.

SUMMARY

To succeed, great advertising must rely on sound marketing strategies. Therefore, in order to aid one's understanding of advertising, a number of basic marketing terms are defined in this chapter.

Briefly, marketing is the performance of business activities that direct the flow of goods and services from producers to consumers. Markets are groups of people who are willing to spend their purchasing power in the service of their needs. In order to pass goods and services to the consumer in the most effective manner, a marketing concept develops. This theory is based on consumer orientation, profit, and coordination of the internal organization in the service of consumers. Product differentiation and market segmentation are two basic marketing strategies. Under product differentiation, marketers direct their activities toward an entire market, distin-

[25]Robert M. Pirsig, *Zen and the Art of Motorcycle Maintenance* (West Caldwell, New Jersey: Morrow, William & Co., Inc., 1972).

[26]Jack Trout and Al Ries, "The Positioning Era Cometh," *Advertising Age*, 24 April 1972, 35–38; "Positioning Cuts Through Chaos in Marketplace," *Advertising Age*, 1 May 1972, 51–54; "How to Position Your Product," *Advertising Age*, 8 May 1972, 114–16.

guishing their products from competitors by minor product features and advertising claims. Under market segmentation, marketers isolate one or more segments of a total market and direct their activities toward these segments. A useful device for segmenting markets is the concept of product space, an abstract space bounded by relevant product attributes. Attributes used in constructing a product space may be tangible aspects of the product or imputed psychological characteristics.

Marketing communications is a process used to present a product position within a product space (referred to as a product concept) to consumers. It encompasses all marketing activities visible to consumers and its purpose is to translate a product concept into an appealing brand image in the minds of consumers.

Advertising is a major form of mass communications. Technically, advertising is defined as any paid form of nonpersonal presentation and promotion of ideas, goods, or services by an identified sponsor. Because this definition fails to capture the spirit of advertising, others examined are: (a) advertising as information; (b) advertising as a substitute for personal selling; (c) advertising as value added; and (d) advertising as a translation of product concept into consumer benefit.

Marketing is a complex activity that requires the participation of many organizations. The industry is composed of four groups—advertisers, advertising agencies, media organizations, and collateral services—whose activities are outlined in a marketing plan. Due to the diverse temperaments and responsibilities of the individuals involved, conflicts often arise which require skillful handling by management personnel.

REVIEW QUESTIONS

1 Explain the statement "Advertising is the tip of the iceberg." What does this have to do with the effectiveness of advertising?
2 Identify the three components of the generic definition of a market.
3 Explain the marketing concept. What are the implications for a business that adopts it?
4 Distinguish between product differentiation and market segmentation.
5 Identify and explain the necessary conditions for successful market segmentation.
6 Distinguish between tangible and imputed product attributes. Give examples.
7 Define product space, product position, product concept, and brand image.
8 Identify ways a marketer can shape the brand image.
9 Using the definition of advertising as "a translation of the product concept into a consumer benefit," explain why it is compatible with the other definitions of advertising given in this chapter.
10 Identify the major participants in the advertising industry and the extent of their responsibilities in terms of identifying potential customers, developing products to meet customer needs, pricing, promotion, physical distribution, and personal selling.

DISCUSSION QUESTIONS

1 In the text, marketing is treated as a business activity. Since the early 1970s, there has been a movement to expand the term "marketing" so that it applies to nonprofit organizations such as charities, churches, and government. How does this affect the marketing concept?

2 Select a product of your choice. Construct a product space and identify a product position for a new brand. What advertising appeals might be used to translate this product concept into a brand image?

3 Select an advertisement for a brand that uses imputed product attributes to appeal to consumers. Do you believe this appeal is effective? Why or why not?

PROBLEM

Frank Breckett, a product manager for a major consumer goods company, has been given the assignment of defining a product position for a new brand of toothpaste. An analysis of five leading brands (A, B, C, D, and E), rated on a scale of 1 to 10 (10 being high and 1 being low), indicated the following characteristics and results.

Attribute	A	B	C	D	E
Prevents cavities	10	9	7	7	8
Freshens breath	3	10	5	8	9
Whitens teeth	4	3	9	10	3
Pleasant flavor	6	5	8	6	10

The company's research and development department has reported that it can develop any combination of these characteristics. Consumer research has developed the following information on the toothpaste market.

Brands	Share of Market	Share of Advertising
A	30%	32%
B	10%	12%
C	8%	10%
D	12%	6%
E	18%	19%
All other brands	22%	21%
Total	100%	100%

Percent of user groups who believe all brands are equally effective in preventing cavities (1980 versus 1983):

User Groups	1980	1983
Parents with children under 12	40%	45%
Married, no children	52%	58%
Young singles (18–25)	68%	88%
Teenagers (12–17)	63%	85%
Children (under 12)	64%	81%

Attributes sought in toothpaste by user groups (10 = high; 1 = low):

User Groups	Prevents Cavities	Freshens Breath	Whitens Teeth	Pleasant Flavor
Parents with children under 12	10	4	5	8
Married, no children	7	8	9	5
Young singles (18–25)	7	10	9	5
Teenagers (12–17)	6	10	10	7
Children (under 12)	8	6	5	10

Research has also revealed that, in 80 percent of the families with children under 12, the female head of the household bought the toothpaste.

ASSIGNMENT

1 Define the position the product should hold in order to have the greatest chance of success.
2 Identify the target market(s).
3 Suggest a product name.
4 Should any other research be done?

2

The Advertiser and the Marketing Budget

TRUTH AND FICTION HAVE A LOT IN COMMON

Robert Glatzer, in his book *The New Advertising,* tells the following fictional story to emphasize the tenuous relationships that exist between advertisers and their advertising agencies.

Once upon a time, in the bad old days, the president of Procter & Gamble came to New York from his headquarters in Cincinnati to pay a visit to his advertising agencies. He stopped first at 347 Madison Avenue, headquarters of Dancer-Fitzgerald-Sample, where he indirectly controlled the careers of 112 people working to promote Oxydol, Dreft and Thrill detergents—all Procter & Gamble products. He told them he was not very satisfied with their work.

Then he walked down the street to 285 Madison Avenue to visit Young & Rubicam, where he met sixty-three people devoting their lives to advertising Cheer—another Procter & Gamble detergent. He told them he was not very satisfied with *their* work either.

That afternoon, he stopped in at Grey Advertising, over on Third Avenue, where he listened to reports on Top Job, Joy and Duz—all of them P&G detergents. Joy was outselling Thrill, but Dreft was beating Duz. He said he was pleased with Joy, but unhappy about the others.

Back on Madison Avenue, he visited Compton Advertising, where 217 people worked on P&G's Dash, Tide and Ivory Liquid detergents. He learned that Tide was beating Oxydol, but that Cheer was outselling Dash, Tide and Ivory Liquid. He told Compton that he might have to take the account away and give it to Young & Rubicam.

Early the next morning, he caught the company jet to Chicago, where he dropped in on Tatham-Laird & Kudner, to check up on Bold and Mr. Clean. He was told that Mr. Clean was holding his own, but that Bold was losing out to Dash, though still ahead of Cheer, Tide, Oxydol, Joy and Duz. He told them to dig in and get creative, or else.

The next day he went home to Cincinnati, gave the Thrill account to Compton, the Tide account to Grey, the Top Job and Bold accounts to Young & Rubicam, and the Dreft account to Tatham-Laird. Then he rested from his labors.

Ninety-four people were fired as the result of his trip, not counting media buyers and secretaries, and sixty-one were hired from other agencies to bring new "creative" blood to the accounts. Most of the ninety-four found jobs sooner or later at other agencies, but a few gave up entirely, retiring as "failures" from the business.[1]

If this is fiction, the truth is not much different. Nine of the top twelve United States airline companies changed advertising agencies in the two year period from January 1980 to January 1982.[2] Every issue of *Advertising Age* reports a number of account changes. Each year, usually in March, this publication devotes an issue to advertising agencies, giving brief profiles that include the clients each has gained and lost. These profiles read like a game of musical chairs, and the reasons behind many of the agency switches are arbitrary, political, and capricious. Consider the following examples:[3]

Benton & Bowles
Accounts gained: Blistex, Emory Worldwide, First Bank, Jos. Garneau Co. (Ambassadore Scotch, Cella Wines, and Martell Cognac), Magic Pan Restaurants, Pinkerton Tobacco, RCA Music Service, Richardson-Vicks (Syntex), Showtime, and Texas Commerce Bancshares.
Accounts lost: AMF-Leisure Products, Continental Airlines, Fiat, Holland America, Jacobson, and Kitchens of Sara Lee.
Campbell-Mithun Inc.
Accounts gained: Fred S. James Co., Mass Feeding Corp., Melville Corp., Woolbridge Footwear, Kellwood Co., Ashley's Outlet Stores, McGraw-Edison Company Lighting Products Division, Kohler, Republic Airlines, 3M Co. (corporate), Galleria Retailers Assn., North Dakota Tourism, Personnel Publishing, Tombstone Pizza,

[1]Robert Glatzer, *The New Advertising* (New York: The Citadel Press, 1970), 9. Copyright © 1970 by Robert Glatzer. Published by Citadel Press, a division of Lyle Stuart, Inc.

[2]Robert Raissman, "WRG Flies the Way Pan Am Wants to Fly," *Advertising Age,* 18 January 1982, 3ff.

[3]*Advertising Age* (March 24, 1982); examples taken from alphabetical listing of agency profiles.

Golden Skillet, Air Chicago, Dow Chemical (Peladow), Quaker's Food Service, General Mills (Nature Valley Light & Crunchy)
Accounts lost: Coca-Cola Foods, IDS, Munsingwear, Toro Co., Ada Temporary Service, Blue Cross/Blue Shield of Illinois, The Management Group, and Air Chicago.

J. Walter Thompson
Accounts gained: Genesco, Hewlett-Packard Co., Home Federal Savings & Loan, Lowes, Inc. (Kitty Litter), Munsingwear, Inc., The Nestle Co., Inc., Northern Telecom, OTC Net, Inc., 6 Flaggs over Georgia, Southern Pacific Communications, Teison Co. (Snack Candies), Castle & Cooke Foods, Sears, Roebuck and Co. (L.A. & the Southwest Group), N.Y. City Opera, Christian Dior, Duro-Test Corp., Knomark (TY-D-Bol), Bendex Corp., Harris Group, Penn Central Corp., and Southern National Resources.
Accounts lost: Southland Co. (7-11 stores), Bausch & Lomb, Blue Cross of Southern California, California Milk Advisory Board, Mentholatum Co., Salida Foods, Teledyne Inc. (Water Pik).

Similar patterns exist for other agencies listed in this issue of *Advertising Age.* All are top notch agencies, quite capable of providing good advertising and marketing services for the clients they lost as well as the ones they gained. So, you see, truth and fiction have a lot in common; but the truth hurts more.

100 LEADING NATIONAL ADVERTISERS

In 1981 the 100 leading advertisers spent an estimated $13 billion, 39 percent of all national advertising and almost 22 percent of total estimated advertising expenditures in the United States. Among the biggest spenders were:

1	Procter & Gamble Co.	$659,600,000
2	Sears, Roebuck and Co.	$599,600,000
3	General Foods Corp.	$410,000,000
4	Philip Morris, Inc.	$364,600,000
5	R. J. Reynolds Industries, Inc.	$298,500,000

Of particular interest is that Hershey Foods, which first began advertising in 1970, ranked 93 in the 100 leaders list with an expenditure of $41.3 million.[4]

BRAND MANAGERS— GOOD OR BAD?

Ever since its popular acceptance as a form of advertising organization, the brand manager system has been a topic of dissension. Although it is well established in many companies, critics are still vocal. In the 1960s, an account supervisor from Leo Burnett, Incorporated, a major Chicago-based advertising agency, gave a talk titled "It's Amateur Night in the Ad Game." The advertising executive complained that the influx of business school graduates and M.B.A.s into brand management positions hurt marketing creativity. These young managers, inexperienced in advertising, biased by

---

[4]Marion Elmquist, "100 Leaders Hit $13 Billion Mark," p. 1ff. Reprinted with permission from the September 10, 1981 issue of *Advertising Age.* Copyright © 1981 by Crain Communications, Inc.

their own narrow views of the world, and insensitive to the subtleties of consumer motivation, rejected excellent advertising campaigns simply because they did not like them.

In 1981 an advertising agency president stated,

> "From my experience, the greatest obstacle to effective advertising is the product manager system used by many of our clients. Product managers very rarely have previous advertising experience . . . Their commitment to advertising is perfunctory, since this is only a stepping stone to a more prestigious (in their eyes) position. . . ."[5]

Even advocates of the brand manager system recognize that it has faults. An *Advertising Age* survey of product managers concluded that the product manager system can work if it corrects flaws such as "being sometimes too theoretical and too green in marketing's front-line trenches, occasionally pressing for short-term results at the expense of long-term growth and at times needing more creative and media advertising savvy."[6]

These arguments have been used to dramatize three aspects of the advertisers' side of the business: (a) Advertising is a volatile business in which account losses and gains are a way of life. (b) It's a big and highly concentrated business, with the 100 leading advertisers spending almost 22 percent of the total advertising dollars. (c) Internal organization often inhibits advertising creativity, thereby diminishing the very activity that contributes so much to marketing success.

In this chapter, we will look more closely at the advertiser, examining the nature of the industry, the advertiser-advertising agency relationship, advertiser organization, the advertising department, and the advertising and marketing budget.

THE ADVERTISER— AN OVERVIEW

No one is more important to the advertising industry than advertisers. They develop and produce the products that are marketed to consumers, industries, and government. They provide the funds that make advertising possible. In the final analysis, they make the decisions on what advertising will or will not be used.

Basically, advertisers are businesses.[7] *Statistical Abstracts* defines a **business firm** as a business organization under a single management which may include one or more plants or outlets. Thus, a giant retailer such as Sears, Roebuck and Company is a single business firm, as is a "mom and pop" grocery outlet. Exxon, with receipts of over $100 billion, is a single business firm, as is a small gasoline station operated by a man and his wife. Under this definition, over 14 million business firms in the United States are engaged in marketing products or services. Eighty-four percent have

---

[5]Merle Kingman, "Product Manager: Adman's Friend or Foe," *Advertising Age*, 17 August 1981, 43.

[6]Ibid., 43.

[7]Non-business organizations, such as churches, charitable organizations, public universities, and government agencies, also use advertising. However, the bulk of all advertising is done by commercial businesses; it is this segment of the advertising industry that's the primary focus of this text.

receipts of less than $100,000 and account for only seven percent of all business revenues; four percent have earnings of over $500,000 and account for almost sixty percent of all business revenues.

Therefore, while over 14 million business firms operate in the United States, they are highly concentrated in terms of size. Although any firm can benefit from a systematic approach to its marketing and advertising activities, very few of them bother. Only a minute percentage employ an advertising agency, and only a fraction of those develop a formal marketing plan. Yet, this tiny group is the dominant force in the United States economy, and it floods our national media with advertising messages.

THE ADVERTISER— ADVERTISING AGENCY RELATIONSHIP

Most major business firms in the United States use the service of an advertising agency, although some may handle their own advertising through an **in-house agency,** owned and controlled by the business firm itself. Some major firms, such as Ralston Purina and General Electric, operate in-house agencies for some of their products and employ independent advertising agencies for others.

Our primary concern is with companies that employ independent advertising agencies because this type of client-agency relationship is the most prevalent.

The extent to which an advertising agency is used depends upon the desires of the company management as well as the agency's capabilities. Many advertising agencies, particularly the larger ones, are eminently qualified to develop an entire marketing program because they employ qualified marketing planners and specialists in the fields of marketing research, pricing, distribution, packaging, sales promotion, and public relations as well as advertising. For example, when Nebraska Consolidated Mills, a regional producer of flour and other milling products, first introduced Duncan Hines mixes, its advertising agency was given the responsibility of establishing a network of food brokers to represent the company. When demand for Jack Daniel's liquor exceeded production capacity, its advertising agency was asked to recommend an equitable plan for allocation. Advertising agencies often work closely with their client organizations in defining product positions, identifying product concepts for new products, and developing sales presentations for retail and industrial accounts.

The client organizations that rely extensively upon their advertising agencies for marketing counsel do so because they respect their agencies' competencies and value the outside, independent judgment that an agency can bring to marketing decisions. Most companies badly need to become aware of another point of view. Too often they view their marketing activities from the standpoint of their internal preoccupations rather than that of the consumer.

At the same time, most agencies are eager to become involved in basic marketing decisions even though these decisions are the ultimate responsibility of the client organization. Advertising agencies are acutely aware that the success or failure of a product depends upon the entire marketing effort—not advertising alone. A faulty market forecast, weak product concept, inadequate product, ineffective packaging, poor distribution, noncompetitive consumer pricing, insufficient distributor margins, ambiguous instructions on the package, and paltry advertising and sales promotion funds can mortgage the product's future to the extent that no amount of advertising creativity can salvage the marketing program.

Yet, the client-agency relationship is a tenuous one, based on mutual respect and confidence. Unfortunately, confidence is a fragile commodity that is difficult to build and easy to destroy. Interpersonal relationships between client and agency are exceedingly important, and real or imagined slights of client personnel by agency representatives sometimes rupture the relationship. In addition, advertising agencies are not always selected for sound business or professional reasons. Friendship, rather than competence, is often the main criterion. In 1982 the advertising agency Doyle Dane Bernbach reported that it lost the $35 million Pan American World Airways account to Wells, Rich, and Greene, an equally competent agency, simply on the basis of friendship.[8] An account may also be lost because the wife of an executive in the client company is offended by a commercial or an inappropriate comment made at a cocktail party. Finally, advertising agencies sometimes become careless in their service and do not provide a particular client with the level of creativity or marketing services that it pays for and deserves. For all of these reasons, the client-agency relationship is an unstable one that produces an industry permeated by a certain aura of fear.

Not all client-agency relationships are unstable; some have endured more than 50 years. But, they are the exceptions. Advertising is a highly competitive business. Large sums of money are at stake. The field is filled with bright, ambitious people. Personal reputations are on the line, and there are no sure answers. The reasons products succeed or fail are sometimes obscure, and the role advertising plays is not always clear. Most client organizations are looking for miracles. When a miracle is not forthcoming, they sometimes seek a scapegoat. Often, that scapegoat is the advertising agency.

THE USE OF MULTIPLE ADVERTISING AGENCIES

Many large advertisers that market a number of products retain several advertising agencies, sometimes shifting products back and forth in order to get a fresh creative approach or a specialized service. For example, in 1982 Procter & Gamble (P&G) divided its $649.6 million in billing among ten agencies. Table 2–1 lists these agencies and the individual products they handle.

The use of multiple agencies, while providing diversity of counsel and flexibility for the client organization, also creates supervisory and coordination problems. Most media offer cumulative discounts on the volume and frequency of advertising insertions bought by client companies. By coordinating the media used for its different products, a major advertiser such as Procter & Gamble or General Foods can save millions of dollars in media costs.

The burden of coordinating the media selections of multiple agencies generally falls on the client company's advertising department. This is often handled by appointing specific agencies to coor-

---

[8]Raissman, "WRG Flies the Way Pan Am Wants to Fly," 3.

CHAPTER 2 | THE ADVERTISER AND THE MARKETING BUDGET

TABLE 2–1 Procter & Gamble's advertising agencies and the individual products handled by each

Advertising Agencies	Products Handled
Benton & Bowles, Inc. (New York)	Bounce, Charmin, Crest, Dawn, Ivory Snow, Pampers, Scope, Wondra, Zest, Attends, Ivory shampoo
Leo Burnett Co. (Chicago)	Cheer, Era, Camay, Lava, Lilt, Secret, Gleem, Abound
Compton Advertising, Inc. (New York)	Tide, Cascade, Crisco, Top Job, Comet, Ivory (bar and liquid), High Point, Duncan Hines (cake, brownie, and muffin mixes), Pert, Pace
Cunningham & Walsh, Inc. (New York)	Folger's, Crush, Hires, and Sun Drop
Dancer Fitzgerald Sample, Inc. (New York)	Bounty, White Cloud, Oxydol, Dreft, Luvs, and Solo
Doyle Dane Bernbach, Inc. (New York)	Coast, Gain, Puritan
Grey Advertising (New York)	Downy, Joy, Bold 3, Jif, Puffs, Duncan Hines (cookie mix)
Tatham-Laird & Kudner (Chicago)	Biz, Head & Shoulders, Mr. Clean
Wells, Rich, Greene, Inc. (New York)	Pringles, Safeguard, Sure, Prell
Young & Rubicam, Inc. (New York)	Dash, Spic & Span, Brigade

Source: *Advertising Age,* 10 September 1981, 126.

dinate media use among all of the firm's agencies for a particular media. Thus, one agency will be responsible for coordinating spot television expenditures; a second, network television expenditures; a third, coordinating magazines; a fourth, coordinating newspapers; and so on.

Although this coordination of media expenditures can lower costs, problems in developing the optimum media program for individual products can be created. For example, an advertising agency may be forced to compromise media selection for a particular product in order to maximize the media discounts that are available. How much damage, if any, is done to the advertising schedule for that product is open to question.

SELECTING ADVERTISING AGENCIES

As pointed out earlier, advertising agencies are sometimes selected for strange and wonderful reasons. One midwestern advertiser selected a New York agency because the advertising manager wanted a legitimate excuse to visit New York on a periodic basis. He liked the bright lights, nightclubs, and legitimate theater.

Many advertisers use more appropriate ways to select an advertising agency. Let us assume you are the advertising manager for a company that has a sound business reason for changing advertising agencies. Perhaps you need more experienced creative talent, specialized help in sales promotion, or a wider range of agency services or marketing counsel than your present agency can provide. In such instances, you should use the following procedures:

1   Carefully define the kinds and level of services you want from the new agency. In developing these criteria, consult other people in the company who will be working with the agency and have need of its services.

2   Notify the current advertising agency, by personal conversation and a formal letter of intent, that a change is being considered. Sometimes, client-agency problems can be resolved at this stage, and the search process can be halted. Agency changes are expensive and disruptive; therefore, they should not be made if they can be reasonably avoided.

3   At this point, you have several alternatives. You may: identify three or four agencies whose reputation and work you admire, and invite them for a preliminary meeting to discuss your needs; notify advertising trade publications such as *Advertising Age*; or, discreetly disclose your intention to one or more media representatives. The grapevine in the advertising industry is a miracle of modern communications. Regardless of how the word gets out, within twenty-four hours your intentions will be common knowledge in every advertising center in the country.

4   Screen the applicants. If your account is an important one, you will be deluged by agencies. If the account is less prominent, you will still be deluged, but by smaller agencies. Eliminate the agencies that do not meet the established criteria; tell them they have been eliminated and why.

5   Narrow the list to no more than six agencies. Check these agencies further by talking to some of their clients, examining their creative work, and interviewing their representatives.

6   Select three or four agencies to make a presentation showing how they would handle your account. Give them a specific problem to see how they would approach it. If any agencies are eliminated at this stage, notify them and explain why they have been eliminated.

7   Meet the key agency people that would be assigned to your account. Talk with them. Reach agreement on expectations and compensation.

8   Select an agency. Notify the other agencies of your selection and the reasons for it.

9   Once you have selected an agency, treat it with care. By the time you have gone through this process once, you won't want to do it again.

ADVERTISER ORGANIZATION

Advertisers may organize their marketing effort in any number of ways. The particular form of organization is dictated by the size of the company, number of products it markets, nature of the industry in which it is engaged, and marketing philosophy of its management. Responsibilities may be divided by categories, such as function, geographic area, and end user (for example, industrial products versus consumer products). A number of different organizational patterns are often employed simultaneously, with some forms superimposed over others. For example, an organization may be structured in terms of geographic divisions. Each division, however, may be organized along functional lines. General Motors is organized in terms of product divisions—Chevrolet, Pontiac, Buick, Cadillac. Each of these product divisions is organized along functional lines—accounting, manufacturing, marketing, personnel, design, and so on. The sales force, which is a part of marketing, is organized on a geographic basis.

Instead of trying to describe all of the possible organizational variations, we will focus on the advertising manager and the major ways this role is integrated into the overall marketing organization. In the following material, three forms of organization for a multiple product advertiser are described. The first is that of a company organized by function; the succeeding two represent forward steps in integrating the marketing effort and emphasizing the importance of the basic marketing function. Note that the role of the advertising manager, or director, changes in each organizational form.

ORGANIZATION BY FUNCTION

Figure 2–1 shows a simplified chart for the traditional form of **organization by function.**

Marketing activities are split along functional lines; advertising, sales promotion, and publicity activities fall within the domain of the advertising manager. The advertising manager occupies an important position, although this person is often subordinated to the sales manager insofar as many marketing decisions are concerned. The advertising manager is basically responsible for all promotional activities except sales, works closely with the company's advertising agency or agencies, and develops the company's overall promotional budget.

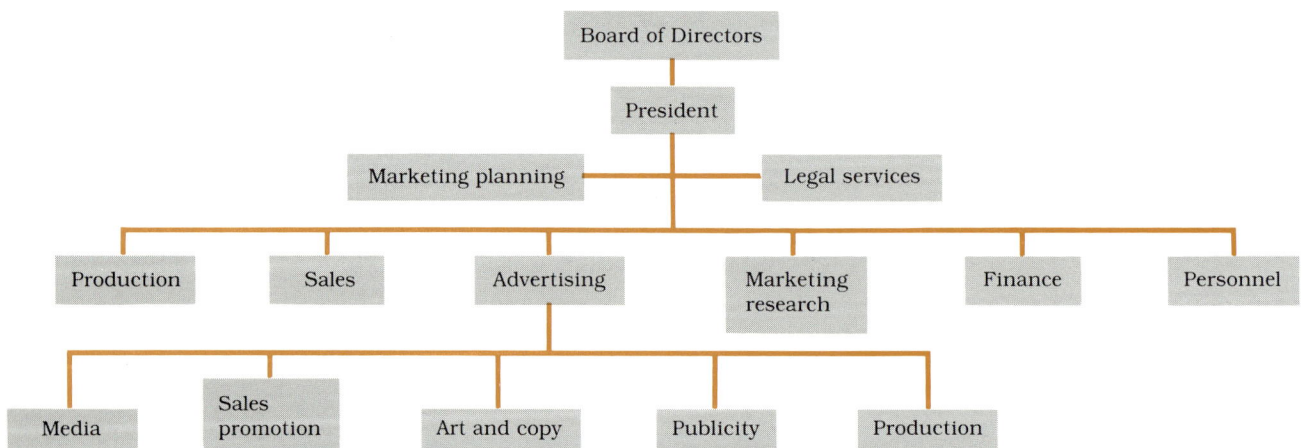

FIGURE 2–1 Advertiser organization by function

The problem with this structure is coordination and responsibility. Major marketing functions are split into different departments, and no single department is specifically responsible for the welfare of individual products. Decisions are centralized, and the entrepreneurial spirit, so essential to successful marketing, is often lost.

PRODUCT MANAGER ORGANIZATION

Figure 2–2 shows a simplified **product manager organization.** This approach is intended to accomplish three objectives: (a) coordinate marketing activities by placing them under the overall supervision of a marketing director; (b) decentralize decision making by assigning individual product managers to each product and charging them with the profit responsibility for the product; and (c) introduce entrepreneurship into the organization by letting the product managers compete for company resources.

In this form of organization, the functions formerly associated with the advertising manager are transferred to the individual product managers; product planning, insofar as it occurs, is delegated to the product management group. The advertising manager's role is decreased in importance (the primary function is in an advisory capacity), although this individual may have the authority to override product management decisions relating to creative work submitted by the company's advertising agency.

While the product manager organization accomplishes many of its objectives, it also exhibits some shortcomings. For example: (a) Product managers often lack the knowledge and experience in

FIGURE 2–2 Product manager organization

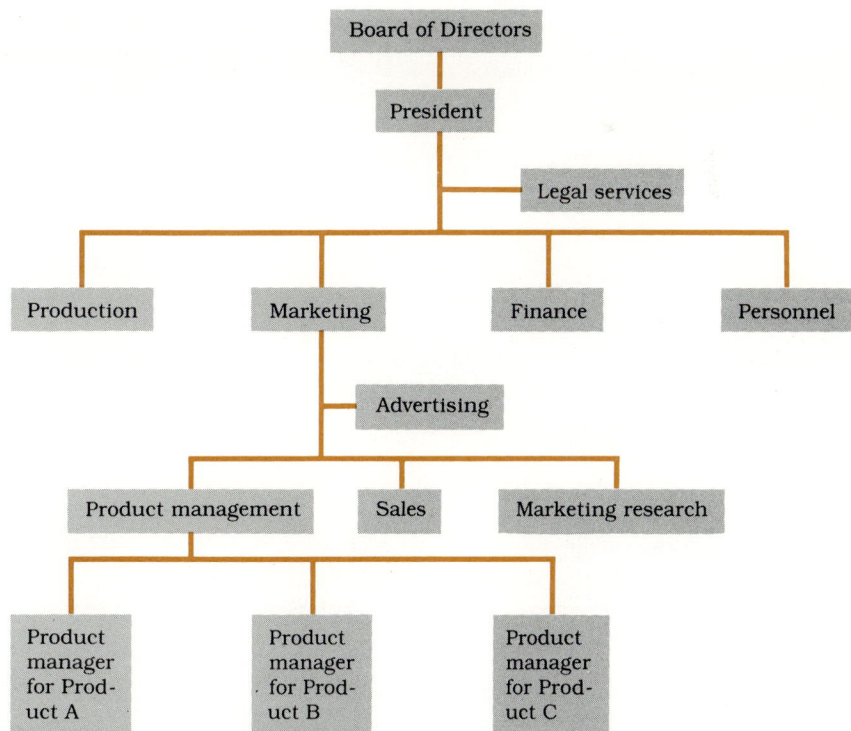

CHAPTER 2 | THE ADVERTISER AND THE MARKETING BUDGET

advertising, sales promotion, media, production, and publicity to deal with these areas effectively. (b) Short-term planning and day-to-day problems of supervising and coordinating activities on individual products often preclude long-range planning. (c) The persuasive and effective manner of individual product managers competing for company resources may lead to misallocation. Thus, a product with little long-range profit potential may receive more company resources than a product with a greater profit potential. These problems have led to the third form of organization, referred to as a coordinated product manager system.

COORDINATED PRODUCT MANAGER SYSTEM

The **coordinated product manager system** is diagrammed in Figure 2–3. Although it retains most of the features of the product manager system, it is modified in two major respects: (a) Planning is removed from the product group and installed as a staff function responsible to the marketing director. (b) The advertising manager's role has been enlarged and staff specialists installed in an advisory capacity under her direction. In addition, an agency coordination function is added to the advertising manager's responsibilities in order to obtain maximum media discounts without losing quality.

The entire thrust of the organizational progression from a functional organization to a product manager system to a coordinated product manager approach is to increase marketing effectiveness. First, individual product managers are held responsible for planning and coordinating all marketing activities for specific products. Then, staff specialists, who report to the advertising manager, counsel the product managers. At the same time, long-range planning is taken away from the product managers and established as a separate function, removed from competition with the day-to-day activities of managing existing products.

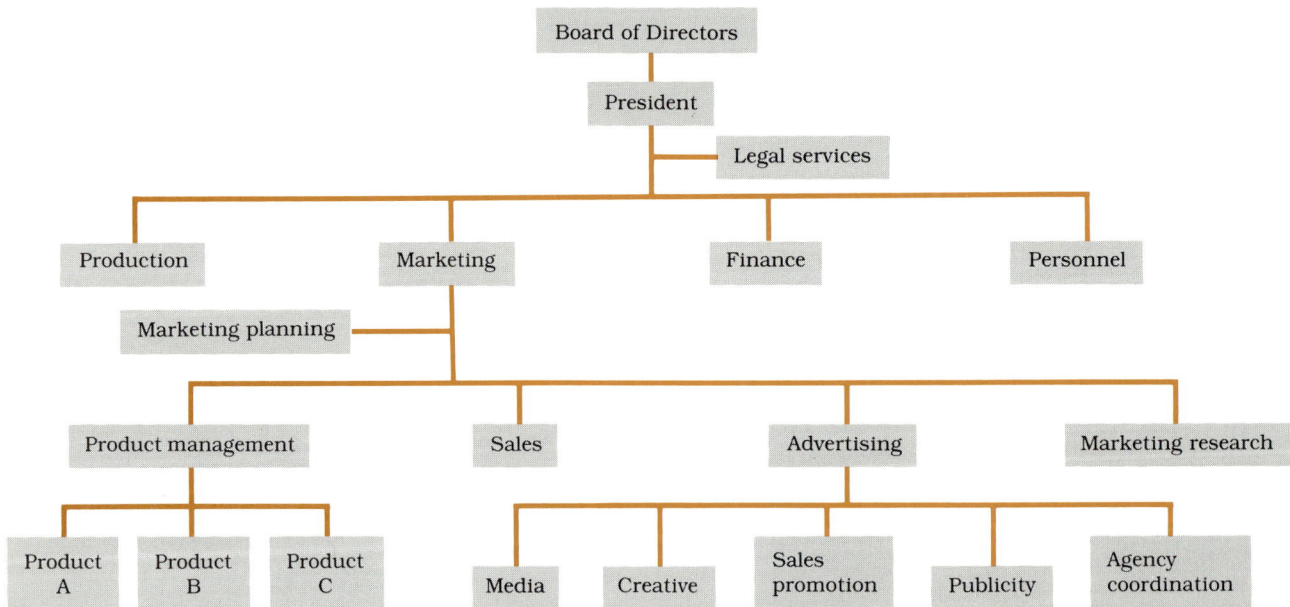

FIGURE 2–3 Coordinated product manager organization

RETAIL ADVERTISER ORGANIZATION

The foregoing discussion of advertiser organization dealt with manufacturing companies—companies that make products sold through retail stores or other outlets. Retailers also advertise, however. Most retailers' advertising is local rather than national, although retailers such as Sears, Roebuck & Company and K mart are exceptions. The organizations of these large, national retailers may be quite complex, involving advertising functions at national, regional, and local levels. At national and regional levels, such companies may use independent advertising agencies.

Large, local retailers, such as major department stores, usually have large advertising departments and seldom use agencies. One reason is the nature of the retail business and the advertising it requires. Retailers often operate on short deadlines; they don't have time to have advertising agencies prepare their daily or weekly specials or sales campaigns. A major department store also has thousands of items, supervised by a number of department heads or merchandising people. The store's advertising department must work closely with all of these people in order to coordinate their advertising activities. The nature of the retail business requires customer contact and sensitivity to consumer buying patterns. Contact is maintained through sales clerks and the daily movement of goods. It would be virtually impossible for an independent advertising agency to provide the same feedback. A second reason is the differing rate structures of advertising media. Local media generally have a national, or general, rate for national advertisers and a retail, or local, rate for retail stores. The national rates are higher and advertising agencies are compensated by commissions. Local rates are lower and not commissionable.

Small retailers have special problems. Most are not large enough to afford an advertising department. As a consequence, they must find other ways to handle their advertising problems. Many use small, local advertising agencies that specialize in small retail accounts, and compensate the agencies on a fee basis for the work done. Often, the owner or manager prepares the advertising with help from local media in writing and design. Some hire free-lance specialists on a part-time basis; others buy syndicated services that provide a general format the retailer can use to insert feature products and prices.

Because of the diversity, complexity, and specialized nature of retail advertising, the focus of this text will remain on the advertising and advertising departments of manufacturing organizations, always recognizing that many advertising principles also apply to retail stores.

THE ADVERTISING DEPARTMENT

The size and functions of a company's advertising department depend upon a variety of factors: (a) the importance of advertising in promoting the company's products (advertising plays a more important role in the marketing of consumer goods than industrial products); (b) the number of products marketed; (c) how sales promotion, trade shows, and collateral materials are used; (d) if the company develops its own advertising and sales promotional materials rather than obtaining them through advertising agencies or outside suppliers; and (e) how much cooperative advertising is used.

Some large companies, such as John Deere & Company and Ralston Purina, distribute company magazines through their dealer organizations. Those marketing technically complex products such as automobiles, farm equipment, and expensive electronics produce elaborate, four-color brochures describing their equipment's operation and maintenance. Other companies operate an in-house advertising agency. In instances such as these, advertising departments are large and employ a number of specialists in a variety of fields.

Because of diversity in size and functions, company advertising departments are organized in several ways. Perhaps the most common is organization by function. This form is widely used because it: (a) is fairly simple, straightforward, and easy to administer; (b) permits the development of trained professionals in highly specialized areas; (c) lends itself to the formation of temporary work groups (members are recruited from the functional areas) for special projects; and (d) is easy to expand or contract by adding and eliminating functions as they are required or no longer needed.

Figure 2–4 shows a basic advertising department, organized by function, for a large consumer products company and demonstrates how easily the department may be expanded horizontally and vertically as responsibilities increase and new functions are added.

THE COMMUNICATIONS BUDGET

The budgeting process begins with a forecast of sales. The sales forecast serves as the basis for planning levels of production, amounts of raw materials required, capital investments made, salary budgets, and expenditures in marketing. If the forecast is too high, unnecessary expenses will be incurred and company resources dissipated. If the forecast is too low, sales and profit opportunities will be irretrievably lost. Forecasting is not an exact science. Misjudgments are made. Even under the best of conditions, an accurate forecast is often a delicate balance of errors.

Forecasting is a top management responsibility. Although the mechanics of forecasting can be delegated to the marketing or research departments, management retains the ultimate responsibility. Therefore, the final forecast, used in planning company activities, carries the sanction of management.

DETERMINING THE COMMUNICATIONS BUDGET

The purpose of forecasting is to reach a sales projection that will enable a company to compute its income, expenses, communications budget, and profit. Two groups make up a company's marketing budget. One group consists of **fixed** and **semifixed expenses** such as salaries for personnel, office space, warehousing, depreciation, and utilities. These items are relatively stable from year to year and do not vary sharply with increases or decreases in marketing activity. A second group of items, referred to as **variable expenses,** are more discretionary in nature and are subject to special appropriations each year. These include expenditures for advertising, sales promotion, package design, and marketing research. The marketing manager has the greatest control over the second group of

(a) Basic functional organization

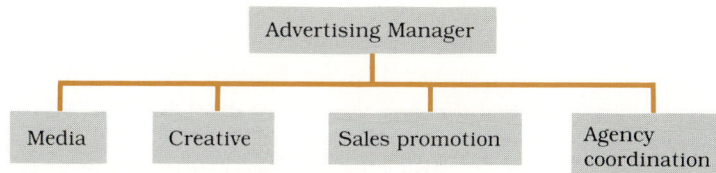

(b) Expanded department as new responsibilities and specialization are added

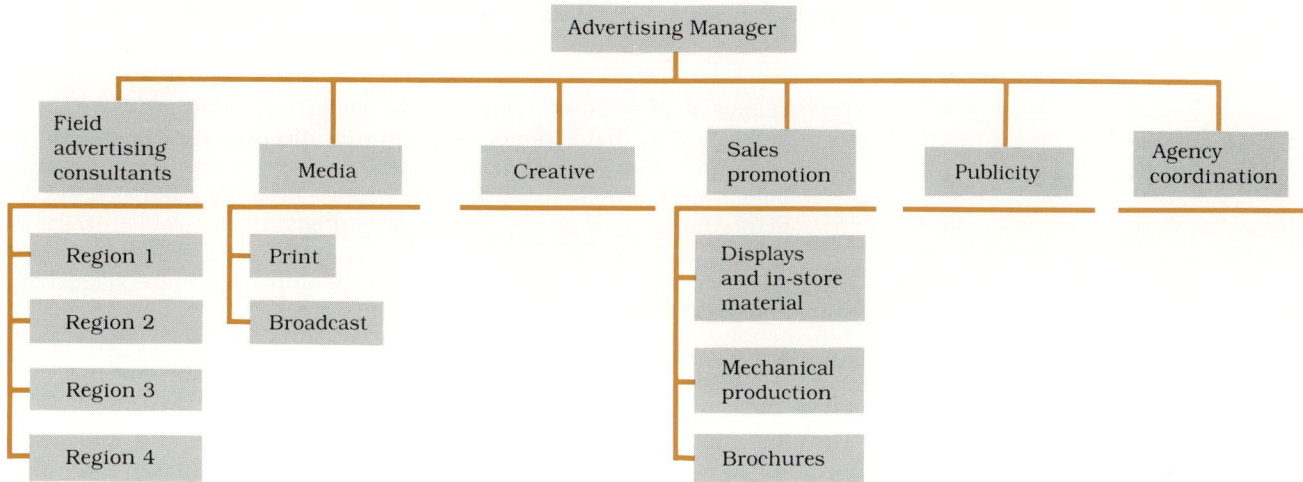

FIGURE 2—4 Two stages in the development of a company advertising department organized by function

expenses because these planned expenditures are designed to accomplish specific communication objectives.

Table 2—2 shows a simplified pro forma budget for a hypothetical company. After all expenses *except* variable marketing expenses have been subtracted from income, the $9,033,000 residual is often

TABLE 2—2 Pro forma operating budget

Sales (1000's cases)	6,230,000	
Income ($8.60 per case)	$53,578,000	
Minus: cost of goods		
(including packaging)	36,892,000	
Gross margin		$16,686,000
Expenses		
Sales expense (including sales force,		
freight, and warehousing)	3,682,500	
Administrative overhead	2,162,000	
Other fixed and semifixed expenses	1,808,500	
Total expense		7,653,000
Contribution to profit		9,033,000
Less: Marketing expense (60%)		5,419,800
Profit before taxes		$3,613,200

CHAPTER 2 | THE ADVERTISER AND THE MARKETING BUDGET

referred to as **contribution to profit.** The contribution figure is the amount of revenue the company has to promote the brand and make a profit. Obviously, the more that is spent for marketing, the less the profit will be. In this particular instance, 60 percent of the contribution has been allocated for marketing, leaving a profit before taxes of $3,613,200.

In this case, is $5,419,800 the proper amount to spend for marketing? That depends upon the nature of the market and the level of competitive activity; how much profit the company needs; the company's objectives; and the effectiveness of the company's programming and persuasiveness of its creative effort. In short, there is no easy answer. Eldridge has pointed out:

> Management is called upon to make no decisions that are more important, or that can more significantly affect the health, growth, and profitability of the business than those involving the marketing budget. In many companies whose success depends upon effective marketing programs, the cost of marketing is the largest controllable expense; in some companies the cost of marketing a product is even greater than the cost of producing it—including raw materials, labor, and packaging costs.[9]

A number of methods are used to establish the communications appropriation; some better than others, but none wholly satisfactory. However, each speaks to some aspect of the allocation process. Four such methods, along with their advantages and disadvantages, are discussed below.

THE AFFORDABLE METHOD

One of the least effective methods to determine the advertising and sales promotion budget is to spend what the company can afford. Generally, the deciding factor is the profit level required by the company. In such cases, management earmarks a given amount for profit, and any excess funds in the contribution portion of the budget may be spent for marketing communications. Joel Dean, an economist, has puckishly suggested that everything above a respectable return on capital could be spent for advertising ". . . since excess earnings have low utility to management as such, compared with the *possible* contribution of continuous advertising to the eternal life of the firm."[10] Generally, this approach is most likely to be used in companies where advertising objectives are poorly defined and serve a general public relations function, as is sometimes the case with public utilities.

The affordable method fails to take into consideration the marketing job that has to be done. Consequently, the appropriation for advertising and sales promotion may be excessive or sadly inadequate.

---

[9]Clarence E. Eldridge, *The Marketing Budget and Its Allocation in the Advertising Budget* (New York: Association of National Advertisers, Inc., 1967), 25.

[10]Joel Dean, *Managerial Economics* (Englewood Cliffs, New Jersey: Prentice-Hall, Inc., 1951), 368.

At the same time, this approach tacitly recognizes the role of budget constraints. Profit *is* a necessary function of a firm. Without an adequate profit level over the long term, businesses simply do not survive. True, the required amount of profit may vary year to year, and on some occasions, a firm may forego profit entirely because of investment requirements or marketing demands. Nonetheless, the profit requirement normally places an upper limit on the marketing appropriation.

PERCENTAGE OF SALES METHOD

Many companies prefer to set their communications budget as a percentage of sales or a fixed amount per case or unit. Automobile manufacturers typically budget a certain amount per car, and oil companies tend to set their communications budget as a fraction of a cent for each gallon of gasoline sold. Similarly, packaged goods manufacturers often appropriate a certain amount per case.

When such appropriations are based on projected or forecast sales, the approach appears to have a certain merit—the greater the forecast, the greater the expenditure. Conversely, during times of depressed forecasts, communications expenditures are cut. In addition, when by tacit agreement all factors in the industry utilize a similar percentage, advertising wars are averted and the industry incurs a certain stability.

Although many companies use this approach, it does have major limitations. First, appropriations are set by anticipated sales or availability of funds rather than marketing opportunities. Second, the percentage spent or the amount allocated per unit is often arbitrary and may bear little relationship to the amount needed to develop the total market effectively. Finally, competitive positions tend to become fixed because all competitors are using similar advertising to sales ratios, and real competition is at a minimum.

On the positive side, this approach recognizes the need for a minimum expenditure level to keep abreast of competition. As demand increases, competitive appropriations increase; the firm that fails to keep pace may anticipate a decline in share. Thus, a firm can establish a standard expenditure rate based on a percentage of sales or a fixed allocation per unit *provided* it recognizes that marketing opportunities and problems may require a deviation from this standard. One advantage of having a standard is that it enables the firm to evaluate deviations in terms of the costs involved in pursuing a particular marketing opportunity.

SHARE OF ADVERTISING METHOD

A truism in marketing states that "all other things being equal, share of market will equal share of advertising." And, while "all other things" are seldom equal, this concept serves as the basis for the share of advertising method of allocating advertising expenditures. J.O. Peckham, executive vice-president of the A.C. Nielsen Company in the mid-1960s, offered this approach, based on empirical studies in food and drug fields. Peckham observed that, over time, a relationship between share of market and share of advertising forms. If a marketer keeps his product and advertising appeals competitive with the rest of the field, the best insurance for maintaining or increasing market share is to keep share of advertising at a point somewhat ahead of share of sales. For *new* brands being introduced into the market, Peckham found that the initial rate of expenditure should be approximately double the share of sales desired. For example, assume a new brand is being marketed in a product field in which annual sales are $60 million and annual advertising expenditures are $8 million. Also assume the market share objective for the new brand is 25 percent. Then

Annual sales goal (25 percent of $60,000,000) = $15,000,000

Annual advertising allocation (50 percent of $8,000,000) = $4,000,000

The disadvantages of this approach are: (a) All other variables are seldom equal. (b) Focus on advertising to the exclusion of other marketing variables exists. (c) Profit needs are not taken into consideration.

Its advantages are that it: (a) emphasizes the need to be aware of competitive activity as one aspect of market performance; (b) deals with measurable quantities and provides a rough basis for setting the advertising appropriation; and (c) provides a rough diagnostic tool. For example, if market share consistently lags significantly behind share of advertising, some other aspect of the marketing mix (copy appeals, media selection, product, price, distribution, package, and so on) is out of kilter and should be re-examined. Or, a greater market share than advertising share may signal an opportunity to improve market position through an increase in advertising expenditures.

OBJECTIVE AND TASK METHOD

In the objective and task method, the firm establishes a sales goal, asks what tasks need to be done to achieve this goal, estimates the cost of each task separately, and then totals these costs to arrive at the marketing allocation required. This method's logic and appeal account for its growing popularity. Charles Mortimer, who rose through advertising and marketing to the presidency of General Foods, has stated the following:

> The task method is built brick by brick; not pulled out of a hat, or devined with a willow wand. . . . It is based on a concrete estimate of the job to be done. It uses extensively past advertising experience— all that is available—but never accepts any rule of thumb or past statistical relation as a sufficient guide for expenditures without reexamination of the nature of the task and the most promising method of accomplishing it *this* year—not *last* year. It involves constant awareness of what the competitors are doing with respect to advertising themes and expenditures, but it does not blindly follow the competitor's program.

The only safe assumption to make in determining advertising expenditures is that each year—or campaign—involves a task that is *new* in some important respect. Old measurements and old answers, accepted uncritically, are not good enough.[11]

On the surface, the task and objective method appears to be ideal; but it's not. Its major strengths are emphasis on situational analysis, recognition of the dynamic nature of marketing, and identification of the job to be done. This method introduces a note of realism into marketing allocations by relating the marketing tasks' variety and magnitude to the size of the allocation.

On the negative side, the objective and task method: fails to consider the need for profit and if a particular objective is cost-effective; and oversimplifies the difficulty of determining how much effort will be required to accomplish a given task. Marketing is filled with risks; that is one of its charms. However, the best laid plans do not always accomplish intended goals; that is one of its frustrations.

A POINT OF VIEW

From a practical point of view, most sophisticated companies use all of these methods in reaching their marketing allocation.

1 As in the affordable method, the availability of funds and the need for profit *is* a consideration.
2 As in the percentage of sales method, management does identify a standard or normal rate of expenditure based on a percentage of sales or a fixed allocation per unit or case.
3 As in the share of advertising method, management does recognize a relationship between share of market and share of advertising, and often uses this rough relationship in determining the marketing appropriation.
4 Finally, all of these approaches are consolidated in the task and objective approach which specifically examines the variety of tasks that must be done in order to accomplish marketing objectives.

To look at how a sophisticated company might apply this pragmatic approach, three new terms must be introduced: **return on investment (ROI)**, **economic profit**, and **payout plan**.

Return on investment.   Return on investment (ROI) is a profit criterion frequently used by firms to determine whether they should compete in a particular product field. ROI is a ratio between the capital investment required to enter a business and the annual amount of profit the business will produce. Use the simplified operations statement in Table 2–2 (see page 43) to demonstrate this concept. The sales income is $53,578,000. Assume the company spent

---

[11]Charles Mortimer, Jr., "How Much Should You Spend on Advertising?" in *Advertising Handbook*, Robert Barton, ed., (Englewood Cliffs, New Jersey: Prentice-Hall, Inc., 1950), 113–15.

$10,000,000 in capital investment to build the plant and buy the equipment needed to produce this product. The firm requires an annual ROI of 20 percent before taxes. In order to meet its profit requirements, the $53,578,000 in sales must produce a profit of $2,000,000 ($10,000,000 × .20 = $2,000,000). This $2,000,000 may be considered a cost of doing business since this level of profit is a policy requirement for making the necessary capital investment.

Economic profit. Economic profit refers to the profit a firm makes over and above its minimal profit requirements. The firm in Table 2–2 made a contribution to profits of $9,033,000. Since the firm only needs $2,000,000 in profits to meet its ROI objectives, it is earning an *economic profit* of $7,033,000 ($9,033,000 − $2,000,000 = $7,033,000) *before* marketing expenses. This $7,033,000, referred to as **available funds,** is the amount the firm has available for economic profit and marketing expenditures.

Now, assume the firm normally expects to realize 30 percent of the available funds for economic profit and to allocate 70 percent of these funds for marketing. Then, normal expenditures for a sales level of $53,588,000 would be $4,923,100. These relationships are shown below:

Sales (1000s cases)	6,230,000
Income from sales	$53,578,000
Contribution to profit	9,033,000
Less: required ROI	2,000,000
Available funds ($1.13/case)	7,033,000
Less: economic profit (30%)	2,109,900
Normal marketing allocation (70%)	4,923,100
Normal marketing allocation as a percent of sales:	9.2%
Normal marketing allocation per case	$0.79

As long as the marketing request for funds falls within the area of $0.79 per case or 9.2 percent of sales, the marketing department and top management will not have any problems; provided the marketing forecast appears realistic, the brand is doing reasonably well, the strategies and plans seem to be well conceived, and the creative approach doesn't offend anyone. From management's point of view, the marketing appropriation is in the *normal* range of the cost of doing business and the company is making its profit.

But now, let us suppose the market is in a real turmoil. A major competitor has just come up with a smashing creative approach; another competitor has launched what appears to be an extremely effective sales promotion program; the company we have been discussing has developed a product improvement that marks a real opportunity for increased sales. In short, the price of doing business has just gone up, and in the judgment of marketing management, a significant increase in the marketing expenditure is required. This leads us to the concept of payout plans.

Payout plan. Payout, as it is used here, refers to the length of time it requires a firm to recover an *investment* in marketing. A **payout plan** is a projection into the future that shows funds available, funds spent, and the resulting economic profit. Payout plans may be for any length of time, although they seldom exceed three years because of the difficulty of projecting sales and income with reasonable accuracy beyond this period. Generally, the length of payout plans has been decreasing during the past decade because technology and competitive response have shortened the length of time that a product or marketing advantage can be maintained. For example, in the 1950s and early 1960s, three year payout plans were common. More recently, one and two year payout plans have become the norm. Table 2–3 illustrates the mechanics of a three year payout plan using the figures we have developed thus far. In this table, total *available funds* for the entire three year period are allocated for marketing expenditures; substantial investments in the first two periods cause losses to be incurred. In the third year, marketing expenditures have returned to normal ($0.79 per case), and the investment has been recovered. For the entire period, no economic profit is earned. However, at the end of the three year period, the firm holds an increased share of an expanded market, and future economic profits will be substantially greater than they have been in the past.

The purpose of the payout plan is to clarify three things for management: (a) the amount of money that will have to be invested to achieve desired results; (b) the length of time the investment must be made; and (c) the benefits that will accrue from the investment. With this information, management can determine whether the risks and potential gain are worth the required investment. The payout approach is commonly used by sophisticated marketers for all new products as well as other major marketing investments such as business-building tests.

The mechanics for developing a payout plan are listed below.

1 Estimate the total market for each year of the payout plan.
2 Estimate the brand's market share for each year.
3 Compute company sales in cases for each year.

TABLE 2–3 Three year payout plan (units and dollars in thousands except for cost per case)

Payout Plan	Year 1	Year 2	Year 3
Total market (1000s cases)	31,150.0	32,695.7	34,669.9
Estimated company share	20.0%	23.1%	25.0%
Company forecast (1000s cases)	6,230.0	7,552.7	8,667.5
Funds available ($1.13 per case)	$7,039.9	$8,534.6	$9,794.3
Expenditures	9,950.0	8,571.5	6,847.3
Economic profit/loss	(2,910.1)	(36.9)	2,947.0
Cumulative economic profit/loss	(2,910.1)	(2,947.0)	–0–
Cost per case	$1.60	$1.13	$0.79

4 Determine funds available for each year by multiplying expected company sales in cases by funds available per case.

5 Add the funds available in each year of the payout plan to obtain *total* funds available.

6 Determine the planned expenditure for the last year by multiplying the estimated company sales in cases during this year by the *normal* expenditure per case.

7 Subtract the planned expenditure in the last year from the total funds available to determine how much is available for the preceding years. Allocate this amount over the preceding years on the basis of judgment.

8 Compute economic profit or loss and cumulative profit or loss by subtracting the expenditures in each year from the funds available for each year.

9 Compute cost per case for expenditures for each year.

HEDGING THE MARKETING BUDGET

Forecasting and budget determination are central considerations in the development of marketing plans. Although sophisticated quantitative models are sometimes used in making these determinations, the dynamics of the marketing situation precludes total reliance on such mechanical approaches. Consequently, experience, judgment, and a sense of marketing opportunity make budget determination as much an art as it is a science.

Since there is always some uncertainty in the marketing forecast, many firms choose to hedge their marketing allocation. A common way of doing this is to hold some amount of the budget—say 10 percent—in reserve, with the stipulation that this reserve will be spent *provided* sales are on forecast after the first six months of the fiscal year. This procedure minimizes the necessity of cutting back the marketing program in order to meet profit objectives if sales lag somewhat behind forecast.

ALLOCATION OF THE MARKETING BUDGET

Thus far we have talked about determining the total marketing budget. This total budget will be allocated to particular marketing activities based on strategic considerations and the tasks to be done. For most consumer goods, the bulk of the budget is normally allocated to advertising and sales promotion. Where special objectives and strategies are an important part of the marketing plan, substantial expenditures may be made in research, market tests, or other activities.

Problems in allocation. In addition to those expenditures identified above, there are other company expenditures which, technically, are marketing expenditures but are not normally charged to the marketing budget. Packaging is a case in point. For consumer goods, packaging often serves three functions: (a) product protection; (b) display; and (c) dispensing. Frequently, marketing will require display and dispensing features which substantially increase packaging costs. These increased costs are clearly marketing expenditures, although normally they are charged to the manufacturing department's budget as product costs. One packaging expenditure generally recognized as a marketing expense is a new package design required for marketing considerations.

Within the marketing budget, there is still a problem of allocating expenses into various functional categories such as advertising, sales promotion, publicity, marketing research, package design, and test marketing. Unfortunately, there is no consistent pattern followed in making such allocations. Table 2–4 identifies three lists of activities that are sometimes charged to advertising. The first list, referred to as the "white" list, clearly belongs in the advertising budget. The second (the "gray" list) is made up of borderline items that, depending upon the circumstances, may appear in the advertising budget. The third (the "black" list) consists of items that should not appear in the advertising budget, but sometimes do.

All too frequently, the advertising budget becomes a catchall for expense items that more properly should be charged to other departments such as finance, personnel, or public relations. Such misallocations distort advertising expenditures, and the lack of standard allocation procedures makes it difficult to compare advertising expenditures from the figures given in company operations statements.

SUMMARY

No one is more important to advertising than advertisers, or clients. They develop products, provide funds for marketing, and decide what advertising and marketing activities will be used. The majority of advertisers in the United States are some of the 14 million business firms in this country. Business firms tend to be highly concentrated in terms of size, with about four percent accounting for almost 60 percent of all business receipts. Only a small percentage of firms use advertising agencies, and only a fraction of those develop systematic advertising and marketing plans.

Advertising agencies are used depending on the desires of company management and capabilities of the firm's advertising agency. Many major firms rely heavily upon their advertising agencies for a wide variety of marketing counsel. The client-agency relationship is a tenuous one based on mutual respect and confidence. Interpersonal relationships are extremely important, and advertising accounts are often gained or lost because of personal friendships, politics, and interpersonal conflicts. Many large companies use a number of advertising agencies simultaneously for their various products. Although multiple-agency relationships provide client organizations with a diversity of counsel and flexibility, they also create problems of coordination. Although many agency selections are made in a haphazard manner, this selection is an important decision that should be approached carefully and systematically.

Advertiser organizations may be structured in a number of ways. The particular form of organization selected depends upon the size of the company, number of products it markets, nature of the industry within which it operates, and management's marketing

TABLE 2–4 *Printers' Ink* guide to allocation of advertising appropriations (sometimes called the "white, black, and gray list")

White list (These charges belong in the advertising account.)

Space
(paid advertising in all recognized mediums, including:)
Newspapers
Magazines
Business papers
Farm papers
Class journals
Car cards
Theater programs
Outdoor
Point of purchase
Novelties
Booklets
Directories
Direct Advertising
Cartons and labels (for advertising purposes, such as in window displays)

Catalogs
Package inserts (when used as advertising and not just as direction sheets)
House magazines to dealers or consumers
Motion pictures (including talking pictures) when used for advertising
Slides
Export advertising
Dealer helps
Reprints of advertisements used in mail or for display
Radio
Television
All other printed and lithographed material used directly for advertising purposes

Administration
Salaries of advertising department executives and employees
Office supplies and fixtures used solely by advertising department
Commissions and fees to advertising agencies, special writers or advisers
Expenses incurred by salesmen when on work for advertising department
Traveling expenses of department employees engaged in departmental business
(Note: In some companies these go into special "Administration" account)

Mechanical
Artwork
Typography
Engraving
Mats
Electros
Photographs
Radio & TV production
Package design (advertising aspects only)
Etc.
Miscellaneous:
Transportation of advertising material (to include postage and other carrying charges)
Fees to window display installation services
Other miscellaneous expenses connected with items on the white list

Black list (These charges do not belong in the advertising account, although too frequently they are put there.)

Free goods
Picnic and bazaar programs
Charitable, religious, and fraternal donations
Other expenses for goodwill purposes
Cartons
Labels
Instruction sheets
Package manufacture
Press agentry
Stationery used outside advertising department
Price lists
Salesmen's calling cards
Motion pictures for sales use only
House magazines going to factory employees
Bonuses to trade

Special rebates
Membership in trade associations
Entertaining customers or prospects
Annual reports
Showrooms
Demonstration stores
Sales convention expenses
Salesmen's samples (including photographs used in lieu of samples)
Welfare activities among employees
Such recreational activities as baseball teams, etc.
Sales expenses at conventions
Cost of salesmen's automobiles
Special editions which approach advertisers on goodwill basis

Gray list (These are borderline charges, sometimes belonging in the advertising accounts and sometimes in other accounts, depending on circumstances.)

Samples
Demonstrations
Fairs
Canvassing
Rent
Light
Heat
Depreciation of equipment used by advertising department
Telephone and other overhead expenses, apportioned to advertising department
House magazines going to salesmen
Advertising automobiles

Premiums
Membership in associations or other organizations devoted to advertising
Testing bureaus
Advertising portfolios for salesmen
Contributions to special advertising funds of trade associations
Display signs on the factory or office building
Salesmen's catalogs
Research and market investigations
Advertising allowances to trade for cooperative effort

Note: This chart is based on the principle that there are three types of expenses that generally are charged against the advertising appropriation.
The first charge is made up of expenses that are always justifiable under any scheme of accounting practice. These have been included in the white list of charges that belong in the advertising account.
A second type consists of those charges which cannot and should not under any system of accounting be justified as advertising expenses. These have been placed on the black list.
There is a third type of expense which can sometimes be justified under advertising and sometimes not. Frequently the justification for the charge depends upon the method used in carrying on a certain activity. These charges have been placed in a borderline gray list.
The chart is the result of the collaboration of the editors of *Printers' Ink* and several hundred advertisers. It has been revised for a third time with the aid of advertising and accounting men. It may be considered, therefore, to represent sound, standard practice.

philosophy. One key problem of organization is the way marketing is integrated into the company. In recent years, there has been a trend toward product management forms of organization, supplemented by a strong advertising department that provides counsel and support for marketing managers.

Retail organizations, such as large department stores, often require special forms of organization. Such stores seldom use advertising agencies. Instead, most of their advertising is handled by a large advertising department. Large advertising departments are necessary because retail stores must move quickly to respond to customer needs and local market conditions. In addition, the rate structures of media do not encourage the use of advertising agencies by retail organizations.

Advertising departments in manufacturing companies vary in size and function depending upon the importance of advertising in the company, number of products marketed, how much sales promotion is used, and if the company develops collateral materials and engages in cooperative advertising. The most common form of advertising department organization is by function because it is relatively easy to administer, permits the development of highly skilled specialists, lends itself to the formation of temporary work groups for special projects, and expands or contracts easily as functions are added or eliminated.

Determination of the marketing budget is a difficult task. A number of methods may be used—affordable, percentage of sales, share of advertising, and objective and task method. All have advantages and disadvantages. Sophisticated advertisers generally use a combination of these methods as well as the concepts of economic profit and return on investment when determining their communication budgets. Payout plans are often used when planning unusual investments in marketing in order to show the length of time required to recover an investment. A properly prepared payout plan enables management to review the amount of money that will have to be invested, length of the investment, and benefits if the investment is successful.

Even after a total marketing budget has been established, problems may arise in how the budget will be allocated to various marketing activities. Often, the advertising portion of the budget becomes a catchall for miscellaneous items, many of which should not be a part of the advertising budget.

REVIEW QUESTIONS

1 What are the major criticisms of the brand management system of organization?
2 Why are advertising agencies generally anxious to become involved in marketing activities other than advertising?
3 What are the primary disadvantages of a simple, functional organization for a producer of consumer products?
4 How does the product manager form of organization improve on the functional form? What are its disadvantages?

5 Diagram a coordinated product manager system. What are the key ways it differs from the product manager form of organization?
6 Explain why major local retailers, such as department stores, do not use advertising agencies?
7 What are the advantages of organizing an advertising department by function?
8 What are the advantages and disadvantages of the affordable method, percentage of sales method, share of advertising method, and objective and task method of determining marketing appropriations?
9 Explain what is meant by the terms *return on investment, economic profit,* and *available funds.* How are these concepts used in arriving at the marketing appropriation?
10 What is the purpose of a payout plan?

DISCUSSION QUESTIONS

1 Visit a small local retailer and find out how it handles its advertising.
2 Visit a major local department store and find out how its advertising department is organized.
3 Examine the advertising of retailers in your local newspaper and the advertising of manufacturers in magazines. What are the similarities and differences between these two kinds of advertising? What implications do these differences have for how advertising can best be handled?

PROBLEM

Mark Linden, product manager for Cook's Choice instant pudding mix, was preparing a marketing plan for the next fiscal year. The pudding market was a relatively stable market, and Cook's Choice held a dominant share. Sales and brand share for the past five years are shown in Table 2–5.

Instant pudding mixes, popular for puddings and pie fillings because of their ease of preparation, were considered by many consumers to be inferior in texture and flavor to regular puddings which took longer to

TABLE 2–5 Five year sales and brand share data for Cook's Choice Instant Pudding Mix

Brand Share	1979	1980	1981	1982	1983
Total market (1000s cases)	32,460.0	33,433.8	34,369.4	35,366.2	36,427.2
Cook's Choice (1000s cases)	7,303.5	7,556.0	7,767.5	8,063.4	8,268.9
Market share	22.5%	22.6%	22.6%	22.8%	22.7%

PART I | THE SETTING

prepare. These shortcomings had put a ceiling on the pudding market. Cook's Choice's research and development department had been working on an improved formula for several years and, in 1982, had developed an instant pudding product that was comparable to regular puddings in richness, texture, and flavor.

In 1983, the new mix was introduced as a "new and improved" product in three test markets. There were some variations in performance on a market by market basis, but the overall results were very encouraging. The funds available for instant pudding mix were $1.20 per case, of which 60 percent was normally allocated to advertising and sales promotion and 40 percent was retained as profit. In the test markets, however, the company had spent at double the normal rate. A comparison of test market sales to sales in the rest of the country is shown in Table 2–6.

Mark had to determine, on the basis of test market results, if he should recommend a national program of investment spending to introduce the new product nationally in 1984. If so, how long a payout should he recommend?

He knew that competition had been alerted to the product change by the 1983 test markets. However, discussions with research and development personnel had partially assured him that the competition would need at least eighteen to thirty months to duplicate the new product because it involved changes in formula, the way the dry milk ingredient was processed, and cooking temperatures. Even after competition had duplicated the process, it would take them at least six months to acquire the special manufacturing equipment required to manufacture in volume.

Based on the relative consistency of the three test markets, consumer tests, and his own evaluation of the new product, Mark felt pretty confident about the test market results.

ASSIGNMENT

Develop a forecast and spending plan for the national introduction of the new product, recognizing that some kind of a payout plan will be required.

TABLE 2–6 Comparison of Cook's Choice test markets to rest of country

Brand Share	Combined Test Markets		Rest of Country	
	1982	1983	1982	1983
Total market (1000s cases)	707.3	763.9	34,658.9	35,663.3
Cook's Choice (1000s cases)	159.8	207.8	7,903.6	8,061.1
Market share	22.6	27.2	22.8	22.6

3

The Advertising Agency

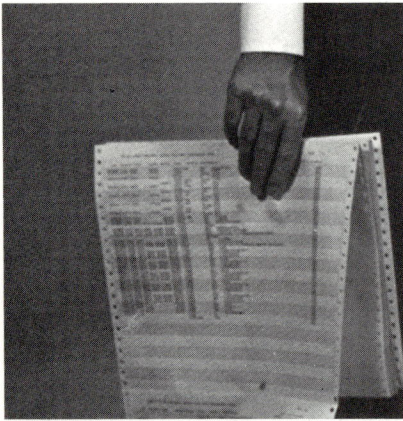

THE SUPERAGENCY

Advertising was once known by the men and women who created it—great names like Albert Lasker, J. Sterling Getchel, Manny Gilliam, Fairfax Cone, Victor Schwab, John Caples, Bruce Barton, Charlie Brower, Charles Adams, Draper Daniels, Rosser Reeves, David Ogilvy, Raymond Rubicam, William Bernbach, and Mary Wells. Many of them founded advertising agencies that still bear their names.

There was a time when advertising agencies were fairly small, intimate, personal organizations. A major agency billed no more than $50 million and employed no more than 500 employees.

As a result of natural growth, mergers, and inflation, the superagency has come of age. These agencies issue billings in excess of $2 billion, manage worldwide operations, and employ over 12,000 people. The great names and small agencies that made advertising history are being replaced by gray, faceless corporations. Many believe that advertising is the less for it.

1 + 1 + 1 + 1 = 1

Bruce Barton described the status of the advertising professional by stating, "God so hated advertising men that he never made a whole one." Tom Dillon, former chairman of the board of Batten, Barton, Durstine & Osborn (BBDO) echoed this same thought: "I think it highly unlikely that any individual can in a lifetime acquire all the skills needed to qualify as a complete advertising person. I don't think the human skull would hold that much. I can guarantee that mine won't."[1]

Figure 3–1 indicates that 1 part creative + 1 part executive + 1 part research + 1 part media = 1 complete advertising professional. Further, a complete advertising person should be a psychologist, expert in interpersonal relations, cost accountant, financial genius, raconteur, and gracious host.

---

[1]Tom Dillon, "Why God Never Made a Whole Advertising Man," *Advertising Age*, 28 September 1981, 49.

THE COMPLETE ADMAN

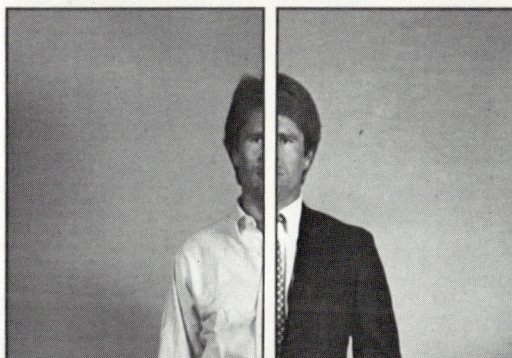

Creative

Executive

Research

Media

MANAGING AN ADVERTISING AGENCY

In *Confessions of an Advertising Man*, David Ogilvy makes the following observations about managing an advertising agency.

> Running an agency takes vitality, and sufficient resilience to pick oneself up after defeats. Affection for one's henchmen, and tolerance for their foibles. A genius for composing sibling rivalries. An unerring eye for the main chance. And morality—people who work in advertising agencies can suffer serious blows to their *esprit de corps* if they catch their leader in acts of unprincipled opportunism.
>
> Above all, the head of an agency must know how to delegate . . . the act of delegation often results in interspersing a foreman between the agency boss and his staff. When this happens, the employees feel like children whose mother turns them over to the tender mercies of a nanny. But they become reconciled to the separation when they discover that the nannies are more patient, more accessible, and more expert than I am.[2]

These examples reflect three of the many dimensions of the advertising agency business. First, the agency business is changing from relatively small, intimate organizations to superagencies that resemble giant corporations. Second, advertising is a complex task requiring diverse skills that cannot be handled effectively by one person. Third, managing an agency is a difficult job, made more so because many advertising people are ambitious, temperamental, and insecure.

Let's take a closer look at advertising agencies, the people and their jobs, and the organizational structures.

ADVERTISING AGENCIES— AN OVERVIEW

The approximately six thousand advertising agencies in the United States range in size from Young & Rubicam, with billings of over $2.3 billion and a 1981 gross income of $353 million, to small operations whose total billings are less than $50,000 and gross incomes are barely able to cover their principals' meager salaries.

Table 3–1 summarizes a report, covering 821 advertising agencies with a combined gross income of over $5.4 billion, on agency operations for 1981.[3] Less than 12 percent of the agencies account for over 84 percent of the agency gross income, pointing up the concentration of business that exists in the advertising industry.

Advertising agencies differ in other ways. For example, some agencies specialize in industrial products, consumer products, or fashion advertising. The smaller ones specialize in retail accounts, real estate, or financial advertising. In short, advertising agencies often carve out highly specialized niches for themselves. However, most major agencies handle a variety of accounts, cutting across the specialty spectrum.

---

[2]David Ogilvy, from *Confessions of an Advertising Man* (New York: Atheneum Publishers, 1963), 16. Copyright © 1963 by David Ogilvy Trustee. Reprinted with permission of Atheneum Publishers.

[3]John J. O'Connor, "1981 Income Tops $5 Billion," *Advertising Age,* 24 March 1982, 1ff.

TABLE 3–1 United States advertising agencies classified by size group

Gross Income	Agencies		Income (Millions)	
	Number	Percentage	Income	Percentage
Over $5 million	97	11.8%	$4,568.4	84.3%
$1–$5 million	296	36.1%	$ 660.6	12.2%
Under $1 million	428	52.1%	$ 189.2	3.5%
Totals	821	100.0%	$5,418.2	100.0%

Source: Compiled from *Advertising Age,* 24 March 1981.

Estimated expenditures for advertising in current dollars have mushroomed from $5.7 billion in 1950 to $54.6 billion in 1980. Figure 3–2 shows the growth in advertising expenditures for each ten year period from 1950 to 1980.

This dynamic growth has brought with it a number of changes; not all have been beneficial.

MORE AGENCY FUNCTIONS ARE BEING ASSUMED BY ADVERTISERS

As advertising costs have increased, client organizations have assumed traditional agency functions in order to save money and obtain value for any money spent. Corporate advertising departments have assumed a more direct role in supervising media buying, creative development, sales promotion, and other advertising activities. Critics think this direct involvement in the creative process has introduced an unwarranted caution that has been injurious to the product.

In-house advertising agencies have become more common, and traditional methods of compensating advertising agencies have undergone a revolution. Agency charges, always a sensitive point of contention between clients and their agencies, have become even more critical in the client-agency relationship. An article in *Advertising Age* on agency compensation states:

FIGURE 3–2 Estimated advertising expenditures in the United States in billions of dollars. (Redrawn and reprinted with permission from the September 14, 1981 issue of *Advertising Age.* Copyright © 1981 by Crain Communications, Inc.)

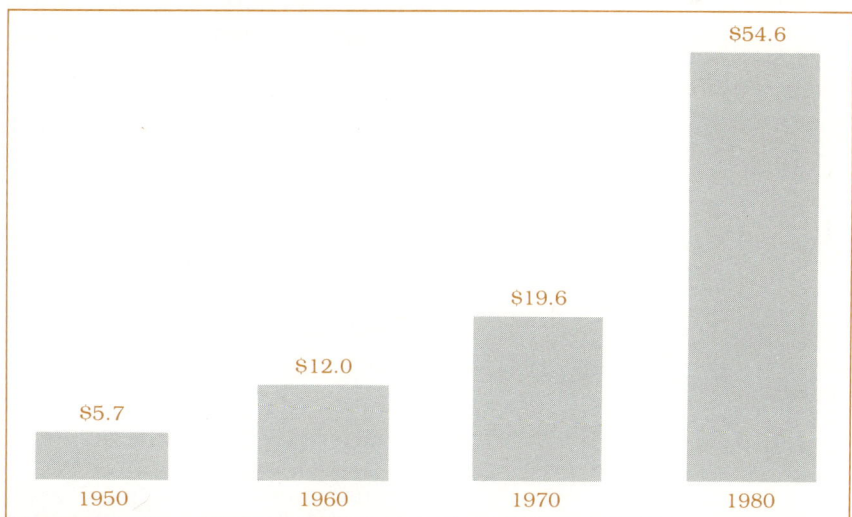

CHAPTER 3 | THE ADVERTISING AGENCY

Agency compensation is, understandably, an issue never far from the consciousness of company marketing executives and the managers of advertising agencies of all sizes throughout the country.

While open controversy about how an agency should be compensated infrequently flares into public quarrels, the issue is struggled with almost continually by members of the advertising community.

Two major trade associations—the Assn. of National Advertisers representing clients and the American Assn. of Advertising Agencies representing agencies—have each issued major documents within the past year-and-a-half or so dealing with the subject. . . .

These reports show that, as complicated and sophisticated as the formulas and adjustments become, the underlying problem remains a very simple yet long-lived one: How equitable and broadly applicable is the traditional 15% media commission as a means of paying agencies for the contributions they make to their clients' operations? If it makes sense for the $5,000,000 to $10,000,000 nationally advertised brand account, can it also make sense for a regional specialty assignment billing only $150,000?

In spite of the growing practice of adjusting the standard commission to achieve a mutually satisfactory arrangement, there's little doubt renewed stress is being felt today because of inflation. As media costs (and consequently advertising budgets) escalate rapidly, the raw commission technique looms more insistently than ever as a concern of conscientious advertisers trying to control one of their costs of doing business.

On the other side of the fence, the heads of large, medium and small agencies are all struggling with unprecedented cost pressures themselves (soaring downtown office rentals to note a particularly excruciating problem right now). Thus, they're working harder than ever to pare costs and expenses wherever possible within the bounds of expected revenue potential in order to assure a reasonable and continuing profit.[4]

This problem is far from resolved and undoubtedly will have a profound effect on advertising agencies in the future.

ADVERTISING AGENCIES BECOME MORE BUSINESS ORIENTED

Traditionally, advertising agencies have not been considered highly business oriented. Whether this criticism was true in the past is debatable; it is not true today. Financial pressure alone has caused agencies to take a hard look at their internal business practices, as well as those of the clients they serve.

Less than twenty years ago, advertising agencies required ten employees for each million dollars in billing. Thus, an agency billing $40 million would have approximately 400 employees (10 × 40 = 400). Today, the ratio is more like four to five employees for each million dollars in billing. Although this reduction in personnel undoubtedly represents a more efficient operation, it also signals a sharp reduction in the quality and quantity of agency service.

---

[4]Herb Zeltner, "Sounding Board: Clients, Adman Split on Compensation," p. 63ff. Reprinted with permission from May 18, 1981 issue of *Advertising Age.* Copyright © 1981 by Crain Communications, Inc.

Sharper business practices on the part of advertising agencies have resulted in a decrease in agency loyalty to their clients. An unwritten rule in the agency business implies that an advertising agency should not handle competitive accounts. For example, an advertising agency should not handle competitive brands of cake mix produced by different companies.[5] No one has been more diligent in enforcing this unwritten rule than client organizations. Because of this practice, advertising agencies traditionally had not solicited competitive accounts. Furthermore, resigning an account in order to accept a more profitable competitive one was considered bad taste and disloyal.

This is no longer true. A common practice for an advertising agency is dropping a longstanding account in order to accept a larger, more profitable competitor. Undoubtedly, this makes sense from a business standpoint. Yet, from the standpoint of personal relations, loyalty has been lost in the process.

A DECLINE IN ADVERTISING CREATIVITY

Some reasons for a possible decline in advertising creativity involve talent, advertising volume, and bureaucracy.

Failure to develop creative talent. When advertising agencies had to decrease their number of employees from 10 to less than 5 per million dollars in billing, certain activities had to be given up. One of the first to go was developing people for the future. William Tyler, a longtime contributor to *Advertising Age*, laments this lack of foresight in the following comment.

> It looked a little too good to be true. And sure enough, it was. I'm talking about the way agencies have been getting along the last few years with only half as many people per dollar billed. They claimed they did it without reducing the quality of their services. Short term, they were probably right. But now it's long-term time—time to take another look.
>
> On the alter of profits, we've sacrificed the development of new creative talent to take the place of the old ones now gone. And now we're paying the price: a critical shortage of mature creative people.
>
> What's the answer? Agency training programs? Okay, but necessarily superficial. Frantic raiding and trading? I'm afraid so, until we go back to the time-honored apprentice system, by hiring promising youngsters and bringing them along the slow and costly way by putting them under experienced hands (where they will learn more from their own errors than their successes, that being the nature of the business).
>
> We're facing an era of wildly escalating creative salaries to make up for the ones we didn't pay the last few years. We dealt the golden goose an almost mortal blow. And she'll be in intensive care for quite a while yet.[6]

---

[5]Advertising agencies sometimes handle competitive brands produced by the same client. Such assignments are made at the discretion of the client organization, however. Handling competitive brands in different geographic areas may occur because the marketing areas differ.

[6]William D. Tyler, "Agencies Return to Time-honored Apprenticeship for Young Creatives," p. 50. Reprinted with permission from August 17, 1977 issue of *Advertising Age*. Copyright © 1977 by Crain Communications, Inc.

The volume of advertising precludes quality control. As the volume of advertising has increased, it has become more difficult to exercise control over the quality of the creative process. J. Walter Thompson, the advertising agency for Ford Motor Company, turns out over 5000 ads a year for Ford and its dealers. It is hardly reasonable to expect a high level of quality control over 5000 ads.

Agencies have become more bureaucratic. As agencies have become larger, they have become more bureaucratic and cautious—hardly a recipe for advertising creativity. A *Fortune* article provides the following comment on this problem.

> It is a question whether the founding fathers, the men whose names still hang on the agencies' doors, would now feel at home in the business they helped invent. Many of those creative types have died, or stepped aside. David Ogilvy lives in a chateau in France, and while he recently took over Ogilvy & Mather's Frankfurt office, he only rarely visits New York headquarters. Leo Burnett died eight years ago. Bill Bernbach still comes to work, but he no longer runs the agency and his colleagues, Maxwell Dane and Ned Doyle, have retired. They have been replaced by a new generation that is more bureaucratic than entrepreneurial. Says William Phillips, Ogilvy & Mather's president: "The people who run the business today are technocrats."[7]

GIANTISM CAUSES AGENCY MANAGEMENT TO LOSE TOUCH

In the past 20 years, mergers have resulted in more than fifty of the nation's top one hundred agencies disappearing from the advertising scene. The significant independent agencies on the West Coast have disappeared, gobbled up by superagencies based in New York and Chicago. An article in *Advertising Age* notes:

> In just 20 years, Marion Harper's little old McCann-Erickson (now the Interpublic Group of Cos.) grew 15-fold, from billings of $200,000,000 to more than $3 billion, from offices in New York and Chicago to one or more offices in just about every major city in the world. The huge Interpublic mantle now embraces several of the nation's once best known independent agencies like SSC&B, Campbell-Ewald, Marschalk and Erwin-Wasey. It is not uncommon for three or four Interpublic agencies to be soliciting the same account.
>
> Recently addicted supergiants Young & Rubicam and Ted Bates are typical of the trend. The former have grown 10-fold since 1960, from $200,000,000 to $2 billion with its 1979 acquisition of $365,000,000 Marsteller; Bates from $120,000,000 to more than a billion. Within weeks, the latter announced the purchase of Campbell-Mithun and Stern Walters/Earle Ludgin, both with active Chicago offices. Typical among the aspirants to giantism, Bozell & Jacobs now owns 13 affiliates, marking a 30-fold increase in billing to its current $380,000,000.[8]

---

[7]Peter W. Bernstein, "Here Come the Super-Agencies," *Fortune*, 27 August 1979, 50.

[8]M. S. Garfield, "The Fallacies of Giantism," p. 51. Reprinted with permission from the June 1, 1981 issue of *Advertising Age*. Copyright © 1981 by Crain Communications, Inc.

No evidence exists that increased size has improved creativity or increased agency service. Client dissatisfaction with advertising agencies appears to be approaching an all-time high. Since the mid-1960s the number of agency switches among major clients has increased to approximately 250 per year. Clients are dissatisfied with the excessive personnel turnover, inability to adhere to schedules, an agency's need for too much lead time, and limited involvement by senior management. These criticisms are characteristic of large, bureaucratic organizations. After all, how can a president of a $3 billion advertising agency, with offices in most major cities of the world, possibly find time to get involved in the advertising of a single client?

How do the superagencies see themselves, and how are they seen by their competitors? Table 3–2 shows the results of a 1979 *Fortune* survey. Although there have been minor shifts in their rankings, and two (SSC&B and Campbell-Ewald) have become a part of Interpublic, the fifteen largest agencies in 1979 were still the fifteen largest agencies in 1981.

What will become of the advertising agency in the future? Perhaps they will become too big, cumbersome, and unadaptable to survive in their present form. If so, they will probably change because the industry has always been a highly flexible one, adapting to the demands of advertisers and offering whatever array of services their clients required.

TYPES OF ADVERTISING AGENCIES

Since the early 1960s, the advertising industry has been in a turmoil because advertisers, in an effort to obtain better service and reduce costs, have insisted that agency services be tailored to their specific needs. The following material briefly describes the major types of advertising agencies that are currently serving the industry.

FULL-SERVICE AGENCIES

A **full-service advertising agency** is one that provides a broad, if not totally complete, range of marketing services. Its development was a process of evolution. Beginning in the early 1880s as space brokers (agents that bought newspaper and magazine space in bulk quantities from publishers and resold it to advertisers in individual units), advertising agencies gradually added additional services as competitive strategies to attract clients and facilitate growth. Today, a full-service agency is generally staffed to handle the entire gamut of marketing counsel, with the exception of personal selling and public relations, although some full-service agencies also undertake public relations functions.

In addition to the necessary internal functions such as management, finance, accounting, personnel, and new business acquisition, full-service agencies generally provide functions such as account service, creative services, traffic, media, and marketing research.

Account service. Account service, or account management, is the liaison between the advertising agency and its clients. The responsibilities of the account manager, usually referred to as an account

TABLE 3–2 How selected major advertising agencies see themselves and how they are seen by their competition

Advertising Agency	How They See Themselves	How Competition Sees Them
J. Walter Thompson	Very sound and strong everywhere. Produces effective advertising. We're going through a renaissance.	A great gray mass. Invisible work. Fuddy-duddy. Not the leaders they were. Still sorting out management.
McCann-Erickson Worldwide	A reawakened giant that's gaining momentum. Unique position worldwide.	Dominated by Coke, Exxon, and Miller. More creative than given credit for. Weak in packaged goods.
Young & Rubicam	Aggressive. Creative. The best in total commercial persuasion worldwide. Benefited from planning.	The best and hottest agency. Spurts of brilliant work. Expanded too fast. Over-emphasis on new business.
Ogilvy & Mather	We combine creative brilliance with marketing discipline. A good place to work.	Classy outfit. Everyone dresses right. Image deteriorated recently. End product slipping.
Ted Bates	Most underrated agency. Businesslike and account-oriented. We create advertising that is meant to sell.	Hard-headed packaged goods agency. Run by a tough guy. Second rate creative. Buying things willy-nilly.
BBDO	Changing with new strong management. Not as creative as we ought to be. Strong in TV, slipped in print.	Better-than-average, stuffy agency. Very profitable. Without identity. Not attracting enough new clients.
Leo Burnett	Informal. Closely involved with clients. Too much self criticism. Shaken by some account losses.	Heartland agency. Lost its luster since Leo Burnett's death. Management problems. Built on Chicago only.
SSC&B/Lintas	Sensational. The professional's professional. Lack high visibility because we are so busy with client's business.	Well-disciplined packaged goods agency. Big and dull. No personality. Just as well they're selling to Interpublic.

Source: Peter Bernstein, "Here Come the Super-Agencies," *Fortune*, 27 August 1979, 46–47.

executive or account supervisor, are twofold: (a) working with the client on a day-to-day basis and being responsible for understanding the client's business needs and interpreting them to agency personnel; (b) working closely with agency personnel in developing plans and recommendations and being responsible for presenting and obtaining client approval for agency recommendations. The account manager is the focal point of agency-client relations and supervises internal agency activity.

In some agencies, the account manager is an experienced and knowledgeable marketer who carries the major responsibility for market planning the client's product by writing the client's marketing plan and working in close coordination with the client organization. In other agencies, the account manager does not bear the brunt of planning, but works closely with those who do in both the client and agency organizations.

Creative services.   The creative services department of an advertising agency is responsible for the creation and execution of advertise-

TABLE 3-2 (continued)

Advertising Agency	How They See Themselves	How Competition Sees Them
Foote, Cone & Belding	Conservative. Disciplined. Got started late in international but catching up. One hell of a creative operation.	Stodgy. Slow but competent. Work a nine-to-five day. Run as three fiefdoms in New York, Chicago, and L.A.
Grey Advertising	A marketing agency par excellence. Strong business orientation. High-quality creative work that produces results.	They have the right name. Hard-muscled marketing agency. A one-man band. Not a lot of fun.
D'Arcy-MacManus & Masius	Marketing oriented. We appeal to people's beliefs. Want to be one of the top three New York agencies.	An animal without a head or tail. Separate agencies trying to become one. Built size through merger.
Doyle Dane Bernbach	The most creative agency. Successful transition from first- to second-generation management. Ethical.	Still enamored of the mystique of creativity. Second rate at mass market products. Successful management change.
Benton & Bowles	Aggressive. Well managed. Blue-chip client list. Strong on marketing strategies for new products.	Know what they want to be. Highly marketing oriented. Tough and intelligent leadership. Well managed.
Compton Advertising	Competent package goods agency. Pretty square. Incredibly disciplined. Wants to rank higher in the top 15.	Dominated by P&G. Dull creative product. Trying to get its act together.
Campbell-Ewald Worldwide	Sound, stable, and conservative. The best automotive advertising. Experts in the durable goods business.	Nice, midwestern agency. Captive of Detroit. Part of General Motors. Not much of a reputation.

ments, commercials, and often for package design, point-of-sale material, or other forms of promotion. Creative services generally include four functional areas: copy, art, print production, and radio and television production. These areas may exist as separate departments, although the trend is to merge these groups into a single department in order to facilitate collective thinking and provide a closer integration of these areas in the creative process. Regardless of how the various creative service functions are organized, they have the following responsibilities:

1 *Copy.* Copywriters are generally assigned to specific accounts and are responsible for conceiving ideas for advertisements and writing the headlines, subheads, and body copy; they also write copy for broadcast media. Copywriters may also prepare a rough visual layout for an advertisement or a television storyboard, even as an art director may contribute copy ideas. In any case, copywriters work closely with art directors and those responsible for print and broadcast production.

2 *Art.* Artists in an advertising agency are responsible for the advertisement's design (the layout) and for its pictorial elements. In the case of television, the layout is known as a storyboard and depicts the sequence of action that makes up the commercial. In general, artists are responsible for the visualization of all artwork, execution of layouts and storyboards, preparation of mechanicals (detailed instructions for the production of advertisements), and type specifications, although this latter function may be handled by specialists known as typecasters. Since little finished artwork is actually produced by advertising agencies, at least one art buyer is responsible for locating and contracting with free-lance artists, independent art studios, and photographers for the finished work.

3 *Print production.* After copy, layout, artwork, and mechanical specifications have been completed and approved, advertisements must be produced. Since advertising agencies do not actually produce finished advertisements, the production group acts as a purchasing agent to select and oversee outside suppliers. The print production specialists also work closely with copywriters and artists, counseling them on the limitations and flexibility of the various graphic art techniques.

4 *Television and radio production.* In the early days of radio and television, broadcast producers in advertising agencies often originated the format and content of programs. Today, this activity is largely handled by the networks, individual stations, or independent producers. As a consequence, the primary responsibility of broadcast producers in an advertising agency is supervising the production of commercials. In this capacity, agency producers select independent production studios. Using the storyboard as a blueprint, the agency producer will generally supervise casting, selection of props and settings, editing, and the thousand-and-one details that go into the production of commercials. In the case of live commercials, where there is no filming or recording, agency producers simply supervise the commercial part of the program. Copywriters and art directors may also participate in the production process.

Traffic. As agencies become larger and more complex, coordination becomes a major problem. To insure coordination, a traffic department is established and given the responsibility for meeting schedules and closing dates. Closing dates are deadlines for submitting advertisements and commercials to media. The traffic department may be a part of the creative services group or a separate department in the agency.

Media. Advertisements and commercials are of no value to the advertiser until they appear in broadcast or print media. The media department analyzes, plans, selects, and contracts for the media that will be used in the advertiser's marketing program. It is a Herculean task. Media departments employ print and broadcast buyers who analyze an enormous amount of data concerning the various media and their audiences in making final recommendations and preparing schedules. The activities of the media department must be closely coordinated with those of the creative department and the client's budget restrictions. Often, media limitations—the inability of a medium to create a particular mood or portray some aspect of the product—have a major influence on the creative effort.

Marketing research. The marketing research department gathers, analyzes, and reports information that will be helpful in preparing the marketing plan and developing advertising. Their activities range from consulting with the client organization to preparing forecasts, including: analyzing sales data; conducting surveys and product tests; and testing advertising concepts, headlines, layouts, and finished advertisements and commercials. Although most major clients have their own marketing research departments, the agency research department is a valuable asset to the advertising agency and its management.

Other functions. The foregoing functions are the central activities of most full-service agencies. Many large agencies are also organized to perform other marketing functions. For example, some advertising agencies have sales promotion (sometimes called *merchandising*) departments that specialize in designing point-of-sale material, product display racks, contests, retail presentations, and other promotional materials. Others have home economics departments that develop and test recipes to be used on packages and in advertisements for the agency's food clients, work with the copy department in simplifying instructions for recipes and package directions, and supervise the preparation of food for photography and live broadcast commercials. A number of agencies also have public relations and product publicity departments.

Another reason for the development of full-service agencies is that advertising agencies sought to gain more control over the success or failure of their clients' marketing programs by involving themselves more deeply in all aspects of the effort, such as sales promotion, marketing research and strategy, pricing, and product planning. The agencies developed the people, departments, and skills that qualified them to participate in their clients' entire marketing programs. After developing these capabilities, advertising agencies provided these skills as a "packaged deal" whether their clients wanted them or not.

The 1960s saw a rebellion on the part of advertisers who, in an effort to cut costs and improve service, wanted to dispense with some of these services and shop around for others. For example, an advertiser might want to buy the creative service of one agency, media expertise of another, research capabilities of a third, and so on. A number of major agencies refused to participate in this process and lost clients; other agencies yielded to the pressure. This resulted in the modular advertising agency.

MODULAR AGENCIES

A **modular,** or a la carte, **advertising agency** is a full-service agency that sells its services on a piecemeal basis. Thus, an advertiser may commission an agency's creative department to develop an advertis-

A DAY IN THE LIFE OF AN ACCOUNT SUPERVISOR

Gail Foster is a far cry from the stereotype of an advertising account supervisor. The mother of two, she worked for 7 to 8 years as a secretary in the advertising departments of Pet, Inc., and Ralston Purina. She left Pet, Inc., to take a job in account service in a small St. Louis advertising agency, Advertising Associates, where she had an opportunity to combine a secretarial position with that of account service. Overnight, she found herself writing copy and becoming involved in the thousand and one activities of a small advertising agency.

After eight years with Advertising Associates, Gail joined D'Arcy-MacManus & Masius, where she is serving as a vice-president and account supervisor on Ozark Airlines and Shelter Insurance.

Gail is a strong advocate for small agency experience. "It is," she says, "the best place in the world to learn about advertising."

6:30

My day starts when I get in the shower. Mentally, my mind starts planning the things I have to take care of as soon as I arrive at the office. If something absolutely has to be done that day, I better do it first thing because once the day has started, plans seem to go astray.

Today I made a mental note to check with the broadcast Traffic Department to be sure the two, 2-inch television tapes I need for my insurance client have been ordered; call the Finance Department to get the year-end sales and earnings analysis; call Bob in the Outdoor Department to see if the stadium sign contract has been worked out for my airline client; and make sure the master for the new insurance radio tapes has been sent to Studio D for future use.

8:40–9:30

Arriving at the office, I find three phone messages waiting and the television tapes I ordered. That saves me one call, but I have three new ones, so I've added two to my list.

The first call is from Stan, the ACD (associate creative director) on the airline account, which is very busy at the moment, so it takes priority. Stan tells me he is ready to present the new air cargo mailing piece and trade ad, and asks for a meeting sometime this morning. This is a "hot" project, so we agree to get everyone involved together at 9:30. Hopefully, this will give me enough time to make my calls.

My call to the Outdoor Department is disappointing. Bob is out of town and will not be back for two days. This will delay my letter to the client, but it can't be helped. It is always frustrating to be ready to complete a project and have it delayed because one step in the procedure depends on someone who is not available. Will put this on my calendar for Thursday SURE.

Next, I decide to go see Gloria in Financial to pick up the S&E (Sales & Earnings) report. I'm anxious to see if we made forecast. I think we did, but will feel better when I know for sure. Hooray! We made it. Of course, this means I have what I need to complete a budget report and that is a task that I do not look forward to doing. It comes with the job. Supervisors are responsible for reports. It will have to wait until later in the day (week . . . month?). It is getting close to 9:30 and I still have three calls to make. I eliminate a call from a newspaper representative and ask Cindy, my assistant, to call him and tell him to contact Bernie, the media planner on the airline. I also give Cindy the job of calling the studio to make sure the radio tapes are on file.

One call to go and it's 9:25 and it's busy. Well, I tried. Now to collect Mike (account executive on

the airline) and head for the Creative Department.

9:30–10:30
Stan and Ed (art director) submit copy and layouts for the air cargo mailing piece and trade ad. The copy is right on, but minor revisions are needed on the illustrations. Client meeting set up for the next day to present to the air cargo manager who is hard to please. This meeting is over and it's 10:30. Time to get a few more things out of the way before lunch.

10:30–12:00
Back to my office and two more calls are on my desk. One from Jan (insurance client) and one from Ron (airline client). Call Jan first because it will be a shorter call.

Jan is checking on television tapes and I tell her they're on the way. Jan and I attended a company district sales meeting last week to present the television spots, and we compare notes on the success of the presentation. Jan agrees that the reaction was great and the district managers will be able to sell the campaign to the local agents as part of the new co-op program. I review the status of the co-op newspaper ads and request a copy for the local agents list, by state, for use in organizing slides to be used when the Media Department makes the television buy in March. We review a proposal made by the Research Department and decide it would be best to delay action until next fall. This is an out of town client and much of the business is handled by phone and mail with approximately one or two trips a month to the client's office.

One more call before lunch. Too late! Mike just came in with a problem. It seems the art sent to the outdoor operators for a new outdoor board design is not to scale and will delay the painting of the boards. I have asked Mike to meet with Stan and Ed to determine how this happened and, more important, to make sure it doesn't happen again. A slight error, but one that will cost us valuable time and money. The boards in question were on a tight posting schedule to begin with.

12:00–1:30
Today is the day the agency serves lunch to management in the executive dining room if you make a reservation. It is a good way to see people from other departments whom you don't get a chance to see or talk to on a regular basis. Account supervisors who work on other accounts, for instance. Lunch is usually good, too.

1:30–3:00
Back from lunch. Now to a few more phone calls. An account supervisor's job would be a lot less hectic if we didn't have a phone. Of course, pigeons would take a lot longer.

I talked to George (ACD on the insurance account) about the possibility of changing the end of the new corporate television spot. The president of the company has questioned the appropriateness of showing the agent's sign on a corporate spot. George and John (the producer) have reviewed the situation and there are several alternatives open to us. However, they both feel it is a better spot left the way it is. I asked George to put this in writing so I will have the details to give to the client.

Ron (airline) called with up-to-date information on fares to be featured in a newspaper campaign promoting Florida and to postpone the second insertion of a "Kids Fly Free" campaign. A competitor is lowering fares in our client's markets which is prompting many last minute revisions in our ads.

The next step is to call the print production manager with the latest changes and hope her patience lasts through this latest crisis. This is not an easy job and I know it is terribly frustrating to have ads ready to go and a phone call means holding everything up at least one more day.

3:00–4:45
It's 3:00 and time for another meeting. This one is with Rita (creative director), who is part of the special group that worked on a project involving marketing to women. Meeting lasted longer than I anticipated, but we resolved several problems relating to the assignment of creative personnel to the special group. Part of the problem is that this project is in addition to everyone's current work load. A follow-up meeting was scheduled for next week.

4:45–6:00
It's getting close to quitting time. That's when I get a lot of paperwork done. I usually stay an hour after most people go home. It's surprising how much you can get done when the phone stops ringing. Especially if you're working on a year-end report filled with figures for the client.

Contributed by D'Arcy-MacManus & Masius, St. Louis.

ing campaign, while obtaining other agency services elsewhere. Or, an advertiser may hire an agency's media department to plan and execute a program for advertising that another agency has developed. In each case, a fee is charged for the service provided; the size of the fee is negotiated in terms of the amount of work done.

IN-HOUSE AGENCIES

The **in-house agency,** owned and operated by the advertiser, provides all of the media and creative functions of a full-service agency at a lower cost because all of the profits are pocketed by the advertiser. This not only saves money, it also stabilizes the people working on the account and gives the advertiser greater control over agency activities.

The economic advantages of an in-house agency are particularly apparent in new product work. The development of marketing plans, product names, packages, advertising, and sales promotion is time-consuming and expensive. Since new products provide no revenues during this period, advertising agencies often charge additional fees for this work. An in-house agency can do much of this preliminary work at a lower cost.

Critics of in-house agencies argue that advertisers lose the benefit of experience and an objective viewpoint that independent advertising agencies can provide, creative groups grow stale working on the same product lines, and in-house agencies are unable to attract comparable creative personnel. There is merit in these arguments. Nonetheless, in-house agencies appear to be growing in popularity and will probably continue to grow as advertisers attempt to gain greater control over the spiraling costs of advertising.

CREATIVE BOUTIQUES

During the 1960s, increasing competition led to renewed interest in advertising creativity. Some advertisers felt that full-service agencies were emphasizing other marketing services at the expense of creativity. Simultaneously, members of agency creative services departments felt that their creativity was being hampered by management and some of their best ideas were not being presented to clients because of excessive caution on the part of account mangement. As a result, some highly respected copywriters and art directors (often with covert arrangements with leading clients) left full-service agencies to set up their own shops, known as **creative boutiques.** The creative boutique performs only the creative function, usually for a fee or percentage of the media expenditure.

Creative boutiques reached the peak of their popularity in the late 1960s but had lost much of their appeal by the early 1980s. A number of clients, who were intrigued by the idea of a purely creative shop, found that they still wanted traditional agency services. As a consequence, many of the original boutiques became full-service agencies, as it became apparent that advertising must be coordinated with the rest of the marketing effort. At this point, the future of the creative boutique is uncertain; although in any industry as volatile as the advertising business, they will probably continue as a viable alternative to full-service agencies for some advertisers and creative projects.

ADVERTISING AGENCY COMPENSATION

Advertising agencies are compensated for their services in a way that has been a subject of controversy for years; no evidence suggests the controversy will diminish.

THE AGENCY COMMISSION SYSTEM

Traditionally, advertising agencies have been paid a percentage of the gross billing charged by media and other suppliers. This commission has been 15 percent of gross billing (although outdoor advertisers generally give 16⅔ percent, and some trade publications offer 20 percent). Other commissions may be charged, but 15 percent is almost universal in the United States. Table 3–3 shows how the commission system works. Assume an advertising agency spends $100,000 for an advertiser in television, magazines, or some other media offering the standard 15 percent commission. After the advertisement has run, the media will bill the agency $100,000 *less* 15 percent commission, *less* 2 percent cash discount if the bill is paid within ten days.[9]

Agencies generally pass the 2 percent cash discount along to their clients. Assuming the agency and the client pay promptly, the agency will bill the client $100,000 less the 2 percent cash discount on the net amount, or $98,300.

Historically, commissions from media provided about 65 percent of agency income, although the larger the agency, the higher the proportion of income from media commissions. Even among the

TABLE 3–3   Example of agency commission system

Media charges agency	$100,000
Less: agency commission of 15%	15,000
Equals: cost of media	85,000
Less: 2% cash discount for payment within ten days	1,700
Agency pays media	83,300
Agency charges advertiser	100,000
Less: 2% cash discount	1,700
Advertiser pays agency	98,300
Agency compensation	
Advertiser pays agency	98,300
Agency pays media	83,300
Agency compensation for work	$15,000

[9]The ostensible purpose of the 2 percent cash discount is to encourage prompt payment and reduce the cash requirements of the media. It also serves as a gauge of the financial stability of the advertising agency. The liquidity of agencies that do not pay their media bills in time to qualify for the cash discount is suspect. As a consequence, most media associations actively encourage their members to offer a 2 percent cash discount and use it as an early warning signal.

largest agencies, however, 10 to 25 percent of income came from sources other than media.

In addition to income received from media, advertising agencies also receive direct payment from clients for materials and services such as finished art, comprehensive layouts, television storyboards, supervision of production for outside suppliers, research, design of point-of-sale material, and package design. Generally, the extra charges will be proportionately greater as the size of the agency (and advertiser) decreases, because media commissions are not sufficient to cover the costs of preparing advertising. In some cases, these additional charges are based on agency costs (for example, cost of materials), a flat fee or hourly rate (for point-of-sale material or package design), or a commission on outside services such as commercial production. The particular schedule of charges varies by agency, but is spelled out in the advertiser-advertising agency contract.

Qualification for agency commissions. The commission system is a functional discount paid to advertising agencies for performing services that benefit the media. From media's standpoint, the agency performs the following functions: (a) centralize the servicing of accounts and reduce billing costs; (b) reduce credit risks by screening clients and guaranteeing payment; (c) reduce the media's publication cost by providing materials that meet the media's mechanical specifications; and (d) promote advertising as a form of marketing communication.

Traditionally, media commissions were only granted to *recognized* agencies. To gain recognition, an advertising agency had to have acceptance by individual advertisers and their trade associations.[10] Acceptance was gained by meeting four general criteria: (a) The advertising agency must be a bona fide agency (not owned or controlled by advertisers or media). (b) It must keep all commissions and not rebate to either media or advertiser. (c) The agency must have personnel with the experience and ability to service its clients and promote advertising. (d) The agency must have the financial resources to meet the commitments it makes to media.[11]

Although media observance of these standards was purely voluntary, trade association support carried considerable clout. One consequence was to make it difficult for in-house agencies to gain recognized status since they obviously rebated their commissions to the advertisers who owned them. This restriction did not eliminate in-house agencies, but it did introduce a certain amount of obscurity and deceit into the nature of their financial ownership.

Challenges to the commission system. Despite its widespread use, a number of advertisers and advertising agencies believed that

---

[10]The leading trade associations involved in recognizing advertising agencies were: American Newspaper Publishers Association (ANPA), for most newspapers; Periodical Publishers Association (PPA), for consumer magazines; American Business Press (ABP), for most trade and industrial publications; and Agricultural Publishers Association (APA), for most farm papers.

[11]C. H. Sandage and Vernon Fryburger, *Advertising Theory and Practice*, 9th ed., (Homewood, Illinois: Richard D. Irwin, Inc., 1975), 634–35.

the commission system was inherently wrong because a relationship between the amount of work done by an advertising agency and the compensation it received was not always equitable. For example, two advertising campaigns might require the same amount of agency work to create and produce. Yet, one of the campaigns would spend $100,000 to generate $15,000 in agency commissions, while the second campaign might spend $3 million to generate $450,000 in agency commissions.

In 1955 the Department of Justice brought civil suit against the American Association of Advertising Agencies (the 4 A's) and five leading media associations. The suit alleged that the defendants were violating the Sherman Antitrust Act by: (a) promulgating uniform standards for recognition of advertising agencies; (b) withholding commissions from agencies not recognized; (c) charging gross rates to advertisers, while charging only net rates to advertising agencies; and (d) fixing the commission at 15 percent of the gross rate. In 1956 a consent decree was entered in the U.S. District Court in New York City enjoining and restraining the 4 A's from engaging in the alleged practices. Similar consent decrees were later entered for the media associations involved in the suit. The Department of Justice's suit dealt only with associations of advertising agencies and media; it did not prevent individual media from establishing criteria for the recognition of advertising agencies. Nonetheless, the court action made it possible for advertisers and agencies to work out any compensation agreement they saw fit.

The consent decree on agency compensation was handed down in 1956. Fifteen years later, 45 percent of the leading advertisers were still using the commission system.[12] Current practices in the field involve a variety of compensation systems. Advertisers may use the commission system, negotiate a flat fee with their agencies, apply a cost plus system, or combine commissions and fees. It is not unusual for a given advertising agency to have several different compensation systems with its various clients.

At the heart of the compensation problem is the question of what constitutes a reasonable profit. Unfortunately, there is little agreement on this point. A survey of advertisers and advertising agencies indicates that the majority of advertisers think agencies should have an operating profit before taxes of 10 to 20 percent; others thought 10 percent was too high. On the other hand, advertising agencies considered operating profits of 20 percent and over appropriate.[13] It is doubtful that the question of what constitutes a reasonable profit for advertising agencies will be easily resolved.

NEGOTIATED COMMISSIONS

Some advertising agencies still insist upon a 15 percent media commission; some advertisers refuse to pay it. Young & Rubicam, at one point, resigned the $30 million Bristol-Meyers account because it claimed that their 8.5 percent commission was insufficient to cover costs and produce a profit.

---

[12]*The Gallagher Report*, Vol. 19, (November 1971).
[13]Herb Zeltner, "Sounding Board: Clients, Adman Split on Compensation," 66.

Negotiated commissions take the form of: (a) a stipulated flat reduction in media commissions by advertiser and advertising agency; (b) sliding commissions that are reduced as billing increases beyond a given amount; and (c) commissions with a floor and ceiling profit percentage. When agency profits drop below a specific amount (floor), commissions are increased; when profits rise above a stipulated amount (ceiling), commissions are decreased.

Presumably, negotiated systems take into consideration the needs of the advertisers and advertising agency. In practice, they still present problems because of disagreements regarding the level of agency profits and a reluctance on the part of agencies to reveal their costs as a basis for negotiations.

FEE AND COST-PLUS COMPENSATION SYSTEMS

Fee and cost-plus systems are generally advantageous to the advertiser (client) when substantial sums are spent in relatively high cost media (national consumer magazines and television) and the agency provides few additional marketing services (market planning, research, and preparation of point-of-purchase, or in-store, materials). Such systems are advantageous to the advertising agency when consumer media expenditures are relatively low and substantial noncommissionable marketing services are required.

Fee systems. In a fee system, the advertiser and its agency negotiate a flat sum to be paid to the agency for all work done. The advertising agency estimates the cost (in terms of agency payroll and out-of-pocket expenses) of serving the client during the coming year and adding in a desired profit margin. This total is submitted to the client who either accepts it or starts negotiating. During negotiations, some agency services (for example, marketing research) may be eliminated or the client may agree to have fewer account executives assigned to the account. Negotiations continue until an agreement is reached.

One major advertiser was spending approximately $20 million in major media. Its agency was compensated 15 percent of this amount, or $3 million, through commissions. After negotiating a fee system, the client paid the agency a flat $2 million in fees, and all media commissions were rebated to the client, effecting a savings for the client of $1 million annually. The agency, in this particular instance, was able to negotiate a reduction in service in the areas of: (a) the account group; (b) marketing research; (c) development of sales aids for the sales force; and (d) reduced participation in developing sales promotion materials. As a result, agency costs were substantially reduced so that agency profits, while smaller than before, were still significant. This example points up one major advantage of a fee system: It forces both the client and the advertising agency to reexamine the services provided and reach agreement on the role the advertising agency will play in the client's marketing effort. There are two major disadvantages in a fee system: (a) It gives client management a critical look at the agency's internal compensation and management practices, causing the agency to lose some operating independence. (b) In the name of economy, it sometimes leads to the elimination of services that the client can ill afford to lose.

Cost-plus systems. Cost-plus systems are most often used when media billings are relatively low and a great deal of agency service is required. This happens most often with industrial accounts, new products being prepared for marketing, and circumstances requiring a disproportionate amount of agency help such as preparing brochures, catalogs, and other noncommissionable marketing activities.

In a cost-plus system, the client agrees to pay the agency the cost of its work (employee costs as well as out-of-pocket expenses) plus a certain percentage of this amount (often 25 percent) to cover agency overhead and profit. In practice, the agency and client estimate the amount of work that will be required during the coming year and estimate its cost, usually on a quarter by quarter basis. The client then makes monthly payments against this estimate and periodically (usually quarterly) reviews the estimate with the agency to make sure that actual costs are in line with the estimate. In some cases, the estimate will be revised upward or downward as the year progresses. Table 3–4 shows a simplified cost-plus schedule of charges for an agricultural product account.

The advantages and disadvantages of a cost-plus system are similar to those of the fee system. On the positive side, it forces the

TABLE 3–4 Example of a cost-plus system for an agricultural account

Agency Service		Cost
Corporate management (plans board)		2,250
Account service		94,256
Creative department		126,677
Advertising	76,227	
Collateral material	50,450	
Production		48,450
Inside time	10,670	
Out-of-pocket	37,780	
Media		21,367
Marketing research		5,490
Administrative services		9,236
Supplies		270
Communications (telephone)		2,260
Travel		21,090
	Total	383,886
Plus 25% for unallocatable overhead and profit		95,972
	Total charge	$479,858

Notes:
1. Hourly charges for inside time include salary, fringe benefits, and payroll taxes. Time cards, with a minimum time interval of 15 minutes, were kept by all agency personnel working on the account.
2. Administrative services include accounting, data processing, personnel, agency library, office services, local telephone charges, etc. Charges based on an hourly rate or agreed upon formula.
3. Travel is relatively high because the client was an out-of-town company, and weekly trips to the client's home office were required.

CHAPTER 3 | THE ADVERTISING AGENCY

client and agency to critically examine agency services in relation to client needs. On the negative side, the agency's independence is eroded as the client becomes privy to internal agency cost figures.

Regardless of how the agency is paid—by commissions, a flat fee, cost-plus, or a combination of these methods—the whole area of agency compensation is both sensitive and complex. The creative work of an advertising agency does not roll off of an assembly line like so many Barbie Dolls with a neat price tag affixed to each unit. A creative idea may take a week to develop, or it may take three months of intensive work. A marketing plan may pull together quickly or take months of effort. Because of these variables, mutual trust and respect are essential ingredients in the client-agency relationship. When the client starts to worry that the agency is making too much money, mutual trust is turning sour and the agency is in trouble.

ADVERTISING AGENCY ORGANIZATION

There is a story about a former president of J. Walter Thompson who was reluctant to approve a formal organization chart for the agency despite extreme pressure from the board of directors and key agency executives. A number of organization charts had been submitted to him, but he had rejected them all because he felt they made the agency look like a complex of departments with no regard for the employees.

Finally, he was presented with an organization chart that seemed to answer his objections. The names of virtually every employee in the agency were shown on the chart, with solid lines showing areas of direct authority and dotted lines showing lines of communications.

The president studied the chart for a long time, nodding his head in apparent satisfaction. Then he said, "This is the best organization chart I've seen. It shows our people, and that's what our agency is all about. It's almost right. All we have to do is take out all of those solid and dotted lines."

Although advertising agencies may be organized in different ways, a basic structure underlies most large agencies.

In the very small agency—the one and two person shop—there is no need for departmentalization; the principals do everything. As agencies increase in size, specialization starts to appear in the form of various departments. Hierarchies in management begin to form. Generally speaking, advertising agencies are relatively flat organizations with few levels of management. A major reason is that most advertisers want the top managements of their advertising agencies to be personally involved with their products. As agencies become larger, such intimate involvement becomes impossible. To give the illusion that top management is directly involved, agencies are filled with vice-presidents. The account supervisor on most major products (and many minor ones) carries this title. Some agencies, embarrassed by the profligate use of the title of vice-president, call their key contact personnel *associates* or *partners* in an attempt to imply that they are agency principals. Advertising agencies are not alone in this deception, of course. Law firms, investment houses, banks, and other institutions in which personal contact with clients is a major ingredient of business success follow the same practice.

The widespread use of the title of vice-president among members of the client contact group creates a certain amount of unrest and dissatisfaction with mundane job titles throughout the rest of the agency. Everyone wants to be a vice-president.

Figure 3–3 shows the typical functional organization for a medium-sized to large advertising agency. Several comments need to be made about this form of organization. First, this diagram represents the *formal* organization for purposes of staffing and salary administration. The actual working arrangements consist of a series of informal groups organized around clients' products. For example, assume that account group *A* represents a detergent advertiser. Depending upon the size and importance of the client, the account group may consist of a single account executive or an account supervisor plus a number of account executives. The account executive or supervisor will serve as the coordinator of an informal group, consisting of one or more representatives from each of the agency's functional departments. The resulting work group is diagrammed in Figure 3–4. The account manager has no formal authority over anyone in the group. It is a group of equals, each a specialist. This alone leads to conflict and tension. Since the account manager is ultimately responsible for coordination and meeting deadlines, this person often *assumes* a role of authority which is resented by other members of the group. For this reason, skill in democratic forms of leadership and sensitivity to interpersonal relations are essential.

Second, the creative service division may also be organized in the functional departments shown in Figure 3–3. There is a growing tendency, however, to abolish departments and organize creative service personnel into work groups that contain all of the creative functions.

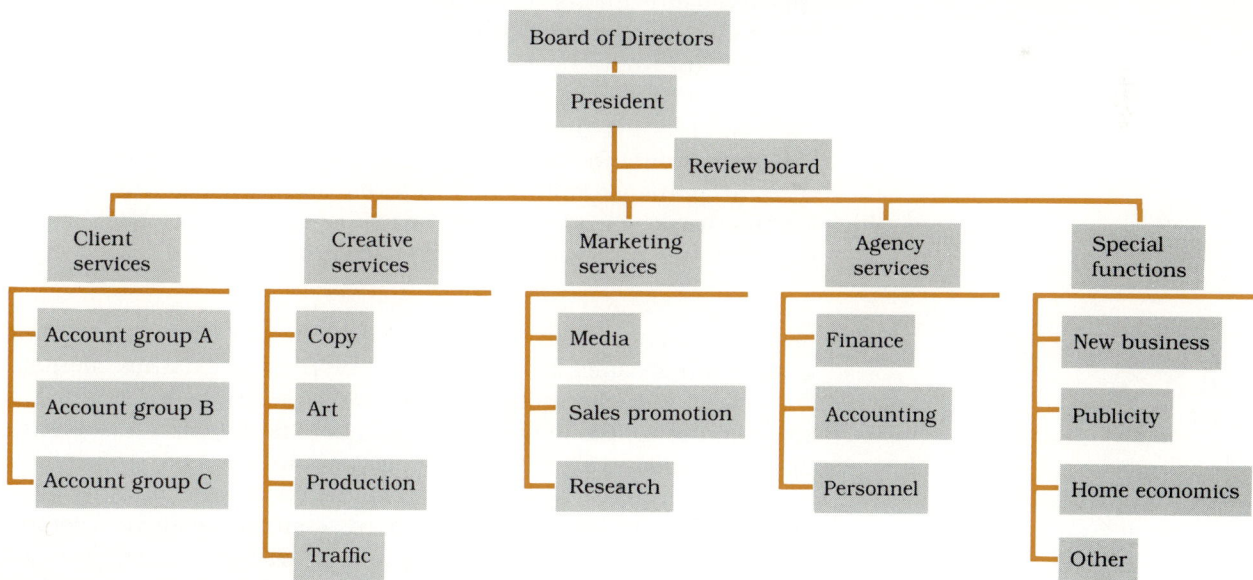

FIGURE 3–3 Typical agency organization by function

CHAPTER 3 | THE ADVERTISING AGENCY

FIGURE 3–4   Agency work group

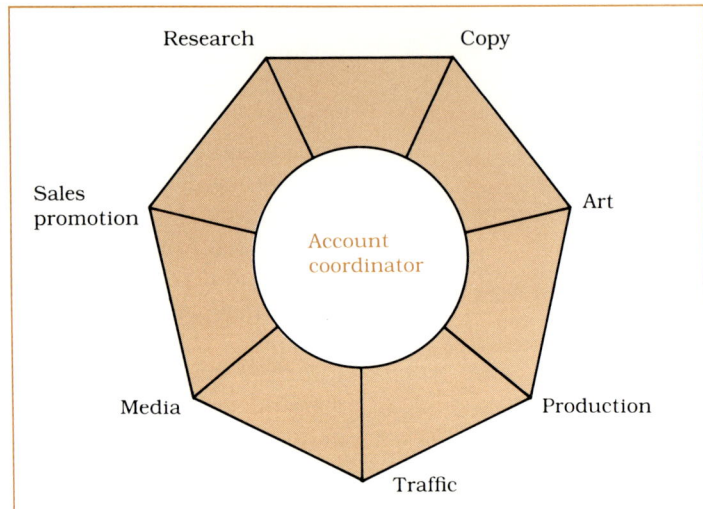

Third, the review board, often called the plans board, generally consists of the agency president and the directors of client, creative, and marketing services. The members review all major plans and creative material prior to its presentation to the client.

Fourth, since the agency works in informal groups, there is a great deal of flexibility in forming new groups as they are needed, and dissolving groups whose tasks have been completed.

Fifth, no hard and fast rules impede who does what in an agency work group or how jobs get done. The emphasis is on performance with little regard to the niceties of organizational protocol. If conflicts and disagreements cannot be resolved in the work group (which is where they should be resolved), they are taken to the directors of the agency divisions. If not resolved there, they are taken to the plans board. In most agencies, anyone in the work group can appeal disagreements to a higher level for resolution. But personnel who consistently resort to this form of conflict resolution generally find that they have no future in the advertising agency business.

The advertising agency work group is a loose organization of experts, all doing their own jobs, tied together by a personal sense of responsibility for their own contributions and coordinated by the account manager and the strictures of the marketing plan. The group's work sounds casual, but it is demanding, backbreaking, and governed by performance and accountability.

HOW AGENCIES SOLICIT BUSINESS

New business is the lifeblood of advertising agencies. Although growth often comes from increased billings of existing clients, the fragility of the client-advertising agency relationship is such that sole reliance on the long-term growth of existing clients is a tenuous basis for plotting an advertising agency's future.

This problem is further complicated by the scarcity of outstanding talent, keeping experienced, competent agency personnel in demand. While it is hard for a person without experience to find a job in an advertising agency, it is easy for someone with agency experience to move to another agency or client organization, often at a higher salary. This has led to intense competition for able, experienced people, particularly in the creative area, and agency salaries have escalated at a rate well above inflation. As a consequence, agency growth is required to create the career opportunities and salary advancements necessary to retain experienced personnel.

Although there is no set pattern for acquiring new clients, essential steps are: (a) obtaining leads; (b) cultivating potential clients; and (c) making a formal presentation.

OBTAINING LEADS

Obtaining leads means identifying clients who are considering, or might consider, an agency change. Sources of leads are as broad as the agency business itself. Common sources are:

1 *Agency principals.* Advertising agency executives are constantly alert for new business opportunities. Through participation in social and civic organizations, they meet business leaders, and they use these contacts to acquaint potential clients with their agency's services and capabilities, build friendships, and cement interpersonal relations. Civic committees and lunches, social games of golf, and participation in charitable organizations often lay the foundation for the active solicitation of a new account.

   Family relationships may also play a role in gaining new business. Advertising is a highly personal business, and it is not uncommon for an advertising account to be given to an agency because of a family connection.

2 *Agency clients.* Satisfied clients recommend their advertising agency to business acquaintances. Often, a company will acquire a subsidiary and arrange for its agency to make a presentation for the subsidiary account.

3 *Agency reputation.* Agencies with a reputation for outstanding creative and marketing skills are constantly approached by clients who are dissatisfied with their present agencies. Thus, a highly successful and widely publicized advertising campaign will inevitably result in inquiries from disgruntled clients of other agencies.

4 *The trade press.* Trade publications, such as *Advertising Age*, regularly report shaky client-agency relationships and publicize major client organizations that are actively seeking a new agency relationship.

5 *Media representatives and other suppliers.* Through their frequent calls on agencies and client organizations, media representatives and other suppliers develop an uncanny sensitivity to evidence suggesting that an agency and its clients are having problems. They report this information to their other customer agencies.

6 *New business groups.* Most major advertising agencies have a new business group, consisting of an agency executive and support personnel, that systematically seeks out and establishes contacts with client organizations their agency would like to serve.

7 *Advertising.* Strange as it may seem, few agencies use advertising to attract clients. However, advertising may be a source of leads for the few that do. The main reasons most agencies do not advertise are: (a) agency service is highly personal and can best be communicated through personal selling. (b) Agency profit margins are relatively low and do not allow for the cost of a major advertising campaign.

Some advertising agencies use an organized system to identify and pursue leads; others handle the issue on a sporadic basis.

CULTIVATING POTENTIAL CLIENTS

Once a lead has been identified, the next step is to cultivate the potential client. This may be as simple as meeting with a client in order to formalize a working agreement for an account that has been proffered, or as complex as planning a systematic campaign to become acquainted with key client personnel and impress them with the scope of the agency's services and accomplishments. The ultimate purpose is either to ask directly for the account or for an opportunity to make a formal agency presentation. Sometimes, the agency does such a thorough job at this point that, even though they are invited to make a competitive presentation against other agencies, the outcome is a foregone conclusion. Agencies have also been known to become overconfident, offer a disappointing presentation, and lose the account.

MAKING A FORMAL PRESENTATION

Once an agency has received an invitation to make a formal presentation, the real work begins. The two types of agency presentations are: agency and speculative.

The agency presentation. In an **agency presentation,** the advertising agency presents information about itself, emphasizing those aspects of its operation that judgment and research indicate will be of most interest to the potential client. Such presentations are often elaborate explanations of how the agency operates and how the account will be staffed. The agency shows examples of its past successes, explains its philosophy of advertising, and details how the unique skills and talents of its staff will be put to work for the client organization.

The speculative presentation. In a **speculative presentation,** the agency shows specifically how it will solve client problems. These presentations involve a great deal of research designed to identify problems of the industry and the client in question. Commercials and print advertising are prepared and produced in rough or finished form. Packages may be designed (if appropriate), and sales promotion programs developed. Preparation for such presentations requires thousands of dollars and untold hours by agency personnel.

The American Association of Advertising Agencies frowns on speculative presentations, but most agencies make them because most clients expect them.

Once a new client has been acquired, a detailed working agreement, specifying responsibilities and methods of compensation, is negotiated and a contract signed. Client-agency contracts are usually open-end contracts that can be cancelled by either party, after providing a 30- or 90-day notice.

SUMMARY

Advertising agencies range in size from superagencies with billings of over $2 billion to small operations with total billings of less than $50,000. The business is highly concentrated, with less than 5 percent of the agencies accounting for over two-thirds of agency gross income.

A number of changes have taken place in the advertising agency business within the past two decades: (a) Corporate advertising departments have taken over more traditional agency functions in order to reduce costs. (b) Advertising agencies are becoming more business oriented. (c) A failure to develop creative talent has caused a decline in advertising creativity. (d) A trend toward giantism is underway.

Since the 1960s, some advertisers have insisted that agencies tailor services to client needs. This has given rise to the following agency forms: (a) full-service agencies that offer a wide range of marketing services; (b) modular agencies, which are full-service agencies that sell their services on a piecemeal or a la carte basis; (c) in-house agencies, owned and controlled by client organizations; and (d) creative boutiques that provide only creative services, usually for a fee or an agreed upon percentage of media billing.

Traditionally, advertising agencies were compensated by commissions paid by media, usually 15 percent of billing. Media and advertising agency associations supported this form of compensation. In 1955 the Department of Justice brought suit against leading advertising and media associations for violation of antitrust, and in 1956 a consent decree was obtained abolishing standard commission practices. Since then, a variety of compensation systems have emerged. The most common ones involve some combination of negotiated commissions, fee systems, and cost-plus arrangements. Many agencies operate on various compensation systems with different clients, or may use several compensation systems with the same client organization.

Most advertising agencies are formally organized on a functional basis. However, the actual work in an advertising agency is usually done in informal work groups that are coordinated by an account manager and contain representatives of the various functional groups in the agency.

New business is the lifeblood of advertising agencies. The steps to follow to acquire new clients are: (a) obtaining leads; (b) cultivating potential clients; and (c) making a formal presentation. When a new client has been acquired, a working agreement is negotiated and a contract signed.

REVIEW QUESTIONS

1 Identify and explain the changes that are taking place in the advertising agency business.
2 What are the reasons for the decline in advertising creativity?
3 Identify and describe the major types of advertising agencies that are currently serving the market.
4 What are the advantages and disadvantages of in-house advertising agencies?
5 An advertising agency spends $300,000 for a client in a medium that pays a 15 percent commission and a 2 percent cash discount for payment within ten days. The agency pays the medium within the prescribed cash discount period. How much does the agency pay the medium? How much does the client pay the agency? What is the agency's compensation for its work?
6 Explain why many people consider the traditional 15 percent commission system inequitable.
7 Briefly explain the major forms of agency compensation.
8 Identify the conditions under which fee and cost-plus compensation systems are advantageous to the advertiser. To the advertising agency.
9 What are the primary advantages and disadvantages of fee and cost-plus systems of compensation?
10 Distinguish between the formal organization used by most advertising agencies and agency work groups.

DISCUSSION QUESTIONS

1 Assume you are the personnel director of an advertising agency interviewing graduates on a university campus to fill a position as an account executive. What kinds of personal characteristics and educational background would you look for in applicants?
2 Assume you are the president of an advertising agency that has had a good client-agency relationship with a regional soft-drink advertiser for fifteen years. You are invited to make a presentation for the account of a large, national soft-drink advertiser. Media billings for the national account are several times larger than those for your current client. How would you handle the situation?
3 Assume you are the president of an advertising agency that is considering a merger in order to increase billings and gain an office in a major city in which you are not now represented. What are some of the major factors that should enter into your decision?

PROBLEM

In 1981 *Advertising Age* selected Henderson Advertising of Greenville, North Carolina, as the agency of the year for "its daring concept of building an agency with big city talents and handling major national accounts—far away from the big city."

Henderson Advertising was founded as a one-man shop by Jim Henderson in 1946. Prior to going into business for himself, Henderson worked in sales promotion and advertising for General Foods, and as an account executive for an advertising agency in Denver.

Today, Henderson Advertising bills $54 million, double its 1978 amount. The agency employs 135 people, many of whom came from major

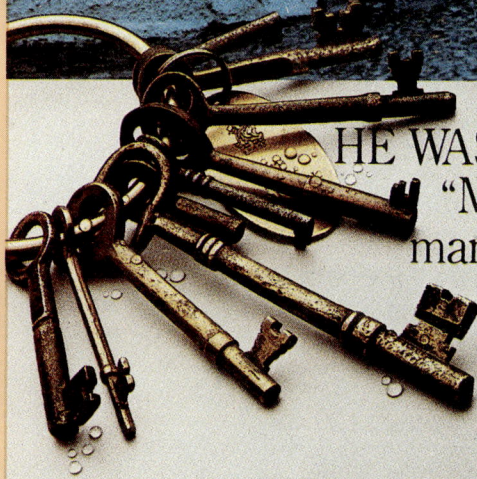

HE WAS never elected. But every night "Mayor" Orlo McBain is the last man to walk the streets of Culross, Scotland. He checks a knob, closes a gate and goes his way. The good things in life stay that way.

Preferred for smoothness, Dewar's® never varies.

Authentic.
The Dewar Highlander

BLENDED SCOTCH WHISKY · 86.8 PROOF · © 1981 SCHENLEY IMPORTS CO., N.Y., N.Y.

PLATE 1 Mood and tradition are used to emphasize the never-changing quality of Dewar's White Label. (Courtesy Schenley Imports Co.)

PLATE 2   Public service and devotion to the performing arts are the themes of this corporate advertisement by Phelps Dodge. (Courtesy Phelps Dodge Corp.)

PLATE 3   In this ad, Volkswagen Jetta capitalizes on the styling and advertising of a great German car—the BMW. (Courtesy Volkswagen of America, Inc.)

PLATE 4 Perrier is represented as a delicious drink that can be used in a variety of ways, not only a mineral water. (Courtesy Great Waters of France, Inc.)

PLATE 5 The setting, people, and crystal remind us that true elegance is simplicity. (Courtesy Lenox China)

PLATE 6 A traditional name and symbol, along with a tradition of excellence, are used to introduce Budweiser Light. (Courtesy Anheuser Busch Co.)

There are only two reasons to buy Laurent Perrier:

You have acquired a taste for exquisite champagne.

You want your friends to know it.

Imported by Almadén Imports Sole U.S. Agents
©Almadén Vineyards, Inc. 1980, San Jose, Ca.

PLATE 7   Rich colors and two simple phrases blend quality and prestige into a dramatic ad. (Courtesy Almadén Vineyards, Inc.)

PLATE 8   Whirlpool offers a clear, simple statement of a corporate philosophy that promises quality. (Courtesy Whirlpool Corp.)

PLATE 9   The reference figures in this ad are not celebrities; however, they represent the target market for Rums of Puerto Rico. (Courtesy Rums of Puerto Rico)

PLATE 10   The photograph tells the story of America's Storyteller. (Copyright © Eastman Kodak Company. Reprinted courtesy of Eastman Kodak Co.)

PLATE 11   Luxurious styling, price, and technology are skillfully woven together in this Timex ad. (Copyright © Timex Corporation. Used by permission of Timex Corp.)

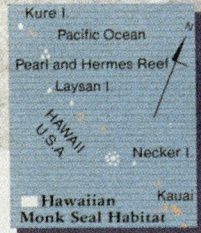

Photographed by David Cavagnaro. *Hawaiian Monk Seal: Genus: Monachus Species: schauinslandi Adult weight: Approximately 172kg (male); 272kg (female). Adult size: Approximately 2.1m (male); 2.3m (female). Habitat: Only among Leeward Hawaiian Islands, a string of tiny coral and rock islets extending over 1,000 miles northwest from the main islands. Surviving number: About 500.*

Wildlife as Canon sees it: A photographic heritage for all generations.

The Hawaiian monk seal is one of the world's few true living fossils. Unaffected by evolution for 15 million years, these shy creatures now survive only on remote rocky Pacific islets far from civilization. And they are in very real danger of disappearing.

There would be no way to bring the Hawaiian monk seal back if it were to vanish from the face of the earth. Photography offers a way to record and help save this living fossil and the rest of wildlife for posterity.

As a scientific research tool, photography can show how the Hawaiian monk seal lives in its natural habitat, thus giving wildlife conservationists the information they need to save it.

Perhaps more important, photography is an effective way to convey to people the rare beauties of creation. Words alone can never equal the contribution to a deeper understanding of wildlife evident in this dramatic natural habitat photograph of a Hawaiian monk seal mother and pup.

And understanding is perhaps the single most important factor in saving the Hawaiian monk seal and all of wildlife.

New F-1

New FD 300mm F/2.8L

Canon
Images for all time

PLATE 12   A superb, detailed photograph says all there is to say about the Canon telephoto lens. (Courtesy Canon, Inc.)

PLATE 13 A well-selected reference figure (Orson Welles) and a memorable slogan—"Paul Masson will sell no wine before its time" — tie in and reinforce a successful television campaign. (Courtesy Paul Masson Vineyards)

"Experts say Paul Masson Cabernet Sauvignon is a mature, complex wine, with nice wood. What they're trying to say is . . . it tastes good."

Paul Masson will sell no wine before its time.

Paul Masson Vineyards, Saratoga, California © 1980

PLATE 14 An excellent example of a long-running campaign in which DeBeers makes diamonds the symbol of love. (Courtesy DeBeers Inc.)

A diamond isn't the only thing about us that sparkles.

I know love is supposed to be something personal, just between the two of us. But we can't help sharing it with the world. Sometimes we even try to hide our feelings. Especially in a crowd of people. But as soon as our eyes meet, there's a certain way we smile at each other. And anyone can look at us and tell we're head over heels in love. So we really didn't need a diamond to say what's in our future. We wanted one because it says what's in our hearts.

A diamond is forever.

To give you some idea of diamond values, the half-carat ring shown here (enlarged for detail) is worth about $670. Diamond values will vary according to color, clarity, cut and weight. Ask your jeweler for the free booklet, "A Diamond Is Forever." De Beers Consolidated Mines, Ltd.

WHEN AMERICAN BUSINESS HITS THE ROAD,
AMERICAN BUSINESS PROFITS AT HILTON.

HILTON
AMERICA'S BUSINESS ADDRESS™

PLATE 15   Luxury is combined with masculinity as Hilton zeroes
in on the business market. (Courtesy Hilton Hotels Corp.)

agency centers such as New York and Chicago. The agency handles a number of local, regional, and national accounts, including the Homelite Division of Textron, Shakespeare Sporting Goods, Texize, and the 3-M Company's Jack Rabbit photo finishing.

In describing the philosophy that has guided his agency, Henderson says, "I'm a perfectionist that can't stand mediocrity."

ASSIGNMENT

1 Based on the information given, what personal beliefs and characteristics do you think Henderson has that have contributed to his success?
2 Do you believe that Henderson could have been equally successful in establishing an advertising agency in any town of comparable size to Greenville, North Carolina? If not, what characteristics do you think Greenville has that contributed to the success of Henderson's agency?
3 Henderson started his agency in 1946. Due to the changes taking place in the advertising business today, do you believe it would be possible for someone with comparable experience to establish a one man agency in 1983 and achieve comparable success? Why or why not?

4

The Marketing Plan

THE CRUCIAL ELEMENT—PLANNING

President Kennedy is reputed to have said, "Planning is everything."
In the practice of marketing, this often seems to be the case. Unfortunately, not all plans are well conceived nor well executed, and even
the best can turn to ashes because of uncontrollable variables. Yet,
planning is a crucial element in marketing success. Successful products don't just happen. Neither do great advertisements. Products
become successful through a careful assessment of marketing opportunities and the thoughtful use of company resources.

GENERAL MILLS

General Mills spends over $170 million a year advertising its consumer products. The importance of developing advertising plans is
summarized in the following quotation.

> At virtually every company with a product-management system,
> product managers are responsible for formulating an annual plan for
> their brands. At General Mills, planning is a three-month process
> that begins with an exercise familiar to every business-school
> graduate—identification of key issues. (How can we get the most for
> our advertising dollars? How do we continue to resist the inroads
> from private label brands?) Then comes a major business review—an
> analysis of all the research data on the brand and competition . . .
> Out of the key issues and business review comes the plan—a budget,
> really, that includes a marketing overview, the brand's competitive
> position, a sales forecast, an itemization of the costs it will take to
> meet it, and the creative, advertising, pricing, and trade tactics. The
> final part of the plan spells it all out in dollars.
>   The product manager submits the plan to—and negotiates it
> with—his boss, a marketing director, who has several product
> managers reporting to him, and his boss's boss, a division manager.
> These upper-level marketers make sure that the plan is reasonable
> and workable and that together with other plans in their purview
> meets the company's larger goals. . . .

Once a plan is approved, executing it and accomodating it to any changes in the marketplace becomes the product manager's responsibility.[1]

How much importance does General Mills' management place on the planning and execution functions of their product managers? Consider the following:

When General Mills completed a ten-story tower at its suburban Minneapolis headquarters last summer, the company discovered that not all the telephones could be installed at once. "Hook up the product managers first," a senior executive ordered. "The business can't run without them."[2]

What are the results of this emphasis on planning? General Mills achieved over $4.8 billion in sales and advertising through products exemplified by the introductory advertisement for Betty Crocker International Noodles shown in Figure 4–1.

PROCTER & GAMBLE

Crest toothpaste burst into the dental care market with all the subtlety of an atomic bomb. Spearheaded by massive door-to-door sampling, publicized by heavy consumer advertising extolling the benefits of fluoride, and supported by the endorsement of the American Dental Association, Crest made American consumers cavity conscious. "Look, Mom! No cavities" became a national byword. But it didn't happen by chance.

Procter & Gamble carefully identified cavities and expensive dental work as a major consumer concern. They developed a product containing fluoride, a compound effective in inhibiting cavities; then they postponed the product introduction while they carefully amassed the clinical tests necessary to obtain the approval of the American Dental Association for their advertising claims. The success of Crest is an outstanding example of thorough planning.

---

[1]Ann M. Morrison, "The General Mills Brand of Managers," *Fortune*, 12 January 1981, 102–3.
[2]Ibid., 99.

Nor is Crest an exception in Procter & Gamble's stable of products. Charmin, Ivory, Scope, Cheer, Camay, Secret, Gleem, Tide, Cascade, Crisco, Comet, Duncan Hines, Folger's, Oxydol, Pampers, Head & Shoulders, Sure, and Spic & Span are household words. Success seems to be such a habit at Procter & Gamble that many believe P&G has a secret. They do. An article published on the subject states:

> That secret, in a word, is thoroughness. Procter & Gamble manages every element of its business with a painstaking precision that most organizations fail to approach. Thoroughness extends to the careful and tenacious recruitment of employees, the development of a much admired executive corps, the design of manufacturing facilities, and the creation and testing of products. By the time a product gets to

the marketing stage, the thorough preparation through all the prior stages has already endowed it with an edge on competition.[3]

Every P&G product is developed and guided into the marketplace by a thorough marketing plan.

THE SCOPE OF PLANNING

Few topics in marketing and management have received as much attention as planning. In most management texts, planning is treated as one of the primary functions of management. Too frequently, the planning is haphazard, and many so-called plans represent little more than the thoughtless perpetuation of past management errors. This point is dramatized in Theodore Levitt's well-known and often quoted essay, "Marketing Myopia."[4] Leon Winer has pointed out: "The biggest problem in marketing is *planning*. Many companies have a marketing 'plan,' yet few of these plans represent any real planning."[5]

Much of the literature on marketing deals with top management decisions that are based on the strategy a company should use to determine its competitive markets, internal organization, and application of resources to insure survival and growth. Thus, Peter Drucker emphasizes the importance of determining what business a company is, or should be, in.[6] Alfred P. Sloan, Jr., generally considered the architect of General Motors' success, is quoted as claiming he made only three important decisions in his years at General Motors: organization of the company; financial controls; and product policy.

Another side to marketing occupies most of the time and energy. It is the planning, development, and execution of marketing activities for existing products. Advertising and other mass communication activities are rooted in this planning, and this activity determines the success or failure of the products that fill retail shelves. The product marketing plan, with its objectives, strategies, and tactics, gives direction to the day-to-day marketing activities that influence consumers in their buying practices.

THE PRODUCT MARKETING PLAN

Since the marketing plan is essentially a mass communications document, it is generally prepared or supervised by the marketing manager. Although the sales plan is usually a separate document that details the activities of the sales force, technically it is a part of the product marketing plan. One major reason the two documents are prepared separately is that many companies market a number of products that are handled by the same sales force. Thus, there may

---

[3]Peter Vanderwicken, "P&G's Secret Ingredient," *Fortune* (July 1974): 75ff.

[4]Theodore Levitt, "Marketing Myopia," in *Modern Marketing Strategy*, E. C. Bursk and J. F. Chapman, eds. (Cambridge, Massachusetts: Harvard University Press, 1964), 24–48.

[5]Leon Winer, "Are You Really Planning Your Marketing," *Journal of Marketing* (January 1965): 1–8.

[6]Peter Drucker, *Management* (New York: Harper & Row, Publishers, 1974), 86–91.

be a number of marketing plans (one for each product) but only one sales plan, which allocates sales activity to the various products as needed. As a result, the marketing manager for one product may be competing with the marketing managers of other company products for sales force attention. Ultimately, if this competition becomes too strong and makes excessive demands on the sales force's time, top management must decide how to best allocate sales force time. In a single product company, the sales plan may indeed be a part of the basic marketing document.

THE TIME FRAME

Marketing plans may be either long-range or short-term documents. Long-range plans often cover a period of five or more years; plans of less than five years are considered short-range. In this text the marketing plan is a short-range plan, usually covering a one-year period. Some marketing practitioners believe the plan should cover at least a three year period and be updated and extended on an annual basis. This would provide continuity for the marketing program; and by forcing the planner to look further ahead, it would encourage a more careful consideration of marketing decisions. A new planning period always brings pressure for change, and successful advertising themes may be prematurely discarded. Nonetheless, since marketing conditions change so rapidly, most marketing practitioners opt for a one-year plan because they consider a three-year plan a time-consuming waste of effort. Plans extending beyond one year tend to be inflexible and become difficult to change even though the marketing situation may require a redirection of effort.

Regardless of the time frame chosen, all marketing plans require constant reexamination to make sure that environmental changes have not made them obsolete.

THE FUNCTION OF THE MARKETING PLAN

While the purpose of the marketing plan is to provide guidance for future marketing activities, it also serves several other functions within the organization.

1 Brings together all important facts, conclusions, and operating decisions which bear on the marketing problem and its solution.
2 Provides a complete operating guide for all personnel working on the product, within the advertiser's organization and participating organizations, such as the company's advertising agency.
3 Provides a summary of basic facts and conclusions for review by new personnel as well as those who are not directly involved in the preparation or implementation of the plan.
4 Establishes benchmarks for judging marketing and advertising accomplishments.

In addition to these key functions, the preparation, at least once each year, of a comprehensive marketing plan offers these additional values.

1 Encourages clear and logical analysis of marketing problems by bringing various elements of the problems and their solutions into an orderly sequence—problem definition to the setting of objectives to proposed solutions and the selection of means to achieve objectives.

2 Provides a framework for viewing problems objectively.

3 Forces the author, or authors, of the plan to dig deeply into the product, its market, and the product's problems and opportunities.

4 Helps identify gaps in available information, or weak links in the chain of logic leading to recommended actions.

5 Sets apart each major decision or judgment upon which the detailed plan is based, facilitating critical appraisal of each element and decreasing the danger of continuing past activities without careful, periodic review.

The product marketing plan serves as a control center for the effective management of all aspects of a company's marketing activities.

A NOTE ON TERMINOLOGY

No universal terminology can be used to describe the concepts in a marketing plan. Instead, the profusion of terms include: goals, objectives, strategies, plans, tactics, copy platform, image, program, promotion, sales promotion, and merchandising. Some are used interchangeably, and some have unique, highly idiosyncratic meanings. To avoid confusion, some terms used in the following material are defined below.

☐ **Objective** is the end result that is to be achieved in a specific period of time. The statement of objectives at any level (that is, marketing objectives, media objectives, sales-promotion objectives) always identifies *what* is to be accomplished, not how it is to be accomplished. Objective and **goal** are often used synonymously.

☐ **Strategy** is a decision explaining *how* the objectives are to be accomplished. Thus, strategy statements communicate the principles used in selecting and utilizing various marketing techniques or devices (for example, marketing strategy, media strategy, and copy strategy).

☐ **Plan** can be used in two ways. When preceded by the word *marketing*, it refers to the entire document. When it is preceded by such words as *advertising, media,* or *copy*, it refers to the detailed presentation of recommended action. This latter use of the word *plan* is synonymous with the term **tactics**. (Academicians tend to use the word *tactics*, while practitioners tend to use the word *plan*.)

☐ **Sales promotion** is the provision of special incentives to consumers, the trade, the sales force, or to other activities designed to stimulate action by one of these groups (excluding advertising, packaging, publicity, and normal pricing). Point-of-purchase material is considered sales promotion. By convention, advertising agencies often use the word *merchandising* when they mean sales promotion, but this is technically an improper use of the term. *Merchandising* refers to the activities of merchandise houses, the original term for department stores. Its original meaning referred to the selection, pricing, display, and promotion of the goods, or merchandise, offered by these stores. The retail trade still uses it in this way. However, advertisers and advertising agencies have appropriated the word and use it as a synonym for sales promotion.

☐ **Advertising** includes only paid media advertising, including direct mail.

☐ **Publicity** is a form of promotion. It differs from advertising because it is not paid for at standard rates, and the sponsor is not identified. Usually, publicity appears (unidentified as such) in the editorial or news columns of printed media or the noncommercial portion of radio or television programs.[7] Another term, *public relations*, is not used in connection with the marketing of a product, but is often used in describing the communications activities of a company. It is a broader term than publicity and involves a variety of practices designed to build good relations between a company and the various publics with which it deals. Public relations may involve publicity, advertising, or a number of other techniques in accomplishing its objectives.

A NOTE ON STYLE

The main body or text of the marketing plan should be as concise as possible—neither an outline of key points nor a written transcript of an oral presentation. Style and organization should be uniform throughout. Language should be clear and specific and should avoid clichés or jargon that are unique to advertising, marketing, or the particular field for which the plan is written. It is a document of communication that should be comprehensible to readers who may not have the unique background or specialized knowledge of the marketing plan's author.

The plan should *flow* smoothly from one point to the next and from one section to the next. Formal structuring of the text, using subheads and titles, is usually the best way to achieve a clear progression of ideas without excessive wordiness at transition points.

Finally, the marketing plan is *not* a "sales pitch." Its persuasiveness should arise from its real strengths—knowledge, analysis, logic, incisiveness, and imagination—not from irresponsible one-sided enthusiasm.

CONTENT OF THE MARKETING PLAN

The marketing plan is a systematic document that proceeds from the general to the specific—from an assessment of the marketing environment (referred to as the **market review** or **situational analysis**) to a detailed summary of the marketing budget. Each step logi-

---

[7]S. W. Dunn and A. M. Barban, *Advertising: Its Role in Modern Marketing* (Hinsdale, Illinois: The Dryden Press, 1974), 9.

cally leads to the next, and each specific marketing recommendation is firmly rooted in the material that precedes it.

A marketing plan is not a long document. In most cases it does not exceed fifteen to twenty single-spaced, typewritten pages, including tables and exhibits. The main text of a relatively simple plan can usually be handled effectively in less than ten single-spaced pages. The marketing plan represents a distillation of the relevant marketing facts and judgments that influence the marketing program. A great deal of data may be examined in order to filter out what is relevant, but only that material which bears directly on marketing decisions will find its way into the marketing plan. A single table, for example, may result from an analysis of many work sheets of basic data. These work sheets are usually included in a back-up marketing facts book that serves as supportive data, should it be needed. This marketing facts book becomes a repository for the detailed history of the market and the product's performance in that market.

The marketing plan for an established product usually contains the following parts:

1 Market review
2 Problems and opportunities
3 Marketing objectives
4 Marketing strategy
5 Advertising objectives
6 Advertising strategy
7 Copy strategy
8 Copy plan
9 Media strategy
10 Media plan
11 Sales promotion strategy
12 Sales promotion plan
13 Special objectives, strategies, and plans
14 Budget summary
15 Schedule of activities

The special objectives, strategies, and plans section (item 13) refers to marketing variables such as product, packaging, pricing, publicity, and marketing research that may not be a part of the marketing plan for an established product. If the product is a new product, the marketing strategy section should be followed by sections devoted to product objectives, strategy, and plan; or packaging objectives, strategy, and plan; and so on. With an established product, these variables are usually givens; unless they are to be changed in some significant way, there is no need for objectives, strategies, and plans for them.

In the following material, each major section of the marketing plan will be described and clarified. This material, designed to show you how to write a marketing plan, should be approached in three ways: (a) Read it all the way through in order to get an impression

CHAPTER 4 | THE MARKETING PLAN

of the various parts and how they fit together. (b) Study each section of the market plan in order to understand its purpose and construction. (c) Use this material as a guide for preparing a marketing plan of your own.

The only way to learn to write marketing plans is to write them, again and again. Appendix 1 at the end of the book shows a marketing plan for a fictitious product. From this example, you can see how the various parts of the plan fit together, and how the material flows from section to section.

THE MARKET REVIEW

The market review is the first section of the marketing plan, providing the factual basis for the definition of problems and opportunities, marketing objectives, and marketing strategies that follow it. Its purpose is to summarize the relevant information that will shape marketing decisions.

The preparation of a marketing review is not simple and routine. This part of the marketing plan is critical, and its value depends wholly on the analyst's ability to select those facts needed to understand the current situation, be objective in selecting and reporting these facts, and report them in a concise, intelligible manner for a reader who is not intimately involved in marketing the product on a day-to-day basis.

Generalizing about the content of the marketing review section is difficult. The dynamics of individual markets vary widely for different products, and there are major distinctions in the kinds and amount of information available to the marketing analyst. For example, the analyst for a grocery or drug store product that has access to A.C. Nielsen data will have information on: (a) bimonthly national and regional sales for the industry and for selected competitors; (b) market share data nationally, and by region, county size, and store type; (c) pricing, promotions, and retail inventories; and (d) special analyses such as the effect of shelf facings on market share. By contrast, the analyst who does not have access to the A.C. Nielsen service may have only company sales records, rough estimates of market share, and possibly local reports of product performance provided by media surveys of brand preferences in major markets. Similarly, the marketing planner who has recently completed a test market, promotion test, or major consumer survey will have relevant data to include in the market review section that will not be available to the planner who has not conducted such activities.

The first step in preparing the marketing review is the development of a checklist from which relevant information can be selected. Such a checklist is given in Appendix 2.[8]

The purpose of the marketing review section is to describe the current marketing situation. Historical data should be summarized and used only if it explains or highlights the present market condition and trends. For example, an analysis of historical data may show that the total market or the brand share is increasing or de-

---

[8]Herbert West, *Advertising Agency Magazine*, 10 May 1957.

creasing at a regular, accelerating, or decelerating rate. This fact may have a profound effect on forecasts of the market and on brand performance. Generally, however, the marketing review concentrates on developments in the market since the last marketing plan, thereby focusing on developments of the past year.

The following outline shows the major areas of interest from which relevant facts are extracted in the preparation of the marketing review section.

THE MARKET

1 Definition of the relevant market. For example, if the marketing plan is being prepared for a dog food product, it should explain what part of the dog food market is considered relevant. Is it the total market for dog food, or a specific segment such as canned, moist, or dry dog foods? If it is dry dog food, is the marketer primarily concerned with baked products, meals, kibbles, snacks, or some combination of these types?
2 Market size and growth trends.
3 Forecast of market growth.
4 Makeup of market by product type, brand, package size, price, and other relevant characteristics.
5 Distribution of the total market by region, season, city or county size, sales by outlet type, and so on.
6 Significant trends or changes in any of the above areas.

COMPETITIVE POSITION

Frequently, key points can best be emphasized by contrasting the brand's strengths or weaknesses with that of competition. Relevant considerations are:

1 Product quality, both technical and as judged by consumer tests.
2 Pricing, sizes available, and packaging features.
3 Distribution of the product category in retail outlets as well as the distribution for individual brands and the various package sizes.
4 Brand shares of market and/or per capita consumption data. If possible, this information should be examined for the total market (outlet type, geographic regions, and so on).
5 Trends or recent changes in any of the above areas.

THE CONSUMER

1 The size of the consumer market in terms of persons, households, or families (whichever is the most relevant).
2 Frequency of purchase, usage rates, trial, repurchase rates, and so on.
3 Definition of the consumer market by socio-economic groups and by socio-psychological characteristics. This data, combined with usage rates, serves to identify target markets.

CHAPTER 4 | THE MARKETING PLAN

4 Consumers' knowledge and/or attitudes toward the product category and individual brands.

5 Consumer usage habits. This includes such things as how, when, and where it is used, where the product is consumed, and so on.

6 Factors influencing brand selection. Who within the family selects, purchases, and uses the product? What are the decision patterns for the brand?

7 Trends or recent changes in any of the above factors.

DEALERS, DISTRIBUTORS, BROKERS

1 Buying patterns, including such characteristics as "seasonal loading."

2 Attitudes toward the company, its product, pricing, advertising, and other aspects of the company's marketing program.

3 Mark ups, promotional practices, and so on.

4 Trends or new developments in the above areas.

ADVERTISING HISTORY

This information should be obtained for the company's brand as well as for competition.

1 Advertising expenditures, in total, per unit or case, and as a percentage of sales. If possible, this information should be broken down by markets, regions, seasonal periods, package sizes, and other relevant considerations such as flavor, models, and so on.

2 Copy. An analysis and comparison should be made of basic appeals, claims, themes, and the mood or tone of presentation.

3 Media. An analysis should be made of the major media used, media mix, coverage, reach, frequency, scheduling, selectivity among primary target groups, and media efficiency.

4 Advertising results. Analysis should be made of any copy tests, media tests, research findings on awareness, registration of specific selling point, attitudes, and so on.

SALES PROMOTION

Again, this information should be analyzed for the company's own brand as well as for competition, insofar as competitive information is available.

1 Types and amounts of sales promotion activity.

2 Estimated promotional expenditures in total (item, region, and season).

3 Traceable results of past promotions in terms of trade and sales force comments, special pricing, displays, retail advertising, and consumer action.

4 Trade attitudes toward various forms of promotion for the product category.

Earlier, it was pointed out that the marketing review should be objective. This point is worth reemphasizing. The marketing review is not the place to defend a recommended course of action or to be overly optimistic, enthusiastic, or persuasive.

PROBLEMS AND OPPORTUNITIES

This section of the marketing plan is linked directly to the marketing review section and consists of the conclusions derived from it. It appears as a separate section for two reasons: (a) to highlight key findings by setting them apart from the background analysis; and (b) to allow additional latitude for interpreting the meaning and implications of these findings.

The problems and opportunities section provides the bases for the marketing objectives as well as major points of marketing, advertising, copy, media, and promotion strategy. Points appearing in this section generally fall into one of the following three groups: (a) identification of specific marketing problems; (b) identification of specific marketing opportunities; and (c) basic conclusions or judgments that have a major bearing on the action that will be recommended in later sections.

This section of the report should be quite brief. All major points can usually be made concisely on a single page since they have been mentioned in the marketing review section and represent key conclusions from the foregoing analysis.

Examples of the kinds of conclusions that might be drawn in this section are shown below in terms of: general marketing, advertising, and sales promotion.

General Marketing Conclusions

We conclude that investment spending in behalf of the product in 19xx is not warranted because of: (a) competitive weaknesses in the product itself; and (b) disappointing results of the heavy spending tests in Nashville and Tulsa last year.

Analysis of retail distribution indicates that there is an attractive profit opportunity in the introduction of a new package size in the 12- to 18-ounce range. This conclusion is augmented by the facts that: (a) 50 percent of consumer purchases are of multiple packages; and (b) a package in this size range introduced by a major competitor last year has achieved widespread distribution and currently accounts for 30 percent of their sales.

The results of the pricing test in Des Moines has, thus far, failed to provide evidence that increased distribution and market share will result from a permanent price reduction.

There is an opportunity to increase sales through investment spending in this market. This conclusion is based on the findings that: (a) only 25 percent of the target market has tried the product; (b) repeat purchases among those who have tried the product exceed 50 percent; and (c) there is no strongly entrenched competitor in this field.

Advertising Conclusions

Results of an advertising awareness test conducted during October indicate that the new "moistness you can see" campaign has performed well above expectations in registering key selling points and increasing "intention to buy" attitudes among consumers.

An analysis of the audience of our television effort indicates a need to strengthen coverage in: (a) the Southeastern region; and (b) families with incomes over $12,000 in all areas.

Sales Promotion Conclusions

The results of last year's national in-pack coupon effort fail to justify the use of this technique as a device for improving the repurchase rate.

A comparison of monthly sales figures and actual retail movement for the July–December period indicates that the free-case offer during July and August did stimulate trade loading, but did *not* have a measurable effect on brand share in the two test regions.

The conclusions section of the marketing plan is an excellent place to identify important gaps in marketing information. It is not the place, however, to develop a research proposal for gathering this information. If such a proposal is to be included in the marketing plan, it should be described briefly in the section for *special objectives, strategies, and plans* and the details of the proposal should appear in a separate document.

MARKETING OBJECTIVES

The marketing objectives section follows immediately after the conclusions section. The objectives section should be brief and spell out the commitment made to management in return for the allocation of resources that is requested. At a minimum, the objectives section specifies sales for the marketing period and the amount of money that will be spent in obtaining the sales objective.

If relevant, other objectives may also be included in the objectives section. For example, the commitment to develop a new package, introduce new flavors or a new model, and initiate product improvements or a major research project may appear in the objectives section.

Marketing objectives should always be specific, actionable, and achievable. If they do not meet these three criteria, they provide little guidance for marketing activity and no basis for evaluating the marketing program. Examples of marketing objectives are shown in the following material.

Market Share Objective

The objective for 19xx is to achieve an average market share of 22.5 percent, with an expenditure for advertising and sales promotion of $3,250,000.

The objective for 19xx is to achieve a market share of 23.5 percent by the end of the fiscal year with an expenditure for advertising and promotion that does not exceed $2,400,000.

Sales Volume Objective

The sales objective for 19xx is to invoice 1.2 million equivalent cases of 24's during the fiscal year with an expenditure for promotion of $800,000. (Note: The concept of equivalent cases is often used when more than one package size or more than one case size is being marketed. Thus, all units are converted to a single case size for analytical convenience.)

Size of Market as an Objective

A major objective for fiscal 19xx is to sufficiently stimulate new trial and increased usage rates for the product category as a whole so that industry sales will increase from 10,300,000 equivalent cases of 24's to 10,920,000 cases, an increase of approximately 6 percent.

Introduction of New Flavors as an Objective

A major objective of the brand during fiscal 19xx is to introduce the new strawberry and lime flavors throughout the Eastern region, as a first step toward national distribution of these items.

Research as an Objective

It will be an objective of the brand during fiscal l9xx to complete a national, random sample survey of consumers in order to develop more complete information on consumer demographics, product preferences, and usage patterns.

Note that each of these objectives is specific (so that it is subject to measurement) and actionable (specific activities can be undertaken in order to achieve it). The achievable criterion simply means that, in terms of the company's resources and present marketing position, the objective appears reasonable. Although this marketing plan is a short-term plan, it can refer to a long-range plan that is in existence when the long-range plan has a direct bearing on strategy for the current period. In such cases, a long-range objective is usually best handled as a lead-in thought for an objective for the current period. For example: "In view of the long-range objective of completing national distribution by the end of 19xx, it will be a primary objective of the current fiscal year to introduce the three basic package sizes into at least 30 percent of the U.S."

MARKETING STRATEGY

The marketing strategy section stands at the heart of the marketing plan as the basic statement of *how* the various marketing variables will be used in order to achieve the marketing objectives. Strategy statements define the roles of advertising, sales promotion, pricing, packaging, distribution, and even personal selling.

Marketing strategy is the first real test of the competence of the marketing planner. To this point, the planner has analyzed the current situation and set objectives. The marketing strategy is the test; it brings together understanding, imagination, vision, and decisiveness to give direction to the entire marketing effort. If the marketing strategy is ill-conceived or ambiguous, there is little chance the plan will be successful. While a well-conceived strategy can be sabotaged

97

by inept execution, it is at the strategy level where key decisions are made that can spell the difference between a brilliant marketing program and just another mediocre one.

The marketing strategy section of the marketing plan is closely related to the problems and opportunities section. In fact, there should *always* be one or more strategy statements for each problem and opportunity that has been defined. There is no point in defining problems and opportunities unless one intends to devise specific marketing strategies to deal with them.

Marketing strategy provides the framework within which specific strategies and plans are developed for each area of marketing activity. An important part of this framework is the clarification of the interrelationships between the various elements in the marketing mix: advertising and sales promotion, distribution and pricing, product and packaging. In the following material, several areas of strategy have been identified and examples of strategy statements given.

How total marketing resources will be allocated among various activities, especially the relative emphasis given to advertising versus sales promotion:

Sales promotion expense will be held to a maximum of 20 percent of the total marketing budget ($300,000) in view of the need to offset competitive claims with a strong advertising program.

Total marketing expenditures will be allocated between advertising and sales promotion in the ratio of 70 percent for advertising and 30 percent for sales promotion. This ratio is based on: (a) general practices within the industry; and (b) the judgment that the brand cannot compete effectively with private label brands without strong advertising support.

During fiscal 19xx, 40 percent of the advertising-sales promotion budget will be spent in promotion. This is a departure from the normal promotional expenditure of 20 percent of the total budget because of the need for an extensive sampling program to induce consumer trial of the improved product.

How total marketing weight will be distributed in place, time, or among several target groups in order to achieve the marketing objectives:

Since historical patterns indicate peak competitive activity during the January–June period, 70 percent of the advertising and sales promotion budget will be spent during this period in order to dominate competitive activity.

It is recommended that total advertising and sales promotion weight be concentrated in the product's top twenty-five volume markets. These markets account for nearly 80 percent of total sales, yet they include less than 40 percent of the population in the entire distribution area. Thus, concentration of funds in these markets will: (a) make the most efficient use of media funds; and (b) permit an effective program within the constraints of a limited budget.

What the basic role(s) of advertising is to be in terms of what is to be advertised, to whom, and for what purpose:

Advertising will be employed as an important, but secondary, technique for creating familiarity with the company and its product lines among the estimated 2000 key purchasing agents and management personnel who comprise the primary target group.

The major portion of the marketing budget will be devoted to consumer advertising directed at current and prospective users. These users are housewives between the ages of 24 and 35, with family incomes of over $15,000, and with children under the age of six.

In view of the reduced profitability of the basic flavors, advertising and promotion support will be devoted to the three new flavors.

How a packaging change will be used to meet a specific objective:

In order to stimulate trade and consumer interest in the recent product improvement, basic marketing strategy for fiscal 19xx will be to introduce a completely redesigned line of packages by October 1.

During the first six months of the fiscal year, advertising will feature the advantages of the new convenience package. During the second half of the year, advertising will revert to an emphasis on product claims, and the new package will be given a prominent, but secondary, position in our advertising communications.

How pricing will be used to meet company objectives:

Average selling price will be increased approximately 10 percent in order to: (a) meet the company's profit objectives; and (b) generate marketing expenditures competitive to the case rate employed by competition.

Average selling price will be maintained at current levels, despite the 10 percent increase in ingredient costs, because of recent consumer resistance to price increases in the industry.

How sales promotion will be used in order to accomplish objectives such as increasing market share or increasing trade purchases:

The primary use of sales promotion during fiscal 19xx will be to obtain consumer trial of the improved product.

Sales promotion expenditures will be devoted primarily to obtaining retail distribution for the new, economy package size.

The preceding examples are general. They do not attempt to specify what media will be used, what specific sales promotion devices will be employed, or precisely how the advertising will be written. This is left to the experts in these fields. The strategy statements do place certain constraints on the experts, however. Boundaries are given for how much money may be spent for a particular activity, the kinds of people to be reached, and the areas of the country in which media is to be used. Within these constraints creative groups, sales promotion experts, and media buyers are free to exercise their imagination, judgment, and experience.

ADVERTISING OBJECTIVES

Advertising objectives are an extension of the general marketing strategy. The purpose of this section is to define further the role of advertising in the total marketing effort and establish specific advertising goals for the current planning period. Advertising objectives should not repeat anything that has been stated in the marketing strategy. Instead, the advertising objectives section should add new dimensions to the advertising part of the marketing plan and provide the primary basis for future evaluations of advertising effectiveness.

Since advertising is only one of the controllable marketing variables that affect sales results, advertising objectives should usually be communications objectives. They should not be defined in terms of sales results or other direct consumer action such as product trial, product satisfaction, or purchase rates. The whole area of evaluating advertising is covered in Chapter 22.

The advertising objectives section will ordinarily be quite brief. Since it is supported by separate copy and media strategies and plans, it should cover only those decisions which affect copy and media. Normally, advertising objectives do two things: (a) Define the target group(s) in terms of *who* they are and *where* they are. (If these definitions have been made in the marketing strategy section, they should not be repeated in this section.) (b) Advertising objectives provide specific, measurable communication goals such as awareness of the product or its advertising, knowledge of product attributes, or attitudes toward the product. Thus, effective advertising objectives are usually based on research measurements. The following examples of advertising objectives are those typically found in a marketing plan:

☐ To increase awareness of product attribute X from its present level of 20 percent to 30 percent among U.S. urban housewives in the 20 to 45 year age group.

☐ To create awareness of brand advertising among at least 50 percent of the primary target group—namely, adult males in the 40 to 65 year age group.

☐ To increase favorable attitudes toward the product (as defined in the 19xx attitude study) from 50 percent to 60 percent among U.S. housewives in the 25 to 35 age group.

☐ To direct consumer advertising to adult women who are full-time housewives in families of average or larger size since they constitute the primary purchase group for the product type.

The advertising objectives section should always make provisions for measuring how well the proposed advertising accomplishes its objectives. This provision may be handled by a prefatory sentence introducing the section. For example, "Consumer research will be used to measure how well the advertising program accomplishes its stated objectives." Or, it may be treated as one of the advertising objectives, per se. For example, "The objective of the print advertising effort will be to achieve a Starch seen-associated score of 20 percent or higher."[9]

Sources of information for evaluating advertising effectiveness may include such things as coupon returns, unsolicited consumer letters, press comment, trade comments, or response from the company's sales force. These are generally weak measures, however, and every effort should be made to develop more sophisticated techniques for measuring the advertising program, preferably periodic consumer studies.

The details of the techniques for measuring advertising effectiveness need not be spelled out in the objectives section. These details can be spelled out briefly in the *special objectives, strategies, and plans* section of the report.

ADVERTISING STRATEGY

The advertising strategy section is an optional section in the marketing plan to be used for an established product. It is generally more appropriate in the case of a new product or where unusual conflicts between copy and media objectives need to be reconciled. If it leads to redundancy, don't include it. Statements that might be reflected in the advertising strategy section are given in the following examples.

The way in which the advertising budget will be apportioned between two or more communication tasks or between two or more target groups.

The first priority in allocating the advertising budget will be given to consumer advertising. Insofar as funds are sufficient for this purpose, second priority will be given to influencing the retail trade through advertising directed to retail grocers.

Ways in which the total advertising effort will be distributed in place and time.

Advertising support will be sustained throughout as much of the year as possible in order to: (a) capitalize on the rapid growth of the market by reaching new users who will be coming into the market throughout the year; and (b) achieve initial trial by the large number of users who purchase products in this category infrequently.

The way in which advertising will be related to other marketing activities, since these relationships may either affect advertising timing or require a change in the copy approach.

Forty percent of the media and copy support will be concentrated during the final quarter of the year to support the consumer sampling program planned for September.

Further clarification of what is to be advertised in terms of such factors as the allocation of advertising among products in a line.

---

[9]Starch testing is a method of measuring advertising effectiveness. (See Chapter 22.)

CHAPTER 4 | THE MARKETING PLAN

Advertising support will be apportioned within the product line according to individual product sales forecasts.

Advertising support will be concentrated on the deluxe model, with other models being referred to in body copy only.

Which of two considerations—media or copy—will govern the overall advertising program. Spectacular units might be used for advertising impact at the sacrifice of reach, frequency, or advertising continuity.

In order to achieve maximum concentration of advertising support during the four-week periods preceding Christmas and Mother's Day, media considerations of continuity will be subordinated to the need for major copy units such as multiple-page spreads or full program sponsorship in television.

COPY STRATEGY

When the product is advertised to two or more groups, a single marketing plan may contain two or more separate copy strategies. For example, a cereal product might be advertised to both children and mothers, using different appeals for the two groups; or, one advertising campaign might be directed to consumers, the other to the retail trade. Separate strategies may also be required when a product is being advertised for two or more uses. For example, a soap or detergent that is used for both laundry and dishes; or an evaporated milk that is used for infant feeding, cooking, and creaming coffee. In instances of multiple product use, the copy strategy should indicate the relative importance that will be given to each use.

A well-written copy strategy will normally contain four statements regarding: (a) the principal benefit offered by the product; (b) the principal characteristics of the product—why the benefit exists; (c) the character or personality of the product to be reflected in the mood, tone, and overall atmosphere of the advertising; and (d) what the product is, and what it is used for.

Product claims or benefits should always be stated in competitive terms. For example, the claims should be expressed as "superior to" or "better than" competition. Failure to do this can lead to pale, washed-out copy. Examples of copy strategy points are given below. None of these statements represents a complete strategy for a single product.

Brand X evaporated milk will be presented to consumers as an ingredient item that is *superior* to competitive products in terms of richness, creaminess, and blending qualities.

Brand Y detergent will be advertised on the basis of its *greater* versatility for a wider range of fabrics than competitive products.

Brand Z lawn mower is easier and more economical to use than competitive mowers because of our exclusive feature *A* which guarantees easy starting and reduces maintenance costs.

The mood or tone of the advertising for Brand C headache remedy will be clinical, so as to associate it with the medical profession.

Product B is a harmless, tasteless powder that is used to tenderize meat.

COPY PLAN

The copy plan explains how the copy strategy will be executed in a specific advertising campaign. It is a short-term document that records the decisions and rationale used to create a recommended copy unit. The copy plan is prepared *after* the copy itself has been written in order to give creative groups the maximum freedom to develop a persuasive copy approach. Thus, the chief role of the copy plan is to explain *why* the copy was executed as it was. Copy that lacks logical support is usually highly vulnerable to attack and criticism. The copy plan also formalizes the creative approach and provides a pattern for the development of further commercials or advertisements. A separate copy plan is required for each creative strategy statement and each medium employed. The same plan can seldom be used for both magazines and television because the two media require different presentation techniques.

The copy plan typically covers the following areas, although these are not exhaustive.

The specific product claims (or facts) that are to be communicated.

The phrase, "Gets clothes cleaner than ever before," will be featured in all copy as the articulation of the basic selling proposition. This claim will be supported by a testimonial from a "typical" user who will be featured in the advertising.

The relative degree of emphasis to be given to various claims that may be used.

Primary emphasis will be given to "natural flavor," with secondary emphasis given to convenience of preparation and economy.

A specification of the media units to be employed along with a justification for the choice.

All commercials will be 60 seconds because this commercial length is needed to develop the basic copy story and to show consumer satisfaction.

Visual devices that will be used to communicate key ideas.

The solubility claim will be supported visually in the following ways: (a) print copy, by a time-lapse photo sequence; (b) television, by means of a continuous-action demonstration using direct side-by-side comparisons with the leading competitive product which will be referred to as Brand X.

The way in which copy or action is used to capture attention or achieve believability.

For a dog food commercial, the copy plan might state: The dog(s) used in the feeding scenes on television will always be shown "jumping eagerly" in anticipation of being fed.

103

Ways in which the "tone" or "mood" specified in the copy strategy will be achieved.

Settings will be informal, featuring happy social groups at a barbecue or picnic.

The way in which the product itself will be presented, including such considerations as the model or package size that will be shown or how special problems in illustrating the product or package will be handled.

The large-sized package will be featured in all advertising because of its: (a) superior legibility; and (b) more favorable size impression relative to other visual elements.

The ways selective appeals will be used to increase copy effectiveness among specific subgroups of the target audience, or how a series of different appeals will be featured in a series of related ads or commercials.

Real people rather than professional models will be used, and in successive ads, they will be chosen from different occupational groups and shown in a setting that will clearly identify their occupations.

If the copy plan is truly well written, a new creative group, with no previous experience with the product, could use the copy plan to develop advertising that would fit smoothly into the campaign.

MEDIA STRATEGY

The media strategy is subordinate to the marketing and advertising strategies, which have already established general media constraints such as the amount of money available, definition of the target group(s) of consumers, the relative emphasis to be given to various target groups, and when (during the year) advertising support is to be delivered. The basic function of the media strategy is to show how media will be selected and used to meet these general objectives.

The marketing and advertising strategies may not provide a complete statement of the factors affecting the media plan. In such cases, the media strategy statement lists additional factors which will influence the final media plan. To avoid the redundancy that usually results from separate statements of media objectives and media strategy, these clarifying factors can usually be linked directly to a strategy statement. Three examples are: (a) Spot radio will be purchased on an alternate week basis to extend advertising support throughout the peak buying season. (b) Local spot television will be employed to fill gaps in major market network coverage. (c) On judgment, it is believed that the media program must provide effective message reach among at least 50 percent of the primary male user-group in order to achieve the penetration specified under advertising objectives.

Media strategy statements generally cover the following areas:

The use of local versus regional versus national media and the reasons for these decisions.

Media plans will use local media exclusively since: (a) local media satisfy the creative requirements of the advertising; and (b) provide the flexibility required by marketing objectives.

The use of print versus broadcast media, and the reasons for this choice.

Spot television will be used as the primary medium because it offers the optimum combination of mass coverage, cost efficiency, flexibility in time and place, and meets the creative requirements.

The selection of a specific kind of media within the broad categories of radio, television, magazines, newspapers, and so on.

Black and Spanish-language radio and television will be used to bolster coverage of these target groups because basic coverage of these groups by magazines is deemed inadequate.

The way each medium selected will be used to meet requirements of reach, frequency, cost efficiency, or other factors influencing media scheduling.

Spot television will be scheduled in three, twelve-week flights spread over the entire year in order to provide year around coverage within the budget restrictions.

The particular time or space units that will be used.

In print advertising, all ads will be full page, four-color, bleed units in order to meet creative requirements.

The way in which factors such as seasonality of sales, timing of promotion, or availability of copy will affect media scheduling.

Thirty percent of the budget will be spent in August and September in support of the "back-to-school" promotion.

The ways in which two or more media will be combined to meet specific marketing and advertising objectives.

Since magazines do not provide the depth of coverage required in the Southeastern region, coverage in this area will be supplemented by local newspapers in major markets.

The ways in which specific broadcast time periods or space positions will be used to achieve advertising objectives.

News programming on network radio will be used during the 5:00 P.M. to 6:00 P.M. "drive-time" periods in order to reach adult males.

The way in which the media plan compromises between optimum reach and frequency and the use of large space units.

Since the complexity of the advertising message requires relatively large space and time units, reach and frequency will be subordinated in order to provide full-page, four-color print units and 60 seconds for television commercials.

MEDIA PLAN

The media plan shows how the media strategy is to be executed in terms of specific purchases. Since the media strategy sets forth the principles upon which the media plan is based, the media plan itself shows how these principles are brought to bear in individual buying decisions. However, the media plan as it appears in the marketing plan is a summary statement, not a detailed one. Necessary rationale or other background discussion should be relegated to separate support documents. The following types of statements are characteristic of the media plan:

The recommended media plan provides for 50 percent sponsorship of "Hill Street Blues." This show was selected over alternatives because of: (a) overall cost efficiency with adult audiences; (b) concentration of coverage of the target market group; (c) key geographic coverage. An analysis of the "Hill Street Blues" audience is available in a separate media document.

Six one-half pages are recommended in *Good Housekeeping* magazine because it: (a) provides concentrated coverage of the target market; (b) has minimal duplication with other media recommended; and (c) is believed that the *Good Housekeeping* seal of approval is a decided asset in this product field.

The media plan calls for 39 weeks of spot television in 63 key markets. These markets include all U.S. markets of 100,000 or greater population in which industry per capita consumption exceeded 4.0 units during the past year. The proposed market list is shown in Appendix 1. The recommended spot program will provide coverage of 77 percent of all U.S. households and 89 percent of industry sales. Message penetration is estimated to be: (a) 45 percent of total homes, one or more times during each four-week period; and (b) an average frequency of 2.1 times during each four-week period.

SALES PROMOTION STRATEGY

The section on sales promotion should be founded on one or more points in the marketing strategy section; these points should identify the role to be played by consumer or trade promotions. Thus, the marketing strategy establishes the sales promotion objectives. Typically, the sales promotion strategy will contain the following kinds of statements.

Statements of the promotional techniques that offer the most effective and efficient means of meeting the marketing objectives.

Primary emphasis will be given to consumer-oriented promotions since experience has shown that trade incentives have failed to stimulate dealer cooperation in the past.

The recommended sales promotion program will utilize a direct mail coupon to encourage consumer trial following the introduction of the new package in August. Direct mail couponing is recommended in preference to other alternatives because experience has shown that it: (a) achieves broad reach in a relatively short period of time; and (b) generates greater retailer display activity than other trial-getting devices.

A statement of how total promotion weight will be allocated by product, marketing area, season, and so on.

All trade support for the product line will be concentrated on the large package size because this package size: (a) is most profitable; and (b) has the greatest effect on retailer cooperation.

Generally, the selection of a particular sales promotion technique to accomplish a particular marketing objective is based on: (a) company experience; (b) traditional practices in a given industry; and (c) the results of specific promotion tests. Chapter 19 discusses sales promotion techniques and the unique values of each.

SALES PROMOTION PLAN

The sales promotion plan explains how the promotion strategy will be executed in terms of specific offers or other activities, geographic areas of application, key audiences to which the sales promotion will be addressed, and specific times during the marketing year that promotions will be used. In addition to outlining the details of the recommended sales promotion activities, the sales promotion plan also summarizes the estimated cost of the promotions.

SPECIAL OBJECTIVES, STRATEGIES, AND PLANS

The final section of the marketing plan text is devoted to recommendations in areas such as the product itself, packaging, pricing, research, test marketing, and publicity. Marketing plans for established products will not deal with these areas unless the marketing review section has identified specific problems or opportunities relating to these variables. However, if the marketing review reveals weaknesses in any of these areas, they should be dealt with by recommending consumer tests, initiating developmental work, revising packages, or engaging in other appropriate activity.

Often, weaknesses in one or more of the controllable marketing variables will be detected during the course of the marketing year—that is, between plans. Such developments often result from competitive activity such as a product improvement, redesigned package, or change in pricing practices. In such cases, the marketer cannot afford to delay action until the next formal planning period. Instead, existing objectives, strategies, and plans must be reexamined immediately, and any necessary adjustments must be made. For this reason, every marketing plan should contain a budget reserve. The budget reserve is a contingency fund that may be used to defray the expenses of unanticipated events so that the planned profit contribution will not be reduced. Even under the best of conditions, the market planner cannot anticipate all of the contingencies that may arise in a competitive marketing situation. It is this factor that surrounds marketing with an aura of uncertainty; it is also what makes marketing an exciting, dynamic occupation.

BUDGET SUMMARY AND SCHEDULE OF ACTIVITIES

At some point in the marketing plan, all recommended expenditures should be brought together to enable the reader to grasp quickly the full implications of what has been proposed and show the relationship of the various parts of the marketing plan. This summary usually works best at the end of the plan because the material that precedes it provides its justification. The budget summary should be limited to a single page. Major related expenditures should always be grouped together so that the outline of the spending plan is clear. An example of a budget summary appears in Table 4–1. Following the budget summary, it is helpful to provide a calendar of marketing activities in order to give a visual picture of how the various activities fit together. An example of such a calendar is shown in Figure 4–2.

TABLE 4–1 Budget summary

Advertising

1. *Consumer Magazines* 6 to 9 four-color bleed pages in each of 8 magazines: total circulation of 38.5 million. Net unduplicated coverage of 56% of U.S. households		$940,000
2. *Spot Television* 60 to 100 Gross Rating Points weekly for 26 weeks in 38 markets		720,000
3. *Spot Radio* 15 to 20 sixty-second commercials weekly for 39 weeks on estimated 26 Black stations in 21 major markets		173,000
4. *Production, Preparation* Magazines: Television: Radio:	$15,000 8,000 4,000	 27,000
	Total advertising	$1,860,000

Sales Promotion

1. Major tie-in promotion based on 50¢ per case display allowance; national magazine support		$200,000
2. February-March: Repeat fall tie-in promotion		200,000
3. "Pay Day" Black promotion—SE region		40,000
4. Promotion materials		30,000
	Total promotion	470,000

Reserves

1. For test marketing two new packages		$125,000
2. General reserves (5% of budget)		125,000
	Total reserves	250,000
	GRAND TOTAL	$2,580,000

	A	M	J	J	A	S	O	N	D	J	F	M
Consumer Magazines: (Page 4-C Bleed)												
LHJ	x	x	x			x	x	x	x	x		x
GH	x	x	x			x	x	x	x			x
Redbook	x	x	x			x	x	x	x		x	x
FC	x	x	x			x	x	x	x		x	x
WD	x	x	x			x	x	x	x		x	x
Ebony	x	x				x		x		x		x
TS	x	x				x		x		x		x
MR	x	x				x		x		x		x
Spot Television GRP Weekly	60	60	-	-	-	100	100	60	-	-	100	100
Spot Radio 15-20 Spots—Wk.	x	x				x	x	x	x	x	x	x
Fall Tie-in Promotion						x	x					
Winter Tie-in Promotion											x	x
Black "Pay Day" Promotion (S.E. region only)						x	x	x	x	x	x	x

FIGURE 4–2   Calendar of marketing activities

SUMMARY

The marketing plan is the central document used in organizing, integrating, and developing the advertising and promotion activities of a company. It is a mass communications document and seldom includes a sales plan, which is a major ingredient in the company's marketing effort. Instead, the sales plan is usually a separate document prepared by the sales manager. The two documents are prepared separately because many companies market a number of products that are handled by the same sales force. Thus, there are a number of marketing plans (one for each product), but only one sales plan.

Although it is recognized that a marketing plan may be long-range (five years or more) or short-range (less than five years), prevailing industry practice is to prepare an annual marketing plan that covers the forthcoming fiscal year.

The functions of the marketing plan are to bring together the key facts and conclusions bearing on marketing decisions, provide an operating guide for marketing personnel, and establish benchmarks against which marketing and advertising accomplishments can be judged. In addition, the marketing plan encourages clear and logical thinking, forces the author of the plan to examine the product and its marketing opportunities, and helps identify gaps in information.

In order to outline an in-depth discussion of the marketing plan, the following terms were defined: objective, strategy, plan, sales promotion, and publicity.

CHAPTER 4 | THE MARKETING PLAN

Subsequent sections of the book deal with the various parts of the marketing plan, primarily focusing on advertising and its relation to other marketing activities.

REVIEW QUESTIONS

1 Distinguish between the marketing plan and the sales plan. Explain why they are usually separate documents.
2 What are the arguments for a three year versus a one year marketing plan? Why does it make little practical difference which time frame is used?
3 What are the functions of the marketing plan?
4 Distinguish among advertising, sales promotion, and publicity.
5 What are the major areas of interest in the *marketing review*? Why are they important?
6 At a minimum, what should be specified in the *objectives* section of the marketing plan? What are the three basic criteria that objectives should meet? Explain why these criteria are important.
7 Distinguish among *objectives, strategies,* and *plans.* Give an example of each.
8 Explain the relationship between the *marketing strategies* and the *problems and opportunities* section.
9 What does unnecessary redundancy have to do with the marketing plan? How can it be avoided?
10 Why is the *special objectives, strategies, and plans* section of the marketing plan important? What might normally be included in this section of the marketing plan for an established product?

DISCUSSION QUESTIONS

1 Why is market planning a necessary step for the development of effective advertising?
2 The marketing plan is supervised by the marketing manager. Could it be supervised by the advertising manager instead? Why or why not?
3 A single marketing plan may contain two or more separate copy strategies when the product is advertised to two or more groups. Select a product, such as cereal, that is advertised to two different groups of people, using different appeals. Write a copy strategy for each market.

PROBLEM

Select an advertisement from a magazine. Make sure the advertisement has body copy that states a reason why the product is superior to competition. Write a copy strategy and a copy plan for this advertisement.

Did you have difficulty finding an advertisement you could use to write a copy strategy? If so, why? What are the implications for effective advertising?

II
Marketing Analysis and the Marketing Mix

Marketing analysis is the starting point in preparing a marketing plan. Facts and figures are developed making it possible to set realistic objectives and devise effective strategies and detailed plans. The value of marketing analysis depends largely on the marketer's ability to: (a) select those facts that are relevant to understanding the current marketing situation; (b) be objective in selecting and reporting these facts; and (c) report facts in a manner that is concise, yet fully intelligible to a reader who is not intimately involved in marketing the product on a day-to-day basis.

The world is full of facts about markets, products, product performance, consumers, and other marketing variables. The marketer must sift through these variables, selecting some and discarding others, until those that have a direct bearing on the success of the product have been isolated. There is no way of knowing beforehand which facts will be relevant.

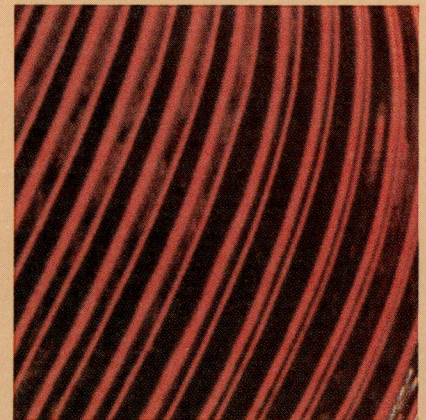

Specific procedures and disciplines help the marketer make these decisions. This section examines some of these procedures and disciplines.

Chapter 5 deals with marketing analysis and marketing research. It focuses on those aspects that are of special interest to people who are actually involved in the preparation of advertising. These topics include the product, its market position, consumer demographics, decision processes, purchasing patterns, motivational appeals, advertising analysis, media

practices, and advertising expenditures.

Chapter 6 explores consumer behavior. This chapter considers the concept of motivation—the basis for all advertising appeals—and relates the psychological concept of need to the economic concept of demand. It summarizes basic conclusions about motivation that can be drawn from academic research, and reviews the major social and interpersonal variables that influence motivational patterns.

Chapter 7 turns its attention to the product, brand, and package—three key marketing variables that are intimately related to advertising. A good product is essential to successful advertising, and the brand name and package should reinforce the product concept.

Chapter 8 discusses pricing and distribution. Although they play key roles in marketing success, these two variables are often neglected in texts on advertising. Price is frequently used as a basis for market segmentation, and symbolic pricing is often used in advertising as a surrogate indicator of product worth. Without adequate distribution, advertising is a waste of company resources. Sometimes, a major task of advertising is to provide dealer listings so that consumers can find the advertised product.

Taken together, the information in these chapters forms the background required for advertising strategies and plans to be conceived and developed.

5
Marketing Analysis and Research

WHAT'S WRONG WITH THE DOGS?

One day while I was still in the advertising agency business, Noel Digby, the creative director, called me on the phone.

"Ken," he asked, "can you spare some time this morning to look at dog chow commercials? Our commercials aren't coming off right, and I don't know what the problem is. I've scheduled the viewing room for 10 o'clock and asked the television department to pull together all of the dog chow commercials we've made in the past three years. If you and I view them in the order they were made, maybe we can find out what the problem is and when it started."

"Sure," I answered. "I have nothing scheduled that I can't cancel. See you at 10."

Before becoming creative director, Noel had been creative supervisor on the Purina account. He had developed the advertising campaign we were currently using. After being named creative director, he was replaced by another copy supervisor in the Purina creative group.

Noel and I started watching commercials. At one point, Noel commented, "This is the last commercial I made. The rest were supervised by Joe."

Joe's commercials were good. They were well planned and written. The audio and video were well coordinated and cast, and the production work was excellent. After watching about four or five of Joe's commercials, Noel asked, "Ken, do you notice anything about the dogs?"

"Yeah," I said. "They're not excited about eating Purina Dog Chow."

"That's it!" Noel said.

In all of Noel's commercials, the dogs literally danced with anticipation at the prospect of being fed Purina Dog Chow. Noel had obtained this effect by scheduling his shooting before the dogs' normal feeding time. They were hungry and their eagerness to get to the dog food was obvious. Joe, on the other hand, had scheduled his shooting later in the day; the dogs had been fed and weren't hungry. As a result, they sat patiently while the dog food was being prepared. It made all of the difference in the world. Joe's commercials simply didn't convey the excitement and appetite appeal of the product, whereas Noel's did.

As a result, the copy plan was rewritten, specifying that the dogs should show excitement—dancing, jumping, quivering—in anticipation of being fed Purina Dog Chow.

OHRBACH'S

In 1923 Ohrbach's department store opened on 14th Street in New York. Later, it was moved to 39th Street, and opened branches in suburban New York, Newark, and Los Angeles. It became known as a fashion leader, and the distributor of low cost copies of Paris originals. Ohrbach's was an anomaly compared to other department stores; it offered no deliveries, wrapping service, C.O.D.s, mail or phone orders, or alterations. In short, Ohrbach's offered few of the services that department stores customarily use to woo customers. Instead, it offered high fashion, high quality, and low cost.

An analysis of Ohrbach's strengths and weaknesses enabled its advertising agency, Doyle Dane Bernbach, to develop some of the finest creative advertising in the retail field. One of these 1957 ads, "I found out about Joan," is shown in Figure 5–1.[1]

This ad is considered a classic in retail advertising and helped earn Doyle Dane Bernbach a reputation as a hot, creative agency. Using a skillful blend of artful illustration and cattiness, this ad's body copy creates a powerful registration of Ohrbach's strengths.

> The way she talks, you'd think she was in Who's Who. Well! I found out what's what with *her*. Her husband own a bank? Sweetie, not even a bank *account*. Why that palace of theirs has wall-to-wall

[1]Robert Glatzer, *The New Advertising* (New York: The Citadel Press, 1970), 38–45.

FIGURE 5–1 (Courtesy Ohrbach's, Inc.)

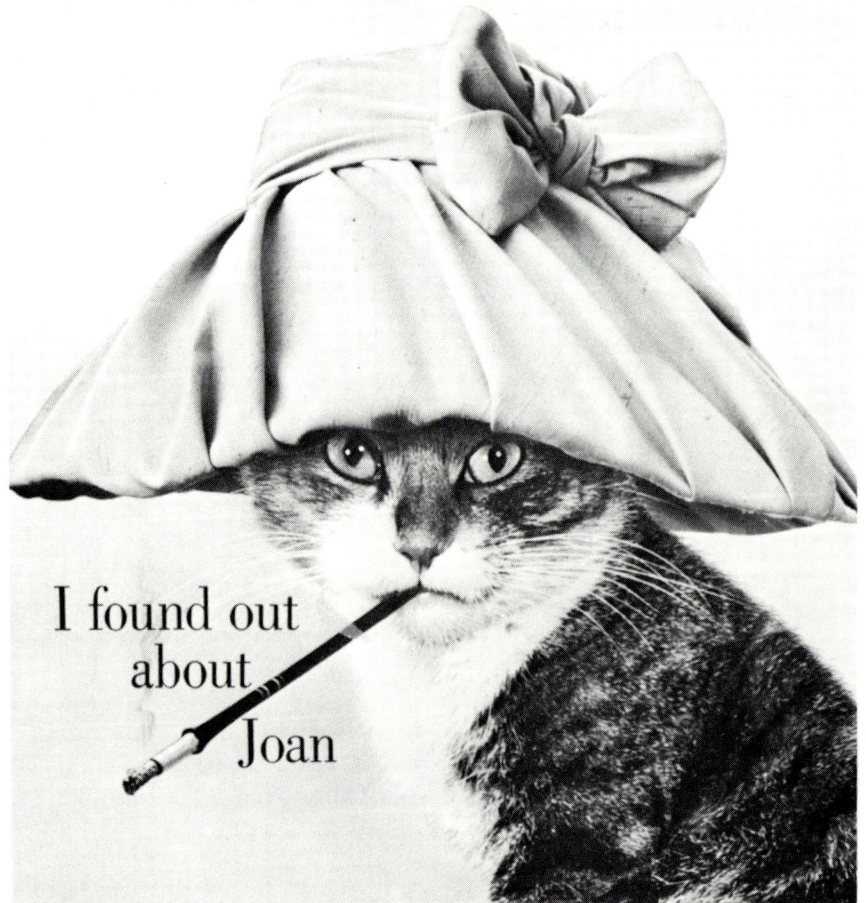

The way she talks, you'd think she was in Who's Who. Well! I found out what's what with *her*. Her husband own a bank? Sweetie, not even a bank *account*. Why that palace of theirs has wall-to-wall *mortgages!* And that car? Darling, that's horsepower, *not* earning power. They won it in a fifty-cent raffle! Can you imagine? And those clothes! Of course she *does* dress divinely. But really...a mink stole, and Paris suits, and all those dresses...on *his* income? Well darling, I found out about that too. I just happened to be going her way and *I saw Joan come out of Ohrbach's!*

Ohrbach's

34TH ST. OPP. EMPIRE STATE BLDG. · NEWARK MARKET & HALSEY · "A BUSINESS IN MILLIONS, A PROFIT IN PENNIES"

mortgages! And that car? Darling, that's horsepower, *not* earning power. They won it in a fifty-cent raffle! Can you imagine? And those clothes! Of course she *does* dress divinely. But really . . . a mink stole, and Paris suits, and all those dresses . . . on *his* income? Well, darling, I found out about that too. I just happened to be going her way and *I saw Joan come out of Ohrbach's!*

KNOWING WHAT TO SAY

Marketing research has received both its share of plaudits and criticisms from the advertising industry. Most people who are charged with the responsibility for creating advertising are avid users of research, eager for the insights into consumer motivation and behavior that marketing research can unearth. Far too often, however, they complain that advertising research is used to evaluate completed advertisements rather than provide the information necessary for developing advertising in the first place. Many marketing research people agree with this criticism. Thus, John A. Fiedler, senior vice-president and executive director of research at Ted Bates Advertising in the early 1980s, has asserted, "There should be far greater effort devoted to the determination of what will motivate prior to the writing of final copy."[2] R. F. Chay, director of marketing at Johnson Wax in the early 1980s, endorsed this statement with the observation, "The industry should be spending far less time testing copy executions and more time finding the right things to say before commercials are written."[3]

These three examples have been selected to emphasize the importance of analysis and marketing research in the development of advertising. The Purina Dog Chow example demonstrates how a simple, comparative analysis of different commercials in a campaign identified a weakness that had crept into creative execution. In the case of Ohrbach's, an analysis of company strengths resulted in imaginative *and* persuasive advertising. The example on marketing research points up the need for research to help creative groups find out what to say *before* they start writing the advertising.

In this chapter, we will direct our attention to the role of analysis and marketing research in preparing advertising. Throughout, our focus will be on advertising and those aspects of analysis and research that are most relevant to its preparation.

THE ROLE OF ANALYSIS

Marketing research and analysis form the bases for effective marketing plans and persuasive advertising. The marketing review section of the marketing plan is an exercise in analysis to identify problems and opportunities faced by the brand. Once they have been identified, strategies can be developed to exploit them.

Proper analysis investigates every aspect of the market and the marketing program. Not all analyses, however, are of equal value to the people responsible for creating advertising. In the following material, we will highlight some of the areas of analysis that are of particular value to the creative team. These areas will be explored more fully in Chapter 11.

THE PRODUCT

All advertising starts with a product and its inherent consumer benefits. It is not hard to develop good advertising for a product that has clearly identifiable consumer benefits, such as American Tourister luggage with its "rugged steel frame" (Figure 5–2) and Alpo dog food, containing real beef (Figure 5–3). It is exceedingly hard to develop good advertising for a product that is indistinguishable from

---

[2]"Leaders View the Problems," *Advertising Age,* 20 October 1980, 5–9.
[3]Ibid., 5–9.

FIGURE 5–2   (Courtesy American Tourister, Inc.)

**American Tourister.
No matter where you take it, it can take it.**

Our soft-sided American Tourister luggage is built to survive any trip, tumble or fall.
    To be flung around, in all the far-flung corners of the world.
    That's because we make it with a rugged steel frame, a tough durable exterior and wheels that roll with the punches.
    Of course, we also make it look good.

We style it in rich colors like navy, camel and mahogany, and give it handsome stitched panels and strong clean lines. The result of all this is luggage worthy of the name American Tourister.
    Luggage you can take anywhere.
    Even downstairs.
**It's not just how good it looks.
It's how long it looks good.**

competition. This is one reason so much of today's advertising appears bland and pointless—full of empty claims and implying non-existent differences.

This is why product analysis is so important for the creative team. Within the product itself, or from performance tests or methods of production, one can often find justification for a consumer benefit that will appeal to potential customers.

MARKET POSITION

Product position is often a key factor in influencing the kind of advertising to be used. Market position is usually measured in market share, or share of mind (the percentage of consumers who are aware of it). Thus, a little known brand may benefit by comparing its quality to a widely used brand, whereas a brand that is well-known and

FIGURE 5–3 (Courtesy Allen Products Company, Inc.)

"**Dogs love real beef. That's why they love ALPO.®**"

"Every dog's a natural-born beef eater. Beef has the taste they love and the protein they need. And beef is where a balanced diet begins. That's why every can of ALPO Beef Chunks Dinner is packed with this much real beef.

Give the dog you love the real beef he loves. Give him ALPO.

After all, dogs don't thrive on love alone."

Lorne Greene

ALPO® With all the beef dogs love to eat.

©1982 Allen Products Company, Inc.

has a high market share has nothing to gain by comparison advertising.

A classic example of associating a relatively unknown brand with leading competitors was used by J. Sterling Getchell in an advertisement that is widely recognized as one of the all-time greats.

The time was 1932; the product field—automobiles. Chevrolet had outstyled and outsold the Model A Ford, and held a dominant position in the market. Ford plants had been out of production for almost a year while Henry Ford tooled up to produce a radically new model—the V-8. The automobile trade press and the newspapers had been giving tremendous publicity to the forthcoming, marvelous car from Ford. Plymouth, in its third year of production, was ignored, neglected, and virtually unknown. Getchell's advertising problem was how to bring the Plymouth out of obscurity and into the limelight. His answer is shown in Figure 5–4. "Look at all three" launched Plymouth into the marketplace as a major competitor and made advertising history.

CONSUMER ANALYSIS

Consumers are the third key area of analysis for the creative team. Four dimensions are particularly fruitful when analyzing consumers: consumer demographics, purchasing patterns, decision patterns, and motivation.

Consumer demographics. Demographics describes consumers in measurable terms such as age, family size and structure, income, education, geographic distribution, ethnic and cultural groups, and so on.

A first step in consumer analysis is identification of the demographic characteristics of the target consumers. This is helpful in

FIGURE 5–4 Source: Julian Lewis Watkins, *100 Greatest Advertisements* (New York: Dover Publications, Inc., 1959), 108.

"Look at All Three!

BUT DON'T BUY ANY LOW-PRICED CAR UNTIL YOU'VE DRIVEN THE NEW PLYMOUTH WITH FLOATING POWER"

"It is my opinion that any new car without Patented Floating Power is obsolete."

THOUSANDS of people have been waiting expectantly until today before buying a new car. I hope that you are one of them.

Now that the new low-priced cars are here (including the new Plymouth which will be shown on Saturday) I urge you to carefully *compare* values.

This is the time for you to "shop" and buy wisely. Don't make a deposit on any automobile until you've actually had a demonstration.

It is my opinion that the automobile industry as a whole has never offered such values to the public.

In the new Plymouth we have achieved more than I had ever dared to hope for. If you had told me two years ago that such a big, powerful, beautiful automobile could be sold at the astonishing prices we will announce on Saturday . . . I'd have said it was absolutely impossible.

I have spent my life building fine cars. But no achievement in my career has given me the deep-down satisfaction

A STATEMENT BY WALTER P. CHRYSLER

that I derive from the value you get in this 1932 Plymouth. To me, its outstanding feature is Floating Power. We already know how the public feels about this. Last summer it was news, but today it is an established engineering achievement.

It is my opinion, and I think that of leading engineering authorities, that any new car without Floating Power is obsolete. Drive a Plymouth with Patented Floating Power, and note its utter lack of vibration . . . then drive a car with old-fashioned engine mountings and you will understand what I mean. *There's absolutely no comparison.*

We have made the Plymouth a much larger automobile. It is a BIG car. We have increased its power, lengthened the wheelbase and greatly improved its beauty.

In my opinion you will find the new Plymouth the easiest riding car you have ever driven. Yet with all these improvements we have been able to lower prices.

Again let me urge you, go and see the new Plymouth with Floating Power on Saturday. Be sure to look at all THREE low-priced cars and don't buy any until you do. That is the way to get the most for your money.

FIRST SHOWING NEXT SATURDAY, APRIL 2nd, AT DESOTO, DODGE AND CHRYSLER DEALERS

formulating appeals, selecting models for advertisements, and devising settings for illustrations. Beer, for example, is consumed primarily by the 18 to 36 age group; diet foods are used primarily by women; family settings are appropriate for a wide range of products dependent upon family consumption; peanut butter is consumed in families with children; inexpensive, sturdy furniture finds its largest market among young families; and vacations and luxury items are purchased by those with discretionary incomes.

Media audiences are described in terms of their demographic characteristics, and insofar as is possible, advertising should reflect the demographic characteristics of the media in which it appears.

Purchasing patterns. Different products are purchased in different ways. Frequently purchased, inexpensive items may be bought purely on the basis of advertising with little or no comparison shopping. Other products, such as furniture, carpeting, expensive electronic equipment, automobiles, and major clothing articles, often involve extensive shopping. As a consequence, the kinds of information presented and the types of advertisements used may play a critical role in advertising effectiveness. Research, for example, has shown that buyers of expensive furniture want to study furniture in room settings—look at it over and over again, think about it, and imagine how the furniture would look in their homes. As a consequence, magazine advertising is more effective than television because the consumer has time to study the setting in the magazine and is able to refer back to it.

Decision patterns. When various family members participate in the decision process, purchases involve shared consumption. In some instances, particularly for routine food items, toiletries, and kitchen supplies, the female head-of-household is the primary decision maker. For other purchases, such as distilled spirits, insurance, automobiles, and lawn and garden products, the male head-of-household may be more important in making the purchase decision and selecting the brands bought. Children may also have an important role in decision making; or the decision process may be shared with their parent.

In any event, the patterns of decision making within the family will determine the audiences that advertising should address and the appeals it should use. As a consequence, analysis of family decision patterns is a prerequisite for effective advertising.

Motivation. In Chapter 6 the role and diversity of consumer motives will be discussed. At this point, only note that the same generic product type may be purchased for many reasons. Watches, for example, may be purchased for reasons of economy, style, accuracy, durability, different functions (alarms, dates, underwater use, laptiming capability), and status. Beneficial toothpaste attributes include economy, decay prevention, teeth whitening, breath freshening, or flavor. Other products may exhibit a similar or even wider array of motivational appeals.

Finding the appropriate motivational appeal is often the most difficult task, therefore motivational analysis is a necessary step in developing effective advertising.

CHAPTER 5 | MARKETING ANALYSIS AND RESEARCH

ADVERTISING ANALYSIS

Advertising analysis involves a comparison of one's own advertising to that of the competition on the basis of appeals employed, media used, total advertising expenditures, size of space units, and advertising effectiveness. Often, analyses will signal a need for a change in one or more of these dimensions.

Appeals employed. Advertising appeals need to be examined on a regular basis to make sure they retain their uniqueness. Downy fabric softener is a case in point. The advent of detergents created a problem for consumers and an opportunity for marketers. Although detergents cleaned clothes better than soap, they left clothing harsh and rough to the touch. Downy was introduced as a laundry additive to soften fabrics, and was highly successful. Its success attracted many competitors to the field; soon, the field was inundated by brands making identical claims. An analysis of competitive advertising indicated that Downy's advertising had lost its uniqueness. As a consequence, the product was reformulated and a freshener—an ingredient that makes clothes smell fresh and clean—was added.

TABLE 5–1 Comparison of content and format of two dry dog food advertisements

	Gravy Train	Mealtime
Product:	Gravy Train	Mealtime
Headline:	"Dogs prefer the taste of new improved Gravy Train 3 to 1"	"Mealtime. It's just what your dog's been waiting for."
Illustration:	Side by side illustrations: (1) dog ignoring Gravy Train (2) three dogs eating new improved Gravy Train	Dog on porch, standing over empty food bowl
Claims:	(1) Palatability (2) Natural beef flavor	(1) Palatability (2) Meat protein (3) Available in two different sized pellets
Support:	(1) Close-up illustration of texture difference between particles of "old" and "new" Gravy Train (2) Reference to tests in which dogs preferred "new" to "old" Gravy Train 3 to 1	Dogs love meat; "Tail-waggin'" taste
Package Illustration:	Lower, right-hand corner	Two packages, lower center—one for large crunchy bite pellets and one for small crunchy bite pellets

Downy's advertising was changed, using both *softness and freshness* as advertising appeals. This change reinstated Downy in the market as a unique product, different from and superior to competition.

A simple format for comparing advertising appeals is shown in Table 5–1, using two dry dog food brands as an example. The advertisements are shown in Figures 5–5 and 5–6.

Media comparisons.   Media comparisons simply examine the specific media used by competition, patterns of use employed, and how some media are dominated by competitive advertising. An analysis may be conducted to ascertain whether competitors are exploiting media opportunities that the agency is missing. Competitors' brand share increases, or decreases, are sometimes accompanied by a ma-

FIGURE 5–5   (Reproduced with permission from General Foods Corp.)

CHAPTER 5 | MARKETING ANALYSIS AND RESEARCH

FIGURE 5–6 (Courtesy Kal-Kan Foods)

jor shift in their media emphasis. A brand that has always used one form of media for the bulk of its advertising may find that a shift to another may enhance its advertising effectiveness. For example, while working on a cold remedy account, an agency observed a sharp share increase by a major competitor in the New York area. During the winter season, cold remedy advertising is quite sensitive to advertising pressure, yet there was no evidence of significant increases in competitive advertising spending. In fact, a particular competitor had decreased its advertising in radio and television in the New York market. An examination of the media this competitor was using revealed the competitor had shifted significant funds from broadcast media to car cards in the New York subway system. Apparently, the crowded conditions and stuffy atmosphere of subway trains made consumers particularly conscious of and responsive to cold remedy advertising.

Total advertising expenditures.   All things being equal, share of market should equal share of advertising. Although all things are seldom equal among competitive products, the importance of examining the relationship between share of market and share of advertising must be emphasized. Table 5–2 shows a hypothetical comparison of share of market and share of advertising that could easily occur in an industry. On the surface, it would appear that Brand C is underspending both in total and on a per case basis and that an increase in advertising might reasonably be expected to result in an increase in market share. Such a conclusion is only tentative and could be revised by an examination of competitive pricing, sales promotion, and distribution. However, if we assume that these factors are relatively equal for leading brands in the market, then Brand C (possibly because of product quality, package, positioning, media pattern, or the effectiveness of its copy appeals) is a reasonable candidate for increased advertising expenditures, at least in a business-building test. The decision to increase advertising on this brand, however, must be weighed against company objectives and the profit contribution of the brand.

In the case of Brand A, the relatively unfavorable relationship of advertising and market share *may* result from the brand's high share. Products in a dominant market position often find that increased advertising expenditures become marginally less effective as the brand approaches the limit of those consumers to whom its marketing program is appealing. In this instance, it is possible that a reduction in advertising expenditures would increase the brand's profit contribution while having a negligible effect on its market share position. The relatively unfavorable relationship between advertising and sales for Brand D may well signal weakness in some other aspect of its marketing program and should alert the marketer to search for the area or areas in which corrective action needs to be taken. A comparison of share of market against share of advertising raises a number of possibilities that need to be explored and may well be an important determinant in developing both marketing objectives and strategies.

Obviously, a comparison of these two variables requires a relatively accurate measure of competitive market share and competitive

TABLE 5–2   Comparison of share of advertising and share of market for a hypothetical consumer product

Brands	Advertising Expenditure in 1000s	Share	Sales Cases of 1000s	Share	Expenditure Per Case
A	$ 7,388.0	40%	8,971.2	34%	$0.823
B	3,694.0	20	5,804.8	22	0.636
C	2,770.5	15	6,860.3	26	0.404
D	4,617.5	25	4,749.4	18	0.972
Totals	$18,470.0	100%	26,385.7	100%	$0.70

CHAPTER 5 | MARKETING ANALYSIS AND RESEARCH

advertising. As pointed out earlier, reasonably accurate measures of market share are obtainable from national store audits such as those provided by A.C. Nielsen, from national consumer panels such as the one maintained by Market Research Corporation of America (MRCA), or from services that compile warehouse withdrawal records. Estimates of competitive advertising expenditures are available from a number of industry sources. The better known ones are Leading National Advertisers-Publishers' Information Bureau (LNA-PIB) and Simmons for magazines; Media Records for newspapers; Bureau of Advertising Research (BAR) network television, Target Group Index, and Simmons Selected Markets for network television; BAR Barcume and Rorabaugh for spot television; BAR Radio and Radio Expenditure Report for network and spot radio; and LNA Outdoor for outdoor advertising. Major advertising agencies subscribe to most of these services and smaller agencies often have access to them through affiliation arrangements with larger agencies.

Size of space units. In some instances, a simple examination of total advertising expenditures and schedules for competitive brands will suggest a creative direction. It is a common occurrence for minor brands in a competitive field to be heavily outspent by the leading brands. These leading brands are able to afford large space and time units in a wide variety of media. If the minor brand attempted to emulate these major competitors, it would dissipate its advertising effort and be overshadowed in all media in which it appeared.

By using smaller space or time units and concentrating expenditures in a single medium (for example, a single magazine), a minor brand may be able to achieve advertising dominance against a significant portion of the total market.

Advertising effectiveness. Advertising effectiveness is a major consideration in analysis because it can double or halve the value of media expenditures. Many problems are involved in gauging the effectiveness of advertising (see Chapter 22), but some form of advertising evaluation is essential in comparing one's own marketing effort to competitors. Many advertisers and advertising agencies conduct this kind of research through their own marketing research departments. Others retain independent copy testing services. When independent testing services are used, the service often provides average performance scores for the product type so that the performance of one's own advertising can be checked.

Many other forms of marketing analysis are performed; any or all may make a specific contribution to the development of advertising. The areas discussed are areas of analysis that are generally of particular interest to the creative team.

The basic data used for analyzing markets and advertising is derived from marketing research.

MARKETING RESEARCH

Since marketing research is the primary tool used to gather relevant marketing information, we need to examine the scope of the discipline in order to recognize the major areas in which it can be used.

Marketing research is the gathering, recording, and analyzing of facts about problems relating to the transfer and sales of goods and services.[4] Within this definition, the activities of a marketing research department are limited only by the information needed, imagination and ethics of the research personnel who devise ways of obtaining needed information, and budget considerations. Because of its versatility, marketing research offers many values for market planning and the determination of marketing and advertising strategies. As a result, marketing research personnel are often a functional part of the marketing group. Table 5–3 provides insight into the variety of tasks undertaken by marketing research departments, listing thirty-two different research tasks, divided among five major research areas.

MARKETING RESEARCH AND THE CONSUMER

One form of marketing research that is particularly important to advertising is sometimes referred to as **consumer research,** so as to distinguish it from sales analysis, forecasting, store audits, and other impersonal forms. In the area of consumer research, three broad research traditions differ in their focus or emphasis. These three traditions have been referred to as the distributive, morphological, and analytical approaches.[5]

Distributive research.   Distributive research focuses attention on the outcomes of consumer behavior and is essentially concerned with *who* buys and *what* is bought. The emphasis is on demographics—geographic and sociological characteristics of customers. It builds profiles of buyers and nonbuyers by determining such factors as age, income, marital status, family size, and geographic location, and computes per capita and per family consumption rates for relevant products and brands. The distributive approach is quantitative, descriptive, and the beginning of marketing wisdom.

The value of distributive research.   Distributive research is the starting point to understanding the consumer. More sophisticated approaches are simply refinements or supplements to the distributive approach. Because of its relatively simple and straightforward research techniques, distributive research is usually less expensive than other forms of consumer research. The results can also be compared with U.S. census data in order to estimate market potentials and project future trends. Distributive research determines the geographic allocation of advertising dollars and media selection; it often provides a rough guide for creative development. This is particularly true when income, family life cycle, or social class are key dimensions influencing product use and consumption rates.

The limitations of distributive research.   Despite its values, distributive research has three major limitations.

---

[4]"Report of the Definitions Committee," *Journal of Marketing* (October 1948): 210.

[5]J. W. Newman, *Motivation Research and Marketing Management* (Boston: Harvard University Graduate School of Business Administration Division of Research, 1951), 228.

CHAPTER 5 | MARKETING ANALYSIS AND RESEARCH

☐ It is purely descriptive and fails to deal with the decision process behind purchases. Unless the decision process is understood, sound marketing strategies cannot be developed. Buying a carpet, for example, involves a completely different decision process from buying a pound of coffee. Since different sources of information, shopping behaviors, and influence patterns characterize these two purchases, the marketer of carpeting and the marketer of coffee must allocate their marketing resources differently,

TABLE 5–3   Research activities of 798 companies

Activity	Percentage conducting research
Advertising research	
Motivation research	48%
Copy research	49
Media research	61
Studies of ad effectiveness	67
Business economics and corporate research	
Short-range forecasting (up to one year)	85
Long-range forecasting (over one year)	82
Studies of business trends	86
Pricing studies	81
Plant and warehouse location studies	71
Acquisition studies	69
Export and international studies	51
MIS (Management Information Studies)	72
Operations research	60
Internal company employees	65
Corporate responsibility research	
Consumers' "right to know" studies	26
Ecological impact studies	33
Studies of legal constraints on advertising and promotion	51
Social values and policies studies	40
Product research	
New product acceptance and potential	84
Competitive product studies	85
Testing of existing products	75
Packaging research: Design or physical characteristics	60
Sales and market research	
Measurement of market potentials	93
Market share analysis	92
Determination of market characteristics	93
Sales analysis	89
Establishment of sales quotas, territories	75
Distribution channel studies	69
Test markets and store audits	54
Consumer panel operations	50
Sales compensation studies	60
Promotional studies of premiums, coupons, sampling, deals, etc.	52

Source: Dick Warren Twedt, ed., *1978 Survey of Marketing Research* (Chicago: American Marketing Association, 1978), p. 41.

each developing a marketing mix that is appropriate for the specific product. While the differences in the decision process for carpets versus coffee appear obvious, other products have important distinctions that are not immediately apparent.

☐ The distributive approach fails to deal with the dynamics of behavior. In order to understand consumers and communicate effectively with them, the marketer must know something about their motivational patterns, media and promotional susceptibilities, and the relative importance of various psychological and sociological influences. In short, one needs to know why consumers behave as they do. Distributive research does not provide this kind of information.

☐ As markets become more competitive, segmentation along demographic lines becomes less adequate for purposes of product positioning. In order to remain competitive, the marketer must look to psycho-social dimensions as possible bases for segmentation.

Morphological research. The morphological approach starts where distributive research stops. After consumers are identified and described, the morphological approach focuses on the ways products are bought by different groups of people (for example, by social class or stages in the family life cycle). Morphological research might be described as "how" research because it concentrates on how decisions are made.

In the carpeting versus coffee example given earlier, the purchaser of carpeting will visit several outlets in order to see competitive carpeting samples and gather information. The person may consult consumer reports to learn more about fibers, talk with friends who have purchased carpeting recently, be strongly influenced by retail sales personnel, and share the final decision with the spouse. The decision process will tend to be drawn out over a period of time, possibly several weeks. By contrast, the buyer of coffee will probably rely on judgment and experience, augmented by advertising and recommendations from friends. Obviously, the marketer of carpets has different points of influence from the marketer of coffee. However, each must know the consumer's points of influence before recommending proper use of company resources.

Analytical research. Analytical research, like the morphological approach, starts where distributive research stops. It differs from morphological research because it involves causal assessment, determining *why* consumers purchase the products and brands they do. Causal assessment may reveal that the purchase was based on apparent product differences or influenced by psycho-social aspects of the product's image.

Generally, analytical research is the most difficult to obtain and assess and contains more ambiguity and error than the other forms of marketing research. Because of this, a number of indirect techniques have been developed to determine consumer motivations.

The example of carpets and coffee may help distinguish between morphological and analytical research. In the case of carpeting, our hypothetical consumer visited carpeting dealers, read consumer reports, talked with friends, was influenced by sales personnel, and discussed the decision with a spouse. This is a morphological description of *how* the consumer went about making the decision, but it doesn't indicate which information source was most influential or why the consumer chose the purchased brand of carpeting. Analytical research, on the other hand, might reveal that the consumer bought: (a) a particular type of carpeting because the fiber was resistant to stain and quickly recovered from crushing; (b) the brand chosen because of the fashion appeal used in the advertising; (c) the carpeting because it was from a high prestige store; and (d) from the salesperson who provided reassurance in choice of colors and patterns. By contrast, in the case of coffee, the consumer may have purchased a particular brand because of a celebrity's endorsement, particular advertising claim such as Folger's "mountain grown" slogan, appealing package design, price-off coupon offer, or a variety of other reasons.

Distributive, morphological, and analytical research answer different types of questions.

☐ Distributive research asks: "Who?"
☐ Morphological research asks: "How?"
☐ Analytical research asks: "Why?"

These questions are important, and marketing managers should consider all of them when developing a marketing plan.

PRIMARY vs. SECONDARY RESEARCH

Marketing makes a distinction between **primary** and **secondary research.** This distinction is not always clear. Primary research is data originated in view of a specific need. Secondary research already exists in some organized form, having been searched, organized, and stored by someone else. For example, if *Time* magazine were to undertake a survey to define their subscribers' demographic characteristics, the study would be primary research. This same information would be secondary research if it was provided to advertisers and advertising agencies because they did not originate the data.

Primary research. Primary research does not rely on published data. Original data is developed through some form of experimental or survey design. Essentially, it is collected in three ways (although each may appear in a variety of forms or in combination to solve a particular research problem)—observation, experiments, and surveys.

Observational techniques. Many marketing questions can be answered by simply observing some aspect of the marketing process at work.

☐ A major magazine regularly concealed a television camera in its waiting room to observe which magazine articles people read while waiting to see someone in the company. The intent was to find out which articles commanded the greatest attention.

☐ Investigators set up a hidden television camera in the ceiling of a supermarket to follow shoppers as they walked through the store. The object was to develop generalizations on the customer flow pattern that would lead to a more effective arrangement of merchandise and increased customer purchases.

☐ Twenty-four sheet poster (billboard) companies regularly observe traffic flow in various parts of major cities to develop statistics about the number of automobiles passing billboard sites.

The opportunities for observation are endless. Pantry or garbage can checks, concealed microphones that reveal how sales representatives respond to questions, and other observational methods can be employed when they are appropriate, and provide insights into consumer behavior.

Observation, however, is restricted to overt behavior and provides only inferential material about the consumer's thoughts. It also tends to be expensive and requires careful observation by the investigators.

One criticism of the observational technique is the question of ethics. Normally, consumers are not aware that they are under observation; therefore, such observations may be considered an invasion of privacy. Not all of the observational techniques constitute an invasion of privacy, but some do. At this time, legal guidelines are ambiguous, and the researcher must formulate personal standards of ethical conduct.

Experimental designs. Another problem of the observational method is that behavior usually takes place under natural, uncontrolled conditions. Drawing meaningful conclusions or testing a marketing hypothesis is difficult. In order to test hypotheses about some marketing stimuli or behavior, the experimental method may be employed by introducing experimental controls. It involves systematically introducing selected stimuli into a marketing situation and carefully measuring the effects these stimuli exert on the dependent variable. Extraneous factors that might influence experimental results are controlled by experimental design, statistical analysis, or both.

A simple example of a marketing experiment would be an in-store test of a product display's effectiveness in generating additional sales. One approach would be to use two groups of stores, **control** and **experimental.** The control and experimental stores might be given the treatment shown in Figure 5–7.

The product's unit sales would be measured during the pretest, test, and posttest periods in both control and experimental stores. In the control stores, the conditions would be the same in all three periods. By contrast, the display in experimental stores would be erected during the test period. The display's effectiveness in generating additional sales would be determined by comparing the sales patterns in the control stores to those in the experimental stores and testing the significance of the statistical differences found.

FIGURE 5–7 A simple design using control and experimental stores

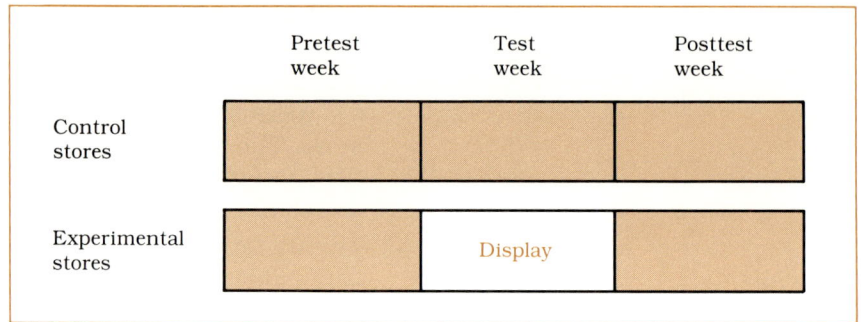

This example is a simple experimental design for a controlled experiment in marketing. Others could have been used for the same experiment; some would be more sophisticated and others less sophisticated. The highly sophisticated experimental design is not always the best, nor is the relatively crude design necessarily the worst. The nature of the problem, data, and decision are always the deciding factors. Marketing managers should have at least some training in experimental design and scientific methodology so that they can evaluate the design's adequacy and assess the validity of its results.

Surveys. The most common method for developing consumer information is the survey. Compared to direct observation and experimental designs, surveys are more versatile, produce a wealth of information, and are applicable to a greater variety of research problems. Surveys may be used to develop distributive, morphological, and analytical data and are the workhorses of consumer research.

Since surveys are so widespread and their use so commonplace, people often assume that surveys require no great skill to design and execute. This is not true. The design of the survey, development of the questionnaire (sometimes referred to as the **schedule**), identification of the appropriate population, selection of the sample, interviewing procedure, and data coding and analysis constitute one of the most demanding and technically advanced areas of marketing research. The survey's design and execution require a great deal of skill and judgment.

Because of the complexity of planning, executing, and analyzing surveys, extensive literature has been written detailing procedures and cautioning against common errors. One of the references is McGraw-Hill's *Handbook of Marketing Research,* a good portion of which relates to surveys.

Although surveys may employ a variety of specific techniques, there are three basic methods of collecting survey data: personal interviews, mail surveys, and telephone interviews. Each method has different problems in terms of sample design, interviewing flexibility and control, and cost; therefore, each interviewing method has unique advantages and disadvantages (Table 5–4). As a consequence, the method chosen will depend upon the types of data to be collected, population to be sampled, time restrictions, and budget available.

TABLE 5–4 Summary of major advantages and disadvantages of personal interviews, mail surveys, and telephone interviews

Survey Method	Advantages	Disadvantages
Personal interviews	Can be used with individuals and groups. Can accommodate long and complex questionnaires. Skilled observations and probes can develop more complete data than other methods. Sample selection can be well controlled.	More expensive than other methods. Interviewer bias can contaminate responses. Reliability depends upon the skill of the interviewer. Requires more training and is difficult to supervise. Some respondents are difficult to contact.
Mail surveys	Relatively inexpensive compared to personal interview surveys. Interviewer bias is eliminated. For major, geographically dispersed surveys, it usually saves time. Control can be centralized. It is versatile, so a wide variety of data can be obtained.	No opportunity to probe or clarify answers. Not possible to develop a random sample because of nonresponse problems. Tends to undersample in lower and upper income groups. Limited length and complexity of the survey questionnaire. Inappropriate for very short deadlines. Restricted to people who are literate.
Telephone interviews	Fast and convenient. Relatively economical. Can often reach people difficult to contact by other methods. Opportunity for limited probing. Interview is easy to control and supervise.	Difficult to use for long or complex questionnaires. Opportunities for probing more limited than in personal interview surveys. Possibility of interviewer bias. Telephone universe does not include all respondents.

Secondary research. An immense amount of useful secondary data pertaining to industries, markets, products, advertising, and consumers is available in the United States. One of the most useful sources is Sales Management's *Survey of Buying Power*, an annual publication that provides a plethora of population, household, and income statistics, as well as data on retail sales for selected merchandise groups. Data is broken down by geographic regions, states, counties, selected cities, and metropolitan county areas. A number of bibliographies of marketing information sources are also available. Among the better source bibliographies is the *Encyclopedia of Business Information Sources,* containing over 20,000 entries in 1300 subject categories, including references to source books, periodicals, organizations, directories, handbooks, and bibliographies. In addition, the U.S. Bureau of Census publishes data on population, housing, retail and wholesale trade, manufacturers, mineral industries, agriculture, transportation, and other areas. Trade associations, media, and a variety of commercial services also gather and organize marketing data on a number of industry and product groups.

Obtaining secondary information is primarily a matter of digging it out. With perseverance, information can be found relevant to almost any marketing problem that can be defined. However, secondary data is often not specific enough to the immediate problem and must be supplemented by primary research.

As we have seen, there are a variety of ways to collect consumer data. Secondary sources are often not specific enough for the information required. Observational methods, experimental designs, and various survey techniques all have unique advantages and disadvantages. No single approach is adequate. The secret of good research is using the proper technique for the proper problem at the proper time.

Good consumer research is rigorously systematic and wholly empirical. Although it employs a variety of mathematical techniques, it is an art as much as a science. Identifying appropriate population universes, designing questionnaires, and selecting samples are not absolute procedures. Budget constraints inevitably force compromises—choices among research techniques, problems to be researched, and precision of the acceptable answers.

Research professionals do not agree about the usefulness of available research techniques or the value of the mathematical models that are employed. When defining a competent research practitioner, creativity and judgment augment technical skill. Market managers and advertising specialists, however, should not be alienated by the lack of agreement in the field. They do need to learn enough about research to understand the disagreements and recognize when consumer research may be of value.

MAJOR AREAS OF RESEARCH JUDGMENT

Before leaving the general realm of consumer research and turning our attention to specific research techniques of interest to those responsible for the development of advertising, we need to discuss three critical areas of the research process: research objectives, questionnaire design, and sampling.

RESEARCH OBJECTIVES

Good research is not done on a haphazard basis. It requires organization, planning, and careful execution. At the heart of the research process are its objectives.

All research should start with a clear statement of the objectives, indicating not only what is to be learned, but also what kind of decision will be made on the basis of the findings, and the budget constraints. Without this information, it is not possible to select the appropriate research techniques, design a research instrument, and select an adequate sample.

Most disappointing research findings probably arise because the objectives were not sufficiently clear. When this occurs, marketing managers and advertising specialists have no one to blame but themselves. They alone know the nature of the decisions they have to make, can specify the information they need to make a decision, and can communicate this information to the market researcher.

QUESTIONNAIRE DESIGN

Few aspects of surveying are more critical than the design of the questionnaire. The art of writing questions may seem simple, but it is full of pitfalls for the naive and unwary.

Lorie and Roberts relate a story about measuring the readership of *Gone With the Wind.* When respondents were asked "Have you read this book?" more "yes" replies were received than were known to be possible. When the question was rephrased to "Do you intend to read *Gone With the Wind?*" only those who had read it indicated so, and the affirmative response was much lower.[6] Those who had not yet read it could respond without losing face by saying that they intended to read it.

Many instances of misleading results arise from poorly worded questions. The type of questions asked,[7] wording of the questions,[8] and question sequence[9] can have a profound effect on survey results.

Questions sometimes produce unintentional information. The simple, apparently straightforward question "Why do you use Trend detergent?" is actually three questions. Consumers might give answers such as: (a) It gets the clothes clean. (b) It's easier on my hands. (c) My neighbor recommended it. The first answer tells why the consumer used a detergent; the second tells why she prefers Trend to competitive products; and the third explains how she happened to start using Trend.[10] Questions that may be answered in several ways are called **multielement questions** and often lead to ambiguous results.

Guidance in the development of questions is available from a variety of sources, although Stanley L. Payne's *The Art of Asking Questions* is one of the best.[11] Questionnaire development is no job for the amateur, and even the pen of the experienced practitioner

---

[6]B. Schoner and K. P. Uhl, *Marketing Research,* 2nd ed. (New York: John Wiley & Sons, Inc., 1975), 237.

[7]B. S. Dohrenwend, "Some Effects of Open and Closed Questionnaires on Respondents' Answers," *Human Organizations* (Summer 1965): 175–84.

[8]D. Rugg, "Experiments in Wording Questions: II," *Public Opinion Quarterly* (March 1941): 91–92.

[9]E. J. Gross, "The Effect of Question Sequence on Measures of Buying Interest," *Journal of Advertising Research* (September 1964): 41.

[10]H. W. Boyd, Jr. and R. Westfall, *Marketing Research: Text and Cases,* 3rd ed. (Homewood, Illinois: Richard D. Irwin, Inc., 1972), 290.

[11]Stanley L. Payne, *The Art of Asking Questions* (Princeton, New Jersey: Princeton University Press, 1951).

A DAY IN THE LIFE OF A MARKETING RESEARCH SUPERVISOR

Bob Bohle brings to marketing research the academic background and the practical experience that make a well-rounded marketing research professional. A graduate in business administration at Berkeley, he gained a year's experience in purchasing and accounting before earning a degree in international business from the Thunderbird School of International Business in Phoenix, Arizona. Bob then spent a summer in Mexico, polishing his Spanish, before joining Purex as assistant manager of operations. Four years later, he became an assistant product manager in the International Division of Colgate-Palmolive, and shortly thereafter spent two years as a product manager in Germany. Returning to the United States, Bob gained additional experience in product management with General Foods, in the New Venture Department of Ralston Purina, and as a marketing research consultant before joining D'Arcy-MacManus & Masius as a marketing research supervisor.

Bob not only uses his marketing research skills in business, but also contributes them to civic organizations such as the Citizens Advisory Council for the Lindberg School District in St. Louis County, Missouri.

7:30–8:00

Thought I'd be the first one in, but Paul is here already. There's a major client presentation in Florida Friday morning.

Planned day . . . Checked with Bill (an account supervisor) to see if anything is needed today. Nothing yet.

8:00–10:15

Started to review tapes of focus groups conducted last week to pretest a new television campaign for the phone company.

. . . Have got to control the groups more effectively—too many people talking at once.

. . . Got some good insights though, they talk freely.

. . . Taking notes for content and quotes.

. . . Comparing impressions gained from listening to the groups to the notes written at the conclusion of each group that summarized my impressions for that group session . . . pretty close, need more detailed explanations.

. . . I hate listening to these groups again; besides being boring, it's painful to hear the mistakes you've made moderating the groups . . . but I've learned something.

10:15–10:35

Bill called. . . . Client wants a proposal for an awareness study for the new campaign that will be aired starting next month. Target group will be housewives between the ages of 25 to 49 with a minimum family income of $20,000 (that keeps going up).

Need to call Media to find out what the media timetable is going to be, if all markets will be subject to the same media pressure, and when we'll have accumulated a minimum of 600 GRPs (Gross Rating Points).

10:35–11:05

Tom (Creative) called. The TV commercials are done—the one's we pretested some eight weeks ago. Wants me to look at them.

They're good. It bothers me though that they did not quite catch the mood needed to influence our target audience to the maximum effect.

Our segmentation study completed six months ago indicated that our target, the "Rational Businessman," was influenced by the more subtle selling approaches. These commercials may be somewhat too dramatic, perhaps emotional is a better word for it.

I wonder if I'm letting my own preferences dictate my reaction.

. . . I didn't say anything to Tom about my concerns. . . . Too late to do anything about it; besides, they are really good commercials.

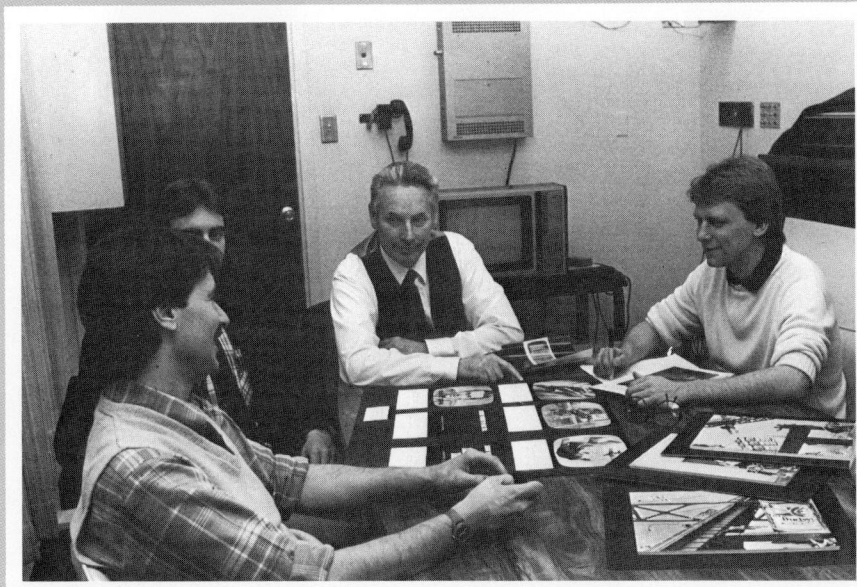

11:05–11:15
Phil (my boss) returned my report on the charcoal exploratory study to me. Thought it was a good job, but made a few notes on it. I'll have to rewrite a small section of the report. The point I made about outdoor cooking being a "macho" thing with men needs clarification.

11:15–11:30
Back to the focus groups. Will do about anything to get out of listening to these things over again. Maybe I'll let my secretary transcribe them for me. . . . She didn't particularly like the idea. . . . Can't blame her.

11:30–12:15
Tim (New Business) called. Can I come to a meeting with a potential new client? We have an opportunity to pitch the account. . . . A new frozen food item. Just what I was waiting for. I said, "Yes!"

Prospect is willing to underwrite research and creative costs. A most generous offer. We're in competition with three other agencies who shall remain nameless. My task is to determine what research is needed in order to provide our creatives with the information needed to do a good job.

Meeting breaks up. Everyone is very enthused about the opportunity to work on this business. Potential is between $15–$20 million per year.

Went back to my office. Flushed out a few ideas, then talked to Phil to brief him and to get his thinking. We agreed to ask the client for whatever research he may have. No sense duplicating work done already. Proposal will have to wait until we have this information.

12:15–1:45
Tom D. called; "Want to have lunch?" You bet. Always interesting. Tom works for a small marketing consulting firm. Between stories about his family's sessions with the psychoanalyst and his employer's idiosyncrasies, I am thoroughly entertained.

1:45–4:45
Listened to tapes again. A three-hour grind. At last finished. Time to start on the report.

4:45–5:00
I dig through the files for the research proposal. It's times like these I'm thankful that I've been taught the value of writing a good proposal. I change the tense of the verbs and a few words here and there, and I've completed the first three sections of the report (Background, Objectives, and Method).

The rest of the report is also not too difficult to write, since the time spent preparing for the research assured me that all the issues were thoroughly covered during the conduct of the study. Nothing worse than incomplete data.

5:00–6:50
Have to put off completing the job. Linda F. from Creative came by. She's concerned about the pretest. Are we going to probe for the right kinds of issues? I asked her to give me the issues she's concerned with and why. Linda leaves an hour later, somewhat reassured that her creative effort will not be violated through misunderstanding. I gained a better understanding of creative people's needs. The project will be better off for it.

6:50
It's later than I thought. Time to go home.

Contributed by D'Arcy-MacManus & Masius, St. Louis.

slips occasionally. Every questionnaire should be pretested to determine how well it works and the kinds of information it develops.

SAMPLING

Sampling is one area of consumer research that can be pursued with firm guidelines and scientific precision. However, scientific precision is frequently considered to be too expensive, slow, and unnecessary. Before a sample is drawn, the following things must be determined: (a) the type of information to be collected; (b) how this information will be used; and (c) how precise the results need to be. A scientifically drawn sample is recommended if the information being collected is statistical in nature, it will be used to make forecasts or draw firm conclusions about the past, the measuring instrument is valid, and precise information is needed. If one's purpose is less rigorous and the measuring instrument provides only gross measurements, a scientifically drawn sample is unnecessary.

Sampling is an essential part of marketing research. It is based on a well developed theory, an efficient way to estimate a universe, and an accurate and pragmatic way to obtain empirical data. Suppose a marketing manager wants to know the proportion of people eighteen years of age and over that drink coffee. If he had the time and money, he might interview all of them. Of course, if he used a thousand interviewers, interviewing twelve hours a day, and completing an interview every ten minutes, he could complete the task in about six years. On the other hand, he could obtain an excellent estimate from a carefully drawn sample of only a few hundred respondents.

Many people are skeptical that one can describe the reactions of several million people by interviewing only a few hundred. Yet, it is done all of the time with remarkable precision. A few hundred grocery stores are audited to determine the brand shares of grocery products; two or three hundred people may be used in a comparative taste test of two food products to predict the preferences of the U.S. population; and a carefully drawn sample of 1500 voters can approximate how the body politic will vote in a national presidential election.

Not all samples are equally reliable in reflecting the characteristics of the population universe. The size of a sample is a factor in determining its accuracy. But, the precision used to draw the sample is often a much more critical consideration. The key word in sampling is **representativeness.** A sample must be representative before a marketing manager can be confident that it will provide a valid reflection of the relevant characteristics of that population.

A detailed discussion of sampling is far beyond the scope of this text. The American Marketing Association has published a monograph, *The Use of Sampling in Marketing Research,* that outlines sampling theory in clear language and provides a bibliography for the student who wishes to pursue the area further.[12]

Type and size are two aspects of sampling that determine the representativeness of the sample.

---

[12]W. P. Dommeruth, *The Use of Sampling in Marketing Research* (Chicago: The American Marketing Association, 1975).

Types of samples.   Basically, there are two types of samples—probability and nonprobability. In a **probability sample,** every unit in the universe being sampled has an equal and known probability of being included. Although there are a variety of techniques for drawing probability samples, the essential characteristic is that no unit has a greater or lesser chance of being included in the sample. Representativeness can be assured with a probability sample, and statistical techniques can be used to determine the magnitude of the probable sampling error.

Generally, there are three kinds of **nonprobability samples.** The **convenience sample** contains respondents selected on the basis of convenience. Interviewing passers-by on a street corner or in a shopping center is an example. In the **judgment** or **purposive sample,** the researcher chooses respondents believed to be representative of the entire population. An example of a judgment sample would be to select a sample of supermarkets from various sections of town and various chains and independent organizations to measure the sales of a food product. The stores would not be selected on a random basis, but would be chosen because of size and location. In the **quota sample,** the researcher selects sampling units to fill a quota for certain known parameters of the general population. For example, if 20 percent of the population had incomes of over $30,000, then 20 percent of the sample would have incomes of over $30,000. If 10 percent of the heads of households were over sixty years of age, then 10 percent of the sample heads of households would be over sixty years of age. A quota sample is usually more elaborate than other forms of nonprobability samples, but it resembles them in that factors other than chance determine sample inclusion.

Nonprobability samples are frequently criticized because there is no way to guarantee that they will be representative of the population being sampled, nor is it possible to calculate the magnitude of the sampling error. Nonetheless, they are used extensively because: (a) They are less expensive in terms of time and money than probability samples. (b) For some research techniques, there is no feasible way of drawing a probability sample because units in the population are uncooperative.

Because of costs and feasibility, nonprobability samples are widely used in marketing research. There is nothing wrong with their use provided: (a) The user of the research is aware of the sample's limitations. (b) Reasonable judgment has been exercised in avoiding gross sampling errors. Nonprobability samples are often used in the early stages of a research project when the market researcher is simply searching for ideas or attempting to develop hypotheses for testing, in obtaining consumer reaction to advertising and package designs, and are commonplace among various motivational techniques. The use of probability versus nonprobability samples only becomes critical during the infrequent occasions when a high degree of accuracy is required in research data.

Sample size.   The size of the sample required to represent a population is determined by the complexity of the population rather than the size of the population itself. A relatively small sample may be used if the population is known to be homogeneous. If the population is known to be complex (as in the case of the U.S. population, with its diversity of ethnic, religious, income, and special interest groups), the sample size needs to be relatively large to provide representation of the various population segments.

Generally, an appropriate sample size is somewhere between thirty units and five percent of the population. Actual size, however, will depend upon the complexity of the population and the size of the sampling error that is acceptable. Specific decisions on the sample's size for a particular survey must be made by the researcher on a project by project basis, with the final decision often being a compromise between the precision desired and the funds available for the project.

MARKETING RESEARCH AND THE DEVELOPMENT OF ADVERTISING

Although all forms of marketing research may prove valuable in the development of advertisements and commercials, creative groups are often more interested in analytical research because it deals directly with consumer motivation—*why* consumers buy the products and brands they do. One reason analytical research is often the most difficult to conduct and more subject to ambiguity and error is that consumers' answers sometimes produce misleading survey results. For example, when questions are asked about brands of beer, it is not uncommon for survey results to indicate that people drink more Michelob than Anheuser Busch produces. Respondents think they gain prestige in the eyes of the interviewer by claiming a premium beer as their regular brand even though they usually drink a popular priced beer. Similar misrepresentations occur in other product fields.

Misrepresentations are particularly numerous when the questions are of a personal nature, or causal questions are used. Consumers do use products for reasons they are unwilling to admit. Sometimes they will fabricate plausible, partially true explanations to protect themselves from embarrassment, while still satisfying the interview requirements. In some cases, the consumer honestly does not know why he or she uses one brand instead of another and will give a trivial or stereotyped response.

As a result, a number of research techniques, many borrowed from the social sciences, have been developed to determine why consumers behave as they do. They are generally referred to as **motivational research.** In the following material, two types of motivation research, **projective techniques** and **extended interviews,** will be discussed briefly.

PROJECTIVE TECHNIQUES

Projective techniques, long used by psychologists for clinical diagnosis, have been adapted to a wide variety of marketing problems. The theory behind marketing's use of projective techniques is that consumers will reveal their own need-value systems when they are asked to respond to a relatively unstructured stimulus. Projective techniques are of special value in disguising the purpose of an interview and eliciting information that might normally be withheld by consumers or overlooked by more traditional research procedures. Some of the more frequently used projective techniques are briefly described in the following material.

Word association. Word association is one of the best known and most widely used forms of the projective techniques. It is relatively easy to apply and can be used effectively to screen brand names for negative connotations or uncover consumers' feelings about new products, packages, designs, illustrations, or communications themes. Typically, the respondent is asked to give the first word that comes to mind in response to each of a list of unrelated words or some other stimulus. In some cases, the consumer is asked to respond with a series of words; this modification is referred to as **chain** or **successive word association.** The name search for Standard Oil of New Jersey used word association to explore the connotations of the word "Exxon" among consumers.

Sentence completion. An incomplete phrase is given to consumers, and they are asked to add words in order to complete the sentence. For example, respondents may be asked to complete the thought "When I have a headache. . . ." A consumer might respond by saying ". . . I want to be left alone," ". . . nothing seems to help," ". . . I take Excedrin," or a variety of other responses. An analysis of responses often leads to a product claim or communications theme that can be developed in advertising. For example, a bank used the stimulus "When I go into a bank. . . ." Analysis of the results showed a disproportionate number of responses such as: "I am ignored," "I'm treated like a number," "I feel I'm imposing on them," "I feel all they want is my money." These results led to the development of a communications theme stressing "personal attention" and "concern for customers," as well as a training program for tellers and bank officers designed to improve their interpersonal skills in dealing with customers.

Picture and visual methods. In this approach, a cartoon or picture serves as the stimulus object. There are a number of variations of this technique, such as: (a) The subject may be shown a picture of a marketing situation or a product in use and may be asked to tell a story about it. (b) One character in a cartoon may be making a statement or asking a question, and the subject is asked to formulate an answer. (c) Two cartoon characters may be shown disagreeing on some point, and the subject will be asked to indicate with which she agrees and why. The picture method is highly flexible because the visual stimulus can be adapted to the marketing question at hand.

One advantage of this approach is that subjects seem to enjoy working with pictures, and this helps build rapport with the interviewer. This factor undoubtedly contributes to the quality of the information that can be gained from the interview.

Situational methods. Situational methods differ from visual techniques in that a verbal rather than a visual stimulus is used. In a situational approach, respondents will be asked to describe in detail the kind of person who uses a particular product or shops at a particular store. G. H. Smith cites a study in which young women were asked to write a personality sketch of the type of person who buys Brand X deodorant and who buys Brand Y. Analysis showed that the Brand X user was seen as more lax in her cleanliness standards, less intelligent, and less popular with boys than the user of Brand Y. Some respondents rationalized their negative perceptions of the Brand X user by saying she was thrifty, wanted to save time, and preferred a less messy deodorant. These findings led to the recommendation that Brand X exploit thriftiness, saving time, and tidiness as advertising themes, and the product name be given a positive connotation by linking it to these desired product features.[13]

The situational method is extremely flexible, easy to work with, and limited only by the imagination of the researcher.

Other projective techniques. A number of other projective techniques are used infrequently because they are difficult to use, require highly trained people to gather and interpret the data, and do not lend themselves to the collection of data from large samples. One example is **psychodrama,** in which participants are asked to act out situations. As the participants become involved in their assigned roles, it is believed that they will express their true feelings and beliefs. Another example is **graphology,** the analysis of handwriting. These and other projective techniques are cumbersome and have found limited favor with marketers.

EXTENDED INTERVIEWS

Extended interviews is an approach that can be used with either individuals or groups to obtain qualitative data about consumers' motivations, feelings, and beliefs. Variously referred to as *qualitative, unstructured, depth,* or *focused interviews,* the approach differs from traditional interviewing approaches in the following ways.

☐ The interview is relatively unstructured. Instead of using a formal questionnaire, the interviewer has a list of topic areas that may be introduced in a variety of ways. The interview is more of a discussion than a question and answer encounter, with the interviewer encouraging respondents to discourse widely over a variety of related and relevant topics. When used with groups, the interview evolves into a group discussion of relevant topics introduced by the interviewer or brought up by group members. It requires skillful leadership to keep the discussion pertinent, and to exhaust one area of discussion before moving to others.

☐ The interview is qualitative. It emphasizes feelings, experiences, and anecdotes rather than tabular and quantifiable responses. How something is said (the tone) and what is left unsaid (avoided) are often more important than *what* is said.

---

[13]George H. Smith, *Motivation in Research and Marketing* (New York: McGraw-Hill, 1954), 229.

- [ ] The elicited information tends to be more profound, detailed, and comprehensive than that normally garnered from traditional interviewing techniques.
- [ ] Interviews tend to be longer. Extended interviews last for several hours in their efforts to explore all aspects of a given subject.
- [ ] The interviews are usually recorded. Tapes are usually made of the interviews so that a complete transcript is available for analysis.

Since the extended interview approach is relatively expensive, small samples are generally used; and since extended cooperation is required, the sample is generally nonrepresentative. Interpretation is time-consuming, difficult, and often highly subjective. Despite these limitations, extended interviews are widely used because they provide insights into behavior that would otherwise be overlooked. Members of the creative team often sit in on the interviews or observe them through a one-way mirror in order to gain firsthand experience of the ways in which consumers express themselves and react to the topics under discussion.

Extended interviews are particularly useful in providing hypotheses that can be translated into product ideas or marketing communications that can be tested by more traditional survey techniques for verification or rejection.

SUMMARY

Marketing research and analysis makes effective marketing and persuasive advertising possible. Certain areas of analysis are of primary interest to advertising's creative teams, namely the product, market position, consumer, and advertising.

Marketing research is used to gather relevant marketing information. Three broad research traditions dealing with the consumer are distributive, morphological, and analytical.

A distinction is often made between secondary and primary research. Secondary research deals with published data, whereas primary research is concerned with originating new data. Observation, experiments, and surveys are three basic techniques used in gathering primary data. Of these three, surveys are the most versatile and widely used. The three basic survey techniques are personal interviews, mail surveys, and telephone interviews. Each has unique advantages and disadvantages.

In developing primary research, there are three key areas of research judgment: (a) definition of research objectives; (b) questionnaire design; and (c) sampling. The definition of research objectives is the starting point of effective research. Poorly defined objectives result in disappointing research findings. Questionnaire design is another critical area of the research process. Misleading results arise from the questions asked, their wording, and the question sequence. Sampling is the third critical area of research judgment. There are two basic types of samples—probability and nonprobability. Although nonprobability samples have many limitations, they are frequently used in marketing and advertising research because of cost considerations, and the absence of a feasible way to devise a probability sample. The adequacy of a sample depends upon its type and size.

Although all forms of marketing research are of value in the development of advertising, creative groups are often more interested in analytical research because it deals directly with consumer motivations—why consumers buy the products and brands they do. This type of research is the most difficult to conduct because consumers will sometimes give false or misleading answers. As a consequence, a number of special research techniques, called motivation research, have been developed to determine *why* consumers behave as they do. Two primary types of motivation research are projective techniques and extended interviews. Projective techniques use a relatively unstructured stimulus to elicit consumer responses. Extended interviews involve long, relatively unstructured interviews with individuals or with groups.

REVIEW QUESTIONS

1 Why does much of today's advertising appear bland and pointless?
2 In discussing consumer analysis, the text suggests four areas of analysis that are particularly fruitful for people who are responsible for developing advertising. What are these four areas and why are they helpful?
3 The following table shows a hypothetical comparison of share of market and share of advertising. What is the basic premise underlying this comparison? What tentative conclusions about the advertising expenditures of each brand might be drawn from this table?

Brand	Share of Market	Share of Advertising
A	35%	45%
B	15%	5%
C	30%	29%
D	20%	21%

4 Identify the strengths and weaknesses of distributive research.
5 Distinguish between primary and secondary research. What are the strengths and limitations of secondary research?
6 Explain what is meant by observational techniques. What is the main limitation of this approach?
7 Define a marketing problem and construct an experimental design to answer it.
8 What are the advantages and disadvantages of: (a) personal interviews; (b) mail surveys; and (c) telephone interviews?
9 Distinguish between probability and nonprobability samples. In view of their shortcomings, why are nonprobability samples often used?
10 Explain why motivation research is used. Explain what is meant by projective techniques and the assumption upon which they are based. Explain how extended interviews differ from more traditional interviews.

DISCUSSION QUESTIONS

1 Comment on the possible value of motivation research in dealing with each of the following situations.

- ☐ Reasons for buying designer jeans.
- ☐ Finding out what new forms of cake mixes consumers would be interested in.
- ☐ Why a widely advertised brand of beer has not been successful among heavy beer drinkers, although taste tests indicate that they are unable to distinguish it from their preferred brands.
- ☐ Reasons for buying private label shaving cream.

If motivation research is applicable in these instances, which form—projective techniques or extended interviews—do you think would be most appropriate? Why?

2 Assume that you have been assigned to write advertising for a new furniture account acquired by your advertising agency. The client company has done no marketing research into the characteristics of its market. You are told that a limited budget has been approved for a marketing research study. Knowing that the research funds available will not be sufficient to answer all of your questions, set up a list of priorities for the types of research that you would like to see done.

3 The text points out that extended interviews often take two forms: (a) interviews with individuals; and (b) interviews with small groups (perhaps six or seven people in a group). What do you think the advantages and disadvantages of these two approaches would be?

PROBLEM

Select two competitive advertisements for the same type of product. Compare these two advertisements using the format suggested in the text. After you have analyzed the two advertisements, write a copy strategy for each of them. What conclusions can you draw from this experience?

6
Consumer Behavior

'THE KID IN UPPER 4'

During the early days of World War II, the New Haven Railroad ran the advertisement in Figure 6–1. Unlike most advertising, it promised no benefit. Instead, it asked for sacrifice and understanding (see copy in Figure 6–1). Rationing was a national policy, and everything was in short supply, including railway travel. Airline transportation, an infant industry, was virtually nonexistent. Commercial travel between cities was almost exclusively train or bus. Troop trains crisscrossed the nation, severely limiting the supply of coach seats and sleepers available for civilian use. It was a time of inconvenience, hardship, frustration, and complaint. The New Haven ad was pure emotional impact at a time when emotions ran deep.

The response that greeted this advertisement was probably

> . . . the greatest slug of publicity ever accorded any advertisement, anywhere, at anytime. It was read on leading radio programs by the stars themselves, made into a song, pinned to thousands of bulletin boards, reproduced free in leading magazines and newspapers, read from pulpits, published in prisons, picked up abroad . . . and Joseph B. Eastman, Director of Defense Transportation, asked the railroad to run it all over the country.
>
> A rival railroad—the Pennsylvania—asked for 300 posters to display in its stations. MGM made it into a movie short, and it won the highest award for outstanding copy in 1942. . . .[1]

'MY FRIEND, JOE HOLMES, IS NOW A HORSE'

George Gribbin, one of the greatest copywriters in advertising's history, wrote the advertisement in Figure 6–2. It is in direct contrast to the New Haven ad. Instead of asking for sacrifice and understand-

---

[1]Julian Lewis Watkins, *100 Greatest Advertisements* (New York: Dover Publications, 1959), 149.

FIGURE 6–1 [Source: Julian Lewis Watkins, *100 Greatest Advertisements* (New York: Dover Publications, Inc., 1959), 148.]

FIGURE 6–2 [Source: Julian Lewis Watkins, *100 Greatest Advertisements* (New York: Dover Publications, Inc., 1959), 132.]

My friend, Joe Holmes, is now a horse

JOE always said when he died he'd like to become a horse.

One day Joe died.

Early this May I saw a horse that looked like Joe drawing a milk wagon.

I sneaked up to him and whispered, "Is it you, Joe?"

He said, "Yes, and am I happy!" I said, "Why?"

He said, "I am now wearing a comfortable collar for the first time in my life. My shirt collars always used to shrink and murder me. In fact, one choked me to death. That is why I died!"

"Goodness, Joe," I exclaimed, "Why didn't you tell me about your shirts sooner? I would have told you about Arrow shirts. *They never shrink.* Not even the oxfords."

"G'wan," said Joe. "Oxford's the worst shrinker of all!"

"Maybe," I replied, "but not *Gordon,* the Arrow oxford. I know. I'm wearing one. It's Sanforized-shrink-proof. Besides, it's cool. Besides, this creamy shade I chose is the newest shirt color, *bamboo.*"

"Swell," said Joe. "My boss needs a shirt like that. I'll tell him about Gordon. Maybe he'll give me an extra quart of oats. And, gosh, do I love oats!"

If it hasn't an Arrow Label it isn't an Arrow Shirt

ARROW SHIRTS
Sanforized Shrunk — a new shirt free if one ever shrinks
Made by CLUETT, PEABODY & CO., INC.

ing, it offers physical comfort; instead of trading on emotions, it trades on humor. Yet, it too is a great advertisement.

'THE PENALTY OF LEADERSHIP'

The advertisement in Figure 6–3 is about quality. It expresses a product philosophy that has made the brand name Cadillac synonymous with excellence. In commenting on this advertisement, Julian Watkins, author of *100 Greatest Advertisements*, says:

> The list of famous advertisements selected for this book is not entirely my own. When the work began, I wrote to perhaps fifty leading advertising men explaining my belief in the need and usefulness of a volume like this and asked them to name some of the

FIGURE 6–3 (Courtesy General Motors Corp.)

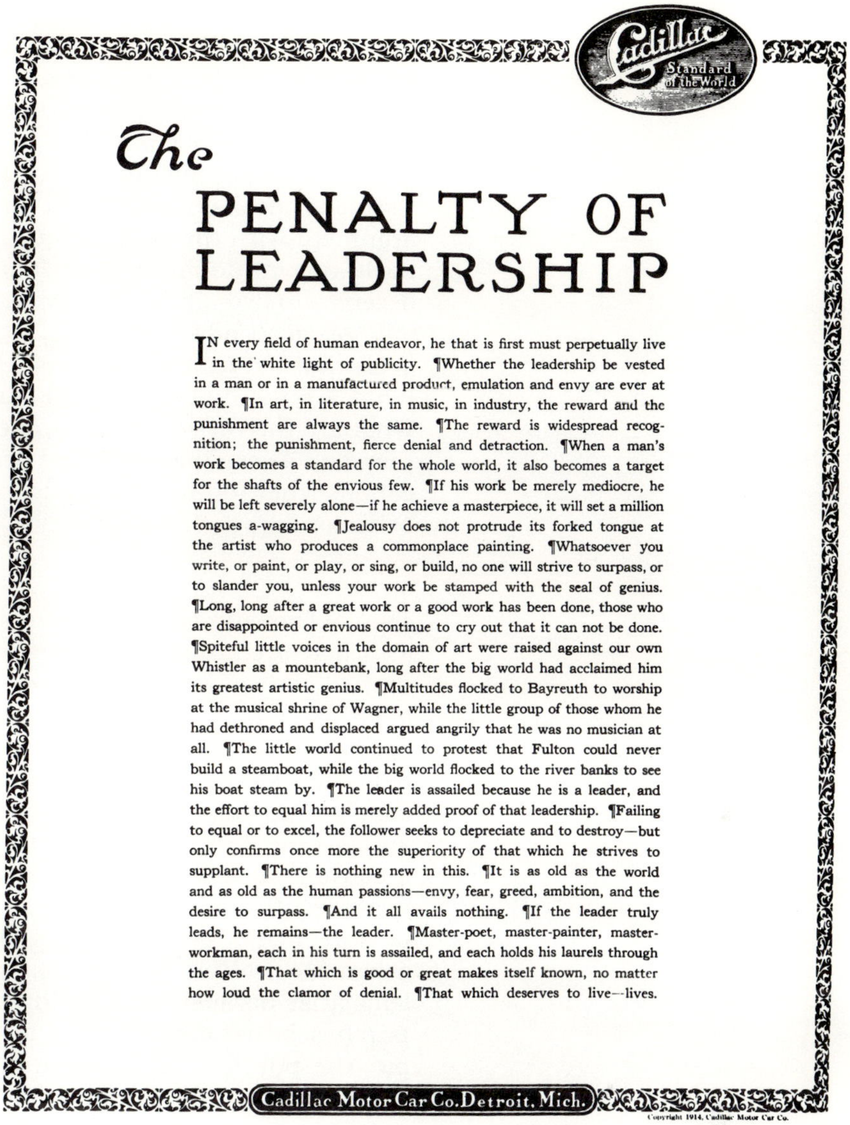

The

PENALTY OF LEADERSHIP

IN every field of human endeavor, he that is first must perpetually live in the white light of publicity. ¶Whether the leadership be vested in a man or in a manufactured product, emulation and envy are ever at work. ¶In art, in literature, in music, in industry, the reward and the punishment are always the same. ¶The reward is widespread recognition; the punishment, fierce denial and detraction. ¶When a man's work becomes a standard for the whole world, it also becomes a target for the shafts of the envious few. ¶If his work be merely mediocre, he will be left severely alone—if he achieve a masterpiece, it will set a million tongues a-wagging. ¶Jealousy does not protrude its forked tongue at the artist who produces a commonplace painting. ¶Whatsoever you write, or paint, or play, or sing, or build, no one will strive to surpass, or to slander you, unless your work be stamped with the seal of genius. ¶Long, long after a great work or a good work has been done, those who are disappointed or envious continue to cry out that it can not be done. ¶Spiteful little voices in the domain of art were raised against our own Whistler as a mountebank, long after the big world had acclaimed him its greatest artistic genius. ¶Multitudes flocked to Bayreuth to worship at the musical shrine of Wagner, while the little group of those whom he had dethroned and displaced argued angrily that he was no musician at all. ¶The little world continued to protest that Fulton could never build a steamboat, while the big world flocked to the river banks to see his boat steam by. ¶The leader is assailed because he is a leader, and the effort to equal him is merely added proof of that leadership. ¶Failing to equal or to excel, the follower seeks to depreciate and to destroy—but only confirms once more the superiority of that which he strives to supplant. ¶There is nothing new in this. ¶It is as old as the world and as old as the human passions—envy, fear, greed, ambition, and the desire to surpass. ¶And it all avails nothing. ¶If the leader truly leads, he remains—the leader. ¶Master-poet, master-painter, master-workman, each in his turn is assailed, and each holds his laurels through the ages. ¶That which is good or great makes itself known, no matter how loud the clamor of denial. ¶That which deserves to live—lives.

Cadillac Motor Car Co. Detroit, Mich.

Copyright 1914, Cadillac Motor Car Co.

advertisements which, over the years, had made a profound impression on them. "The Penalty of Leadership" appeared on every list!

Much has been written about this perhaps greatest of all advertisements, the conditions which prompted it, etc., but the significant fact to me is this: the advertisement, contrary to popular belief, appeared but once: January 2, 1915 in *The Saturday Evening Post*, yet after more than thirty years, hardly a week goes by that either Cadillac or its agency, MacManus, John & Adams, Detroit, do not get requests for one or more copies. Millions have been distributed.[2]

These three examples, all considered advertising classics, have been chosen not only because they are examples of good advertising,

[2]Ibid., 23.

CHAPTER 6 | CONSUMER BEHAVIOR

but also because they demonstrate that good advertising thrives on a variety of motivational appeals.

The New Haven advertisement uses an emotional appeal to explain inconvenience and accept sacrifice; the Arrow Shirts ad uses humorous body copy to sell the idea of comfort; the Cadillac advertisement speaks of quality in an intellectual vein, summing up its argument with the observation: "That which is good or great makes itself known, no matter how loud the clamor of denial. That which deserves to live—lives."

All good advertisements, past and present, are rooted in appeals that motivate consumers. How does one appeal to consumers? What are the differences and commonalities of the buying public? What are the variables that influence consumers to behave the ways they do? These questions are at the heart of marketing communications; they indicate a need to examine the entire area of consumer behavior.

AN OVERVIEW OF CONSUMER BEHAVIOR

Think of consumers as problem solvers wherein a problem is defined as a perceived difference between an existing state of affairs and a desired state of affairs. Thus, consumers' needs, wants, and desires often present problems that consumers try to solve by purchasing goods and services. The housewife who needs a dessert for a dinner party may solve this problem by purchasing a cake. A newly married couple needs a place to live; they may solve this problem by renting an apartment or buying a house. Or, a young executive, who needs a convenient way to carry documents and establish himself in his new executive role, buys an attaché case. When a consumer's supply of a regularly used product has been exhausted, the individual solves the problem by purchasing more of that product. Other problems arise because of changing needs, improved financial status, or purchases that create a need for additional acquisitions. For example, the purchase of a house gives rise to the need for furniture, carpeting, appliances, and other household objects. But in every case, consumers are solving what appear to them to be problems.

Obviously, where the purchase of goods or services is concerned, problems can be solved in different ways. Consumers are faced with many choices, urged upon them by manufacturers insisting that their product is the best solution. Clairol, Revlon, Max Factor, Elizabeth Arden, Charles of the Ritz, and Helena Rubenstein are but a few of the alternatives available in the cosmetics and personal care field. Ford, Chevrolet, Plymouth, Pontiac, Oldsmobile, Chrysler, Volkswagen, Datsun, and Subaru hardly begin to enumerate the alternatives available among automobiles. Other product fields offer a similar array of choices.

Each manufacturer, through product design, packaging, pricing, advertising, and other communication variables, is attempting to motivate consumers to choose its particular product. Those that are successful in this endeavor prosper; those that are unsuccessful do not. It is little wonder that motivation is a buzzword in marketing and consumer behavior is a subject of intense interest. In this chapter, we will isolate consumer behavior as a subject of study and briefly examine human motivation and the variables that influence it.

MOTIVATION

Motivation is one of the more complex areas of human behavior. Most of us have difficulty defining the term, even though we know what we mean when we use the term ourselves. When faced with the problem of motivating someone to behave in a particular way, we often do not know what to do. Employers worry about motivating employees; teachers fret about the lack of student motivation; and advertisers spend an inordinate amount of time and money trying to find effective ways to motivate consumers to buy their products.

One of the problems is the ambiguity of the words we use to discuss motivation. We use the terms *motivation, motives, needs, drives, wants,* and *goals,* mixing technical and popular language and confusing both ourselves and others. To complicate matters further, we sometimes make distinctions between *conscious* and *unconscious* motives, *rational* and *irrational* motives, and *needs* and *wants.*

A second problem is that motives cannot be directly observed. Only behavior can be observed. For example, we observe someone eating and we *infer* that the person is hungry. Yet, hunger may not be the reason for eating at all. Most of us have had the experience of joining someone for a sandwich and a cup of coffee not because we are hungry, but for social reasons. We want companionship. Sometimes we eat just because it is time to eat. By virtue of our daily routine, we usually eat at a particular hour, whether we are hungry or not. Then there is the compulsive eater—the person who eats continually because of some psychological conflict, thereby endangering health and gaining unwanted weight.

In the following material, we will do four things: (a) Define motivation. (b) Suggest some terminology that can be used to eliminate ambiguity when discussing the subject. (c) Discuss some of the key issues relating to motivation. (d) Identify some of the conclusions that can be drawn about motivation.

DEFINITION OF MOTIVATION

Generically, **motivation** is a theoretical construct involving an internal need state (sometimes referred to as an **energizing force** or **tension system**) that gives impetus to behavior, and a directional component that gives general direction to a variety of responses serving the same general function for the organism.

Although there are many theories of motivation, most agree with the stipulations in this definition. Let's look at these stipulations more closely.

☐ *Theoretical construct.* Motivation is a theoretical construct that cannot be directly observed. We cannot see inside people's heads. We can only observe behavior from which we *infer* motives. Thus, a motive is an abstraction intended to explain behavior.

☐ *Internal need state.* Generally, the concept of motivation requires an internal energizing force that causes us to act. Further, this need state may vary in intensity.

☐ *Directional component for a variety of behaviors.* Generally, a motive provides direction for a variety of behaviors. The emphasis on a directional component for a variety of responses suggests that motivated behavior is adaptive and influenced by environmental and personal variables. The child who is unable to gain attention by tugging at a parent's hand may do so by having a temper tantrum. The student who cannot achieve recognition through scholarship or athletic prowess may do so through antisocial behavior.

Similarly, a safety motive could be used to explain the purchase of flight insurance, acquisition of steel-belted radial tires, installation of a smoke detector, purchase of a burglar alarm, retreat in the face of danger, or aggressive behavior used to subdue an observed threat.

With this definition of motivation, let us turn to the language of motivation. In the process, we will relate the psychological concept of motivation to the economic concept of demand because, ultimately, advertising practitioners are interested in consumer demand. Consumer motivation is of concern to advertisers only insofar as it creates demand for their products.

THE LANGUAGE OF MOTIVATION

Inherent in the concept of motivation is the concept of a goal. The need states in our definition of motivation are internal. Yet many, if not most, of our need states must be satisfied through things in the external world. These external things that have the capacity to satisfy internal need states are called **goals,** and much of our behavior is directed toward their attainment. A goal may be an object, such as food, water, or a product; or a state of affairs, such as an occupation, marriage, or admiration and esteem from others.

The intent of marketing is to persuade consumers to perceive products and services as goals that will satisfy their needs. As marketing succeeds in this task, it transforms psychological needs into the economic concept of demand.[3] This transformation takes place through the following four stage progression: internal need states; need recognition; product identification; and product demand.

Internal need states.   This is what we normally mean when we use the term *need*—the hypothetical need state referred to in our definition of motivation. At this stage the need state (or need) is nonconscious in the commonsense use of the term, and broad enough to accept a variety of related goals or solutions. An example of such a need state might be the general safety of the individual.

---

[3]Johan Arndt has suggested that, for clarity of thinking in marketing, a conceptual distinction should be made between the concepts of needs, wants, and demand. See Johan Arndt, "How Broad Should the Marketing Concept Be?" *Journal of Marketing* (January 1978): 101–3.

There is no universal agreement and no way of experimentally validating the precise nature or number of internal need states. However, the late Abraham Maslow, an eminent psychologist, suggested that man has five basic needs—physiological requirements, safety, affiliation, esteem, and self-actualization. Let us assume that these five basic needs are substantially correct; then the general safety of the individual may be considered a need state.

Need recognition.   This is what we normally mean when we use the word *motive*. At this state, the need appears as a conscious, identifiable idea. The particular form in which the need manifests itself in consciousness will be influenced by the individual's psychological characteristics and factors in the external environment. Thus, for someone living in a high crime area, the need for safety might surface in consciousness as a fear that one's home will be burglarized. In this instance, the motive would be to take action to prevent this eventuality from occurring. With a different individual, or under different environmental conditions, the internal need for safety might appear in consciousness as a concern for health, fear of injury from an automobile accident, fear of flying, or some other concern.

Product identification.   This is what we usually mean when we use the term *want* in connection with marketing.[4] At this stage, a product or service is identified that appears to offer a solution to the conscious motive that has emerged. In the example we are using, a number of alternatives are available to help protect oneself from burglars—additional locks on doors and windows, security service, burglar alarm, watchdog, gun, and so on.

Product identification may occur at different levels of specificity. The first level is generalized; a protection device is desired. At a second level, after thinking about it or preliminary investigation, specific alternatives are identified. Finally, a specific alternative—perhaps a security service—is chosen because of its procedures, personnel, and cost.

Product demand.   At this point, a want is converted into economic demand by the act of purchase. To continue our example, a particular security service is chosen, and a financial commitment is made.

The progression reflected in the foregoing discussion is shown graphically in Figure 6–4. In this diagram, we can see how a need for safety might be converted into demand for a particular security service. With a different individual or under other environmental circumstances, the need for safety could have taken another form and resulted in different market behavior. Further, each of the other basic needs may also give rise to a variety of motives, wants, products being considered, and demand outcomes.

Although successful advertisers should have a basic concept of what constitutes internal need states (Stage 1 of the progression), the effects of marketing activity are most apparent at Stages 2, 3, and 4. For example, an individual's need for affiliation (an internal

---

[4]Psychologists tend to use the words *peripheral needs* or *instrumental needs* when referring to this motivational level.

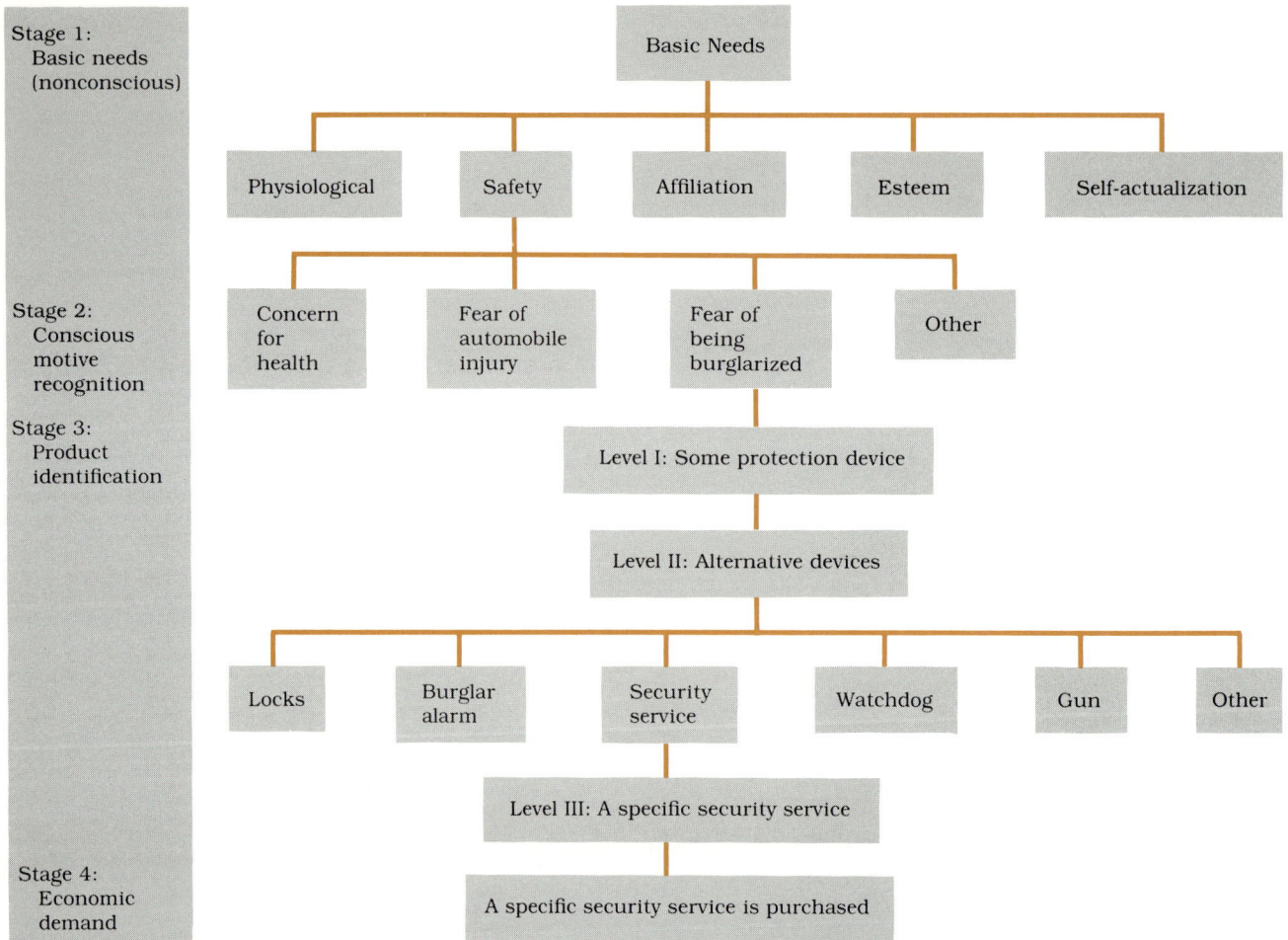

Stage 1:
  Basic needs
  (nonconscious)

Stage 2:
  Conscious
  motive
  recognition

Stage 3:
  Product
  identification

Stage 4:
  Economic
  demand

Basic Needs

Physiological Safety Affiliation Esteem Self-actualization

Concern for health Fear of automobile injury Fear of being burglarized Other

Level I: Some protection device

Level II: Alternative devices

Locks Burglar alarm Security service Watchdog Gun Other

Level III: A specific security service

A specific security service is purchased

FIGURE 6–4   Progression of a "need for safety" to the purchase of a security service [From Kenneth E. Runyon, *The Practice of Marketing* (Columbus, Ohio: Charles E. Merrill Publishing Co., 1982), 182.]

need state) may appear in consciousness as a desire "not to offend" (a motive). The advertising for a particular brand of deodorant may create a preference (a want) by promising "long lasting" protection as evidence of its superiority over alternative deodorant soaps, colognes, and other brands of deodorant. When this brand is purchased, demand is created.

KEY ISSUES RELATING TO MOTIVATION

Two issues relating to the subject of motivation are of particular interest to advertisers: (a) the number and nature of the basic needs; and (b) the intensity of motivated behavior.

Basic needs.   Earlier, we pointed out that there is no universal agreement upon and no way of experimentally validating the precise number and nature of basic needs or internal need states. Different psychologists suggest different answers. In Chapter 11 we will point out that highly successful copywriters develop their own lists of needs. Abraham Maslow has one formulation. Maslow has described human beings as "wanting" animals and has suggested that human needs are insatiable; as quickly as one set of needs is satisfied, another set arises.

Maslow postulates that human beings have a hierarchy of needs, and that lower level needs must be largely satisfied before higher level needs become salient. This hierarchy, arranged from lower to higher, is summarized below.[5]

☐ *Physiological needs.* If the organism is to survive, physiological needs must be met. Essentially, these biological needs are hunger, thirst, waste elimination, and so on.

☐ *Safety needs.* Included among the safety needs are security, protection, avoidance of pain, and order and structure in the environment.

☐ *Affiliation needs.* These are social needs. Human beings need warm and satisfying relationships with other people—needs for association and affection.

☐ *Esteem needs.* These are needs for recognition and self-respect. There are two kinds of esteem needs: (a) achievement, personal adequacy in dealing with the environment and other people, confidence, and independence; and (b) reputation, respect, attention, and appreciation.

☐ *Self-actualization needs.* These are needs for self-fulfillment; the need to become relatively independent from environmental demands and to develop all of one's abilities.

At a primitive level, where no needs are being met, physiological needs dominate human behavior. The other needs remain unrecognized until physiological needs are largely met. Once physiological needs have been largely satisfied and no longer exert an influence on behavior, the next higher order needs, those of safety, emerge. This level of need satisfaction then becomes predominant and remains so until it is largely fulfilled. The same progression follows down through the hierarchy.

When needs at a particular level are frustrated, or only partially satisfied, they persist as an influence on the individual's motivational patterns. Unfortunately, the circumstances of human existence often prevent the satisfaction of all lower order needs, so relatively few people ever become self-actualizers, although most of us engage in some self-actualizing behavior.

A key point in Maslow's theory is that our needs are never satisfied. As needs at a particular level in the hierarchy are satisfied, other higher order needs emerge to take their place. According to this theory, marketing does not create needs. Diverse and emerging needs are a unique human experience. Marketing may contribute to the creation of *wants* by portraying products as instrumentalities that can be used to satisfy basic needs. However, material products and services only partially satisfy most human need states, so human motivational patterns remain remarkably persistent.

---

[5]Abraham Maslow, *Motivation and Personality*, 2nd ed. (New York: Harper & Row, Publishers, 1970), 35–36.

CHAPTER 6 | CONSUMER BEHAVIOR

A second implication of Maslow's theory is that lower order needs are largely met in an affluent society such as the United States. Accordingly, the higher order needs—affiliation, esteem, and self-actualization—should be prepotent. An examination of commercials and advertisements quickly shows the importance of higher level needs in product design and motivational appeals. We seldom buy food *just* because we are hungry. We have many choices in what we eat; even the most mundane food products use a variety of social and personal appeals.

The intensity of motivated behavior. A second issue relating to motivation lies in the recognition that some motives require more energy to be expended in their service than others. We may spend a great deal of time and energy to satisfy some of our motives, while devoting relatively little time and effort to satisfy others. In addition, people differ dramatically in the effort they put forth to achieve what appears to be the same motive. For example, let us assume that two people of similar ability and means express desires to become medical doctors. One, through self-discipline, hard work, and long hours of study, eventually is graduated as an M.D. The other, unwilling to make the personal sacrifices or put forth the effort required, drops out of the program. In comparing their behaviors, most people would agree that the student who completed the program was more highly motivated toward becoming a doctor than the one who did not.

In order to explain the differences in intensity that characterize motivated behavior, cognitive psychologists often invoke the concept of central and peripheral needs.

☐ **Central needs** are those needs closely related to our sense of identity and survival. In our definition of motivation, they are termed basic need states and include physiological, safety, affiliation, esteem, and self-actualizing needs.

☐ **Peripheral needs,** sometimes referred to as *instrumental needs* or *wants,* consist of the preferences one has for alternative means of satisfying central needs.

For example, a minimum amount of liquid is required for survival (a central need). A variety of liquids will satisfy this minimal requirement—water, beer, tea, coffee, fruit juices, and so on. The individual's preference order for each of these alternative liquids represents a personal order of instrumental needs or wants. Even though one liquid is preferred, if it is not available, another will suffice.

Similarly, from a psychological standpoint, status may represent a central need. Status may be satisfied in a variety of ways—money, housing, excellence in any variety of activities, becoming a member of a profession, holding office in an organization, and so on. An individual's particular order of preference for these alternatives represents a hierarchy of peripheral needs and, if the preferred alternative is unobtainable, the next alternative is acceptable, although perhaps not as satisfying.

The distinction between central and peripheral needs is important to marketing. Central needs tend to be absolute and not subject to substitute satisfactions. Thus, prestige is no substitute for food and food is a poor substitute for prestige. On the other hand, peripheral needs or wants *are* subject to substitute satisfactions. Pork will serve the same function as beef in alleviating hunger and promoting the survival of the individual. Athletic prowess and academic success are alternative ways of gaining prestige.

For the normal person commercial products and services are merely alternative ways of satisfying peripheral needs or wants. Many products and services are interchangeable in their ability to satisfy consumers' wants and desires. As a consequence, marketing activities—advertising, packaging, pricing, and sales promotion—can be effective devices in persuading consumers to purchase one product or brand rather than another.

A theory of motivation requires an energizing force that varies in intensity to accommodate the empirical observation that motives vary in strength. The exact nature of this energizing force is uncertain. For some psychologists, affect (emotion) is the energizing factor.[6] Thus, needs of high centrality will be accompanied by strong emotional commitment, while peripheral needs are invested with less. Thus, J. Sterling Getchell, one of advertising's great copywriters, insisted that a good advertisement not only stated a logical justification for the purchase, but had an emotional "hooker" that attracted our attention.

A survey of motivational theories and research permits us to draw certain generalizations about motivation that are relevant to marketing and advertising.

☐ Consumer behavior is purposeful, goal-directed activity.

☐ Basic consumer needs are diverse, including physiological, safety, affiliation, esteem, and self-actualizing needs.

☐ Consumer needs are insatiable. As needs at one level are largely satisfied, higher order needs come into play. In addition, products and services may only partially satisfy basic human needs. As a consequence, these needs are never wholly satisfied, and continue to exert an influence on behavior.

☐ Needs vary in intensity, with the basic or central needs generally having a greater influence on behavior than instrumental or peripheral needs (referred to as *wants* in the popular language).

☐ Since most products and services represent wants, many can be substituted to satisfy human requirements. Thus, marketing activities can be used to persuade consumers to accept one product or brand rather than another.

☐ In a relatively affluent society, such as the United States, the higher level needs tend to be prepotent. As a consequence, marketing appeals to these needs tend to be successful.

---

[6]Bernard Weiner, *Theories of Motivation* (Chicago: Markham Publishing Co., 1972), 173–74.

☐ Emotions (affect) are intimately involved in the concept of motivation, and emotional appeals often serve as cues for motivational arousal.

Throughout our discussion of motivation, we have emphasized the diversity of behavior which different individuals may express in the service of the same basic need. We have also noted that the same individual, under different environmental constraints, may exhibit different behaviors in the service of the same motive. One way of expressing these relationships is shown in Figure 6–5. Note that the central or basic needs are filtered through socio-psychological variables, and the emerging motivational patterns are surrounded by environmental constraints which also influence the specific behavior that occurs.

In the remainder of this chapter, we will briefly examine some of the major socio-psychological variables that influence our motivational patterns. Along with motivation, these areas are the subject matter of texts on consumer behavior. Students interested in exploring some of these areas should refer to the library for any number of excellent texts on consumer behavior.

VARIABLES INFLUENCING BEHAVIOR

Motives are diverse and complex. If the author of marketing communications expects to compete successfully, he cannot afford to underestimate the complexity of consumer motivation or be unaware of the variables that shape behavior. The remainder of this chapter will identify some of the major behavioral variables and briefly characterize their importance.

The variables that will be identified are not monotonically related to behavior; that is, they are not independent of one another. However, we often don't know how these variables are interrelated

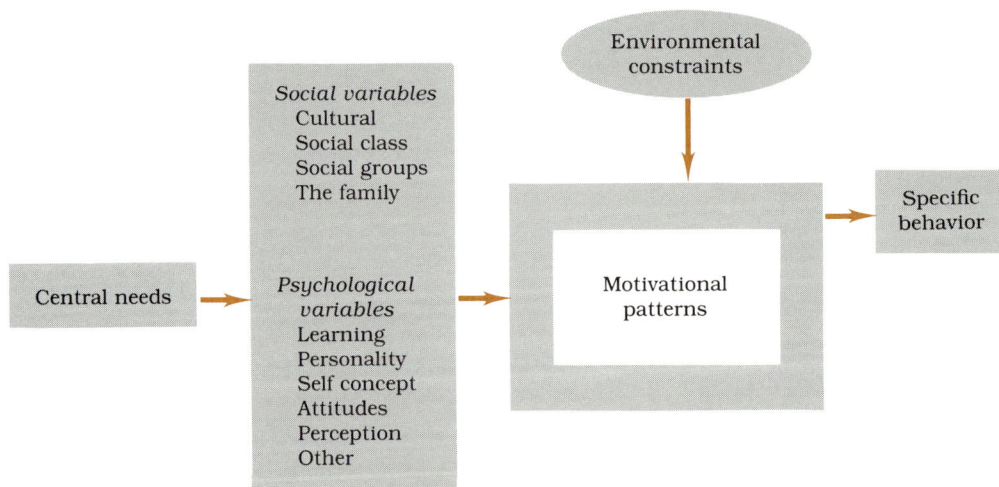

FIGURE 6–5 Graphic representation of central needs filtered through socio-psychological variables and environmental constraints before emerging as behavior [From Kenneth E. Runyon, *The Practice of Marketing* (Columbus, Ohio: Charles E. Merrill Publishing Co., 1982), 186.]

or which will be dominant in a given situation. Nonetheless, a knowledge of these variables can often provide insights into behavior that help us to segment markets or devise an advertising appeal that will be successful for an established product.

SOCIAL VARIABLES

Thorstein Veblen, an economist of the early twentieth century, is generally credited as the pioneer of **social determination** in human behavior. Veblen questioned the Victorian assumptions that behavior is primarily the result of economic forces; he theorized that behavior is the consequence of social competition and emulation. He coined the term **conspicuous consumption** to describe the behavior of consumers and argued that we purchase products in order to enhance our social prestige. Veblen's influence turned attention to culture, reference groups, and family as prime determinants of consumption patterns.

CULTURE

Every society has a cultural heritage that prescribes certain broad patterns of behavior. These patterns extend to such diverse areas as sexual roles, dress, food habits, recreation, patterns of authority, status symbols, artifacts, attitudes, motivation, use of space, and meaning of language. We are accustomed to the practices and configurations of our own culture and, when deprived of them, are often unable to deal effectively with our environment. Alvin Toffler refers to the phenomenon of **culture shock** as the psychological effect of suddenly finding ourselves without our accustomed cultural support.

> Culture shock is the effect that immersion in a strange culture has on the unprepared visitor. . . . Culture shock is what happens when a traveler suddenly finds himself in a place where yes may mean no, where a "fixed price" is negotiable, where to be kept waiting in an outer office is no cause for insult, where laughter may signify anger. It is what happens when the familiar psychological cues that help an individual to function in society are suddenly withdrawn and replaced by new ones that are strange or incomprehensible . . . it causes a breakdown in communication, a misreading of reality, an inability to cope.[7]

There is a dominant United States culture, but our society is also highly pluralistic, composed of a variety of ethnic and religious groups whose values, languages, and motivations often differ from those of the dominant culture. Some of these groups, such as blacks, Spanish-Americans, orientals, Jews, and Indians, represent significant markets and require special forms of marketing communications. Care should be taken to communicate with these groups in a manner that will not offend or alienate them.

The problem becomes even more acute when a United States marketer is marketing products in a different country. Jack Stone

---

[7]Alvin Toffler, *Future Shock* (New York: Random House, Inc., 1970), 179. Copyright © 1970.

quotes executives of a United States owned affiliate in Canada as commenting: "Possibly half of the United States prepared advertisements are usable in Canada, but almost never without some change being made in copy or one of the illustrations.[8] Edward Hall, in "The Silent Language of Overseas Business," details many of the cultural shoals upon which U.S. advertisers run aground when marketing in foreign countries.[9]

The solution is to utilize marketing research in order to gain an understanding of the values, decision-making processes, buying practices, and motivations of the cultural groups to whom the marketing effort is being addressed, and to use local citizens to interpret and rewrite ads when a foreign culture is involved.

SOCIAL CLASS

All societies are structured in social groups because different societal functions must be performed so that society can survive. Some of these functions are valued more highly than others and, as a consequence, accorded a higher status. Berelson and Steiner observe that

> every known human society, certainly every known society of any size, is stratified. . . . The hierarchical evaluation of people in different social positions is apparently inherent in human social organization. Stratification arises with the most rudimentary division of labor and appears to be socially necessary in order to get people to fill different positions and perform adequately in them.[10]

In a complex society, there may be a number of status hierarchies based on such factors as sex, age, income, occupation, or political position. Social class is one such system of stratification. As the term is used in the United States, it refers to aggregates of persons or families differing in values and behavior and forming a random order of status levels. Social class is a useful concept in marketing because members of different social classes have different values, employ different symbols, and spend their resources in different ways. For example, a college professor and a cross-country truck driver will have similar incomes, but their interests and spending patterns may be vastly different. The emphasis placed on education, savings, insurance, housing, and social consumption will vary by social class. The magazines they read will differ. Thus, the *New Yorker,* a sophisticated publication for high-level social groups, differs significantly from *True Story,* a magazine directed toward lower-level social groups. The editorial content, style of writing, illustrations, artwork, and even humor of these two magazines differ so greatly that they contain material of little interest for social class groups outside those for which the magazines are edited. This

[8]J. R. Stone, "American-Canadian Co-Operation: Key to Successful Advertising," in *Marketing: Canada,* Litvak and Mallen, eds. (Toronto: McGraw-Hill of Canada, Ltd., 1964), 262.

[9]Edward T. Hall, "The Silent Language of Overseas Business," *Harvard Business Review* (May-June 1960): 87–96.

[10]G. A. Steiner, *Human Behavior: An Inventory of Scientific Findings* (New York: Harcourt Brace Jovanovich, Inc., 1964), 460.

is illustrated by Table 6–1, which shows a partial table of contents for an issue of each of these publications.

SOCIAL GROUPS

Groups are the fundamental units of the social system. They are formed to promote survival, carry out work, achieve goals, provide solace and comfort, entertain, and allow their members to relax. We work, learn, play, and buy certain goods in groups. It is little wonder that groups play an important role in influencing the products we use and brands we purchase.

Although groups may be defined and analyzed in many ways (size, structure, purpose, decision processes, cohesion, formal and informal, and so on), the **reference group** holds the greatest interest for marketers. A reference group may be defined as a group with which an individual wants to be associated and whose beliefs, attitudes, values, and behaviors the person will seek to emulate. Sociologists generally speak of reference *groups*, but we may also speak of a reference *person*. A reference person is an individual who serves as an ideal or model and generally embodies the salient group characteristics that are admired.

The influence of reference groups and reference persons on human behavior is confirmed in literature, common human experience, and controlled experiments. The role of social imitation, or **modeling**, as a source of learned behavior is well documented. For these reasons, marketing communications frequently employ reference groups or reference individuals in selling products.

Many advertisers display their products in group settings that consumers can find identifiable. In most soft drink advertising, it is difficult to tell whether the advertiser is selling a product or "lovable people having fun." The same thing can be said for chewing gum, beer, and bank advertising.

Along with using groups in advertising communications, there is a widespread use of reference individuals. Sports figures, television stars, and other celebrities grace the airways and newsstands. During the past decade, the use of star presenters has grown. Today, approximately ten percent of all television commercials use celebrities as spokespersons.[11] The effectiveness of star presenters apparently varies substantially. James Garner and Mariette Hartley are credited with selling two million Polaroid "One Step" cameras and are reported to be outselling competition with Polaroid's higher priced "Sun" cameras.[12] At the same time, McCollum/Spielman & Company, a research firm specializing in advertising research, reports that only 41 percent of the celebrity commercials they have tested have been above average in terms of either increasing brand awareness or influencing attitudes, and only 19 percent have been above average in both of these criteria.[13] This seems to imply that star presenters can be highly successful in promoting products, but

TABLE 6–1 Comparison of parts of the tables of contents of *New Yorker* and *True Story*

New Yorker	True Story
The Glory of the Brooklyn Bridge	How Can We Possibly Go On Living Together?
On Madison Avenue: The Year of Living Safely	Don't Count Me Out Yet!
Theater: Double or Nothing	My Husband Wants to Get Rid of Me!
Music: Shoestring Opera	Dinner On the Double
City Life: Miss Manners	Lunch Box Suggestions
	Beauty Notebook

Source: From tables of contents of *New Yorker*, 30 May 1983, 3 and *True Story* (June 1983): 1.

[11]James Forkan, "Product Matchup Key to Effective Star Presenters," *Advertising Age*, 6 October 1980, 42.

[12]Harry Wayne McMahan and Corwin Mack Kile, "100 Best," *Advertising Age*, 22 February 1982, M–4.

[13]Forkan, "Product Matchup Key to Effective Star Presenters," 42.

care must be exercised and marketing research employed to select the proper presenters.

Reference figures are not restricted to television stars and celebrities. The Puerto Rico Industrial Development advertisement (Figure 6–6) features Kenneth G. Fisher, president and chief executive officer of Prime Computer, Incorporated, as a reference figure that many less successful businessmen would love to emulate.

Some companies, such as General Mills, create their own reference person. Betty Crocker, created in 1921, has reigned for over fifty years as "a sort of 'First Lady of Food,' the most highly esteemed

FIGURE 6–6 (Courtesy Puerto Rico Industrial Development)

Prime Computer, Inc. and Puerto Rico. A partnership that works.

"Our start-up in Puerto Rico beat all forecasts. And we were profitable very quickly."

Kenneth G. Fisher President and CEO, Prime Computer, Inc.

"Our experience in Puerto Rico has been very favorable. So much so that we can do much more there than we originally planned, including very technical things. And that's really a function of the quality of our Puerto Rican employees. They are determined to be our very best producer. In fact, they'd bet on it.

"Everything's been positive in the sense of the people. They're intelligent, hard-working, industrious, punctual. They have a great deal of pride in what they're doing. There's no quality fall-off in Puerto Rico. So our Puerto Rico plant is one of the lowest-cost, most efficient operations in our whole company.

"In just one year, we've made a commitment to triple the work force. We have a number of new

Approved by the Electoral Review Board.

and demanding projects for Puerto Rico. They'll take them in stride. So the issue really is getting the extra floor space. And the Puerto Rican government will help us get that—fast. They are willing, really willing and anxious to pitch in.

"Sure you get the tax break. But the thing a CEO really wants to know is did he get the deal he went for. In Puerto Rico, we got the deal we went for—and then some. Because we got productive people."

Prime's Puerto Rico plant handles every phase of memory board production.

Compare your effective tax rate with this hypothetical profit model.

Sales	$5,000,000
Production Worker Payroll	500,000
Profit Before Tax	500,000
Eligible Incentives	
A. 5% Production Worker Payroll Deduction	$ 25,000
B. Income Tax and Property Tax Exemption at Partial Rates	
Pre-Tax Income	$ 500,000
Production Worker Payroll Deduction	25,000
Adjusted Taxable Income	$ 475,000

ANNUAL INCOME TAX CALCULATION BY PERIOD*

Years	1-5	6-10	11-15	16-20
% Tax Exempt	90%	75%	65%	55%
% Taxable Income	10%	25%	35%	45%
Taxable Income	$47,500	118,750	166,250	213,750
Calculated Tax	$12,475	36,438	56,075	76,163
Effective Tax Rate	**2.50%**	**7.29%**	**11.22%**	**15.23%**

*Duration of tax exemption depends upon geographical zone in which the firm has been established. In addition, note that the U.S. Internal Revenue Code Section 931 lets you bring current profits home without U.S. taxes.

© 1980 Puerto Rico Economic Development Administration

Puerto Rico, U.S.A.
The ideal second home for American business.

For more information: write us on your company letterhead.
Puerto Rico Industrial Development, Dept. FO-13, 1290 Avenue of the Americas, New York, N.Y. 10102 . Or call us toll-free: (800) 223-0699, ext. 223.

home service authority in the nation and a real friend to millions of women."[14] Ann Pillsbury of Pillsbury and Ann Page for A&P are other examples of corporate personalities created to communicate with consumers. Although it is extremely expensive to create a corporate personality, this type of personality could never sabotage the communications program through a public indiscretion.

When used properly, reference groups and individuals spell persuasion, a vital word in the art of marketing communications.

FAMILY

The family is a unique form of reference group that shapes the individual and influences his decision patterns and purchase behavior. It is atypical because: (a) the relationships between family members are more intimate, emotional attachments more intense, and bonds stronger than those normally found in other groups; and (b) shared consumption and joint decision making are characteristic of family living. This latter characteristic is particularly important in marketing.

Since a great deal of family consumption is shared consumption, several family members may participate in the decision to purchase a particular product category or brand. Children may have a major voice in purchases of food and child related items. Figure 6–7 is an example of an advertisement that recognizes the role children play in determining whether parents purchase the product being advertised. In some cases, such as dry cereals or snack items, children may be the primary users, although parents exercise veto power. In other situations, such as buying automobiles, the husband and wife share the decision. In any event, knowledge of family decision patterns is necessary when selecting media and determining the copy appeals that will be developed.

The family is also worthy of study because of the **family life cycle** phenomenon.[15] A family passes through several stages in its development. At each stage, different patterns of object accumulation occur. For example, the newly married couple without children has vastly different needs and purchase patterns than the older family with several children. Demographic information such as age, size, and income of U.S. families is available from the U.S. Department of Commerce and can be used in identifying target markets and estimating market size. A variety of social variables must be acknowledged in developing marketing programs. These variables may often be used as a basis for marketing segmentation or in developing advertising appeals within a market segment. Large numbers of products, such as deodorants, mouthwashes, and cosmetics, are purely social and, since so much of our consumption takes place in social settings, most other products and brands have social implications. Even toilet tissue is produced in different colors so that we may impress guests with the decor of the family bathroom.

---

[14]Watkins, *100 Greatest Advertisements*, 205.

[15]William D. Wells and George Gubar, "Life Cycle Concept in Marketing Research," *Journal of Marketing Research* (November 1966): 355–63.

FIGURE 6–7 (Courtesy Hunt-Wesson Foods, Inc.)

INTRAPERSONAL VARIABLES

Social variables are inadequate to account for all consumer behavior. Consumers express their individuality within the social context of society in a variety of ways. For an understanding of the intrapersonal variables that influence behavior, we must turn to the field of psychology.

Major areas of psychology include learning, personality, self-concept, attitudes, and perception. Each of these areas contains clues that can guide the marketing practitioner in segmenting markets and devising appeals.

LEARNING

Learning theory is central to understanding behavior and devising effective marketing communications. Brand names and product attributes are not engraved in our central nervous systems at birth.

Our knowledge of brands and their attributes is learned, and a major function of marketing communications is to facilitate learning. An examination of leading learning theories identifies certain principles that are useful in helping consumers to learn. Four of these principles—repetition, contiguity, reinforcement, and meaning—are described in the following material.

Repetition. The principle of repetition, the repeated exposure of a product message or brand name, is one of the most widely used learning principles in advertising. It is used both in media scheduling and within the copy of advertisements.

A point of conventional wisdom in the advertising industry is that thirteen insertions a year in a magazine (one every four weeks) represent an optimal media schedule. H. A. Zielske demonstrated experimentally that by the end of the year thirteen exposures, four weeks apart, generated awareness of the advertising among 48 percent of the sample. A higher awareness of advertising can be obtained by using the same number of exposures over a briefer period of time, although the duration of the effect is sharply reduced. Thus, one advertisement a week for thirteen weeks resulted in 63 percent awareness; however, the advertisement had been forgotten by the end of the year.[16] Figure 6–8 is a graphic expression of Zielske's findings.

FIGURE 6–8 Weekly percentages of housewives who could remember advertisements [From H. A. Zielske, "The Remembering and Forgetting of Advertising," *Journal of Marketing* (January 1959): 239–43. Published by the American Marketing Association]

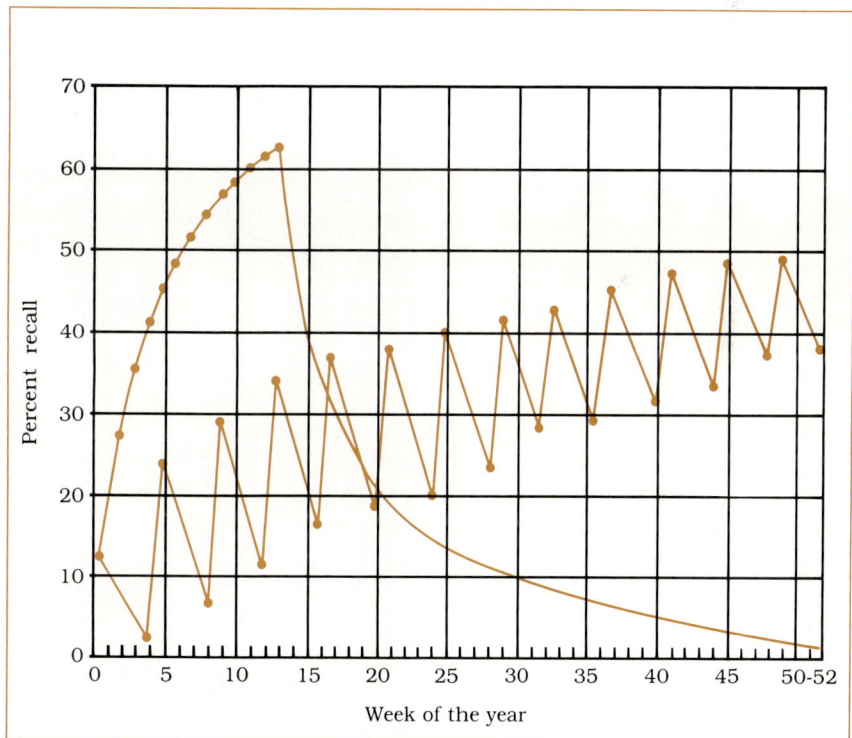

[16]H. A. Zielske, "The Remembering and Forgetting of Advertising." Reprinted from *Journal of Marketing* (January 1959): 239–43. Published by the American Marketing Association.

The use of repetition to register a product name within a single advertisement is demonstrated in the No Nonsense advertisement (Figure 6–9). The name "No Nonsense" appears 14 times within the body of the advertisement.

Contiguity.   Contiguity is most often seen in marketing communications by associating a product with a pleasant situation through spatial or temporal proximity. Beer is shown being enjoyed in a happy social setting; carefully selected models are used in fashion advertising to associate clothing with slim, attractive, sophisticated people; and dozens of products are associated with sex by placing a beautiful and often scantily clad woman in the advertising, even though her presence may have little or nothing to do with product use. Figure 6–10 is an interesting use of contiguity that associates the Triumph Spitfire with power, speed, and sportiness.

FIGURE 6–9 (Courtesy No Nonsense Fashions, Inc.)

FIGURE 6–10 The Triumph Spitfire ad shows an interesting use of contiguity (Courtesy British Leyland Motor Corp., Ltd.)

166

Reinforcement. Reinforcement or reward is the primary learning principle underlying operant conditioning, a leading learning theory. The basic thesis of operant conditioning is that people tend to engage in rewarding activities and avoid punishing situations or activities. In advertising, the reader is usually promised a reward for using a specific brand. While economic, social, and personal rewards are all widely used, the simple promise of a beer that goes well with food is the uncomplicated claim of the Natural Light advertisement shown in Figure 6–11.

Meaning. The concept of meaning is a central pillar in cognitive learning theory. Cognitive theory views the individual as a problem solver who seeks the attainment of personal goals. Applied to marketing, cognitive theory emphasizes subjective feelings and perceptions and provides product information that will enable consumers

FIGURE 6–11 (Courtesy Anheuser Busch, Inc.)

Ahh, the beer with the taste for food!

CHAPTER 6 | CONSUMER BEHAVIOR

to relate the marketer's product to themselves in a meaningful way. John Deere & Company successfully introduced their lawn and garden tractor by marketing it, not as an oversized lawn mower, but as a "Weekend Freedom Machine," a unique piece of equipment that would enable the purchaser to complete lawn and garden chores quickly and enjoy the weekend with family and friends. New Purina Dog Chow was introduced as the dry dog food that "makes dogs eager eaters," thereby allaying consumers' subjective fears that their pets would refuse to eat the dry dog food they purchased.

Many direct applications of learning theory to marketing communications can be made. M. S. Hatwick devotes three chapters of his book *How to Use Psychology for Better Advertising* to this topic,[17] and S. H. Britt summarizes twenty applications of learning theory to advertising communications in an article that first appeared in *Printer's Ink*.[18]

PERSONALITY

All of us are familiar with the term *personality*. We use it frequently in describing other people; many of us have taken personality tests; and to some of us, personality is synonymous with psychology. Despite our familiarity with the term, few of us normally think of personality as an important marketing variable. Yet, it is a subject of keen interest among marketers. Not all attempts to segment markets on the basis of personality differences have been successful, but there are many instances in which personality differences have been successfully exploited in the development of products and devising of appeals.

A classic case of market segmentation that seems to have its roots in personality differences exists in the market for mouthwashes and gargles. Listerine is a straw-colored, astringent, unpleasant tasting mouthwash that is described in its advertising as the "taste you hate two times a day." Scope, by contrast, is deep green in color and pleasant tasting. Both products have the same function, with the only apparent differences being in color and taste. The Listerine user finds it hard to believe that a pleasant tasting mouthwash can be effective. The Scope user cannot understand why people would subject themselves to the taste of Listerine when better tasting alternatives are available. The differences in preferences seem to lie in the personalities of the users. Similar differences appear to apply to the proprietary medicine field; some consumers behave as though medicines must be unpleasant tasting and harsh to be effective, while others prefer a gentler approach to medication.

Detergents, cosmetics, cigarettes, beer, alcoholic beverages, automobiles, clothing, and many other products often play on basic differences in the personalities of consumers in achieving acceptance, and a number of advertising agencies use psychologists and psychoanalysts as consultants to help them develop advertising appeals. Earnest Dichter and his Institute for Research on Motivation

[17]Melvin S. Hatwick, *How to Use Psychology for Better Advertising* (New York: Prentice-Hall, Inc., 1950), chapters 14, 15, and 16.
[18]Steuart H. Britt, "How Advertising Can Use Psychology's Rules of Learning," *Printers' Ink*, 23 September 1955, 77ff.

gained both fame and fortune by identifying unconscious motives which are, by definition, hidden facets of the personality.

Personality has been defined by Allport as "the dynamic organization within the individual of those psychophysical systems that determine his characteristic behavior and thought."[19] Note that there are two aspects to this definition. On the one hand, there is an internal *structure*, referred to as "the dynamic organization within the individual of . . . psychophysical systems." On the other hand, the definition refers to certain behavioral manifestations as "characteristic behavior and thought." These behavioral manifestations are often referred to as *traits.*

The existence of both an internal structure and behavioral traits makes it possible to study personality from either point of view. There are many theories of personality, most of which consider human beings as purposive organisms. Theories differ on a variety of dimensions, such as the weight they give to unconscious factors, reinforcement, structure, heredity, environmental factors, and social influence. One major dichotomy, however, is whether personality is considered primarily in terms of structure or traits.

Structural theory. Structural theories emphasize the internal structure of the person as the determinants of behavior. Freud's psychoanalytic theory and its many variants are among the better known theories of this nature. Since structural theories tend to focus on the differences rather than common traits between people, emphasize unconscious motivation, and not lend themselves to quantitative analysis, they have not been subjected to a great deal of empirical research by marketers.

This does not mean that psychoanalytic theory is not used in marketing communications or that psychoanalytic themes are not employed in advertising and promotion. Motivation research, which reached its peak in the 1950s and has since become accepted as an established field of marketing research, owes its popularity to the Freudian concept of unconscious motivation. The purpose of motivation research is to get below the surface of conscious rationalizations and explore the real reasons for product preferences and use.

In advertising, the widespread use of sex as a vehicle of interest for a broad spectrum of consumer products is a direct reflection of the Freudian stress on sexuality as a repressed dynamic that underlies much of our behavior. Applications of Freudian theory are not restricted to implications of sex, however. Fantasy and wish fulfillment themes are also congenial to Freudian theory. Airlines have offered appealing visions of escape from reality through vacations to exotic places; Schaeffer Beer devotes the better part of one of its commercials to hang gliding, capitalizing on the unconscious symbolism of flying as a universal escape fantasy; and Honda has used an "escape from convention" theme to sell its motorcycles. Because of the universal nature of psychoanalytic symbolism, it is difficult to find an advertisement or commercial that does not contain some psychoanalytic appeals.

---

[19]Gordon W. Allport, *Pattern and Growth in Personality* (New York: Holt, Rinehart and Winston, Inc., 1967), 28.

The problem with psychoanalytic theories, as well as other structural theories, is not their lack of use. They do not lend themselves to tidy formulations; it is often difficult to make the translation from the theoretical concepts to effective communications.

Trait theory. Trait theories stress the response aspect of personality. A trait is a predisposition to respond in a particular way, and personality is described as a particular constellation of traits. A number of scales have been devised to measure the extent to which various traits are present. For example, the Thurstone Temperament Schedule is designed to measure how individuals differ on seven different response characteristics labeled: active, vigorous, impulsive, dominant, stable, sociable, and reflective. Other instruments exist which measure different combinations of traits. Since these scales provide quantitative scores, they lend themselves to marketing analysis and experimentation.

In addition to such standardized scales for measuring traits, tailor-made scales can be devised which measure constellations of traits related to a particular area of activity. For example, I. S. White reports a study in which response traits such as flexible, objective, emancipated, and evaluative were used in relation to household cleaning tasks.[20] The findings were used to segment the detergent market when analysis revealed that housewives could be divided into "modern" and "traditional" groups, which exhibited markedly different preferences for detergent package designs and advertising appeals. For the most part, tailor-made scales such as that used in the detergent study have been much more productive in adapting personality theory to marketing problems than have standardized scales of traits.[21]

Psychographics. Psychographics, sometimes referred to as lifestyle research, or as activity and interest research, is a variation of trait theory that has gained support in the past decade or so. More of a technique than a theory, it attempts to describe the characteristic mode of living of a society, or a segment of it.[22] The basic procedure for gathering psychographic information is to use an Activities, Interests, and Opinion (AIO) questionnaire. The AIO questionnaire is a series of statements that subjects answer with an agree-or-disagree response. Sample statements might be:

I am a swinger.

I am modern.

I like to fish.

I enjoy sports.

I like contemporary music.

---

[20]I. S. White, "The Perception of Value in Products," in *On Knowing the Consumer,* J. W. Newman, ed. (New York: John Wiley and Sons, Inc., 1966), 173–86.

[21]Kenneth E. Runyon, *Consumer Behavior and the Practice of Marketing* (Columbus, Ohio: Charles E. Merrill Publishing Co., 1977), 234–40.

[22]W. D. Wells, "Psychographics: A Critical Review," *Journal of Marketing Research* (May 1975): 196–213.

The number of statements and the variety of dimensions explored are limited only by the respondent's patience and the researcher's imagination. The same questionnaire may be used to gather demographic information and media preferences. The data are factor analyzed to identify various constellations of answers, and the results are used to segment markets and develop appeals. The assumption underlying the psychographic approach is that people who give similar answers to the questions will have similar interests and respond to similar products and advertising.

There is little question that personality plays a significant role in the purchase decisions that consumers make. Some product fields undoubtedly are more amenable to personality analysis than others, and the particular way in which personality variables can be used in a specific case must be determined by systematic analysis and testing.

SELF-CONCEPT

The self-concept or subjective self refers to the way an individual regards himself. Each of us has a self-concept; that is, we have a conscious perception of ourselves as being a certain kind of person, and we reflect the kind of person we perceive ourselves to be by the things we do, clothes we wear, and products we buy. Vance Packard, a critic of advertising, makes the following observation in the *Hidden Persuaders:*

> Studies of narcissism indicated that nothing appeals more to people than themselves: so why not help people buy a projection of themselves? That way the images would preselect their audiences, select out of a consuming public people with personalities having an affinity for the image. By building traits known to be widely dispersed among the consuming public, the image builders reasoned that they could spark love affairs by the millions.
> The sale of self-images soon was expediting the movement of hundreds of millions of dollars worth of merchandise to consumers, particularly gasoline, cigarettes, and automobiles. And the image builders were offering some surprising evidence of the extent to which American consumers were becoming self-image buyers.[23]

Vance Packard intended his observations as a criticism of advertising and pretended shock at the practice of image building for consumer products, but responsible marketers have long considered the self-image a legitimate basis for marketing segmentation. Britt, for example, has observed that

> a consumer may buy a product because, among other factors, he feels the product enhances his own self-image. Similarly, a consumer may decide not to buy a product or not to shop at a particular store if he feels that these actions are not consistent with his own perceptions of himself.[24]

[23]From the book *The Hidden Persuaders* by Vance Packard. Copyright © 1965 by Vance Packard.

[24]Steuart H. Britt, *Consumer Behavior and the Behavior Sciences: Theories and Applications* (New York: John Wiley and Sons, Inc., 1966), 186.

All of us are aware that we do use possessions as a way of making statements about ourselves. The teenager who smokes, or drinks alcoholic beverages, is using these products to say, "I am an adult." The adult who drives a Cadillac or Lincoln Continental is telling others that he is important. The host and hostess who serve imported wine are exhibiting their discriminating taste to their guests. In the automotive field, Leon Piconke, Chrysler's director of marketing services in the mid-1970s, made the following observation:

> The automobile is a piece of communication, and the automobile purchase is a very complex expression. When we do attitude studies we ask the question, "Is that your kind of car?" The subject is deciding whether that car fits his image, the kind of personality he wants to project.[25]

This is not to say that all consumption is determined by the self-images consumers hold. However, it should be recognized that self-concepts do exist and may influence many consumer purchases, particularly for those products that have high visibility and are primarily consumed in social settings.

Few, if any, brands can be all things to all people. Those that try to be run the risk of becoming nothing to everyone. Therefore, the marketer should try to build a strong, unambiguous brand image for the product that a significant number of consumers find identifiable. By doing so, marketers can differentiate their products from competition and gain recognition and sales in the marketplace.

ATTITUDES

Thus far, we have dealt with a variety of variables that exert an influence on consumer behavior. We have identified social factors such as culture, social class, groups, and family. We have recognized intrapersonal influences such as learning, personality, and self-concept. Although all of these variables may exert an influence on behavior, the psychological mechanism through which they operate has not been specified. One useful approach is to consider the concept of attitudes as this mechanism. From this point of view, the net effect of social and intrapersonal variables is to create a structure of attitudes that ultimately govern behavior.

Attitudes may be defined as "predispositions to respond in a particular way toward a specified class of objects." In the context of marketing, the goal of marketing communications is to affect attitudes, thereby creating a predisposition to purchase particular brands. For this reason, the measurement of attitudes toward products is a multimillion dollar business, and changing attitudes is a major preoccupation of the advertising industry.

It is generally recognized that attitudes have three components—affective (feeling), cognitive (knowledge), and behavioral. That is, our attitudes consist of feelings toward an object, knowledge about the object, and a predisposition to behave in certain ways toward the object. Further, these three components tend to be consistent with one another. For example, if we have a favorable feeling

---

[25]Peter Vanderwicken, "What's Really Wrong at Chrysler?" *Fortune* (May 1975): 179.

toward a brand, we generally believe favorable things about it and are inclined to buy it.

It also follows that if we can change one of these components, the others will tend to shift in the same direction. Thus, if we can change an individual's emotional response toward a brand from negative or neutral to positive, the person may start perceiving the brand differently and be persuaded to purchase it. Or, if we can provide favorable information about a product, thereby changing the consumer's knowledge of it, there will be a tendency for feelings to change, and the probability of purchase will be increased. Finally, if we can change a person's behavior—induce the person to use a product he or she has not previously used—then feelings toward the product and knowledge of it will also tend to change.

These three strategies (changing feelings through emotional appeals; changing knowledge by providing information; and changing behavior by inducing trial) are the primary strategies used by marketers to change attitudes. Generally, the more components of an attitude we can affect, the greater will be the probability of attitude change. For this reason, most advertisers use a combination of strategies.

Wind Song perfume, Campbell's soup, and Aunt Jemima Lite Syrup are examples of these three approaches (Figures 6–12, 6–13, and 6–14). The Wind Song ad appeals to emotions. It doesn't talk about the product; it suggests love and intimacy. Its purpose is to associate Wind Song with our deepest emotional expressions. On the other hand, the Campbell's ad is an informational advertisement. It provides information on the nutritional value of Campbell's soups. Finally, the Aunt Jemima Lite Syrup advertisement is a coupon ad. Certainly, it shows the product in an appetite appealing photograph (emotional appeal), and provides information on the calories the product contains (information), but the *focus* of the advertisement is on a trial-inducing coupon to get consumers to change their behavior and buy Aunt Jemima Lite Syrup if they have not already done so.

In any case, the purpose of all three ads is to change attitudes. It is only the strategy that differs. For the student interested in marketing communications, a knowledge of attitudes and how they change is an essential ingredient to success.

PERCEPTION

Each of us perceives the world in somewhat different ways, and behaves in terms of what we perceive. Perception starts with the stimulation of the sense receptors (eyes, ears, nose, skin, tongue, and kinesthetic receptors) by a pattern of energy. Each receptor transforms this energy into a neural impulse that is received by the central nervous system. There it is modified and elaborated to create a meaningful experience. Incoming stimuli are not passively received by the organism; they are organized, interpreted, and given meaning. Thus, perception can be defined as a process through which incoming stimuli are given meaning, or perception is the process through which we make sense of the world. Within the framework of this definition, certain aspects of perception should be noted.

FIGURE 6–12 Wind Song—an
emotional appeal (Courtesy Prince
Matchabelli)

Perception is subjective. Since perception takes place wholly in the mind of the perceiver, it is a subjective experience. No two people see things in precisely the same way. Two prospective purchasers viewing a new refrigerator may focus on different aspects of the appliance. For one person, design or special features may dominate perception to the detriment of other aspects of the purchase. For another person, price or construction details may be predominant. One ends up buying and the other does not, even though they may have comparable incomes, similar financial obligations, and equivalent requirements for refrigeration.

As consumers, we sometimes block out or ignore things we don't want to recognize, emphasizing only the positive aspects of the product. In other instances, we may focus on product defects, ignor-

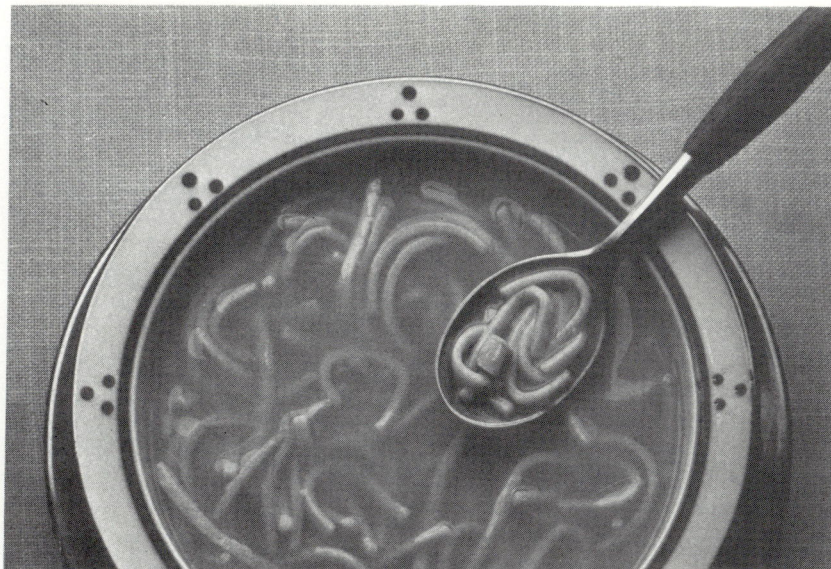
ing positive attributes. We tend to see what we want to see, and hear what we want to hear. It is often said we never see things as they really are; instead, we see things as we want, expect, or need them to be.

Perception is selective. During the course of an average day, we are surrounded by thousands of stimuli. At any moment, it is not possible to attend to all of the stimuli that bombard our senses. Thus, we cannot read, carry on a conversation, and watch television at the same time. When we try, we find our attention shifting back and forth from one source of stimuli to the other with our compre-

"Lite Syrup?
You're kidding.
It's thicker than
our syrup!"

Aunt Jemima® Lite Syrup.
1/3 less calories, high calorie taste.

Aunt Jemima Lite Syrup. It's even thicker than the leading
syrup. With all the rich flavor your family wants, but one-third
less calories! And no artificial sweeteners. Try Aunt Jemima Lite
Syrup. With the high calorie taste.

STORE COUPON

M02 4286

Save 15¢
on Aunt Jemima®
Lite Syrup.

15¢

RETAILER: As our agent you may accept this coupon from retail customers only when redeemed on the specified product(s). Quaker will reim-
burse you for the face value of this coupon plus 7¢ for handling. Any other
use may constitute fraud. Adequate proof of purchase must be submitted upon request.
Customer pays any tax. This coupon is void if transferred, assigned, reproduced, taxed,
licensed, restricted, or wherever prohibited by law. Offer good only in U.S.A. and military
commissaries and exchanges. Cash value .001¢. Only retailers and Quaker authorized
clearing houses send to The Quaker Oats Company, P.O. Box 4106, Oak Park, IL 60303.
TERMS OF OFFER: Redeemable only on the purchase of specified product(s). Any
other use may void all coupons submitted for redemption and such coupons may
be confiscated. Limit one coupon per transaction.

COUPON EXPIRES July 31, 1982

No artificial
sweeteners

hension of each of these activities becoming disjointed and fragmen-
tary. For this reason, we tend to select out of our environment those
stimuli that are most important to us, ignoring the rest.

This point is particularly important for marketing. The United
States consumer is bombarded with advertising messages from a
variety of sources. The marketer's advertising message for a particular product is competing with many others, only a few of which will
be consciously seen. Yet, we do see the advertising for products in
which we have a current interest. Were it not for selective perception, it is doubtful that any advertising would be seen by enough
people to justify its cost. Thus, all marketing communications are
indebted to the phenomenon of selective perception.

Perception and marketing communications. The role of marketing communications is to help consumers perceive particular prod-

ucts in desired ways. We do this by surrounding a product or brand with **cues** that help identify and give it a desired character. Words, colors, shapes, sounds, odors, weight, and other symbols are some of the cues we use. For example, color and texture are used effectively in the advertisement for Ultra Sense (Figure 6–15). Dark, rich colors and an expensive fur coat are used to connote quality and elegance.

Surrogate indicators. Often, consumers are unable to assess the quality of a brand offered for sale. This frequently occurs with fabrics, furniture, carpeting, electronic equipment, or other products where consumers may not have the technical knowledge to distin-

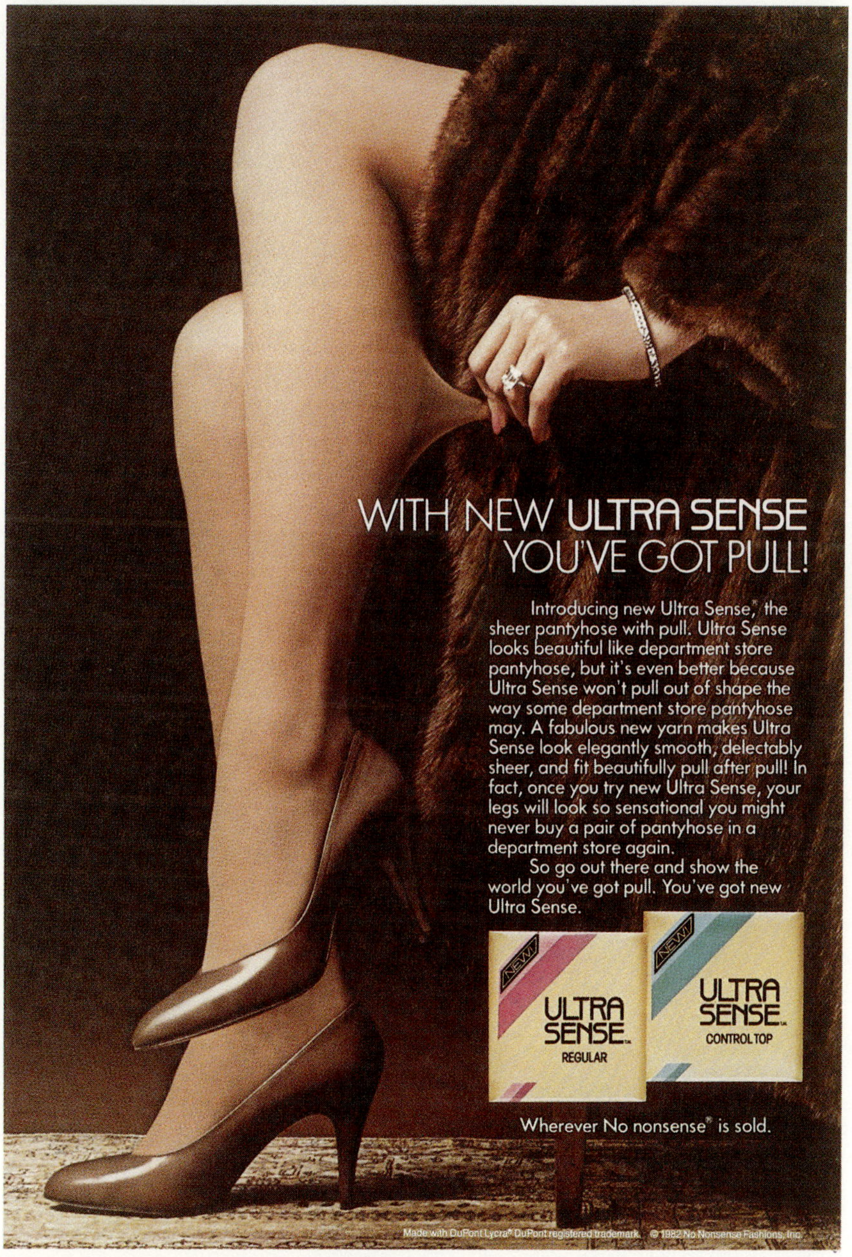

WITH NEW ULTRA SENSE
YOU'VE GOT PULL!
Introducing new Ultra Sense,® the sheer pantyhose with pull. Ultra Sense looks beautiful like department store pantyhose, but it's even better because Ultra Sense won't pull out of shape the way some department store pantyhose may. A fabulous new yarn makes Ultra Sense look elegantly smooth, delectably sheer, and fit beautifully pull after pull! In fact, once you try new Ultra Sense, your legs will look so sensational you might never buy a pair of pantyhose in a department store again.
So go out there and show the world you've got pull. You've got new Ultra Sense.
NEW
ULTRA SENSE
REGULAR
NEW
ULTRA SENSE
CONTROL TOP
Wherever No nonsense® is sold.
Made with DuPont Lycra® DuPont registered trademark. © 1982 No Nonsense Fashions, Inc.

FIGURE 6–15 Color is used effectively in this ad for Ultra Sense. (Courtesy No Nonsense Fashions, Inc.)

guish a superior brand from an inferior one. In such cases, consumers often use surrogate or substitute indicators. Under the assumption that higher priced products tend to be superior, price is often used as a surrogate indicator for quality. This assumption may or may not be true. Suds are often used as a surrogate indicator for detergents, which is why detergents frequently contain sudsing agents even though sudsing has nothing to do with cleaning effectiveness. Blue Cheer is perceived as particularly effective in getting clothes white because "bluing" is associated in consumers' minds with whiteness. The use of the words "blue magic" in blue Cheer's advertising supports the consumers' illusion.

Many other surrogate indicators are used by consumers. Bright, garish colors imply cheapness; dark, rich colors imply quality. One of the more important surrogate indicators used by consumers is the brand name. The brand that establishes a reputation for excellence—such as Toro for lawn mowers, Budweiser for beer, Sara Lee for frozen desserts, Titleist for golf balls, or General Electric for major appliances—has a lot going for it in the marketplace.

There are many ways in which consumers may be helped to perceive products in desired ways so that the image of the brand may be enhanced. A number of techniques may be used to emphasize a product or a product name in advertising. Examples may be found by the way elements are positioned in an illustration, use of photographic effects, or addition of musical punctuation in broadcast media. The advertisement for Vandermint (Figure 6–16) uses soft focus for the background elements to enhance perception of the central figures in the advertisement. It also uses the silhouette of a windmill to reinforce the liqueur's association with Holland.

CONSUMER BEHAVIOR AND COMMUNICATIONS

No one factor that we have discussed holds the key to effective communications. One product may be primarily subject to group influences; another may be more closely tied to personality or the self-concept. Learning, attitudes, and perception are also important aspects of consumer behavior. Generally, consumers are acted upon by a number of these variables simultaneously, and it is the job of marketing and advertising people to sort out what is most significant.

Human behavior is complex, and consumer behavior is no simpler. There are no easy answers, no shortcuts. Knowledge, analysis, sensitivity, intuition, and hard work are all ingredients in the creative process.

SUMMARY

Consumers are problem solvers who perceive their needs, wants, and desires as problems which they often try to solve through the purchase of goods and services. Marketers compete with one another in trying to influence consumers to use their particular products in order to satisfy their needs. Thus, consumer motivation—the study of human desires and strivings—is a subject of intense interest to advertisers.

FIGURE 6–16 Soft focus for the background elements enhances perception of the central figures. (Reprinted with permission of General Wine & Spirits Co.)

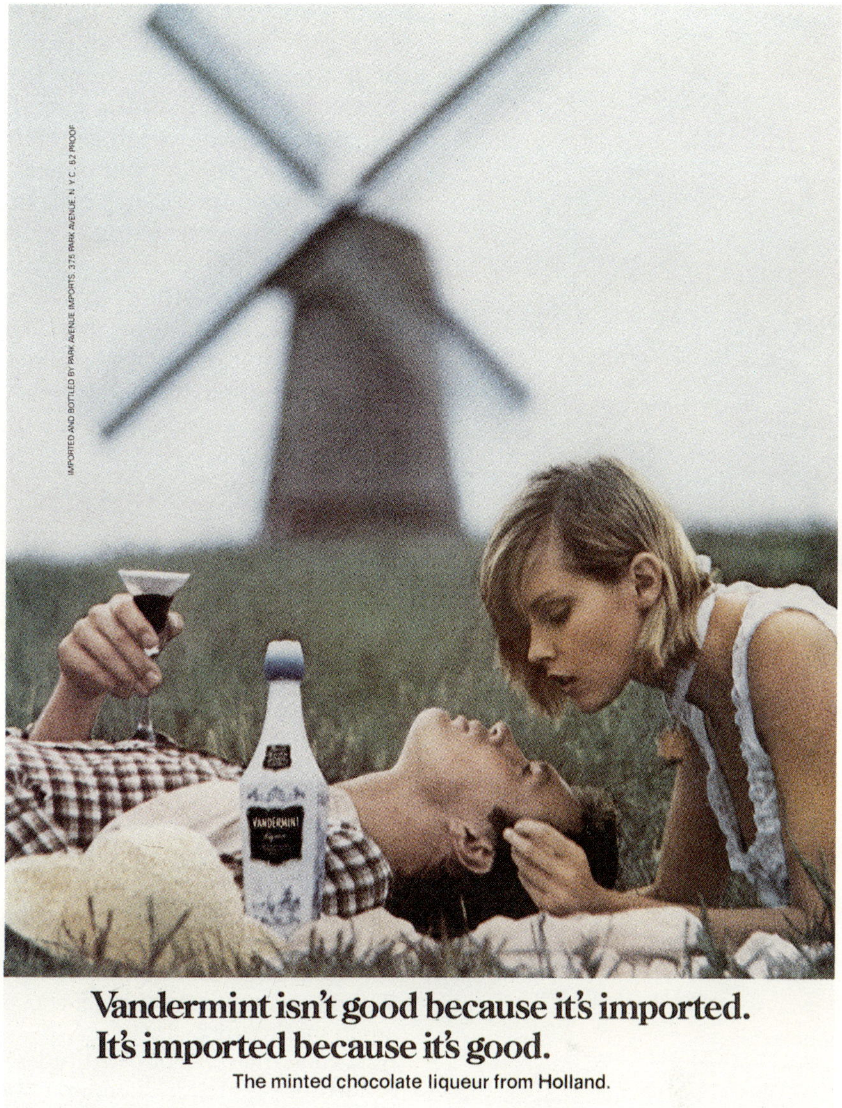
IMPORTED AND BOTTLED BY PARK AVENUE IMPORTS, 375 PARK AVENUE, N.Y.C., 62 PROOF
VANDERMINT
Vandermint isn't good because it's imported.
It's imported because it's good.
The minted chocolate liqueur from Holland.

Motivation is a complex area of human behavior, enhanced by the ambiguity of the words we use to discuss it and the fact that motives cannot be directly observed. Only behavior can be observed. Inherent in the concept of motivation is the concept of goal. The intent of marketing is to persuade consumers to perceive products and services as goals that will satisfy their needs, thereby transforming psychological needs into the economic concept of demand. This transformation can be conceptualized through a four-stage process: (a) internal need state; (b) need recognition; (c) product identification; and (d) product demand. Key issues in motivation concern the number and nature of basic needs and the variations in the intensity of motivated behavior. A survey of motivational theories and research permits us to draw certain conclusions about motivation that are relevant to marketing.

The author of marketing communications who expects to be successful in motivating consumers needs to recognize the complexity of motivational phenomenon and be aware of the variables that shape behavior and give it direction. Although no one of these variables provides a complete explanation of behavior, a knowledge of them often provides insights into behavior that help us in segmenting markets and defining effective advertising appeals.

A number of variables relate to marketing practices. These variables include social phenomena such as culture, social class, social groups, and family. They also include psychological or intrapersonal factors such as learning, personality, self-concept, attitudes, and perception. None of these social and psychological variables hold the key to effective marketing. The importance of a particular variable is dependent upon the product, the function it serves, and the target group of consumers. Knowledge, analysis, sensitivity, intuition, and hard work are necessary in devising product appeals that will be successful in influencing consumers.

REVIEW QUESTIONS

1   Explain the process by which the psychological concept of need is transformed into the economic concept of demand.
2   Summarize Maslow's motivational theory and explain its implications for marketing.
3   Distinguish between central and peripheral needs. Explain why they differ in intensity.
4   Identify and explain the four principles of learning derived from learning theory. Give examples of how they are used in advertising.
5   Distinguish between structural and trait theories of personality and explain why most of the research in the field of marketing has been done with trait theories.
6   What is meant by psychographics? What is the underlying assumption upon which psychographics is based? How is this approach used in marketing?
7   What is meant by the self-concept? Why is the self-concept important in marketing?
8   Define the concept of attitudes. Identify the basic components of an attitude and give examples of how these components are used in marketing.
9   Define perception. How do marketers use the concept of perception in marketing communications?
10   Explain what is meant by surrogate indicators. Give examples of such indicators and explain how they are useful in marketing.

DISCUSSION QUESTIONS

1   Select a product of your choice. Show how this product might be advertised to appeal to: (a) physiological needs; (b) safety needs; (c) affiliation needs; (d) esteem needs; and (e) self-actualization needs. Which of these basic needs do you think would be most appropriate for this particular product? Why?
2   In Maslow's need theory there is no mention of a need for money. Do you think money is a central or peripheral need? Why? How do you

account for the fact that people place so much importance on money in this culture?

3 Bring four magazine ads to class, emphasizing the principles of: contiguity; repetition; reinforcement; and meaning or goals. Which of these advertisements do you think is most effective? Why?

PROBLEM

Select a magazine advertisement or a television commercial. If a magazine ad is used, bring the ad to class. If a commercial is used, prepare a brief description of it. Analyze the advertisement or commercial in terms of: (a) the basic function served by the product; (b) the primary appeal used; (c) secondary appeals employed; (d) the primary and secondary appeals in terms of Maslow's need theory.

7
Product, Brand, and Package

RECIPE FOR SUCCESS

Most marketing success stories follow a similar recipe.

1 Start with a good product.
2 Mix well with a dollop of positioning.
3 Season with a carefully chosen brand name.
4 Stir in a well-tested package design.
5 Add a cup of pricing.
6 Blend in a generous portion of distribution.
7 Bring to a boil with sales promotion.
8 Simmer with a heavy media expenditure.
9 Top off with a consistent sauce of creative advertising.

Voilà! Haute cuisine a la marketing. Nowhere is the use of this recipe for success more apparent than in the story of Procter & Gamble, an $11 billion company whose sales have multiplied more than thirty times since 1945. Six P&G products (Pampers, Tide, Charmin, Bounty, Cheer, and Downy) are among the top ten household products purchased by consumers; Folger's and Crisco are among the top ten in foods; Crest, Head & Shoulders, and Scope are among the top ten in health and beauty aids. Many others are leaders in specific product fields: Cascade, the leading dishwasher detergent; Ivory, the leading dishwashing liquid; Comet, the leading scouring cleanser; and Duncan Hines, the leading baking mix.[1]

How does one account for P&G's record of success? Excellence in planning and execution at every step of the production-marketing operation is a major requirement. Behind it all is a product philosophy that can be summed up in the following quotation by Howard M. Morgens, a former chairman of the board of Procter & Gamble.

> The only way you can succeed in business is with a good product. You can't do it with advertising. It all gets down to the fact that if

---

[1]Carol J. Loomis, "P&G Up Against Its Wall," *Fortune*, 23 February 1981, 99.

you've a good product, you can be successful with a reasonable marketing expenditure, but if you haven't got the product, the surest way to go broke is to pour your money behind it.[2]

NEVER CONFUSE CONSUMERS

A package should always identify, clearly and unequivocally, the product and its purpose. Conversely, a product package should not confuse consumers. Consider the case of Sun Light, a dishwashing liquid introduced by Lever Brothers Company. The product smells like lemons, contains lemon juice, and has a picture of a lemon on the label. Using small type, the package identifies the product as a dishwashing liquid and cautions the consumer against taking it internally. However, consumers do not always read the small print on the label. Thus, on a hot day in Maryland, thirty-three adults and forty-five children became ill when Sun Light was mistaken for lemon juice and added to iced tea. Apparently, the problem wasn't confined to Maryland. When samples of Sun Light were distributed in the San Diego area, the San Diego Association of Poison Control Centers reported that confusion over the Sun Light label and the product's use was widespread.[3]

Since Sun Light is labeled as a dishwashing detergent, Lever Brothers Company is not legally responsible for misuse of the product. A spokesperson for the company has said that it has no intention of changing the label. From a legal standpoint, Lever's position is defensible. However, from a marketing standpoint, it lacks savvy. A package for any dishwashing detergent that enables consumers to confuse its contents with consumable lemon juice is the result of a questionable marketing plan.

To be successful, advertising needs a strong foundation consisting of the other elements of marketing—product, package, product name, pricing, and distribution. However, advertising also con-

---

[2]John S. Wright, Daniel S. Warner, Willis L. Winter, Jr., and Sherilyn K. Zeigler, *Advertising,* 4th ed. (New York: McGraw-Hill, 1977), 81.

[3]Lynn G. Reiling, "Consumer Misuse Mars Sampling for Sun Light Dishwashing Liquid," *Marketing News,* 13 September 1982, 1.

tributes to this foundation. Without advertising, most consumer products would die aborning.

Advertising practitioners in client organizations and advertising agencies are not only interested in the other elements of marketing because they affect advertising, but also because these practitioners are often called upon to contribute to the development of other marketing elements. Specific advertising personnel are: (a) asked to participate in pricing decisions; (b) involved in discussions of product position and attributes; (c) required when determining the design of packages or devising brand names; and (d) needed to participate in decisions concerning distribution. For example, when Contac was first introduced, creative reasons—to give it a clinical, pharmaceutical image—restricted the initial distribution to drug stores. When Duncan Hines cake mixes were first introduced by Nebraska Consolidated Mills, a regional milling company with limited marketing experience, its advertising agency was charged with the responsibility of recruiting a network of food brokers to represent the company.

In this chapter we will examine three elements of the marketing mix—product, brand name, and package.

THE PRODUCT

Without a product, there is no advertising; without a good product, there is little chance of advertising success. The primacy of the product in the marketing enterprise is an act of faith and a fact of life among successful marketers. Yet, the product concept is not a simple one. Consider the advertisement for Mudd in Figure 7–1. According to the illustration, Mudd is a mud pack used for cleansing the skin. The label lists its contents as "water, caprylic/capric triglyceride, glyceryl stearate, propylene glycol, quaternium-22, decyl oleate, mineral oil, lavreth-23, cetearyl alcohol, emulsifying wax, N.F. stearyl alcohol, ceteareth-20, myristyl lactate, imdazolidinyl urea, propylparaben, cetyl alcohol, methylparaben, and dimethicone." For women who buy it, Mudd is a way of obtaining beautiful skin. The advertisement states Mudd is a way women can become pretty for a whole week. What *is* the product?

Broadly speaking, a product might be defined as a bundle of satisfactions. Actually, it is more complicated than that. Every product is really three products—a generic, physical, and psychological product.

THE GENERIC PRODUCT

The **generic product** refers to the basic product type, and the primary function it serves. In the example given, Mudd is a skin cleanser. Consumers have certain general expectations concerning generic products—their primary function, general appearance, and price. A product that does not conform to consumers' general expectations may meet resistance or rejection. Back in the early 1930s, Chrysler introduced a new model called the Airflow. Its streamlined appearance was at least thirty years ahead of every other car on the market. Even though it was an excellent automobile, consumers re-

FIGURE 7–1   (Courtesy Chattem, Inc.)

jected the Airflow because it did not conform to their expectations of how a generic automobile should look. When preemergent herbicides were introduced into the agriculture market, their use violated the generic expectations of how farmers dealt with weeds. Traditionally, farmers waited for weeds to sprout, using up soil nutrients in the process. Then the farmers plowed the weeds under or sprayed them with a herbicide and watched them wither and die. With a preemergent herbicide, farmers had to mix the herbicide into the soil before planting their crops so that it would keep the weeds from sprouting. Since farmers never saw the weeds, they weren't sure whether the herbicide had killed them, or there simply weren't many weeds that year and the use of the preemergent herbicide was a waste of time and money. As a consequence, farmers were slow to adopt preemergent herbicides as an efficient agriculture practice.

Diffusion theory—the process by which a new idea or product is accepted by the aggregate population—indicates that a new product that departs from consumers' generic expectations will be accepted slowly, if at all.

THE PHYSICAL PRODUCT

The **physical product** is the actual physical entity or service that is offered to consumers. It is the tangible object that is sold. In the case of Mudd, the physical product is water, caprylic/capric triglyceride, glyceryl stearate, propylene glycol, quaternium-22, decyl oleate, mineral oil, lavreth-23, cetearyl alcohol, emulsifying wax, N.F. stearyl alcohol, ceteareth-20, myristyl lactate, imdazolidinyl urea, propylparaben, cetyl alcohol, methylparaben, and dimethicone. In short, it is the physical thing manufactured.

THE PSYCHOLOGICAL PRODUCT

The **psychological product** is the physical product along with the entire galaxy of service, warranties, benefits, and psychological overtones that accompany it. In the case of Mudd, the psychological product is the promise of beautiful skin and being pretty.

Few purchasers of Mudd probably know what the physical ingredients are. One would need to be a chemist or a pharmacist to understand its technical composition. Users of Mudd buy the product not for what it actually is, but for what they believe it can do. According to the body copy of the advertisement, it has

> . . . the unique ability to draw out oily dirt and imbedded makeup everyday soap can't reach.
> And Mudd lifts away dry, flaky skin cells that can make your complexion look dull.
> The result is skin so deep-down clean it can really breathe again. Your face will feel tingly, refreshed and alive. It will look pretty for days.

As long as a product meets this expectation in the eyes of its users, consumers will be satisfied with their purchase. This brings up the question of consumer expectations and their relationship to the physical product.

CONSUMER EXPECTATIONS AND PRODUCT SATISFACTION

If the concept of a product is complex, consumer satisfaction is no less so. Two consumers may buy the same brand of a product. Each of the products purchased performs equally well. Yet one consumer is satisfied and the other is not. Consumers may make purchases which initially please them. A few weeks later their initial pleasure turns to dissatisfaction and they regret having made the purchase.

The key to the problem of consumer satisfaction seems to lie in the concept of expectations. Satisfaction often lies less in the actual performance of the product than in the purchaser's expectations of performance. A number of theories of consumer satisfaction and dissatisfaction, all based on the concept of expectations, have been devised.[4] One of the most useful lends itself to advertising analysis and action. It is the two-factor theory suggested by Swan and Combs.

Swan and Combs suggest that consumers judge products on a limited set of attributes. Some are relatively important in determining satisfaction; others are not critical to satisfaction but create dissatisfaction when their performance is disappointing. In making this distinction, the authors speak of two aspects of performance.[5]

☐ **Instrumental performance** refers to a means to a set of ends. This is essentially the performance of the physical product.
☐ **Expressive performance** is the performance that consumers consider an end in itself. It involves psychological attributes such as style and expression of the self-concept.

The determinant attributes of a given purchase may be the expressive ones, while the instrumental attributes may not be an explicit part of the purchase decision. However, inadequate performance of the physical product (instrumental attributes) may lead to dissatisfaction with the purchase. For example, a woman may buy a dress because of its style and be pleased with her purchase. Style, an expressive attribute, is the determinant attribute of her purchase. After she has worn the dress a few times, the material begins to stretch and lose its form, or seams are constantly tearing loose. When making the decision to purchase the dress, she did not consciously consider these factors. She tacitly assumed that the dress was of good quality and would perform well (a generic expectation). However, she became bitterly dissatisfied with her purchase—not because of the style (an expressive attribute), but because of physical deficiencies (instrumental attributes) that were not consciously considered at the time of purchase but were a part of her generic expectations of how a dress should wear.

The instrumental performance of Swan and Combs is equivalent to the performance of the physical product. Thus, Swan and Combs isolate the physical product from the complexities of the generic and psychological product, and they emphasize the role of the physical product in consumer dissatisfaction, although this dissatisfaction may not have been a determinant factor in making the purchase.

Howard Morgens, who was quoted at the beginning of the chapter, was undoubtedly talking about the physical product when he observed: "The only way you can succeed in business is with a good product. You can't do it with advertising." For advertising, this

---

[4]Ralph E. Anderson, "Consumer Dissatisfaction: The Effect of Disconfirmed Expectancies and Perceived Product Performance," *Journal of Marketing Research* (February 1973): 38–44.

[5]John E. Swan and Linda Jones Combs, "Product Performance and Consumer Satisfaction: A New Concept," *Journal of Marketing* (April 1976): 25–33. This theory was anticipated by Irving S. White, who made a distinction between "expressive products" and "utility products" in 1969. See Irving S. White, "New Product Differentiation: Physical and Symbolic Dimensions," in *Marketing in a Changing World*, Bernard A. Morin, ed. (Chicago: American Marketing Association, 1969), 99–103.

CHAPTER 7 | PRODUCT, BRAND, AND PACKAGE

implies that the performance characteristics of the physical product always remain key determinants in product satisfaction or dissatisfaction, regardless of the product's psychological attributes. Thus, the quality of the physical product should *always* be a major concern of advertisers, and those who write advertising must be thoroughly aware of the product's strengths and limitations.

RETAIL STORES AND SERVICES AS PRODUCTS

We have discussed products as though they were tangible objects (a car, refrigerator, baking mix, or detergent) that consumers buy, take home, and use. However, a retail store is also a product, as is a service such as that provided by a doctor, dentist, television repair person, or insurance agent.

A retail store is a product that sells other products. The store itself has tangible attributes and characteristics that cause consumers to form preferences. The location, appearance, depth and breadth of merchandise assortments, name brands carried, courtesy of personnel, credit policies, and pricing practices are all attributes of a store. We speak of a *store image* in the same sense that we speak of a brand image. The Ohrbach's advertisement, used as an example in Chapter 5, shows a retail store attempting to create a store image that makes it a desirable place to shop.

Similarly, a service provided by a doctor or a television repair person is also a product from the standpoint of marketing. Individuals who offer a service succeed or fail based on their abilities to provide consumer satisfaction. As a consequence, the role of advertising for a retail store or service is to translate these underlying concepts into appealing consumer benefits.

STRATEGIES FOR NEW PRODUCTS

New products are the future of business. Without a continuous flow of new products, the marketing system, as we know it, would probably atrophy and die. In his book *New Product Management*, Eberhard Scheuing estimates that ". . . eighty percent of today's products will have disappeared from the market ten years from now, while an estimated eighty percent of the products that will be sold in the next decade are as yet unknown."[6] The development of new products is expensive, and the risks are relatively high. Ford is estimated to have lost $350 million on the Edsel; DuPont lost $100 million on Corfam, a synthetic leather; Scott Paper Company lost $12 million on Baby Scott, a disposable diaper; Procter & Gamble lost over $250 million on Pringles; and Standard Brands spent $6 million in marketing support alone during the brief year that its Smooth & Easy Sauce and Gravy Mixes unsuccessfully struggled for survival. During the early 1970s, the cost for designing and producing a new automobile was estimated to be $750 million. By 1980 Ford had spent $3 billion developing the Ford Escort and Mercury Lynx, Ford's answer to fuel efficient imports; this does not include the high cost of introducing a new entry into the automobile market.[7]

---

[6]Eberhard E. Scheuing, *New Product Management* (Hinsdale, Illinois: The Dryden Press, 1974), 1.

[7]"Detroit's Uphill Battle," *Time,* 8 September, 1980, 46.

Few products are as expensive to develop as automobiles, but all are relatively expensive. A succession of new product failures is enough to depress the profits and weaken the financial structure of even the most vigorous companies. Although few reliable figures are available on new product failure rate, only a tiny proportion of all new products entering the developmental pipeline ever reach the stage of commercialization; of those that do, over a third of them fail.[8] *The Wall Street Journal* has referred to new product development as one of the "highest risk and highest reward activities in the business world."[9]

The most common reason for the failure of new products is the lack of a significant difference in the physical product (as viewed by the consumer) from products already being sold in the marketplace. According to Theodore Angelus, who made a study of 75 new product failures in the food and drug industries, the major cause of failure was the lack of a significant product difference, as viewed by consumers.[10] J. Hugh Davidson supports this conclusion in a study of 100 new products, fifty that failed and fifty that succeeded.[11] The results of this study, summarized in Table 7–1, clearly show that 74 percent of the successful products were better than competition, while most of the products that failed were either no different or worse than competition in terms of the physical product.

These findings, which are supported by the pragmatic experiences of marketing and advertising practitioners, lead to the following broad guidelines for new product strategy.

☐ A new product has the greatest chance of success if it is noticeably better than established products on some dimension that is important to consumers. In introducing food products, for example, the product has the greatest chance if it tastes better or is more convenient to use than competitive brands. The whole history of convenience foods supports this observation. The marketer who has such a product can introduce it with a good chance of marketing success.

TABLE 7–1 Comparison of successful and unsuccessful products

Differences from Competition	Percentage of Successful Products	Percentage of Unsuccessful Products
Better than competition	74%	20%
Same as competition	26%	60%
Worse than competition	—	20%
Total	100%	100%

Source: Adapted and printed by permission of the *Harvard Business Review.* An exhibit from "Why Most New Consumer Brands Fail" by J. Hugh Davidson (March/April 1976). Copyright © 1976 by the President and Fellows of Harvard College; all rights reserved.

[8]C. Merle Crawford, "New Product Failure Rates—Facts and Fallacies," *Research Management* (September 1979): 9–13.

[9]"Seeking a Winner: Success Comes Hard in the Tricky Business of Creating Products," *Wall Street Journal*, 23 August 1978, 1.

[10]Theodore L. Angelus, "Why Most New Products Fail," *Advertising Age*, 24 March 1969, p. 85–86.

[11]J. Hugh Davidson, "Why Most New Consumer Brands Fail," *Harvard Business Review* (March-April 1976): 119.

CHAPTER 7 | PRODUCT, BRAND, AND PACKAGE

☐ If the new product is not better, but distinguishably different from competing brands, it has a reasonable chance of success; however, the risk is higher. If the product is physically different in some way, the marketer has a point that can be featured in advertising, and this apparent difference can sometimes be translated as a tangible consumer benefit.

☐ If the product is virtually identical with competitive products, it has little chance of marketing success. In this case, the marketing risk is extremely high, and a disproportionate burden is placed on the packaging, product name, and advertising. Further, any brand preference that may be formed through heavy promotion tends to be weak and vulnerable to competitive efforts. There is nothing more discouraging than working with an advertising creative group to try to find a reason why consumers should use such a product rather than an established one when there isn't any reason in the physical product itself. The best approach is not to introduce the product.

☐ If the new product is inferior in its physical performance characteristics to products on the market, it has virtually no chance of success. The best advice is to forget it.

These guidelines are not absolute. Exceptions can be found in the marketplace, but they are relatively rare. Sound marketing decisions are based on playing the odds. In the case of the third and fourth guidelines, the possibility of success is increased if the product can be sold at a price substantially under competition, so that it still represents a value to consumers. Even in this case, the product can only succeed as long as a competitor does not undercut the price.

THE PRODUCT LIFE CYCLE

The product life cycle is the simple recognition that products go through various stages: **introduction, growth, maturity,** and **decline** (Figure 7–2). Different stages often require different marketing and advertising strategies.

FIGURE 7–2 Typical four stage product life cycle and profit curve

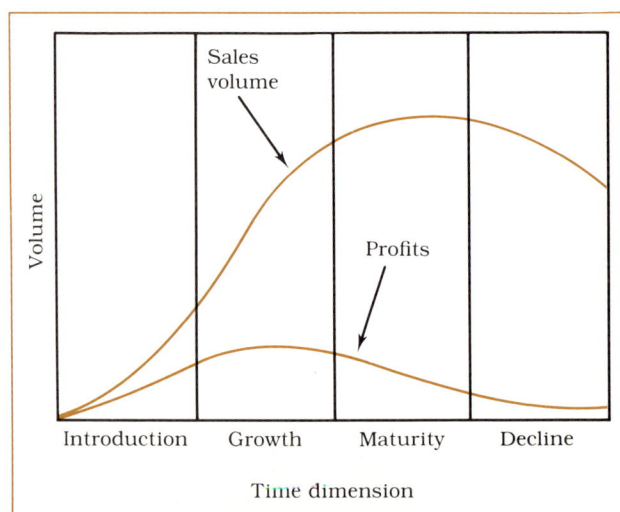

INTRODUCTION STAGE

The introduction stage of a product life cycle is generally characterized by slow growth, heavy promotional expenditures in relation to sales, relatively high prices, and limited product offerings such as flavors, styles, and forms. The role of advertising is to create **primary demand**—educate consumers about the product type and encourage distributors and retailers to stock the product.

GROWTH STAGE

If the introduction is successful, sales start climbing rapidly as distribution increases and consumers are persuaded to try the product. Promotional expenditures remain high; prices tend to remain high unless they are reduced to stimulate demand or discourage competition from entering the field. Competitors enter the field and major product improvements appear as a response to competition. Product differentiation and market segmentation emerge as marketing strategies, and advertising starts emphasizing **selective demand**—specific features of particular products that give it an edge over competition.

MATURITY STAGE

The growth rate slows down when most of the potential customers have tried the product. The reduction in growth exerts a downward pressure on prices, dealer margins, and profits. Weak competitors and less than adequate brands drop out of the market. The maturity stage is marked by increased efforts to find unique, dramatic, and compelling ways of presenting advertising claims. A larger proportion of the advertising budget is devoted to advertising sales promotion activities such as coupons, contests, and sweepstakes.

DECLINE STAGE

Eventually, most product forms and brands enter a period of declining sales. This period may be rapid, particularly in a case where technology devises a new product form that is functionally superior to existing brands. Or, the decline period may continue over a period of years as consumers gradually lose interest and a variety of substitute product forms emerge. More and more companies drop out of the market as the product field becomes unprofitable. Advertising expenditures decrease, and a substantial portion of advertising funds are often devoted to supporting sales promotion activities.

MANAGING THE PRODUCT LIFE CYCLE

For the marketing manager, the major question is whether the product life cycle is inevitable or if it can be managed in such a way that the vitality of the brand is prolonged. Certainly, many brands have lost their luster and disappeared from the marketplace. On the other hand, Ivory Soap has been around since 1878, and Kodak cameras have a similar longevity. Kellogg's cereals, Ford, RCA, Remington typewriters, Folger's coffee, Maxwell House, Hires Root Beer, Coca-Cola, Woodbury's Soap, Cadillac, Hershey, and many other brands seem to defy the life cycle concept and retain their vigor long past the age of reasonable senescence. Some, such as Coca-Cola, have done so while keeping their original form and formula. Others have gone through a variety of brand modifications and marketing strategies.

From the standpoint of product itself, a number of strategies are useful in prolonging the product life of individual brands, including: (a) improving product quality through ingredient and manufacturing changes; (b) line extensions such as adding flavors, new product forms (bar, liquid, tablet, and granular forms of soap, for example), or related products to the line (a cake mix might expand into a line of dessert mixes); and (c) style and feature obsolescence, where new styles or features are added on a periodic basis.

In each of these strategies, advertising has a key role in reaching consumers to inform them about product quality improvements, line extensions, new features, or new styles.

THE BRAND NAME

In the mid-1950s, Anheuser Busch marketed Michelob and Budweiser, both premium priced beers. Yet, 80 percent of the beer market was made up of popular priced beers; the premium segment was only 20 percent of the total. In an attempt to crack the popular priced market, Anheuser Busch, working with the D'Arcy Advertising Agency, test marketed Busch Lager beer in St. Louis. The new product took off with all the snap and crackle of a wet noodle.

Elmer Marschutz, then chairman of the board of the Gardner Advertising Company in St. Louis, sat next to an executive vice-president of Anheuser Busch at a civic luncheon. As a conversation starter, Elmer said, "I understand Busch Lager isn't doing very well."

"It could be doing better," the Anheuser Busch executive admitted, grudgingly.

Then Elmer dropped the bomb. "I know why it isn't selling," he said.

"Why?"

"Two reasons," said Elmer. "First, you named it Busch Lager Beer. Budweiser is also a lager beer, and no one wants to buy a second-rate Budweiser. Second, your advertising theme, 'the talk of the town,' is dull. It doesn't promise the consumer anything."

"Do you think Gardner could do any better?" asked the Anheuser Busch executive.

"I know we could," said Elmer, modestly.

"Could you develop a campaign for presentation within a month?"

"That's plenty of time," Elmer lied.

Back at the office an hour later, Elmer received a call from the Anheuser Busch executive. "Elmer, you have a two o'clock appointment one month from today to make a presentation to Mr. Busch."

Within half an hour of that call, Elmer Marschutz had a short meeting with the agency's department heads to tell them about the assignment. Pandemonium broke loose. Agency personnel had to become knowledgeable about beer; a product concept had to be defined; product characteristics had to be specified; a brand name had to be selected; packages had to be designed; copy had to be created;

point-of-sale material had to be prepared; media had to be identified; and it all had to be assembled into a professional presentation.

The deadline was met, the presentation was made, and Busch Bavarian Beer was born. Busch Bavarian Beer. A new, different kind of beer. Light, refreshing, thirst quenching. A beer like they drink in Bavaria.

Although some marketers have an intuitive knack for sensing the mood of consumers, the quest for brand names that unerringly project the appropriate product concept is a creative act that can and should be confirmed by marketing research. However a brand name is chosen, its importance to the product and its advertising is obvious. The search for appropriate brand names is a multimillion dollar business, the consequences of which are apparent in product group after product group. Consider the following examples:

☐ Dishwashing liquids: White Magic, Cinch, Dawn, Dove, Sun Light, and Joy.
☐ Air fresheners: Glade, Brocade, Twice As Fresh, Air Wand, Wizard.
☐ Paper towels: Truly Fine, Viva, Tuf 'n Ready, Scotch Buy, Hi-Dri, Gala, Brawny, and Bounty.
☐ Dog food: Gaines•burgers, Top Choice, Gravy Train, Kibbles 'n Bits, Tender Chunks, Atta Boy, Come 'N Get It, Mealtime, Tasty Nuggets, Special Cuts, Butcher's Blend, and Chuck Wagon.
☐ Disposable diapers: Huggies, Luvs, and Pampers.
☐ Deodorants and antiperspirants: Mum, English Leather, Old Spice, Brut, Dry Idea, Ban, Soft & Dry, Arrid, Tickle, Secret, Sure, Right Guard, Suave.
☐ Coffee: Brim, Chock Full o' Nuts, Mellow Roast, Master Blend, Yuban, Taster's Choice.

The list is endless. Cars aren't cars; they are Cougars, Thunderbirds, Pintos, Falcons, Rabbits, Cutlasses, and Firebirds. Cosmetics are called Cover Girl, Slim Tint, Liquid Lips, and Skin Principle.

LEGAL CONSIDERATIONS IN SELECTING BRAND NAMES

Before we proceed further in the discussion of brand name strategy, perhaps we should define some of the key terms associated with branding and mention some of the legal requirements that govern the use of brand identification.

DEFINITION OF TERMS

Confusion often arises in the use of terms such as **trade name, brand name, brand mark,** and **trademark,** although each has a distinctive meaning.

☐ *Trade name* The name under which a company conducts its business. General Motors, General Mills, Procter & Gamble, Ralston Purina and Anheuser Busch are all well-known trade names.

CHAPTER 7 | PRODUCT, BRAND, AND PACKAGE

□ *Brand* "A name, term, sign, symbol, or design, or a combination of them which is intended to identify the goods or services of one seller or a group of sellers and to differentiate them from those of competitors."[12]

□ *Brand name* That part of the *brand* that can be vocalized, such as Instant Breakfast, Charlie, Winston, and Pampers. A brand name may be, but need not be, a trade name. For example, Coca-Cola is a trade name that is also the brand name of the company's leading product. Pampers is a brand name, but the trade name of the company that manufactures Pampers is Procter & Gamble.

□ *Brand mark* That part of the *brand* that can be recognized but can not be vocalized, such as a design or symbol, or distinctive coloring or lettering. The Plymouth "ship," the Metro-Goldwyn-Mayer "lion," and the Playboy "bunny" are all brand marks.

□ *Trademark* A brand or part of a brand (a brand name or brand mark) that is given legal protection because it is capable of appropriation. A trademark is a legal concept that protects the seller's exclusive rights to use a brand name and/or brand mark. A product may have several trademarks; Coca-Cola and Coke are both trademarks referring to the same product.

LEGAL REQUIREMENTS FOR A TRADEMARK

Trademarks are normally registered with the U.S. Patent and Trademark Office, although they need not be officially registered in order to be given protection under the 1946 Lanham (trademark) Act. However, the registering of the trademark helps to protect it by establishing priority of use, a major consideration in trademark ownership. A trademark may be registered for a period of twenty years and is repeatably renewable. A number of legal restrictions apply to the use of trademarks; the major ones are identified below.

A trademark must be used in connection with an actual product. A design or name that is only used in an advertisement or on a building does not constitute a trademark within the definition of the law. The design or name must be clearly applied to a particular product and appear on the product itself. If that is not possible, it must appear on the package or dispensing unit such as a gasoline pump.

A trademark may not cause confusion or deceive purchasers as to the source of the product. The Patent Office will not register trademarks that are so similar to existing trademarks that they might cause confusion. The test for confusion is not that the trademarks appear similar when presented side by side, but that the consumer might be confused when making a purchase. For example, the trademark for Promise furniture polish was disallowed because it was confused with Johnson Wax Company's Pledge furniture polish. A list of trademarks that courts have held to be in conflict is shown in Table 7–2.

---

[12]*Marketing Definitions: A Glossary of Marketing Terms* (Chicago: American Marketing Association, 1960).

TABLE 7–2 Trademarks in conflict. According to various tribunals, there is a likelihood of confusion between these trademarks when used in connection with the indicated goods.

Marks of Successful Party	Marks of Unsuccessful Party
AFRIN topical nasal decongestant	FA-DRIN chlorphenpyridamine maleate tablets
AFTER TAN lotion for skin grooming	APRES SUN skin lotion
AIR COMMAND air conditioners and parts	CLIMATE COMMAND heating, cooling and air conditioning units
AIREX cellular material of artificial and natural elastomers and plastomers	SEREX plastic forms for use in insulation
AIRVAC dental aspirators and apparatus	VACUUM/AIRE dental equipment and accessories
ARMALON coated fabrics	ARMALONVEST armored vests
AWAKE frozen concentrate for imitation orange juice	ARISE liquid breakfast drink
BALL PARK frankfurters	BALL GAME wieners
BEER NUTS shelled and salted peanuts	BEER POTATO CHIPS potato chips
BIG BOY stick-candy	BIG BOY! powder for soft drinks
BY GEORGE men's toiletries	GEORGE V toilet water
THE CATTLEMAN restaurant and food services	CATTLEMAN canned chopped beef, luncheon meat, etc.
CHICKEN KING drive-in restaurant services	WHERE CHICKEN IS KING restaurant services
COFFEE-MATE non-dairy cream substitutes	COFFEE BREAK non-dairy cream substitutes
COMSAT satellite communications system	COMCET communications computer
CONDITION beauty pack treatment for hair	CURL & CONDITION permanent waving lotion
CORVETTE automobiles	VETTE fiberglass repair panels for automobiles
DISNEY; WALT DISNEY PRESENTS and DISNEY-LAND motion picture films, educational parks and services	DISNEY AREA ACREAGE, INC. real estate
DOT fasteners, connectors and attaching devices of various types used in construction, etc.	RED DOT DOLLY fastening devices used in construction
DURO-LITE incandescent and fluorescent lamps	DURAGLOBE globes for electric lighting fixtures
DUMPMASTER lifting mechanism for true dumping	TRASHMASTER heavy-duty vehicles
EXECUTIVE razors and blades	EXECUTIVE after-shave, pre-shave lotions
FLECTO protective coatings for paint, etc.	FELCO paint
GALLAHER smoking and chewing tobacco, etc.	GALAHAD cigars
GANT SHIRTMAKERS dress and sport shirts	GHENT on Scroll, design shirts, pajamas, etc.
GP lubricating oil	GP-7 conditioning additives for gasoline, kerosene
HILTON hotels, restaurant and bar services; HILTON HOTELS Scotch whisky, gin, etc. and CONRAD HILTON Scotch whisky and bourbon	HILTON'S gin, vodka, bourbon, etc.
HOLLOWAY HOUSE variety of frozen food products and restaurant services	DOC HOLLIDAYHOUSE pecans
ISI magazine	I.A.I. indexes to books
JVC radio receivers and FM multiplex radio receivers, etc.	IVC magnetic video tape recorders and reproducers
KENTUCKY FRIED CHICKEN CORPORATION restaurants	OLD KENTUCKY HOME FRIED CHICKEN, INC. restaurants
KUD-L-WRAP, KUD-L-DUDS and KUD-L-NAP nightwear for infants and young children	CUDDLER knitted outerwear for infants
LAND YACHT house trailers	SHASTA ROYAL LAND YACHT mobile homes
LAVE soap	LAVANA liquid detergent for fabrics
MAGIC silicone impregnated paper	ITS-MAGIC cleaning pads
MISS MERRY and MY MERRY toy kits	MISS MARY children's tea sets
MISTOMETER metered dose dispensers	METER MIST preparation for asthma
NARCO electronic radio and navigational equipment	NACO radios and tape recorders
NOON HOUR pickled and marinated fish, etc.	12 O'CLOCK dietary food in powder form

TABLE 7-2 (continued)

Marks of Successful Party	Marks of Unsuccessful Party
OCEAN FREEZE frozen seafood	SEA FREEZE and Design frozen seafood
OLD DOUGLAS whiskey	JAMES DOUGLAS blended Scotch whisky
OROGLAS synthetic resinous materials in the form of sheets, rods, etc.	PROGLAS plastics, for synthetic injection molding materials
PENNY WISE and Girl, canned sweet potatoes, hot sauce, etc.	PENNYWISE and Oval Design cookies
PEXENE liquid floor conditioner	TEXENE germicidal cleaner
PLEDGE furniture polish and cleaner	PROMISE dishwashing detergent
PRESCOTT cotton piece goods	PRESSCOTT sweaters, sport and dress shirts, coats, etc.
PRESDFLAKE particle board	CRESFLAKE particle board
Q-TIPS swabs consisting of sanitary absorbent cotton	QUICK TIPS manicure finishing spray
RID-X preparation for liquifying and deodorizing waste materials	RED X insecticides for tobacco crops
SAFGUARD mufflers and exhaust systems for automobile engines	SAFEGUARD automotive engine replacement parts
SANSRUN hosiery	SANS topless footwear
SERENE cold wave permanent kit	CERENA products for care of nails
SI-BONNE fabrics	TRES-BONS hosiery
SPECTRUM decorative paper	SPECTRA gift wrap paper
STOP & SHOP grocery store services	STOP 'N SHOP grocery store services
SUDS WITH MUSCLES detergent	MUSCLE detergent
TARACTAN tranquilizer	TARUXAN preparation for treatment of cardiac insufficiencies
THERMIX magnetic stirrer, hot plate for laboratory use	MIX O THERM magnetic stirrer, hot plate for laboratory use
TIC TAC TOE ice cream and sherbet	TIC TAC candy
TITLEIST and FINALIST golf balls	MEDALIST golf balls
TYGON plastic products for surgical use	TYCRON surgical sutures
UNIFLO oils and greases	OMNIFLO motor oil, lubricating greases
UNIVAC tabulating, record handling, computer, etc.	ANAVAC electrically operated entertainment apparatus
VANISH toilet bowl cleaner	BANISH room deodorant
VO 5 and VO 5 CONDITIONER hair conditioner, shampoo, etc.	CONDITIONER #5 pomade for hair
WHOPPER and HOME OF THE WHOPPER burger-type sandwiches and drive-in restaurant services	WHOPPABURGER sandwiches
ZIRCO catalytic agents	COZIRC driers for paints and varnishes

Source: *The United States Trademark Association Year End Report*, 1970, pp. 8-15.

A trademark may not be deceptive by implying benefits that are invalid. Names that have been legally barred include "Six Months Floor Wax" because the wax shine did not last six months; "Lemon" soap that did not contain lemon; and "Nylodon" for sleeping bags that did not contain nylon.

There are limitations on names that are primarily surnames, geographical names, or merely descriptive names. Many surnames apply to products, such as Chrysler, Ford, and Johnson. Many of these names were in effect before the current trademark laws were enacted. It would be more difficult to get such names approved today. In addition, trademark law does not protect names that are merely descriptive, such as Fresh Bread. Since the word "fresh" is a generic attribute of bread desired by consumers, it may not be used as the name for a particular product of a specific manufacturer. As a consequence, the selection of names that impute the essential quality of the product concept may create problems in trademark registration and need to be checked thoroughly for their acceptability. For example, Sun Oil Company devised a method of blending gasoline at the pump so that the consumer could regulate the octane rating of the gasoline purchased. Sun Oil referred to this innovation as Custom Blended gasoline and spent $30 million over a six-year period advertising Custom Blended gasoline as a Sun Oil Company brand. When the company was challenged in the courts, the court ruled that "custom blended" was a descriptive term that no company could appropriate for its exclusive use.

BRAND NAME STRATEGIES

In choosing a brand name for a new product, marketers have a number of broad strategies that may be employed. For example, they may use one or more of the following four approaches: company name plus product identification; company name plus brand name; brand name plus product identification; or brand name only.

COMPANY NAME PLUS PRODUCT IDENTIFICATION

Among companies following this practice are Campbell's, General Electric, and Sara Lee. Thus, we have Campbell's Tomato Soup, Campbell's Cream of Chicken Soup, Campbell's Clam Chowder, and so on. The company name (trade name) acts as a family name or umbrella and is complemented by the brand's generic product name.

COMPANY NAME PLUS BRAND NAME

This practice is characteristic of the automotive and personal-care industries, where we find Ford Pinto, Ford Mustang, Mercury Cougar, Volkswagen Rabbit, Chrysler Cordoba, and so on. The personal-care industry brings us Revlon's Charlie, Revlon's Sun Jewels, Clairol Herbal Essence Shampoo, Clairol Quiet Touch, Clairol Balsam Color, Helena Rubenstein Skin Dew, Helena Rubenstein Strong and Sheer, and many others. The intent under this strategy is to offer a familiar family name, while providing each brand an opportunity for differentiated communication through individual brand names.

BRAND NAME PLUS PRODUCT IDENTIFICATION

This approach is often found in large companies with several distinct product lines, some of which have been acquired through purchase or merger. It is also characteristic of large retail organizations that have several lines of private labels. Producers following this practice include Betty Crocker baking mixes (General Mills), Duncan Hines mixes (Procter & Gamble), and Jell-O products (General Foods). Among retailers, examples include the Kenmore and Craftsman lines for Sears, Ann Page and White House for A&P, and Lucerne for Safeway. The logic here is similar to the strategy of using a company name plus product identification. However, companies using a brand name plus a product identification are usually so diverse that the company name may be inappropriate for many of its product lines.

BRAND NAME ONLY

Finally, there are those companies that follow a strategy of using only brand names on most of their products. This is common practice in the cigarette field, such as Camel, Tareyton, Pall Mall, Marlboro, and Winston, and in the detergent field, such as Tide, Oxydol, Fab, Duz, Cheer, and All. These manufacturers insist that each brand stand on its own feet with no help from the parent company name. This strategy provides the greatest opportunity for building a distinct and unique brand image for an individual product, unhampered by historic connotations of a company or family name.

The first three strategies are referred to as **brand extension strategies** because an existing brand name is extended to cover other products, often with different product concepts. Although the use of a brand extension strategy inevitably blurs the brand image of the products to which it is applied, to some degree, brand extension confers three benefits:

1 Facilitates the introduction of new products by capitalizing on the halo effect of a well-known and reputable brand. The reputation of the existing brand encourages consumers to try a new product carrying the same brand name.
2 Reduces promotion costs since advertising funds spent on any individual product reinforce the entire line through repetition of the family name.
3 Increases in-store impact because the same brand name appears on a number of products.

These are mixed blessings, however, and the case against a brand extension strategy rests on two arguments. First, the introduction of a less than adequate product under a family name can have a negative effect (negative halo) on the entire line, causing dissatisfied customers to distrust other products in the line. Second, excessive use of a brand extension strategy can dilute the sharpness of brand images and create confusion among customers.

Few hard rules govern whether one should or should not use brand extensions. Their use is always a compromise between dilution of the brand image and possible consumer confusion, and advertising efficiency. Generally, brand extensions make a great deal of sense for a line of products that differ primarily in terms of flavor, such as Betty Crocker cake mixes; and they make some sense for a line of dessert items, such as those marketed by Kitchens of Sara Lee. They make less sense for a diverse line of baking mixes that ranges from commonplace items such as cornbread and pancake mix to petits fours. They make no sense at all for products produced by companies that manufacture both human and pet foods.

If there is a rule for brand extensions, it is a three part rule that says:

1 The more similar two product concepts are, the greater the benefits that will accrue from a brand extension strategy.
2 The more different two product concepts are, the greater the risk involved in using such a strategy.
3 Do not automatically use a brand extension strategy just to save money. It may turn out to be the most expensive money you have ever saved.

SELECTING A BRAND NAME

The actual selection of a brand name is often a time-consuming and frustrating assignment. So much so that Fairfax Cone, in a moment of cynicism prompted by his experience with the ill-fated Edsel, complained: "Naming products is a source of constant and usually fruitless mental exercise in advertising agencies (where the client's wife or a guest at a dinner party usually suggests the name that is finally accepted)."[13]

In the case of the Edsel, his cynicism seems justified. Starting with a list of 16,000 names, judgment and research had reduced the list to four—Corsair, Citation, Pacer, and Ranger. Unfortunately, Ford's board of directors, under a deadline for a name to be used on some vital dies, ignored all recommendations and arbitrarily decided that they would name the new car after the father of the company's president, provided they could obtain the consent of the family. According to Fairfax Cone:

> Consent was forthcoming . . . and so the Edsel was christened in embryo with a name that was at once a surprise and a huge disappointment. As one of our people said, "The name Flab, which had been suggested by a wag in our London office, couldn't have been any less appropriate." Insofar as the public was concerned the name Edsel was devoid of any feeling of action or spirit. It was a proper name, like Elwyn or Ethelbert, and like them, it was faintly effeminate. It had none of the strength of Pontiac or Lincoln, or the spirit of Mercury; nor did it perpetuate a great name in the industry like Chevrolet or Chrysler—or Ford itself.[14]

Fortunately, not all names are selected by boards of directors, client's wives or husbands, or dinner guests. Since the selection of a strong brand name is essentially a creative process bolstered by the judicious use of research, there are few hard and fast rules. Some general guidelines are listed below, although most of them have been violated at one time or another by some of America's best-known products.

1 The brand name should *never* contradict the essential attributes of the brand concept. Ideally, the brand name should be supportive of this concept, such as Slender, Coffee-mate, and Charlie. If

---

[13]Fairfax Cone, *With All Its Faults* (Boston: Little, Brown and Co., 1969), 249.
[14]Ibid., 250.

that is not possible, the brand name should be neutral so that the desired meaning can be created with advertising and promotion.

2 The name should be simple and clear, easy to spell, write, pronounce, and recognize. Purina Dog Chow, Aztec (a suntan lotion), Crest, Ritz, and Hotpoint are good examples.

3 The name should be distinctive and not easily confused with other brand names on the market either by sound or appearance. This avoids trademark infringement and possible consumer confusion.

4 The name should be adaptable to package and label design, retaining its identity even when it is reduced in size for package or commercial purposes.

5 The name should avoid unpleasant connotations that may offend customers. There is no excuse for poor taste—particularly in marketing.

6 The name should not be too cute, clever, or dear. In the search for a distinctive name, the temptation is strong to substitute clever for direct, contrived for simple, and phony for honest.

Finding the appropriate brand name is well worth the effort. Everywhere it appears, the brand name communicates some message about the product; the stronger and more appropriate the message, the better the communication.

PACKAGING

Why is Jack Daniel's whiskey sold in a square bottle? The story people tell in Lynchburg, Tennessee, the home of Jack Daniel Distillery, starts out many years ago, when Jack Daniel was operating a small distillery. A glass salesman approached him with a proposition to supply all of his bottling needs. The salesman used the following approach: "Mr. Daniel, before I came to see you, I wanted to find out what kind of a man you were and what you were like to do business with. So, I called on every tavern and business in this part of the country and asked, 'What kind of a man is Jack Daniel?' To a man, they all said, 'You won't find a better, more honest man than Jack Daniel. You can depend on his word. He's a *square* man to do business with.' Mr. Daniel, that gave me an idea. I think you should capitalize on your reputation. I think you should put your whiskey in a square bottle and call it 'Square Jack Daniel's.' "

AN OVERVIEW OF PACKAGING

Although billions of dollars are spent on packaging each year, it is one of the most neglected areas of marketing. An examination of marketing journal articles indicates that the subject is either totally ignored or treated in an offhand manner. Much packaging is badly designed, cheap, and inconvenient. The marketing concept sometimes appears to have stopped short of packaging. This is unfortunate because packages are everywhere—on retail shelves and in displays, advertising, and the home. It is one of the most obvious channels of communication with consumers. In a speech prepared for the American Management Association's conference on packaging, one speaker said:

> Packaging is the hottest buy in advertising today—and the least understood. First, packaging is the biggest of the advertising media. The message on the package usually reaches far more people than any type of conventional advertising the product can afford. However, businessmen haven't bothered to measure its coverage. Second, it is the least expensive of ad media. Space which costs millions of dollars elsewhere is free on the package; this space is paid for in manufacturing to contain and protect the product. Additional charges to make the package do a better promotional job are usually infinitesimal in relation to audience size. Third, it is the most potentially effective medium. It is seen by those customers who may buy, at the spot where they buy, and at the moment of the buying decision. Packaging has enormous circulation with virtually no waste. Yet, as a marketing tool, it is poorly understood, generally mismanaged, and barely exploited.[15]

Those comments were made in 1965; the situation has not changed much since. A 1980 article in *Advertising Age* notes:

> Old habits die hard, but escalating media costs will spur big advertisers to develop package design as a marketing tool, predicted William J. O'Connor, exec vp, Source/Inc, a Chicago design company.
> Packaging traditionally has been the sort of "fickle love object" of marketers who move away from packaging considerations in good times and toward them in bad, or to save a "murky" product. But, as costs have gone up, attitudes have changed, Mr. O'Connor told an ADVERTISING AGE WEEK workshop. . . .
> In the future, marketers increasingly will look to packaging for innovative presentations of the product form. . . . Package research and testing, a relatively specialized field, will grow in importance in the '80s as more marketers turn to packaging for cost efficiency.[16]

Not all packaging is poorly done. There are many outstanding packages on the market. The Hamilton Beach 'popaire' Electric Hot Air Popper (Figure 7–3) shows the product in use and quickly communicates the selling line "Pop corn the oil-less way using hot air . . . more nutrition, less calories." The Townhouse Instant Mashed Potatoes package uses excellent photography and appetite appeal to show the final product in use, while providing immediate identification of the product type (Figure 7–4). The Country Blend Cat Chow cat food package, with a large picture of a cat against a rural background, emphasizes the reference to "country" in the product name, quickly communicates the variety of flavors in the product (chicken, liver, and cheese), and stands out on the grocery shelf among a welter of other cat food packages (Figure 7–5). The Finish

FIGURE 7–3 Hamilton Beach "popaire" package (Courtesy Hamilton Beach Division, Scovill)

---

[15]Reprinted by permission of the publisher from "How to Calculate Package Audience" by S. M. Barker, p. 28, *Profitability and Penetration Through Packaging* (AMA Bulletin No. 65) © 1965 by American Management Association, Inc. All rights reserved.

[16]"Packaging Seen As Effective Marketing Tool." Reprinted with permission from September 1, 1980 issue of *Advertising Age*. Copyright © 1980 by Crain Communications, Inc.

CHAPTER 7 | PRODUCT, BRAND, AND PACKAGE

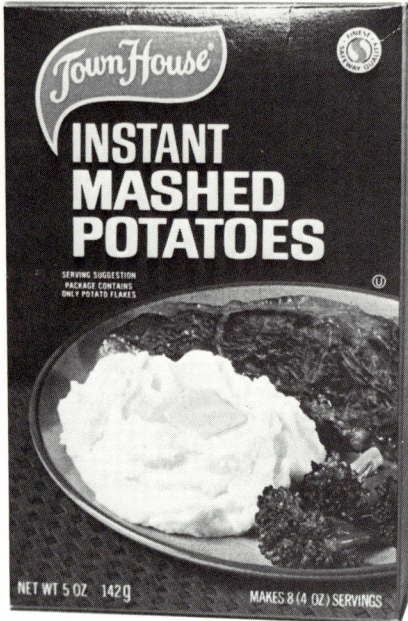

FIGURE 7–4   Townhouse Instant Mashed Potatoes package (Courtesy Safeway Stores, Inc.)

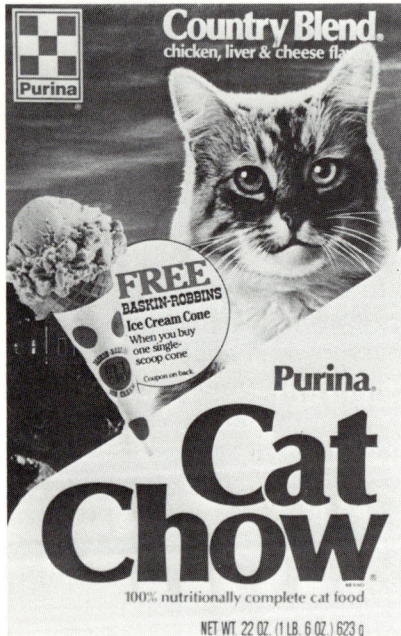

FIGURE 7–5   Country Blend Cat Chow cat food package. (Reproduction of package is used with permission of Ralston Purina Company.)

package is a clean, straightforward package that communicates the product concept at a glance (Figure 7–6).

Packages do not have to be expensive and printed in four-color to be effective. The one for Kingsford Charcoal Briquets is a simple, inexpensive, functional package in red and blue printed on white that is distinctive and quickly communicates the product's function while registering two key selling points: "lights easy and fast" and "easy to open" (Figure 7–7).

Each of the above examples appears to be designed with the product concept in mind; communicates this concept to consumers; provides visibility on the retail shelf; tells its story directly and simply; is adaptable to print and television advertising; and protects the physical product. In short, each of these packages serves several purposes and thereby makes a tangible contribution to the marketing effort.

THE FUNCTIONS OF PACKAGING

Traditionally, packaging has played a minor role in the marketing mix. More recently, this role has been expanded, although not all companies have fully realized its potential. Basically, packages have four functions: **protection, economy, convenience,** and **promotion.**

Protection.   The minimum requirement the manufacturer seeks in packaging is the protection of the product during its passage from manufacturer to warehouse to retailer to consumer. To gain this end, double packaging is used—an outer shipping carton for transportation and delivery to the retailer, and individual packages for shelving and sale to consumers. The package must be sufficiently strong to withstand rough handling and airtight and leak proof to protect the freshness and integrity of its contents.

Economy.   Unfortunately, many manufacturers regard the package primarily as an expense item, without any redeeming marketing features. More than any other reason, this emphasis on cost has retarded the development of the package as a marketing tool and has often led to packaging that is shoddy, unattractive, difficult to shelve, and inconvenient to use. A case in point is the "blister packs" used for table-ready meats and many other small retail items sold through supermarkets, drug stores, and hardware outlets. The blister pack protects the product, keeps it fresh, and is economical; but it is an abomination to open.

Convenience.   A third function of the package is convenience for shipping and shelving and for the consumer. From the standpoint of shipping, warehousing, and shelving, convenience has taken the form of general standardization of shipping carton sizes, easy to open shipping cartons, "price spots" for retail pricing, and the Universal Product Code and Symbols (UPC) for computerized checkouts and inventory control. The UPC promises the elimination of price marking (the price is carried in the computer and scanned at the checkout), reduction of checkout costs and errors (a major expense

FIGURE 7–6 Finish package
(Courtesy Economics
Laboratories, Inc.)

FIGURE 7–7 Kingsford Charcoal
Briquets package (Courtesy The
Kingsford Company)

item for supermarkets), and improved inventory control (inventory status is automatically monitored by the computer). Figure 7–8 shows an example of the UPC, as well as a typical sales receipt that is automatically printed for the customer.

For consumers, convenience has also taken a variety of forms: easy to open packages; pour spouts, aerosol cans, and other dispensing devices; a wide variety of package sizes for different family sizes; multiple packs; heat and serve items; frozen foods packaged in compartmentalized serving trays; coating and baking products; boil in the bag foods; dry mixes that the user can mix in the original package; and reclosable packages. As convenience foods became a big business, the need for convenience packages grew.

Promotion. The package is valuable in enhancing the brand's appeal through typography, colors, and illustrations. It also conveys the desired brand image, describes the product's features, and provides recipes and service suggestions. Often, the package can be designed to be used as an attractive dispenser in the home—on the dining table for food products and in the bedroom or bath for products such as toiletries and facial tissues.

A good package is one that performs all of these functions in an optimal fashion, always being subject to the mutual constraints of each.

PACKAGING STRATEGY

Packaging can be used as a strategic tool in the marketing effort in a number of ways. The strategies should enhance or at least be compatible with the product concept. The more important packaging strategies are based on: size, material, shape, design, convenience, and promotion.

Size strategy. Many markets may be segmented in terms of volume users or product use. Examples of this may be found in the marketing of both "regular" and "family size" packages or the small size produced in some fields for the convenience of travelers.

Size strategy also plays a dual role in new product introductions by encouraging retail stocking and consumer trial. In the first instance, shipping cartons of six or twelve individual packages may be used to minimize the retailer's investment and create the impression of high case movement. The use of this strategy also requires relatively intense sales coverage to avoid out-of-stock conditions. After a new product is well established, the shipping carton can be increased to perhaps twenty-four or forty-eight units to decrease packaging costs. For consumers, an introductory small size package is used generally to minimize consumer risk; larger sizes are introduced later to meet the requirements of volume users and provide additional shelf facings and promotional push.

Material strategy. The material used in a package may play a major role in marketing strategy. For example, packaging materials may be used to impute quality or to insure safety. Examples of quality packaging are tasteful display boxes designed for small luxury goods

CHAPTER 7 | PRODUCT, BRAND, AND PACKAGE

UNIVERSAL PRODUCT CODE AND SYMBOLS

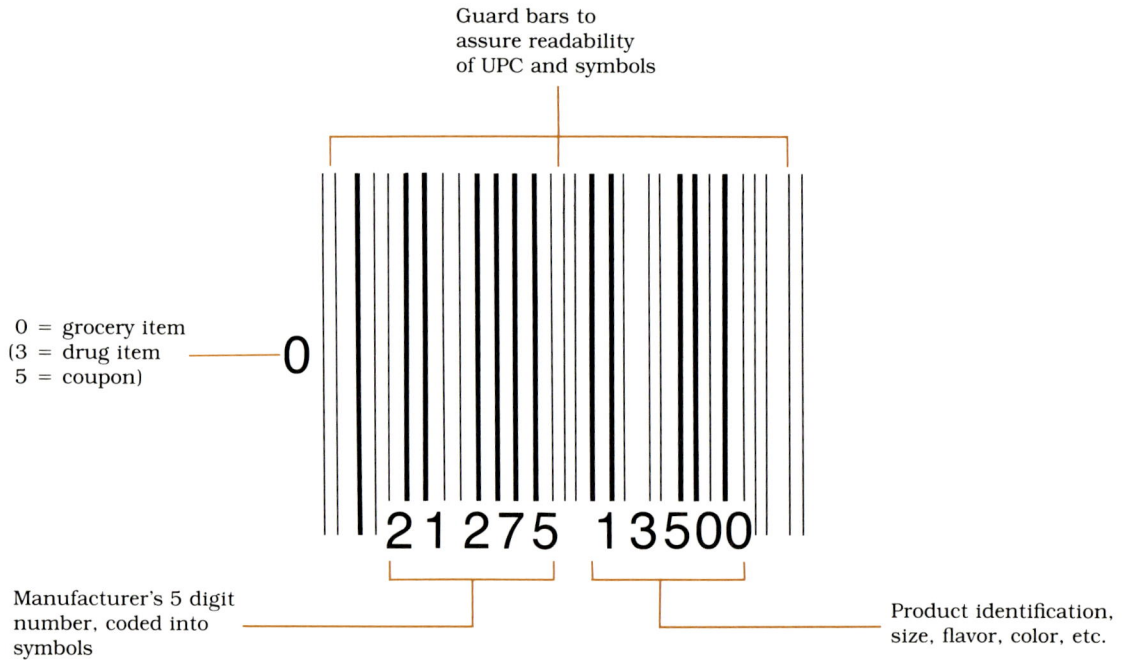

Guard bars to
assure readability
of UPC and symbols

0 = grocery item
(3 = drug item
5 = coupon)

0

21275 13500

Manufacturer's 5 digit
number, coded into
symbols

Product identification,
size, flavor, color, etc.

```
THANK YOU FOR
SHOPPING
ABC FOOD—OUR TOWN                        Store, location
GALLON MILK              1.45            Item description
POST TOASTIES             .89
JOY LIQ DET              1.39T           Taxable item
SIRLOIN STK             3.85
@2/.59 PEAS               .30            First item of 2/59¢
VITA HERRING            1.69
2.46 LB-3LB@.89 BANANA     .73           Produce weighed, rung up
VANISH                    .95T
C. DRY TONIC              .63T
POLIDENT                1.03T
SUCRETS                 1.29
@2/.59 PEAS               .29            Second item of 2/59¢
SKIM MILK QT              .38
CYCLE DOG FD             .39T
NO NON HOSE             1.19T
RISE SHAVE              1.23T
CRANAPPL JC               .79
PLAYTEX TAMP            1.49T
MORTON PIE               .37
EGGS                      .95
LITE-LINE CH            1.29
COUPON                  1.00             Coupon allowance
TAX DUE                   .67            Total tax

TOTAL                  22.36             Total of order

CK TEND                25.00             Amount presented by check

CHG DUE                 2.64             Change due

7/07/77 17:15 140/2                      Store number, checkout lane
COUNT ON US
```

Weight — 2.46 LB-3LB@.89 BANANA

Date, time — 7/07/77 17:15 140/2

FIGURE 7–8 Example of the Universal Product Code and Symbols, and a typical sales receipt [From *Grey Matter* (New York: Grey Advertising, 1977)]

PART II | MARKETING ANALYSIS AND THE MARKETING MIX

such as jewelry or electric shavers. Safety packaging is illustrated by nonbreakable shampoo bottles or closures that make it difficult for children to open packages containing something that may be harmful to them.

Shape strategy. Product shape has long been recognized for its perceptual implications. Smooth, rounded shapes connote femininity; square, solid shapes imply masculinity. Shapes may also be designed to encourage in-home display on the dining table or in another room where the product serves as a visual reminder of the brand. Liquid bath soaps have been packaged in the form of animals, fish, and other objects to provide a pleasant distraction for a child who is being bathed. A number of years ago, Log Cabin syrup was packaged in a miniature log cabin container. This practice was abandoned, presumably because of manufacturing costs and difficulties in shelf stacking.

Design strategy. Of course, design strategy may also involve shapes and materials. But here the emphasis is on colors, typography, pictures, and symbols that enhance the product in the consumer's mind. Design strategy is often used to give identity to a line of packages, such as the Betty Crocker "red spoon," or the picture of a Quaker on The Quaker Oats Company products. Packaging a product as a gift is a standard practice in the expensive chocolate and distilled spirits industry.

Convenience strategy. The world is full of convenience packages designed to make life easier for consumers. When convenience is a relevant consideration in terms of the product concept, it may be possible to use the package to fulfill a part of this convenience objective. Sometimes convenience is not an attribute that consumers really want. For example, people have complained for years about the difficulty of pouring catsup out of the traditional long necked, narrow opening bottle. Yet, when a catsup manufacturer introduced a wide mouthed bottle that made pouring easier, consumers continued to purchase catsup in the traditional bottle.

Promotion strategy. Packages may be designed or redesigned to tie in with major sales promotions. Back or side panels lend themselves to featuring recipes, service suggestions, and special offers. Cents-off and two-for-one offers are often emblazoned on the package face.

All of these strategies are possible through packaging. Therefore, packaging is emerging as a major element in the marketing mix and one that can facilitate or hinder the communication of the product concept.

DESIGNING PACKAGES

A package is not a thing; it is an idea. This thought was aptly expressed by Edward Breck, while president of John H. Breck, Inc., marketer of Breck Shampoo.

> A package is, above all else, an idea. The stronger, the clearer, and the more compelling the idea, the more powerful the package. Many

of us in marketing become too absorbed in the details and complexities of package development to realize how important this core idea is to success. Without it the package fails to convey a single impression; its message becomes blurred, and it cannot possibly function with force.[17]

There is no way to tell someone how to design a package. It is a creative, problem-solving process. However, a package designer should ask certain questions. Starting with a clear understanding of the product concept, Walter Margulies, an executive of a leading package design firm, has suggested the following questions.[18]

- How much emphasis should be placed on the brand name? On the product name?
- Toward what segment of the market should be product's basic appeal be aimed?
- In what way will the packaging system best communicate product appeal?
- Should the graphics try to convey the size, shape, color, in-use applications? If so, how?
- In dealing with a food product, is it advisable to include recipes on the package? Which ones? Should they be changed in accordance with the seasons?
- Are all package panels being used to their best advantage? Will they effectively sell the product regardless of the way the package is stacked on the supermarket shelf?
- Can the basic design be extended to logically encompass other items in the manufacturer's line? Is it flexible enough to permit the addition of new products at some future date?
- Is there ample space for the inclusion of extra copy to announce special sales offers?
- What about price marking? Has a specific place been set aside where the product can be priced easily by the retailer so as not to mar the total look of the package?
- Is the design flexible enough to permit the addition of new products?

This list is not intended to be exhaustive, but it is a good starting point.

TESTING THE PACKAGE DESIGN

The finished package should always be tested. Tests of visibility and ease of recognition under different levels of illumination and from different angles of perspective are used to check its adequacy for retail display. Shipping tests may be undertaken to ascertain its durability. Accelerated aging tests are often made to ensure that the package protects product freshness. Consumer tests are employed to determine ease of use and reactions to the overall package design.

---

[17]Reprinted by permission of the publisher from "Function vs. Aesthetics in Packaging" by E. J. Breck, p. 6, *Profitability and Penetration Through Packaging* (AMA Bulletin No. 65) © 1965 by American Management Association, Inc. All rights reserved.

[18]From pp. 47–48 in *Packaging Power* by Walter P. Margulies (World). By permission of Harper & Row, Publishers, Inc.

Sales tests may be undertaken to see how well the package performs under competitive marketing conditions. A package is ready for use only after it has been subjected to these scrutinies.

CHANGING PACKAGES

Normally, a package design will last for a number of years. Yet, packages do require redesigning from time to time. Reasons for change are manifold: repositioning of the product concept; availability of new packaging materials or technology; increased costs of existing materials; competitive innovations; change in consumer attitudes and values; and modernization of the design. Since package is an important part of the brand's communications with consumers, the question of whether a package change should be made depends upon whether the change will help or hurt the brand.

In some fields, package changes are readily accepted by consumers; in others, they are not. Several years ago, *Business Week* prepared a presentation for advertising agencies and distillery managements demonstrating that since the turn of the century, no successful distilled whiskey had made a package design change without suffering a decline in sales. At one point, Camel cigarettes attempted to simplify its package by removing some of the pyramids and palm trees from the package face. Consumer complaints were so vocal that the elements were restored. On the other hand, Ivory Soap has changed the package for its bar soap many times in almost a century of marketing. Many of the changes are almost imperceptible; but in the aggregate, the appearance of the package has undergone a transformation (Figure 7–9).

Stephan Barker, executive of a packaging firm, has offered a checklist of package changes (Table 7–3). Some involve low risk; others involve high risk.

How much a package should be changed and how frequently changes should be made are questions of marketing judgment that must be made on a product by product basis and always in the light of the existing competitive situation.

LEGAL REQUIREMENTS FOR PACKAGING

Within the past few decades, legal restrictions on packaging have grown along with the consumer movement. The Fair Packaging and Labeling Act of 1966 states:

> Informed consumers are essential to the fair and efficient functioning of a free economy. Packages and their labels should enable consumers to obtain accurate information as to the quality of the contents and should facilitate value comparisons. Therefore it is hereby declared to be the policy of the congress to assist consumers and manufacturers in reaching these goals in the marketing of goods.

The Food and Drug Administration (FDA) is responsible for enforcing the law in regard to foods, drugs, cosmetics, and other devices. The Federal Trade Commission (FTC) has jurisdiction over other consumer products.

TABLE 7–3 Packaging threats to a consumer franchise

	Low Risk	High Risk
Change in package graphics	Directions, cautions* Ingredient line, etc.* Other secondary-panel changes Legal copy requirements Temporary premium offer Temporary deal offer	New name New principal color New illustration, photo New logo New style New design shapes Other new design features on main panel Directions, cautions*
Change in package structure	New convenience feature New cap or fitment** New material** Fewer inks** Additional packages† Additional sizes† Temporary premium pack Multipack Sample package Display pack New shipping case New distributor pack New unit load	New type package New shape package Change in only size Obvious but unexplained change in critical material‡

*Risk depends on degree of change.
**If appearance is not dramatically different.
†Line extension.
‡As elimination of protective lining.

Source: Stephan M. Barker, "When To Change Your Package—and When Not To," p. 49. Reprinted with permission from the May 23, 1977 issue of *Advertising Age*. Copyright © 1977 by Crain Communications, Inc.

Since 1970, FDA regulations require manufacturers to submit data on the safety of food, including the packaging materials with which it may come in contact. Regulations also specify precise labeling requirements (including descriptive words that may be used), how quantities and volume must be stated, the size and placement of type relating to volume and weight, and background colors. There are rules governing misrepresentation, slack-fill (failure to completely fill the package), health, and a variety of other factors. Obviously, these regulations place restrictions on package design. Some of the restrictions are undoubtedly beneficial; others, merely whimsical. In any case, under today's legislation the package designer should have access to a good lawyer.

Packaging, as well as advertising, is a highly visible marketing element that bears the brunt of communicating with consumers. Most advertising for packaged goods features the package prominently in the ad or commercial. When premiums or promotions are

FIGURE 7–9 Changes in Ivory Soap packages from 1898 to 1965 (Courtesy The Procter & Gamble Co.)

shown on a package panel, the package becomes an extension of advertising. Thus, the basic design of an advertisement must not only be compatible with the product package, but also make provision for how the package will be shown, and where it will be located in the ad.

SUMMARY

Successful advertising is built on a foundation made up of the other elements of marketing—product, package, product name, pricing, and distribution.

Without a good product, there is little chance of advertising success. Every product is really three products: (a) the generic product refers to the basic product type and the primary function it serves; (b) the physical product is what is actually produced; and (c) the psychological product is the physical product plus the psychological overtones that accompany it. Consumers' responses to products depend more upon their expectations of product performance than on actual product performance. As a consequence, the performance of the physical product must always be compatible with their expectations. In the marketing sense, retail stores and services are also products, and the task of advertising is to translate the product concept into an appealing product image.

New products are the future of business; however, new product development is expensive and risky. The most common reason new

CHAPTER 7 | PRODUCT, BRAND, AND PACKAGE

products fail is that the physical product is not better than, or at least different from, products already in the market.

Products go through various stages. This product life cycle is generally divided into four stages (introduction, growth, maturity, and decline), and each stage usually calls for a different balance of the elements in the marketing mix. Useful strategies in prolonging the product life cycle are: (a) improving product quality; (b) line extensions; and (c) style and feature obsolescence.

The search for brand names that project the appropriate product concept is a creative act that can and should be confirmed by marketing research. A number of terms related to branding were discussed in this chapter: trade name, brand, brand name, brand mark, trademark, brand name strategies, and brand extension strategies. Legal requirements applying to trademarks are identified under the Lanham (trademark) Act.

Packaging is one of the more neglected areas of marketing and, traditionally, has played a minor role in the marketing mix. Packaging has four basic functions: protection; economy; convenience; and promotion. Packaging strategies include those relating to size, material, shape, design, and convenience. Package designs should always be tested prior to use and caution exercised before making packaging changes. Since the passage of the Fair Packaging and Labeling Act of 1966, package design is subject to a number of legal requirements. A package designer would be wise to clear new designs through legal counsel.

REVIEW QUESTIONS

1 Distinguish between the generic, physical, and psychological product.
2 Explain the Swan and Combs two-factor theory of product satisfaction.
3 Explain why most new products fail and identify the broad guidelines that should govern the development of new products
4 Explain what is meant by the product life cycle. Briefly characterize each of its stages.
5 Identify and explain each of the strategies defined in the text for prolonging the product life cycle.
6 Define each of the following terms: (a) trade name; (b) brand; (c) brand name; (d) brand mark; and (e) trademark.
7 Identify and give examples of the basic brand name strategies that are used.
8 What are the advantages and limitations of a brand extension strategy?
9 Identify and explain the basic functions of packaging.
10 Identify and explain the packaging strategies outlined in the text.

DISCUSSION QUESTIONS

1 Identify the generic, physical, and psychological product for each of the following products: (a) McDonald's restaurants; (b) Sears, Roebuck and Company; (c) K mart; (d) Cadillac; (e) Marlboro; and (f) Calvin Klein jeans.

2 Select a product field for a grocery or drugstore product. Make a list of the brand names in the product field and evaluate them in terms of the criteria given in the text.

3 Select a product field for a grocery or drugstore product. Examine the brands in the field in terms of packaging and answer the following questions: (a) What is your general impression of the effectiveness of the packaging in the product field? Explain your answer. (b) Select a package that you think is outstanding and evaluate it in terms of the package criteria given in the text. Explain why you think it is outstanding. (c) Select a package that you think is poor and evaluate it in terms of the package criteria given in the text. Explain why you think it is poor.

PROBLEM

Select a product field of your choice. Construct a product space and position a product in this space. Create a brand name for the product, showing how it meets the criteria for brand name selection given in the text. Design a package for the product, showing how it meets the criteria for package design given in the text.

8

Pricing and Distribution

HOG FAT AND PROFITS

The Independent Packing Company of St. Louis, Missouri, had a problem. Under existing pricing practices, the amount of bacon produced exceeded demand, so the packing company had 11 million pounds of bacon in inventory that it couldn't sell. Other parts of the hog, such as ham, pork, roasts, and spareribs, were easily sold. One approach to solving the bacon problem would have been the traditional economist's approach to surpluses: reduce prices, let expanded demand dispose of the surplus, and accept the losses in anticipated revenue with good grace. However, Gardner Advertising Company, the packing company's agency, had a better idea. Change the product and raise the price.

How do you change bacon? Cut it into thick slices, cure it in a heavier than usual smoke, put it into a package designed to simulate a hickory log, and name it Hickory Hill Bacon, "a thick sliced, heavy smoked bacon, with a real country flavor." It worked, and a surplus of hog fat was turned into a surplus of profits.

SAMPLE DISTRIBUTION AND STRATEGIES

More often than not, marketing success depends upon the development and implementation of a successful distribution strategy. There is little point in advertising a product if it is not available to consumers. Many advertising success stories are really stories about distribution. Jafra cosmetics, a Gillette product, grew from $4 million to over $60 million largely because of increases in distribution. The success of McDonald's Corporation was heavily dependent upon its carefully planned franchise system. The growth of Perrier from a specialty product to a beverage that was appropriate for mass consumption was a result of a new product concept joining a new distribution strategy, leading to a successful marketing marriage. Scott's leadership in the lawn care market is a triumph of distribution strategy because Scott's was the first such product to move out of traditional lawn care outlets and exploit grocery, drug, and other convenience stores.

Distribution is not only the concern of marketing managers. Advertising copywriters often need to develop advertising campaigns directed to distributors and retailers. For products with limited distribution, advertising must tell consumers where the products can be found.

The foregoing examples are intended to emphasize the role of pricing and distribution in marketing success. The close relationship between distribution and sales has long been recognized. The role of pricing, however, is more obscure. In this chapter, we will turn our attention to pricing and distribution, two key elements in the marketing program. Without adequate pricing and an effective distribution system, advertising is a waste of company resources.

BASIC ECONOMIC CONCEPTS

Pricing strategy is one of the more complex decisions in marketing. In order to understand its function, we need to examine some of the basic concepts of economics and trace their evolution into today's marketing practices. Historically, economics was founded on the interrelationship of supply and demand, as mediated by the price mechanism. The essentials of this interrelationship are shown in Figure 8–1.

SUPPLY AND DEMAND

Figure 8–1a represents a simplified **demand** curve. It slopes downward and to the right; as price decreases, demand increases because more consumers can afford to buy the product. Figure 8–1b represents the **supply** curve. It slopes upward and to the right. As price increases, more suppliers are attracted to the product field because of the increased opportunity for profits. Figure 8–1c represents the **point of equilibrium,** the point where the supply curve and the demand curve intersect and supply equals demand. A static condition

FIGURE 8–1 Supply and demand curves

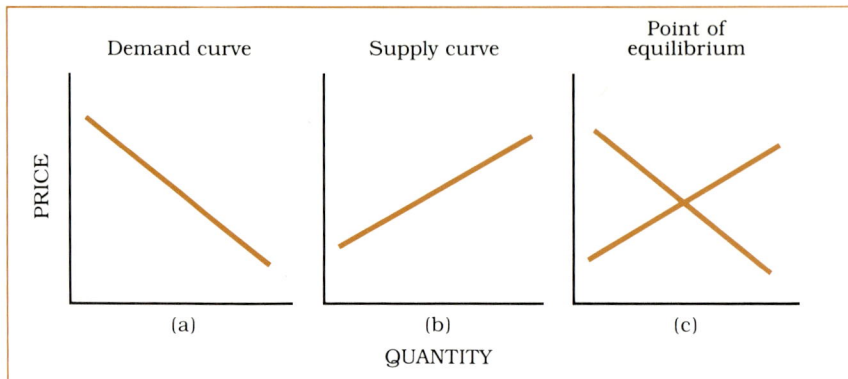

Demand curve   Supply curve   Point of equilibrium

PRICE

QUANTITY

(a)   (b)   (c)

of equilibrium is never achieved because, as prices rise and profit opportunities become more attractive, many suppliers gravitate to the product field and production soon exceeds demand. Then, as prices fall because of excess production, suppliers desert the field in search of more attractive investment opportunities; supply decreases until demand again predominates, and prices start to rise. Thus, the equilibrium point is only a balancing mechanism that keeps supply and demand in an ever-changing relationship. All of us have experienced the effects of supply and demand. When cattle production is high, producers lower prices to dispose of their production; the price of beef drops, and steak is purchased by more consumers. However, as prices decrease, the production of beef becomes less profitable. Production is cut back; marginal producers drop out of the field entirely because they can no longer make a profit; beef becomes scarce. Under the impact of scarcity, demand exceeds supply; prices rise until many consumers can no longer afford to buy beef in the quantities they have in the past, so they purchase fish, poultry, lamb, pork, cheese, or other substitute products. High beef prices encourage new production, and the cycle begins again.

PRICE ELASTICITY

Price elasticity of demand refers to the effect that a change in price has on total income, computed by multiplying price by demand. For example, if the price of a product is $1.00, and demand is 100,000 units, then total income is $1.00 × 100,000 = $100,000. There are four forms of price elasticity: **unitary elasticity, price elasticity, price inelasticity,** and **negative elasticity** (Figure 8–2).

☐ Unitary elasticity (Figure 8–2a). A change in price will be compensated by a corresponding change in demand so that total income remains the same.

☐ Price elasticity (Figure 8–2b). A change in price will yield a relatively large change in demand. As a result, a price *decrease* will result in an *increase* in total income; a price *increase* will result in a *decrease* in total income.

☐ Price inelasticity (Figure 8–2c). A change in price will yield a relatively small change in demand. As a consequence, a *decrease* in price will result in a *decrease* in income, and an *increase* in

FIGURE 8–2 Basic demand curves

price will result in an *increase* in income. A classic example of price inelasticity is insulin, which is used in the treatment of diabetes. If one does not have diabetes, one has no use for insulin. On the other hand, if one has diabetes, one must have insulin regardless of the price. Thus, within a moderate range of prices, the demand for insulin is unaffected by price.

☐ Negative elasticity (Figure 8–2d). Demand moves in the same direction of price. Thus, an *increase* in price *increases* demand and total income, and a *decrease* in price *decreases* demand and total income. Examples of negative elasticity can often be found in the personal care and proprietary medicine fields where a higher price offers assurance of product efficacy and, therefore, makes the product more attractive to consumers. For example, when home permanents were first introduced into the consumer market at a price of 25 cents a package, the product was a colossal failure. Women were simply not interested. The same product was repackaged and introduced at $1.25 a package, and it was a smashing success. Apparently, women were unwilling to trust their hair to a 25-cent product for fear of hair damage. The higher price increased their confidence in the product's safety.

From the standpoint of the individual firm, prices are too high if demand is elastic because a decrease in price would result in an increase in total revenue. On the other hand, if prices are inelastic or subject to negative elasticity, so that an increase in price would increase total income, prices are too low.[1]

TRADITIONAL PRICING

In traditional economic theory, the relationship between supply and demand is wholly a function of price. In practice, it doesn't always work this way; note the examples of Hickory Hill Bacon and home permanents. Nonetheless, price considerations continue to dominate most economic thinking. Philip Kotler has pointed out that

---

[1]This statement is contingent upon the behavior of costs at various levels of production since an increase in total revenue does not necessarily result in an increase in profits. However, for our purposes, we may consider the suggested relationship to be generally valid.

CHAPTER 8 | PRICING AND DISTRIBUTION

there are persuasive historical, technical, and social reasons for economists to emphasize price.[2]

From a historical point of view, economics emerged at a time when production was characterized by commodities such as wheat, cotton, sugar, and other raw materials; even basic foodstuffs and clothing were largely undifferentiated. Branding, packaging, and advertising were virtually unknown. The major factor differentiating one loaf of bread from another or one bushel of wheat from another was price. Since most incomes were low, and luxuries were enjoyed only by the wealthy, frugality was a necessary condition for existence.

From a technical point of view, price was emphasized because it was easily quantified and unambiguous. Thus, it provided an easy tool for analyzing economic activity. Because other considerations such as product quality, brand image, promotion, and customer service were essentially psychological in nature, they were difficult to define and even more difficult to measure.

From a social point of view, price offered a defensible rationale for the operation of the marketing system. Price fluctuations served as a mechanism to control surpluses and scarcities. When surpluses existed, there was a tendency to cut prices to get rid of excess production. The lower prices increased demand and discouraged further production. When scarcity prevailed, there was a tendency to raise prices to increase profits. This, in turn, attracted new producers to the field. Supply and demand, aided by the price mechanism, automatically controlled the economy and kept it in balance.

CHANGING POINTS OF VIEW

Over time, two factors emerged in the United States which conspired to change the traditional role of pricing. First, economic growth gave rise to a large body of relatively affluent consumers. Mere subsistence was no longer the rule; discretionary income became commonplace, and millions of consumers discovered that they had a taste for luxuries. Second, dramatic increases in productive capacity, combined with an increased rigidity of costs brought about by the mechanization of production and the emergence of labor unions, generated a perpetual surplus for many products. Manufacturers found themselves faced with the need to increase demand in order to dispose of their production, and they were unable to lower prices sufficiently to do so and still make a profit. Industry responded to this challenge with the marketing concept and actively began to seek new ways of attracting consumers. Market segmentation and product differentiation became a way of life, and these strategies gave rise to two phenomena: **monopolistic competition** and **symbolic pricing.**

MONOPOLISTIC COMPETITION

Pure competition exists when there are many suppliers and all products are homogeneous. Thousands of wheat farmers offering their

---

[2]Philip Kotler, *Marketing Management*, 2nd ed. (Englewood Cliffs, New Jersey: Prentice-Hall, Inc., 1972), 515.

harvest for sale represent a condition of pure competition. This is one end of the competitive spectrum. At the other extreme is the concept of **monopoly,** where one supplier controls the entire supply of a product that consumers must buy because there are no substitutes. A true monopoly probably does not exist because there are generally substitutes of one sort or another. Nonetheless, the concept of monopoly is still valid. Between these two extremes, there are an infinite number of marketing structures, one of which is monopolistic competition.[3]

In monopolistic competition, the product of each competitor differs in some way from that of other competitors so that, in effect, each manufacturer has a monopoly because an exact duplicate of its product cannot be obtained from any other source.[4] True, there are substitute products. For example, one could buy a Ford instead of a Chevrolet and serve the same purpose. However, if the consumer wants a new Chevrolet, the only supplier is the Chevrolet Division of General Motors. Branding, packaging, style, and advertising claims are used by modern marketers to reinforce the concept of a monopoly and perpetuate the impression that there is no real substitute for the brand being promoted. The major advantage of monopolistic competition for the producer is that it minimizes the need to compete on the basis of price, thereby giving rise to the practice of nonprice competition.

SYMBOLIC PRICING

In monopolistic competition, price is a symbol used by producers to create an impression about their products in the minds of consumers. As a symbol, price need not function in the traditional manner. For many products, a higher price may lead to an increase in demand rather than a decrease as portrayed by traditional economic theory because, in these instances, price serves as a symbol of quality. Similarly, a low price may discourage demand rather than increasing it because the low price connotes inferiority.

PRICING IN CONTEMPORARY MARKETING

Contemporary marketing does not deny the general validity of traditional economic theory. Generally speaking, a lower price does result in an increase in demand. More Chevrolets are sold than Rolls-Royces; when the price of steak skyrockets, most of us purchase hamburger, chicken, or fish; and a price reduction on a popular brand can do remarkable things to the sales curve. However, since product differentiation and consumer psychology can be used to loosen the shackles that traditionally bound supply and demand together in a rigid price relationship, contemporary marketing is no

---

[3]Edward H. Chamberlin, *The Theory of Monopolistic Competition* (Cambridge, Massachusetts: Harvard University Press, 1933).

[4]Economists generally distinguish between *monopolistic competition* and *differentiated oligopoly*. In monopolistic competition, many competitors' products differ sufficiently to justify branding, advertising, and sales promotion. In a differentiated oligopoly, the same situation prevails in terms of product differences, but there are only a few competitors. I have combined monopolistic competition and differentiated oligopoly because my primary focus is on product differences, not the number of competitors.

longer a slave to price. As a consequence, symbolic pricing has joined traditional pricing theory as a marketing tool. Together, they make a formidable team.

There are several reasons why symbolic pricing is an effective marketing tool. First, most consumers believe that there is a necessary relationship between the price of a brand and its manufacturing cost. This belief is often expressed through the cliché "you get what you pay for." Studies by Leavitt,[5] as well as Tull, Boring, and Gonsior,[6] and Gabor and Granger[7] support this observation. Unfortunately, this belief isn't necessarily true. A private label shaving cream that sells for 69 cents often costs no less for product and package than does the advertised brand selling for double the price. The $2.25 proprietary medicine often costs no more than 25 cents for product and package; and the bulk of the cost is in the package. In personal care products, distilled spirits, cosmetics, proprietary medicines, hard goods, home furnishings, art objects, and even in food and clothing, price is often as much a reflection of product positioning as it is of product costs. Morris and Bronson correlated price with the quality ratings of Consumer Union for 48 sets of products (mostly major household appliances) over a period from 1957 to 1968. They concluded that: "Price and quality do correlate, but at so low a level as to lack practical significance." Further, there was no obvious method by which the consumer could identify the set of products for which price as an indicator of quality works.[8]

A second reason for symbolic pricing is that consumers often do not have the expertise required to evaluate product quality. This is particularly true of major appliances, electronic equipment, fabrics, carpeting, furniture, and many other product fields. Packaged goods whose contents are concealed and list of ingredients require advanced degrees in chemistry and pharmacology to decipher also present a problem. In these instances, the consumer is forced to rely on surrogate or substitute indicators such as brand reputation, price, or other extraneous factors.

Another reason for symbolic pricing is that quality is often in the eye of the beholder; it is a psychological phenomenon that follows the path of the self-fulfilling prophecy. Consumers expect to be satisfied with their purchases and, barring some blatant product failure, have their expectations fulfilled.

Still a fourth reason for symbolic pricing is the age-old phenomenon of snobbery. Consumers sometimes buy expensive brands to demonstrate good taste, impress friends and relations, and distinguish themselves from the crowd.

This does not mean that symbolic pricing is completely free from the traditional strictures of the price mechanism or pressure of competition. In fact, studies have shown that consumers often have a range of prices which they consider appropriate for a partic-

---

[5]Harold J. Leavitt, "A Note on Some Experimental Findings About the Meaning of Price," *Journal of Business* (July 1954): 205–10.

[6]D. S. Tull, R. A. Boring, and M. H. Gonsior, "A Note on the Relationship of Price and Imputed Quality," *Journal of Business* (April 1964): 186–91.

[7]Andre Gabor and C. W. J. Granger, "On the Price Consciousness of Consumers," *Applied Statistics* (November 1961): 170–80.

[8]R. T. Morris and C. S. Bronson, "The Chaos of Competition Indicated by Consumer Reports," *Journal of Marketing* (July 1969): 26–34.

ular product type. For example, the Gabor and Granger study found that buyers have two price limits in mind when they consider a purchase: (a) an upper limit above which the product is judged too expensive; (b) and a lower limit below which the quality of the product would be suspect.[9] Similar findings have been reported by Sherif[10] and Wassen.[11]

Nor can symbolic pricing offset the obvious inferiority of a pair of tennis shoes that fall apart within a few weeks of purchase, a television set that spends its life in the repair shop, a garment that tears out at the seams after the first washing, or a thousand other fragilities of a shoddy product. Product performance and price must be generally compatible, and both should project the product concept.

PRICING AND ADVERTISING

Because of its influence on demand and its symbolic character, pricing is often used in advertising as a primary appeal. However, the ways that it is used may differ. Figure 8–3 is an example of what we normally think of as price advertising. It is a direct mail advertisement for Anthony Richards' Leisure Lounger. Although style and quality are portrayed in the illustration, price is featured in the headline.

By contrast, price is used quite differently in the Bijan advertisement (Figure 8–4). Fifteen-hundred dollars for perfume is hardly an economy appeal. Similarly, Black Willow Mink uses a headline that states: "This year, only 80 women in America can afford the luxury of a Black Willow Mink." And, Curtis Mathes, which uses price advertising to guarantee the quality of its television sets, states: "Curtis Mathes is the highest priced television set in America. And it's worth it."

Price cannot be separated from value and often plays a major role in advertising.

PRICING STRATEGIES

The purpose of the foregoing discussion of pricing has been to provide a background for examining pricing strategies. A variety of pricing strategies may be used as a part of the marketing program. The overriding consideration is that they support or at least are compatible with the product concept. Some frequently used pricing strategies are briefly described in the following material.

Market skimming. In market skimming, a new product is introduced at a premium price in order to recover investment quickly. Market skimming is a viable strategy when: (a) the new brand has a clear superiority over existing brands; (b) the brand is protected by

[9]Gabor and Granger, "On the Price Consciousness of Consumers," 170–80.

[10]Carolyn W. Sherif, "Social Categorization as a Function of Latitude of Acceptance and Series Range," *Journal of Abnormal and Social Psychology* (August 1963): 148–56.

[11]Chester Wassen, *Consumer Behavior: A Managerial Viewpoint* (Austin, Texas: Austin Press, 1975), 391.

patents, or lag time for competitors in developing an equivalent product is relatively long because of technological complexities or the need to build new plants and equipment; and (c) the market is price inelastic so that a high price will attract enough consumers to be highly profitable. Normally, market skimming is a temporary strategy because the price will be lowered to a competitive level when other firms enter the field with a comparable product.

Penetration pricing. Penetration pricing is an introductory pricing strategy in which the new brand is priced relatively low to stimulate market growth and capture a large market share. It is a viable approach when: (a) the market is highly elastic; or (b) lag time for com-

FIGURE 8–4 (Courtesy Taylor and Co.)

$1500.

It's a comfort to know not every man will be wearing it.

Created by Bijan.
Blended in France.
Held in signed
numbered Baccarat.
Composed of
the world's rare essences.
This is the definitive
perfume for men.
A few men.

bijan®

designer for men
beverly hills

petitors is short and management wants to discourage competition by establishing a relatively low profit margin for the product field.

Market segmentation. Many markets can be segmented on the basis of price; the automobile market is a prime example. Used in this way, pricing strategy is an effective device for appealing to a particular economic segment of the total market.

Prestige and economy pricing.   As pointed out earlier, consumers in a particular market segment generally have a range of prices that they consider appropriate for the product in question. In prestige pricing, the brand is priced in the upper region of this range. In economy pricing, it is priced in the lower region of this range.

Break-even pricing.   Break-even pricing is a viable strategy when a company has two or more components; one is purchased infrequently, the other frequently. For example, razors are purchased infrequently; razor blades are purchased much more frequently. In such an instance, one might price the razor at break-even or with a slight margin in order to get the product in use. Blades would be priced with a relatively high margin in order to capitalize on the repurchase pattern of sales. A similar strategy could apply to camera and film (if the manufacturer makes both) or any other item that requires special refills.

Multiple pricing.   Multiple pricing is a quantity discount. A lower price is charged if more than one unit is purchased. This strategy is widely followed by retail stores, particularly grocery and drug outlets, in the form of two-for or three-for combinations. Research has consistently shown that two-for and three-for pricing may double or triple sales over single unit pricing, even though the price savings may be negligible. In many instances, multiple pricing probably steals sales from future periods and does not lead to an absolute increase in usage. In other cases, however, it does increase consumption, particularly for products such as soft drinks and beer where availability of the product in the home stimulates use. This is why manufacturers of these products use six-packs or some other multiple packaging unit.

Line pricing.   Manufacturers who market a line of similar products, such as different flavors of cake mix or soup, or a line of diverse but related items, such as pet care products, often find that their manufacturing costs for each item in the line differ. When the differences in cost are substantial, they are reflected in the price of the individual items. When they do not differ significantly, a strategy of **average pricing** is often used. The same price is charged for each item in the line, even though the margins will differ somewhat. On the average, however, the manufacturer achieves the desired margin. The purpose of average pricing is to simplify pricing practices for the consumer and create the impression of comparable quality across the entire line.

Another strategy for lines of products is sometimes referred to as **lead pricing.** In this strategy, the high volume items in the line carry relatively low manufacturer margins in order to gain distribution, facilitate consumer purchase, and develop consumer preference. The low volume or speciality items are priced with substantial margins.

Odd pricing.   Odd pricing, sometimes referred to as **psychological pricing,** is frequently used by retailers, although it may be used by manufacturers when their brands are prepriced (when the price is printed on the package or the manufacturer suggests a list price). Odd pricing is based on the psychological concept that 99 cents is, psychologically, much less than one dollar; or $1.79 is much less than $1.80. One manufacturer of private aircraft consistently suggests odd pricing for its airplanes, such as $24,999 instead of $25,000 and $49,999 instead of $50,000.

Sales promotion pricing.   In sales promotion pricing, a price discount is used to deplete inventories, sample consumers, and stimulate sales. This strategy is used by both manufacturers and retailers and involves a variety of price reductions: two for the price of one, penny sales, various forms of multiple pricing, coupons, and so on. Loss leaders are frequently used by retailers to attract customers. A **loss leader** is usually a high volume, frequently purchased item that is price featured in retail advertising near or below cost. The assumption is that loss leaders will attract customers to the store, and while the customers are there, they will buy other items at the regular price.

Bait pricing.   Bait pricing is usually used for hard goods and durable items. In this strategy, a stripped down model is offered at an attractive, low price. When customers inquire about the bargain, salespeople will attempt to trade them up to a higher priced model with more features and a normal margin. Bait pricing is a defensible technique if customers are permitted to purchase the stripped down model at the advertised price if they wish. Often unscrupulous retailers have no intention of selling the bargain and offer the excuse that they had only a limited number of the sale item, and those have all been sold.

Pricing strategy is an integral part of the marketing plan and needs to be coordinated with advertising and other elements of the marketing program through the strictures of the marketing plan.

DISTRIBUTION

MICHELOB

For many years Michelob, the premium of American beers, was sold only in draft form. It was neither bottled nor canned because both required pasteurization or constant refrigeration. Pasteurization caused subtle changes in the flavor of the product, and constant refrigeration was expensive, cumbersome, and difficult to control under conditions of mass distribution. Anheuser Busch, the brewer of Michelob, opted for limited distribution in draft outlets. The bars and taverns selected for distribution were carefully chosen and rigorously controlled. Not only were rigid standards imposed concerning the handling of the product (the temperature had to be controlled within specified limits, the dispenser had to be cleaned on a periodic basis, and a keg had to be consumed within a specified time), but the brewery imposed standards of cleanliness and appearance on dispensing outlets as well as standards for the use of promotional material. In short, retailers of Michelob were selected and policed in such a way as to guarantee the integrity of the product and enhance the image of the brand.

The strategy of selling Michelob only in draft form was continued until technological developments made it possible to pasteurize the product without altering the flavor. At that point, distribution strategy was broadened to include a bottled product. Control of outlets serving Michelob in draft form, however, remained a strategic concern for Anheuser Busch.

DUNCAN HINES CAKE MIXES

Duncan Hines cake mixes were conceived and introduced by Nebraska Consolidated Mills, a small midwestern milling company, several years before the brand was purchased by Procter & Gamble. The initial introductions by Nebraska Consolidated Mills in the midwest were spectacularly successful. Despite heavy advertising and promotion expenditures, the brand paid out in well under a year, and achieved 40 to 50 percent market shares in the backyards of General Mills and Pillsbury, leaders in the cake mix market.

Dazzled by their success in the midwest, and blinded by dreams of high profits with little effort, the management of Nebraska Consolidated Mills decided to invade the California market on a wave of free publicity and with only a token expenditure for advertising and promotion.

General Mills and Pillsbury belatedly awakened from complacency and countered Duncan Hines's California introduction with promotional devices that included increased advertising, promotional allowances, massive displays, and consumer coupons. As a consequence, Duncan Hines never really got off the ground. In many California markets, it failed to gain the 20 percent share of the cake mix market necessary at that time to maintain widespread distribution and lay the basis for future growth.

Five years after the California fiasco, a review of the national marketing plan for Duncan Hines cake mixes indicated that California was still a problem area due to a weak pattern of distribution and faltering brand share. Thus, five years later the brand was still suffering from a distribution malaise caused by failure to establish a strong distribution base during its introduction.

AVON VS. REVLON

Avon, a highly successful line of cosmetics, is distributed through personal sales representatives who call on customers in their homes. Almost every adult in the United States is familiar with the term "the Avon lady." Revlon, sometimes referred to as the General Motors of the cosmetic industry, makes its annual $2 billion-plus sales through drugstores, department stores, beauty shops, and food stores. Both of these companies are successful, but they use quite different channels of distribution.

These examples were chosen to emphasize the importance of distribution in the marketing of consumer products. Michelob provides an example of the use of selective distribution in order to protect the product and enhance its brand image. Duncan Hines represents a failure to obtain intensive (widespread) distribution in a field where intensive distribution is essential to product success. Avon and Revlon represent two similar product lines that have followed quite different distribution strategies. Revlon has sought intensive distribution in conventional outlets. Avon has used a strategy of independent distribution, bypassing conventional outlets and using personal representatives.

The variety of channel arrangements that are used by producers of consumer and industrial goods to make their products available to consumers makes it difficult to formulate a simple, universally applicable generalization about distribution channels. Some firms, particularly in industrial markets, distribute their products directly to their ultimate customers. Others use company owned stores or franchised outlets. Most firms in the consumer field distribute their products through networks of established wholesalers, distributors, and retail stores.

The way that a company distributes its products often has profound implications for its advertising. In order to understand the relationship between distribution and advertising, we must briefly examine the functions of distribution and its strategy.

FUNCTIONS OF DISTRIBUTION

When we speak of distribution, we think only in terms of product availability. However, availability is only one dimension of distribution. Practically, distribution serves four distinct functions in marketing.

1 It is a mechanism for making a product available to those consumers for whom it is intended.
2 It is a symbolic communication of product worth.
3 It is a guarantor of consumer satisfaction and customer service.
4 It is an invaluable sales tool for products that require demonstration and personal selling, thereby eliminating the possibility of self-service.

Only the first function deals solely with product availability. The other three are concerned with the *type* of retail outlets employed.

The type of distribution used is more important for some products than others because the required amount of retail service and support varies by product type. For example, the first function of distribution (product availability) is often the only essential requirement for low priced, mass distributed, packaged goods such as cigarettes and soft drinks. By contrast, all four functions of distribution are important for a variety of high priced, luxury goods ranging from automobiles to carpeting.

For this reason, any consideration of distribution strategy must recognize that consumer goods may be divided into classifications based on the shopping habits of consumers. There are a number of systems for classifying consumer goods; one of the most widely used was developed by Copeland.[12] Copeland classified consumer goods as convenience, shopping, and speciality goods.

☐ **Convenience goods** are those that consumers purchase frequently, immediately, and with a minimum of effort in comparison and buying. Examples include cigarettes, soap, many food products, and newspapers.

☐ **Shopping goods** are those goods which consumers characteristically compare on such bases as suitability, quantity, price, and style. Examples include furniture, clothing, used automobiles, and appliances.

☐ **Speciality goods** are those consumer goods with unique characteristics and/or brand identification for which a significant group of buyers are habitually willing to make a special purchasing effort. Examples include specific brands and types of luxury goods, stereo components, and photographic equipment.

The goal of all marketers of branded merchandise is to make their particular brands a speciality good so that consumers will seek them out and accept no substitutes. In most product fields, this goal is only partially realized because substitute brands are usually available and acceptable to consumers if their preferred brands are difficult to obtain.

Having identified the functions of distribution, and having recognized that different types of products are purchased in different ways by consumers, we are now ready to examine distribution strategy as a part of the marketing plan.

DISTRIBUTION STRATEGY

The particular distribution system used by a firm depends upon the nature of the markets being served, types of products involved, and resources of the producer. Generally, three distribution strategies are available in the consumer field: **intensive, selective,** and **independent.**

Intensive distribution. In intensive distribution, the marketer seeks widespread availability of the brand, often using multiple channels for this purpose. It is generally appropriate for convenience goods. Cigarettes, candy, and soft drinks are commonplace examples of an intensive distribution strategy; these products are found in grocery stores, drugstores, eating and drinking establishments, and vending machines. There are cases in which intensity is sacrificed for other considerations. For example, a product with a rela-

---

[12]Melvin T. Copeland, "Relation of Consumer Buying Habits to Marketing Methods," *Harvard Business Review,* (April 1923), 282–89. Other systems of classification have been devised by: Leo V. Aspinwall, "The Characteristics of Goods Theory," in *Managerial Marketing: Perspectives and Viewpoints,* revised edition, William Lazer and Eugene E. Kelley, eds. (Homewood, Illinois: Richard D. Irwin, Inc., 1962), 633–43; Gordon E. Miracle, "Product Characteristics and Marketing Strategy," *Journal of Marketing* (January 1965): 18–24.

tively short shelf life may be distributed only in outlets that have high volume turnover in order to protect product freshness. Or, consider proprietary cold tablets that are commonly sold in both food and drugstores. A particular brand in this category that is attempting to project a "clinical" or "prescription" image may adopt a strategy of restricting distribution to drugstores and use this strategy as a device for enlisting the support of registered pharmacists and medical doctors in recommending the brand to consumers. This strategy, in fact, was followed by Coricedin for years. It was also the initial distribution strategy of Contac.

Multiple channels of distribution are often necessary to reach different segments of the same market. Fancy chocolates are a case in point. Fancy chocolates are generally sold through three types of retail outlets: specialty candy shops, department stores, and drugstores. However, many consumers reject "drugstore" candy as inferior or stale and insist on buying in one of the other types of outlets. So, for market coverage, drugstores need to be supplemented with other forms of distribution. Interestingly enough, attempts to sell fancy chocolates in food stores have been unsuccessful, even though many food store customers are also buyers of fancy chocolates. Apparently, food stores symbolize "window box" or inexpensive candies and are an inappropriate source for expensive chocolates in the minds of consumers.

Selective distribution. In selective distribution, the producer does not seek intensive coverage, but elects to distribute through a limited number of outlets that complement the brand image and/or provide the level of personal selling and customer service that is required. This distribution strategy is often critical for shopping and speciality goods where the images of the retail outlets themselves may have a profound effect on the consumer's perception of the brand. For example, a television set that has a marketing emphasis on stylish design, quality performance, and prompt customer service will probably not be sold in an automobile accessories store, even though such a store may be appropriate for more utilitarian television sets. Why? Consumers do not shop for stylish furniture in automobile accessories stores.

Similarly, makers of clothing and other household furnishings that rely on high style, cost, and snob appeal as selling points cannot afford to have their products distributed by retail outlets that do not reflect these same dimensions. The consumer does not expect to find a flawless diamond at K mart or Yellow Front and is likely to be suspicious if these outlets purport to carry such items. On the other hand, one does not go to Tiffany's in search of cheap costume jewelry.

Independent distribution. Independent distribution is a form of selective distribution in which producers bypass existing distribution channels and set up a private system that meets their particular needs. Independent distribution can take many forms. Among the most common are: direct mail and catalog selling, direct sales agents, company owned stores, and franchise distribution.

CHAPTER 8 | PRICING AND DISTRIBUTION

Direct mail and catalog selling are particularly appropriate for speciality items that are infrequently purchased and consumers that are widely but thinly dispersed throughout the general population. A great deal of hobby equipment and supplies is sold in this way, although this approach has also been used by clothing manufacturers, producers of gift cheeses, and book publishers in order to avoid the cost and difficulty of obtaining distribution through conventional channels. A relatively recent development in catalog sales is the offering of a wide variety of nationally advertised brands of durable and semidurable goods at substantial price reductions.

Direct sales agents are used by a number of firms to sell directly to consumers on a door-to-door basis. Avon has successfully used this approach for cosmetics; Fuller Brush Company was a pioneer in this field; Tupperware has developed in-home selling into an art; and the sale of carpet sweepers appears to be moving in this direction.

Company owned stores often sell a particular manufacturer's brands exclusively, although they may also distribute noncompetitive items for other manufacturers. The Delmar Corporation, the retail division of International Shoe, uses this strategy, as do the tire industry and major oil companies.

Franchise distribution uses independent entrepreneurs to make its products or services available to consumers. Under the franchise system, the parent company executes an exclusive agreement with independent business people. The parent company generally provides a protected geographic area, technical service, and managerial help in return for compliance with company standards and capital to establish the local outlet. This strategy has long been used by automobile manufacturers and, in recent years, has found favor in the tourism industry (Holiday Inn, Travelodge, Motel-6), in food service (Kentucky Fried Chicken, McDonald's, Baskin-Robbins, Burger Chef), as well as in a number of other industries.

The primary advantage of an independent distribution strategy is that it guarantees maximum control by the manufacturer at the sacrifice of either immediate service (direct mail and catalog sales) or widespread product availability.

ADVERTISING AND DISTRIBUTION

The type of distribution strategy employed by a firm has a direct effect on the advertising that is run. Generally, distribution presents no problem for the firm whose products enjoy intensive distribution. Advertising is directed at the target market through appropriate media, and consumers who see the advertisement will have little or no problem finding the product in the stores.

On the other hand, firms that use selective distribution must find some way of telling potential customers where their products can be found. Failure to do so may result in wasted advertising. One way of handling this problem is through dealer listings. The Paul Stanley, Ltd. ad (Figure 8–5) is an example of a dealer listing advertisement. Note that there are only 12 outlets in which this fashion

Available at:

Los Angeles
AMES
BULLOCK'S
LANZ

Bellevue, Wash.
CLASSIC CLOTHES

Sacramento, CA.
DE MILLE'S

Denver, Colorado
HANNAH

Houston, Texas
J. METZ

Salt Lake City, Utah
JAK'S

San Francisco, CA.
JOSEPH MAGNIN
LITTLE DAISY

Portland, Oregon
M.WILLOCK

Las Vegas, Nevada
MARSHALL RUSSO

Dallas, Texas
SANDY'S

Billings, Montana
SPINNING WHEEL

Seattle, Wash.
TOTALLY MICHAEL

Paul Stanley, Ltd.

silk blend
herringbone
in natural
jacket 130.
skirt 68.
4 to 14

Executive Offices
2701 S. Main Street, Los Angeles, CA 90007 (213) 749-7960   ●   1411 Broadway, New York, N.Y. 10018 (212) 221-3208

can be found. The outlets' names and cities in which they are located are shown on the left side of the ad.

In other instances, instead of using dealer listings, advertisements will refer readers to the yellow pages of their local telephone directory, give a toll free telephone number, or supply an address, along with the invitation to "call or write for the address of the store nearest you."

In the case of direct mail or catalog advertising, the problem is even more acute. In these instances, the advertisement itself must complete the sale by portraying the product thoroughly and persuasively, giving its price, and telling how the merchandise can be obtained. Direct mail advertising is one of the most difficult forms of advertising to write. There is no better training for the aspiring copywriter than to spend a stint engaged in direct mail selling.

CHAPTER 8 | PRICING AND DISTRIBUTION

SUMMARY

Pricing and distribution are intimately involved in marketing success. Without adequate pricing and an effective distribution system, advertising is a waste of company resources.

Pricing strategy is a complex decision in marketing. Historically, economists have considered pricing as the mechanism that mediates the relationship between supply and demand and emphasized price almost to the exclusion of other marketing activities. However, the rise of consumer affluence and increased productivity has given rise to monopolistic competition and symbolic pricing in the marketing equation. In monopolistic competition, the product of each competitor differs in some way from that of other competitors; thus, each competitor has a monopoly because an exact duplicate of its product is not available from any other source. Symbolic pricing refers to the use of price as a symbol of quality because of a widespread belief among consumers, not supported by fact, that there is a necessary relationship between price and quality. Monopolistic competition and symbolic pricing have loosened the ties that traditionally bound supply and demand together in a rigid price relationship and turned pricing into a formidable marketing tool. Frequently used pricing strategies include market skimming, penetration pricing, market segmentation, prestige and economy pricing, break-even pricing, multiple pricing, line pricing, odd pricing, sales promotion pricing, and bait pricing.

The variety of channel arrangements used by producers of consumer and industrial goods to make their products available makes it difficult to formulate a simple generalization about distribution channels. Distribution serves four distinct functions in marketing: (a) a mechanism for making the product available; (b) a symbolic communication of product worth; (c) a guarantor of consumer satisfaction and customer service; and (d) a sales tool for products that require product demonstration and personal selling. Different types of products often require different distribution strategies, including intensive, selective, and independent. The type of distribution strategy employed by a firm has a direct effect on the advertising. For example, in the case of selective distribution, one task of advertising is telling consumers where the product can be found.

REVIEW QUESTIONS

1 Explain the interrelationship of supply, demand, suppliers, and price.
2 Explain the relationship between total income and price changes under the following conditions of elasticity: (a) unitary elasticity; (b) price elasticity; (c) price inelasticity; and (d) negative elasticity.
3 What are the historical, technical, and social reasons underlying the traditional emphasis on price?
4 Explain what is meant by monopolistic competition and why it is important in marketing.
5 Explain why symbolic pricing is an effective marketing tool.
6 Explain the strategies of market skimming and penetration pricing. Identify the conditions under which each is appropriate.
7 Explain what is meant by prestige and economy pricing, break-even pricing, multiple pricing, line pricing, odd pricing, sales promotion pricing, and bait pricing.

230

PART II | MARKETING ANALYSIS AND THE MARKETING MIX

8 What are the functions of distribution?

9 Distinguish among convenience, shopping, and specialty goods.

10 Explain what is meant by intensive, selective, and independent distribution. Indicate the type of goods for which each is appropriate.

DISCUSSION QUESTIONS

1 In 1980 the market for American-made cars was depressed. Under traditional economic theory, this should have led to a decrease in prices for new American-made cars. Yet, major American auto makers increased the prices of their cars over the previous year. Why do you think this was done?

2 Visit a local supermarket and select several product fields, such as coffee, canned pears, or saltine crackers. Identify the prices charged for three or four brands in each field. How do you account for the differences in prices which you encounter?

3 It has been suggested that house to house selling is the most efficient form of retail selling because it eliminates retailers and wholesalers. Do you agree with this statement? Why or why not?

PROBLEM

A key consideration in pricing a new product is determining the profit contribution that the product will produce at a given level of sales and under a given advertising expenditure. Contribution to profit can be determined in the following way:

1 Determine gross sales. Gross sales are computed by estimating the sales in units and multiplying by the selling price per unit.

2 Determine total gross margin. Total gross margins are determined by subtracting total variable costs from gross sales. Total variable costs are computed by multiplying variable costs per unit by the total number of units to be sold.

3 Compute funds available. Funds available are determined by subtracting fixed costs and variable sales costs from the gross margin.

4 Contribution to profit. Contributions to profit are obtained by subtracting the advertising expenditure from the funds available.

For example:

1 Gross sales
   a. Estimated sales in units   2,000,000
   b. Selling price per unit $2.00
   c. Gross sales (2,000,000 × $2.00) $4,000,000

2 Gross margin
   a. Variable costs per unit $1.00
   b. Total variable costs
      (2,000,000 units × $1.00) $2,000,000
   c. Gross margin
      ($4,000,000 − $2,000,000) $2,000,000

CHAPTER 8 | PRICING AND DISTRIBUTION

3 Funds available
   a. Fixed costs $20,000
   b. Variable sales costs as a percent of sales 10%
   c. Total variable sales costs ($4,000,000 × .10) $400,000
   d. Funds available $2,000,000 − ($20,000 + $400,000) $1,580,000
4 Contribution to profit
   a. Advertising expenditure $1,000,000
   b. Contribution to profit $1,580,000 − $1,000,000 $580,000

You are the advertising manager of a company that sells a wide range of personal care items. The company has recently developed a new suntan oil that represents a technological breakthrough. If applied fifteen minutes before exposure to the sun, it will: (a) permit normal tanning while eliminating the possibility of sunburn; and (b) eliminate the problem of premature aging of the skin and dark spots which may be caused by excessive exposure to the sun.

Factory prices for products currently on the market range from $1.82 to $3.92 for an eight-ounce bottle, the standard size sold. Consumer research has estimated that the product will sell 3,000,000 to 4,000,000 units (approximately 20 percent of the market) at a factory price of $2.50 and an advertising expenditure of $3,750,000.

Variable costs are estimated at $0.80 per unit, including packaging. Fixed costs are estimated at $30,000. Variable sales costs are estimated at 15 percent of factory sales.

There is disagreement among company executives regarding the factory price that should be charged. The president of the company is concerned that a factory price of over $2.50 will discourage purchase at both the trade and consumer level. Further, he says that as the factory price is increased over $2.50, additional advertising dollars will have to be spent in order to achieve a 3,000,000 to 4,000,000 unit sales level.

The marketing director argues that the product's superiority warrants a price near the upper end of the competitive price range, and the advertising appropriation should be increased.

As advertising manager, you have been asked for your recommendation.

ASSIGNMENT

1 Compute the profit contribution at a factory price of $2.50 per unit for estimated sales of 3,000,000 and 4,000,000 units.
2 What price do you recommend and what do you think the advertising appropriation should be at this price level? What will be the contribution to profit, assuming sales of 3,000,000 and 4,000,000 units?
3 Devise a name for the product.
4 Design a package for the product.
5 Would you use price in the advertising? Why or why not?

III
Advertising

Thus far, our attention has been directed to the setting in which advertising occurs, marketing analysis, and key elements of the marketing mix. We now come to the section of the marketing plan that carries the main burden of marketing communications—advertising.

There is probably more disagreement about advertising and the way it should be written than any other area of marketing. It is a highly controversial area encompassing different theories, opinions, and personal likes and dislikes. Yet, effective advertising does not occur by chance. Advertising is a *disciplined* creativity, firmly rooted in marketing and directed by the logic of the task to be done.

Normally, the advertising section of the marketing plan is divided into three parts:

1 Advertising objectives and strategies
   a. Advertising objectives specify the target group or groups to be reached, as well as measurable and realistic communication goals.

   b. Advertising strategy (optional) is only included in the marketing plan when additional specifications for the advertising are required, such as the timing of the schedule, how advertising weight will be distributed within a line of products, and how advertising will be used to support other marketing activities.
2 Copy strategy and plan
   a. Copy strategy reflects basic decisions that will

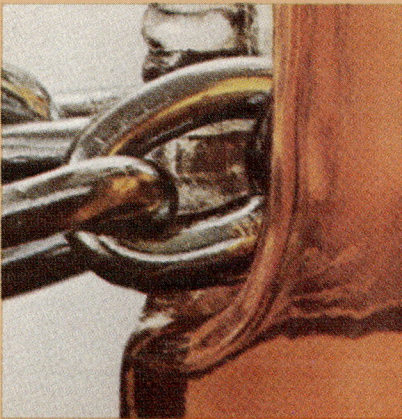

direct and shape the content and form of the advertising copy.
   b. Copy plans detail how the copy strategy will be executed in a specific advertisement or advertising campaign.
3 Media strategy and plan
   a. Media strategy indicates how media will be selected and used in accomplishing advertising objectives.
   b. Media plans detail the specific media that will be used.

Part 3 has been divided into five chapters. Chapter 9 will discuss the nature of advertising. We will deal with advertising and the economy, the morality of advertising, the uses and the effects of advertising. Chapter 10 will address itself to mass communications and theories of advertising, while Chapter 11 discusses how one should approach the task of writing advertisements. Chapter 12 is devoted to print advertising and deals with headlines, illustrations, and body copy. Advertising design, layout, and mechanical

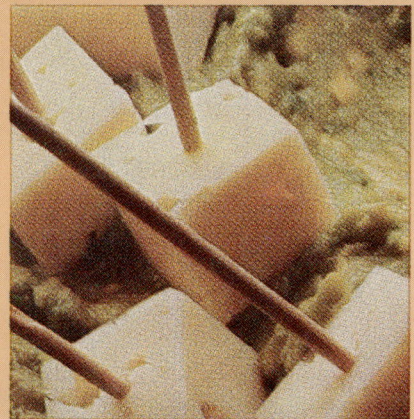

production are discussed in Chapter 13, and Chapter 14 is concerned with broadcast advertising and its production.

Advertising is an art, not a science. There are no hard and fast rules for designing advertisements or writing copy. Yet, it is through the creativity of advertising copy that the product takes wing and systematic strategy statements are translated into persuasive communications. In a sense, advertising creativity is the soul of marketing. Without it, mass marketing is not possible.

9
The Nature of Advertising

ADVERTISING—AN OBJECT OF CONTROVERSY

Advertising has long been an object of controversy—controversy about its effects on the economy, overall effectiveness, and morality. Consider the following examples.

FTC vs. THE CEREAL COMPANIES

In 1972 the Federal Trade Commission filed suits against four cereal companies—General Foods, General Mills, Kellogg's, and The Quaker Oats Company—for restraint of trade. Among the charges cited was one involving advertising. According to government attorneys, the large advertising budgets of the defendants served as a "barrier to competition" thereby discouraging smaller companies from entering the field. The attorneys considered advertising a source of monopoly power. After nine years of litigation, 41,000 pages of testimony, and $27 million worth of legal expenses by the cereal companies, the government dropped its charges upon the recommendation of the trial judge.[1]

WHICH HALF?

John Wanamaker, founder of Wanamaker's department stores, was one of the first merchandising giants who relied heavily on advertising to build his company's sales and reputation. At one point, a critic asked, "Mr. Wanamaker, don't you think that about half of the money you spend on advertising is wasted?"

Wanamaker's famous answer was: "I know that half the money I spend on advertising is wasted, but I can never find out which half."

An example of Wanamaker's advertising, run in 1919, is shown in Figure 9–1.

---

[1]Stanley E. Cohen and Richard L. Gordon, "FTC Tosses Cereal Industry Case," *Advertising Age*, 14 September 1981, 1 ff.

FASHION FIRST!

Wanamaker's

FASHION *Mail Order* **CATALOG**

Yes, it is a "regular" Mail Order Catalog, but *specializing in fashions*, including women's, misses' and children's inner and outer wearing apparel.

Price range? *The happy medium!* Going as low as quality can be bought for. Fifty-eight years of successful store-keeping have established this absolutely trustworthy standard of merchandising.

Can you be sure of *correct and newest fashions?* You couldn't be *more* sure than at Wanamaker's! Our home is in the fashion center of New York and we are in constant touch with our Paris office. We go to press weeks after most of the other Mail Order Catalogs are completed, so for our catalog we are able to choose and design the very *latest* fashions.

If you want a copy of this catalog, please send for it right away because the edition is limited and a delay in writing may lose the chance to get YOUR copy.

P.S. *Letter postage is back to its old rate! A penny postal will bring this catalog today. Please ask for Catalog R. Address.*

John Wanamaker
Mail Order, New York

FIGURE 9–1 Wanamaker's advertisement (1919) (From *Those Were the Good Old Days,* Copyright © 1959, 1979 by Edgar R. Jones. Reprinted by permission of Simon & Schuster, a Division of Gulf & Western Corporation.)

MASS WASTE OR MASS COMMUNICATIONS?

In the introduction to his book *Common Sense in Advertising,* Charles F. Adams observes:

> Most people who create advertising and most people who approve it live in a dreamworld.
>
> They labor endlessly on the finer points of each advertisement and each commercial. They fill it with so many facts that it fairly bulges with information. They argue about color tones and semantic nuances. They fret over phraseology. They have conferences on commas. Their search for perfection is commendable—but they are all too often spending their effort and their time on the wrong thing.
>
> They believe that the audience they have purchased to view their advertising is going to give it the same loving attention that they have lavished on it. And they want it to be absolutely perfect for the careful reading or the detailed viewing that it is going to receive from the tremendous numbers to whom it will be presented.
>
> Their delusion is understandable to anyone who has spent much time in advertising. The money involved is so important and the presentations of media analysts so convincing, that it would be heretical to suggest that advertising planners are involved in mass waste instead of mass communications. After all that careful planning and all that brilliant strategy and all that expenditure and all those endless conferences, who is brave enough to say that no one will notice the ad?
>
> Yet, that is precisely the case. Or, to be more literal, it is all but true for the great majority of ads. Many advertising experts have suspected this for some time, but they have been reluctant to give voice to their thoughts for fear of damaging advertising's reputation and discrediting its powers.[2]

THE MORALITY OF ADVERTISING

Almost any discussion of advertising, whether with students or the general public, finds those who deplore the morality of advertising.

---

[2]Charles F. Adams, *Common Sense in Advertising* (New York: McGraw-Hill, 1965), 3–4.

Criticisms range from the charge that it creates materialism to the contention that it is deceptive and in poor taste. Some of these criticisms are undoubtedly valid; others are ill-conceived. To many of its critics, however, advertising is immoral and should be abolished or rigorously controlled.

Some basic questions about advertising, what it does, and its value are worth examining. Too often, proponents of advertising make exaggerated claims about its powers, while critics belabor its weaknesses. Too seldom do either attempt to look at advertising dispassionately.

In this chapter, we will examine four aspects of advertising: (a) its effects on the economy; (b) morality; (c) the uses; and (d) effects. With this background, we will address ourselves to the subject of mass communications and to theories of advertising in Chapter 10.

ADVERTISING AND THE ECONOMY

Advocates and opponents of advertising hold very different beliefs concerning the role of advertising in the economy.[3]

Advocates believe:

1 Advertising stimulates the Gross National Product (GNP) and contributes to a higher standard of living.
2 Advertising, by providing information, enables consumers to make more intelligent choices.
3 Advertising lowers the cost of goods by stimulating demand.
4 Advertising facilitates competition by making it possible for new products to be introduced.

Opponents believe:

1 Advertising is wasteful and neither stimulates the economy nor leads to a higher standard of living.
2 Advertising, by providing biased and incomplete information, does not enable consumers to make more intelligent choices.
3 Advertising increases the cost of goods.
4 Advertising is a barrier to competition.

Normally, the validity of opposing points of view can be assessed by examining the empirical support for each. Let's look at the empirical support for each of these four opposing sets of beliefs.

ADVERTISING STIMULATES THE GNP vs. ADVERTISING IS WASTEFUL

Although it might be reasonable to assume that advertising stimulates the economy, there is insufficient evidence to support this point of view. Richard Holton, an economist, notes:

---

[3]The affirmative points of view in these four issues are adapted from Richard H. Holton, "How Advertising Achieved Respectability Among Economists (Or Anyhow, They've Heard of It)," p. 56–64. Reprinted by permission from the April 30, 1980 issue of *Advertising Age.* Copyright © 1980 by Crain Communications, Inc.

If advertising does cause the GNP to be greater than it might otherwise be, one would expect advertising expenditures to lead the business cycle, i.e., advertising expenditures would begin to move upward, after a recession, before other indicators of economic activity, especially personal consumption expenditures.

But one of the major difficulties inhibiting investigations of this sort is the absence of satisfactory data on advertising expenditures. The McCann-Erickson monthly index includes only national advertising. Since this may represent only about 30% of all advertising expenditures, it is not completely satisfactory.

None of the attempts to analyze this problem have provided any strong indication that increased advertising causes increases in personal consumption expenditures. And there is at least some evidence that the causality may run in the other direction, i.e., when personal consumption expenditures move up, advertising expenditures follow. . . .

If we set the business cycle aside and ask whether advertising has not led to increased personal consumption expenditures and hence a higher GNP over the long pull, again we find inconclusive evidence. Personal consumption expenditures over time have had a fairly stable relationship to personal disposable income, even though the ratio of advertising to GNP has been rising. Although it is difficult to imagine that advertising has not stimulated demand over the decades, economists simply have not been able to prove or disprove this point.[4]

Thus, the effects of advertising on the economy are unresolved, and either point of view is equally plausible.

ADVERTISING PROVIDES INFORMATION vs. ADVERTISING PROVIDES BIASED, INCOMPLETE INFORMATION

Evidence on this point is disputable. Undoubtedly, advertising does provide some information that helps consumers shorten the search process for commercial goods and services. This is particularly true in the introduction of new products, use of telephone book yellow page advertising and dealer listing advertising that tells consumers where products can be purchased, and advertising that provides specific information on product benefits and features. On the other hand, a cursory examination of contemporary advertising indicates that much of it is virtually devoid of information, particularly when it attempts to establish a mood and when product characteristics are largely, or wholly, ignored.

One problem lies in how "information" is defined. If information is defined primarily in terms of price and performance characteristics, then it must be admitted that a lot of advertising provides little or no information. If information is defined more broadly—including style, appearance, prestige, and the portrayal of the product in an attractive setting—then all advertising provides some information, although it may be both incomplete and biased.

Again, both points of view appear to have validity.

---

[4]Ibid., 58.

ADVERTISING LOWERS PRICES vs. ADVERTISING INCREASES PRICES

Evidence in support of these opposing propositions is mixed. At the level of the individual firm, advertising may indeed lower prices by increasing selective demand and permitting economies of scale. For example, in pricing new products, both costs and prices are usually calculated in terms of different levels of production. Since costs per unit are lower at higher production levels, the price that must be charged to earn a profit is lower. Firms ordinarily set prices on the basis of anticipated levels of production, and since advertising is used to increase demand, it may be argued that the net effect of advertising is to lower prices.

At the macro level, however, the effects of advertising are more ambiguous. Given a limit to demand, an increase in the demand for Brand A (reducing its costs and prices) will result in a decrease in demand for competitive Brand B (increasing its costs) resulting in a rise in the price of Brand B, or the brand will have to be withdrawn from the market. Until it can be demonstrated that advertising actually increases the total level of economic activity, it cannot be demonstrated that in the aggregate advertising lowers prices.

ADVERTISING FACILITATES COMPETITION vs. ADVERTISING IS A BARRIER TO COMPETITION

During the 1960s, these opposing propositions were the focus of considerable debate. In the example of FTC versus the cereal companies at the beginning of the chapter, the FTC charged that heavy advertising on the part of the major cereal companies served as a barrier to competition. The weight of empirical evidence, however, tends to refute this accusation.

If the charge that advertising is a barrier to competition were valid, one would expect to find: (a) little brand switching from well established brands to newly introduced ones; (b) a positive correlation between advertising intensity and the concentration of sales for consumer product industries (advertising expenditures would be high in those industries dominated by a few major companies and correspondingly lower in fields characterized by many competitors); and (c) little evidence of new brands encroaching on the brand sales of entrenched companies. Yet, one does not find any of these things.

Testimony before the U.S. Congress's subcommittee on monopoly indicates that brand switching is rampant.[5] In the detergent industry, as well as the personal care, cereal, automobile, fashion, household appliance, proprietary drug, and other fields, brand switching is a way of life. A study of the correlation between advertising intensity and concentration of sales by economist Lester G. Telser indicated no relationship between the amount of advertising and the number of new products introduced into the field.[6] Finally, evidence of new brands making competitive inroads on well estab-

---

[5]U.S. Congress Subcommittee on Monopoly of the Senate Select Committee on Small Business, *Role of the Giant Corporations*, Part 1-A (July 1969), 923.

[6]Lester G. Telser, "Some Aspects of the Economics of Advertising," *Journal of Business* (April 1968), as reproduced in *Advertising's Role in Society*, John S. Wright and John E. Mertes, eds. (St. Paul, Minnesota: West Publishing Company, 1974), 38–39.

lished leaders in the field is widespread. For example, import automobiles have driven major U.S. car manufacturers to the edge of bankruptcy; Timex has literally taken the watch market away from Bulova; Sony became a major factor in the television market against entrenched competition such as General Electric, Philco, RCA, and Motorola. Miller displaced Schlitz as the number two brewery; Polaroid has had outstanding success in Kodak's domain; Bic has been successful against Gillette; and dozens of other examples could be given.

In a book titled *Advertising and Competition*, economist Jules Bachman concludes that entry into new markets is easier when advertising can be used.[7] In addition, *Fortune* magazine states that economist Harold Demsetz and others have "pretty well disposed of the myth that advertising is a source of monopoly power."[8]

In summary, the weight of systematic research indicates that advertising is not a barrier to entry into new markets. On the contrary, advertising makes entry possible.

In examining opposing points of view about the effects of advertising on the economy, advertising as a barrier to competition is the only instance where empirical evidence clearly supports one point of view over another. In the three other cases, empirical evidence is either lacking or ambiguous. All one can say with confidence is that advertising, as a marketing tool, facilitates the introduction of new products.

THE MORALITY OF ADVERTISING

Criticisms of the morality of advertising usually take one or more of the following forms:

☐ Advertising creates materialistic values.
☐ Advertising makes people buy things they do not need.
☐ Advertising is deceptive.
☐ Advertising is often annoying and in poor taste.
☐ Commercial sponsorship of mass media has resulted in bland, generally poor program content.

Let us examine each of these criticisms more closely.

Advertising creates materialistic values. Advertising focuses on materialistic values; however, does it *create* these values, and is materialism a desirable value for society and individuals?

In answer to the first of these questions, materialism has been preeminent as an American value since the country was founded. Advertising didn't create materialism; it was always here. Early observers of the American society, notably Alexis de Tocqueville (1805–1859) and Charles Dickens (1812–1870), commented on the materialistic character of America over a hundred years before the emergence of modern marketing. It should be recognized, however, that

---

[7]Jules Bachman, *Advertising and Competition* (New York: New York University Press, 1967), 177.
[8]A. F. Ehrbar, "Martin Feldstein's Electric Blue Economic Prescriptions," *Fortune*. Copyright © 1978 by Time, Inc. All rights reserved.

CHAPTER 9 | THE NATURE OF ADVERTISING

advertising helps to perpetuate materialism with its emphasis on products and material satisfactions. Thus, in the process of reflecting the social value of materialism, advertising undoubtedly reinforces its concept.

The second question is more relevant. Is materialism a desirable value for society and individuals? Insofar as material values represent a free choice for society's members, saying that materialism is not a desirable social value is difficult without repudiating the basic concepts of democracy and a free economy.

As American society has become more affluent, a growing number of consumers have begun questioning whether materialism is a desirable social goal. They recognize that it has a cost, such as dissipation of resources, environmental pollution, and diminution of other social values as well as the quality of life.

Unfortunately, the issue of materialism is relative, not absolute. The question is not whether materialism is desirable, but how much materialism is acceptable, and how great a cost are we willing to pay. As irreplaceable resources are exhausted, energy costs increase, and pollution becomes excessive, the limits of materialism will be defined, not by philosophical predilections, but by external environmental considerations.

Advertising makes people buy things they do not need. Advertising can't make anyone do anything. For example, General Motors cannot make a person buy a General Motors car if the person chooses not to do so. Advertising can make a product or a service appealing, but the decision to purchase is always a personal one.

At a more subtle level, this criticism implies that advertising directs consumers' attention away from things they truly need and toward things they merely want. Such a distinction between needs and wants is a subjective judgment. Critics who adopt this point of view are saying that some purchases are more desirable than others according to their criteria. While they can make such judgments for themselves, they cannot make them for others without depriving people of their freedom of choice.

Advertising is deceptive. Advertising is intended to persuade. But, when does persuasion become deception?

Pearce, Cunningham, and Miller have pointed out that there are four dimensions to deception: (a) the intent to deceive; (b) the capacity of the message to deceive; (c) whether the recipient of the message is deceived; and (d) the standard of judgment to be used in determining the extent of deception.[9]

Intent to deceive is subjective and, therefore, difficult to evaluate. Undoubtedly, some advertisements are dishonest and do attempt to deceive. However, business firms that intend to stay in business generally have unequivocal policies against deliberate deception.

The capacity of the message to deceive is heavily dependent upon the nature of the recipient. An advertisement that is not de-

---

[9]M. Pearce, S. M. Cunningham, and A. Miller, *Appraising the Economic and Social Effects of Advertising*, Marketing Science Institute Staff Report (October 1971): 423.

ceptive to its intended audience may be deceptive to a lesser educated audience or to a young child. Further, the distinction between information, persuasion, and deception is ambiguous, according to findings by the National Goals Research Staff of the U.S. Government.[10] Frederick Webster, Jr., has pointed out that the standards used by regulatory agencies have not been particularly flattering to the average consumer, who has been described at various times as gullible, ignorant, easily persuaded, uneducated, and incapable of making sound judgments.[11]

Undoubtedly, some people are deceived by advertising, although the extent to which they are deceived is highly ambiguous and judgmental. A rudimentary knowledge of psychology indicates that some people want to be deceived and will go out of their way to obtain this result. W. C. Fields once observed, "You can't cheat an honest man." In other words, most people who are cheated have a bit of larceny in their own hearts and become victims because they are trying to cheat the cheater. There is some element of truth in this assertion, and it is present in many charges that advertising is deceptive.

Advertising is often annoying and in poor taste. This charge probably has more substance than any of the others. Some advertising is clearly in poor taste. Its intentional use is inexcusable and widely criticized within the industry itself. *Advertising Age* has criticized the use of poor taste in advertising as a device for gaining attention;[12] leading practitioners have consistently campaigned against it. Unfortunately, it still exists.

Commercial sponsorship of mass media has resulted in bland and poor program content. Critics who make this charge have probably never traveled in foreign countries where television programming is controlled by the government. Most decent television in these countries consists of reruns of American programs.

Nonetheless, even the most vociferous defenders of commercial television would probably concede that the average run of American television programs contributes little of cultural consequence, aesthetic value, or dramatic excellence. As one observer of the American scene commented, "No one has ever gone broke underestimating the taste of the mass market."

Defense of television programming rests on, essentially, two significant arguments. First, television stations give the American people what they want to see. When a program fails to achieve an adequate rating, it is replaced. Of course, if one's tastes are somewhat different from those of the mass market, that person may consider commercial television to be an intellectual wasteland. However, the market system is taking care of this problem. As significant

[10]National Goals Research Staff, *Toward Balanced Growth: Quantity and Quality* (Washington, D.C.: Superintendent of Documents, U.S. Government Printing Office, 1970), 139.

[11]Frederick E. Webster, Jr., *Social Aspects of Marketing* (Englewood Cliffs, N.J.: Prentice-Hall, Inc., 1974), 34.

[12]"Shock: A Creative Shortcut," *Advertising Age*, 28 November 1977, 10.

numbers of consumers have become bored with standard television programs, cable television has emerged as an attractive alternative. If a person does not like the offerings of standard or cable television, the person can always turn the set off. Second, commercial television provides a forum for the exercise of free expression, virtually uncontaminated by government control.

Some criticisms of advertising are justified; others are not. Some are self-serving and superficial; others are inspired by genuine concern. Yet, when we examine the criticisms that are made of advertising, none of them justify the blanket charge that advertising is immoral.

THE USES OF ADVERTISING

Different kinds of advertising can serve a variety of advertising objectives. The effectiveness of an advertising campaign depends upon how clearly the objectives are stated. If the objectives are obscure or ill-defined, little productive advertising will result. Broadly stated, there are six kinds of advertising: product, sales promotion, trade, corporate, classified, and retail.

PRODUCT ADVERTISING

Product or **brand advertising** is designed to provide consumers with information about a product or service and translate the product concept into an appealing consumer benefit. Product advertising is sometimes referred to as *display advertising* because it displays the product for everyone to see, or as *image advertising* because it attempts to create a favorable image of the product being advertised. Its general purpose, over a period of time and through repeated exposures, is to affect consumer knowledge, beliefs, and attitudes about a product or service. Most of the advertising appearing on television and in magazines is product or display advertising. Figure 9–2 is an excellent example of product advertising for the Hoover Celebrity. The product and some of its features are illustrated; body copy explains why the product cleans better than other, more expensive canister sweepers. The entire focus of the advertisement is on the product and the benefits it offers.

SALES PROMOTION ADVERTISING

Sales promotion advertising is intended to create immediate actions. It generally carries an urgent message, such as an announcement of a sale, contest, coupon, or some other offer. The consumer benefit is a special offer, usually of a financial nature. Major sales promotion activities (see Chapter 19) are frequently supported by advertising, and the specific objectives of this advertising are determined by the nature of the promotion being used. For example, advertising in support of a consumer contest or sweepstakes is designed to describe the prize structure, rules of the contest, and what consumers must do to enter. If the promotion features a premium, the primary objective of the advertising should be to describe the premium clearly, and tell consumers how they can obtain it.

The Come 'N Get It dog food advertisement in Figure 9–3 is an excellent example of sales promotion advertising. The headline an-

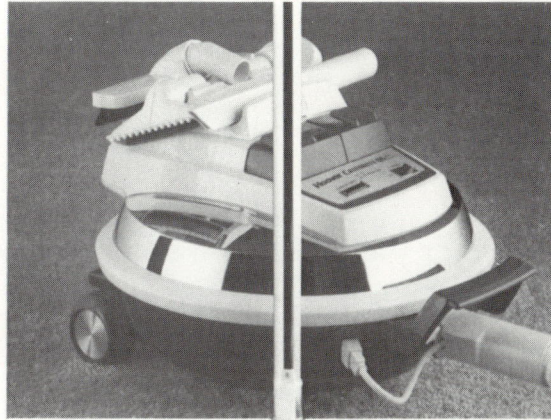

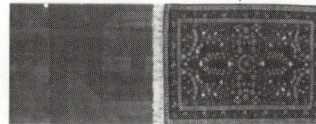

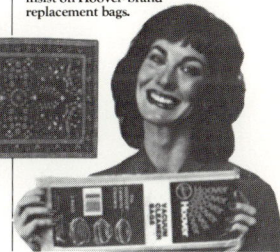

nounces FREE and refers to "details on mail-in offer below." The focus of the advertisement is not on the product but on a book by Barbara Woodhouse, titled *No Bad Dogs* and identified as a $12.50 value. The lower portion of the advertisement contains two coupons—one for the book, the other for fifty cents off the purchase price of any package size of Come 'N Get It. Virtually nothing is said about the product. Instead, body copy is devoted to the offer. Finally, note the urgency of the statement over the coupon: "Take this coupon and start saving now!"

TRADE ADVERTISING

Trade advertising for consumer products is directed to the retail trade and designed to help gain distribution or enlist retail cooper-

FIGURE 9–3 (Courtesy Carnation Company)

ation in a product promotion. In the first instance, such advertising emphasizes the profit (benefit) that the retailer can make by stocking the brand and often offers a *stocking allowance* (a certain amount of money per case) for all initial purchases. In the second instance, trade advertising generally describes the promotion, specifies its dates, indicates the extent of consumer advertising support, and offers a *promotion allowance* for allowing in-store displays during the promotion period. The benefit is the implied promise of increased sales and profits for those channel members participating in the promotion.

Both of these goals—gaining distribution and announcing promotions—are supported by the activities of the sales force. Advertising is used to provide broad coverage of the trade and pave the way for personal sales presentations.

Figures 9–4 and 9–5 are examples of trade advertising. The Dolly Madison advertisement is designed to encourage retailers to

FIGURE 9–4 (Courtesy Interstate Brands Corp.)

stock the Dolly Madison line. Its headline promises profits, and the body copy identifies areas of sales and advertising support offered by the company. Figure 9–5 is strictly a promotional advertisement. It is for a joint or *tie-in promotion* for five different companies. The advertisement emphasizes that 80 million coupons will be distributed and urges grocers to contact the sales representatives of the participating companies to learn the details of special promotional allowances and merchandising materials that will be made available.

CORPORATE ADVERTISING

A clear distinction needs to be made between product advertising and **corporate advertising**. The difference is one of *primary focus*. Whereas product advertising is undertaken in support of a particu-

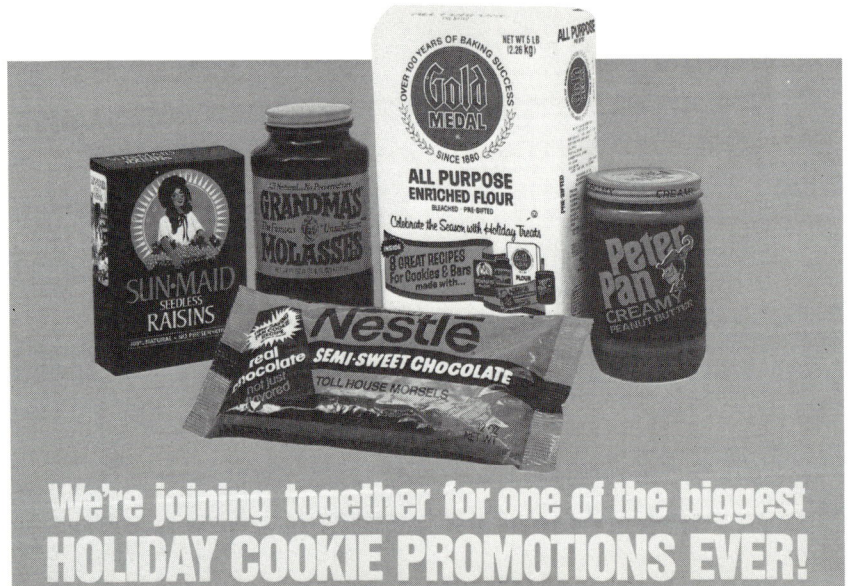

Celebrate the Season with Holiday Treats...

From Gold Medal® Flour, Nestlé® Semi-Sweet Real Chocolate Morsels, Sun-Maid® Seedless Raisins, Peter Pan® Peanut Butter, Grandma's® Unsulfured Molasses and Thematics

We're joining together for one of the biggest HOLIDAY COOKIE PROMOTIONS EVER!

80 million coupons will be distributed through THEMATICS insert in November issues of Ladies Home Journal, Good Housekeeping, Better Homes and Gardens and McCalls

Two page THEMATICS ad will introduce a special holiday recipe.

20 million specially marketed Gold Medal flour sacks will contain 8 delicious cookie recipes using the five participating products

Participating sales reps will contact you with special promotional allowances and merchandising materials

® Gold Medal is a registered trademark of General Mills, Inc.
® Nestlé is a registered trademark of the Nestlé Company, Inc.
® Sun-Maid is a registered trademark of © Sun-Diamond Growers of California
® Peter Pan is a registered trademark of Swift and Company
® Grandma's is a registered trademark of Duffy-Mott Company, Inc.

GET READY AND STOCK UP ON THESE FINE PRODUCTS!

lar brand or brands, corporate, also referred to as *institutional,* advertising is undertaken in support of objectives of the company. Its purpose is to provide information and influence attitudes about the company itself.

Corporate advertising may be undertaken for several reasons, including financial, political, or public relations, and directed to a variety of publics. A survey conducted by the Association of National Advertisers provides the following summary by corporate advertisers of some general corporate advertising objectives.

1 Enhance or maintain the company's reputation or goodwill among specific public or business audiences.

2 Establish or maintain a level of awareness of the company's name and nature of its business.

3 Provide a unified and supportive marketing approach (umbrella) for a combination of present and future products and services.

4 Educate the audience on subjects of importance to the company's future (for example, profits, free enterprise, economics).

5 Establish the company's concern for environmental or social issues.

6 Bring about a change in specific attitudes of the audience toward the company or its products.[13]

Although corporate advertising can have value, many corporate ads are poorly conceived, badly executed, and largely a waste of company resources. Such advertising is often wholly self-serving, and benefits for the audience are either nonexistent or ambiguous.

Figure 9–6 is an example of corporate advertising for National Gypsum Company. No specific product is being sold. The basic message is that despite the home production slump, National Gypsum is undertaking an expansion program in the expectation that the slump won't last; when it ends, National Gypsum will have adequate production facilities. The benefit for the intended audience is that National Gypsum will be prepared to meet their future requirements for material needs.

CLASSIFIED ADVERTISING

The primary purpose of **classified advertising,** as it is used by major corporations, is the recruitment of employees for specific job openings.[14] Classified advertising, sometimes referred to as *nondisplay advertising*, is usually segregated in the back pages or a special section of publications. It consists of small *reader ads* (closely set type in an inch or so of space), or somewhat larger ads using a combination of different typefaces, white space, or simple illustrations to gain attention. Figure 9–7 shows examples of classified ads.

RETAIL ADVERTISING

Retail advertising is not a separate type of advertising; it is a term reserved for the advertising done by retail stores, usually in local media. Retail advertising generally appears in the form of display (image) advertising which focuses on the store as a product, or sales promotion advertising which features prices and sales. Sales promotion advertising accounts for most retail advertising, and the pages of local newspapers are filled with it. Very few retail stores use display or image advertising, although some of the more successful ones do. The Ohrbach's advertisement shown in Chapter 5 (Figure 5–1) is an example of image advertising for a retail store.

---

[13]Harry L. Darling, *Current Company Objectives and Practices in the Use of Corporate Advertising* (New York: Association of National Advertisers, Inc., 1975), 6–7.

[14]Direct mail companies, as well as individuals, often use classified advertising to sell specific products and services. Local, retail businesses, particularly automobile dealers and real estate brokers, also use the classified sections of local newspapers for the same purpose. For most major corporations, however, employee recruitment is the primary purpose for the use of classified advertising.

FIGURE 9–6   (Courtesy National
Gypsum Co.)

Why is National Gypsum building its capacity in the middle of a building recession?

A $200 million investment in the building materials industry is no small piece of change. Especially at a time when home construction is going anywhere but up. But as any construction-industries analyst knows, this situation won't last. And that's exactly what National Gypsum is preparing for now.

The moment the recession in the building industry lets up, National Gypsum will be ready to provide what's needed. Extensive capital improvements have been made to existing plants, mines and equipment in all divisions to increase capacity. Many have expanded by an average of 30 percent with an increased emphasis on the repair and remodeling markets. New plants are being purchased, both at home and abroad, while investments in oil and gas promise to offset gradually National Gypsum's energy costs.

What it all adds up to is a company that's ready—and able—to do business. Write for our annual report and find out more.

National Gypsum Company
A family of companies building for the future.

Dept. PR-FT, 4100 First International Building, Dallas, Texas 75270

National Gypsum is Gold Bond wallboard, ceiling tiles and panels, vinyl siding. American Olean quarry tile, glazed tile, ceramic mosaic tile. Binswanger glass, mirrors, laminated safety and furniture glass, architectural glazing systems. Binning's thermal aluminum doors and windows, patio doors, storm doors and windows. Benchmark, Strahan and Style-Tex wallcoverings and companion fabrics. Huntington House designer and decorative fabrics. Huron and Allentown cements. Biscayne cushioned vinyl flooring. Together, we're a family of companies building for the future.

THE EFFECTS OF ADVERTISING

The goal of advertising is to affect consumer attitudes thereby converting nonbuying consumers into customers. At any given time, however, different consumers may be in various stages of attitude formation. For example, a consumer who is unaware of a particular product is less likely to buy it than one who is aware of it, favorably impressed with its attributes, and considering its purchase. One can, in fact, conceptualize a progression of stages from "unaware of the product" to "purchasing it for the first time."

Several marketing writers have suggested models for this progression. Five such models, referred to as "hierarchy of effects," are shown in Table 9–1.

The similarity between these various models is apparent. They differ only in the number of steps involved and the particular words used to describe the steps. The Association of National Advertisers

FIGURE 9–7 Sample classified ads

commissioned R. H. Colley to develop the DAGMAR model (an acronym for Defining Advertising Goals for Measuring Advertising Results) in an effort to devise a method of measuring advertising effectiveness.[15] The Lavidge and Steiner model conceives of advertising as a force that moves people up through a series of steps in which "the actual purchase is but the final threshold."[16] The AIDA model has traditionally been used by salespeople to visualize the process of moving a prospect along a series of mental steps to the final sale.[17] The Adoption Process model has been borrowed from sociology and is primarily associated with the introduction of new products. Finally, the National Industrial Conference Board developed its model as an aid in visualizing the sales process. The presentation of this model noted: (a) the influence of advertising at each stage depends on the industry, product, and type of advertising as well as factors peculiar to the company, its selling methods, and previous marketing position; (b) the influence of advertising tends to diminish at each successive stage, playing a smaller role in "provoking the sale" than in "awareness;" and (c) much advertising is only intended to achieve some intermediate objective such as increasing awareness or arousing a desire to buy.[18]

In order to examine the hierarchy of effects concept more closely, let us take one of the models and consider it in detail. Although any of the models could be used equally well, let us use the National Industrial Conference Board model since: (a) its terms are relatively unambiguous; (b) it has an intermediate number of steps that seem to parallel the stages that consumers often go through; and (c) it explicitly recognizes that the importance of advertising may diminish as consumers move up the scale in terms of their familiarity with the brand and their propensity to purchase it.

This scale, like the others, assumes that the progress from awareness to purchase is a laborious one taking place over a period

TABLE 9–1 Hierarchy of effects models

Dagmar	Lavidge-Steiner	AIDA	Adoption Process	National Industrial Conference Board
Action	Purchase	Action	Adoption	Provoking sale
Conviction	Conviction	Desire	Trial	Intention to buy
Comprehension	Preference	Interest	Evaluation	Preference
Awareness	Liking	Attention	Interest	Acceptance
	Knowledge		Awareness	Awareness
	Awareness			

[15]R. H. Colley, *Defining Advertising Goals for Measured Advertising Results* (New York: Association of National Advertisers, 1961).

[16]R. L. Lavidge and G. A. Steiner, "A Model for Predictive Measurements of Advertising Effectiveness," *Journal of Marketing* (October 1961): 59–62.

[17]K. K. Cox and B. M. Ennis, *The Marketing Research Process* (Pacific Palisades, California: Goodyear Publishing Company, Inc., 1972), 41.

[18]H. D. Wolfe, J. K. Brown, and G. C. Thompson, *Measuring Advertising Results.* Studies in Business Policy, No. 2. The National Industrial Conference Board (1962), p. 7.

of time, the consumer moves one step at a time, and each step upward increases the probability of purchase. Although these assumptions may hold true in many cases, they are not inviolate. If the consumer benefit is strong and relevant to needs that are prepotent, one may traverse the ladder from awareness to purchase in a single leap. Kristian Palda has questioned the assumption that each step up the ladder leads to an increased probability of purchase.[19] Certainly, one can imagine situations in which Palda's criticism is valid. For example, one can clearly progress from "awareness of" to a "preference for" a Rolls-Royce with no increase in the probability of ever buying one. The person may not only lack the money, but the thought of spending over $100,000 for an automobile may violate the person's sense of propriety. This simply means that advertising often has effects on individuals who are outside the intended target market.

Aside from these exceptions, the hierarchy of effects model seems reasonably descriptive and offers a way to monitor advertising as it progresses beyond the role of providing information toward achieving its goal of translating the product concept into an appealing consumer benefit. Let us appraise each of the steps in the National Industrial Conference Board model to see how it works in practice.

AWARENESS

As a first step in the purchase process, broad awareness among relevant consumer groups is critical. Few brands are positioned to appeal to an entire market; each, on some basis, identifies a target segment to which it is directed. How much brand awareness is achieved can be measured fairly simply through market surveys of the appropriate user groups.

Awareness is often difficult to attain because it means breaking through the fog of lethargy, apathy, and distraction that surrounds consumers. In order to create awareness, the advertisement or commercial must first attract attention, and this usually requires a dramatic device. In magazine advertising, the advertiser has only a fraction of a second to arrest the attention of the reader before he flips the page. Dramatic headlines, provocative illustrations, and the ostentatious use of color are all used to attract attention. This is undoubtedly one of the reasons for the excessive use of scantily clad or provocative women in advertising illustrations, even though it is not always clear what they have to do with the product or its use.

In broadcast advertising, it is generally believed that the first five seconds of the commercial must capture the active attention of viewers. Otherwise, their minds will wander; they will flip to another channel; or they will engage in some other activity. This premium on developing attention-getting devices tests the ingenuity of advertising writers and illustrators.

Preoccupation with gaining attention can become so single-minded that inadequate thought is given to other tasks that the advertisement should perform. Thus, some brands' advertisements

---

[19]K. S. Palda, "The Hypothesis of Hierarchy of Effects: A Partial Evaluation," *Journal of Marketing Research* (February 1966): 13–24.

have achieved wide awareness, but have done little to move the consumer to the next step in the hierarchy, acceptance.

ACCEPTANCE

When a product has gained acceptance, it is seen as an alternative brand, one that might be bought if the preferred brand is not available. In some product fields where leading brands are seen as similar, gaining acceptance may be about as much as advertising alone can accomplish. In the gasoline industry, for example, it is generally recognized that brands with which consumers are familiar fall into two groups. The *golden circle group* includes brands that are considered acceptable and interchangeable. An individual will use any brand in his golden circle without concern and with equal confidence. The *off-brands group* includes those brands about which the consumer is a little suspicious and will avoid using if possible.

The level of acceptance requires greater familiarity and more information than the level of awareness. Familiarity and information are often achieved through "reason why" copy or by showing the brand in appropriate use situations. Sometimes, sheer repetition of the brand name may move it to the level of acceptance. This expensive way to gain acceptance is used because the logic of some consumers seems to be: "I've seen that brand name so often, it must be all right. If it wasn't, the manufacturer couldn't sell enough to justify its continued advertising."

Reason why copy may take many forms. It may take the form of a secret ingredient such as "the mysterious beauty fluid" in Oil of Olay that "works with your skin's own natural moisture to quickly ease away dryness, leaving your skin feeling soft and smooth." A product endorsement by a celebrity is another form of reason why copy; thus, Everynight Astringent Shampoo by Helene Curtis has Chris Evert, the tennis star, saying: "It super cleans oily hair without drying it out." It may take the form of demonstrations or simple reassurances. Whatever form it takes, reason why copy enables the consumer to make this subjective decision: "This brand is all right. I won't go too far wrong if I use it."

PREFERENCE

The goal of most advertising is to bring consumers to the point where they prefer a particular brand over all others. From the standpoint of advertising's capabilities, preference is always tentative; product purchase may result in disappointment, with the product falling back to the bottom rung of the ladder and not being repurchased. When the preference stage is reached, it is quite possible that other factors are entering into the process of product evaluation—factors such as word-of-mouth advertising, exposure to the product through friends or other social occasions, experience of users, and so on. At this point, the contribution of advertising may become severely contaminated by personal experience, experience of others, or other marketing activities.

The advertising techniques used to create preference and to promote acceptance are the same. It must be recognized that an argument or appeal that is sufficient to generate preference on the part of one consumer may only generate acceptance by another and leave a third consumer untouched.

The extent of preference can be measured by marketing research on the bases of the proportion of the target market preferring the brand and preference strength. If consumer research indicates that relatively few consumers prefer a particular brand compared to competition, the problem may lie in the physical product, brand name, packaging, pricing, service, and so on. Only when these other areas have been ruled out, may it be assumed that a new advertising approach needs to be developed. Far too often, advertising is blamed for a lack of consumer interest when the real problem lies elsewhere.

On the other hand, if a brand's share of preference is greater than its share of sales, the evidence is fairly clear that advertising is doing its job, and some other part of the marketing effort needs strengthening. For example, consumer surveys consistently revealed that 40 to 45 percent of the potential customers preferred a brand of household appliance *before* they began shopping for actual purchase. However, the brand obtained less than 30 percent of sales. Investigation indicated that lack of sales support at the retail level was the culprit. The company had neglected retail sales people in their marketing program, and it was these sales people who were switching customers to other brands. Take the case of Alka-Seltzer in the late 1960s. Frequent shifts in advertising direction did little to revitalize a sales curve that had leveled off at about 21 percent of the market. The real problem is not clear, but the brand probably had exhausted that segment of the market that was interested in an Alka-Seltzer type product. Further expansion in the upset stomach– analgesic field could only be obtained through a different product formulation aimed at a different market segment.

INTENTION TO BUY

This stage refers to the consumer's psychological commitment to purchase a particular brand. For many low priced, packaged goods, preference and intention are virtually synonymous. For more expensive items, where price is a limiting factor, intention becomes a critical stage in the buying process.

For relatively expensive products or brands, the advertising of warranties such as "five years or 50,000 miles" for an automobile may move a consumer from the preference stage to a psychological intention to buy. Or, advertising the lifetime guarantee of the J. C. Penney sealed battery may be sufficient assurance. Similarly, the safety emphasis on the advertising for steel-belted radial tires may overcome the price differential and transport the consumer from a state of preference to the committed customer state. In most instances, where intention to buy is a distinct step from preference, the advertising needs to be substantive to cause that step to be taken.

PROVOKING THE SALE

The role of advertising in provoking the final sale will differ widely, depending upon the product class. For relatively inexpensive, frequently purchased items, the development of brand preference is usually sufficient to cause trial. However, for products requiring demonstration or personal selling, such as automobiles, insurance, clothing, furniture, and carpeting, the contribution of advertising in closing the sale is usually minimal. Advertising may make the consumer receptive to a particular brand, but other marketing activities usually occupy the dominant role in closing the sale.

However, the one form of advertising that may be the determining factor in this final stage is promotional advertising that features a major price reduction. If the consumer has already formed a brand preference and made the psychological commitment to purchase sometime in the future, promotional advertising may precipitate immediate action.

It is doubtful that the hierarchy of effects concept provides a pure, unadulterated description of advertising's contribution to marketing; too many other marketing activities also enter into the process. This concept is useful because it suggests that advertising should be evaluated on the basis of that which it does best: namely, creating awareness, acceptance, and preference for a brand. However, the amount of advertising required to achieve a given level of awareness, acceptance, or preference depends on the nature of competition, strength of the product concept, and effectiveness of the advertising.

SUMMARY

Advertising is one of the more controversial areas of marketing. In this chapter, we examined four aspects of advertising: (a) its effects on the economy; (b) definitions of what advertising is; (c) the uses of advertising; and (d) its effects on consumers.

Advocates and opponents of advertising hold very different views concerning the effects of advertising on the economy. Advocates contend that advertising stimulates the GNP and contributes to a higher standard of living, provides information that enables consumers to become better buyers, lowers prices, and facilitates the introduction of new products. Opponents of advertising disagree on all of these points.

For the most part, these opposing points of view cannot be resolved through an examination of empirical evidence because such evidence is either unavailable or ambiguous. One exception is the effect of advertising in the introduction of new products. Economic and competitive analysis indicates that advertising does, in fact, facilitate the introduction of new products.

Critics of the morality of advertising argue that advertising is deceptive, creates materialistic values, makes people buy things they do not need, is often annoying and in poor taste, and results in bland, poor program content due to its commercial sponsorship of mass media. Examination of these charges indicates that they tend to be oversimplifications and do not substantiate the charge that advertising is immoral.

Different kinds of advertising can serve a variety of advertising objectives. The effectiveness of a given advertising campaign is directly dependent upon how clearly the objectives are stated. Broadly stated, the six kinds of advertising are product, sales promotion, trade, corporate, classified, and retail. All are examined in the chapter.

The goal of product advertising is to affect consumer attitudes. At any given time, however, different consumers are in various stages of product familiarity and attitude formation. Several models, referred to as hierarchy of effects models, have been devised to describe these stages. The typical steps consist of awareness, acceptance, preference, intention to buy, and provoking the sale. Although advertising may be helpful at any stage, it is generally most effective in the early stages of the progression.

REVIEW QUESTIONS

1   What are the four opposing points of view concerning the effects of advertising on the economy? What does empirical research show in response to these points of view?
2   How does the text deal with the charge that advertising creates materialistic values?
3   Distinguish between product advertising and sales promotion advertising.
4   Distinguish between product advertising and corporate advertising.
5   According to the text, why is corporate advertising often ineffective?
6   What are the two basic uses of trade advertising?
7   What is meant by retail advertising? According to the text, why isn't retail advertising a separate form of advertising?
8   Explain what is meant by "hierarchy of effects" models.
9   What are the two assumptions underlying hierarchy of effects models? Evaluate these two assumptions.
10   How do hierarchy of effects models relate to the problem of evaluating advertising?

DISCUSSION QUESTIONS

1   How do you think marketing would be affected if advertising were prohibited? Would the cost of marketing be reduced?
2   What is the primary role of advertising for each of the following products? Use the hierarchy of effects mode discussed in the chapter in formulating your answer.
    (a)   gasoline   (d)   insurance
    (b)   cake mix   (e)   expensive camera
    (c)   chewing gum   (f)   automobile
3   Select a magazine advertisement that you think is deceptive. Bring it to class. Explain why you think it is deceptive and whether the deception involved is immoral.

PROBLEM

Select a corporate advertisement. Possible sources are *Time, Newsweek, Business Week, U.S. News and World Report, Fortune,* or one of the financial magazines.

1 Identify the objectives of the advertisement.
2 Identify the consumer benefit for the audience to whom the advertisement is addressed.
3 Do you think this advertisement is a good use of company resources? Why or why not?

10
Mass Communications and Advertising

THE SQUEAK THAT WAS HEARD AROUND THE WORLD

In a time of multibillion dollar corporations and multimillion dollar advertising budgets, Wall Drug Store could hardly be considered one of the big time spenders. Yet, the proprietors of this unlikely merchandising phenomenon used a basic concept of service and hokey advertising to parlay a $3,000 investment into a $4.6 million a year enterprise. As *Time* magazine tells it:

> Only the signs and billboards along interstate 90 break the monotony. They beckon to motorists heading west toward Mount Rushmore and Yellowstone or east toward Sioux Falls and the industrial midwest. The pitch is tantalizing: BE A WALL FLOWER. HAVE YOU DUG WALL DRUG? WALL-EYED AT WALL DRUG.
>
> The signs lead to a drugstore and soda fountain three-quarters of a block long that has grown into an oasis of friendly commercial hurdy-gurdy in the middle of the sparse prairie. The Wall Drug Store in Wall, S. Dakota (pop. 800), 50 miles east of Rapid City, is a three generation family business that this year celebrates its 50th anniversary. Its standing offer of free ice water, and coffee at 5¢—as much as you can drink of both—helps attract as many as 20,000 customers on a busy summer day, maybe a million a year.
>
> The whole improbable enterprise was started in the depth of the depression by a 28-year-old Nebraska pharmacist named Ted Hustead. He had a $3,000 stake, a wife, a child of four, and the brass of a born capitalist. . .
>
> The story of how his wife Dorothy penned some doggerel ("Get a soda, get a beer, turn next corner, just as near, to Highway 16 & 14, free ice water, Wall Drug") to attract thirsty motorists has assumed Arthurian dimensions in South Dakota. Remembers Ted: "We hardly got back to the store from putting the sign up before people started turning in." Before long, billboards sprouted along the highways in every direction; someone once counted 53 along a 45 mile stretch. G.I.'s tacked up Wall Drug signs as they made their way through Europe in World War II. The same thing happened in Korea and Vietnam. The store is covered with photographs of tourists, soldiers,

and scientists displaying Wall Drug signs everywhere from Antarctica to the Taj Mahal. The drugstore has even paid for advertising in Amsterdam, Paris, and London. . . . Despite its chintzy tourist baubles, Wall Drug has a homeliness that makes customers spend with a smile. Perhaps a young Connecticut man, heading west with his new bride (but passing up the FREE COFFEE AND DOUGHNUTS TO HONEYMOONERS), puts it best: "They don't try to make a lot of money off a few people, just a little money off a lot of people."[1]

COMMUNICATIONS IS SOMETHING COMMUNICATED

According to the *American Heritage Dictionary*, one of the definitions of communications is "something communicated." Often, when we think of communications, we think of *verbal* communications. Yet, some of our most effective communications do not involve words at all. The illustrations in the Pledge advertisement (Figure 10–1) are powerful pieces of communication. Through these two pictures, the basic claim of Pledge furniture wax, i.e., a shine so brilliant that one can see one's reflection, is communicated directly and simply.

CHIVAS REGAL vs. JACK DANIEL'S

Consider the two advertisements in Figures 10–2 and 10–3—one for Chivas Regal; the other for Jack Daniel's. Both are distilled spirits; both are relatively expensive. It is obvious that these two companies have different theories about how one appeals to consumers through advertising. The Chivas Regal ad is a four color, full page, bleed advertisement showing a chain affixed to the bottle and the headline "Who could blame you?" There is no body copy. The approach is modern, sophisticated, clever, and indirect; the implication is that a bottle of Chivas Regal is to be valued.

The Jack Daniel's ad is a two-thirds page, black and white ad in a picture-caption format. It is homey, emphasizes tradition, and

[1]"In South Dakota: Buffalo Burgers and Wall Drug," *Time*, 31 August 1981, 8. Copyright © 1981 Time Inc. All rights reserved. Reprinted by permission from TIME.

"How do I get clearly more beautiful wood?"

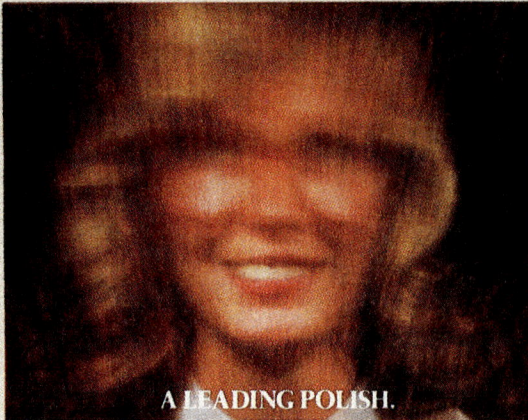

A LEADING POLISH.

PLEDGE.

Unretouched photography

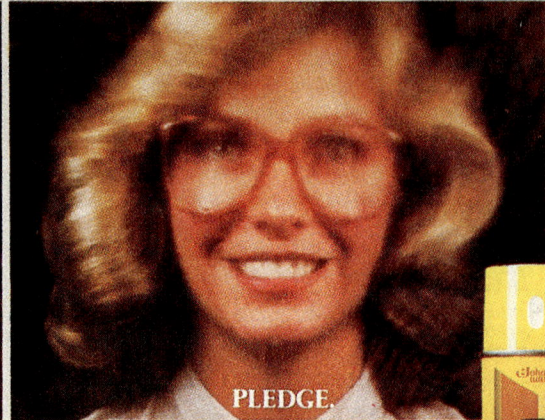

"I side with Pledge."

"My wood is special to me. So I always dust with Pledge. Other products may say they work on wood, but they just don't give my furniture the clear, beautiful shine that Pledge does. That's because Pledge is made especially for wood. And that's what my wood deserves!"

Doesn't your wood deserve Pledge?

LEMON pledge

Waxed Beauty Instantly As You Dust

©1981 S.C. Johnson & Son, Inc.

FIGURE 10–1 (Courtesy S. C. Johnson & Son, Inc.)

carries body copy which speaks of a manufacturing process (charcoal mellowing) that makes the product "uncommonly smooth." The product slogan, featured in all Jack Daniel's advertising, states "Charcoal mellowed—drop by drop."

These examples illustrate three different dimensions of mass communications. Wall Drug Store, a small drugstore on the prairies of South Dakota, generated word of mouth communications from Europe to Asia. Pledge furniture wax uses nonverbal communications in an effective advertising technique. Chivas Regal and Jack Daniel's use very different approaches to communicate with consumers. Communications! It is a complex process, achieved through many different means.

Communications is the quintessential nature of advertising. In the final analysis, all advertising effects are communications effects. As a consequence, people engaged in the development of advertising should have a thorough understanding of the process of communications.

In this chapter, we will review briefly nine aspects of mass communications and advertising: (a) the nature of communications; (b) nonverbal communications; (c) the communications process; (d) research in persuasive communications; (e) multiple channels

FIGURE 10–2 (Courtesy General
Wine & Spirits Co.)

of communications; (f) identifying advertising appeals; (g) keeping
in touch with consumers; (h) theories of advertising; and (i) selected
dimensions of advertising.

THE NATURE OF COMMUNICATIONS

Advertising is based on ideas, but it communicates these ideas
through signs—words, phrases, pictures, and actions—that give
rise to meaning. A **sign,** as it is used in communications, is merely
a stimulus, or label, that represents an object or an idea. The sign
apple, for example, means a familiar kind of fruit. The sign *run*
means a certain kind of action. Signs gain their meanings through
learning, and insofar as two people have the same learning experience they use the same signs to represent the same things. Without
common signs there can be no communication; anyone who has

If you'd like a wall poster of our distillery's founder, drop us a line.

MR. CLAYTON TOSH has more good tales about Jack Daniel than most folks can ever believe.

He'll tell you that Mr. Jack promised marriage to two girls at once in 1875; that nobody ever saw him without a coat and tie; and that he perfected a way of manufacturing his whiskey (called charcoal mellowing) that made it uncommonly smooth. Of course, there's no one living who can vouch for the first two tales. But after a sip of Jack Daniel's, most everyone goes along with the third.

CHARCOAL MELLOWED
◊
DROP
◊
BY DROP

Tennessee Whiskey • 90 Proof • Distilled and Bottled by Jack Daniel Distillery
Lem Motlow, Prop., Inc., Route 1, Lynchburg (Pop. 361), Tennessee 37352
Placed in the National Register of Historic Places by the United States Government.

FIGURE 10–3   (Courtesy Jack Daniel Distillery)

traveled in a foreign country without knowing the local language knows how awkward communications can become.

People reared within the same culture have certain common experiences, in home, school, and society at large, that facilitate their communication. Because no two people ever have an identical history of experience, even common signs may become distorted. For example, the sign *mother* has a core meaning in our culture that is shared by most people. Even this sign will have a somewhat different meaning to two people if the mother of one was loving and concerned and the mother of the other was uncaring and critical. To the first person, the sign *mother* will give rise to feelings of affection; to the other, it will trigger feelings of hostility and resentment. Since even common signs can have somewhat different meanings, communications are seldom perfect. The problems that arise are represented in Figure 10–4.

The sender of a message can communicate with the receiver of the message to the point where their fields of experience overlap. Signs that fall outside the area of shared experiences will not be understood or will be misinterpreted. Since signs may have different meanings to different people, we need to more closely examine the concept of meaning. Generally, signs have four kinds of meanings: (a) **denotative;** (b) **connotative;** (c) **structural;** and (d) **contextual.**

DENOTATIVE MEANING

Through learning we associate signs with objects, actions, and ideas. The sign *chair* denotes a particular class of objects with certain characteristics which, by common agreement, is called *chair.* Denotative meaning involves a relatively simple sign-object relationship. Words high in denotative meaning most often refer to concrete objects. The dictionary definition of a word refers, essentially, to its denotative meaning.

CONNOTATIVE MEANING

Many objects and ideas are more complex than that represented by a simple sign-object relationship. The idea or object becomes surrounded by a complex constellation of meanings so that the sign's meaning varies somewhat among different people. *Communism, socialism,* and *capitalism* all have a denotative meaning as a form of economic organization. At the same time, these words have rich connotative meanings which differ among different people and are

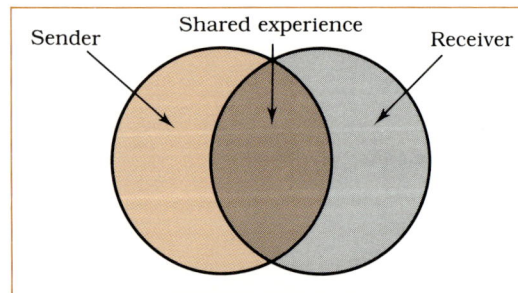

FIGURE 10–4   Fields of experience of the sender and receiver of a message. Only signs that fall within the region of shared experience will be understood.

often associated with strong feelings. Many people, for example, respond to *communism* as bad, threatening, oppressive, and undesirable. Others respond to it as good and desirable, and perceive it as a reasonable attempt to introduce rationality, equity, and justice into economic relationships. Sometimes, words that have the same denotative meaning may have somewhat different connotative meanings. For example *naked* and *nude* denotatively mean to be without clothing. Yet, connotatively, *naked* is a masculine word and *nude* is a feminine word. When great precision in communication is desired, one should try to use words that are high in denotative meaning and low in connotative meaning. Conversely, when persuasion is the object of communications, words high in connotative meaning become more important. For example, in trying to persuade a recent university graduate to come to work for a particular company, it would be more persuasive to describe the company as an *organization* rather than a *bureaucracy*. For the same reason, Cadillac dealers are urged not to refer to their used Cadillacs as *used* Cadillacs, but as *previously owned* Cadillacs.

Since the object of advertising communications is persuasion, words high in connotative meaning are its basic tools. Herein lies a danger in the communications process. Words should be chosen to complement each other. When words with noncomplementary connotative meanings are used together, confusion and ambiguity mar attempts at communication. There is generally a "right" word to express every thought, and the careless use of a single word can destroy a carefully constructed argument.

Advertising writers must be adept with words, sensitive to their nuances, and conscious of their power.

STRUCTURAL MEANING

Single words are insufficient for most communications. Normally, we need to use combinations of words to express our meanings. Syntax and grammar provide the rules for stringing words together in a meaningful relationship. These rules permit us to express complex ideas through sentences and paragraphs. The receivers of messages respond to sentences in the same way they respond to individual words. A sentence has a coherent unity if it is properly constructed.

Writers of advertising sometimes deliberately violate the rules of syntax and grammar in order to gain impact and euphony. "Winston tastes good like a cigarette should" is grammatically incorrect. It should read "Winston tastes good as a cigarette should." Yet, this grammatical violation adds force to the slogan, even though it may offend some grammarians. Violations of syntax and grammar need to be used judiciously, if at all. When syntax and grammar are used carelessly or ignorantly, the intended meaning may be lost or the reader may be confused.

CONTEXTUAL MEANING

Signs often derive their meanings from the context in which they occur—that is, from the signs that surround them. Consider the following sentences:

We crossed the river on the *bridge* north of town.

I have never played worse *bridge* in my life.

It was a difficult billiard shot. Even with the *bridge*, I could hardly reach the cue ball.

Did the dentist have to install a *bridge?*

I'm having trouble building a *bridge* between the key ideas of the presentation.

In each case the word *bridge* has a different meaning, depending upon the context of the sentence.

Context is extremely important for advertising. The meaning of a sign is often clarified and sometimes enhanced by the sentence's context. The context may be other words, a picture, an object, or an action. In the California Avocado Advisory Board ad (Figure 10–5), the headline is meaningless without the illustration. The refrigerator that carries the sign *General Electric* is a very different refrigerator from the one that carries the sign *Hickory Hollow Manufacturing Company.*

NONVERBAL COMMUNICATIONS

Thus far, we have dealt primarily with words as signs, although some of the previous examples indicate that signs can also be nonverbal. Pictures, actions, colors, and shapes are signs. The Eagle Printing Company printed the following suggestions for enhancing the appetite appeal of food illustrations.

> Orange is one of the dominant hues of high appetite appeal. The color is rich and luminous. Avoid yellow-orange. Clear yellow, however, slightly warm in tone, is savory. But again avoid the goldenrod cast (which appears rancid) and the greenish cast (which appears raw).
>
> Among the reds, use bright vermillion, suggestive of porterhouse steaks and ripe apples. Purplish reds seem "tough" and unfit for human consumption.
>
> As for greens, select clean ones, crisp and clean in quality. Avoid yellowish greens which are bilious and bluish greens which seem poisonous.
>
> Your other colors will then consist of warm browns and tans, remindful of well-cooked meats and breads. For a definitely "sweet" color choose pink. For wines and liquors choose transparent purples. This is the appetite pallette. Blues may be used to set them off, for while blue is not a good food color it does seem to suggest cleanliness and freshness.
>
> However, purples, grays, magentas, chartreuse greens, and the like are to be avoided. We would not care to "eat" them—so why should they feature any products meant for our tables?[2]

Shapes are also used for communications. Classic examples lie in the styling of automobiles, furniture, and appliances. Some shapes are heavy, bulky, and masculine; others are graceful, deli-

---

[2]Eagle Printing Company, "What Colors Look Good Enough to Eat?" No. 5, *Facts from the Research Department of the Eagle Printing Company,* 100 Sixth Avenue, New York, N.Y.

Jack and Avocado get together for a dip.

Tired of the same old chip dip? Here's an idea guaranteed to wow you. Brightly seasoned avocado dip scooped up on tasty morsels of Monterey Jack cheese. It's a natural. The mellow flavor of Jack and the nutlike taste of avocados were made for each other. So whip up the recipe and invite some friends over for a dip. They'll flip.

Guacamole (Classic Avocado Dip)
4 California avocados, mashed & pureed, 1 teaspoon seasoned salt, 2 tablespoons lemon or lime juice, 1/2 teaspoon Worcestershire, 1/8 teaspoon Tabasco, 1 medium tomato, chopped fine. Combine and chill all ingredients. Serve with cubed Monterey Jack cheese speared on picks.

CALIFORNIA MONTEREY JACK CHEESE
Manufacturing Milk Producers of California
LOVE FOOD FROM CALIFORNIA
©1973 California Avocado Advisory Board

cate, and feminine. Consider the two shapes in Figure 10–6. If you were asked to assign the term *rikrak* or *oola* to each of these shapes, you would have no trouble doing so because the sounds and appearance are more appropriate to one shape than the other.

Even something as simple as a line can be used for communication purposes. For example, McNeal notes:

Some lines are strong and decisive, some weak and timid, and still others, thin and precise. Thus, without forming any representational object, a line may still be descriptive of an idea or mood. For example, dark angular lines are generally recognized as being symbolic of strength. Smoother flowing lines symbolize femininity. Straight lines

FIGURE 10–6 Which term, *rikrak* or *oola*, applies to each of these two shapes?

convey a feeling of formalism, while kinky lines represent an informal situation.[3]

McNeal further points out that vertical lines symbolize growth and life, horizontal lines express stability and repose, and diagonal lines are symbolic of action.[4]

In addition to colors, shapes, and lines, we may also use objects, animals, and people to convey ideas and meaning. The Rock of Gibraltar, used by the Prudential Insurance Company as a trademark, is intended to convey strength and dependability. The cougar used by Mercury automobiles symbolizes power and speed. People are used in various ways by marketers: babies to suggest innocence and softness; children and teenagers to convey vitality; couples to communicate intimacy; and elderly people to communicate calmness, wisdom, and serenity.

Words, colors, lines, shapes, objects, animals, and people are all instruments that convey meaning, and all are used lavishly in marketing communications.

THE COMMUNICATIONS PROCESS

We can describe communications in a variety of ways, depending upon purpose, method, and number of persons involved. The form of communication of particular interest to advertisers is mass communications.

Effective communication takes place when the receiver of the communication perceives the message that was intended by the sender. If the message is not perceived the way it was intended, communication has failed. Mass communications are subject to failure because the lack of face to face contact between the sender and receiver eliminates or delays feedback that indicates the message is being received, misread, or ignored.

A MODEL FOR MASS COMMUNICATIONS

A mass communications model is shown in Figure 10–7. The model has eight elements: (a) sender; (b) intended message; (c) transmitted message; (d) channel; (e) received message; (f) receiver; (g) response; and (h) feedback.

---

[3]James U. McNeal, *An Introduction to Consumer Behavior* (New York: John Wiley & Sons, Inc., 1973), 102.
[4]Ibid., 103–4.

FIGURE 10–7 A mass communications model

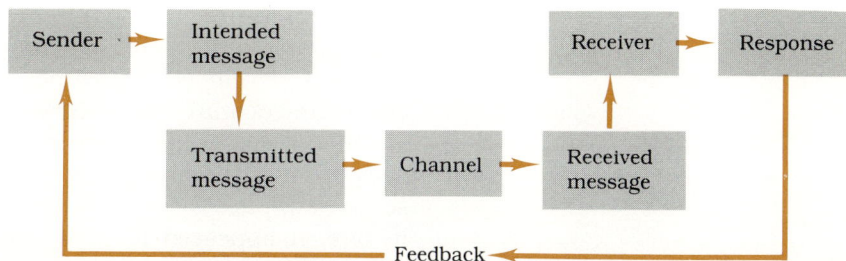

Sender → Intended message

Transmitted message → Channel → Received message

Receiver → Response

Feedback

Sender.   The sender in mass communications is the originator of the message—in this case, the advertiser of a consumer product. The purpose of the communication is to reach a particular group of consumers with a message that will predispose them to buy it. Assuming the marketing concept has been followed, this communication should not be difficult because the product has been designed with the interests of this group of consumers in mind.

Intended message.   The intended message is the product concept, including the physical and psychological attributes that are appropriate for the target market. The goal is to create a brand image that will appeal to the intended market segment.

Transmitted message.   Before the intended message can be sent, it must be put in a transmittable form that is appropriate to the channel of communication being used. If the channel is radio, the transmittable form will be sounds—words, music, and sound effects. If the channel is a magazine, the transmittable form will be visible—printed words, colors, and pictures. Message form always involves symbols that stand for thoughts the sender wishes to transmit. If sufficient care is taken in translating the intended message into the transmitted one, a reasonable correspondence between the two will probably occur. Most of us have had the experience of being unable to express an idea or describe something as precisely as we experience it. The more abstract the idea or the more personal the experience, the more difficult it is to communicate. By definition, brand concepts are abstract and personal, thereby challenging precise communication. To guard against this problem in advertising, communications specialists, such as copywriters, artists, and package designers, compose the transmitted message.

Channel.   The channel is the medium or carrier of the message. Marketing communications employ a number of channels simultaneously. Commercial media, such as radio, television, magazines, newspapers, and outdoor posters, are the most widely recognized channels of communication because they are used for advertising. However, point-of-sale material, the package, product name, and product itself are also channels. The same message must be sent over each channel used; otherwise, confusion by the receiver is inevitable.

Received message.   The received message may not be the same as the intended message because the channel influences message content. Sometimes, the channel influence is simply the result of poor message reproduction. For example, a four-color newspaper advertisement developed for Duncan Hines Chocolate Cake featured a chocolate-coconut icing. Great care was taken to obtain a photograph that conveyed appetite appeal. Unfortunately, not all newspapers are capable of high quality color reproduction. As a result, in some newspapers the cake illustration was decidedly unappetizing; in one, it appeared to be a nauseating purple lump, covered with bilious green worms.

Aside from poor message reproduction, channel character may profoundly affect the persuasiveness of the message. Early experiments in message effectiveness exposed matched groups of subjects to an identical argument about a controversial subject. One group would get the argument in the form of a personal lecture; another would hear it on the radio; a third would read it in print. Each group was tested to see what attitude changes had taken place. In experiment after experiment, the results were consistent; the face-to-face lecture was more persuasive than radio, and radio was more persuasive than print.[5] Subsequent experiments have shown that television and film are superior to radio, but still less effective than personal contact.[6]

The editorial setting of a medium may make it more appropriate for some messages than others. For example, *New Yorker* magazine's urbane, sophisticated, eastern seaboard orientation, provides quite a different environment for product advertising than does *Sunset*'s provincial, West Coast, home-service view of the world. Media analysts are acutely conscious of these editorial differences and select media compatible with the product and specific message.

Receiver. The receiver also influences the perceived message because of expectations, situational factors, or inattentiveness. For example, a division of the Bell System prepared a newspaper advertisement to encourage use of the yellow pages. The advertisement showed a worn shoe with a hole in the sole. The headline and body copy urged the consumer to save time and shoe leather by using the yellow pages to locate needed goods and services rather than engaging in wasteful, trial and error shopping. However, advertising research revealed that a large number of consumers, who only glanced at the advertisement, interpreted the worn shoe as an appeal for a rate increase. Thus, the advertisement not only failed to communicate the intended message, but also raised the delicate subject of increased telephone rates.

Response. Receivers may respond in a variety of ways to a message; they may show interest, accept, reject, question, resent, or ignore it entirely. Yet, for the one sending the message, the response is often critical and an integral part of the whole communications

---

[5]James T. Clapper, *The Effects of Mass Communications* (New York: Free Press, 1960), 106.

[6]P. M. Sandman, D. M. Rubin, and D. B. Sachsman, *Media* (Englewood Cliffs, New Jersey: Prentice-Hall, Inc., 1972), 231.

process. In marketing, a message is only effective when it gives rise to some positive response, either overt or covert.

Feedback. Feedback is the response that flows to the sender from the recipient and serves as a control mechanism for the accuracy of the communication. Ideally, feedback occurs quickly and in the form of questions requesting clarification, or evidence that the message is or is not being received. In marketing communications, feedback typically occurs in the form of letters of satisfaction or complaint, product purchase, returned merchandise, and lack of sales. Feedback, if received and properly interpreted, provides a basis for evaluating the effectiveness of the communication and making changes in the message.

Unfortunately, marketing feedback is often delayed, misleading, or ambiguous. Few consumers express their satisfactions or complaints directly to the producer, and those who do are frequently not typical of the target market. Consumers are more inclined to express satisfaction and dissatisfaction by purchasing or not purchasing the product. After all, this is the ultimate weapon of the consumer. As a measure of communications effectiveness, sales changes are often inadequate because sales may be influenced by factors other than communications, and inventories at different levels in the distribution chain may delay recognition of shifts in consumer buying practices. For these reasons, the marketer of consumer goods must initiate and maintain independent and continuing research to monitor consumer responses to various parts of the marketing program.

NOISE IN THE COMMUNICATIONS SYSTEM

Noise refers to any type of interference with the communications process. It can occur anyplace in the system. For example, the product concept may be fuzzy or ambiguous. Noise may occur because the intended message is improperly encoded, channel is distorted, channel and message are incompatible, or receiver is distracted or disinterested. In short, anything that interferes with communications is considered noise.

The difficulty of mass communications and the threat of noise within the system has led Schramm to identify conditions that are essential to communication success:

1. The message must be so designed and delivered as to gain the attention of the intended destination.
2. The message must employ signs which refer to experience common to source and destination in order to "get the meaning across."
3. The message must arouse personality needs in the destination and suggest some ways to meet these needs.
4. The message must suggest a way to meet these needs which is appropriate to the group situation in which the destination finds himself at the time he is moved to make the desired response.[7]

---

[7]Wilber Schramm, *The Process and Effects of Mass Communications* (Urbana, Illinois: University of Illinois Press, 1954), 13.

CHAPTER 10 | MASS COMMUNICATIONS AND ADVERTISING

A fifth condition should be added to the four identified by Schramm: The message should be communicated via an appropriate channel that is compatible with and reinforces the content of the message.

RESEARCH IN PERSUASIVE COMMUNICATION

The centrality of communications in human intercourse has prompted extensive empirical research on the variables that influence persuasive communications. An excellent summary of relevant studies, prepared by McGuire, appears in *The Handbook of Social Psychology*. Table 10–1 is compiled from McGuire's article and identifies some research variables that relate to the major components of the communication system—source, message, channel, and destination (receiver).

Sample findings on persuasive communications include the following observations.

SOURCE VARIABLES

Substantial evidence indicates that the source of the message has an effect on its persuasiveness.

TABLE 10–1 Variables influencing persuasive communication

Source Variables	Message Variables	Channel Factors	Receiver Variables	Destination Variables
Credibility (expertise, trustworthiness) Attractiveness (similarity to receiver, familiarity, liking) Power (control over sanctions)	Type of appeal (rational, emotional, fear) Message style (clarity, skill in presentation) Inclusions and omissions (implicit versus explicit conclusions, refuting versus ignoring opposing arguments, repetition) Order of presentation (conclusions first or last, ordering with respect to agreeability, refuting counter-arguments before or after giving supporting arguments)	Direct experience with object versus communication about it Effects of communication modality (voice only, visual only, combination of sense modalities) Media effectiveness (mass media, face-to-face communications)	Active versus passive role Demographic factors (age, sex) Personality factors (self-esteem, general susceptibility, intelligence)	Temporal decay in attitudes Factors influencing rate of decay Delayed action effects

Source: William J. McGuire, "The Nature of Attitude and Attitude Change," from Lindzey/Aronson, *The Handbook of Social Psychology*, © 1969. Addison-Wesley, Reading, MA: 172. Reprinted with permission.

Source credibility. High credibility sources cause more opinion change than low credibility ones, but do not increase learning. By contrast, neutral sources produce an intermediate amount of opinion change, but increase understanding of message content.[8] Thus, as long as the receiver knows whether the source's credibility is high or low, he or she can apparently evaluate the conclusion without having to pay much attention to the arguments.[9] For example, the advertising trade press has noted that Walter Cronkite, because of the credibility he has developed over the years as a commentator for CBS, Inc., could easily command $5 million as a product spokesman.

Similarity between source and receiver. People are more easily persuaded by sources they perceive as similar to themselves.[10] This phenomenon has been exploited through the use of ordinary people instead of professional actors or models in television commercials and print advertising. Leo Burnett, founder of the Leo Burnett Company in Chicago, is considered a pioneer in this form of advertising.

Expertise. A source's socially desirable dimensions, such as knowledge and professional attainment, increase persuasiveness. Studies have shown that these dimensions affect persuasiveness even when the area of expertise is irrelevant to the subject at hand.[11]

MESSAGE VARIABLES

Findings on message variables include rational versus emotional appeals, implicit versus explicit conclusions, and use of fear appeals.

Rational versus emotional appeals. Little evidence suggests whether logical or emotional appeals are more desirable; both can be effective.[12]

Implicit versus explicit conclusions. Persuasive messages are more effective if the source explicitly draws the conclusion rather than leaving it to the receiver. McGuire observes:

> It may well be that if the person draws the conclusion for himself he is more persuaded than if the source draws it for him; the problem is that in the usual communication situation the subject is either insufficiently intelligent or insufficiently motivated to draw the conclusion for himself, and therefore misses the point of the message to a serious extent unless the source draws the moral for him. In communication, it appears, it is not sufficient to lead the horse to water; one must also push his head underneath to get him to drink.[13]

[8]William J. McGuire, "The Nature of Attitude and Attitude Change," in *The Handbook of Social Psychology*, Vol. E, Gardner Lindzey and Elliot Aronson, eds. (Reading, Massachusetts: Addison-Wesley Publishing Co., 1964), 182.

[9]R. A. Bauer, "A Revised Model of Source Effect," Presidential address of the Division of Consumer Psychology, American Psychological Association Annual Meeting, Chicago, 1965.

[10]McGuire, "The Nature of Attitude and Attitude Change," 187.

[11]Ibid., 192.

[12]Ibid., 202.

[13]Ibid., 209.

Use of fear appeals.   Some research studies indicate that the use of fear appeals is an ineffective persuasive device; others indicate the opposite is true. Another philosophy suggests that the relationship between fear appeals and persuasion takes the form of an inverted "U". That is, neither low nor high levels of fear arousal lead to the desired response; rather, moderate levels are optimal for persuasion. Finally, additional findings indicate that the optimal level of fear arousal depends upon the desired response. For example, high fear arousal may be more effective in getting subjects to reduce their amount of smoking, but low fear arousal is more effective in getting subjects to take X rays to check the possibility of lung cancer.[14]

CHANNEL FACTORS

Although there is little empirical research to support this conclusion, McLuhan and Fiore argue that the employed medium has more impact than the message content itself.[15] Much of the research on media factors is ambiguous and inconclusive. The superiority of one medium over another is uncertain and may depend upon the subject matter of the message. For example, if demonstration is an important element in persuasion, television and film can be particularly effective. On the other hand, a complex technical argument may be more effective in print.

RECEIVER FACTORS

Research in this area is ambiguous, however, it does suggest a relationship among persuasibility, age, and sex, and one between persuasibility and the receiver's involvement with the message.

Age and sex.   Generally, maximum suggestibility to persuasion increases up to the age of eight or nine. Thereafter, it tends to decline. Some evidence indicates that females are more persuasible than males. The reason is uncertain, although there is some evidence that females pay more attention to and are better able to comprehend details than males.[16]

Involvement of the receiver.   Herbert Krugman suggests that the extent of receiver involvement influences the communications process.[17] If the receiver is highly involved, the message gives rise to a cognitive change, leading to a change in attitude and behavior. Under conditions of low involvement, the cognitive change is followed by a change in behavior with no real change in attitude. Krugman describes the low-involvement process in the following way:

> As trivia are repeatedly learned and repeatedly forgotten and then repeatedly learned a little more, it is probable that two things will happen: (1) so called "overlearning" will move some information out of short term memory and into long term memory systems, and

---

[14]Ibid., 204–5.

[15]M. McLuhan and Q. Fiore, *The Medium Is the Message* (New York: Bantum, 1967).

[16]McGuire, "The Nature of Attitude and Attitude Change," 187.

[17]Herbert E. Krugman, "The Impact of Television Advertising: Learning without Involvement," *Public Opinion Quarterly* 29 (1965): 39–56.

(2) that we will permit significant alterations in the structure of our perceptions of a brand or product but in ways which may fall short of persuasion or attitude change.[18]

In marketing, high product involvement is present when consumers have strong brand preferences, there are clearly distinguishable differences between brands, and the decision to change brands is a deliberative process. With high involvement products, the role of advertising is to provide information, and the weight or frequency of advertising is of secondary importance.

By contrast, low-involvement products are those comprised of weak brand preferences, trivial brand differences, and where product trial is the primary information source concerning product performance. Convenience products and routine purchases fall within this category. In these instances, advertising weight is more important than informational content.[19]

While some findings are unequivocal, many are controversial. Few unchallenged, simplistic statements can be made about what is or is not persuasive. Persuasion seems to be dependent upon the source, message, channel, and receiver. The relationships among these variables are not linear and defy easy descriptions. This leaves the creative team somewhat adrift in their search for scientifically supported communication principles upon which to base advertising. As a result, much of advertising's persuasion is rooted in the industry's conventional wisdom and the creative group's inherent skills rather than the laboratories of communication theorists.

MULTIPLE CHANNELS OF COMMUNICATIONS

When more than one channel of communications is employed to reach a receiver or group of receivers, extreme care must be exercised to make sure that the same message is being delivered through each channel. If different channels transmit different messages, only confusion can result.

Although our focus in discussing communications has been on advertising, it must be remembered that advertising is only one of the communication channels used to reach consumers. Indeed, broadly defined, marketing communications consists of all activities undertaken by the marketer that are visible to consumers and may have an effect upon their buying behavior.

Therefore, in addition to advertising, the product itself, product name, package, pricing, sales promotion activity, and product's retail outlets may also be considered channels of communication; they, too, are visible to consumers and thereby play a role in the communications process.

Advertising's message must be carefully coordinated with those of other visible marketing activities or consumer confusion will occur, and the effectiveness of the total marketing effort will be diminished.

---

[18]Ibid., 39–56.
[19]Thomas Robertson, "Low Commitment Consumer Behavior," *Journal of Advertising Research* (April 1976): 19–24.

IDENTIFYING ADVERTISING APPEALS

Within the framework of motivation theory (see Chapter 6), a consumer benefit is anything that will help consumers solve problems or achieve goals. For example, if a consumer is concerned about a dry skin condition, Oil of Olay or any number of other moisterizers will help solve the problem. Copy taken from an Oil of Olay package states

> Discover the secret of Oil of Olay . . . shared by women around the world. This mysterious beauty fluid works with your skin's own natural moisture to quickly ease away dryness, leaving your skin feeling soft and smooth. An abundance of pure moisture, tropical oil and emollients impart a renewed radiance and glow to your skin. Oil of Olay is remarkably fast penetrating, with no greasy after-feel. Gentle it on every morning and night to help your skin live in its own moist climate. And it's marvelous under makeup, too.

Does it work? Apparently millions of women believe that it works and solves their problem within the framework of their expectations. The product promises and delivers a consumer benefit.

Of course, dry skin is only an apparent problem. The real problem—or goal—is probably a desire for beauty or confidence in one's appearance; the elimination of dry skin is an instrumental way of achieving this goal.

The bases for all advertising promises or claims lie within the motivational structure of the individual consumer. Some needs or motivations may be universal; others may be highly idiosyncratic. Because a knowledge of consumer motivation is an integral part of marketing, advertising practitioners, as well as psychologists, have sought to identify a list of basic motivations or needs that will enable them to understand the apparent vagaries of consumer behavior.

Attempts have been made to draw up a list of basic needs that would provide guidance to understanding and influencing behavior. Melvin S. Hattwick, a psychologist, spent a number of years in the advertising field with BBDO and Needham, Louis and Brorby, Inc. In 1950 Hattwick wrote a book titled *How to Use Psychology for Better Advertising,* and he listed eight basic wants that characterize consumer behavior: (a) food and drink, (b) comfort, (c) freedom from fear and danger, (d) superiority, (e) companionship of the opposite sex, (f) welfare of loved ones, (g) social approval, and (h) a long life.[20] In addition to these basic appeals, Hattwick identified a number of secondary appeals that are learned or acquired and not as powerful as the basic appeals. These secondary appeals included such things as: bargains, information and education, cleanliness, efficiency, convenience, dependability and quality, style and beauty, economy and profit, and curiosity.

Victor Schwab offers a somewhat longer list which is divided into four major divisions.

> People want to *gain* . . .
> (1) Health, (2) Time, (3) Money, (4) Popularity, (5) Improved appearance, (6) Security in old age, (7) Praise from others,

---

[20]Melvin S. Hattwick, *How to Use Psychology for Better Advertising* (New York: Prentice-Hall, Inc., 1950), 89.

(8) Comfort, (9) Leisure, (10) Self-confidence, (11) Personal prestige.
They want to *be* . . .
(1) Good parents, (2) Sociable, hospitable, (3) Up-to-date,
(4) Creative, (5) Proud of their possessions, (6) Influential over
others, (7) Gregarious, (8) Efficient, (9) "First" in things,
(10) Recognized as authorities.
They want to *do* . . .
(1) Express their personalities, (2) Resist domination by others,
(3) Satisfy their curiosity, (4) Emulate the admirable, (5) Appreciate
beauty, (6) Acquire or collect things, (7) Win others' affection,
(8) Improve themselves generally.
They want to *save* . . .
(1) Time, (2) Money, (3) Work, (4) Discomfort, (5) Worry,
(6) Doubts, (7) Risks, (8) Personal embarrassment.[21]

While he was executive vice-president of a major advertising agency, Charles F. Adams drew up a much shorter list of advertising appeals. His list and comments about the importance of having convictions concerning consumer motivation follow.

1. *First, the Promise of Economy and Greater Financial Ease.* This does not necessarily imply cheapness, but rather a sound purchase and excellent value received for the money spent. And, of course, it embraces freedom from service and maintenance. The dependability of the product is also of great importance.
2. *Second, the Promise of Self-improvement.* Everyone wants to be liked, if not admired. Anything you can tell the prospect about what your product will do to enhance his image in his own eyes or in the eyes of others and add to his community standing and prestige should have a telling effect.
3. *Third, the Promise of Self-gratification.* This concerns the creature comforts of life, health, the satisfaction of hunger, bodily comfort, relief from physical labor and effort. Obviously any appeal to these needs will be soundly based.
4. *Fourth, the Promise of Increased Family Happiness.* Anything that will add new zest to living, a spirit of togetherness for the people the prospect loves and needs, will put your presentation on solid ground.

My own list of appeals has stood me in good stead over the years, but whatever list the admaker prefers, he should at least *have* one. If he does not, he should then either create one of his own or borrow someone else's. For if his advertisements or commercials do not appeal in some way to at least one of these mainsprings of human action, then they will probably not sell anything. And it is also true that no amount of semantic dexterity or graphics ingenuity can take the place of such an appeal.

I have gone through this brief explanation for a very definite purpose. For it is my belief that modern admakers are coming more and more to rely on their mechanical and technical skills, and less and less on their understanding of what sells things.[22]

---

[21]Specified excerpt from p. 47 in *How to Write a Good Advertisement,* by Victor O. Schwab. Copyright © 1962 by Victor O. Schwab. Reprinted by permission of Harper & Row, Publishers, Inc.

[22]Charles F. Adams, *Common Sense in Advertising* (New York: McGraw-Hill, 1965), 70–72.

Other successful admakers will have other lists; some items will be the same, some different. There is no magic in any particular list of consumer motivations. The lists simply imply that the admakers have some understanding and convictions about consumer motivations. Without this understanding and conviction, there is little chance that effective advertising will be written. The successful admaker never loses sight of what people worry, think, and dream about because that's what produces effective advertising.

KEEPING IN TOUCH WITH CONSUMERS

In Chapter 6, reference was made to Abraham Maslow and his contention that human needs are insatiable; as fast as one set of needs is satisfied, another set of needs arises. Changing economic conditions and societal values may give certain needs greater prepotency at one time and other needs greater prepotency at another period. For example, needs of security and economy may become more important in times of social and economic stress. Similarly, the women's movement may change many consumer benefits to which women will respond. As more women enter the work force, opportunities for broader participation in society increase, and sexual freedom becomes more explicit, traditional appeals to women consumers may have to be modified if advertising effectiveness is to be maintained.

Most successful copywriters are good at writing advertisements for the particular kinds of people that they themselves are. As copywriters become more successful, they go through a changing process called **psychological mobility.** Higher income and a different standard of living start to insulate them from the consumers for whom they are writing. It is difficult to write about bargain basement sales with understanding if you buy all of your clothes at Brooks Brothers or Saks Fifth Avenue. You quickly lose empathy for lunch box dining when you become accustomed to martini lunches at "21" or the Four Seasons. It's a different world. An admaker can try to keep pace with target consumer groups by reading research findings, but the facts and figures fail to capture real life experience. As a consequence, most successful advertising writers seek other methods of keeping in touch with the pulse of the market. A copywriter may read Ann Landers' column in the daily newspapers, devote some leisure time working at a check out counter in a supermarket, or conduct personal interviews on his or her assigned products. Advertising writers often attend group interviewing sessions conducted by the agency research department in order to get the firsthand experience of listening to consumers express their likes and dislikes, feelings and frustrations, and expectations and disappointments.

Consumer motivation is the fuel that fires successful advertising, and the search for viable product concepts and advertising appeals is an endless preoccupation of successful advertising practitioners.

THEORIES OF ADVERTISING

Advertising, unlike its associated disciplines of economics and marketing, has shown little interest in theory. This may be because of a lack of academic traditions, the success or failure of an advertising campaign being so confounded by uncontrollable variables that experimentation is difficult, or because those who are most deeply involved in advertising are less concerned with discovering abstract truths than in gaining short-term, competitive advantages. Whatever the reason, one can review texts on advertising and never encounter the word **theory.**

Nonetheless, theory does exist in advertising. In this section, we will examine five theories, often referred to as *philosophies* of advertising. Each theory is associated with a successful agency, and each grew out of that agency's experience. Ted Bates Advertising developed the concept of U.S.P.; Ogilvy, Benson, and Mather promoted image advertising; Norman, Craig, and Kummel emphasized empathy; Doyle Dane Bernbach, Inc., stresses execution; and the Leo Burnett Company focuses on inherent drama.

THE UNIQUE SELLING PROPOSITION

The **Unique Selling Proposition (U.S.P.)** is a unique difference in a product or its use that distinguishes it from competition. It is an identifiable consumer benefit. According to Rosser Reeves, there are three criteria for a successful U.S.P.:[23]

1 It requires a specific promise that if consumers buy a particular product, they will get a specific benefit.
2 The U.S.P. must be unique in the sense that the competition is not using the same idea. Ideally, the product should have a unique characteristic that is not possessed by competitive products. However, it may be a preempted claim—a claim that could, but has not been, used by competitive products. An example is the Wonder Bread statement "Wonder Bread helps build strong bodies 12 ways." Any enriched bread could have made that claim, but none had done so until Wonder Bread preempted the claim as its own.
3 The Unique Selling Proposition must sell. It must be a benefit that is important to consumers, not something trivial that consumers don't care about.

The U.S.P. may be stated directly or implied. For example, the Wonder Bread U.S.P. is a direct, clear statement. On the other hand, the highly successful Toni campaign line "Which twin has the Toni?" implies that a Toni permanent looks like natural hair without saying so directly. In fact, Reeves suggests, words may not be necessary as long as the U.S.P. can be projected without them.

Figure 10–8 is an excellent example of Ted Bates Advertising's use of U.S.P. This campaign helped Colgate earn a 50 percent share of the toothpaste market. Colgate's dominant position was finally overthrown by Crest's even stronger U.S.P. "Look Mom . . . no cavities!"

The effectiveness and logic of a strong Unique Selling Proposition is undeniable. Unfortunately, the Federal Trade Commission (FTC) demands that specific claims be supported by scientific research. The Bates agency has spent millions of dollars in clinical and laboratory tests attempting to provide scientific evidence for product

[23]Rosser Reeves, *Reality in Advertising* (New York: Alfred A. Knopf, 1961), 69.

CHAPTER 10 | MASS COMMUNICATIONS AND ADVERTISING

FIGURE 10–8 (Courtesy Colgate-Palmolive Co.)

Brush Your Teeth with Colgate's...
Brush Bad Breath Away!

And Colgate's with GARDOL Fights Decay All Day, Too!

Colgate Dental Cream with Gardol stops mouth odor all day for most people . . . with just one brushing! Gives you that fresh-clean feeling that comes from brushing your teeth with Colgate Dental Cream.

And unlike other leading toothpastes,* Colgate's contains Gardol to form an invisible, protective shield around your teeth that fights tooth decay all day . . . with just one brushing!

Gardol's invisible shield fights tooth decay all day . . . with just one brushing.

GARDOL IS COLGATE'S TRADE-MARK FOR SODIUM N-LAUROYL SARCOSINATE.

COLGATE DENTAL CREAM with GARDOL

*THE TOP THREE BRANDS AFTER COLGATE'S.

Colgate's With Gardol CLEANS YOUR BREATH WHILE IT CLEANS YOUR TEETH

claims. In the 1970s, the problem became even more difficult because the FTC ruled that it wasn't enough for a claim to be literally true. The claim also had to make a significant difference in why the consumer should use it; significance is often hard to demonstrate. Further, many brands have foundered in their U.S.P. attempts by touting a unique difference that was trivial in the eyes of consumers.

IMAGE ADVERTISING

David Ogilvy of Ogilvy, Benson, and Mather is often considered the father of **image advertising.** Ogilvy believes that one learns to write great advertising by studying great advertisements and picking the brains of the men and women who wrote them. However, his concept of image advertising is a major departure from the U.S.P. espoused by Rosser Reeves. According to Martin Mayer:

> Few disagreements in any business have been so thoroughly thrashed out as the conflict in viewpoint between Ogilvy and Reeves. They have been brothers-in-law, and over the years have seen a good deal of each other socially. Each regards the other as a great personal salesman; each shakes his head over the way the other wastes his clients' money on bad advertising. When they talk about each other, however, it must be understood they are playing a private game, the rules of which are known to them alone. Competitive with each other both personally and professionally, they conduct their competition within the framework of a mutual admiration society.[24]

In speaking of Reeves, Ogilvy says: "He taught me more about advertising than anybody I've ever known; the pity of it is that I couldn't teach him anything." Scenting a battle, Reeves replies, "If we ever get out of packaged goods and into luxury items, I'll be glad to sit at David's feet and listen."[25]

In describing his theory of advertising, Ogilvy says:

> Every advertisement should be thought of as a contribution to the complex symbol which is the *brand image.* If you take that long view, a great many day-to-day problems solve themselves.
>
> How do you decide what kind of image to build? There is no short answer. Research cannot help you much here. You have actually got to use judgment. (I notice increasing reluctance on the part of marketing executives to use judgment; they are coming to rely too much on research, and they use it as a drunkard uses a lamp post, for support rather than for illumination.)
>
> Most manufacturers are reluctant to accept any *limitation* on the image of their brand. They want it to be all things to all people. They want their brand to be a male brand *and* a female brand. An upper-crust brand *and* a plebian brand. They generally end up with a brand which has no personality of any kind, a wishy-washy neuter. No capon ever rules the roost.
>
> Ninety-five percent of all the campaigns now in circulation are being created without any reference to such long-term considerations. They are being created *ad hoc.* Hence the lack of any consistent image from one year to another. . . .
>
> It takes uncommon guts to stick to one style in the face of all the pressures to "come up with something new" every six months. It is tragically easy to be stampeded into change. But golden rewards await the advertiser who has the brains to create a coherent image and the stability to stick with it over a long period. As examples, I cite Campbell Soup, Ivory Soap, Esso, Betty Crocker, and Guinness Stout (in England). The men who have been responsible for the advertising of these hardy perenials have understood that every advertisement, every radio program, every TV commercial is not a one-time shot, but a long-term investment in the total personality of

---

24Martin Mayer, *Madison Avenue U.S.A.* (New York: Harper & Brothers, Publishers, 1958), 54. Reprinted by permission of Curtis Brown, Ltd. Copyright © 1958 by Martin Praeger Mayer.

25Ibid., 55.

their brands. They have presented a consistent image to the world, and grown rich in the process.[26]

Ogilvy's best work has been done in the area of social products where prestige is important. As Ogilvy says, "It pays to give your brand a *first-class ticket* through life. People don't like to be seen consuming products which their friends regard as third-class."[27]

Figure 10–9 is an early Ogilvy ad that is generally recognized as both a classic and a triumph for the image school of advertising.

EMPATHY ADVERTISING

Norman B. Norman of Norman, Craig, and Kummel rejected both the U.S.P. and image approaches. For Norman, the secret of good advertising is **empathy**—the real, unconscious reason people buy. Trained as a social scientist, Norman's orientation is Freudian. His goal is to ". . . involve customers with the advertised products at the deepest level of their beings. . . ."[28] His theory of advertising is summed up in the following quotation:

> Why does a man use a cologne? To be sexy, of course. Sportsman toiletries came to us; they were using fishing rods in their ads to show they appealed to the outdoor type. What good is that? That girl we gave them has been one of the highest rating ads since it first appeared. Take Veto deodorant. Of *course* it should stop perspiration, people *expect* a deodorant to stop perspiration, the way they expect bread to be fresh. Why advertise what people expect? We gave them a slogan with empathy—"Because You Are the Very Air He Breathes." That got at the heart of the matter.[29]

The Maidenform brassiere ads in the mid-1950s are a classic example of Norman's work (Figure 10–10). Research by a rival agency on the Maidenform ads indicated that housewives were shocked by the ads. "It combines dress and undress. She would be decenter if she were entirely in her underwear."[30] Kay Daly, a copy chief for Norman, Craig, and Kummel, was delighted with these findings. "Housewives," she said, "*should* think those ads are shocking. That's the point."[31]

Many of Norman's most successful advertisements have been in the cosmetics and lingerie fields where the real reasons for purchase are often sexual. Nonetheless, the approach has been applied effectively in other fields. A Norman campaign for Ronson lighters was built upon motivational research findings that indicated flame was a sexual symbol; a campaign for Pabst beer was built around the headline "Pabst makes it perfect," emphasizing the leisure time significance of beer drinking.[32]

---

[26]David Ogilvy, from *Confessions of An Advertising Man* (New York: Atheneum, 1963), 103. Copyright © 1963 by David Ogilvy Trustee. Reprinted with the permission of Atheneum Publishers.

[27]Mayer, *Madison Avenue U.S.A.*, 57.

[28]Ibid., 60.

[29]Ibid., 59.

[30]Ibid., 60.

[31]Ibid., 60.

[32]Ibid., 60.

EXECUTION

For William Bernbach of Doyle Dane Bernbach, Inc., execution is the key to effective advertising. Robert Glatzer observes:

> Perhaps Bernbach's greatest contribution, even more than his individual campaigns, was his recognition that, to the consumer, advertising is as much a part of a product's makeup as its chemical composition. "Businesses are similar, products are similar. What's left is my ability to make the consumer feel something about my product. *Execution becomes content.* You have to say the right things so that people feel it in the gut."[33]

---

[33]Robert Glatzer, *The New Advertising* (New York: The Citadel Press, 1970), 18. Copyright © 1970 by Robert Glatzer. Published by Citadel Press, a division of Lyle Stuart, Inc.

FIGURE 10–10 (Courtesy Maidenform Brassiere Co., Inc.)

I dreamed
I played chess in my maidenform bra

I'm the darling of the chess-set. Pawns, knights, even kings watch my every move. For whether I'm the White Queen or the Black, I rule the board in my Maidenform bra. The dream of a bra: *new* Concerto* Wunderwire, the bra with the deep, deep dress-up plunge. Wired beneath the cups in a wonderful "W"-shape that never pinches or presses, just caresses. Purest white or blackest black in delicate nylon lace. A, B, C and D sizes . . . 5.95. *REG. U. S. PAT. OFF. ©MAIDEN FORM BRASSIERE CO., INC., N. Y. 16, N. Y.

A key concept in Bernbach's theory of advertising is being different.

> Why . . . should anyone look at your ad? The reader doesn't buy his magazine or tune in his radio and TV to see and hear what you have to say . . . What is the use of saying all the right things in the world if nobody is going to read them? And, believe me, nobody is going to read them if they are not said with freshness, originality, and imagination . . . if they are not, if you will, said "different."[34]

[34]Mayer, *Madison Avenue U.S.A.*, 66.

Bernbach believes that every advertisement should have a big idea behind it, and he will search ceaselessly for that idea. After the idea has been found, it must be said in a way that is memorable. Certainly, Bernbach has developed some of the more memorable campaigns in modern advertising history; Volkswagen, Polaroid, Orhbach's, El Al Airlines, and Max Factor are only a few. Figure 10–11, developed for a Jewish bakery in New York that had fallen on evil times and was trying to build its sales by broadening its appeal to a gentile audience, is an excellent example of Bernbach's work.

One danger in the execution is content theory of advertising is that execution or technique may take precedence over the idea be-

FIGURE 10–11 (From *The New Advertising* by Robert Glatzer. Copyright © 1970 by Robert Glatzer. Published by Citadel Press, a division of Lyle Stuart, Inc.)

You don't have
to be Jewish

to love Levy's
real Jewish Rye

hind the advertisement, and one tries to be different purely for the sake of being different. This problem is most prevalent when creative people who are less talented and diligent than William Bernbach develop advertising that is neither memorable nor effective.

INHERENT DRAMA

Leo Burnett, founder of the Chicago-based Leo Burnett Company, believed in **inherent drama advertising**. He thought every product possessed inherent drama.

> Of course we, over and over again, stress this so-called inherent drama of things because there is usually something there, almost always something there, if you can find the thing about that product that keeps it in the market place. There must be something about it that made the manufacturer make it in the first place. Something about it that makes people continue to buy it . . . capturing that, and then taking that thing—whatever it is—and making the thing itself arresting rather than relying on tricks to do it.[35]

The concept of inherent drama is more difficult to explain than the other advertising theories, and it is sometimes difficult to distinguish from them. Thus, the Marlboro Country advertisement, created by Burnett, looks surprisingly like the image advertising of Ogilvy. Nonetheless, much of Burnett's distinctive advertising involves romanticizing and personalizing the product. Examples include: Betty Crocker, created by Burnett for General Foods; Charlie the Tuna; Morris the Cat; the Pillsbury doughboy; Tony the Tiger; the Maytag repairman, "the loneliest man in town"; Allstate Insurance's "You're in good hands with Allstate"; the Keebler elves; and the Jolly Green Giant in "The Valley of the Jolly Green Giant." Figure 10–12 is an outstanding example of inherent drama for an undramatic product. "Harvested by Moonlight" is much more romantic than "packed fresh" or some other such mundane phrase.

None of the advertising approaches discussed in the foregoing material were originated by the associated agencies, but these agencies articulated them as distinct theories of advertising and thereby focused the attention of the advertising industry on formalized concepts of persuasion.

No one approach is equally appropriate to all products under all competitive conditions. Other agencies have adopted different devices for attracting clients, such as total marketing (McCann-Erickson), thorough research (Compton), and corporate experience (J. Walter Thompson). Almost every agency will adopt new ideas that capture the imagination or appear successful. Perhaps the case is best summed up by an officer of BBDO who suggested, tongue-in-cheek: "You can always tell an Ogilvy ad or a Bates ad, but you can't spot a BBDO ad, because we'll steal from everybody."[36]

---

[35]Reprinted with permission from *The Art of Writing Advertising* by Deňis Higgins. Published by Crain Books division of Crain Communications, Inc. Copyright © 1965 by Advertising Publications, Inc., Chicago.

[36]Mayer, *Madison Avenue U.S.A.*, 70.

Harvested in the Moonlight

Whether it's day or night, Green Giant Peas are picked at the fleeting moment of perfect flavor—less than three hours from field to can

Typical night scene at pea viner station in the Land of the Green Giant.

NATURE doesn't punch a time clock. "The fleeting moment of perfection" in the life of Green Giant Peas may come at 9 o'clock in the morning or 11:30 at night. Two or three hours can make a real difference in flavor and tenderness. If the "fleeting moment" comes at 12 midnight we are out to harvest them under the silvery moon or even in the drizzling rain.

Less than three hours later they are sealed in tins ready for your table.

Better to begin with because they're packed from a rare and exclusive breed, harvested at the very peak of their bursting young plumpness, no wonder Green Giant Peas taste so much better.

The new crop is now at your grocer's.

Green Giant Brand Peas are packed only by Minnesota Valley Canning Co. of Le Sueur, Minnesota, and Fine Foods of Canada, Ltd., Toronto, Ontario. Also packers of Niblets Brand Corn, Niblet-Ears Brand Corn (corn-on-the-cob in a can) and Del Maiz Brand Cream Style Corn.

He is a vegetable expert—this Green Giant. Look for him on the next can of peas you buy and be sure of a new thrill in garden peas.

Green Giant Peas

GREEN GIANT GREAT BIG TENDER SWEET PEAS

SELECTED DIMENSIONS OF ADVERTISING

Other important dimensions of advertising are: (a) believability; (b) liking versus disliking; and (c) poor taste.

BELIEVABILITY

Believability is a complex idea. John Maloney makes a sharp distinction between two types of nonbelief, which he refers to as *disbelief* (outright rejection) and *curiosity*. A consumer's statement that an advertising claim is "hard to believe" may mean two different things: "I do not believe that, and I won't try the brand" (disbelief); or "That's hard to believe, but I think I'll try the brand to see if it is true" (curiosity). Maloney's survey indicated that housewives who found an advertising claim "hard to believe" were just as willing to try a brand as those who found the claim "easy to believe." Consequently, Maloney concluded that absolute believability is not an essential ingredient of effective advertising.[37]

This conclusion is consistent with the use of fantasy in advertising. For example, no one believes that a white knight charging around on a white horse and pointing a white lance at a bunch of dirty kids will make them sparkling white. Yet, Ajax's "white knight" advertising was extremely successful. The use of fantasy as a device for overstating claims is a legitimate tool. Even the courts have conceded that fantasy that exceeds the bounds of credibility does not constitute false and misleading advertising.

LIKING vs. DISLIKING

A frequently raised question in advertising is whether advertising itself must be liked in order to be effective. Few advertising writers deliberately attempt to write advertising that consumers dislike, but they sometimes use strident claims, poor taste, or a technique that offends some group of consumers.

The problem of "liking" is a difficult one because the people who are most vocal in their dislike of a particular advertisement are often not the people for whom the advertisement was written. For example, many male college students are vociferously critical of detergent advertising, perceiving it as dull, farfetched, and trivial. However, detergent advertising is written for housewives who are inundated with dirty children, husbands, clothes, linens, and dishes. Further, the "slice of life" technique that is often used in such advertising is not taken from the lives of college students, but from the lives of housewives. As another example, advertisements are often criticized because women are cast in stereotyped roles. Such criticisms are generally valid. However, many women are not offended by these stereotypes and respond positively to them.

Little hard data exists on whether ads that are liked are more effective than those that are not because there is little agreement on how one measures the effectiveness of advertising. However, Maurice Kelly, while vice-president of marketing and planning for Eastern Airlines, stated the following opinion.

> Noisy promotions alienate the consumer. . . . The public today wants to be persuaded softly, not rudely; to be coaxed, not commanded. They're tired of shouting.[38]

On the other hand, Draper Daniels, basing his opinion on thirty years in the advertising business, states:

1. The consumer tends to prefer advertising that does *not* make her remember the name of the product or make her want to buy it.
2. If there is any correlation between how consumers feel about advertising and sales power of advertising, it would appear to

---

[37]John C. Maloney, "Curiosity versus Disbelief in Advertising," *Journal of Advertising Research* (June 1962): 2–8.
[38]"They're Tired of Shouting," *Advertising Age,* 13 April 1970, 3.

indicate that advertising about which consumers most often complain is the advertising most likely to sell them.

3. While highly offensive advertising is frequently highly effective, it is also largely responsible for the rise of Consumerism and the trend toward more stringent government regulation of advertising.[39]

One research study, reported by Treasure and Joyce, used the percentage shift in brand preference before and after exposure to commercials as a measure of effectiveness. The study found that:

1 Specific commercials that are especially well liked or especially disliked are not substantially different in effectiveness.

2 Adjective choices used to describe commercials with high liking scores clustered around entertainment values. Adjectives used to describe highly effective commercials focused more on creative and communication values. This suggests that liking and effectiveness are *not* the same thing.[40]

Perhaps the most balanced view is that suggested by David Ogilvy. "A good advertisement," he says, "is one which sells the product *without drawing attention to* itself. It should rivet the reader's attention on the product. Instead of saying, 'What a clever advertisement,' the reader says, 'I never knew *that* before. I must try this product.' "[41] According to this point of view, the advertisement that is doing its job properly stays in the background, neither pleasing nor offending.

TASTELESS ADVERTISING

Young writers will always face the temptation to shock people in order to gain their attention. Further, it is probably impossible to write anything that will not be offensive to someone, somewhere. Nonetheless, the temptation to shock or offend should be avoided. After all, advertising exists and will continue to exist at the sufferance of the public. The use of tactics that violate good taste is also an open invitation to further government regulation. Fairfax Cone, a respected advertising practitioner, deplores "tastelessness in advertising" and suggests that there *must* be a better way to present the product.[42] In the following editorial, *Advertising Age* echoes this point of view.

Shock: A Creative Short-cut

The double entendre is a perennial industry problem, one that will from time to time belch forth its bad taste and blanket the industry. We see evidence of this each week as readers send us what are called "Ads we can do without," usually ads that play off anatomical features or sexual activities.

---

[39]Draper Daniels, *Giants, Pigmies and Other Advertising People* (Chicago: Crain Communications, Inc., 1974), 252–53.

[40]John Treasure and Timothy Joyce, "As Others See Us," Occasional Paper 17, Institute of Practitioners in *Advertising*, London, 1967.

[41]Ogilvy, *Confessions of An Advertising Man*, 90.

[42]Fairfax Cone, *With All Its Faults* (Boston: Little Brown and Co., 1969), 304.

We recall the commotion that greeted National Airlines' "Fly me!" campaign a few years ago, and the eyebrow-lifting that occurred when the "My men wear English Leather or they wear nothing at all" campaign broke. More recently, we've had the "Flick your Bic" campaign. Such efforts, obviously in questionable taste, nevertheless managed to link product or service to a fresh slogan and thereby earned grudging recognition in some quarters as hard-working creative solutions to marketing problems.

How, then, does one justify the tv commercial for Speidel's new digital watches? Speidel has a prospective groom telling his bride-to-be, "Honey, this is the day. Today, I'm going all the way." The future bride registers shock, unaware that he's only talking about the Speidel watch and watchstrap he has bought. The theme then becomes, "Speidel goes all the way," thus linking Speidel to a phrase that already draws snickers from every boastful adolescent. By attaching its brand name to that expression, Speidel hopes to gain instant recognition and identification for the new entry. Where the budget is weak, the competition strong, and time short, the temptation is to treat the creative short-cut as a creative solution; too bad creative people can't make their talents transcend such temptation.[43]

SUMMARY

Advertising is based on ideas communicated through words, phrases, pictures, and actions that are called signs. Since signs gain their meanings through learning, two people with the same learning experiences will use the same signs to mean the same things. Signs that fall outside the area of shared experience will be misunderstood or misinterpreted. Four kinds of meanings associated with signs are denotative, connotative, structural, and contextual. Although we tend to think of signs in terms of words, signs can be nonverbal, such as colors, shapes, lines, people, animals, and actions.

Communication takes place when the receiver of the communication perceives the message intended by the sender. The process of communications can be broken down into a series of steps: sender, intended message, transmitted message, channel, received message, receiver, response, and feedback. Noise refers to anything that interferes with the communication process; it can occur at any step in the system.

Research on persuasive communications has focused on areas such as source, message, channel, and receiver variables. While some of the research findings have been unequivocal, much of the research is ambiguous.

Marketing communications involves simultaneous communications through a number of channels. Each visible marketing activity—the product itself, brand name, package, price, advertising and promotion, and place of sale—represents channels marketers use to communicate with consumers. Consumer confusion will result if each channel does not transmit the same message.

Since a key role of advertising is to translate the product concept into a consumer benefit, the copywriter needs to understand what is meant by a consumer benefit. Basically, it is anything that

[43]"Shock: A Creative Short-cut," p. 10. Reprinted with permission from the November 28, 1977 issue of *Advertising Age*. Copyright © 1977 by Crain Communications Inc.

will help consumers solve problems and achieve goals. The basis of all consumer benefits lies in the motivational structure of the individual consumer. Attempts have been made to draw up a list of basic consumer needs, but none is wholly satisfactory. Nonetheless, successful advertising practitioners usually have a list containing research information that might persuade consumers to purchase products.

Although the advertising industry has shown little interest in theory, certain theories of advertising are broadly recognized, including: (a) Unique Selling Proposition; (b) image advertising; (c) empathy advertising; (d) execution advertising; and (e) inherent drama. Each theory has been associated with a particular advertising agency; while each has value, none is universally applicable to all products in all competitive situations.

Other dimensions of advertising, such as believability, liking versus disliking, and poor taste, are also important. Believability is a complex concept that may take the form of active disbelief or curiosity. The second form of disbelief is no barrier to product trial. Liking or disliking advertisements has no apparent relationship to advertising effectiveness. However, a good advertisement is probably one that calls attention to the product rather than to itself. Tasteless advertising is a perennial industry problem. Too often, advertising writers use shock to call attention to their products rather than using their talents to transcend this temptation.

REVIEW QUESTIONS

1 Explain what is meant by signs and shared experience in communications.
2 Distinguish among denotative, connotative, structural, and contextual meaning.
3 Explain what is meant by noise in the communications process. In which steps of the process does it occur?
4 Identify the essential conditions for successful communications.
5 Identify the channels of communications employed in marketing. What are the implications of using multiple channels?
6 What are the essential conditions for a successful U.S.P.?
7 What are some of the problems involved in using a U.S.P.?
8 What is meant by: (a) image advertising; (b) empathy advertising; (c) execution advertising; and (d) inherent drama?
9 Discuss the concept of believability in advertising.
10 Discuss the concept of liking versus disliking in advertising.

DISCUSSION QUESTIONS

1 Distinguish between the denotative and connotative meanings of the following signs: capitalism, communism, labor union, Michelob, welfare, Cadillac, bureaucracy, and advertising.
2 Select a magazine advertisement and bring it to class. In what ways have nonverbal signs been used to communicate with consumers?

3   The text lists the basic motivational appeals that have been suggested by Melvin S. Hattwick, Victor Schwab, and Charles F. Adams. Draw up a list of five basic appeals that you think are most important.

PROBLEM

Go through a consumer magazine and select advertisements that represent each of the five theories of advertising discussed in the text: (a) U.S.P.; (b) image; (c) empathy; (d) execution; and (e) inherent drama. Bring the advertisements to class and explain why you selected these particular advertisements.

11
Advertising Creativity— the Preparation

VARIETY IN ADVERTISING

CONTAC

Contac was introduced into the market in September, 1961, at the beginning of the cold season. In three months, it was being distributed in 90 percent of all United States drugstores. The product concept behind Contac was a "time pill" consisting of hundreds of tiny pills that were designed to dissolve at different rates, providing continuous medication. The name, a contraction of "continuous action," was selected to reinforce the product concept. To gain druggists' support, Contac's initial distribution was restricted to drugstores because discount houses and food stores were pirating sales from drugstores by selling competitive products at discount prices. The advertising was clear, straightforward, and concise; it consisted of a dominant headline and short body copy (Figure 11–1). Note the body copy references to "600 tiny 'time pills'," "keep on working up to 12 hours," and "get Contac at your pharmacy." The package is the only illustration in the advertisement, reinforcing the product concept by prominently featuring a close up of a capsule with hundreds of tiny time pills.

WOLFSCHMIDT

The Wolfschmidt advertisement (Figure 11–2) is very different in format from the Contac ad. Wolfschmidt used a dominant illustration that conveys the product image of an upper class, prestige product. Its headline and body copy refer to a historic time and associate the product with royalty, luxurious living, and dignity. Reference is made to a tradition of excellence which "elevated it to special appointment to his Majesty the Czar and the Imperial Romanov Court."

LYSOL SPRAY DISINFECTANT

Consider the Lysol Spray ad (Figure 11–3). The headline, illustrations, and body copy tell the same story. The headline announces

Here comes Daddy with a cold for everybody.

A few sneezes here and there and suddenly your whole family could be sharing Daddy's cold. Which is good reason for keeping Contac® on hand. Because a single Contac capsule works fast to help check your sneezes, stop your sniffles, and clear your stuffy nose. And the 600 tiny "time pills" inside keep on working up to 12 hours.

You get gentle relief all day or all night from the good medicine in just one Contac capsule. And when you're not sneezing and sniffling and blowing, you're not spreading as many cold germs. And you'll be a family hero for that. Get Contac at your pharmacy.

CONTAC

FIGURE 11–2 (Courtesy Seagram Distillers Co.)

"Six reasons why even the cleanest homes need Lysol Spray." These six reasons are then illustrated by product-in-use pictures that are clearly numbered. The body copy clarifies each of the illustrations and signs off with the consumer benefit: "Lysol Spray kills household germs, including germs that cause odors." It is a hardworking advertisement that features the product, and shows how easy it is to use and how it deals with a common household problem.

Each of these advertisements does its job in a different way. They use different headline approaches, illustrations, and layouts. Yet, each clearly and simply translates the product concept into a consumer benefit that can be understood and appreciated by its intended audiences.

STRATEGY AND STYLE

Every advertisement starts with an idea; but ideas can be executed in a variety of ways. Given the Contac, Wolfschmidt, or Lysol Spray assignment, ten separate creative groups would probably produce

Six reasons why even the cleanest homes need Lysol Spray.

Even the cleanest homes have germs and odors. That's why it's so important to keep Lysol Spray on hand.

Lysol Spray kills household germs, including germs that cause odors. Make Lysol Spray the important final step in cleaning—every day.

1. Get rid of smoke and stale odors trapped in fabrics.
2. Clean the air of cooking and other odors.
3. Kill the germs that cause odors in garbage cans.
4. Eliminate pet odors.
5. Kill athlete's foot fungus on shower floors.
6. Kill mold and mildew and their odors on the shower curtain.

Lysol Spray kills household germs, including germs that cause odors.

ten different executions of the basic idea. Some might be more effective than others in communicating with consumers, yet all of the ads would be written within the framework of the copy strategy. For example, Ted Bates Advertising once tested four of its own commercials for the same brand of cigarettes. All of the commercials used the same U.S.P., expressed in the same words, but the advertisements were written differently. The copy tests indicated that the commercials varied widely in their ability to register their message with consumers. The best commercial was fifteen times more effective than the worst.[1] Thus, creative execution can make a substantial difference in carrying out copy strategy.

[1]Rosser Reeves, *Reality in Advertising* (New York: Alfred A. Knopf, 1961), 92.

COPY STRATEGY

In Chapter 4, it was pointed out that the copy strategy contains four elements. All may not appear in every copy strategy, but they should; they provide basic guidance for the execution of copy. These four elements are:

1 A statement of the *principal benefit* offered by the product.
2 A statement of the *principal characteristics* of the product—the "reason why" the benefits exist.
3 A statement of the *character or personality* of the product which will be reflected in the *mood, tone, and overall atmosphere* of the advertising.
4 A statement of *what the product is,* and *what the product is used for.*

Precisely *how* these four strategy dimensions are reflected in a particular advertisement or campaign is a question of execution and style. Sometimes the principal benefit is explicitly stated in words, illustrated, or strongly implied. In a good ad, the principal benefit is always presented. Let's see how these strategy elements were executed in the Lysol Spray advertisement.

The principal benefit. Lysol Spray cleans, disinfects, and removes unpleasant odors from homes. These benefits are stated or implied in several ways: the headline; the name Lysol, an established disinfectant; the body copy which specifies six areas of effectiveness; and the graphics on the package.

The principal product characteristic that provides this benefit. Lysol Spray kills household germs that cause odors. This assertion appears in the body copy and secondary headline at the bottom of the page. The advertisement could have specified the particular ingredients that cause Lysol Spray to kill germs, but the writer chose to make a direct assertion instead. Generally, consumers are not interested in the anatomy of products; they are more concerned with what the product does.

The mood, tone, or overall atmosphere of the advertising. The advertisement is straightforward and businesslike, yet informal. It uses models and a home setting that are easily identifiable to consumers. It could have been funny, sexy, chic, sophisticated, clinical, threatening, moody, or exuberant; but it isn't. Those moods would not have been appropriate for this product.

The product and its use. Lysol Spray is a spray disinfectant and germ killer, and it is used for cleaning and eliminating odors. The advertisement states this information in a number of ways. Further, the product's ease of use and versatility are reflected in the illustrations and body copy.

Use these same dimensions to examine the Wolfschmidt and Contac advertisements. These elements will be explicitly stated or clearly implied in all good ads. Use of a written copy strategy simply guarantees that what is stated or implied will always be the same, even if expressed in a different writing or artistic style.

STYLE

Style refers to an artist's or writer's unique way of expression. Most good writers and artists have a style of their own. It is not a formula; it is a characteristic mode of expression. Edward Buxton quotes Paula Green, a partner in the Green Dolmatch advertising agency in New York, on the question of style:

> *Interviewer:* How did you—or how do you—think creative people develop a style of their own?
>
> *Green:* (Before answering she picks up a doll from a nearby table. It is a sad-sweet, old-fashioned doll called Holly Hobby. Paula is currently preparing an advertising campaign to launch the doll). Maybe this is part of the answer. It is a curious thing—the creator of this doll, a young woman, looks exactly like her doll. She recreated herself—or a fantasy of herself. Creative people are like that. I used to see it during my years at Doyle Dane. Art directors always drew themselves in their layouts. There is always something of the creator in all creative work.[2]

George Gribbin, a copywriter who later became chairman of Young & Rubicam, recalls that when he first joined the agency he was assigned to the Packard account and told to write the way his predecessor, Jack Rosebrook, had been writing. Gribbin says:

> I got lost in the minutiae of it, imitating Rosebrook. In six weeks they took me off the Packard ads. I said to myself, "Well, maybe I can't write the Packard account. I don't know. But what I do know is that I can't write like Rosebrook. I've got to write like Gribbin." Over the years, I've learned that if we have a writer and we tell him, "Do it in this particular style," we'll get less good advertising.[3]

Most of us express ourselves best when we express ourselves naturally. When we try to use someone else's words, style, or format, we become awkward, stilted, and unconvincing. In an advertisement, this would cause the death of effective communications.

DEVELOPING ADVERTISING

When trying to come up with an idea for an advertisement or campaign, there is no rigid division of labor. All members of the creative group work together, contributing their ideas and talents to a common venture. The importance of coordinating these talents from the outset is dramatized by the following quotation:

> It is possible to leave a piece of copy on an art director's table, go away, and hope that something good will come of it. Sometimes it does; more often it doesn't.

---

[2]Edward Buxton, *Creative People At Work* (New York: Executive Communications, Inc., 1975), 155.

[3]Judith Dolgins, "Because He Loves the Feel of Words," in *Advertising: an Omnibus of Advertising* prepared by *Printers' Ink* (New York: McGraw-Hill, 1963), 118.

CHAPTER 11 | ADVERTISING CREATIVITY—THE PREPARATION

It is possible for a copywriter to sketch an ad *exactly* the way she wants it to appear. With the copy attached to the sketch, the copywriter hands it to the art director with the instruction, "Just clean this up a little for me, will you?" Something good may come of this. Usually it doesn't.

Of all the important moments in the birth of an ad, the one we arrive at now can be the *most* important: the moment when art director and copywriter sit down together to discuss what the ad is going to look like.

This is important for you to understand. Because if it does not happen, your chances of getting an attractive, hard-selling ad are going to be greatly reduced. The fact is that often this meeting of the minds does *not* take place. As we mentioned earlier, many of the smaller agencies in your city do not have art directors. By choice they rely on an art service to make their layouts for them. The busy copywriter may find it inconvenient to drive across town to the studio, or he or she may feel that some scribbled instructions on the copy sheet are enough. Often it is not.

When you have something to say about your company's advertising, you will be doing everyone a favor if you insist that the art director and the copywriter get together—even if you have to take them to lunch.[4]

Because of this need for coordination, the term *admakers*—be they copywriters, art directors, or creative groups—will be used in the following discussion on the developing of advertising.

William Bernbach has said, "Properly practiced creativity can make one ad do the work of ten."[5] Properly practiced creativity doesn't come easily, however. John Crawford, author of a text on advertising, says that the admaker's job consists of two parts:

1. *A never-ending search for ideas*—the "what to say" in an advertisement that provides the brilliant answer to an advertising problem, and
2. *The never-ending search for new and different ways to express those ideas*—the "how to say it" and "how to show it" techniques of preparing an advertisement that provide the brilliant execution of the ideas the copywriter wants to convey.[6]

Not all advertising is brilliant, of course. Some of it is downright dull. When advertisements fail to live up to their expectations, it is often because the admaker lost patience and failed to expend the required effort.

THE SEARCH FOR FACTS

Good advertising begins with all of the facts that one can gather. Some will be trivial and of little value; but at the outset, it isn't possible to know what is dross and what is gold. "Lynchburg (Pop. 367), Tennessee" is a fact about Jack Daniel's whiskey; it's the location of the distillery. As a fact in and of itself, it is completely triv-

---

[4]James S. Norris, *Advertising* (Reston, Virginia: Reston Publishing Co., Inc., 1977), 158.

[5]William Bernbach, "Advertising's Greatest Tool," in *Speaking of Advertising*, John Wright and Daniel S. Warner, eds. (New York: McGraw-Hill, Inc., 1963), 313.

[6]John W. Crawford, *Advertising*, 2nd ed. (Boston: Allyn and Bacon, 1965), 173.

ial. Yet, it has been made important in Jack Daniel's advertising as a symbol of the tradition and care that go into the making of the product. This exemplifies a curious characteristic about facts in advertising: No fact is important until someone makes it so. Advertising practitioner Charles Adams emphasizes this point with the observation: "Before you pick up the pencil, pick up the facts. Detachment is fine, but ignorance is inexcusable."[7]

Depending on the nature and variety of sources used by the admaker, the gathering of facts can become complex. A primary source of facts is the client organization. Before starting work on a new project, one admaker had over a hundred questions that he submitted to the client.[8] Beyond this, relevant research studies are conducted by the agency, client, and media. Often, a substantial amount of secondary or published research is available through the government or trade associations. Facts can be obtained from the account group and contact with consumers and the wholesale and retail trade. Appendix 2 lists 278 questions that might be asked. Not all of these questions are equally important or relevant for all writing assignments, but they do serve as a comprehensive reference list. At the very least, the admaker should become a repository of information about the product, people who use it, marketing practices in the product field, and the past and present advertising of the product and its competitors.

THE PRODUCT

The starting point for any advertising campaign is the product. Some of the more important questions about the product are identified below.

What is the product? This may sound like an obvious question, but the answer is sometimes complex. Before it became a brand of coffee, Brim was the brand name of a powder that made a delicious drink when mixed with milk. Since four servings of Brim met all of a person's daily nutritional requirements and contained approximately 900 calories, the product could have been a liquid diet food, dietary supplement, beverage to drink with meals, or between meal snack. Since the makers of Brim were unable to decide, its advertising reflected this confusion, and the product failed in test markets. Carnation Company developed a similar product, called it Instant Breakfast, advertised it for people who did not have time for a regular breakfast, and built a multimillion dollar market.

When dealing with a complex product, it may be difficult to define precisely what the product is. When Gaines·burgers was first introduced into test markets, the product performed poorly because pet owners weren't sure whether the product was a snack or a complete nutritional dinner. The advertising wasn't clear on this point, and neither were consumers. The product did not succeed until it was clearly positioned as a complete nutritional dinner.

Claude Robinson, one of the founders of the Gallup-Robinson copy testing service, remarked that advertisers frequently overlook

---

[7]Charles Adams, *Common Sense in Advertising* (New York: McGraw-Hill, 1965), 20.
[8]Ibid., 15.

the obvious and make grievous mistakes by doing so. Never make the mistake of assuming what the product is. Ask what it is; that's the beginning of product knowledge.

What does the product do? Most products have more than one function or use, such as makeup that is a skin moisturizer; shampoo that is a conditioner; all-weather topcoat that provides warmth and protection from rain; fabric softener that is a freshener; and detergent that bleaches and cleans. These examples are of products that have more than one instrumental function. Products also have expressive functions; products permit us to make a statement about ourselves. Thus, a sportscar is *more* than transportation; a fashion by Dior is *more* than a dress; Chateau Haute Brion is not just another dinner wine; and Marlboro is as much an image of masculinity as it is a cigarette.

The admaker must determine whether the essential product benefit is instrumental or expressive and not let it become lost in a swarm of secondary and tertiary claims.

What is it made of? A product's ingredients may offer the key to its advertising. Crest's fluoristan prevents tooth decay; Coors beer is made with clear mountain water; Dial soap contains AT-7, which attacks skin bacteria that causes body odor; Shell gasoline gets better mileage because of TCP; and Contac has tiny "time pills."

Although consumers generally don't get too excited about product ingredients, occasions arise when an ingredient provides a justification for the primary product benefit which otherwise would be a hollow claim. For example, Purina Puppy Chow contains *extra* protein to help puppies grow stronger; Alpo canned dog food is *all* meat; and the flavor of Tareyton Lights is improved by charcoal, if one happens to like charcoal filter cigarettes.

Services also have ingredients, such as raw materials, courtesy, and special features. Burger King makes your hamburger the way you like it; American Airlines offers fine dining; and Avis Rent A Car tries harder. In any case, the admaker should know what the ingredients in the product are and what they do. After all, steel-belted radial tires revolutionized the tire industry.

How is it made? The process used to make a product may inspire an advertising approach or provide support for a product claim. Budweiser floats beechwood chips through its brewing vats, and Jack Daniel's whiskey is "charcoal mellowed drop by drop." In fact, much of Jack Daniel's successful advertising is based on the process used to make the product. The process not only gave distinction to the brand, but also resulted in a new classification of charcoal mellowed whiskeys as competitors attempted to capitalize on Jack Daniel's success.

One of the classic advertising campaigns for beer was developed by Claude Hopkins, who based the campaign on a process that was only marginally related to the product. While touring the Schlitz brewery, Hopkins was unimpressed by the brewing process, but when he saw the empty bottles being sterilized by live steam he came alive. His campaign theme, "Our Bottles Are Washed with Live Steam," was a blockbuster because, at the time he wrote the campaign, consumers wondered if sanitation would be affected by the use of returnable bottles. Sanitation was a relevant consumer benefit. Today, the same campaign would probably have all of the impact of a stifled yawn.

Or, consider the advertisement for Henry Weinhard's Private Reserve beer (Figure 11–4). The headline is provocative: "Some comments about Henry Weinhard's from a man who drinks beer for a living." For beer lovers who think of themselves as experts on their favorite brew, the headline is an irresistible temptation to read further.

The body copy is a personal statement by Michael Jackson, who qualifies himself as an authority on beer.

FIGURE 11–4 (Courtesy of Blitz-Weinhard Brewing Co.)

SOME COMMENTS ABOUT HENRY WEINHARD'S FROM A MAN WHO DRINKS BEER FOR A LIVING.

by Michael Jackson

And while some brewers patch up their products with an additive here and a chemical there, Mr. Daniel uses only the best natural ingredients, like Cascade hops and two-row malting barley. Henry's is made with more of these costly ingredients than any other beer I know of.

If you prefer quality to quantity, I recommend that you try Henry Weinhard's Private Reserve. It's one of the things I enjoy every time I make a visit to your country.

You might say that beer is my bread and butter. I write about beer for a newspaper in London, I talk about beer on British radio, and I even published a whole book on the subject called *The World Guide to Beer.*

In the course of my research, I've sampled more than a thousand beers, and I'm always looking for something new. It's especially rewarding, in this age of mass production, to find beers of individuality and quality that are still made the old-fashioned traditional way. An excellent example is Henry Weinhard's Private Reserve, made by a small

brewery in Portland, Oregon.

While some beers seem to be produced by computers, Henry's is the product of an honest-to-goodness brewmaster who personally supervises and tastes each bottling. His name, believe it or not, is Jack Daniel.

Some brewers look for short-cuts in the brewing process, but the people who make Henry's have gone in the opposite direction—back to the slower methods of the last century. These days, for example, many brewers hardly bother to mature their beer, but Henry's is aged and mellowed for weeks.

ABOUT OUR BREWERY

The Blitz-Weinhard Brewing Company was one of the first brewing establishments in America, and is the oldest continuously-operated brewery west of the Mississippi River.

Founded in 1856 by German master brewer Henry Weinhard, the brewery's original location was near Fort Vancouver in the Oregon Territory. Henry's beer enjoyed an overwhelming popularity among the cavalrymen garrisoned at the fort, as well as with the loggers, trappers, and other pioneer settlers of the area. A newspaper of the period described the beer as "unsurpassed by any other native product of its kind."

With success came expansion, and in 1861 Mr. Weinhard moved his brewery to its present location in Portland. Since then, fine beer has been brewed using the premium hops and barley's grown in the Northwest, and pure, fresh water from the Cascade mountain range.

THE BLITZ-WEINHARD BREWING COMPANY OF PORTLAND, OREGON

Creative Director: Hal Riney; Art Director: Jerry Andelin; Copywriter: Dennis Foley; Agency: Ogilvy and Mather, San Francisco

You might say that beer is my bread and butter. I write about beer for a newspaper in London, I talk about beer on British radio, and I even published a whole book on the subject called *The World Guide to Beer.*

In the course of my research, I've sampled more than a thousand beers, and I'm always looking for something new. It's especially rewarding, in this age of mass production, to find beers of individuality and quality that are still made the old-fashioned traditional way. An excellent example is Henry Weinhard's Private Reserve, made by a small brewery in Portland, Oregon.

Jackson then commends the Henry Weinhard product because it is personally brewed and tasted by an "honest-to-goodness brewmaster," takes no shortcuts in the brewing process, is carefully aged and mellowed, and uses only costly, natural ingredients.

This body copy refers to ingredients and the brewing process to validate the superior quality of the Henry Weinhard product.

The company is small. The product is only sold on the West Coast. But, in my opinion, their advertising is the finest beer advertising running in America today.

How does it compare with competition? Advertising takes place in a competitive environment, not a vacuum. Branded products may be similar; few are identical. This is what is meant by monopolistic competition. The admaker should know the strengths and weaknesses of the product and those of competition. For example, one cold tablet may have a more effective analgesic for easing aches and pains; another may have a more effective ingredient for reducing fever; and still another may have a more effective antihistamine for relieving nasal congestion. One cold tablet may work more quickly or longer than another. One detergent may be more effective for getting out stains, while another is safer for delicate fabrics. One brand of paper towels may be more absorbent, while another is stronger.

In some cases, the admaker may not find a difference in the brand itself, but in consumers' perceptions of the brand. Bayer aspirin is perceived by millions of consumers as being more reliable and efficacious than other brands of aspirin, although from the standpoint of analgesic qualities, all aspirin is the same. Yet, Bayer continues to dominate the aspirin market because of its "quality" story. If there are no differences between brands and consumers perceive different brands as the same, the admaker is dealing with a commodity. Writing advertising for a commodity is a thankless task. Through a dramatic technique or sheer advertising weight, one commodity may be made better known than another. However, this is seldom a profitable undertaking. At this point advertising has reached the limits of its persuasion, and other marketing activities, such as pricing, reciprocity, and trade deals, become the most effective mode for generating sales. The admaker must have the courage to say, "This brand has nothing to sell." Then attention can be paid to how the brand can be changed to become suitable for advertising.

Few brands are completely hopeless. However, an admaker does require the imagination and will to improve a brand that has sunk into the quagmire of commodities.

How can it be identified? Most product advertising is concerned with the stimulation of **selective demand** (demand for a particular brand) rather than **primary demand** (demand for a product type). When a particular brand dominates a market, greater attention may be given to the stimulation of primary demand because the dominant brand will be the principal beneficiary if the entire market grows. However, even in this case selective demand is seldom totally neglected. Sometimes, trade associations such as the American Dairy Association or an association of citrus growers will assess its members for funds to develop an industry-wide promotion to increase the use of dairy products or orange juice, but most product advertising is concerned with the selective demand for individually branded items.

One of the admaker's jobs is to determine how the brand can best be identified at the point of sale. Prominently displaying the package or trademark in the advertisement is the usual method. Sometimes, a unique color is used. For example, the John Deere tractor is painted in a special shade of green with the John Deere name emblazoned on a yellow swatch. In any case, the copywriter must decide what there is about the brand that will make it easily identifiable. The Duncan Hines "old English" sign is an identifying symbol that works on the package and in advertising.

What does it cost? Price is a basis for market segmentation and is used symbolically to position a product vis-à-vis competition within a particular market segment (see Chapter 8). The role of price in display advertising depends largely on the importance of price as a relevant strategic consideration. When price is a critical factor in product positioning, some reference to price should appear in the advertising. The Chrysler New Yorker featured price in its introductory advertising even though one could hardly describe the New Yorker as an economy car (Figure 11–5).

For most competitively priced packaged goods, price is ignored in advertising because it isn't a relevant consideration. Nonetheless, the admaker should be familiar with the price of the product as well as that of competition. Sometimes, this knowledge will serve as a basis for an economy or snob appeal.

Quoting a specific price in display advertising usually isn't possible because freight rates and retail prices will vary somewhat by geographic region. This difficulty can be overcome by using a list price as in the New Yorker ad, indicating a suggested retail price, acknowledging that the brand is "less than" or "more than" competitive products, or indicating a price range.

In sales promotion advertising, particularly for a retail store, a knowledge of price is critical because this type of advertising relies on bargains for its appeal. Obviously, the admaker must be familiar with the regular price of an item in order to communicate the magnitude of the savings.

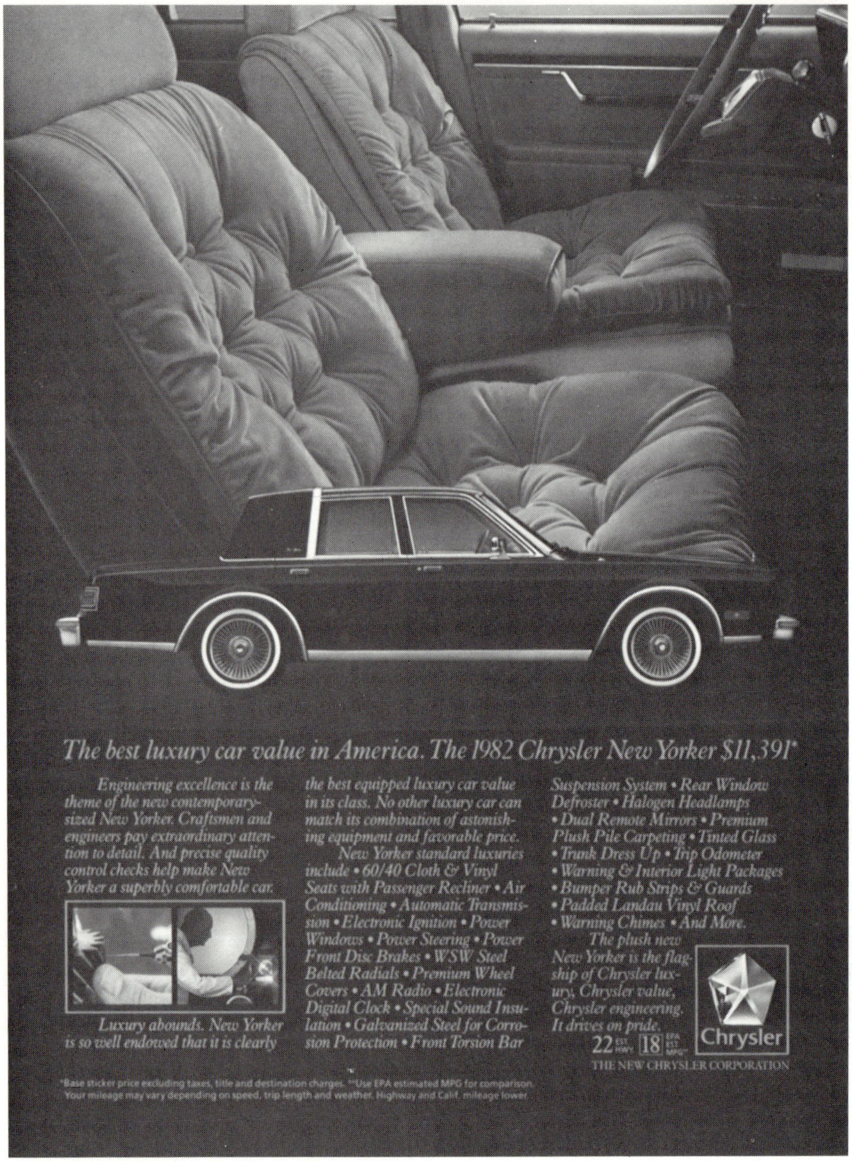

FIGURE 11–5 (Courtesy Chrysler Corp.)

THE CONSUMER

An almost endless array of questions can be asked about consumers. Five key question areas are recognized in the following material.

Who uses it?   The admaker must identify the target market. Is the product used by men? Women? Children? Families? Who are the primary users? For example, both men and women use diet foods, but women account for 80 percent of the market. Special K is an adult cereal, and Cocoa Puffs is for children. Peanut butter is for children; toothpaste is for the entire family; and shaving cream is used by men. Beer is drunk by both males and females, but no brewery has ever succeeded by advertising beer primarily to women because men are the heavy beer drinkers, and the male ego apparently shrinks at the thought of drinking a "woman's" beer. Not too long ago, cigarettes were advertised primarily to men; today, a significant market for cigarettes is among women.

Age groups are also important. Most beer is consumed by young adults, while scotch whiskey is consumed by older people. Teenagers account for an estimated 90 percent of the single record sales and 50 percent of the albums other than classical music. Most products have a target age range, and the family life cycle (see Chapter 6) is often used as a guide to the existing patterns of object accumulation. Thus, the newly formed family is a primary market for refrigerators, ranges, and inexpensive, durable furniture. Families with young children are heavy buyers of washing machines, dryers, baby furniture, baby foods, and so on. The family with grown children is an excellent market for tasteful furniture, travel, recreation, self-education, and hobbies.

Other socio-economic considerations, such as income and social class, are also important. The admaker needs to know for whom the product is intended so that the appropriate appeals and signs may be used in advertising communications.

Who influences brand choice? The user of a product or brand may not be the one who makes the purchase or specifies the brand. About 73 percent of all United States dwelling units are occupied by families. Individual family members purchase products for their personal use as well as for other family members. The question "Who uses the product?" generally has to be supplemented by two other questions: (a) Who specifies the brand? (b) Who actually makes the purchase? These questions are necessary because brand influence can occur at any stage of the decision process.

Both men and women use shampoo, but in most families, the woman selects the brand. Many children's products must be approved by parents, usually the mother. As a consequence, many children's products require a dual appeal—a direct appeal to children and a secondary appeal to the mother to enable her to rationalize the purchase. This dual requirement often demands two different advertising campaigns.

Table 11–1 shows the results of a buying influence study for a selected group of products. This study, jointly supported by five magazines, was made available to client organizations and advertising agencies. One of its shortcomings is that this study does not deal with child influence. It does indicate, however, that both husbands and wives exert an influence on the types of products used and on the particular brands purchased, and that the extent of husband-wife influence varies greatly.

How and where is the product used? Some products are used in social situations; others are used in private. Products such as cars, clothing, cosmetics, and home furnishings are highly visible; others, such as deodorants, shaving cream, shampoo, and underclothing, are seldom seen by others. The advertisement by Soflens (Figure 11–6) is an interesting approach because it shows a close-up of an invisible product that is worn in public, but is not meant to be seen.

FIGURE 11–6   (Courtesy Bausch & Lomb, Inc.)

Highly visible products are used by consumers for their expressive as well as instrumental functions. They are used to make a public statement about the user, whether we are talking about the blue jeans of a college student or the Lincoln Continental of a surgeon. The admaker needs to understand the importance of that public statement in order to surround the brand with the proper symbols.

If a product is a highly social one, such as beer, it is usually desirable to show it in a social setting. If the product is an intimate

TABLE 11–1 Relative buying influence between husbands and wives (percentage of influence)

Product	Purchased by		Direct Influence Product		Direct Influence Brand		Indirect Influence Product		Indirect Influence Brand	
	W	H	W	H	W	H	W	H	W	H
Cereals:										
Cold (unsweetened)	84	16	74	26	71	29	65	35	67	33
Hot	84	16	67	33	67	33	63	37	59	41
Packaged lunch meat	73	27	60	40	64	36	56	44	57	43
Peanut butter	81	19	70	30	74	26	65	35	68	32
Scotch whiskey	35	65	18	82	18	82	22	78	23	77
Bar soap	85	15	65	35	64	36	60	40	61	39
Headache remedies	67	33	67	33	67	33	64	36	65	35
Cat food (dry)	66	34	75	25	81	19	80	20	80	20
Dog food (dry)	76	24	60	40	59	41	60	40	61	39
Fast-food chain hamburgers	68	32	55	45	55	45	53	47	52	48
Catsup	75	25	68	32	68	32	60	40	62	38
Coffee:										
Freeze-dried	68	32	57	43	62	38	56	44	59	41
Regular ground	74	26	65	35	65	35	58	42	60	40
Mouthwash	72	28	56	44	56	44	52	48	53	47

Share of influence

Product	Purchase Decision Influence Product		Brand		Initiation Product		Brand		Purchase Product		Brand	
	W	H	W	H	W	H	W	H	W	H	W	H
Vacuum cleaner	60	40	60	40	80	20	69	31	66	34	65	35
Electric blender	59	41	53	47	67	33	50	50	53	47	52	48
Broadloom carpet	60	40	59	41	82	18	74	26	72	28	69	31
Automobiles	38	62	33	67	22	78	21	79	18	82	18	82

Source of data: "Purchase Influence Measures of Husband/Wife Influence on Buying Decisions." Haley, Overholser & Associates Inc., New Canaan, Conn., January, 1975. Percentages reflect relative purchase activity, direct and indirect influence of husbands and wives in the sample. For durables and services, percentages reflect relative activity in purchase decision, initiation of idea to purchase, and the gathering of information.

Source: "Buying Study Called Good Support Data," p. 52. Reprinted with permission from the March 17, 1975 issue of *Advertising Age*. Copyright © 1975 by Crain Communications, Inc.

one, it should convey intimacy. An outdoor product belongs outdoors; an indoor product belongs in the house; and most food products belong on the table or in the kitchen. Effective advertising seldom blazes new trails in the realm of social mores; it bows to the prevailing values and conventions of society. For attention value, products are sometimes shown in bizarre settings. When it works, the bizarre setting usually has some relevance to dominant product attributes.

How is the product purchased? Frequently, packaged goods are generally bought without too much thought or conflict. On the other hand, carpeting and expensive furniture involve considerable information gathering, shopping, comparison, and uncertainty. Advertising should be adapted to its role in the consumer decision process. Advertising for expensive furniture should display the furniture's elegance in a handsome setting, surrounding it with symbols of quality and discriminating taste. The facts of construction, durability, fabric, and price may be better left to retail sales personnel or point-of-purchase brochures. For Hamburger Helper, a simplified "how to prepare it" approach may be more meaningful. If the admaker doesn't know how a product is purchased, the advertising probably will not be used in the most effective way.

Why is the product purchased?   Some successful advertising practitioners, such as Rosser Reeves, prefer direct, straightforward, conscious reasons, firmly embedded in tangible product characteristics. Others, like David Ogilvy, insist that ". . . it is almost always the total *personality* of a brand rather than *trivial product differences* which decide its ultimate position in the market."[9] Norman B. Norman goes even further by saying that conscious suggestions are usually a waste of the advertiser's time and money; what is meaningful is the unconscious suggestion. This latter point of view is purely psychoanalytic and suggests that sex, aggression, power, fantasy, and security underlie all consumer behavior.

Each of these practitioners probably has a vision of the truth, but none see it in its entirety. Some reasons for buying a particular product or brand are undoubtedly conscious; others are merely conscious rationalizations of obscure motivational dynamics. J. Sterling Getchell said: "People buy for emotional reasons, and then justify their purchases with rational reasons why." The purchase of a Lincoln Continental may be clearly understood by the buyer as an expression of prestige and power. On the other hand, it may be a compensation for unconscious feelings of personal inadequacy. A motorcycle may be bought for its convenience and economy, or it may be an expression of an unconscious wish for self-destruction—the Freudian death instinct.

Since there may be many motivational bases for the purchase of a particular product, the admaker should know as much about them as possible. Whether the admaker ultimately chooses the route of conscious or unconscious motivation, or a combination of the two, is a matter of choice. In order to make a choice, however, one must be aware of alternatives.

THE MARKETING SITUATION

Another group of facts that are relevant to the admaker concerns the brand's marketing position and its distribution.

What is the brand's marketing position?   Whether a brand is the leader in its market, a major contender, or a poor performer may, in itself, be a source of advertising inspiration. The self-confidence of Budweiser's dominant position in the beer market is reflected in the television advertising jingle that accompanies the use of a beer wagon drawn by the company's Clydesdales. The opening words of the jingle are: "Here comes the King! Here comes the King! Here

---

[9]Martin Mayer, *Madison Avenue U.S.A.* (New York: Harper Brothers, Publishers, 1958), 58.

When you're only No. 2, you try harder. Or else.

Little fish have to keep moving all of the time. The big ones never stop picking on them.

Avis knows all about the problems of little fish.

We're only No. 2 in rent a cars. We'd be swallowed up if we didn't try harder.

Avis can't afford to relax.

There's no rest for us.

We're always emptying ashtrays. Making sure gas tanks are full before we rent our cars. Seeing that the batteries are full of life. Checking our windshield wipers.

And the cars we rent out can't be anything less than spanking new Plymouths.

And since we're not the big fish, you won't feel like a sardine when you come to our counter.

We're not jammed with customers.

FIGURE 11–7 (Copyright © 1964, Avis, Inc.)

comes the big number one." Deliberate use of market leadership is summed up in the slogan "Budweiser, the king of beer."

Only one brand can occupy the dominant position in a market. In 1962 Avis lagged far behind Hertz in the car rental field. The company was losing money and had been for a number of years. A new president of Avis was given the task of turning the company around. As an effort in this direction, he hired Doyle Dane Bernbach to develop an advertising approach. The advertisement shown in Figure 11–7 is the beginning of the "We try harder" campaign that took its cue from Avis's market position and the new management's dedication to upgrading the entire operation.

New management and its advertising were successful. In 1962 Avis's revenues were $34 million, with a loss of $3,200,000. In 1964 revenues were $44 million, with a profit of $3 million. Anyone who didn't have a "We try harder" button wasn't really in style.

How is it distributed? Contac is an example of a brand whose method of distribution played an integral role in its advertising. Reference to getting Contac at your pharmacy was used to give an ethical connotation to the brand, enlist the support of pharmacists, and direct consumers to the place of purchase. For many products with selective distribution, telling consumers where the brand can be found is an important function of copy. While everyone may know that Plymouths are sold by Plymouth dealers, many people may not know that Opels are sold by Buick dealers, Fiestas by Ford dealers, Johnny Miller menswear at Sears, or that Elancyl (a shampoo massage) is available at Saks Fifth Avenue. Some advertisers with limited distribution, such as De Weese Designs (swim and sun fashions) or Pantene (a specialty shampoo), list a toll free number in their advertising so that consumers may call to find the location of the nearest outlet. Since cosmetics, as well as many other products, can be purchased in drugstores, department stores, variety stores, supermarkets, or some combination of these outlets, the least the admaker can do is to direct consumers to the appropriate places of purchase.

ADVERTISING HISTORY OF THE BRAND AND ITS COMPETITORS

The admaker should be thoroughly steeped in the past advertising approaches of the brand and its competitors as well as the strengths and weaknesses of these approaches, as measured by research or sales results. Creating an advertising appeal that has been preempted by competitive brands or repeating a campaign that has not distinguished itself in the past has little virtue.

On the other hand, there is little profit in replacing a highly effective advertising campaign simply for the sake of doing something new and different. Constant use does wear out advertising campaigns, but not as quickly as most advertisers think it does. Contact with a campaign idea from its inception may cause an admaker or advertiser to become bored with the idea by the time it makes its first appearance in consumer media.

CHAPTER 11 | ADVERTISING CREATIVITY—THE PREPARATION

THE STORY THAT COULDN'T BE TOLD

THE WAY IT IS

The development of brand advertising doesn't always flow smoothly. Sometimes the process is characterized by misjudgments, false starts, and disagreement.

The real story of how advertising campaigns are often developed is seldom told in advertising text books. It is for this reason that the following case history has been summarized.

This case is not represented as being typical of campaign development. However, having spent almost 20 years in advertising agency management, I know that situations like this occur more often than I would like to think. This case does yield some insights into the dynamics of marketing and of the client-agency relationship.

The name of the brand and its product class have been omitted, as have the names of the people involved, in order to avoid personal embarrassment to some very able and dedicated people. Doing this makes it possible to tell a story that, otherwise, couldn't be told.

THE BRAND'S HISTORY

The brand was first introduced as a high prestige consumer product with limited distribution. During the first few years, volume grew to approximately $12 million.

In the 1960s the strategy of selective distribution was abandoned, and a national advertising campaign emphasizing the high prestige and exclusivity of the product was launched. During the next few years, sales volume grew to over $25 million.

At this point, a slight change was made in the brand's advertising strategy. The high prestige and exclusivity of the brand was retained, but the focus was shifted to using the brand as a way of impressing one's friends. In the first phase of this campaign, sales climbed to almost $70 million. In the second phase, sales reached over $120 million.

The next major campaign change continued to reinforce the high prestige of the brand, but associated it with "special" situations. Sales climbed to $200 million in less than five years.

Thereafter, although the brand continued to grow in sales, its rate of growth declined. At this point, a critical decision was made. It was decided to broaden the appeal of the brand and direct its advertising to a broad consumer audience instead of a selective one. Over the next two years, the dollar sales of the brand increased slightly because of price increases, but its actual unit sales declined by almost 10 percent.

A history of the brand's sales growth is shown in Figure 1.

PROBLEM ANALYSIS

Analysis of a consumer tracking study, which was a part of the continuing marketing research on the brand, enabled members of agency ac-

FIGURE 1 Brand's sales growth

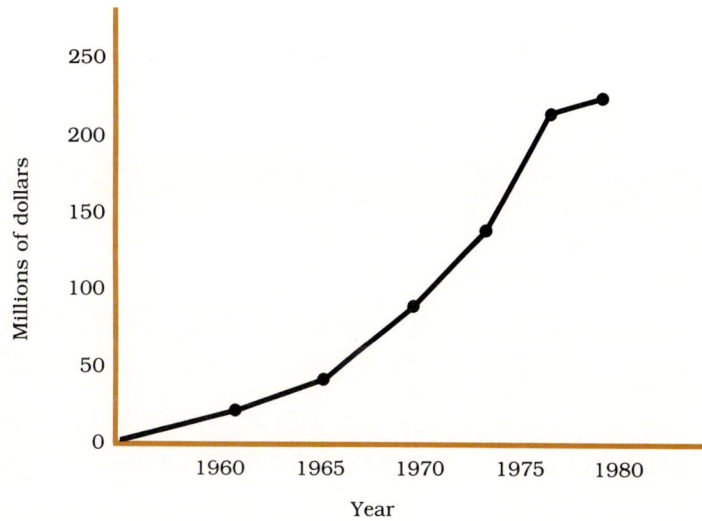

count management to identify what it believed to be the source of the problem. The consumer tracking study consisted of periodic consumer surveys designed to provide information on brand awareness, reported purchases, brand appeal, and brand image.

Analysis of this data suggested that the brand was losing its special appeal. In the attempt to broaden the brand's market, the brand image had become tarnished. Figure 2 is a simplified diagram of what had happened to consumers' perceptions of the brand following the attempt to broaden its appeal. Observation 1 was made immediately before the campaign. Observations 2, 3, and 4 were made sequentially during the two years in which sales had begun to lag. At the same time this was happening, the brand's percentage price differential was also declining, so that consumers did not perceive it as being more expensive than competitive products.

Client brand management did not agree with the agency's diagnosis, but attributed the decline in unit sales to increased competitive activity. It took almost two years after the first evidence of sales leveling before client brand management conceded that something besides competitive activity was affecting the brand's sales. In the meantime, agency suggestions that the brand's advertising be changed were rebuffed.

CREATIVE DEVELOPMENT

Once agreement was reached between the agency and client brand management on the nature of the brand's problem, a full-scale effort involving marketing research, creative, and account management was undertaken. The basic objective was to reestablish the brand as a high prestige, special product. This basic decision received the full support of agency management and the vice-president of marketing in the client

FIGURE 2 Consumers' perceptions of the brand

```
                                    Special people
                                         │
                                         │
                                         │
                                         │
                                         │       2
                                         │          1
                                         │   3
                                         │
Ordinary                                 │                        Special
product  ────────────────────────────────┼──────────────────────  product
                                         │  4
                                         │
                                         │
                                         │
                                         │
                                         │
                                         │
                                    For everybody
```

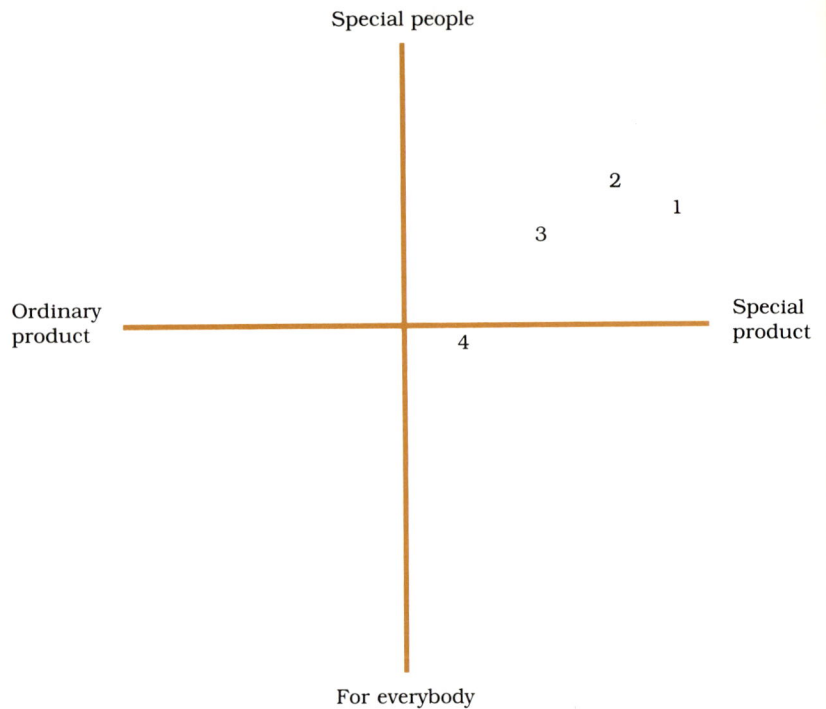

organization. The new campaign development effort proceeded in a number of stages.

Stage 1 Initial creative development centered around associating the brand with up-scale, prestigious individuals and symbols. There was a difference of opinion within the client organization over this strategy, but rather than rejecting it, the client agreed that the idea be developed, subject to testing. Over the next six to nine months, several executions of this strategy were developed and tested in local media tests. The results of the research indicated that, although there was a definite improvement in brand image, there was also some consumer confusion about what specific message was being communicated. As a consequence, the whole strategy was shelved.

Stage 2 While the initial campaign was being developed, the client asked for a number of backup campaigns. At the same time, the client expressed dissatisfaction with the creative group assigned to the account, and requested additional creative help. A request such as this from a client is not really a request—it is a command performance. A great deal of pressure was put on the creative director to come up with a solution. He responded to this pressure by calling in several additional creative groups both from the agency's local office as well as from agency offices in other cities.

Most of what was produced by this massive effort was unsatisfactory to both the agency account group and the client.

And, time was running out.

Stage 3 A new idea came out of a creative review meeting. The agency management supervisor on the account suggested that they focus on the product and glorify it. The immediate response from the creative director and the group creative director was that it was a dumb idea and would lead to dull advertising. However, the associate creative director was intrigued by the idea and thought that it could be done. Nonetheless, the idea was shelved in the search for another solution.

When nothing better was offered during the next hour of discussion, the management supervisor again suggested that they focus on the product.

Patience and persistence often pay off in advertising as well as in other fields. This time, the associate creative director said that he thought he could pull it off, and asked for a chance to try. Management, for the lack of a better alternative, gave its approval.

The results were some outstanding product shots and some arresting background music.

Stage 4 Everyone liked the visuals and the music, but copy was a problem. It didn't do anything. At about this time, the creative director was assigned to some other accounts, and a new creative director was brought in. He assigned a group of senior creative people to the problem, but all of the copy alternatives they developed were rejected.

Finally, five senior creative people took a hotel room for a couple of days to get away from the agency and to "live with" the problem.

They returned with a copy theme that they enthusiastically sold to account management and the client.

Stage 5 The new commercials were tested in focus groups with consumers. The focus group participants were enthusiastic about the visuals and music, but lukewarm toward the copy.

Other copy alternatives were written. These were tested in subsequent focus groups and received a highly positive reaction.

THE RESULTS

Commercial copy testing of the final commercials showed significant improvements in consumers' perceptions of the brand, particularly among the brand's target audience. When the commercials were presented at the client's annual sales meeting, the sales force was enthusiastic.

But, best of all, when the commercials appeared on television, brand sales started climbing again, and the brand appears to be on the road to new highs.

Moral Campaign development isn't always fun—but it can be rewarding.

Frequently, a product that starts out with a unique consumer benefit finds itself inundated by competition with similar products and look-alike advertising. Initially, the brand may benefit from the competitive advertising, particularly if it has advertised heavily enough to have preempted the product benefit in the eyes of consumers. Eventually, its primary association with the benefit may be eroded by the competition's advertising. At this point, either the product concept needs to be modified, or a fresh and distinctive advertising campaign has to be developed. In any event, an active file of past and current advertising should be maintained to keep abreast of competitive activity and changes occurring in the field.

The search for facts is an important part of the admaker's job, but it is only the starting point. No fact is important until it is translated into a consumer benefit that will attract attention and persuade consumers to try the product. This point is demonstrated by the following anecdote related by Charles E. Scripps when he was board chairman of the Scripps-Howard newspaper chain:

> "Gentlemen," said the sales manager, "I want to show you the very latest thing out of our laboratories." At this point he paused and took from his pocket a small twist drill, the kind everyone uses to drill holes in wood or metal. "I want you to know all about this," the sales manager continued enthusiastically. "This is a 5/8" drill. It's exactly 6-3/4" long. It's made of a new secret alloy that will outlast anything on the market." He went on and on, describing how their research department had determined just the right degree of twist, the angle at the point, the strength and hardness. Then he said, "Gentlemen, there are 3.5 million 5/8" drills sold in the U.S. every year. Every garage mechanic, carpenter, machinist, plumber, electrician, home mechanic—everyone who works with tools—has to have one. But, gentlemen, let's just keep one thing in mind: *Not a single one of those people want a drill. What they want is holes.*"[10]

In this case, the job of the creative admaker is to translate drills into holes by persuading consumers that one particular drill will make holes better than competitive brands.

THE CREATIVE PROCESS

The development of advertising is a creative process that takes place within the constraints of the problem and under the pressure of time. Unfortunately, not all creative ideas solve the problem at hand, and good ideas cannot be programmed to arrive precisely when they are needed. As a consequence, effective creativity demands a discipline that some consider foreign to the creative act itself. A systematic procedure is also required, although many sophisticated advertising people resent step-by-step procedures. Many good admakers have developed a systematic procedure of their own that is so thoroughly integrated into their normal work habits that they don't think of it as systematic.

Traditionally, the creative process has been divided into the three steps beautifully described by Charles Adams:

---

[10]Charles E. Scripps, "Money, Media and Minutes," an address before the Advertiser's Club of Cincinnati, January 7, 1959.

First, there should be a period of *ingestion*. Drink in all the facts and information you can about the subject. Acquaint yourself with the purposes and objectives of the campaign. Familiarize yourself with competitive efforts. Look at the history and the track records of previous efforts for this advertiser. Familiarize yourself with the product. Make yourself as informed as possible. Generally immerse yourself in the advertising challenge.

The second stage I call *incubation*. This is the period during which you put the problem aside. Or, metaphorically, you let it simmer on the back burner. You don't ask for a solution or even for an intelligent analysis. You let it stew, or as has been said, you "just walk around it" for a while. But you will be surprised and delighted to find it coming to the surface every now and again, almost involuntarily. And when it does surface, it will probably be showing some new side or sparkling in some new way in the light of your current thoughts and experiences.

The final stage might be termed *inspiration*. Here you try in earnest to come up with a solution. You force yourself into action, lay the problem out in the open, search avidly and determinedly for the answer. And, usually, if you give it enough time and effort, it comes—that moment of insight, that triumph over ignorance that makes the total effort worthwhile. It may be something as simple as a phrase—something as complicated as a new photographic process. But whatever it is, you will know it when you find it. And then you will shelter it, nourish it, elaborate on it, change it, and polish it until it reaches that point where it is presentable, salable, and workable.

This, in endless variation, is the creative process. It is essentially a lonely task, a private agony. And it is best not hurried.[11]

While not rejecting the three stages of the creative process summarized by Adams, Walter Joyce is more specific in suggesting ways to put the creative process to work. Joyce identifies eleven steps that are helpful in stimulating ideas and gaining new insights into the problem.[12]

1 *Define the problem.* Since creativity in advertising is a problem-solving activity, the first step is to identify the problem. If the problem is improperly defined, there is little chance that an acceptable solution will be found. Is the problem one of identifying the primary consumer benefit of the product or service? Or, is it one of dramatizing this benefit? Is the problem one of gaining name registration? Or, is it one of demonstrating a unique brand feature? Is the problem one of developing a rationale to support the central claim? Or, is it one of overcoming consumer apathy?

2 *Consciously question every accepted assumption of the problem.* Most of us enter a new situation with a mass of preconceptions. Our heads are filled with beliefs that are true, partially true, and patently false. The admaker is also exposed to members of the client organization and other people who have had experience with the product. They, too, have questionable pre-

---

[11]Adams, *Common Sense in Advertising*, 142–44.
[12]Walter Joyce, "Care and Feeding of the Idea," in *Advertising: an Omnibus of Advertising* prepared by *Printers' Ink*, p. 113.

CHAPTER 11 | ADVERTISING CREATIVITY—THE PREPARATION

conceptions that they are willing to share as the literal truth. Because of this, the admaker needs to adopt an honest skepticism, a willingness to question one's own beliefs as well as those of others.

3 *Get involved with the problem.* Creating good advertising is an engrossing proposition. The admaker can't be a dilettante. Each assignment must be the most important thing there is to be done. It may be difficult to get totally involved with a cake mix, jar of peanut butter, or box of soap, but the talent, or skill, of total involvement is a necessary ingredient in the creative process.

4 *Begin to ask questions.* Asking questions is the road to new insights. Some of the answers we get may be trivial, but many will not be. Through questioning, new information is developed and new perspectives gained. The right question may open a totally new line of inquiry. For example, when Ralston Purina was trying to find a way to get a profitable share of the growing dry dog food market, the planning group kept wrestling with the question, "How?" They were getting nowhere. One day, a member of the planning group said, "Instead of asking, 'How can we get a major share of the market?' we should be asking, 'What does the consumer want in a dry dog food?' " This broke the logjam.

5 *Consciously begin to adopt new assumptions or try to renovate old ones.* This is a major step in breaking out of our preconceptions. Here, we deliberately try out new beliefs and new ways of thinking. In short, we start playing the game of "What if . . .?" and begin to question our new assumptions.

6 *Consciously let the inductive process start to work.* In this step, we start to look for new relationships that have not been articulated before. Let imagination flow freely; speculate; go beyond the facts.

7 *Begin to form a judgment.* Ultimately, a creative idea is a judgment. It is a personal conclusion about what is important, drawn from one's own experience and exploration. Sometimes this judgment is called a *hunch*, sometimes an *intuition*. Whatever it is called, it is something unique that the individual brings to the situation.

8 *Try to make a prediction.* At this point, Joyce says, ". . . try to see if there is a new unity in the world that surrounds your problem." Another way of expressing this thought is to ask if the problem is being seen in a new light. Do the ideas make sense? Do they have a natural coherence, a logic of their own? Are they too complex or involved? Good ideas have a logic and coherence of their own, and the test of their usefulness is often their simplicity.

9 *Now take action.* Once an idea that makes sense starts to take shape, try it out. It may have to be tried a dozen ways before it comes out right; ultimately, it has to be committed to paper. If it has any value, it will survive this test. This is often a traumatic experience for admakers because it means they have to

venture outside their private world and expose their fledgling ideas to the harsh realities of criticism. While few people can create a good ad, critics are legion. Everyone is an expert.

10 *Develop the drive, the competence, to demonstrate the validity of the new theory.* In other words, develop the guts to survive criticism, fight for an idea you believe is right, and to remain confident even when others disagree.

11 *Be ready, however, to question the new hypothesis—and to start all over again if it doesn't solve the problem.* There is a difference between defending an idea and being blind to its faults. Criticism is often justified; it points up flaws and short-comings. Sometimes these weaknesses are not serious, and honest criticism gives rise to modifications that strengthen the concept. On the other hand, some flaws are fatal. At this point, the difference between the amateur and the professional comes to light. The amateur self-righteously continues to defend a lost cause; the professional literally goes back to the drawing board.

Creativity is highly idiosyncratic. The foregoing guidelines only represent an approach that recognizes that creativity requires factual data, fluidity of thought processes, and an ability to change perspectives. Gathering data, asking questions, deliberately taking another point of view, and engaging in imaginative speculation are only techniques that are helpful. Most people who make their livings by exploring new ideas bring an innate curiosity to the process. Having an assignment and a deadline only gives the admaker an opportunity to be curious in a defined area.

PITFALLS OF ADVERTISING CREATIVITY

Although advertising thrives on new ideas, it is often inhospitable to them. New ideas are not really popular in business, and there are good reasons for this. Most businesspeople are fairly conservative. A business enterprise requires major investments in plant and equipment, people, organization, and training. It functions best in a somewhat stable environment where forecasts can be made with reasonable confidence, plans can be laid and carried out with a minimum of revisions, and risk is reduced to an acceptable level. A stable world is one in which decisions can be programmed, rules and formulas can be devised and followed, and sensible caution will avoid catastrophe.

New ideas always involve risk, and there is constant temptation to avoid the new for the sake of the safe. Edward Weiss, chairman of Edward H. Weiss & Company, has summed up this thought with the observation that: "The greatest danger in modern technology isn't that machines will begin to think like men, but that men will begin to think like machines."[13] Therefore, the first pitfall for the admaker is falling victim to formula advertising that is defensible because it has worked in the past.

The second pitfall is that of substituting techniques for ideas. Such substitutions may take the form of a dramatic photographic

---

[13]Ibid., 105.

treatment, bizarre illustration, humor, sex, exaggerated claims, news, rhetoric, or a dozen other attention-getting devices. Nothing is wrong with any of these devices, provided they are secondary elements and enhance the consumer benefit. When they take precedence over the consumer benefit or ignore it, mediocrity is the inevitable consequence.

A third pitfall is poor taste. The use of vulgarity in order to gain attention is inexcusable. Granted, values change, but the world is still full of people who are uncomfortable with many of these value changes. In the sale of mass consumer goods, these people are customers.

Fourth, never fall into the trap of assuming that consumers are witless pawns who can be manipulated and beguiled. Consumers may have many faults, and they often act unwisely, but they are not stupid.

Finally, beware of losing touch with the consumer. Advertising people talk to advertising people, and the business tends to develop its own idiom. Outside the advertising business, millions of people have problems and concerns and don't talk the way advertising people do. They are called *customers*.

SUMMARY

The chapter is introduced by three examples of advertisements, each doing its job in a different way. Effective advertising comes in different forms of headlines, illustrations, body copy, and formats that are determined by strategy and style.

Strategy provides basic guidelines for the execution of copy and generally contains four statements regarding: (a) the principal benefit; (b) product attributes or characteristics; (c) the character or personality of the product; and (d) what the product is and its use.

Style refers to the unique way individual writers express ideas easily and naturally.

Unless the coordination of writing, illustrations, and production is consciously undertaken at the outset, the possibility of developing an effective advertisement is appreciably diminished. The development of advertising is a never-ending search for ideas and new and different ways of expressing these ideas. Fundamental to this search are the search for facts upon which to base ideas and the creative process itself.

The first step in developing advertising is to search out all of the facts one can find about the product, consumer, marketing situation, and the past and present advertising of the product and its competitors.

The creative process is divided into three stages: ingestion, incubation, and inspiration. The chapter outlines eleven steps that are often helpful in stimulating ideas and facilitating the creative process. Five common creative pitfalls include: temptation to avoid risks and "play it safe;" substitution of techniques for ideas; use of poor taste in order to gain attention; assuming consumers are naïve and gullible; and losing touch with consumers. These temptations are ever present and all are destructive to the creation of effective advertising.

REVIEW QUESTIONS

1 What are the four elements that should be included in the statement of copy strategy?
2 Distinguish between strategy and style. What is the key to effective style?
3 What are the two parts of the admaker's job?
4 What determines whether a fact is important or trivial in developing advertising?
5 Discuss the role of ingredients and manufacturing processes in developing advertising.
6 Discuss the role of price in developing advertising. What are the functions of price?
7 Explain the statement: "Writing advertising for a commodity is a thankless task."
8 Identify and describe the three stages in the creative process.
9 What is the first step in the creative process? Why is it important? Use examples to explain your answer.
10 Identify and explain the five creative pitfalls that the admaker should avoid.

DISCUSSION QUESTIONS

1 Locate two advertisements for competitive products. Analyze them by describing differences in the appeals they use. What is the basis for their appeals? Which do you think is more effective? Why?
2 According to the text, "effective advertising seldom blazes new trails in the realm of social mores; it bows to the prevailing values and conventions of society." Why do you think this statement was made? Can you think of any exceptions to it?
3 In recent years, a number of advertising campaigns have been charged with using poor taste. Among these have been: (a) United Airlines' "We move our tails for you" campaign; (b) English Leather's "My men wear English Leather or they wear nothing at all"; and (c) Bic disposable lighter's "Flick your Bic." Do you agree that these advertising campaigns were in bad taste? Why or why not?

PROBLEM

Sun Light is a dishwashing detergent produced by Lever Brothers Company and is used to wash dishes by hand. One of its ingredients is real lemon juice. Product tests against Ivory dishwashing liquid, the leading competitive product, have demonstrated that Sun Light cleans dishes better. In one test, a casserole dish was coated with an even layer of gravy and baked until the gravy formed a hard crust. The casserole dish was then cut in half. After equal soaking and cleaning, the Sun Light half was sparkling clean while the leading brand's side was still dirty. The following copy strategy has been written for Sun Light.

1 Sun Light dishwashing liquid is superior to competitive products in its ability to remove baked-on grease and other foods from dishes and cooking utensils.
2 The reason for its superior cleansing power is real lemon juice, an essential product ingredient.

3 The mood of the advertising will be down-to-earth and straightforward.
4 Sun Light is a dishwashing liquid used to wash dishes and cooking utensils by hand. It may also be used safely to wash fine fabrics.

ASSIGNMENT

Go to a supermarket and see what the Sun Light package looks like. Using this copy strategy, develop an advertisement for Sun Light.

12
Print Advertising

DRAMATIC DIFFERENCES IN PRINT ADVERTISING

Figures 12–1, 12–2, and 12–3 are print advertisements that communicate an idea clearly and forcefully, yet are dramatically different.

VOLKSWAGEN

The Volkswagen advertisement is nothing but a headline with white space where one would normally expect to find an illustration or body copy. However, the white space tells the headline story more clearly than any illustration or body copy could. The advertisement takes a single feature of the product—its air cooled engine—and turns the feature into a consumer benefit that supports the basic idea behind the Volkswagen; namely, the concept of a car that is economical, dependable, and trouble free. This advertisement is effective because the basic concept of the Volkswagen had been established through previous advertising. Standing alone, without this background, much of the advertisement's impact would have been lost.

VAN CLEEF & ARPELS

In contrast to the Volkswagen example, the Van Cleef & Arpels advertisement depends wholly on the illustration. It has no headline in the traditional sense, only the store's name at the bottom of the page. The body copy consists only of the addresses and telephone numbers of store locations. The advertisement is stark in its simplicity, yet it conveys wealth, style, and prestige through a direct visual experience.

ZAREH

The third advertisement has neither headline nor illustration. It is all body copy, tightly set. In form, it is a newspaper column, but the success of this advertisement is vindicated by the following quota-

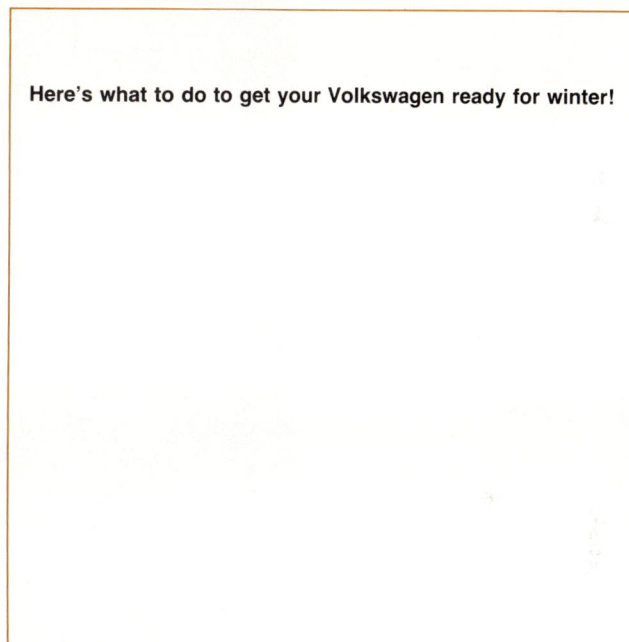

Here's what to do to get your Volkswagen ready for winter!

tion from a *Fortune* magazine profile on Zareh Garabed Thomajan, the proprietor of Zareh. Thomajan referred to himself as "the thief of State Street."

Zareh's column is probably the most widely read advertising copy in Boston and environs. At State Street he receives a steady stream of visitors who, if they do not come to buy, come to seek his advice in advertising their own products. A few of his fan letters are "scurrilous" like the one he got recently that began, "Zareh, you cur." Magazines and trade journals have run articles on his copy. The *New Yorker* reprinted one of his ads featuring a "positively insulting" scarlet corduroy loafer coat. Little, Brown & Co., publishers, asked him to write a book, and finally, he has been propelled into after-

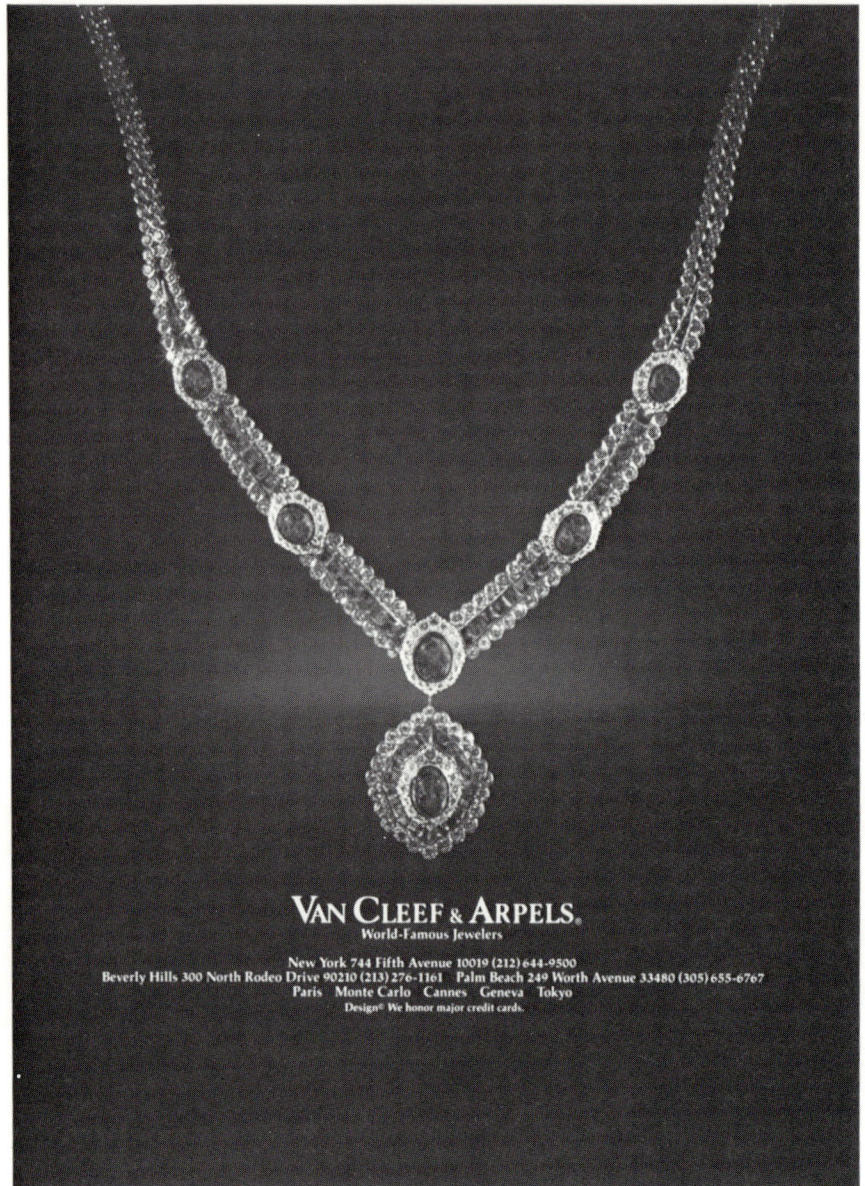

dinner speaking. He must have been the only haberdasher ever to
address a group of 1,000 genuine Boston notables.[1]

Admittedly, these three advertisements represent extreme
cases. Few advertisements are all headline, all illustration, or all
body copy. Taken together, they emphasize the point that advertising need not be forced into a mold or written by formula in order to
be effective. The ultimate test of a good advertisement is whether it
communicates the intended idea in such a way that it reaches and
influences its target audience. Many literary and visual devices can
be used to convey an idea. The job of the admaker is to discover and
use those devices.

[1]"Zareh Garabed Thomajan," *Fortune* (November 1947): 148.

EXECUTING THE IDEA BEHIND THE ADVERTISEMENT

All advertising starts with an idea, and finding the right idea is often a frustrating task. However, James Webb Young, in a treatise titled *A Technique for Producing Ideas,* suggests that the execution of an idea, the final step in the creative process, may be the most difficult one. Specifically, he says:

> In this stage you have to take your little newborn idea out into the world of reality. And when you do, you usually find that it is not quite the marvelous child it seemed when you first gave birth to it.

Z

I'll never forget the first time he came into our shop about a year ago. He was a little man in a green elevator operator's uniform, oldish and very shy. We were quite busy that day, but he awaited his turn patiently and then asked to see some "fine sweaters." Now "fine sweaters" in this shop means twenty or thirty dollars, so I showed him some for ten, thinking that by so doing I could save him some embarrassment and still meet his requirements. He said they were "nice," but would I please show him our "best" ones. So I did, some Scotch cashmeres, in the meantime making a mental note never again to judge a man by his jacket. He selected one at $27.50 and then asked if I would "lay it aside" and accept "$2 weekly" until it was paid for. I said I would and he came in every Saturday for a month and lived up to his agreement. On his fourth payment he asked to see some more "fine sweaters," selected one at $25, and then asked if I'd lay this aside, too. He wanted still to pay $2 a week (not $4) and pick up both sweaters when the whole amount, $52.50, had been paid. I consented only after I had tried to dissuade him from spending so much money. I didn't know what his income was, but I suspected $52.50 was most of two weeks' wages. Believe it or not, after about six more payments he propositioned me again. It seems we

had *four* English alpaca sweaters in our State Street window and would I please lay these aside, too! Well, this was obviously ridiculous. While we had nothing to lose (*all* his selections would remain in our hands until *all* were paid for, and this by his request), I felt I had to do something if my unusual client wasn't to go into hock for life. But it wasn't easy. This gentleman was obviously the sensitive type. I told him, and as gently as I could, that our arrangement was a bit top heavy, that there was no need to buy so many sweaters because the foreign markets were opening up again, that even prices might soon come down, and finally, I suggested something that was really none of my business—that he was spending too great a part of his income for things he could do without. He was very courteous. He listened intently to everything I said but could he still have the sweaters? He said he didn't drink or smoke, that $2 a week was no hardship, and that if I was worried he could pay $2.75 or $3 weekly! I got nowhere. I asked him then if he would at least take out a couple of sweaters and enjoy wearing them while he was paying me. He said, "No, thanks," that he expected to pay his total bill by the following August, at which time he'd take them out in time for his two-weeks' vacation in Nova Scotia, his childhood home. Right after he left, Tim came up and informed me that, contrary to my belief, Mr. "C" now had *thirteen* sweaters in the "hold" department instead of the seven I had believed. It seems our little friend had bought half a dozen more in the weeks past while making his Saturday payments to other clerks!

So I called my boys together. What to do without offending our passionate friend. It was finally agreed I should go to his place of employment, and, as gently as possible, call the deal off and refund his payments or, if that proved too difficult, settle for the first three sweaters that were now paid for in full. Well, partly because I was very busy, but chiefly because I dreaded the job, I did nothing for a few weeks more. Finally, one Saturday afternoon, I asked my bookkeeper to give me Mr. "C's" account. It was— 13 sweaters totalling $284, 39 payments totalling $78. Roxy also told me something that wouldn't be significant ordinarily but which was in this instance—no payments had been made these past four weeks. I walked up to the building where our friend worked, and, not seeing him about, asked the starter where I could find him. Possibly you have guessed the rest. Mr. "C" had died suddenly just four weeks before and was there anything he could do? No, there wasn't. I trudged back to the store and told the boys. Everybody felt low. About the only consolation we could find in the whole affair was my failure to deliver the ultimatum we had planned.

I shall be grateful for that failure as long as I live.

P.S.—What happened to the $78? Mr. "C" 's heirs have been reimbursed in full.

Zareh
INC.
25 STATE ST.

FIGURE 12–3   (Courtesy Zareh Men's Clothing Inc.)

It requires a deal of patient working over to make most ideas fit the exact conditions, or the practical exigencies, under which they must work. And here is where many good ideas are lost. The idea man, like the inventor, is often not patient enough or practical enough to go through with this adapting part of the process. But, it has to be done if you are to put ideas to work in a work-a-day world.[2]

In addition to starting with an idea, a good advertisement is a **gestalt,** a single, unified impression. Demand for a single, unified impression places two restrictions on the creation of ads. First, limit the number of things that are placed into the advertisement. Too many ideas will start to get in the way of each other so that none of them comes through clearly. A central idea, adequately buttressed with validation, is about all that a single advertisement can handle. Consider the advertisement for Scotchgard carpet cleaner (Figure 12–4). The central idea is embodied in the subhead "Makes carpets stay cleaner longer so you shampoo less often." The rest of the ad addresses this point. Second, all elements of the ad should fit together like the pieces of a jigsaw puzzle. Note the illustration immediately under the subhead; it compares Scotchgard with a leading brand. The first paragraph of the body copy provides supportive evidence of the basic product claim, and the second paragraph invites consumers to try it and see the benefits themselves. The product package picks up the central idea with the phrase ". . . so carpets stay cleaner longer." Finally, a coupon is offered to encourage consumer trial.

Most advertisements are like the Scotchgard ad in that they have four elements: (a) a headline and, possibly, subheads; (b) one or more illustrations; (c) body copy; and (d) a logo or brand identification. Some advertisements do not use all four of these elements, as was demonstrated in the Volkswagen, Van Cleef & Arpels, and Zareh ads. If all four elements are used, they are not always given the same weight or importance. Nonetheless, each element makes a specific contribution to an advertisement, and together, they provide a logical sequence or progression of the idea being communicated. The admaker should thoroughly understand the functions of each element because only then is it possible to make a judicious decision regarding which element or elements to emphasize or eliminate entirely. If one is eliminated, its function must be assumed by the remaining elements of the ad.

THE HEADLINE

The headline generally has three functions. First, it is a device that arrests the reader's attention when leafing through a magazine or newspaper. Therefore, writers often try to capture the essential idea of the advertisement in the headline. For example:

Wella Balsam Shampoo not only conditions your hair, it even repairs split ends.

or

The April Honda: lowest priced car in America.

---

[2]James Webb Young, *A Technique for Producing Ideas* (Chicago: Crain Communications, Inc., 1970).

FIGURE 12–4 (Courtesy 3M Co.)

Second, the headline is often used to select the target audience by appealing to a particular group of people, as the following examples do:

> More and More small shippers are discovering we're the Cargo Coddlers.
>
> or
>
> As the head of a business, I read Barron's to keep ahead.

The first headline identifies small shippers as the target audience. The second singles out heads of businesses.

Third, the headline, often assisted by a subhead, is used to entice the reader into the text or body copy of the advertisement. The following headlines are deliberately designed to lead the readers into the body copy of the ad.

8 great ways a Playboy Club Key turns the finer things your way.

or

A significant breakthrough in the fight against the effects of aging.

The headline assumes added importance when it is recognized that 80 to 90 percent of the audience never read more than the headline. David Ogilvy, for example, states:

> The headline is the most important element in most advertisements. It is the telegram which decides the reader whether to read the copy.
>
> On the average, five times as many people read the headline as read the body copy. When you have written your headline, you have spent eighty cents out of your dollar.
>
> If you haven't done some selling in your headline, you have wasted 80% of your client's money. The wickedest of all sins is to run an advertisement *without* a headline. Such headless wonders are still to be found; I don't envy the copywriter who submits one to me.[3]

ILLUSTRATIONS

In addition to headlines, most advertisements contain illustrations. Like headlines, one of the functions of the illustration is to attract attention. As an attention getting device, however, the illustration should be relevant to the ad's basic idea and not simply a source of **borrowed interest,** the use of irrelevant illustrations of high interest value. Properly used, illustrations not only attract attention, but also reinforce the headline, demonstrate the product, convey abstract ideas that are hard to express in words, and set the tone or mood for the entire advertisement.

BODY COPY

Copy is a somewhat ambiguous term that often applies to all of the words appearing in an advertisement, including the headline and subheads. When the term "copy" is modified by the word "body," it refers to the text of the ad, excluding headlines, subheads, illustration, and logotype. Body copy provides information about the product, develops support for the headline, and persuades readers to use the product being advertised. It is sometimes referred to as the advertisement's "reason why" because it permits the writer to develop reasons why the product should be used, rather than competitive products.

LOGOTYPES AND BRAND IDENTIFICATION

Logotypes (logos), or signature cuts, are special designs of the advertiser or its products which are used to facilitate identification. The logo in a particular ad may be a name, trademark, package, or some combination of these elements. There is no rule as to where a logo

---

[3]David Ogilvy, from *Confessions of An Advertising Man.* Copyright © 1963 by David Ogilvy Trustee. Reprinted with the permission of Atheneum Publishers.

should be placed. The logo is the only element that always appears in an advertisement. Headlines, illustrations, or body copy may sometimes be dispensed with, but the logo always appears to identify the advertiser.

WRITING HEADLINES

Not all advertising practitioners are as adamant about headlines as is David Ogilvy, who was quoted earlier. Most will agree that the headline is a major element in the advertisement. All advertisers deplore the empty, or hollow, headline that is a weak or meaningless statement. However, many headlines convey no information or inherent interest. Consider the following headlines:

Power Pal (a hairdryer)
So French you can feel it (a cosmetic)
Don't interrupt life's great performances (a cassette deck)
How very you (luggage)
It tastes like today (a soft drink)
Strip to our bare essentials (shoes)
Unsurpassed (a cleaner)

In some cases, these headlines were rescued by an arresting illustration; in most cases, they were not. When we consider that 80 to 90 percent of magazine readers only see the headline, we must question how much selling was done by these examples, how effective they would be in drawing readers into the body copy, and what they contribute to registering the name of the product being advertised. By way of contrast, consider the following headlines:

World's only dog food that makes its own gravy (Gravy Train)
How to *fix* any part of *any* car (Motor Book)
Charlie, I just love what your makeup does for my skin. Even after I take it off. (Charlie)
Why is any size headache The Excedrin Headache? (Excedrin)
This remarkable makeup gives you a fresh look that stays fresh all day. (Maybelline)

These headlines will not be of interest to everyone. They aren't meant to be because the products they advertise aren't for everyone. However, they do say something to those consumers who have an interest in the product fields they represent.

If there are any rules, perhaps the first rule of headline writing is that the headline should *do* something. It should state a benefit, create interest, identify the brand, give information, or select the audience. One obvious difference between the headline examples that said something and those that did not is that the former were longer than the latter.

HEADLINE LENGTH

A headline should be long enough to say something. Generally, one can say more in five words than in one word, more in ten words than in five. However, the point of diminishing returns is reached where the cost of reading the headlines exceeds the value of what it has to say. Consumers glance at an ad. The headline should be short enough to be read in this glance. Most writers strive for relatively short headlines. This is sound practice provided the headline doesn't become so short that it becomes meaningless. A short headline may have enough intrigue or be so well integrated with the illustration that it retains its power. Generally speaking, however, more sins are committed with short headlines than with long ones. One agency writer, Whit Hobbs, wrote this seventy-word headline:

> I seem to spend my whole day picking up; picking up the laundry and the groceries and the mail; picking up Jim at the station and the children at school—and picking up after them all! Sometimes I feel like a squirrel in a cage . . . running in circles all day and never getting a chance to collect my thoughts and take a look at what's going on in the world.

Why seventy words? Mr. Hobbs's answer was, "Because it took 70 words to say what I wanted to say."[4]

By contrast, one of the most effective advertisements ever run by an advertising agency has a single word headline (Figure 12–5). Much of the headline's power derives from the illustration. Raymond Rubicam acknowledges this point in the following quotation:

> Vaughn Flannery, then our art director, Anton and Martin Bruehl, photographers, and I worked long and hard to make that ad register as well as say *"Impact"* in every detail. Oddly, the very first picture idea that we rejected was a picture of two prize fighters, one getting a good sock in the jaw. Before we came back to it, we tried at least 20 other ideas, none of them with sufficient *"Impact."* It was only when Bruehl posed two negro fighters instead of two white fighters that the picture took on the fresh and dramatic character we wanted.
>
> I had the same kind of trouble, but perhaps not so much of it, with the text. It had to be short, it had to be emphatic, it had to be conclusive. So I adopted the device of two definitions of the word *"Impact,"* and stopped there.[5]

Subheadlines. Sometimes the problem of long headlines can be solved by the use of subheadlines (subheads), which may explain, qualify, amplify, or develop the headline in some way. A subhead is subordinated to the main headline but distinguished from body copy by being separated from it physically and shown in larger type. For example:

Headline: More Than Gentle!
Subhead: Earth Born Baby Shampoo combines a fresh honey-
suckle fragrance with a low pH, non-alkaline formula!

---

[4]S. W. Dunn and A. M. Barban, *Advertising,* 3rd ed. (Hinsdale, Illinois: The Dryden Press, 1974), 327.

[5]Julian Lewis Watkins, *100 Greatest Advertisements* (New York: Dover Publications, Inc., 1959), 97.

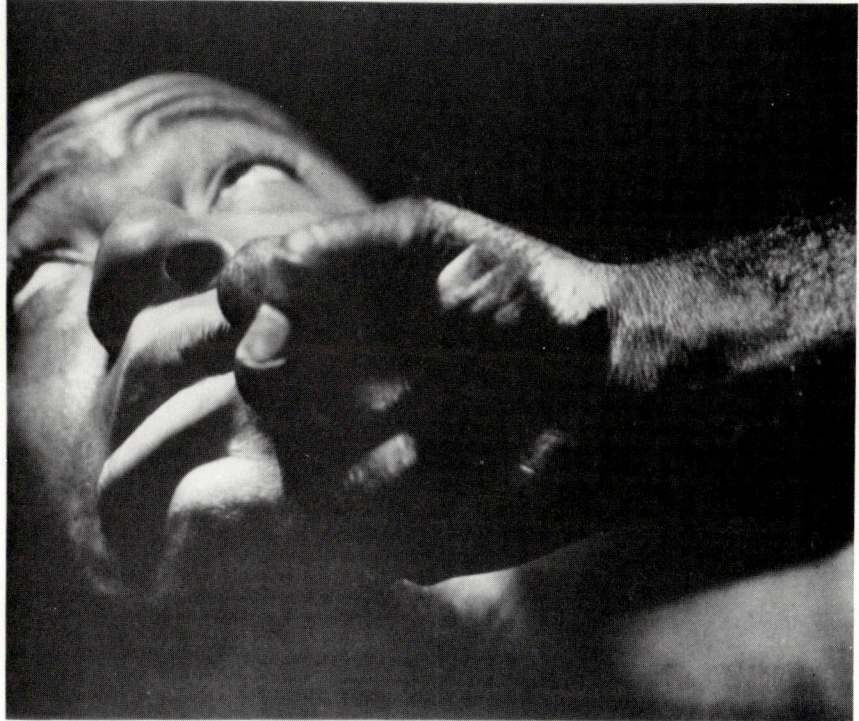

FIGURE 12–5 (Courtesy Young & Rubicam, Inc.)

Headline: Flatter your Filet!
Dramatize your dessert!
Glorify your goulash!
Subhead: Introducing Pyrex Fireside.

Headline: The beauty secret that keeps Royal Velvet Towels young.
Subhead: Our secret is invisible. It's locked in the weave.

Many short headlines have worked well; many long ones have worked also. On balance, though, about six to twelve words is the optimum length for a headline. Fewer than six words runs the danger of becoming telegraphic jargon. If more than twelve words are required, the idea may be too complex to be expressed in a headline. Margot Sherman, who gained recognition throughout the advertis-

CHAPTER 12 | PRINT ADVERTISING

ing industry as a copywriter at McCann-Erickson, touches on the real basis for judging the length of headlines with the following questions about advertising in general:

> Ask yourself, If I were a flesh and blood human being instead of an advertising thinker, would there be any reason in God's earth for reading or listening to this message? Is there really something here for me?[6]

DIRECT AND INDIRECT HEADLINES

Two ways headlines may be classified are as *direct* or *indirect*. Direct headlines identify the principal message of the ad; indirect ones are designed to arouse curiosity and lead the reader into the body copy. Two examples of direct headlines are given below. Both are relatively long—seventeen to eighteen words. In each instance, the body copy amplifies the headline, but the basic message is delivered by the headline itself.

> Max Factor creates
> Mistake-proof nail enamel.
> Pre-measured for perfect application.
> In the plastic shatter-proof bottle.

The headline not only identifies the consumer benefit ("mistake-proof"), but also provides reasons for this benefit ("pre-measured" and "shatter-proof bottle"). In addition, it identifies the manufacturer, Max Factor. Such headlines are often referred to as *hard-working headlines* because of the amount of information they convey relatively quickly.

The following direct headline from a Pioneer advertisement sums up the primary sales point in the headline.

> MOST $600 RECEIVERS SOUND AS GOOD AS THIS ONE. UNFORTUNATELY FOR THEM THIS ONE SELLS FOR UNDER $300.

The following headline from a Joy Manufacturing Company corporate advertisement is indirect almost to the point of misdirection:

> Think about what the world needs now.

Yet, it provides a focus for the advertisement and is appropriate in terms of its content (Figure 12–6).

These examples suggest that the type of headline depends largely on the purpose of the advertisement and the nature of the message. If the advertisement's primary purpose is to register the brand name or express the consumer benefit in a few words, then a direct headline is preferable. If the message is too lengthy or complex to be expressed in the headline, then the headline must be written

---

[6]*Advertising:* an Omnibus of Advertising prepared by *Printers' Ink* in its 75th year of publication (New York: McGraw-Hill, 1963), 316.

FIGURE 12–6 (Courtesy Joy Manufacturing Co.)

Think about what the world needs now.

Think about coal.
And think about the fact that JOY is the number one producer and servicer of underground coal mining equipment—including conventional, continuous and longwall mining systems—in a world where high oil costs and new coal export markets could increase U.S. production more than 30% in the next 5 years.

sors of all types and other air machinery in a world where the cost of delivering power is as critical as the power itself.

Think about pollution control.
And consider JOY's state-of-the-art dry scrubbers, wet scrubbers, precipitators, bag houses and cyclone collectors in a world inevitably headed towards syn-fuels, coal fuel conversion and a new generation of power plants and steel mills.

Think about key minerals.
Like chromium, cobalt and manganese, and JOY's firm foothold in hard rock drilling, ore extraction and various processing industries that are vital to supplying the future demand for these strategic minerals.

Think about oil.
And how JOY's petroleum equipment sales rose 45%—to $192 million dollars—in fiscal 1981.

Think about air power—the 4th Utility.
And think of JOY's leadership in supplying and servicing compres-

For more information about JOY and all we do, write Joy Manufacturing Co., Oliver Building, Pittsburgh, PA 15222. Or call J. Strauss, Investor Relations, at (412) 562-4518.

The world needs what we do. Right now.

JOY MANUFACTURING COMPANY
Pittsburgh, Pa. And around the world.

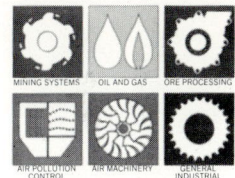

in such a way that it will attract readers to the body copy. In this instance an indirect headline may be required.

Often a direct headline may be provocative by the simple addition of a word. For example, consider the following headline for Bavarian Motor Works (BMW).

PEOPLE WHO DRIVE A BMW ENJOY
DRIVING MORE THAN YOU DO.

The headline is direct because it communicates the product name and makes a statement about people who drive a BMW. As it stands, it might draw some people into the body copy, but it has all of the characteristics of a "brag and boast" headline—all air and little content. Now examine the headline as it actually ran, with one word added.

WHY PEOPLE WHO DRIVE A BMW ENJOY
DRIVING MORE THAN YOU DO.

When the word *why* is introduced, the headline takes on substance, suggests that there are valid reasons for the claim, and implies that these reasons will be explained in the body copy.

When a headline lures readers into the body copy, the body copy had better be worth reading. It should say something worthwhile to compensate readers for their time and effort. Otherwise, the entire ad may be rejected as being irrelevant, and the product will have lost a chance to create a customer.

OTHER TYPES OF HEADLINES

In addition to being classified as direct or indirect, headlines may be classified in terms of content (the type of appeal or consumer benefit offered) or grammatical form (questions, statements, exclamations, or conversations). The following headline from a Pampers advertisement is conversational:

"I wouldn't use anything but Pampers. I've been
through this before."

There is little evidence that one form of headline is more effective than another. Effectiveness depends on the ad and what the headline is supposed to do. Some practitioners argue that, at least in product advertising, the brand name should always appear in the headline. Others disagree.

Many writers insist that one should avoid clichés in the headline. Ogilvy disagrees:

The two most powerful words you can use in a headline are FREE and NEW. You can seldom use FREE, but you can almost always use NEW—if you try hard enough. . . . Other words and phrases which work wonders are HOW TO, SUDDENLY, NOW, ANNOUNCING, INTRODUCING, IT'S HERE, JUST ARRIVED, IMPORTANT DEVELOPMENT, IMPROVEMENT, AMAZING, SENSATIONAL, REMARKABLE, REVOLUTIONARY, STARTLING, MIRACLE, MAGIC, OFFER, QUICK, EASY, WANTED, CHALLENGE, ADVICE TO, THE TRUTH ABOUT, COMPARE, BARGAIN, HURRY LAST CHANCE.

Don't turn up your nose at these cliches. They may be shopworn, but they work. That is why you see them turn up so often in the headlines of mail-order advertisers and others who can measure the results of their advertising.[7]

Some of the more frequently used forms of headlines are described in the following material.

---

[7]Ogilvy, *Confessions of An Advertising Man*, 105–6.

PART III | ADVERTISING

News headlines. Most consumers are interested in news about products: new developments, styles, or ways of doing things. The news headline takes advantage of this interest. Facts about a product are news as long as a large number of potential consumers are unaware of them, but the news headline always implies that these facts are of recent origin. Sometimes, the news headline contains the word *new*, but there are many ways of saying this without using the word. For example:

"Now there's a small copier that's not short on features." (Xerox)

or

Answers to the most asked questions about cigarettes. (The Tobacco Institute)

or

FINALLY, A REAL CHOICE (Citicorp)

or

ANOTHER FIRST (Boeing)

or

Introducing Andrea Swirl Off.
The instant nail polish remover (Andrea)

or

AT LAST. DIET FOOD THAT'S GOOD ENOUGH TO EAT. (Weight Watchers)

or

It's here! The new, soft undie in Undie-Leggs. (Undie-Leggs)

or

Arriving Soon. Royal's Non-Stop Copier. (Royal)

or

A NEW GENERATION OF BIO-TREATMENTS TO HELP COUNTERACT THE EFFECTS OF AGING. (Chanel Beauty)

All nine of these headlines are news headlines, even though only two of them use the word *new*.

Question headlines. Psychologically, a question demands an answer. A provocative question generates a psychological tension that is only removed by finding the answer. Many headlines attempt to take advantage of this phenomenon by raising questions, then answering them in the body copy. Some examples:

WHY CAN'T OTHER SHAMPOOS BE PERT? (Pert)

or

Why isn't a better airline more expensive? (swissair)

or

How do I get clearly more beautiful wood? (Pledge)

or

Is your child gifted? (Resources for the Gifted, Inc.)

or

Is Your Microwave Oven As Safe As It Should Be? (The Seeker)

Obviously, the more provocative the question, the greater the interest in the answer.

Command headlines.   A command headline tells consumers to do something, often to try or buy a brand. Properly used, they can be effective. Two interesting examples of command headlines are shown below.

NOW THAT YOU'VE SEEN THEIR
FIRST GENERATION
TAKE A LOOK AT OUR THIRD (Apple)
                    or
Drive a car that impresses people who aren't
easily impressed (Volvo)

More often, a command headline gains effectiveness when it is stated in some other way. Consider how the following command headline can be modified so that it gains effectiveness.

Meet your copier-duplicator needs.

As a command headline, it is weak and offers little of interest to the reader. Interest can be enhanced by making it into a "how to" headline through the addition of three words:

6 ways to meet your copier-duplicator needs.

The headline becomes even more provocative as it actually appeared in an advertisement.

Kodak Offers
6 ways to meet your
copier-duplicator needs.

Headlines often require work and rework before they say precisely what we want them to say in the way we want them to say it.

Testimonial headlines.   Testimonial headlines provide personal testimony about a product or service. Experts are often used to lend credence to advertising claims for products ranging from automobiles to zircons. Sometimes celebrities are used to give prestige to a brand, even though they have no expertise in the particular product field. Plain, ordinary people are often used simply to give assurance of product satisfaction. For example, a businessman, sports figure, and consumer are used in the following three headlines:

"We may not be ICG's biggest customer, but they treat us as if we were." (Anthony M. Santone, Vice-President—Distribution, Allied Tube & Conduit Corporation)
"Short & Sassy is just perfect for my hair." (Dorothy Hamill, figure skating champion)
"I stopped using aspirin the day the hospital gave me Tylenol." (Mrs. Alma Treadway, Scottsdale, Arizona)

Other ways to classify headlines include: *benefit* headlines, identifying a consumer benefit; *comparison* headlines, drawing a comparison between the brand being advertised and competition; and *how to* headlines, telling consumers how to do something (fix a car, lose weight, retire at age 50).

The various forms of headlines are only techniques, and a technique is only useful insofar as it has relevance in a particular situation. Frequently, young copywriters try to use a cute, funny, or creative technique that gets in the way of the idea; mediocrity is the result.

GUIDELINES FOR EFFECTIVE HEADLINES

Each advertisement is different and the requirements of the headline vary with the situation. The following guidelines should be thought of as a checklist of elements to consider.

1 The headline should have content and state the consumer benefit inherent in the brand. Avoid generalizations that could apply to any brand.
2 The headline should employ words that will help select the target market.
3 Brevity is desirable, but not at the sacrifice of saying something meaningful.
4 The headline should be provocative and draw the reader into the body copy.
5 It should be written in the language of the intended consumer.
6 The headline should be coordinated with the other elements of the advertisement.

ILLUSTRATIONS

In some advertisements, the illustration is the most important feature of the ad. The Van Cleef & Arpels advertisement used at the beginning of the chapter is a case in point. More often, the illustration amplifies the headline.

EFFECT OF ILLUSTRATIONS

Normally, the illustration contributes to the overall effect of print advertising by: (a) attracting the attention of the target audience; (b) communicating relevant product ideas or benefits; (c) stimulating interest in the headline and body copy; and (d) expressing ideas and feelings that are difficult to express in words. In a well conceived advertisement, the illustration often accomplishes all four of these functions.

Attracting the target audience.   There are many ways to attract attention with an illustration: run it upside down or sideways; use bizarre settings; shoot through filters; use dramatic subjects; employ action shots; or resort to pornography. Simply attracting attention is not the purpose of an illustration. A good illustration is one that attracts the attention of the relevant target audience in a relevant way. A cliché in advertising states that if you want to attract the attention of women, use the picture of a baby. If you want to attract the attention of men, use a picture of a puppy. If you want to attract the attention of everyone, use both a baby and a puppy. Sometimes babies and puppies are appropriate, as in the Gaines Puppy Choice advertisement (Figure 12–7); but for most products, they are not.

Examine a copy of *Fortune* magazine. Many of the advertisements use illustrations that may seem to be devoid of interest. Now, assume that you are a business person faced with a variety of operational problems, such as production, marketing, transportation, packaging, insurance, data processing, and finance. Reexamine the illustrations from this point of view to see if they do not assume added relevance.

Communicating relevant product benefits.   An illustration can often be used to communicate a product benefit. Thus, the Cascade advertisement (Figure 12–8) shows the results of washing glassware in Cascade.

FIGURE 12–7   (Copyright © 1977 General Foods Corporation. Reproduced with permission of General Foods Corporation)

FIGURE 12–8 (Courtesy The Procter & Gamble Co.)

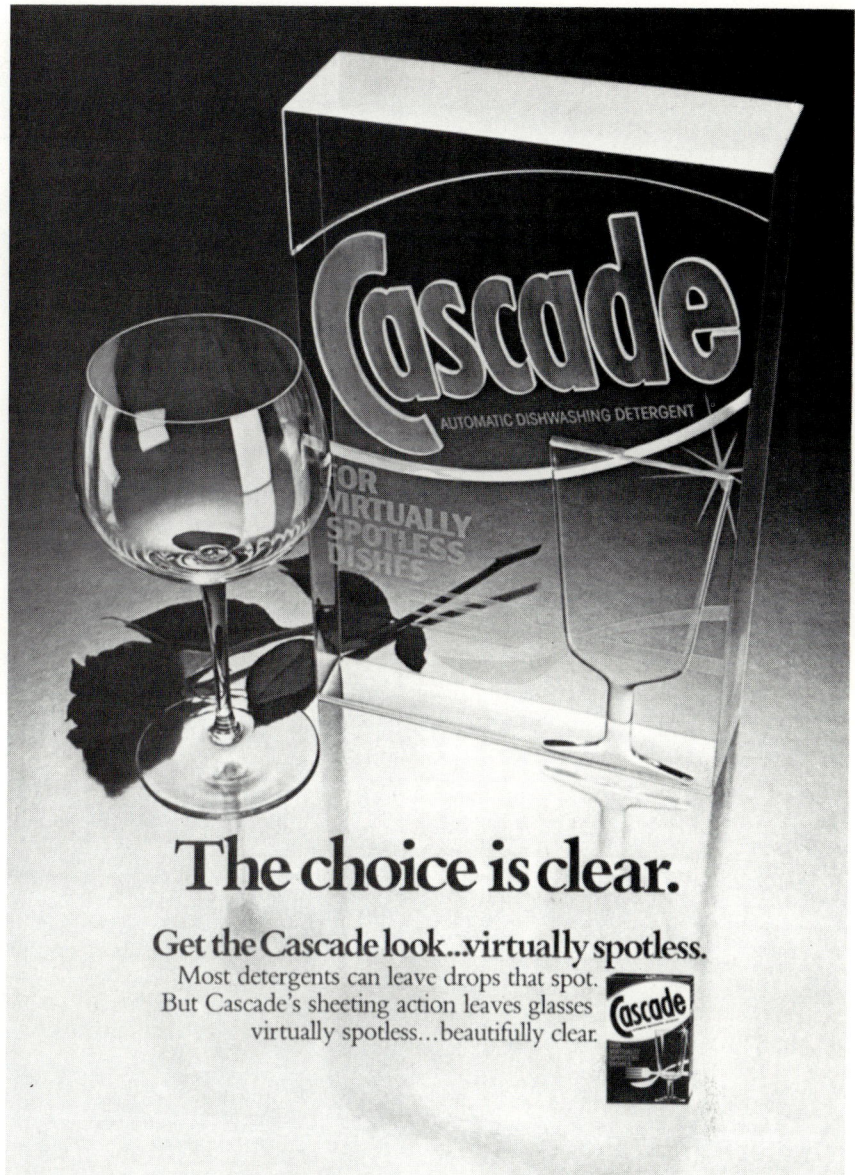

An appetite appeal photograph can enhance the attractiveness of a food product (Figure 12–9); a before and after photograph may be used to show the results of a diet plan; a simplified one-two-three demonstration of a product's use may dramatize product convenience; a fashion shot can reveal the beauty and style of apparel; and tastefully decorated rooms enable the reader to visualize how carpeting, floor tile, draperies, or furniture will look in an actual setting.

The end benefits of products such as fashions, home furnishings, and cosmetics are easier to illustrate than others. Once a principal benefit has been defined, however, finding ways of visualizing it is sometimes the admaker's most challenging job. Volkswagen used a series of illustrations of the Bug being driven through snow, mud, water, and over rocky terrain, summing up with the caption: "Few things in life work as well as a Volkswagen." Volvo demon-

FIGURE 12–9 (Courtesy Banquet Foods)

strated the strength of its roof construction by showing seven Volvos stacked on top of one another; Sound Guard, a dry lubricant for protecting phonographic records, used a magnified illustration of stylus damage to show the difference in wear between an unprotected record and one protected by Sound Guard.

Stimulating interest in headline and body copy. In addition to attracting the attention of the target audience, an illustration should intrigue readers so that they want to know more about the product. Usually, the illustration and headline work together in this respect: the headline makes a statement or asks a question; together, they dramatize a product benefit and create curiosity on the part of the reader.

Contrary to general opinion, women are interested in seeing photographs of women in the advertising they read, and men are interested in seeing photographs of men, because people are interested in themselves and those with whom they can identify. Research conducted by George Gallup for the movie industry has demonstrated that moviegoers are more interested in actors of their own sex than in actors of the opposite sex, and analysis of dreams has shown that male characters outnumber female characters in men's dreams by a ratio of two to one.[8]

Expressing ideas and feelings.　Feeling and mood can often be expressed more dramatically and communicated more quickly in an illustration than in words. Happiness, serenity, confidence, concern, as well as other emotions, can be expressed in words; poets and novelists do it all the time. However, it often takes several paragraphs or pages to do so. Because instant communication is required to capture reader interest, print advertising doesn't have the luxury of using several paragraphs to establish a feeling. Instead, it relies on the illustration for this purpose. An action photograph, quizzical look, intimate scene, fresh complexion, sad face, or happy gathering can be grasped instantly by the reader and can create empathy and curiosity about the advertising message.

ILLUSTRATION TECHNIQUES

The admaker can work with a variety of illustration techniques, such as photographs, original artwork, cartoons, and line drawings. Although the subject of the illustration is more important than the technique, experience indicates that photographs are far more effective than other forms of illustration in attracting reader attention and involvement. Ogilvy states:

> Over and over again research has shown that *photographs* sell more than *drawings*. They attract more readers. They deliver more appetite appeal. They are better remembered. They pull more coupons. And they sell more merchandise. Photographs represent reality, whereas drawings represent fantasy, which is less believable.[9]

The findings of Gallup-Robinson, a firm that has specialized in copy research, support Ogilvy's endorsement of photographs as more effective than other illustration techniques. Perhaps the most convincing evidence is that the advertising industry uses those techniques that tend to work best. Pick up any magazine, and note the large proportion of photographs compared to other forms of illustration. A number of reasons why photographs are more effective than other art forms follow.

1. *Realism:* People like to see the "real thing" in their ads. Good color photography does wonders for all kinds of products, from gleaming motor cars to steaming bowls of soup. Just look at the food photography in any homemaker's magazine!

---

[8]Ibid., 119.
[9]Ibid., 18.

2. *The feeling of "it's happening now":* Photographs—particularly news type photographs—put you right on the spot when it is happening. You are standing on the goal line when the touchdown is scored. You get involved. Remember, one of our big objectives in advertising is to put the reader "in the driver's seat" . . . to make him relate and see himself in that same situation.
3. *Making the "cartoon effect" come alive:* Photographers have done some wonderful things in taking "cartoon situations" and giving them the added dimension of realism. A drawing of the eye-patched Hathaway man, for instance, simply wouldn't come off.
4. *The beauty and sensitivity of film:* Photographers are sometimes able to achieve a high artistic level with their pictures. A photograph can carry a tremendous emotional wallop.
5. *Photographs make excellent "convincers":* What better proof do you need than the unretouched photo of the weight reducer, before and after?[10]

These are all consumer oriented advantages for the use of photographs. In addition, speed, flexibility, and economy are some practical advantages photography has for the admaker. A drawing or painting takes longer to complete than a photograph. Further, a variety of shots can be taken in the same session, and stock photos can be purchased inexpensively.

This does not mean that other illustration techniques should never be used. Photographs do not reproduce well on the coarse paper stock used by newspapers. Here, original artwork and stylized drawings may be more effective. Department stores use original artwork and line drawings to a great extent when depicting clothing, furniture, and other products in their newspaper ads. Original artwork has been used effectively on high gloss paper stock that lends itself best to photographic reproduction. For example, the Container Corporation ran a highly effective corporate campaign using nonrepresentative illustrations by artist Walter Paepcke; Massachusetts Mutual Insurance Company successfully used a series of Norman Rockwell paintings to convey a feeling of warmth and friendliness and imply that the company was concerned with simple, homey virtues. Similarly, graphs and charts may be used effectively in illustrations to convey important information quickly and dramatically. The point is not that nonphotographic illustrations should never be used, but when reproductive quality is not a problem, nonphotographic illustrations should be used cautiously because research has indicated that photographs are far more effective in attracting reader attention and gaining consumer involvement.

SIZE OF ILLUSTRATION

Marplan, a totally owned subsidiary of The Interpublic Group of Companies, a group of advertising agencies, analyzed over 250,000 advertisements, using the Starch "noted" score as the criterion for attention value. Findings indicated that single, large, well-structured illustrations with a single focal point were more effective than other illustrations in attracting attention. The Leo Burnett

---

[10]Stephen Baker, *Advertising Layout and Art Direction* (New York: McGraw-Hill, 1959).

Company confirmed this finding in a review of recent studies of advertising.[11] The use of the Starch "noted" score as the measure of attention may be a relatively superficial measure of readership. However, Gallup-Robinson used the more rigorous "recall" readership measure and made similar findings.

One limitation of these studies is that they only measured general recognition or recall, not the recognition of the specific target group. Nonetheless, the findings are probably valid for the target groups as well because the basic question is how much work the reader has to do in order to understand the advertising message. A complex illustration, or several illustrations in the same advertisement, signal work; work involves time. In the busy world of most consumers, an advertisement that demands a great deal of time will tend to be ignored. Instead, consumers will note and read those ads in which the main elements of the message can be grasped quickly. Robert Pliskin, while vice-president in charge of art for Benton & Bowles, looked into the future of advertising illustrations and predicted:

> Eventually, of course, print ads will be all picture, like TV, the bigger and brighter the better. And, maybe at the bottom somewhere, there will be a small line of type . . . .[12]

THE USE OF COLOR

The first full color advertisement appeared in 1937. Since then, the use of color has grown steadily; today, a majority of full page advertisements are printed in color, as well as many fractional page units. There are a number of reasons for using color in print advertising:[13]

1. Attracting attention to an advertisement.
2. Representing objects, scenes, and people with complete fidelity.
3. Emphasizing some special part of the message of the product.
4. Suggesting abstract qualities appropriate to the selling appeal.
5. Creating a pleasant first impression for the advertisement.
6. Creating prestige for the product, service, or advertiser.
7. Fastening visual impressions in memory (partly because of the performance of the other functions listed above, and partly because of inherent power to stimulate interest).

These are all persuasive reasons, but they do not mean that color should automatically be used. Color costs more than black and white, commanding a premium of up to 30 percent; it is not equally important for all products. Consider the three ads in Figures 12–10, 12–11, and 12–12. Both the Waterford and Grosvenor ads require full color. The drama and impact of these advertisements would be lost without it. By contrast, color is not an essential ingredient of the Panasonic ad. In fact, color would probably detract from it.

---

[11]Donald Wayne Hendon, "How Mechanical Factors Affect Ad Perception," *Journal of Advertising Research* (August 1973): 39–43.

[12]Robert Pliskin, "Some of the Most Carefully Chosen Words Are Pictures," in *Advertising:* an Omnibus of Advertising prepared by *Printers' Ink*, 113–46.

[13]Thomas B. Stanley, *The Technique of Advertising Production*, 2nd ed. (New York: Prentice-Hall, Inc., 1954), 59.

FIGURE 12–10 (Courtesy Waterford)

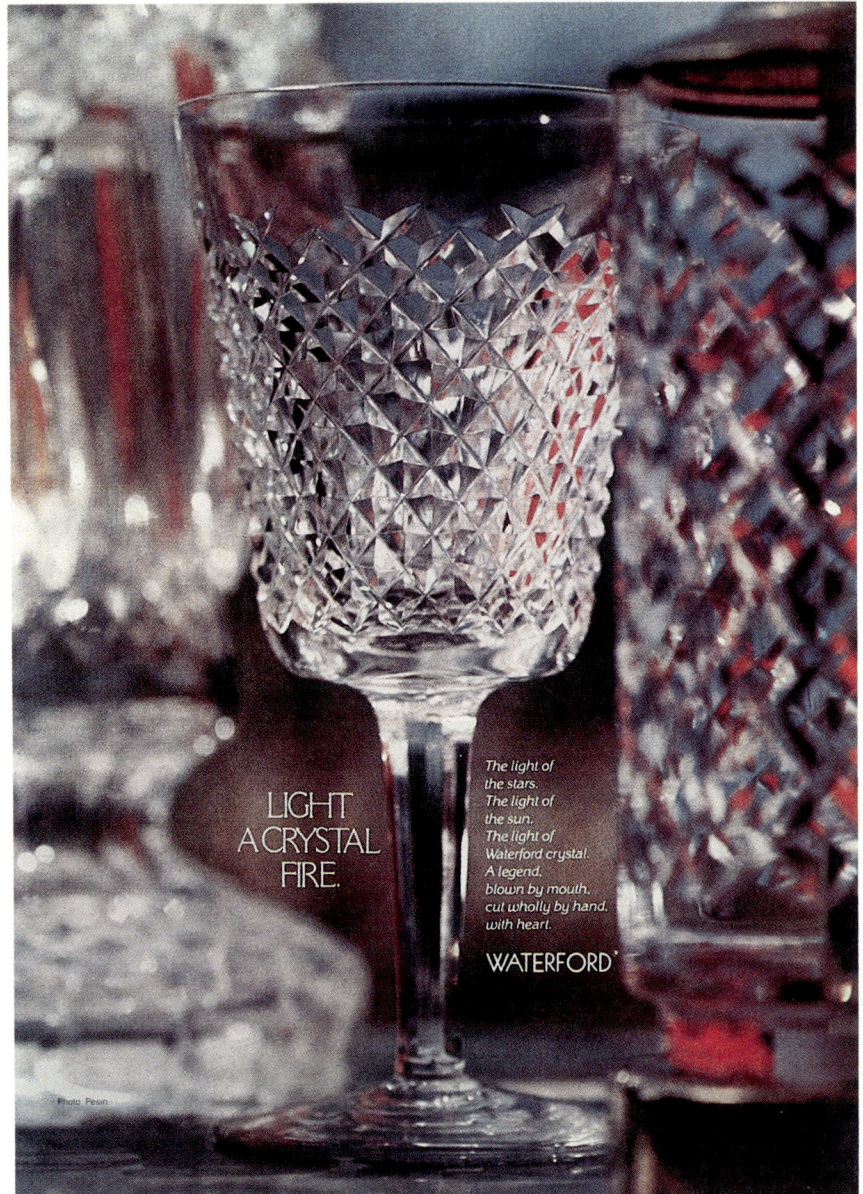

LIGHT
A CRYSTAL
FIRE.

The light of
the stars.
The light of
the sun.
The light of
Waterford crystal.
A legend,
blown by mouth,
cut wholly by hand,
with heart.

WATERFORD

When considering the use of color, the creative group can use a four-color process that will provide a complete range of color reproduction or a more limited, and less expensive, range of color such as: black and one color; two colors; black and two colors. When only one or two colors are used, they are generally used to attract attention or to highlight a part of an otherwise black and white ad. Such limited use of color often defeats its own purpose. Gallup-Robinson has found that when color is used functionally, such as showing green grass in what is basically a black and white ad for lawn seed, it may increase readership. However, when color is used nonfunctionally, such as a color headline or a splash of color for attention value only, it tends to reduce readership.

FIGURE 12–11 (Courtesy D. H. Grosvenor, Inc.)

In 1967, Daniel Starch revealed the findings of a study of 25,081 advertisements in seven product categories in national magazines.[14] The table below summarizes a comparison, based on the Starch "noted" score, of the various uses of color. Each column should be read separately. If the average number of readers noting a black and white, half page ad is indexed at 100, then the average number of readers noting a two color, half page ad will be 2 percent greater (index 102), and the average number of readers noting a four color, half page ad will be 87 percent greater (index 187). For full page ads, the average number of readers noting a two color ad is

---

[14]S. W. Dunn and A. M. Barban, *Advertising*, 375.

8 percent less (index 92) than the average number of readers noting a black and white ad, while the average number of readers noting a four color ad is 52 percent greater than those noting a black and white ad.

	Half page	Full page	Two page
Black and white	100	100	100
Two color	102	92	100
Four color	187	152	149

In the final analysis, the use of color in advertisements is a creative decision. For example, when Jack Daniel's began advertising in the 1960s, virtually all advertising for distilled spirits was full page, four color. Against this competitive background, the Jack Daniel's creative group deliberately decided to use black and white, fractional pages. This decision was made to: (a) set Jack Daniel's advertising apart from competition; (b) communicate the simple, rustic setting in which the product was made; and (c) broaden coverage with a limited advertising budget. This same Jack Daniel's campaign is still running and has been highly successful for almost twenty years (Figure 12–13).

Colors have many connotations and can be used to express a variety of feelings and moods. Blues and greens are cool and relaxing; red is exciting; pastels are feminine; dark browns are masculine; white is pure; black is the color of mourning; golds and purples are rich and expensive. However, colors need to be used thoughtfully, and some are hard to control. The Pet Milk Company devised a campaign for evaporated milk built around the headline "Start cooking with a golden spoon. Start cooking with Pet." Research indicated that the symbolism of a "golden spoon" was highly effective and reinforced the inherent richness of evaporated milk. Advertising

FIGURE 12–13 (Courtesy Jack Daniel Distillery)

IF YOU'RE EVER in need of an experienced photographer, Mr. Joe Clark is your man.

Mr. Clark was born and reared right over in Cumberland Gap, a Tennessee town that's even smaller than ours is. And, since about 1954, he's been taking just about all the pictures that appear in our ads. Over the years, Joe's good snapshots have told you a lot about Jack Daniel's Whiskey. But, as even he would admit, one sip will tell you a whole lot more.

CHARCOAL MELLOWED

DROP

BY DROP

Tennessee Whiskey • 90 Proof • Distilled and Bottled by Jack Daniel Distillery
Lem Motlow, Prop., Inc., Lynchburg (Pop. 361), Tennessee 37352
Placed in the National Register of Historic Places by the United States Government

illustrations featured a golden spoon, as well as appetizing food photography. Unfortunately, gold is a somewhat ambiguous color which ranges from a light yellow to a burnished bronze, and its color fidelity is difficult to control. The same advertisement, appearing in different magazines, reproduced a wide range of gold colors; some were absolutely unattractive. Pet Milk's advertising agency dispatched an art director to the printing plants of all of the magazines on the media schedule to work with printers in selecting the right combination of inks to produce a uniform gold color. After a year of frustration, Pet Milk's advertising manager insisted that the campaign be discontinued because of the inability to reproduce a consistent gold color.

TYPES OF ILLUSTRATIONS

Illustrations may also be classified in terms of their subject matter. A typical classification along these lines is shown below:

1 The product itself.
2 The product package.
3 The product in use.
4 The benefit derived from using the product.
5 The consequences of not using the product.
6 Comparisons—"before and after", as well as comparisons with competitive products.
7 Testimonials about the product.
8 Dramatizations of a situation.
9 Illustrations that create a feeling or mood.

Obviously, the list is not complete. The types of illustrations are limited only by the imagination of the admaker. Many illustrations can be classified in more than one way, and multiple illustrations can be used to show different product attributes or benefits.

Visualization of the major product benefit is often difficult. Robert Pliskin comments on the difficulty encountered in developing a campaign for the Glass Container Manufacturers Institute:

> The objective of the advertising: Demonstrate the superiority of glass over other packaging materials. Most glass, of course, is transparent, almost invisible. Glass also adds beauty and dimension to anything it contains. How do you make an invisible product highly visible on a printed page?
>
> Peaches. Peaches are packed in glass. Photograph a jar of beautiful, halved peaches—you will discover that the peaches simply take over the ad. Women will look at the pretty peaches, drool a little, and pass on to the next page. Worse yet, the peach packers may do the same thing. We want them to drool over the glass. How do you flag the inattentive reader? How do you tell him the ad is for glass containers and not peaches?
>
> Here are some thumbnails we tried.
>
> Why not do the obvious? Simply say GLASS loud and clear. Give the ad a logo, make the logo as big and important as possible. Not bad. But can we say it with imagination, a new way? Try setting the

word "glass" and putting it inside a glass jar, to make the distortion created by the glass enhance the meaning of the word. We run smack-dab into a problem here. We did not want to distort to that degree that would suggest a flaw in the material, but when we distorted the word only a little, we lost the effect we were after.

But the word "glass" alone is dull. We thought of glass letters, or of making the letters look like glass. Tallyho. The idea.

Use the word "glass" very large like a masthead, subdue the values so that it does not detract from the picture values, keep the copy to an absolute minimum.[15]

Figure 12–14 shows what happened.

A key point that emerges from the above quotation is that headline, copy, and illustration cannot be developed independently. They must work together to create a single, overall impression.

CHARACTERISTICS OF EFFECTIVE ILLUSTRATIONS

Effective illustrations often have the following characteristics:

1 The illustration visualizes the central idea or benefit underlying the advertisement.
2 It works with and reinforces the headline; it does not compete with it.
3 Large illustrations are generally more effective in attracting attention than small ones.
4 Illustrations with a single focal point are preferable over illustrations with multiple focal points.
5 When multiple illustrations are used, they should be used purposefully and in an orderly fashion.
6 Color is effective in generating readership when it is used functionally.
7 Photographs attract consumer interest and readership more than other illustrative techniques.

BODY COPY

The primary purposes of the body copy are to satisfy the curiosity of the reader, answer relevant questions about the brand, and persuade the reader to try the product. Littlefield and Kirkpatrick have suggested that good copy follows the pattern of a well-planned presentation and develops along a sequence of these organized steps:

1. Recognize a buyer problem or a buyer desire. This recognition is usually made in the headline so as to get maximum attention of prospects. The problem or desire should be true to life and present the prospect's own experience.
2. Recommend the product being advertised as the best solution or best answer to the problem or desire. The emphasis here is on the product as a solution—not on the product itself. The problem or desire is still the major consideration.
3. Promise benefits and advantages. Spell out in adequate detail and in attractive terms the satisfaction to be had.

---

[15]Pliskin, "Some of the Most Carefully Chosen Words Are Pictures," 134.

CHAPTER 12 | PRINT ADVERTISING

FIGURE 12–14 (a) Thumbnail sketches save time and require no refinement or execution. When the marriage of art and copy is consummated, these layouts are born. They become larger roughs, then comps, and eventually are rendered; some of these ideas become magazine ads. (b) Comprehensive proofs show the development of the advertising campaign beyond the stage of roughs and before the finished ads are produced. (c) The finished ads demonstrate the ideas of freshness, clarity, and uniform flavor in one picture. (Left photo by Ben Rose; top, by Stone-Langley; bottom, by Irving Penn. Courtesy Glass Packaging Institute)

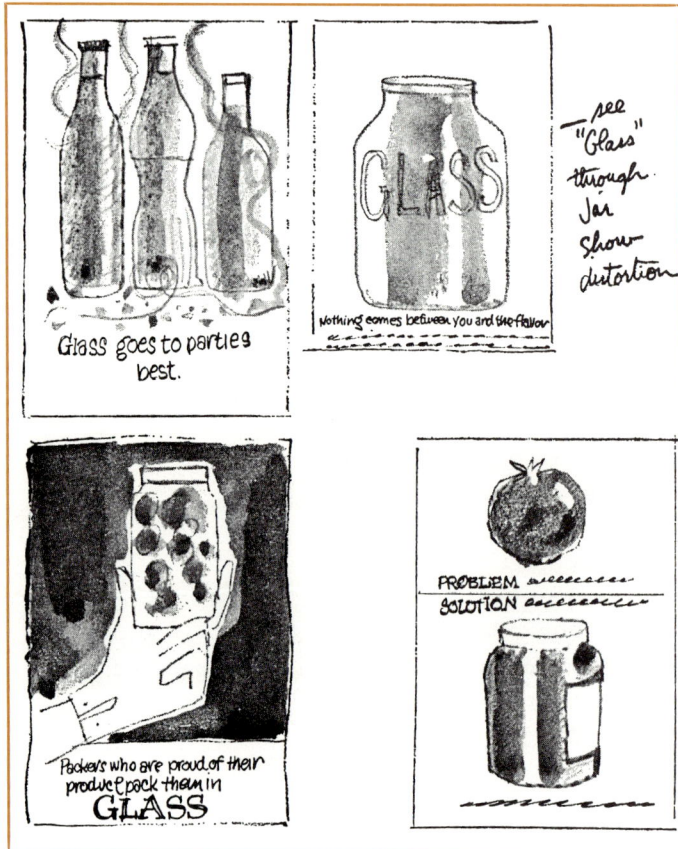

(a)

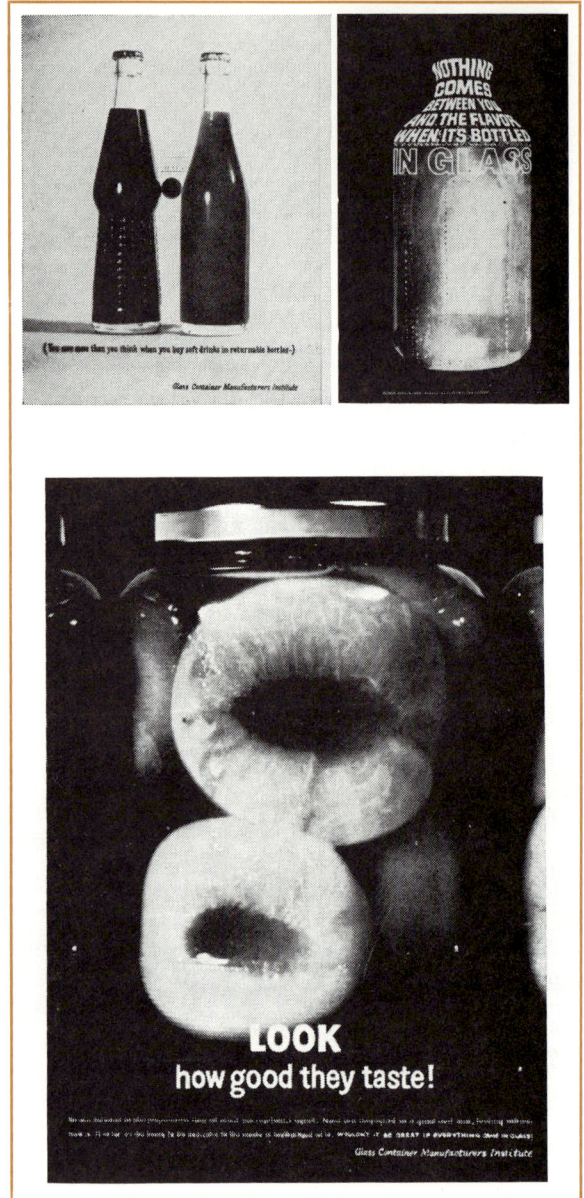

(b)

4. Personalize these benefits and advantages if possible. Reassure the reader that the satisfactions to be had are available to *him,* that he will benefit *personally,* that the satisfactions are designed for *his* situation and for *his* circumstances. Specific information is especially helpful here.
5. Offer proof of the advantages claimed, the benefits claimed, and the benefits promised.
6. Ask for action. Be absolutely and completely clear to the reader about what he is to do. Tell him *where* the product can be found and its *price* if those bits of information are appropriate. If there is a particular reason why the reader should act now, include it.[16]

---

[16]James E. Littlefield and C. A. Kirkpatrick, *Advertising, Mass Communication in Marketing* (Boston: Houghton Mifflin Co., 1970), 178.

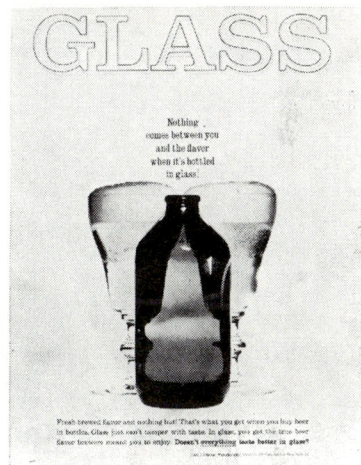

(c)

Not all copy performs these steps in the same way. Nonetheless, good copy carries out the spirit of these suggestions. To a large extent, the content of the copy is determined by the headline, which flows from the advertisement's central idea. Consider the following Pepto-Bismol copy. The headline makes a statement about the product benefit. The body copy amplifies this statement in clear, understandable terms (Figure 12–15).

Headline: (Interest)	Clinical study proves Pepto-Bismol is a good thing for too much of a good thing.
Body Copy: (Personalized)	Eating and drinking too much is one of the most frequent causes of upset stomach.

FIGURE 12–15 (Courtesy The Procter & Gamble Co.)

And among the most common symptoms of upset stomach are nausea, queasiness, and a stuffed, bloated feeling which can make you uncomfortable for hours.

(Benefit) PEPTO-BISMOL RELIEVES THE MOST COMMON SYMPTOMS OF UPSET STOMACH, OFTEN WITHIN 30 MINUTES.

(Proof) But now a clinical study has proved something that's been common knowledge for years. Pepto-Bismol relieves these symptoms fast. Often within 30 minutes.

These were the findings of a medical team after a study of Pepto-Bismol's effectiveness against symptoms of upset stomach associated with over-indulgence in food and drink.

So even though you've known it all along, now you know for sure. A good thing for too much of a good thing is good old Pepto-Bismol.

(Ask for action)   Read and follow label directions.

In this case, the proof is a clinical study. In other instances, it might be an ingredient, testimonial, reference to product reputation, or simply an assertion.

Body copy must always be tailored to the demands of the idea behind the advertisement, and it must be coordinated with the headline and illustration.

CLASSIFICATIONS OF BODY COPY

Among the various ways body copy can be classified include reason why, human interest copy, or humorous. The copywriter sets out with a clear understanding of the advertisement's purpose, a massive array of information about this product and its uses, and with the basic questions: How can I make this copy interesting? How can I make this copy persuasive? How can I make this copy believable? When the job is done, the copy can be classified as reason why, human interest, or humorous. Even copywriters are sometimes surprised with the final copy.

Reason why copy.   This is a broad classification of body copy that starts off with a consumer benefit or statement about the brand and explains why it is true. The Pepto-Bismol copy shown earlier fits easily into this classification. Sometimes, we think of reason why copy as being a straightforward, unemotional recitation of facts about the product. It needn't be. The following example is reason why copy, but it is also human interest, narrative, emotional, conversational, and humorous. It is an outstanding advertisement used by the Travelers Insurance Company.

The Greatest Reason in the World

"Why did you buy life insurance?" I asked him.

"Well," he said, "it was because once I met a young person coming up the stairs of an apartment house with her arms full of packages, one of them dangling from a slender string. I didn't think she'd mind, so I offered to help her. At the door of her apartment, I saw that she was quite pretty. She still is.

"Because late one night, while she and I were waiting at a dimly lighted railway station for the Owl to take me home, I said, 'We could live on the money I'm spending for railroad fares! What do you say we try it?' We did, and it worked.

"Because one day I was offered a job by another company, and when I told my boss, he promised me ten dollars more a week if I'd stay. When I told *her* of the boss's generosity, she said, 'What do you mean, generous? If he knew you were worth that much to him, he should have paid it to you before he had to.' So I quit and took the new job.

"Because one night she woke me up and said, 'I think I'd better go.' We went, and the last I saw of her that night, she was being trundled down a long corridor in a wheelchair, in spite of her protests that she could walk. When I saw her the next morning, she was lying very still and white with the sweetish smell of ether on her breath. A nurse came in and asked, 'Wouldn't you like to see him?' But I wasn't interested in babies just then—not even our own.

"Because one autumn evening, while we were driving leisurely along a country road, we came upon a small white cottage, its windows ablaze with the light of the setting sun. She said, 'What a place this would be for us!' Yes, what a place it has been for us!

"It's because of these memories, and many others that I wouldn't tell you and that wouldn't interest you even if I did, that I bought life insurance.

"And if the premiums could be paid in blood, instead of money, pernicious anemia would be a pleasure."

Moral: Insure in the Travelers. All forms of insurance. The Travelers Insurance Company, The Travelers Indemnity Company, The Travelers Fire Insurance Company, Hartford, Connecticut.

Copy like this is hard to write. That's one reason not much of it is seen. The copywriter has to be a bit of a playwright. The copy is also long, but it enjoyed high readership.

Humorous copy. Humorous copy is also difficult to write well; however, a trend seems to be appearing toward the use of wry humor in advertising. In his book *Humor in Advertising*, Donald Herold defends the use of humor in the following way:

> By humor in advertising I don't mean jokes.
> I don't mean gags.
> I don't mean gimmicks.
> Maybe I don't even mean humor . . .
> By humor in advertising, I mean a quiet and sensible and legitimate use of amusing copy and/or cartoons, or perhaps amusing illustrations or photographs, to do a job of merchandising—first by attracting attention in a relevant way, then by imparting pleasant information and making a soft sell, all in a mixed atmosphere of relaxation and integrity.[17]

Agency head Draper Daniels identifies four rules for using humor in advertising but suggests that these rules are only guides until the copywriter acquires the experience and judgment that makes them unnecessary.

1. In most cases humor is better for selling a low-priced product than it is for selling a high-priced one.
2. Humor is an effective way to put new life and memorability into an old story.
3. Humor is effective in telling a simple story in a memorable manner.
4. Humor is effective in driving home the ridiculousness of an outmoded practice which militates against the use of a new product or method.[18]

---

[17]Donald Herold, *Humor in Advertising* (New York: McGraw-Hill, 1963), 1.

[18]Specified excerpt from "Humor in Advertising" by Draper Daniels in *The Copywriter's Guide*, edited by Elbrum Rochford French. Copyright © 1958, 1959 by Elbrum Rochford French. Reprinted by permission of Harper & Row, Publishers, Inc.

The Volkswagen Bug made good use of humor in its attacks on both the size and yearly model changes of American cars. Maytag uses humor effectively in its story of the Maytag repairman, "the loneliest man in town." The Leo Burnett Company developed the following copy for Del Maiz Niblets Corn:

1. A very wealthy man had once forgotten everything about his early life except the name of the town he came from.
2. He had not given a thought to his dear mother for twenty years, being too busy stacking up the shekels.
3. One night his cook sprang a new one on him. It looked like a dishful of gold. It had a big glob of butter melting on it. He took a helping and tasted—lo! it was "Corn-on-the-cob-without-the-cob." It was Del Maiz Niblets Corn.
4. That big-kerneled, tender corn made scenes of his boyhood flash before his eyes. The old home. His mother standing over the washtub. The red-checkered table cloth. The big platter of sweet, golden ears of corn he used to love.
5. The man ate and reminisced—and vice versa. He was a boy again. So the very next morning he dropped his mother a postcard with a picture of Radio City on it.

Humor is not applicable to all products and may be offensive in some instances. Serious problems, illness, misfortune, and death are obviously inappropriate for humorous treatment.

Testimonial copy. Provided the reader can identify with the individual giving the testimony, body copy written in the form of personal testimony can provoke interest and be highly persuasive. Professional athletes are often used to give expert testimony in support of a brand. Celebrities with no particular expertise are used to attract attention and gain brand acceptance. However, indiscriminate use of celebrities may give rise to incredulity on the part of readers. It is difficult to believe that a leading actress keeps her hands soft and smooth by washing dishes with a particular brand of soap. Therefore, testimonials should be given by someone who is relevant, and with whom readers can easily associate the brand being advertised.

The following body copy from an Avon advertisement demonstrates this point. The purpose of the advertisement is to recruit Avon representatives. The spokeswoman is Cynthy Gravitt, a housewife in Tustin, California.

"I'm not the aggressive type, and I'm shy about meeting new people. But selling Avon cosmetics really is a friendly business. My customers are happy to see me and make me feel welcome. It's amazing how much confidence I've built up since I became an Avon Representative.

And running my own business gives me so much freedom. I'm able to work Avon around my family life. If my son Chad gets a cold, I can be with him as long as he needs me. That's the beauty of being your own boss.

CHAPTER 12 | PRINT ADVERTISING

All in all, Avon has made a beautiful difference in my life. It keeps me fresh and young. I'm more conscious of the way I look. And I've made a lot of new friends. Best of all, Avon has taught me I can just be myself, and everything else falls right into place."

If Cynthy Gravitt's story interested you, why not find out how *you* can become an Avon Representative. Simply call 800-325-6400 (toll free) and someone from Avon will be in touch with you as soon as possible to answer all your questions. Of course, there is no obligation.

Other forms of body copy are conversational, descriptive, and question and answer. The form is not as important as the content. If there is nothing worthwhile to say in the body copy, then the advertisement is better off without it.

LENGTH OF COPY

Generally speaking, short copy will attract more readers than long copy. Long copy spells work insofar as the reader is concerned. However, if readers are interested in a product, they will often read long copy avidly in search of more information. One of the biggest mistakes the copywriter can make is to leave out relevant information purely for the sake of avoiding long copy.

Illustrations and headlines can make long copy unnecessary. Marlboro advertising is a case in point. The picture *is* the idea behind Marlboro. Body copy is not necessary because there is nothing more to say. On the other hand, long copy is sometimes necessary to develop key selling points, tell the product story, or establish a mood. The only sound advice on copy length can be summed up in two admonitions: (a) Try to keep it brief, but don't sacrifice relevant content for the sake of brevity; and (b) Say what you have to say, then shut up.

GUIDELINES FOR WRITING BODY COPY

There are no hard and fast rules for writing body copy, but some guidelines may be useful to the novice copywriter.

Make the first paragraph of the body copy short and interesting. The first paragraph is the reader's introduction to the body copy. Unless this introduction is worthwhile and provocative, there is little incentive to proceed further. Consider these examples:

Now you can make Chinese-style fried rice in less time than it takes to cook ordinary rice. (Minute Rice)

Puppies, like babies, have special nutritional needs. But, unlike a baby, a puppy does 90% of his growing and developing in only one year. (Gaines Puppy Choice)

Sears Superplush towels are Sears' thickest towels. As thick as towels that usually cost much more. (Sears)

Let's say you are looking for a new car. And, just for the sake of argument, let's also suppose that, like many people, you're in the market for a midsize. (Buick Regal)

Each of these examples invites the reader to continue reading because each provides some information and implies that more is forthcoming.

If the copy is long, open it up with captions or white space between paragraphs.   Closely set, densely packed copy can be foreboding. The use of captions to separate copy blocks helps make long copy less formidable. The Conrail advertisement (Figure 12–16) is an example of this technique.

Keep the copy simple.   Copy may be written at different levels of sophistication for different audiences. For example, the vocabulary used for an advertisement in *Junior Scholastic* will differ from that used in an advertisement for the *New Yorker.* However, the presentation of ideas should be clear and easily understood. Most ideas can be presented simply with a little effort; jargon and telegraphese should be avoided. Ideally, copy should flow smoothly, containing no words that interrupt the reader's train of thought. Few consumers have advanced degrees in English literature, and it is unreasonable to expect the remainder to keep a dictionary at hand while reading advertising.

Keep the copy concise.   Every word in an advertisement should work. Excessive verbiage adds nothing to the persuasiveness of copy. The writer should get to the points quickly, without beating about the bush. Conciseness should not be confused with brevity. *Brevity* refers to the length of the copy; if there are a number of points to be made, there is no way to make them with short copy. *Conciseness* refers to how directly each point is made. Consider the following copy for Christian Brothers' Sherry. It is spare, lean copy that makes its points simply and directly.

> There is a wine to enjoy after the dinner is over.
> Creamy. Smooth. Rich. This is a wine to serve with fruit and cheese, desserts, or to offer with coffee.
> Of course, many people enjoy its delicious flavor on other occasions as well. Whenever you serve it, you will always find the quality and care that is there in each bottle from the Christian Brothers Cellars.

Make the copy specific.   Consumers are not interested in generalities. They read body copy to find out specifically what the product will do for them. If an automobile battery is guaranteed to give forty-eight months service, say so. Don't say "it's long lasting." Contac's statement that its "600 tiny time pills give relief up to twelve hours" is a specific statement about product performance. Avoid empty superlatives, generalities, and platitudes. Be factual. Meaningless statements are evidenced when a gasoline extolls the "joy of driving," a beer promises "know the joy of good living," a whiskey informs us it's a "gift in good taste," a tire is a "marvel of engineering," and a liqueur is "splendor in a glass." An effective advertisement tells the reader to buy this product and get these specific benefits.

"We want your freight business. Here's how we're going to fight to get it."

—L. Stanley Crane, Chairman, Conrail

"We've got to be competitive.

"If there's a profit in your business, we'll compete at every level to get it—with *competitive* prices and service you can count on. If you want to know what we can do for you, read what we've done for others."

You can count on Conrail

"We've made great strides in making Conrail as reliable as any railroad in America. We're getting good marks from our present shippers.

"The quality of our plant and equipment is second to none. And, for the year to date, we're in the black (see the financial chart at right). We're earning a profit despite adverse traffic conditions."

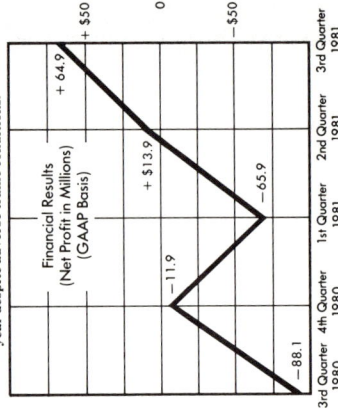

We're right on schedule

"Conrail *has* changed. Here's proof: Today, almost 85% of all freight cars moving on Conrail arrive within 24 hours of the published schedule. Conrail freight trains also boast an *on-time* reliability record that can

stack up to any other railroad in the country.

"In fact, over the past five years, Conrail's on-time performance has improved by 300%.

"Look at the chart on the next page to see just how much things have changed."

We're trimming the fat

"We're trimming down our system and are closing unprofitable routes. That means we can serve our *core* routes more effectively.

"Our goal is to create a core system that serves the industrial heartland of America, offering our present and potential shippers more efficient, reliable service."

We give you the competitive edge

"Rail deregulation opened up new opportunities for the rail industry, and Conrail is capitalizing on them.

"We've implemented 20 new contracts with shippers and we're negotiating another 35 right now. These contracts offer significant benefits including guaranteed rates, service and equipment, tailored to individual needs and requirements. Marketplace competition has forced the rail cost of shipping perishables down. As a result, our shipments of perishables are up. We're carrying 33% more perishable tonnage than last year.

"We also offer substantial discounts through our Econo-Rate programs and our Super Saver discounts. So call us and give us a chance to give you the competitive edge."

We're in the private sector to stay

"We're running a business like you are. We're making a profit, and our shippers are complimenting us for good service. We've developed new marketing solutions to shipper transportation problems.

"For an unprecedented second year in a

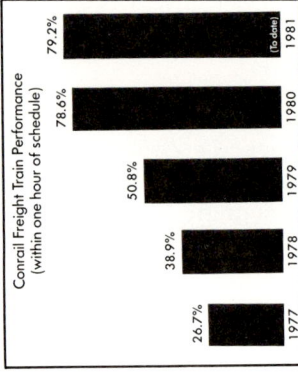

row, we've won the industry-coveted Golden Freight Car award for marketing achievement."

"We're an aggressive, innovative company. We're hungry for your business—your coal, your grain, your chemicals, your steel, your metals, all your shipments in the Northeast and Midwest.

"We promise you competitive prices and service you can count on. And if we don't live up to it, I want to hear about it. Write to me personally at 6 Penn Center Plaza, Room 1040C, Philadelphia, PA 19104."

**Write directly to me.
The buck stops here**

CONRAIL
"We've got to be competitive."

Conrail Freight Train Performance
(within one hour of schedule)

1977	1978	1979	1980	1981
26.7%	38.9%	50.8%	78.6%	79.2% [To date]

Financial Results
(Net Profit in Millions)
(GAAP Basis)

3rd Quarter 1980	4th Quarter 1980	1st Quarter 1981	2nd Quarter 1981	3rd Quarter 1981
−88.1	−11.9	−65.9	+13.9	+64.9

+$50, 0, −$50

Search for the right words. In Chapter 10, reference was made to the connotative meanings of words. A word may produce a positive or negative effect quite different from its literal meaning. "Half empty" and "half full" have the same literal meaning, but the first phrase reflects concern; the second phrase does not. "Inexpensive" and "cheap" have quite different connotations. Few people object to belonging to a large organization, but most people do object to being part of a bureaucracy. Usually, there is a right word to express a particular thought. Be diligent in searching for that word.

Be truthful. With all of their faults, consumers are not stupid. They are quick to spot the spurious or frivolous claim. Say what you have to say honestly, and stick to the facts.

Make every advertisement a complete sales pitch for the product. It is unreasonable to expect consumers to read a series of advertisements to find out about a product. Their time is precious to them, and they have little interest in serialized copy.

LOGOS AND BRAND IDENTIFICATION

The final element of most print advertising is the logotype (logo), which identifies the brand and/or the advertiser. The logo may be a name, trademark, package, or some combination of these elements. Generally, the logo appears in the lower, right-hand corner of the page, although there is nothing inviolate about this position. When the logo is a package, it may appear elsewhere in the advertisement as well. It should be sufficiently prominent so as to be easily seen and should be used to identify the advertiser and facilitate recognition at point of sale.

SUMMARY

There are no hard and fast rules about how an advertisement should be written. The major elements of a print advertisement are the headline, illustration, body copy, and logo.

The headline is often considered the most important part of the advertisement because it is the most frequently read part of the ad. Optimal headline length is about six to twelve words. Several types of headlines are direct, indirect, news, question, and testimonial.

When using illustrations, the advertiser must consider functions, techniques, size, use of color, and the types of illustrations frequently used. A checklist of the characteristics of effective illustrations may be helpful.

The purposes of body copy are to satisfy the curiosity of the reader, answer relevant questions about the brand, and persuade the reader to try the product. The particular type of body copy used will depend upon the purpose of the advertisement. Although brevity in body copy is desirable, relevant content should not be sacrificed merely for the sake of brevity. General guidelines for writing body copy are also outlined.

Each ad has a logo or signature. The logo should be used to identify the advertiser and to facilitate recognition at the point of sale.

1 What are the four basic elements of a print advertisement?
2 Why is it important that the admaker thoroughly understand the elements of an advertisement? What must be done if one element is deliberately left out?
3 What are the functions of: (a) headlines; (b) illustrations; (c) body copy; and (d) the logo?
4 Discuss the question of headline length.
5 What are the guidelines for writing effective headlines?
6 In print advertisements, why are photographs more effective than other art forms?
7 What are the reasons for using color in print advertisements?
8 What are the characteristics of effective illustrations?
9 What is the sequence of steps recommended for body copy?
10 Identify the guidelines for writing body copy.

DISCUSSION QUESTIONS

1 Select a headline from a current magazine advertisement and analyze it using the guidelines for effective headlines. Do you believe that this is an effective headline? Why or why not?
2 Select an illustration from a current magazine advertisement and evaluate it in terms of the primary functions of an illustration. Do you believe that it is an effective illustration? Why or why not?
3 Select a current magazine advertisement and analyze the body copy on the basis of the functions it should perform. Do you believe the body copy is effective? Why or why not?

PROBLEM

The Blitz-Weinhard Brewing Company is a small, regional brewing company in the northwestern region of the United States. A decision has been made to run an advertising campaign in the West Coast edition of *Time* magazine.

Copy Strategy
1 Henry Weinhard's beer is superior in quality to other premium beers.
2 The reason for its superiority is that it is made from more costly ingredients, using premium hops and barley grown in the Northwest and pure fresh water from the Cascade mountain range.
3 The content and tone of the copy will be informal but informative.
4 Henry Weinhard's is a premium, pilsner beer that may be drunk for pleasure or with meals and snacks.

Copy Plan for Print Advertising
1 Print advertising will consist of a testimonial from someone who is an authority on beer.
2 Advertising will be a full page unit.
3 A two-thirds page, square, four-color photograph of the person giving the testimonial in an appropriate setting will appear in the upper left-hand corner of the advertisement, immediately below the headline.
4 The remainder of the advertisement will be copy, black on white, in three columns.

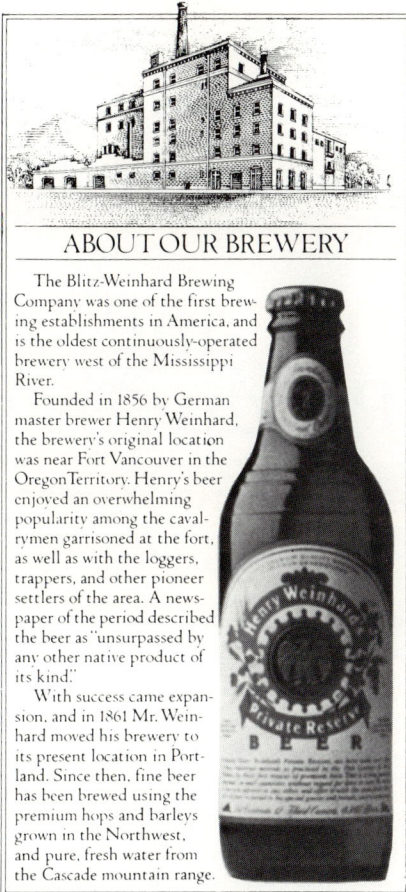

ABOUT OUR BREWERY

The Blitz-Weinhard Brewing Company was one of the first brewing establishments in America, and is the oldest continuously-operated brewery west of the Mississippi River.

Founded in 1856 by German master brewer Henry Weinhard, the brewery's original location was near Fort Vancouver in the Oregon Territory. Henry's beer enjoyed an overwhelming popularity among the cavalrymen garrisoned at the fort, as well as with the loggers, trappers, and other pioneer settlers of the area. A newspaper of the period described the beer as "unsurpassed by any other native product of its kind."

With success came expansion, and in 1861 Mr. Weinhard moved his brewery to its present location in Portland. Since then, fine beer has been brewed using the premium hops and barleys grown in the Northwest, and pure, fresh water from the Cascade mountain range.

FIGURE 12–17 (Courtesy Blitz-Weinhard Brewing Co.)

Creative Director: Hal Riney; Art Director: Jerry Andelin; Copywriter: Dennis Foley; Agency: Ogilvy and Mather, San Francisco

5 The lower half of the last column will contain the cut shown in Figure 12–17.
6 The following line will appear across the bottom of the advertisement: The Blitz-Weinhard Brewing Company of Portland, Oregon.

You have just joined Blitz-Weinhard's advertising agency as a novice copywriter. Your group supervisor has given you the foregoing material and asked you to develop a magazine advertisement.

ASSIGNMENT

1 Describe the illustration.
2 Write a headline.
3 Write body copy.

Suggestion to students: If you wish to see an example of Henry Weinhard's advertising, you may find one in Chapter 11, Figure 11–4. Other examples can be found in other 1982 issues of *Time*. For the purpose of this assignment, you may select or make up an authority. In either case, the body copy should qualify the authority.

13

Design, Layout, and Mechanical Production

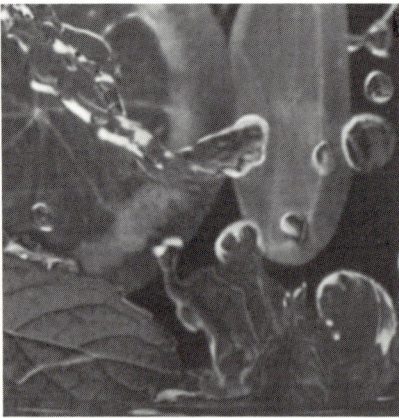

EFFECTIVE DESIGN

Design in print advertising refers to the arrangement of the elements in the space available. Effective design is highly subjective. Consider the following issues.

PICTURE-HEADLINE FORMAT

One point of view is the editorial format, showing a dominant illustration at the top of the page, followed by a headline, body copy, and logo. The Mary Kay ad (Figure 13–1) uses this format. Marplan, following the analysis of the Starch "noting" scores of 250,000 advertisements, supports this point of view.[1] Similar findings have been reported by other research organizations.

An examination of advertisements in any current magazine will reveal that many ads violate this rule. Art directors often insist that the editorial format places too many restrictions on the design of advertisements, hinders the creative expression of ideas, and results in a monotony of design that makes all advertising look alike. Rudy Czufin, former art director of the Gardner Advertising Company, expressed his contempt for the editorial format by charging: "If that's good advertising design, you don't need an art director. All you need is a straightedge and a photograph."

OVERPRINTING AND REVERSE TYPE

Two controversial practices that are widely used in contemporary advertising involve overprinting and reverse type. In **overprinting,** the headline, body copy, or both are printed on the illustration instead of being segregated from it. This practice economizes on space and permits the use of a larger illustration. It also allows greater flexibility in arranging elements in an ad and may help draw attention to the headline. Nonetheless, on the basis of its research,

---

[1]Donald Wayne Hendon, "How Mechanical Factors Affect Ad Perception," *Journal of Advertising Research* (August 1973): 39–43.

Gallup-Robinson cautions against this practice, and Ogilvy states that it reduces the attention value of advertisements by an average of 19 percent.[2]

Overprinting tends to clutter up the illustration, reducing its clarity and communication value. As a result, the headline and illustration compete for attention. Opponents of overprinting argue that the illustration and headline should never compete in a well-constructed advertisement; they should complement each other. Critics suggest that admakers should take their cue from newspaper and magazine editors. They seldom hide their illustrations behind their headlines, and their practices shape the reading habits of consumers.

The second controversial practice, using **reverse type,** is particularly prevalent in contemporary advertising. Reverse type is printing the headline, body copy, or both in white against a dark background instead of following conventional practices and using black type on a white background. A probable reason for the widespread use of reverse type is the growing tendency to use larger illustrations. If the illustration fills the entire advertising space, overprinting must be used. If the same illustration uses dark colors, the advertising designer must use reverse type in order for the headline and copy to be read.

Critics argue that consumers are unaccustomed to reading reverse type because books, magazines, and newspapers do not use it. They further contend that the effect of using reverse type is "arty" and signals to the reader that the communication is just another ad. Kenneth Roman and Jane Maas point out that reverse type may look attractive, but it reduces readership. As an example, they refer to the Save the Children Foundation advertisement, which used white type on a black background when soliciting funds. When the organization tested black type on a white background, the conventional way of printing, contributions increased 65 percent.[3]

---

[2]David Ogilvy, *Confessions of An Advertising Man* (New York: Atheneum, 1964), 125.
[3]Kenneth Roman and Jane Maas, *How to Advertise* (New York: St. Martin's Press, 1976), 36.

FIGURE 13–1 (Courtesy Mary Kay Cosmetics)

LEARN HOW BEAUTIFUL A LITTLE SELF-CONFIDENCE CAN MAKE YOU.

You don't have to look like a model to look beautiful. When you believe in yourself, value yourself, have a positive feeling about yourself, people are just naturally attracted to you.

Mary Kay's professional Beauty Consultant will show you how good you can feel about who you are. She'll give you a beauty show right in your home.

You'll learn which skin care products will make your skin radiant.

You'll learn which cosmetics will bring out your best features.

You'll learn how to apply all Mary Kay's beauty products yourself so you won't just look terrific for a day, you'll know how to look terrific every day.

You'll learn how much you have going for you. And with Mary Kay, that's more than a beautiful face. It's a beautiful feeling.

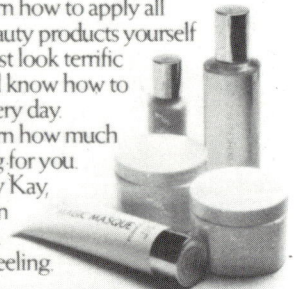

THAT'S THE BEAUTY OF MARY KAY.™

Look in the Yellow Pages under Cosmetics/Retail, or call 800/527-6270 toll-free. In Texas, call collect 214/630-8787. In Canada, 416/624-5600.

COUPONS

Traditionally, advertisements that include a consumer coupon place the coupon in the lower right-hand corner of the ad. In their admonitions to admakers, Roman and Maas suggest that the advertiser who is planning a coupon ad should request a right-hand page position and place the coupon in the lower right-hand corner where it can easily be torn out. On the other hand, Ogilvy says: "When your advertisement is to contain a coupon, and you want maximum returns, put it at the top, bang in the middle. This position pulls

80 percent more coupons than the traditional outside-bottom of the page."[4]

With such conflicting advice it is little wonder that ad designers often just do what seems right to them. Because of a number of reasons, conflicting advertising practices are rampant. First, the basic strength of a good advertisement lies in the idea. If the idea is strong, this strength can overcome many of the limitations of a weak presentation. However, if the idea is weak, good advertising design will probably reveal the idea's weakness by drawing attention to it. Second, different ideas may well require different treatments. A design that works well for one idea may be poorly adapted for another. Third, some poor designs may be redeemed by a powerful headline or compelling illustration that can overcome the inadequacies of an awkward design. Fourth, most research studies are based on large numbers of ads; some are well read, partly read, or not read at all. These studies only conclude that certain design features tend to be more effective than others. Fifth, most research studies of advertising design are based on general readership rather than target audiences. An ad that is usually not read by the general public may still have high readership by those consumers who represent key prospects.

This ambiguity makes advertising design a complex undertaking and leads to the conclusion that effective advertising is more of an art than a science.

DESIGN CONSIDERATIONS

Three terms that are sometimes used ambiguously in advertising design are *visualize, layout,* and *design.* To visualize refers to the mental picture that a copywriter or art director has of an advertisement before anything is put on paper. In the process of developing an idea, its originator begins to imagine or visualize how the advertisement will look in its final form. Because many details have to be worked out, this visualization can be quite specific or fairly general. This "picture in the mind" is the starting point for getting something down on paper.

The term *layout* is an advertising colloquialism that is used as a verb or a noun. As a verb, it refers to the actual process that is involved in translating the admaker's idea into a finished product. As a noun, it is the result of this process. Thus, an art director may layout an ad (referring to work to be done), or produce a layout for an idea (referring to the result of work that has been done). In the layout process, the art director arranges and rearranges the elements of the advertisement until a satisfactory design is obtained.

The design of an advertisement is the final result of visualization as developed and modified through a number of layouts.

SPACE UNITS

Certain pragmatic considerations influence the final design of the advertisement. One of these, the space unit available, is often influenced by budget considerations. If the advertisement can afford a

---

[4]Ogilvy, *Confessions of An Advertising Man,* 125.

two page spread, the art director has more flexibility than having to work within the constraints of a single page, half page, or single column. Further, some page and multiple page advertisements are *bleed ads,* with the illustration extending beyond the normal margins to the edge, or *trim line,* of the page. In a two page spread, the advertisement may bleed across the gutter, e.g., the illustration, type, or both may run across the center binding of the magazine. Other advertising units are: *gatefolds,* double and triple pages that fold out to reveal one advertisement; or *dutch doors,* pages that partially cover each other to lend interest or create a particular effect.

The most frequently used page and multiple page units are exemplified by: (a) Pall Mall's advertisement (Figure 13–2), a con-

FIGURE 13–2 (Courtesy The American Tobacco Co.)

FIGURE 13–3 (Courtesy Thomas
J. Lipton, Inc.)

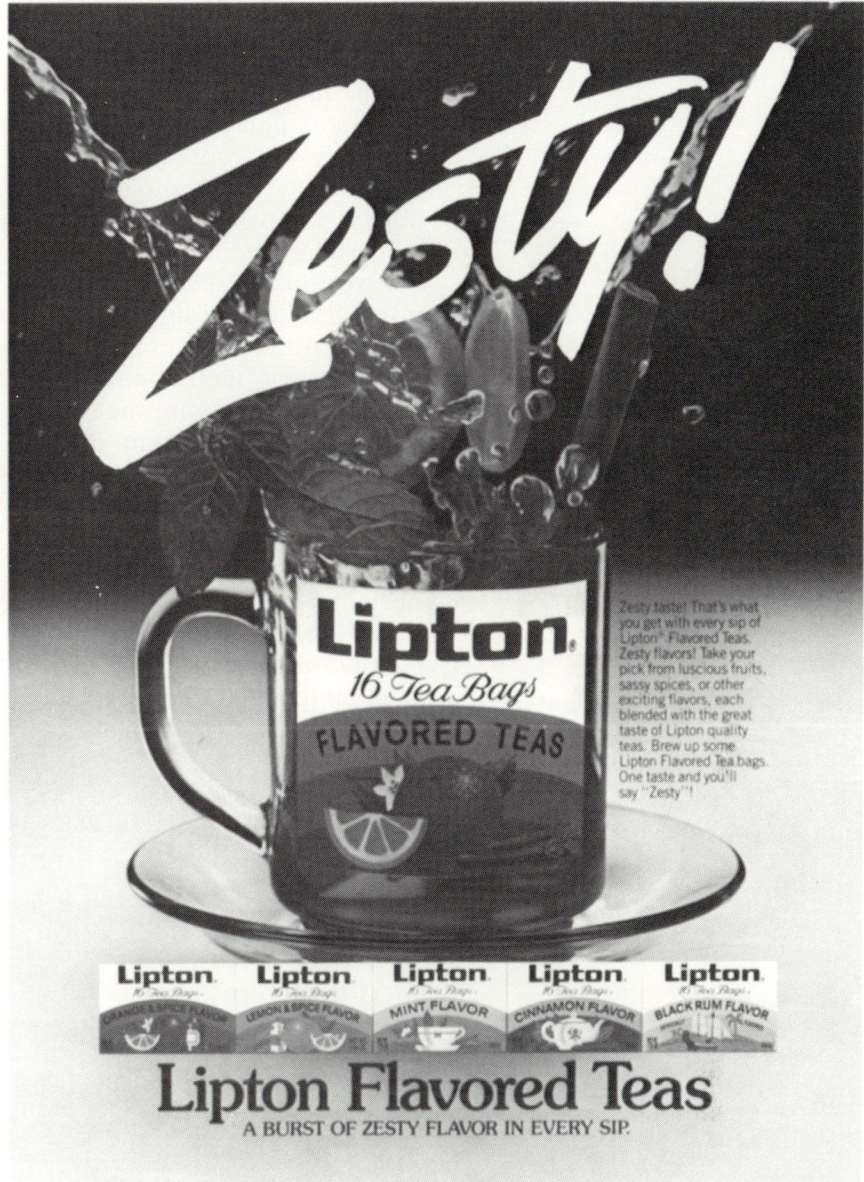

ventional page unit in which the illustration and print areas
arè surrounded by white, trim space; (b) Lipton Flavored Teas' ad
(Figure 13–3), a single page, bleed ad; and (c) a double page ad
that spans the gutter and occupies facing pages (see Figure 12–16,
page 358).

Since nonconventional page units generally carry a premium
price, their use frequently stumbles against the harsh reality of the
advertising budget. For example, a single page, bleed ad usually
costs 15 to 20 percent more than a standard page.

Most consumer magazines usually offer a variety of page units,
ranging from gatefolds and dutch doors to vertical and horizontal
fractional pages, as well as other unusual units. The art director
must always work within the confines of the affordable as well as
available space units.

TYPES OF DESIGNS

In a major space unit of one page or more, the elements of an advertisement may be laid out in any number of ways. One may use a dominant illustration or a number of small illustrations arranged vertically, horizontally, diagonally, or randomly on the page. Using a combination of dominant and smaller illustrations is also acceptable. Headlines and logos may appear anywhere on the page.

The particular design used is important only insofar as it dramatizes the advertisement's main idea. The designer should keep in mind that the design should always be subordinated to the idea being communicated; the purpose of design is to focus attention on the idea, not dominate it. Most advertising practitioners are highly critical of advertising that is designed as art without consideration of its business function. Rosser Reeves suggests that we should always be suspicious of such advertising because it usually obscures the product message.[5]

CHARACTERISTICS OF EFFECTIVE DESIGN

Although print advertisement may be designed in many ways, good designs have several things in common. Some of the more important characteristics include focal point, movement, clarity of presentation, simplicity, and arrangement of headlines.

FOCAL POINT

A well designed ad has a single focal point that attracts the consumer's attention. The focal point is generally the headline or illustration. It draws the reader into the ad and provides a logical place to start. A cluttered design with several focal points often appears confusing, spells work to the reader, and reduces reader interest.

MOVEMENT

Movement refers to the way the reader's attention flows from one element of the advertisement to another. An effective design generally has a dominant or logical focal point and is constructed so that the reader's gaze is drawn successively through the major elements of the ad. A number of devices may be used to obtain this effect.

A logical sequence of elements. Through constant exposure to magazine and newspaper editorial material, most readers have become accustomed to proceeding from the top down and from left to right. This method of presentation seems logical. Thus, advertisements laid out along these lines are easy to read and tend to sustain a higher than average readership. The Shake 'n Bake ad (Figure 13–4) follows this design. The dominant appetite appeal photograph is the focal point, or starting place, for the ad. The reader's gaze flows easily from headline, to package, body copy, and slogan at the bottom of the page.

Pointing devices. Hands, arrows, lines, blocks of type, and numbers can also be used to lead the attention of readers from one part

---

[5]Rosser Reeves, *Reality in Advertising* (New York: Alfred K. Knopf, 1961), 122–23.

"See how Shake 'n Bake keeps chicken more moist and tender."

Fried chicken can be dry.
Baked chicken can be dry.
But chicken made with Shake 'n Bake® coating mix comes out more moist and tender—because the crispy coating seals in the juices.

"With Shake 'n Bake® coating mix you get crispy chicken at its tender best."

© General foods corporation 1977. Reproduced with permission of General Foods Corporation.

of the advertisement to another in a sequential fashion. In the Shake 'n Bake advertisement the chef is pointing to the package. The Eastman 910 Adhesive advertisement (Figure 13–5) uses numbers to direct eye flow. While this advertisement contains many elements, the numbering device helps the reader sort out and dwell on each of them.

Gaze motion. Research studies show that eyes direct other eyes. Gaze motion involves placing persons or animals in such a way that they are looking toward an important element of the advertisement. Although this device is not widely used, the KitchenAid advertisement (Figure 13–6) uses this approach to: (a) focus attention on the product being advertised; and (b) draw attention downward into the ad and toward the body copy.

CLARITY OF PRESENTATION

The art director is responsible for seeing that the elements of the advertisement work together to give a single, unified impression. This becomes particularly important when the advertisement con-

CHAPTER 13 | DESIGN, LAYOUT, AND MECHANICAL PRODUCTION

Here's the adhesive you can count on.

1 One drop of Eastman 910® adhesive can hold up to 2½ tons.

2 And it forms strong bonds in just seconds to minutes.

3 With a variety of materials like rubber, metal, glass, most plastics, ceramic and hardwood.

4 GLASS RUBBER METAL PLASTIC
Or combinations of these to one another.

5 The least Eastman 910 adhesive that will cover the area to be bonded works best—one drop per square inch is usually about right.

6 And there's seldom any need for clamps or holding devices other than simple fingertip pressure.

7 This remarkable adhesive has been proven in industrial use for nearly 20 years.

8 Eastman 910® adhesive, the tool in a tube, is available in stores nationwide.

910
Eastman 910 adhesive
1 drop holds up to 5,000 lbs.

Eastman 910 ADHESIVE

One drop is stronger than you are.

Eastman Chemical Products, Inc. Plastics Products Division
Kingsport, Tennessee 37662

Kodak

With KitchenAid, the dishes come out clean no matter who loads them.

The KitchenAid® Load-As-You-Like Dishwasher.

Loading a KitchenAid dishwasher is so easy anyone can do it.
That's because there are wash arms above and below both racks. Which means you can put pots and pans in either rack and know they'll come out thoroughly clean because of the up and down, all-around scrubbing action.
The top rack on the KitchenAid Superba adjusts to 16 different positions so there's plenty of room for big things above and below.
A built-in Soft Waste Disposer means you don't have to pre-rinse.

And the KitchenAid Superba has a Soak 'n Scrub™ pot cleaning cycle that gets dirty pans and casseroles really clean.
With all this, the KitchenAid dishwasher is the most energy efficient we've ever built.
People who own dishwashers say KitchenAid is the best. So, for quiet, dependable dishwashers, see your KitchenAid dealer. Or write KitchenAid Division, Department 7DG-3, Hobart Corp., Troy, Ohio 45374.

KitchenAid®
People say it's the best.

number of design elements. Although the Ivory Liquid ad (Figure 13–7) contains several illustrations, it does not violate this principle.

SIMPLICITY

Simplicity in design sounds easy, but it is usually violated by trying to include too many elements or ideas in a single communication. The use of several typefaces to attract attention or highlight copy or printing headlines and body copy in different colors creates unnecessary complexity. The ad designer should always remember that reading advertisements is not a major preoccupation in the

FIGURE 13–7 (Courtesy The Procter & Gamble Co.)

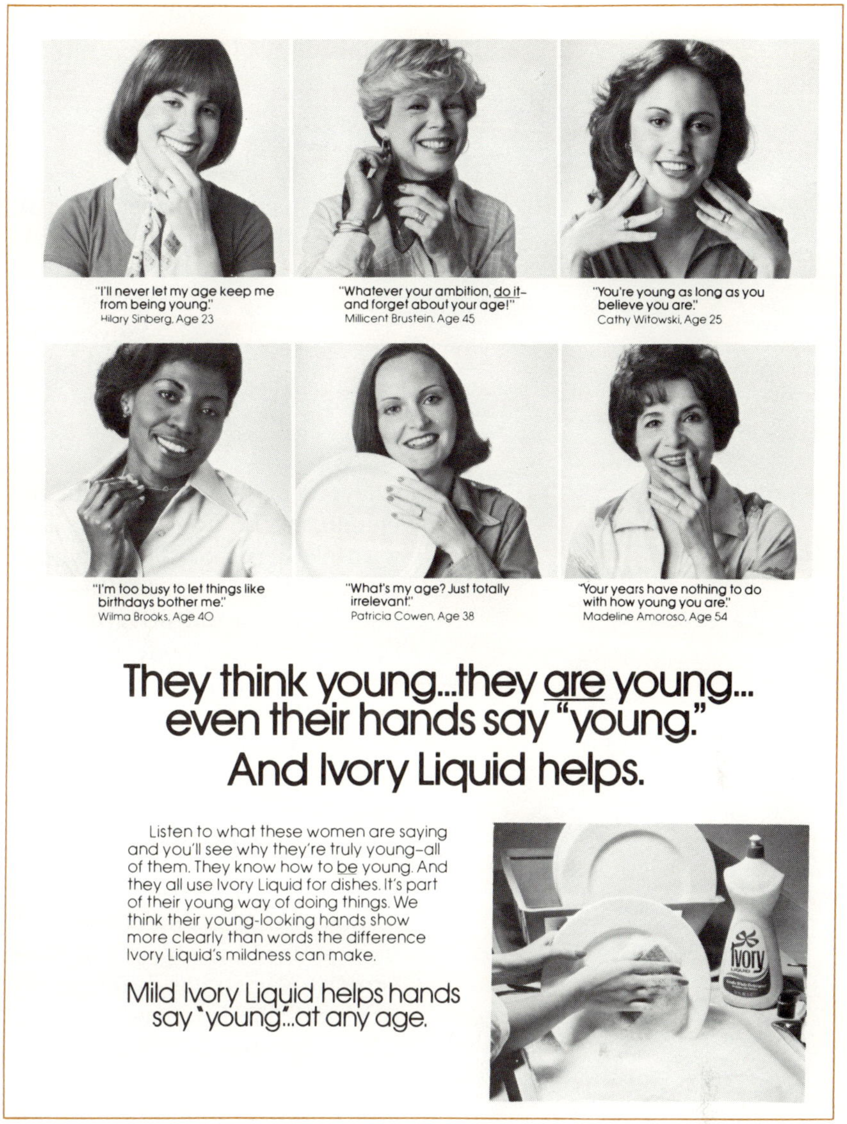
"I'll never let my age keep me from being young."
Hilary Sinberg, Age 23
"Whatever your ambition, do it–and forget about your age!"
Millicent Brustein, Age 45
"You're young as long as you believe you are."
Cathy Witowski, Age 25
"I'm too busy to let things like birthdays bother me."
Wilma Brooks, Age 40
"What's my age? Just totally irrelevant."
Patricia Cowen, Age 38
"Your years have nothing to do with how young you are."
Madeline Amoroso, Age 54
They think young...they are young... even their hands say "young."
And Ivory Liquid helps.
Listen to what these women are saying and you'll see why they're truly young–all of them. They know how to be young. And they all use Ivory Liquid for dishes. It's part of their young way of doing things. We think their young-looking hands show more clearly than words the difference Ivory Liquid's mildness can make.
Mild Ivory Liquid helps hands say "young"...at any age.
Ivory

lives of consumers. Few consumers will waste time on an unduly complex ad.

ARRANGEMENT OF HEADLINES

Headlines need to be arranged to facilitate reading. This can be accomplished by grouping words in meaningful sequences, on different lines. Take the following heading from a Pledge ad, for example:

LET'S FACE IT. PLEDGE MAKES A BEAUTIFUL DIFFERENCE

Although the headline contains only eight words, its readability is enhanced by breaking it into three lines, as it actually appeared:

LET'S FACE IT.
PLEDGE MAKES
A BEAUTIFUL DIFFERENCE

Written in the following form, Maybelline's ad is fairly formidable and difficult to grasp.

> This remarkable makeup gives you a fresh look that *stays* fresh all day.

When it actually appeared, the headline was divided into three distinct, easily graspable thoughts:

> This remarkable makeup
> gives you a fresh look
> that *stays* fresh all day.

TYPES OF LAYOUTS

A layout begins as a rough, preliminary sketch of how the admaker visualizes the ad. It moves through a number of successive stages, with elements of the ad being modified and shifted around until a satisfactory design is obtained. Before starting a layout, the artist usually has a tentative headline, good idea of how much space will be required for body copy, and general agreement on the subject matter of the illustration. Although some layout stages may be omitted in the development of a particular ad, the major layout stages are: **thumbnail sketches, rough layout, finished layout,** and **working layout.**

THUMBNAIL SKETCHES

Frequently, the artist begins with a number of small, rough sketches of possible layouts. These sketches are usually about one-eighth to one-quarter the size of the finished ad and provide a quick and convenient way to get different design ideas down on paper. The headline and illustrations are roughed in, and the location of the logo and body copy are indicated. The artist may prepare two, three, or several thumbnail sketches before arriving at one that holds promise for further development. Figure 13–8 shows four thumbnail sketches for a magazine advertisement for Kellogg Company.

ROUGH LAYOUT

In the second step of the layout process, the thumbnail sketch or sketches selected for further development are roughed out to the actual size in which they will appear. For example, if the advertisement is to appear in *Woman's Day, Time,* or a similar sized magazine, the rough layout will measure 7-1/16 inches wide and 10 inches deep. Some artists prefer to start with a rough layout, bypassing the thumbnail sketch stage. The system one uses depends on personal preference and how clearly the advertisement is visualized prior to the layout stage. One or more rough layouts may be prepared. Rough layouts are crude. Illustrations are hastily sketched; headlines are roughed in; and body copy is indicated by wavy lines. However, these crude layouts help the experienced eye evaluate the appearance of the final ad. A rough layout, developed from one of the thumbnail sketches for Kellogg Company, is shown in Figure 13–9.

FINISHED LAYOUT

The finished layout is much more detailed and carefully drawn than the rough layout. The style of the illustration is indicated; headlines are carefully lettered as they will appear in the final advertisement; the logotype is carefully executed; and body copy is neatly ruled in lines and blocks of copy of varying lengths to indicate indentation and paragraphs. The finished layout is virtually a facsimile of the finished ad. This layout is generally shown to the client for approval. A finished layout of the Kellogg Company's ad is shown in Figure 13–10.

Finished layouts are usually mounted on cardboard and covered with cellophane when being presented for approval. However, a layout should be designed for the publication or publications in which the advertisement will appear, and its design should be compatible with the graphic appearance of these publications. As a consequence, a layout can best be evaluated when it is pasted in the publication. That's the way consumers see it, and that's the way it should be seen prior to its final approval.

WORKING LAYOUTS

Working layouts, sometimes referred to as **mechanicals, keylines,** or **paste ups,** are not actually layouts. They are blueprints for pro-

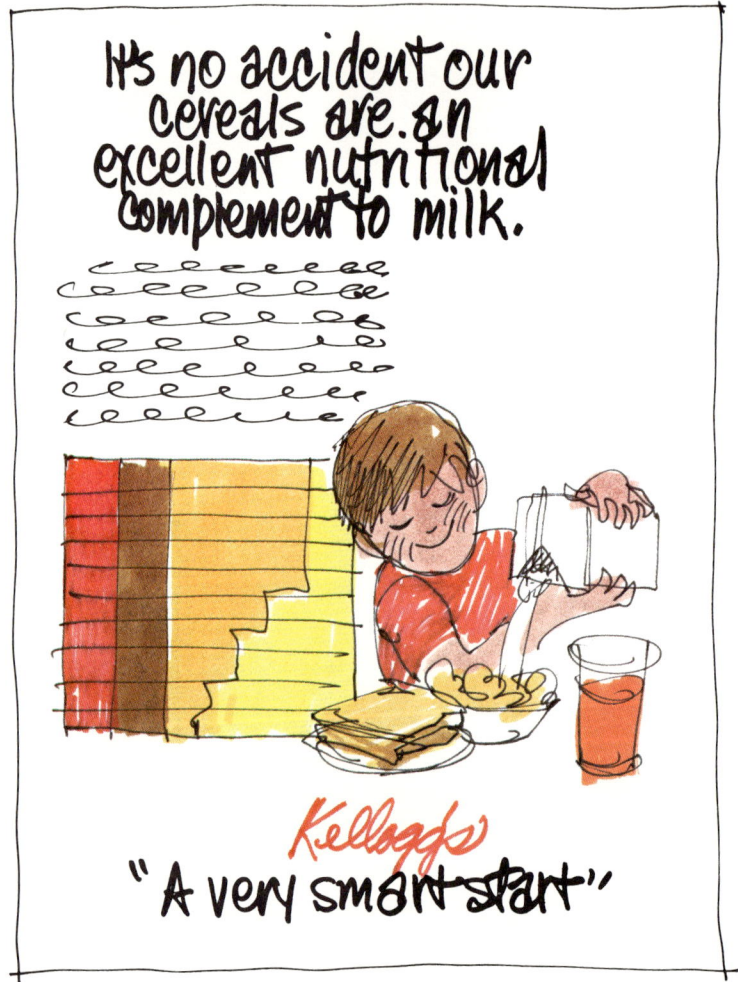

duction. The working layout indicates the exact placement of all the elements in the ad, specifies typeface and size, and includes relevant instructions for the typographer and engraver. The final advertisement is prepared from the working layout. The finished ad for the Kellogg Company example is shown in Figure 13–11.

PRINT PRODUCTION

The production of print advertising is handled by specialists in the advertising agency and outside suppliers. Nonetheless, anyone who works closely with advertising, such as agency account executives and supervisors, client product managers and advertising personnel, or sales promotion managers, should have at least a rudimentary knowledge of advertising production.

The job of the print production department in an advertising agency is to work with the creative groups in translating the working layout into the finished advertisement. In carrying out this function, the production department selects suppliers, instructs them, and reviews their work to make sure that it meets agency standards. Type specification is often handled by the production department in consultation with the art director, or it may be handled by a type specialist, a **typecaster,** who is a member of the art department.

FIGURE 13–10 Finished layout
(Courtesy Kellogg Company and
Leo Burnett Company)

FIGURE 13–11 Finished ad
(Courtesy Kellogg Company and
Leo Burnett Company)

THE PRODUCTION PROCESS

After an advertisement has been approved, a series of production operations still have to be performed. The design and size of type are specified, and a typographer sets the type to fit the working layout. **Type proofs** are returned to the agency for correction or approval. Artwork or photographic material for the illustration and other graphic elements of the advertisement are sent to the engraver, along with instructions on size, screen, type of engravings to be made, and other specifications. The job of the engraver is to reproduce the photographs or artwork. Some colors are difficult to reproduce with modern inks and high-speed presses, and some black and white photographs lack enough contrast for good reproduction. As a consequence, it is usually desirable to discuss any potential problems with the engraver and make needed modifications. When proofs are approved, they are sent along with the engravings to the typographer. The typographer assembles them in a form with the type, following the specifications on the working layout. Proofs of the completed advertisement are then made for final approval and correction, and **printing plates** or **mats**, also called *matrices,* are made for shipment to the media.

This procedure describes the basic steps in the production of advertisements printed by the **letterpress** process. Many publications use **offset lithography** or **gravure** processes. For these processes, the medium is supplied with a paste up, or **camera ready** copy, instead of printing plates. Line artwork and proofs of type are cemented into the exact positions they are to appear in the final ad. They are then photographed and **line negatives** are obtained. Photographs and other continuous tone art are usually submitted separately. This material is photographed through a screen and stripped into position with the line negatives. The stripped-in negatives are used by the publications to make offset and gravure printing plates. In all printing processes, however, each step needs to be carefully proofed and corrected in order to assure accuracy and quality reproduction.

PRODUCTION SCHEDULING

Advertising is a business of deadlines. The **closing date** is the day print advertising material must be received by the publication. This date ranges from a few days before publication date for newspapers to two or three months for consumer magazines. Therefore, creative work must often start several months before the publication date of the magazine in which the advertisement is to appear. The following production schedule is typical for a four color advertisement appearing in a monthly, consumer magazine.

Date of issue	September
On sale date	August 15
Closing date	July 10
Plates must be shipped by	July 5
Engravings go to electrotyper	July 1
Engraver should deliver final proof	June 26
Engraver should have first proof	June 21
Material should go to engraver	June 4

Art and mechanical layout should be ready by	May 28
Type and mechanical layout should be ordered by	May 22
Finished artwork should be delivered by	May 21
Finished artwork should be ordered by	May 1
Creative work should be approved by	April 30
Creative work should start by	April 10

In this example, over four months elapse between the time the creative work starts and the magazine carrying the ad appears on the newsstand. This schedule is based on no delays; this seldom happens. Few ads proceed from conception to appearance without at least one emergency. If the closing date cannot be met, the order can usually be cancelled anytime before the closing date. In the case of back cover positions and unusual space units, however, the cancellation date may be as much as three months prior to the closing date. Failure to meet production schedules does not build client confidence in its agency. If the agency is running only a few days behind schedule, closing date extensions can usually be obtained by calling the publication's production manager.

Since advertising is often prepared on tight schedules, a production order is issued to keep it on track. A sample production order, often referred to as a requisition, is shown in Figure 13–12. Armed with the production order, the traffic department of the agency shepherds the advertisement through its various stages.

TYPOGRAPHY

Typography refers to both the selection and arrangement of type. Type differs in style, known as typeface, and size and can be used to create different effects. Some typefaces are delicate and feminine; others are bold and masculine. They can be modern, old-fashioned, easy to read or difficult. Since readability is a prerequisite for advertising, typefaces that are difficult to read are used sparingly, usually to create a special effect. Generally speaking, **lowercase type** (small letters) is easier to read than **uppercase type** (capital letters).

TYPE GROUPS

There are over one thousand different typefaces, with new faces being created all of the time. Many of these typefaces are similar enough in appearance to be regarded as a group. These broad classifications are widely used: **roman, block, cursive** or **script,** and **ornamental.** These groups are often divided into subgroups, but for our purposes, consideration of these major groups is sufficient.

Roman.   The most popular type group is roman. This group probably contains a larger number of designs than the other three groups. The two most distinguishing features of roman type are: (a) the small lines, or **serifs,** that cross the ends of the main strokes; and (b) variations in the thickness of the strokes themselves.

This line is set in roman.

FIGURE 13–12 Production order

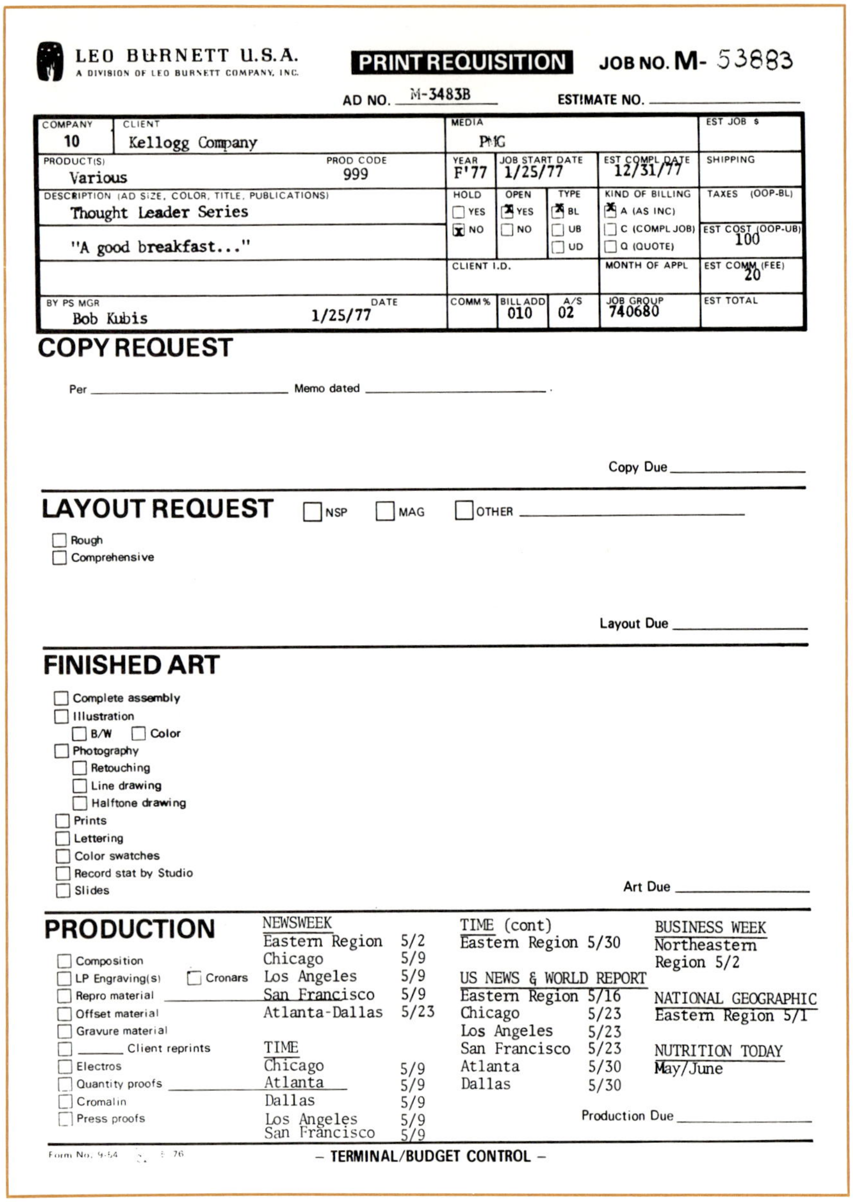
LEO BURNETT U.S.A.
A DIVISION OF LEO BURNETT COMPANY, INC.

PRINT REQUISITION

JOB NO. M- 53883

AD NO. M-3483B ESTIMATE NO. ____

COMPANY	CLIENT	MEDIA	EST JOB $
10	Kellogg Company	PMG	

PRODUCT(S)	PROD CODE	YEAR	JOB START DATE	EST COMPL DATE	SHIPPING
Various	999	F'77	1/25/77	12/31/77	

DESCRIPTION (AD SIZE, COLOR, TITLE, PUBLICATIONS)
Thought Leader Series
"A good breakfast..."

HOLD: ☐ YES ☒ NO
OPEN: ☒ YES ☐ NO
TYPE: ☒ BL ☐ UB ☐ UD
KIND OF BILLING: ☒ A (AS INC) ☐ C (COMPL JOB) ☐ Q (QUOTE)
TAXES (OOP-BL)
EST COST (OOP-UB) 100
CLIENT I.D.
MONTH OF APPL
EST COMM (FEE) 20

BY PS MGR	DATE	COMM %	BILL ADD	A/S	JOB GROUP	EST TOTAL
Bob Kubis	1/25/77		010	02	740680	

COPY REQUEST

Per ____ Memo dated ____.

Copy Due ____

LAYOUT REQUEST ☐ NSP ☐ MAG ☐ OTHER ____

☐ Rough
☐ Comprehensive

Layout Due ____

FINISHED ART

☐ Complete assembly
☐ Illustration
☐ B/W ☐ Color
☐ Photography
☐ Retouching
☐ Line drawing
☐ Halftone drawing
☐ Prints
☐ Lettering
☐ Color swatches
☐ Record stat by Studio
☐ Slides

Art Due ____

PRODUCTION

☐ Composition
☐ LP Engraving(s) ☐ Cronars
☐ Repro material ____
☐ Offset material
☐ Gravure material
☐ ____ Client reprints
☐ Electros
☐ Quantity proofs ____
☐ Cromalin
☐ Press proofs

NEWSWEEK
Eastern Region 5/2
Chicago 5/9
Los Angeles 5/9
San Francisco 5/9
Atlanta-Dallas 5/23

TIME
Chicago 5/9
Atlanta 5/9
Dallas 5/9
Los Angeles 5/9
San Francisco 5/9

TIME (cont)
Eastern Region 5/30

US NEWS & WORLD REPORT
Eastern Region 5/16
Chicago 5/23
Los Angeles 5/23
San Francisco 5/23
Atlanta 5/30
Dallas 5/30

BUSINESS WEEK
Northeastern Region 5/2

NATIONAL GEOGRAPHIC
Eastern Region 5/1

NUTRITION TODAY
May/June

Production Due ____

– TERMINAL/BUDGET CONTROL –

Roman type varies in size and contains a number of subclassifications that vary in terms of the: (a) thickness of the strokes; (b) amount of variation in the thickness of the strokes; and (c) size and regularity of the serifs.

Block. The block letter type is sometimes referred to as **gothic, sans serif, contemporary,** or **uniform strokes.** It also has two distinguishing characteristics: (a) The lines forming the strokes are of uniform thickness. (b) It lacks serifs, hence the term sans serif.

This line is set in block.

A form of type called **square serif** is generally classified as a block type, although it is a combination of block and roman. Like block type, the lines forming the strokes are of uniform thickness. It has serifs like roman, but the serifs have the same thickness and weight as the main strokes. Block type is not as readable as roman because of the uniform width of the strokes in the typeface and the general lack of serifs. Nonetheless, the simple, clean lines of block type give it a modern appearance that is often desirable in advertising.

Cursive or script.   The cursive, or script, group includes a number of typefaces that resemble handwriting. Although script is attractive, it is somewhat difficult to read.

This line is set in script.

In some varieties of this group, the letters appear to be joined together; in others, they are discrete. Script conveys a feeling of formality and femininity. Its use in advertising is generally restricted to emphasizing names and short phrases.

Ornamental.   A large number of type designs do not fit into any of the foregoing classifications. Although these typefaces differ widely in appearance, they are all ornamental or decorative in nature.

This line is set in ornamental.

Some of these designs are extremely difficult to read. When used, they are selected to create a feeling of antiquity, mystery, another culture, or different era.

TYPE FAMILIES

There are type families within each of the major type groups. A type family consists of a related group of designs identified by such names as Bodoni, Caslon, or Futura. The basic design remains the same within the family of type, but the weight, width, and angle of the characters will vary. These differences provide for contrast and emphasis within the same basic type design. The most common variations include bold, extra bold, condensed, extended, and italic, although all of these variations may not be available in a particular type family. Figure 13–13 shows a number of variations in the Helvetica family.

While each variation is set in the same size in terms of height (30 point type), the number of letters that can be printed in a given space varies because the characters vary in width.

TYPE MEASUREMENT

Even a brief discussion of type measurement may be helped by some familiarity with basic type terminology. Figure 13–14 shows a **slug** of type, with its anatomy labeled. Some key terms of type measurement are defined on the following pages.

Helvetica Light

The Helvetica family of type

Helvetica Light Italic

The Helvetica family of type

Helvetica Regular

The Helvetica family of type

Helvetica Regular Italic

The Helvetica family of type

Helvetica Bold

The Helvetica family of type

Helvetica Bold Italic

The Helvetica family of type

Helvetica Heavy

The Helvetica family of type

Helvetica Heavy Italic

The Helvetica family of type

FIGURE 13–13   Variations in the Helvetica family of type

Point.   The size of type (height) is measured in points. There are 72 points to an inch, so a point is 1/72 of an inch. The most common type sizes used in advertising are 6, 8, 10, 12, 14, 18, 24, 36, 42, 48, 60, 72, 84, 96, and 120 points. The smaller sizes, 6 to 14 points, are generally used for body copy; the larger sizes are reserved for headlines and subheads. Figure 13–15 shows a variety of type sizes for comparative purposes.

Beard

Height to paper .918 in.

Point body

Feet — Groove →

Serif

Counter

Face

Serif

Shoulder

Set width

Nick

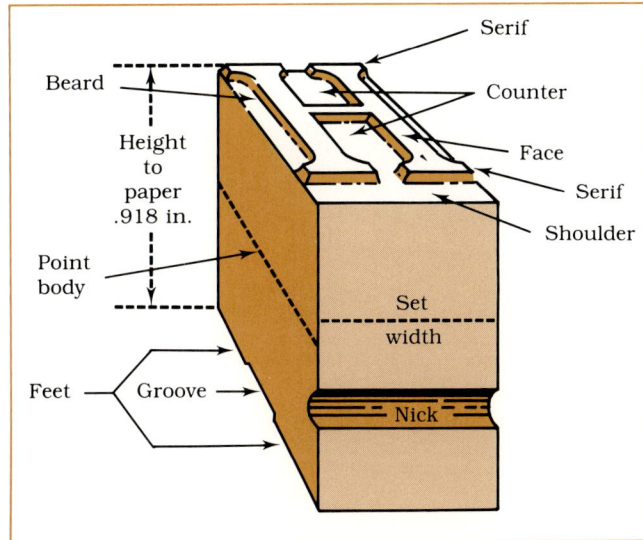

Pica.   A pica is the unit of measure used for designating the width of lines. A pica is 12 points wide, so there are six picas to an inch.

Agate line.   An agate line is a vertical measure of space in which type may be set. It is generally used in referring to fractional space in newspapers and magazines. An agate line is one column wide; there are 14 agate lines to an inch. Thus a newspaper or magazine advertisement that is two columns wide and three inches deep would contain 84 agate lines ($2 \times 3 \times 14 = 84$). Since the agate line is a measure of space only, regardless of the type size used, the foregoing example would still be 84 agate lines, whether it were blank, contained only one line of type, or contained several lines of type.

MAKING TYPE READABLE

Not only are some typefaces more readable than others, but readability can be improved by the way in which type is set. There is a small amount of space between lines of type because the type character is slightly smaller than the metal block on which it is cast. This difference between the size of the character and the metal block is called the **shoulder** (see Figure 13–14). When lines of type are set without any additional space between them, they are said to be set **solid.** To increase readability or adapt the body of type to the space allotted, additional space between lines is desirable. This may be accomplished in two ways: (a) The compositor may cast the characters on a larger block of metal, thus increasing the shoulder and the space between lines. (b) Thin metal strips called **leads** (pronounced "leds") are inserted between the lines. Leading is specified by adding its value in points to the size of type. For example, 12 point type set with two points of space between lines would be specified as "12 on 14" or as 12/14.

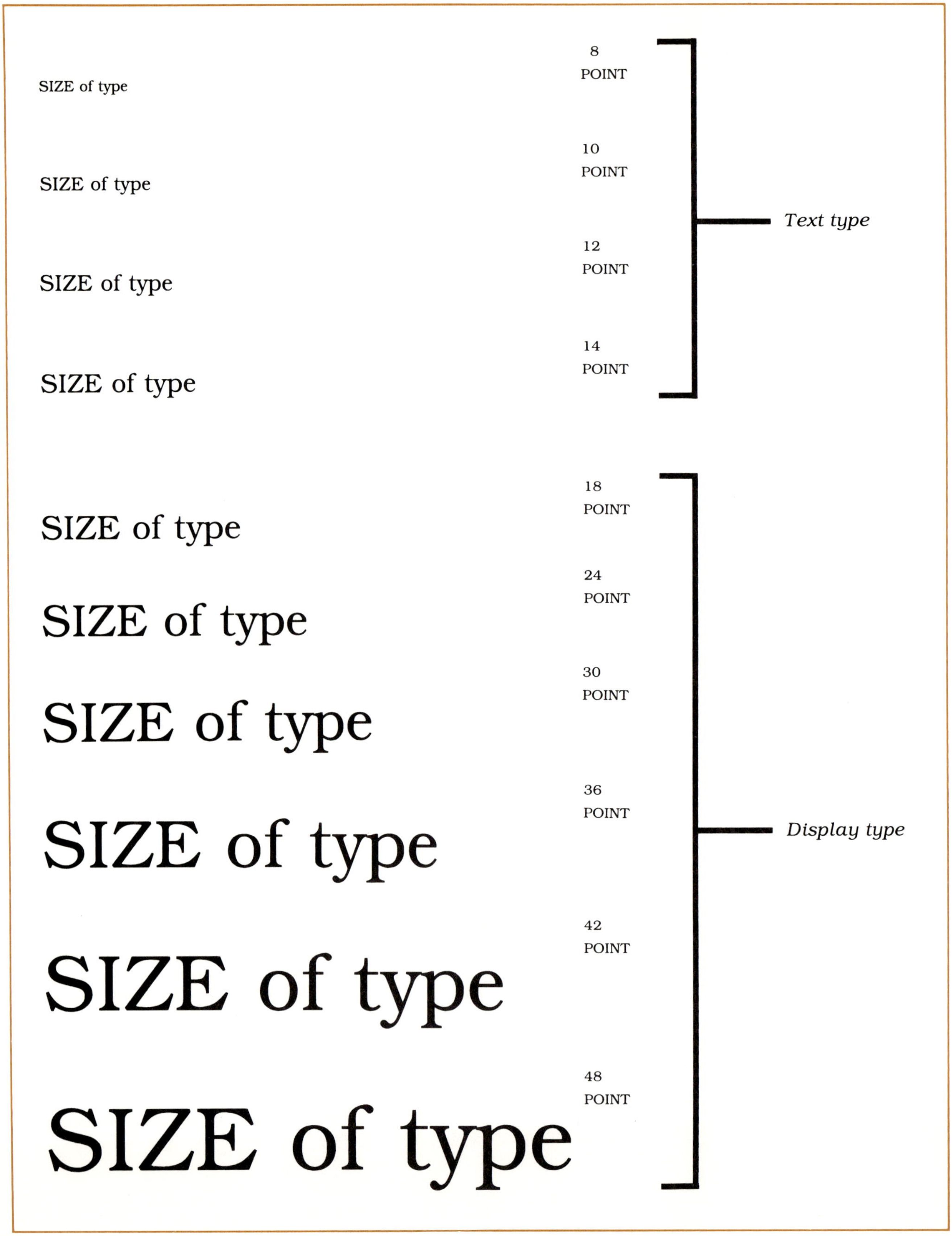

SIZE of type
8 POINT

SIZE of type
10 POINT

SIZE of type
12 POINT

SIZE of type
14 POINT

Text type

SIZE of type
18 POINT

SIZE of type
24 POINT

SIZE of type
30 POINT

SIZE of type
36 POINT

SIZE of type
42 POINT

SIZE of type
48 POINT

Display type

FIGURE 13–15   Sample variations in type size

SPECIFYING TYPE

A number of considerations should be taken into account when specifying type for an advertisement. One of the primary ones is readability. An advertisement that is hard to read, or looks hard to read, will attract few consumers. A second consideration is appropriateness. Since typefaces can create impressions such as masculinity, femininity, modernity, tradition, and exoticism, the typographer needs to select type that is appropriate to the overall impression that the advertisement is intended to create. A third consideration is harmony. It is generally unwise to use too many type styles in an advertisement because a number of styles gives the appearance of clutter and suggests difficulty in reading. One or two styles is usually enough. Contrast can be achieved by using heavier weights for the headline, subheads, and captions than is used for body copy. Key words and slogans can be emphasized by using italics.

When specifying type, the typographer needs to provide the following information: (a) type size and leading; (b) typeface by name; and (c) type width in picas. When specifying type, a number of guidelines facilitate readability.

1 Solid lines of capital letters or italics are difficult to read. However, both can be used effectively to emphasize individual words, names, or slogans.

2 Leading between lines helps increase readability.

3 Sizes below 8 point are usually difficult to read. Don't forget that many consumers either wear or should wear reading glasses.

4 Readability is improved and the body copy is opened up by allowing more white space between paragraphs than between lines in the same paragraph.

5 Short paragraphs and lines are easier to read than long ones. This is why copy is often set in columns with thirty or forty characters to the line.

6 Spacing between words should be watched carefully. If characters are jammed together, they are difficult to read. Similarly, if characters are too far apart, words tend to lose their integrity, and it is difficult to tell where one ends and another begins.

TYPESETTING

There are a number of methods for setting type, arranging letters to form words, sentences, and paragraphs. Each has certain advantages and disadvantages; all can be broadly classified as **hand setting** or **machine setting.**

Hand setting. Hand setting is the oldest form of setting type. In this process, the compositor selects letters individually from a **type font** or **case,** where each letter of the alphabet is assigned to a separate compartment. The letters are placed in a three-sided, metal box referred to as a **composing stick.** After it has been set, the type is transferred to a metal form and locked together. Upon completion of setting, the form is unlocked, and the letters are returned to the appropriate compartments in the type case.

Although hand setting is slow and expensive, it provides wide latitude in spacing and design and is easy to correct since individual characters can be replaced with minimum effort. Because of its expense, hand setting has generally been replaced by various forms of machine setting, although it is sometimes used for handbills and small jobs.

Machine setting. A number of forms of machine setting are widely used in commercial printing because of their speed, economy, and versatility. Major methods are described below.

☐ **Monotype** is a mechanical method of casting letters or characters one at a time. A monotype system consists of two machines. The first uses a typewriter keyboard which produces perforations on a ribbon. The ribbon is fed into a typecaster that casts and assembles the letters one at a time. Since the letters are cast and assembled individually, corrections can easily be made by replacing a single letter. All types of faces may be used, and spacing between words is easy to adjust. Because of these advantages, monotype is frequently used for tables, charts, and certain kinds of fine book work.

☐ **Linotype** is a machine setting process that casts type a line at a time. The linotype operator types out the material on a keyboard that resembles a typewriter. When a line has been typed, it is cast into a metal slug with the complete line of type on its printing edge. When the slugs have been used, they are returned to the machine's melting pot for reuse. Linotype is faster than hand setting or monotype. However, it is more difficult to correct because the entire line in which the correction occurs must be recast. Irregularly shaped type areas may be difficult to set by linotype, so while linotype is quicker and less expensive than monotype for routine work, monotype may be less expensive for complicated jobs or tabular composition.

☐ **Ludlow** is really a combination of hand setting and machine casting. The type matrices (brass molds for each character) are set by hand and locked in a frame. The entire line is then molded by machine. The Ludlow process insures clean, sharp reproduction because it provides new type for each job. Since it is essentially a hand setting process, Ludlow tends to be slow and relatively expensive. It can be used for setting small type, but its primary use is in casting headlines for newspapers and magazines.

☐ **Photocomposition,** also called **cold type,** is the most prevalent form of typesetting in use today because of its sharpness, clarity, greater choice of type sizes and faces, faster reproduction, and lower costs. The basic process involves a letter keyboard that operates an electric camera and a film printing device that makes a photographic negative, or a **reproduction proof.** Photocomposition is primarily used for offset and gravure printing, but it can also be adapted for publications that print by the letterpress method.

Cold type composition can also be produced by equipment such as the IBM Executive typewriter, Varityper, and Justowriter. These machines, which offer a variety of typefaces and spacing variations, produce a printed image from which plates can be made. All three offer greater speed and economy than conventional typesetting processes. They are often used for catalogs, direct advertising material, and house organs.

METHODS OF PRINTING

Four basic printing methods are used in advertising. **Letterpress, gravure,** and **lithography** are widely used for magazine and newspaper reproduction. The fourth form, **silk screen,** is a relatively simple process used primarily for limited production runs, such as posters and point of sale material. Letterpress, gravure, and lithography are generally printed from special plates made by a photoengraving process. Letterpress can print directly from set type. In the high-speed printing required for metropolitan newspapers and magazines, and for printing illustrations, a special plate is required. The basic process involves photographing completed artwork and type and transferring the negative to sensitized metal plates made of zinc or copper.

The basic principle underlying all four of the major printing processes is the transfer of an inked image from one surface to another. However, the methods by which this transfer takes place differ dramatically.

LETTERPRESS

In letterpress, the ink is transferred from a raised surface to the paper. The process is similar to the use of a rubber stamp. The letters or image to be transferred are in relief and backward. The stamp is pressed on an inked pad and then pressed on a piece of paper or other surface to transfer the image.

When letterpress is printed from plates rather than type, the raised printing surface is obtained by etching a metal plate with acid. The parts of the plate to be printed are protected by an acid resistant coating so that they are not affected. The acid eats away the nonprotected part, leaving the areas to be printed on a raised surface. Figure 13–16 diagrams the principle of the letterpress process.

The three types of modern letterpress equipment are **platen, cylinder,** and **rotary presses.** The **platen press** transfers the impression by bringing two flat surfaces together. The **cylinder** or **flatbed press** rolls a cylinder of paper across a flat surface or bed which contains the printing plates. The **rotary press,** which is particularly suited for large quantity, high-speed work, uses a curved printing plate wrapped around a rotating cylinder. Another revolving cylinder carries the paper. Printing is transferred by rotating the cylinders against one another.

FIGURE 13–16 Basic printing processes. These diagrams illustrate the basic principles of the major printing processes. "A" represents the printing plate or screen; "B" is the printing ink; and "C" is the surface on which the design is to be printed.

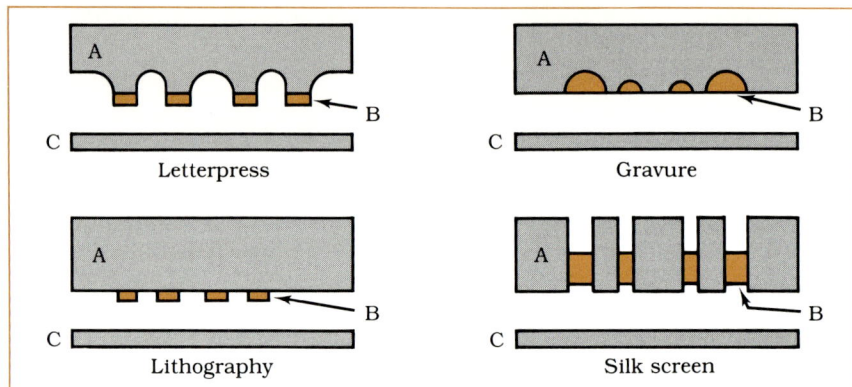

Letterpress is used by most newspapers as well as many magazines and books. It produces a sharper, cleaner image than the other methods and is an excellent process for halftone and color printing. Although relatively expensive, it can be economical when printing large quantities.

GRAVURE OR INTAGLIO

The gravure process prints from a depressed surface (see Figure 13–16). The design is etched into a metal plate, leaving depressions. The surface of the plate is inked and then wiped clean with a metal blade, leaving ink in the depressions. When printing takes place, the depressions give up their ink, transferring the design from the plate to the paper.

The primary value of gravure is its excellent reproduction of color illustrations and tonal effects, even on soft, inexpensive papers. It is generally used by newspapers for special sections and color printing. However, compared to letterpress, its reproduction of type is a little fuzzy. Since the process is relatively expensive, it is used primarily for long production runs.

LITHOGRAPHY

Lithography, as opposed to letterpress and gravure, prints from a smooth surface (see Figure 13–16). The principle underlying lithography is the incompatibility of oil and water; ink, which is oily, will not adhere to a wet surface. The design is deposited on a plate, either by hand or photographically, with a greasy crayon or ink. The nonimage areas of the plate are treated with a stain that retains water. A water roller is then applied to the surface. Since grease and water are incompatible, the design area rejects the water while the nondesign areas are dampened. An ink roller is then passed over the surface. Since the ink is oily, the design area accepts it. Because the nondesign area is dampened, it will not accept the ink.

The two forms of lithography are direct and offset. In **direct lithography,** the printing plate prints directly on the paper. In **offset lithography,** the plate transfers the image to an intermediate rubber surface called a **blanket.** The blanket then transfers the image to the paper. Offset lithography provides a richer effect than direct lithography and is frequently used for long production runs. In contrast to letterpress and gravure, lithography is relatively inexpensive, although obtaining the proper balance of ink and water is sometimes tedious. In addition, offset lithography will print on almost any surface. It is especially suitable for printing on metal; for this reason, packages such as soft drink and beer cans are printed by the lithographic process.

SILK SCREEN OR SERIGRAPHY

Silk screen is one of the oldest and simplest methods of reproducing printed materials. The process operates on the stencil principle and requires no printing plates. A special screen, originally silk, is stretched tightly on a frame over the surface on which the message or image is to be printed. A stencil, prepared by hand or photographic process, is used to block out areas that are not to be printed. A rubber roller is used to force ink through those portions of the screen not blocked out by the stencil (see Figure 13–16). Today, printing screens are usually made of nylon or stainless steel mesh rather than silk. With photographically produced stencils, tonal qualities similar to those obtained from lithography are possible.

Originally, silk screening was a hand process, but today fully automated presses are available. Since silk screening does not require printing plates, the process is economical for small quantity production. In addition, it can be used to print on virtually any surface, from bottles to barrels to sweatshirts. It is particularly useful when short production runs are required, there are severe time and cost limitations, or an unusual printing surface makes other processes impractical.

CHOOSING A PRINTING PROCESS

When preparing advertising material for commercial media such as magazines or newspapers, advertisers have no choice. They must prepare the material for the process used by the particular magazine or newspaper. When preparing brochures, catalogs, inserts, point of sale, and other promotional material, the choice of printing process will depend on such things as cost and time restrictions, quantity, quality, and material on which the message is to be printed. Table 13–1 summarizes some of the major characteristics of each method.

PHOTOENGRAVING

In modern, high-speed printing, photoengraving is used for both type and illustrations. Technically, photoengraving is the process for making plates for letterpress printing. The following description of the process is based on this use, although the same process, with minor variations, is used for the other printing methods as well.

Photoengraving involves a photochemical process using a camera to make a negative. The negative is then transferred to a sensitized metal plate of zinc or copper and etched to create the printing surface. The photoengraving process may be used to obtain either line or halftone engravings.

CHAPTER 13 | DESIGN, LAYOUT, AND MECHANICAL PRODUCTION

TABLE 13-1 Summary of comparative printing methods

Printing Method	Cost	Appearance	Paper Stock	Quantity
Letterpress	Relative high cost of plates, but less waste than lithography. No delays in obtaining proper water/ink balance.	High quality color reproduction. More body and brilliance than other methods. Inks glossier, and less problems with metallic inks.	Works particularly well with high quality paper and special stock.	Almost no limits on quantity; but small sample runs are more expensive than offset.
Gravure	Relatively expensive plates. Economical only on runs of 100,000 or more.	Rich color effects, particularly on cellophane, acetate, and metallic foils.	Can use softer paper than letterpress, but fails to reproduce in as sharp detail.	Ideal for long production runs for periodicals, catalogs, or package wraps.
Offset lithography	Lowest plate cost, but complete new plates required for changes or corrections.	High quality even on rough surfaces.	Sensitive to moisture changes. Problems of paper curl and dimensional stabilities.	Good for both long and short runs and is often used for books and folders. Widely used for promotion materials and direct mail.
Silk screen	Low cost since there are no plates involved.	Good quality, but not as good as can be obtained by other processes.	Extremely versatile. Can be printed on all sorts of material, and on any thickness.	Best for small quantity runs. Recently, high speed machinery has made it feasible for some long run work.

Line engravings are the simplest, since line plates produce only solid tones. They do not produce shades or gradations of color. If continuous tones such as solid black through various shades of gray are desired, the **halftone engraving** process must be used. Intermediate shades of a color are produced by breaking up solid lines and areas in the artwork into minute dots of different sizes. Each dot becomes a printing surface for carrying ink. Whereas line cuts print from solid lines or areas, halftone engravings print from dots.

The same basic photochemical process is used in the production of both line and halftone engravings. However, in making halftone engravings, the original artwork is photographed through a halftone screen, consisting of a sheet of glass or plastic film on which fine black lines have been drawn at right angles to one another so that they form little boxes of clear glass or plastic. The number of lines to the inch in the screen will vary with the degree of fineness the printing requires. Coarse paper, such as that used in newspapers, requires a coarse line screen, usually 65 lines to the inch. On high quality paper, such as that used in magazines, a finer screen may be used. Reproduction becomes better and more detailed with a finer screen. The most frequently used line screens are 55, 65, and 85 for newspapers and 110, 120, or 133 for magazines. Extremely smooth paper can accept up to 150 to 200 line screens without blurring.

The halftone screen is placed between the lens of the camera and the artwork to be photographed. Light from the artwork passes through the screen and spreads on its way to the film negative. The dot pattern on the negative is determined by the amount of light reflected from various areas of the artwork. Dark, solid areas reflect little light and show up on the negative as large dots; bright areas or highlights reflect a greater amount of light and show up as widely scattered, small dots. Whereas the number of dots will depend on the fineness of the screen, the *size* of the dots will depend on the amount of light reflected by the artwork being photographed. Figure 13–17 shows a greatly enlarged halftone showing the effect of screening.

Occasionally, it is desirable to combine the clarity of line engravings with the tonal qualities of halftones in a single plate. This can be done by using a combination of line and halftone negatives that are stripped together to make a composite or combined unit.

PRINTING COLOR

The most common process for producing full color advertisements with tonal values seen in most magazines is the four color process. All colors can be reduced or decomposed to the three primary colors—magenta (red), yellow, and cyan (blue). When black is added to these three colors, detail strength and neutral shades of gray are obtainable. Color artwork is photographed through filters: green filter for red; violet filter for yellow; orange filter for blue; and a special filter for black. This decomposes the artwork into four separate negatives referred to as **color separations.** After the color separations have been corrected for color accuracy, the separations are photographed through a halftone screen to make four halftone plates, one for each color. In photographing the color separations, the halftone screen is rotated to a different angle for each separation. When the four plates are superimposed and printed, the resultant dots do not completely overlap, thereby reproducing a faithful rendition of the

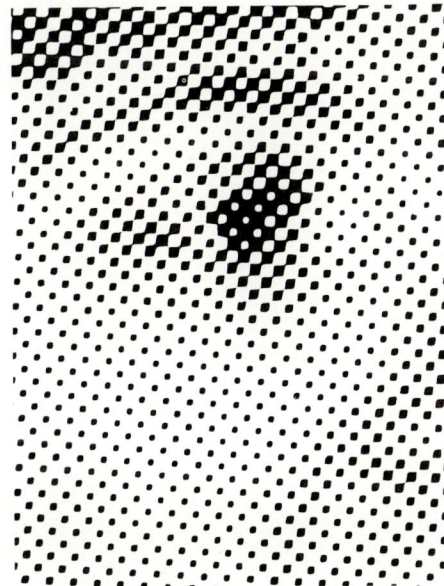

FIGURE 13–17 Enlarged halftone of an eye showing the effect of screening

CHAPTER 13 | DESIGN, LAYOUT, AND MECHANICAL PRODUCTION

(a)

FIGURE 13–18 Progressive proofs are separate and combination proofs of all color plates. They indicate color quality. The proofs shown here are seen in the following order: (a) yellow; (b) red; (c) yellow and red; (d) blue; (e) blue, yellow, and red; (f) black; and (g) final combination of four colors. (Courtesy Aynsley Bone China)

(d)

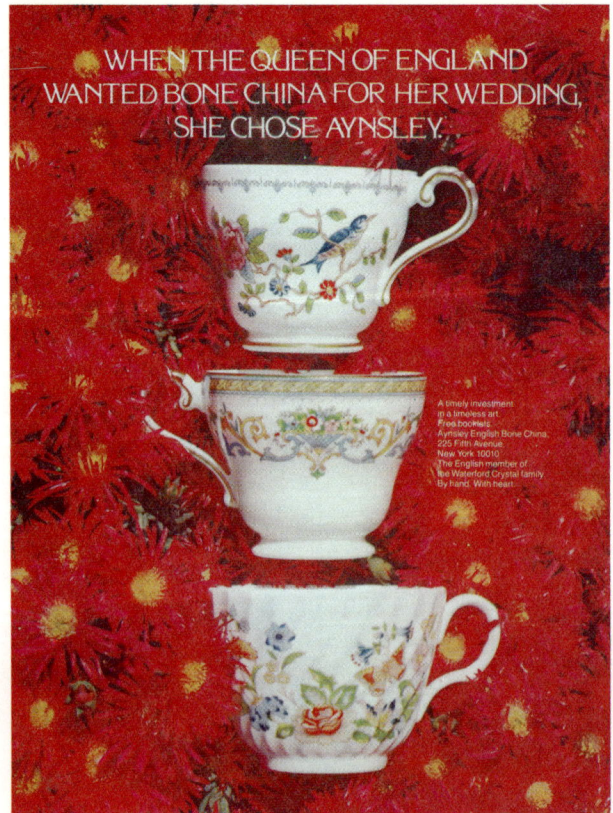

(e)

WHEN THE QUEEN OF ENGLAND
WANTED BONE CHINA FOR HER WEDDING,
SHE CHOSE AYNSLEY.
A timely investment
in a timeless art.
Free booklets.
Aynsley English Bone China,
225 Fifth Avenue,
New York 10010
The English member of
the Waterford Crystal family.
By hand. With heart.
(b)

WHEN THE QUEEN OF ENGLAND
WANTED BONE CHINA FOR HER WEDDING,
SHE CHOSE AYNSLEY.
A timely investment
in a timeless art.
Free booklets.
Aynsley English Bone China,
225 Fifth Avenue,
New York 10010
The English member of
the Waterford Crystal family.
By hand. With heart.
(c)

WHEN THE QUEEN OF ENGLAND
WANTED BONE CHINA FOR HER WEDDING,
SHE CHOSE AYNSLEY.
(f)

WHEN THE QUEEN OF ENGLAND
WANTED BONE CHINA FOR HER WEDDING,
SHE CHOSE AYNSLEY.
A timely investment
in a timeless art.
Free booklets.
Aynsley English Bone China,
225 Fifth Avenue
New York 10010
The English member of
the Waterford Crystal family.
By hand. With heart.
(g)

original colors. The most commonly used screen sizes for magazines are 133 lines for yellow, and 120 line screens for the other color plates. The color plates are printed separately, usually in the sequence of yellow, red, blue, and black, using transparent inks. The transparent inks mix the primary pigments and result in a color blended illustration. The illustrations in Figure 13–18 (see pages 390–1) show **progressive proofs** of a four color, halftone advertisement.

SUMMARY

The heart of the controversy over what constitutes effective design in advertising is based on four issues: picture-headline format; overprinting; reverse type; and coupon placement in coupon ads.

In any discussion of design, three terms, visualize, layout, and design, need to be clarified. A copywriter or art director visualizes a mental picture of an advertisement before anything is put on paper. Layout can be used as a verb or noun. As a verb, it is the actual process of translating the admaker's idea into a finished product. As a noun, it is the result of this process. The design is the final result of visualization as developed and modified through a number of layouts.

One of the major variables influencing advertising design is the space unit available. A larger space unit allows greater freedom to manipulate design elements.

An effective design has the following characteristics: single focal point, logical progression of eye movement, clarity of impression, and simplicity.

Advertising layouts progress through a series of steps. The major layout stages are: thumbnail sketches, rough layout, finished layout, comprehensive, and working layout.

The actual production of print advertising is handled by specialists in the advertising agency and outside suppliers. After an advertisement has been approved, a series of production operations have to be performed. The design and size of type have to be specified, type proofs have to be made and approved, artwork must be engraved, all elements of the advertisement must be assembled, and printing plates must be made for shipment to media. Because of the complexity of the production process, production scheduling must be devised to coordinate the various activities so that time schedules can be met.

Typography refers to the selection and arrangement of type. Many of the over one thousand different typefaces are similar enough in appearance to be classified as a type group. Four broad type groups that encompass most typefaces are roman, block, cursive or script, and ornamental. Within each major type group, there are type families. A type family is a related group of designs identified by names such as Bodoni, Caslon, and Futura. Because of the many typefaces available, it is possible to select type to convey impressions such as modernity, old-fashionedness, formality, futurity, and mystery.

Terms used in measuring type and the space it occupies are the point and the agate line. An agate line is one column wide and 1/14 of an inch high.

Type may be set either by hand or by machine. The particular typesetting method used will depend upon the individual job since each has advantages and disadvantages for various forms of work.

The four basic methods of printing are letterpress, gravure, lithography, and silk screen. The particular printing method used depends on such factors as the surface being printed, cost and speed considerations, and fidelity required in the finished work.

Modern, high-speed printing uses photoengravings. Photoengraving is a photochemical process in which a camera is used to make a negative of the material to be printed. The negative is then transferred to a sensitized metal plate and etched to create the printing surface. The photoengraving process is used for both line and halftone engravings.

The most common process for producing full color printing is the four color process. Color artwork is photographed through filters, and a separate engraving is made for each of the basic colors in the process—red, yellow, blue, and black. These four engravings are printed separately. They are superimposed over one another using transparent inks, which yield a color-blended result.

REVIEW QUESTIONS

1 What are the reasons given in the text for conflicting practices in advertising design?
2 Distinguish among the terms visualize, layout, and design.
3 Identify the characteristics of an effective design.
4 Identify and describe the different types of layouts.
5 Define the following terms: (a) typography; (b) lowercase; (c) uppercase; (d) point; (e) pica; and (f) agate line.
6 Identify and indicate the major characteristics of the four major type groups mentioned in the text.
7 Briefly describe the following methods of setting type: (a) handsetting; (b) monotype; (c) linotype; (d) Ludlow; and (e) photocomposition.
8 Distinguish among the printing processes for: (a) letterpress; (b) gravure; (c) lithography; and (d) silk screen.
9 Distinguish among the methods of printing for the following processes: (a) platen; (b) cylinder; and (c) rotary.
10 Briefly describe how color photographs are printed.

DISCUSSION QUESTIONS

1 Analyze a current magazine advertisement in terms of the characteristics of effective design. Do you believe it is well designed? Why or why not?
2 Which printing process do you believe would be most appropriate for each of the following situations:
   a. A product brochure to be printed on slick paper in large quantities and requiring sharp detail for some of the illustrations;
   b. High quality reproduction on soft paper, with both long and short runs being required;

    c. An appetite appeal photograph for a food product to be printed on a foil package;

    d. Short runs on a variety of printing surfaces in which quality reproduction is a secondary consideration to cost and versatility.

3 Bring an advertisement to class that contains both overprinting and reverse type. Do you believe that these devices help increase the effectiveness of the advertisement? Why or why not?

PROBLEM

As art director of a copy group, you have been working on an advertisement for the Kodak Colorburst 350 that will appear in *National Geographic* (page size 6½ inches wide by 10 inches deep). You have agreed that: (a) the camera will be shown; (b) two color photographs, one labeled "Take pictures at normal distance" and the other labeled "Or close up," will appear.

    The following headline, subhead, and body copy have been written, but not laid out.

Headline:	Kodak brings the instant closer.
Subhead:	Introducing the Kodak Colorburst 350. The only instant camera with a built in close-up lens.
Body copy:	Our exclusive built in close-up lens and our built in electronic flash let you take beautiful instant color pictures from as close as two feet away—in any light. Color pictures that are sharp, rich, vivid. And, best of all, also built in are 100 years of Kodak experience. The Colorburst 350 is the perfect instant camera for you and the perfect gift. Kodak brings the instant to life.

The ad will also carry the Kodak logo.

ASSIGNMENT

1 Lay out the ad, showing how the illustrations, headline, subhead, and body copy will appear.

2 Write a brief set of instructions for the photographer explaining the effect you hope to create with the illustrations.

14
Broadcast Advertising

COMMERCIALS THAT SELL

Charles Wainwright, former vice-president of the Tatham-Laird & Kudner advertising agency, once said: "Selling commercials come in all sizes and shapes. It's impossible to categorize them except to say that a *selling commercial convinces the consumer to buy the product.*"[1] The following two examples of award winning commercials demonstrate this point.

PRINCE SPAGHETTI

The Prince Spaghetti commercial deals with a family experience. It is a narrative commercial designed to capture the traditional role of the product in an Italian family in Boston. Shot on location, it uses a local family and typical neighborhood activities to provide local color (Figure 14–1).

WORLD BOOK ENCYCLOPEDIA

The "eggs" commercial for World Book Encyclopedia (Figure 14–2) is an entirely different creative problem. In the words of Paul Blustain of the Post-Keyes-Gardner advertising agency:

> In the beginning there was no egg commercial. There was simply this strategy:
> 1. To make an interesting and entertaining commercial that would create high awareness for World Book Encyclopedia.
> 2. To define World Book not just as reference material but as books children enjoy reading.
> 3. To appeal to the parents of young students.
> 4. To produce the commercial with a "reasonable" budget.
>   With these objectives in mind, our conversation centered on the famous people in World Book. The commercial itself grew out of a casual remark that intellectuals have been referred to (by anti-intellectuals) as *eggheads.*

[1]From *The Television Copywriter* by Charles A. Wainwright. Copyright © 1966. Reprinted by permission of Hastings House, Publishers, p. 19.

Here comes Anthony again for Prince on TV, in full color, promoting Wednesday is Prince Spaghetti Day.

Anthony Martignetti lives in Boston, On Prince Street. In the Italian North End.

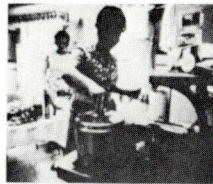

The home, for more than 50 years, of the Prince Spaghetti Company.

Anthony knows a lot about local Italian customs.

And he knows a lot about Prince.

Because that's a local custom, too.

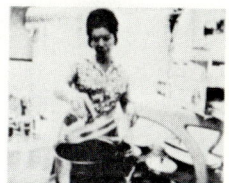

Prince is more than just authentic.

It's something that grows you.

With wheat-germ energy most other pastas leave out.

Most days, Anthony takes his time going home. But not today. Today is Wednesday.

And, as every family in the North End of Boston will tell you...

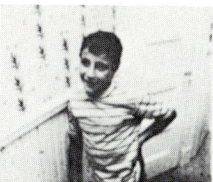

Wednesday is Prince Spaghetti Day.

Prince. Share it with your family.

PRINCE MACARONI MFG. CO., LOWELL, MASS

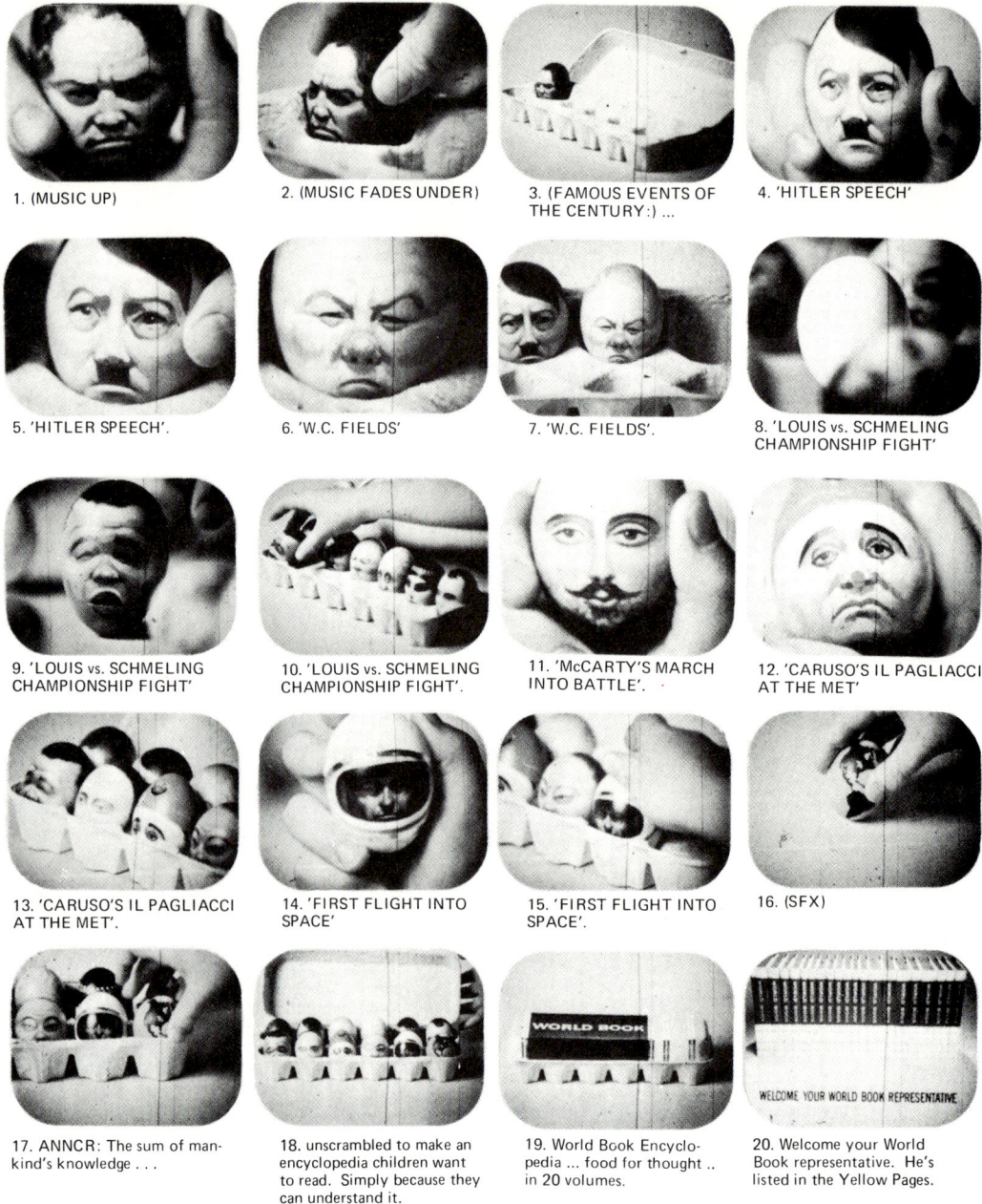

1. (MUSIC UP) 2. (MUSIC FADES UNDER) 3. (FAMOUS EVENTS OF THE CENTURY:) ... 4. 'HITLER SPEECH'

5. 'HITLER SPEECH'. 6. 'W.C. FIELDS' 7. 'W.C. FIELDS'. 8. 'LOUIS vs. SCHMELING CHAMPIONSHIP FIGHT'

9. 'LOUIS vs. SCHMELING CHAMPIONSHIP FIGHT' 10. 'LOUIS vs. SCHMELING CHAMPIONSHIP FIGHT'. 11. 'McCARTY'S MARCH INTO BATTLE'. 12. 'CARUSO'S IL PAGLIACCI AT THE MET'

13. 'CARUSO'S IL PAGLIACCI AT THE MET'. 14. 'FIRST FLIGHT INTO SPACE' 15. 'FIRST FLIGHT INTO SPACE'. 16. (SFX)

17. ANNCR: The sum of mankind's knowledge . . . 18. unscrambled to make an encyclopedia children want to read. Simply because they can understand it. 19. World Book Encyclopedia ... food for thought .. in 20 volumes. 20. Welcome your World Book representative. He's listed in the Yellow Pages.

FIGURE 14–2   (Reproduced with the permission of World Book, Inc.)

We decided to paint eggs with the faces of famous people. We wanted them to be as real as possible, not cartoons or caricatures.[2]

The result is a 120-second commercial. The sound effects (SFX) behind each character reinforced its identification. For example, the introduction to Beethoven's Fifth Symphony was played behind Beethoven, the first character; for Hitler, part of a tape of one of his speeches was played; behind W. C. Fields, a recording of Fields tell-

[2]*CLIO Awards Teacher's Guide* (New York: CLIO Enterprises, Inc.), 31.

ing a humorous story about Philadelphia was used; and so on. The result was a highly dramatic and unusual commercial that executed the creative strategy superbly.

SPECIAL CHARACTERISTICS OF BROADCAST MEDIA

In many respects, creating commercials for broadcast media is similar to creating print advertising. The commercial starts with a product concept—an idea that needs to be translated into a consumer benefit. This idea is expressed in a copy strategy that provides basic guidance for its execution. Like print advertising, broadcast writing requires research and a thorough knowledge of the product. Don Natheson, former president of North Advertising, said:

> When a young man or woman asks me what it takes to be a good television writer, I usually pass out these four suggestions:
>
> 1. BE A DIGGER! Don't live in an "isolation booth." Get out among people and talk to them, find out what they want, what they like about your product—and what they dislike. Check the stores. Talk to the sales clerks. Get their reaction and their customers' reactions. Talk to the research people who created your product. Use the product yourself. Compare it with competitors. Talk to the men who sell your product to dealers. What are they saying and not saying? Read the consumer research reports, especially the un-aided comments. Learn to talk to the consumer in the same language she talks to you.
> 2. BE A SIMPLIFIER! After you have gathered all the facts about your product, simplify. Throw out the unimportant ideas and the bad ones. Keep the good ones. Remember—it only takes one good idea to sell a product. Too much mumbo-jumbo creates confusion. Simplify!
> 3. BE A CONVINCER! Advertising must sell merchandise. That is its purpose. So convert those facts into arguments that will convince people they need and should buy your product. And remember, people are not interested in you or your product. They just want to know what your product can do for them.
> 4. BE AN EXCITER! Facts aren't enough! They're dull, uninteresting. You must embellish facts with pizzazz. Use music, humor, novelty, pace, lighting, atmosphere, camera tricks—anything and everything to attract attention to your convincing arguments.[3]

On the other hand, broadcast media has certain unique characteristics that are not present in print advertising. Whereas print advertising deals with space, broadcast media deals with time. If he is so inclined, the consumer can study a print advertisement, spending as much time as he wishes looking at the illustration, reading the body copy, or relating the product and its benefits to his situation. Broadcast media is different. It's there for a moment, and then it's gone; there are no instant replays. For this reason, broadcast advertising must be kept simple. Writer Hanley Norris has suggested that the broadcast message should be so simple that you should ". . . be able to sum it up in your mind in one sentence—just as you would with a billboard."[4]

---

[3]Wainwright, *The Television Copywriter*, 5.
[4]Hanley Norris, *The Complete Copywriter* (New York: McGraw-Hill, 1966), 153.

At the same time, broadcast commercials often provide a greater opportunity for showmanship than does print advertising. The broadcast medium lends itself to jingles, music, dramatic effects, and a variety of attention getting devices. Broadcast personalities, particularly in radio, are often powerful persuaders.

The audience for broadcast commercials also differs from that of print advertising. The consumer does not have to interrupt the reading of a magazine article to look at an advertisement. Advertising can easily be ignored. In broadcast, however, the advertising is intrusive; the consumer has no choice. Viewing or listening to editorial matter, music, or drama stops when the commercial comes on. It does not resume until the commercial is over. This intrusiveness of broadcast advertising constitutes its greatest strength and its greatest weakness. Although the consumer can always ignore the message or leave the room when the commercial comes on, broadcast commercials obtain the consumer's initial interest more easily. However, intrusiveness is a weakness because commercial interruptions are often unwelcome and viewed with resentment. Most criticism of advertising centers on broadcast media, particularly on television.

Because of its aural character, slogans, key words or phrases, and rhymes are more effective in broadcast media than in print. "You'll wonder where the yellow went when you brush your teeth with Pepsodent," a radio classic, became a national byword. When Busch Bavarian Beer was first introduced, its theme song—replete with yodeling—earned the beer recognition by over 95 percent of adult consumers. The Salem cigarette jingle, "You can take Salem out of the country, but . . . (musical ping)," made it almost impossible for the listener not to complete the phrase.

Rhyme can be used effectively in broadcast, but it can also be overdone. My research for a food client on rhyme versus prose commercials indicated three things:

1 Rhyme commercials were more effective than prose in capturing attention and creating interest.
2 Sales points in rhyme commercials were lost and did not register as well as in the prose version.
3 Listeners became satiated with rhyme commercials more quickly than with prose commercials.

If rhyme is to be effective, it should be used sparingly. A key sales point or slogan stands out and is better remembered if it is couched in rhyme in a commercial that is primarily prose. However, if the entire commercial is in rhyme, sales point recall is reduced.

RADIO COMMERCIALS

In the 1930s and 1940s radio occupied a role similar to that of television today. It was truly a mass media, reaching audiences of millions and providing a leading form of home entertainment. With the advent of television, the decline of radio as a major advertising medium was precipitous. Today, radio is widely used for local and regional advertising; for national advertising, it is often considered a supplemental medium.

Radio presents two major challenges for the copywriter: (a) It is completely an aural medium, and everything has to be accomplished with sound effects. (b) The radio listener is usually doing something else at the same time, such as washing, cooking, cleaning, reading, or driving a car. The burden of capturing and holding the listener's attention is placed on the radio writer. Generally, the commercial must capture the listener's attention in the first eight seconds, or lose him altogether. Thereafter, the commercial's structure and content need to be sufficiently striking to hold interest.

TYPES OF RADIO COMMERCIALS

Kevin Sweeney, former president of the Radio Advertising Bureau, identified four basic forms, or schools of thought, about radio commercials: (a) jingle approach; (b) narrative commercials; (c) straight delivery; and (d) personality commercials.[5]

The jingle approach. In this form, the commercial uses a jingle or rhyme to carry the content of the commercial. Such an approach can be effective for short phrases or ideas, but its excessive use can lead to reduced recall for salient product attributes.

The following radio commercial produced for Kentucky Tourism is a cut above the normal jingle commercial. Using original words and music, it paints an appealing word picture of Kentucky and the pleasures it offers.

> Have you ever seen the sunrise burning off a mist,
> Or a deer drinking water by a quiet stream?
> Ever seen blue skies bluer than blue eyes,
> A mountain that's a thousand shades of green?
> Have you ever daydreamed by the waterside,
> Or laughed with someone till you nearly cried?
> Oh! Kentucky, Oh! Kentucky.

> Have you ever seen your little boy jumping for joy
> 'Cause he caught that fish like he always dreamed;
> Sat by the fire with your heart's desire
> And listened to your whole family sing?
> It's peace of mind like another time,
> You're going to find that you want to say.
> Oh! Kentucky, Oh! Kentucky.
> You'll come to love it in, oh, so many ways.[6]

Narrative commercials. Narrative commercials tell a story, often in dialogue, and frequently with humor. Since most commercials are limited to 60 seconds, careful writing is required to set up the plot, make the sales point or points, and deliver a punch line.

The following example for Minolta Copier demonstrates the structure of a narrative commercial.

Waiter:	I got an order for you, chef.
Chef:	What is it?
Waiter:	Table six wants the blimp cocktail.

---

[5]S. W. Dunn and A. M. Barban, *Advertising* (Hinsdale, Illinois: The Dryden Press, 1974), 406.

[6]William D. Tyler, "The Sounds of Winners: Year's Best Radio Spots," *Advertising Age*, 24 August 1981, 52.

Chef:	You mean shrimp cocktail.
Waiter:	And the beer soup.
Chef:	Bean soup.
Waiter:	And a bowl of the beef glue.
Chef:	What? Let me see that menu.
Waiter:	Okay.
Chef:	Who made this copy. It's all smeared and wrinkled. I can hardly read it.
Waiter:	Booth four wants chicken frisbee.
Chef:	Fricassee.
Waiter:	What the heck is corn on the cat?
Chef:	These copies are terrible.
Waiter:	What do you want from me, our copier jams up all the time.
Chef:	Get me a Minolta.
Waiter:	I don't see Minolta on the menu. Oh, you mean the minestrone.
Chef:	I mean the Minolta EP 310 copier.
Waiter:	Ahhh.
Chef:	The Minolta EP 310 has this incredibly short paper path that virtually eliminates paper jam.
Waiter:	No kidding.
Chef:	And the Minolta EP 310 even has a self-diagnostic system.
Waiter:	How about the bowling banquet in the back room?
Chef:	Yeah?
Waiter:	They want the nude cake.
Chef:	You mean nut cake.
Waiter:	No, nude cake, where the girl jumps out at the . . .
Chef:	Oh, that.
Waiter:	Yeah.
Chef:	That.
Announcer:	The Minolta EP 310 copier. A business partner you can depend on.[7]

Straight delivery.   In this form of commercial, an announcer presents a straightforward message about the product, emphasizes its salient features, and usually ends with a request to "try it." A straight delivery commercial may or may not be accompanied with appropriate sound effects.

The following example of a straight delivery commercial is for the "Save the Whales" movement. Using the sound of whales in the background, the commercial sets out to inform its audience about whales, get listeners to realize how much they have in common with whales, and support the "Save the Whales" organization. As a result of this commercial, contributions increased and whales were probably saved.

Announcer: Greenpeace presents misconceptions about whales. "The whale is a huge fish." Wrong. Whales are typical warm-blooded, air breathing mammals. Their young develop inside the mother's body. They are born alive and are nursed with milk. Whales mate for life and are loving parents. They are extraordinarily sensitive to each other and to their environment. They talk, play, make music and feel emotions. They get ulcers, even tonsillitis. Untypically, however, a whale will risk its own life to save a wounded friend. It will even help

---

[7]Ibid., 54.

a sick animal from another species. A whale's brain is five times bigger than ours. It's the most complex brain of any animal on earth, with the greatest number of active nerve brain cells. Whales do not attack their enemies. They will not fight back this summer when man will mercilessly slaughter 16,000 of them. Greenpeace will fight back. Help us. Contact Greenpeace today.[8]

Personality commercials. This approach gains its strength from a presenter, such as Ed McMahan, Johnny Carson, or local radio personality. In some instances, the personality is given a script to read. In other instances, he or she is simply given a product fact sheet and asked to ad-lib the commercial. Both approaches have advantages and disadvantages. The first controls what is said, but often loses the impact of the personality. The second capitalizes on the presenter's natural style, but often loses control over content. For example, a number of years ago, Arthur Godfrey, using a fact sheet for a peanut butter commercial, started off with: "Ugh! I hate peanut butter. But, if you like peanut butter, Skippy is the best you can buy." Then he went ahead and covered the salient product characteristics.

The following Diet 7•UP commercial capitalizes on the personality of Don Rickles for its attention, humor, and strength.

Announcer:	Look who's turning to Diet 7•UP. Don Rickles and Lynda Carter.
Don Rickles:	I didn't know you were a Diet 7•UP drinker, Lynda.
Lynda Carter:	Well, you learn something new every day, Don.
Don Rickles:	Guess you have to give up a lot to fit into that costume, hah, sweetie?
Lynda Carter:	Oh, Don. I don't know about you, but I don't have to give up anything. Remember, I'm a star. Besides, any diet drink can help me fit into my costume.
Don Rickles:	Oh, really? Well, then, why the Diet 7•UP, Lynda?
Lynda Carter:	Because, when it comes to taste, I don't give up. That's why I like Diet 7•UP. It doesn't have that funny diet taste.
Voiceover:	A lot of people are drinking Diet 7•UP because they won't compromise when it comes to taste. And Diet 7•UP doesn't have a diet aftertaste. It's a crisp, light, delicious diet soft drink.
Lynda Carter:	Why are you drinking Diet 7•UP, Don? Thinking of classing up your act?
Don Rickles:	Hah, funny. I like the taste, too.
Lynda Carter:	That's impossible.
Don Rickles:	Why's that?
Lynda Carter:	Cause you don't have any taste, Donny dear.
Don Rickles:	Oh, you're cute. A real beauty.
Voiceover:	Diet 7•UP. The only thing you give up is calories.[9]

Ross and Landers drew on the Radio Advertising Bureau's library of over 10,000 commercials to devise a classification system that contains seventeen different categories. Their list is shown on the next page.[10]

---

[8]Ibid., 54.

[9]Ibid., 54.

[10]Wallace A. Ross and Bob Landers, "Commercial Categories," in *Radio Plays the Plaza* (New York: Radio Advertising Bureau, 1969), 29.

1. *Product Demo*—Communicating how a product is used, or what purposes a product serves.
2. *Voice Power*—Use of a unique voice adding special qualities to the copy. May blend in other sounds or music, but the power of the commercial is essentially in casting the voice.
3. *Electronic Sound*—Through synthetic sound-making machines or through devices that alter sound, commercial attempts to establish original product-sound associations.
4. *Customer Interview*—A spokesman for the product plus a customer, discussing the merits and advantages of the product or service. Often the most rewarding interviews are those done spontaneously.
5. *Humorous Fake Interview*—Variation of the customer interview in humorous fashion. Has the advantages of preplanning plus the interest the interview generates.
6. *Hyperbole or Exaggerated Statement*—Use of exaggeration, extreme understatement or overstatement to arouse interest in legitimate, often basic product claims that might otherwise pass unnoticed. Can often be a spoof.
7. *Sixth Dimension*—Compression of time, history, happenings into a brief spot. Can often be a sequential narrative, ultimately involving listener in future projections.
8. *Hot Property*—Commercial that latches on to a current sensation. Can be a hit show, a performer, or a song. Hit is adapted for product.
9. *Comedian Power*—Established comedians do commercials in their own unique style. Has advantages of humor and inferred celebrity endorsement.
10. *Historical Fantasy*—Situations or historical characters are revived to convey product message.
11. *Sound Picture*—Sound used to help put the listener into a situation by stimulating his imagination. Sounds are usually easily recognizable to facilitate listener involvement.
12. *Demographics*—Commercial appeals particularly to one segment of the population (an age group, interest group, etc.) through use of music, references.
13. *Imagery Transfer*—Spots reinforce effects of other media through use of musical logos, or other sound associations identifiable with a particular campaign for a particular product.
14. *Celebrity Interview*—Famous person provides celebrity endorsement of the product in informal manner.
15. *Product Song*—Music and words combine to create a musical logo as well as to sell product. In style of popular music with orchestration.
16. *Editing Genius*—Many different situations, voices, types of music, sounds combined in a series of quick cuts to produce one spot. Every cut contributes in some way to strength of message.
17. *Improvisation*—Copywriter conceives situations that might be good backdrop for a product and then allows performers to work out the dialogue extemporaneously. Requires postediting of tapes to make spot cohesive.

Obviously, no classification system can do justice to the variety of effects that can be created with sound. The purpose of identifying these various approaches is simply to emphasize the versatility of radio. The particular approach or combination of approaches must be selected on the basis of the featured product dimensions and impression that is to be created. A number of years ago, the Chrysler Corporation used a series of humorous commercials to advertise the Dodge automobile. The entire approach was inappropriate to the basic image of the car, creating confusion about product position and cheapening the product image.

THE LENGTH OF COMMERCIALS

Since time is the controlling factor, commercial length is a critical consideration. Normally, radio commercials run for 10, 20, 30, or 60 seconds, although longer time segments can be purchased. A few years ago, a con artist used a fifteen minute radio commercial to advertise the "rose of Shangri-la" to aspiring horticulturists. The commercial wove a romantic legend of how explorers, lost in the remote reaches of Tibet, wandered into a hidden valley where they discovered an exotic rose which they imported to the United States at great expense and could be used to turn a routine garden into a place of wonder and beauty. Listeners were urged to create their own Shangri-la by sending their order, accompanied by a personal check, to a post office box number. Those who responded received a species of multi-flora rose, a thorny, sprawling shrub having clusters of small fragrant flowers and widely used as a windbreak in agricultural areas of the Midwest.

If the commercial contains a musical introduction and close, or introduces special sound effects, the length of the product message is correspondingly reduced. Thus, the number of words that may be spoken in a commercial will vary with the commercial's length and structure. The average word count for radio commercials is:

10 seconds	25 words
20 seconds	45 words
30 seconds	65 words
60 seconds	125 words

Since 60-second commercials often include a musical introduction and close as well as identification of local dealers and their addresses, the actual amount of message time is often only 35 or 40 seconds.

GUIDELINES FOR WRITING RADIO COMMERCIALS

Although there are no hard and fast rules for writing radio commercials, the following guidelines can be helpful for the beginning writer.

Keep it simple. Complex verbal messages are hard to comprehend. The listener must grasp the important sales points at the time of presentation. There are no instant replays.

Use a dramatic device or provocative statement early in the commercial. If interest is not flagged in the first eight or ten seconds, the message will probably be lost.

CHAPTER 14 | BROADCAST ADVERTISING

Speak to people in their own language. Unless satire is being used, monologues and conversations should sound natural, not stilted or contrived. Use familiar words, simple sentences, and easily understood references.

Repeat the product name. Use the product name several times in the commercial. If the name is confusing, spell it, more than once if possible.

Be specific. Have something specific to say about product features or consumer benefits. Avoid generalities; they are meaningless.

Choose words carefully. Radio commercials should be sparse and lean. Eliminate unnecessary words, use action verbs, and personalize the message.

Repeat basic ideas. If a sales point is important, repeat it. If it's not important, leave it out. To avoid the sound of redundancy, make the same point in different ways.

Identify the package. Help the consumer visualize the package. If the package is red, say: "Look for the red label." If it has some other identifying characteristic, such as a picture, special shape or material, use this feature to help identification.

Read the commercial aloud. After is has been written, read it aloud to make sure it has no tongue trippers, flows smoothly, and is the proper length.

THE FORM OF RADIO COMMERCIALS

Radio commercials are usually prepared in the form of a script identifying the speakers and sound effects to be used. Figure 14–3 shows a typical radio script for a 60-second commercial.

RADIO PRODUCTION

A radio commercial can be delivered live or prerecorded. Sometimes both methods are combined in a single commercial.

Live commercials. A live commercial is one delivered on the air by an announcer or a station personality. The advantages of live commercials are that they are inexpensive and listeners may have confidence in what local announcers say. A disadvantage is that the announcer may ad-lib or blunder the delivery. When strict control of the presentation is desired, advertisers prefer to use prerecorded commercials.

Prerecorded commercials. Prerecorded commercials may be simple, using an announcer to deliver a straightforward message, or highly complex, using a number of voices, music, and sound effects that require split-second timing. Prerecorded commercials are generally more expensive than live commercials. However, they combine

LEO BURNETT U.S.A.
A DIVISION OF LEO BURNETT COMPANY, INC.
ADVERTISING

PRUDENTIAL PLAZA • CHICAGO, ILLINOIS
312-236-5959

KELLOGG COMPANY
60-Second Live Radio Announcement
("Personality"—Announcer)
"VITAMIN FORTIFIED"
CORPORATE

As Recorded:
Typed: 6/20/78 lkh

L-640-CORP-60

1		(TO BE USED WITH RECORDED "VITAMIN FORTIFIED" RADIO DONUT #0683-CORP-60)
2		(MUSIC UNDER :11)
3	ANNCR: (LIVE WITH MUSIC UNDER)	You might be doing something very smart every morning,
4		and not even know it.
5	SINGERS: (MUSIC TRK.)	YOU OFTEN START YOUR DAY
6		SOME TASTY KELLOGG'S WAY
7		THAT'S SMART, THAT'S VERY SMART.
8		(MUSIC UNDER :21)
9	ANNCR: (LIVE WITH MUSIC UNDER)	If you had a Kellogg's fortified cereal with milk as part of
10		your breakfast this morning, you were smart. Because a
11		typical serving of a Kellogg's fortified cereal with milk
12		contains twenty-five percent of your daily allowance for
13		eight vitamins, plus ten percent of the iron. So
14		if you had a nutritious Kellogg's cereal this morning,
15		congratulations. You're smart.
16	SINGERS: (MUSIC TRK.)	GIVE YOURSELF A BRAVO
17		A GREAT BIG HIP HURRAH
18		KELLOGG'S IN THE MORNING
19		IS A VERY SMART START FOR THE DAY.
20		KELLOGG'S
21		A VERY SMART, VERY SMART . . . START.

FIGURE 14–3 A radio script for a 60-second commercial (Courtesy Kellogg Co.)

the advantages of control with the opportunity to use special effects to increase the impact and effectiveness of the commercial delivery.

When prerecorded commercials are to be used, a radio producer sets up a budget, selects a recording studio, casts the voices, arranges for music and special effects, edits the results, and follows

407

the commercial through to its completion. Music, sound effects, and the spoken message are often recorded separately and then combined on a **master tape** by the recording studio. **Dupes,** duplicates of the master tape, are made for distribution to local radio stations or the radio network. Local dealer identifications are tagged at the end of the commercial and generally dubbed in by a local announcer.

TELEVISION COMMERCIALS

Television commercials are immensely more complex and costly than radio commercials; they also reach larger audiences and are more effective. A fairly complex prerecorded radio commercial may cost $15,000 to $25,000; a simple television commercial of comparable quality may cost $80,000 to $100,000. A recent commercial package for Levi's, consisting of two 30-second and one 60-second commercial, cost $250,000.[11] The advertiser can get almost anything he wants in television, provided he is willing to pay the costs.

In the early days of television, the emphasis was on the product story; **double-spotting,** running two commercials back to back, was the measure of the industry's greed; and the novelty of the medium guaranteed viewer attention. Since then, the cost of television has skyrocketed. **Multiple-spotting,** several commercials run in succession, and commercial clutter has turned the medium into an endless succession of commercials. When Joseph Ostrow was a senior vice-president and director of communications at Young & Rubicam, he charged that "the television industry, and most particularly the networks, seem unable to control their lust for greater and greater profitability."[12] There is a growing concern within the advertising industry that television is pricing itself out of the market.

Rising costs and increased competition on television have had two consequences that affect television commercials: (a) Sixty-second commercials are becoming a rarity, with most commercials being written for 30 seconds or less. (b) There has been an increased emphasis on technique, or presentation, at the expense of the product idea. Hank Seiden has addressed himself to this second point with the following classification of commercials.

> All commercials fall into one of four categories:
> Commercials with bad concepts and bad execution.
> They're the worst.
> Commercials with bad concepts and good execution.
> They're almost as bad.
> Commercials with good concepts and bad execution.
> They're inexcusable.
> Commercials with good concepts and good execution.
> That's advertising.[13]

Despite all of its problems, television is an exciting advertising medium. It is a slice-of-life view of the world in action, color, and

---

[11]"Abel's Technique Lights the Way for Advertising," *Advertising Age*, 22 August 1977, 3.

[12]"Agency Exec Blasts TV Pricing; CBS Blames Sudden Demand," *Advertising Age*, 22 August 1977, 1.

[13]Hank Seiden, *Advertising Pure and Simple* (New York: AMACOM, a division of the American Management Association, 1976), 35.

sound, intruding into the viewer's living room. Because of its versatility, copywriters find television to be an exciting medium.

The development of television commercials parallels the creative process of other media. A commercial starts with an idea; the stronger the idea, the stronger the commercial. It is written within the framework of a copy strategy, but the opportunity for demonstrating the product is infinitely greater than in single dimension media such as magazines, newspapers, and radio.

As in all advertising, a writer's major problems are separating the essential facts and simplifying the basic idea behind the product. One highly successful television writer has described his approach to developing television commercials in the following way:

> Intelligent advertising should begin with the ability to condense a complicated sales message down to its basic form: a headline and a picture. The further we get away from these two elements, the poorer our communication becomes. So, far from being ends in themselves, TV techniques should operate only to make the headline and picture more interesting, more exciting, and more convincing as clearly, quickly, and simply as possible.
>
> With that in mind, I ask you to consider my plan: Every creative team, before starting a TV campaign or commercial, should first rough out a print ad communicating the same message to be communicated in the TV commercial. Needless to say, the team should execute this print ad, consisting of headline, rough visual, and copy points, just for themselves. No one else should see it. To be on the safe side, they should also consider several approaches before deciding on the best way to go. In the end, it's not only conceivable but entirely probable that they'll spend more time on the ad than on the actual television storyboard, because the storyboard will come easily after this basic conceptual groundwork has been laid.
>
> If nothing else, this technique is bound to sharpen creative thinking by forcing a team to determine, first, the single most important point to be made, and, second, how best to make it.
>
> As for the rest, it's easy. The print ad should be used as a blueprint for the TV storyboard and the final execution. All along the way, the storyboard should be judged against this ad to see that the idea hasn't been lost, obscured, or slowed down in translation from print to TV. And it would be a good idea if, in the final production of the commercial, the print ad were prominently displayed so that every time a production technique begins to crush the basic idea, it can be stopped then and there.
>
> As a guide for the final editing, nothing could beat the print ad. It should also be compared to the finished commercial, just to see how closely the technique of one medium has approximated the other.
>
> The print ad, you might say, is ideally suited to serve as the conscience of our industry. If we paid more attention to our consciences, as theologians and thinkers have advised for solid centuries, we would see better and more effective TV commercials in the future.[14]

The forms that television commercials can take are endless. Stand-up presentations, dramatization, song and dance numbers, testimonials, dialogues, cartoons, and fantasy are examples. But the

---

[14]Ibid., 93–94.

CHAPTER 14 | BROADCAST ADVERTISING

real key to the effective use of television is demonstration. Demonstration is television's ultimate weapon. The fact that so many commercials fail to use it suggests that they have nothing to sell or the medium is being misused.

Of course, not all demonstrations are equally effective. The demonstration of a weak idea is the sign of a weak product or a lazy copy group. Substituting technique for content is the bane of television advertising; although advertising is indispensable to modern marketing, it is not marketing. Marketing begins with a consumer benefit and a product concept that provides that benefit. Advertising's job is to present the concept clearly, interestingly, and dramatically.

DEVELOPMENT OF TELEVISION COMMERCIALS

A television script differs from that of radio because it is usually written in double columns, with the audio listed on one side and the video on the other (Figure 14–4). For presentation purposes, the script is rendered in the form of a storyboard which visualizes the action, scene by scene, as it occurs. Figure 14–5 shows how the script in Figure 14–4 was transformed into a storyboard.

Like a magazine layout, the storyboard may be presented in rough, finished, or comprehensive form. The purpose of the storyboard is to permit the client to visualize the commercial, facilitate communication between the writer and producer, and estimate costs.

In describing the action and sounds in a television script or storyboard, the industry has developed its own jargon. Some of the most commonly used symbols and expressions are identified in Table 14–1.

Although these terms are often used in a television script or storyboard to help explain what is happening, their actual use in production of a commercial is usually at the discretion of the producer. As one television writer has pointed out:

> For years advertising copywriters and TV producers have been playing a little straight-faced game in which the copywriter . . . lards his script with all kinds of cuts, dissolves, fades, ECU's and dollies. The producer gravely accepts this script, reads it over, and then goes ahead and shoots the thing as he pleases—which is probably just as well.[15]

The guidelines for writing an effective television commercial are not much different from those for writing an effective radio commercial. Most important, keep it simple. However, certain considerations are unique to television.

Use the video. Don't waste time talking about something that can be more easily shown in a picture. The video should carry the burden of the commercial; the audio serves to interpret and enhance the action.

---

[15]James S. Norris, *Advertising* (Reston, Virginia: Reston Publishing Co., Inc., 1977), 209.

LEO BURNETT U.S.A.
A DIVISION OF LEO BURNETT COMPANY, INC.
ADVERTISING

PRUDENTIAL PLAZA • CHICAGO, ILLINOIS
312-236-5959

KELLOGG COMPANY
30-Second Film
"BUILDING BREAKFAST"
CORPORATE
KLKL6280

Approved for Bidding: 8/17/77

VIDEO		*AUDIO*
OPEN ON KID HOLDING BLOCK WAVING ARM.	KID:	Hey, give us a hand. We're building a better breakfast.
	KID:	What's that?
SHOW KIDS AND BLOCKS IN 4 FOOD GROUPS.	KID:	That's a breakfast with foods from at least three of the four basic food groups.
CU OF KID AND ORANGE JUICE BLOCK.	KID:	I've got orange juice from the fruit and vegetable group.
CU OF KID AND MILK BLOCK.	KID:	Here comes milk from the milk group.
CU OF KID AND CORN FLAKES BLOCK.	KID:	Make room for corn flakes and toast from the cereal and bread group.
KIDS PILING BLOCKS TOGETHER.	KID:	Now that's a well built breakfast.
KIDS ADMIRING BLOCK BREAKFAST.	KID:	Yep! It's got the energy you need for an active day.
	KID:	Build a better breakfast tomorrow.
SHOW 4 BREAKFASTS. SUPER: "KELLOGG'S".	ANNCR:	(VO) This better breakfast message is from Kellogg's.

FIGURE 14–4 Television script (Courtesy Kellogg Co.)

Coordinate the audio and video. Make the audio and video work together. Avoid the inevitable confusion of audio and video tracks that don't relate to one another.

Use action where possible. Ideas can be comprehended quickly in visual form. Action should be used to maintain attention and keep the commercial moving forward. In describing television advertising, Agnew and O'Brien have suggested: "A picture should be simple enough to grasp in five seconds; so, as a rule of thumb, a picture should not be kept static any longer than that."[16]

[16]Clark M. Agnew and Neil O'Brien, *Television Advertising* (New York: McGraw-Hill, 1958), 98.

1. OPEN ON KID HOLDING BLOCK WAVING ARM.
   KID: Hey, give us a hand.

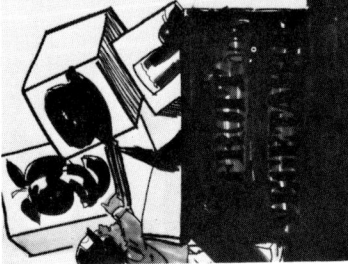

2. SHOW KIDS AND BLOCKS IN 4 FOOD GROUPS.
   KID: We're building a better breakfast.

   KID: What's that?
   KID: That's a breakfast with foods from at least three of the four basic food groups.

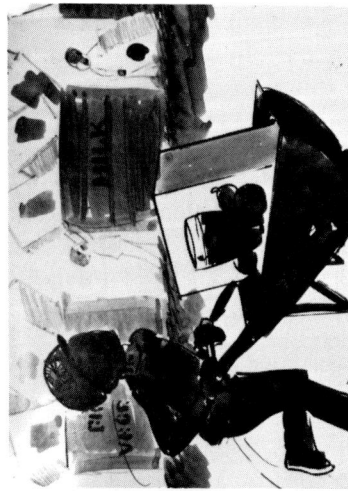

3. CU OF KID AND ORANGE JUICE BLOCK.
   KID: I got orange juice from the fruit and vegetable group.

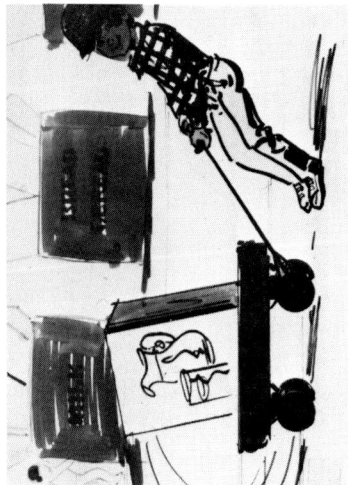

4. CU OF KID AND MILK BLOCK.
   KID: Here comes the milk from the milk group.

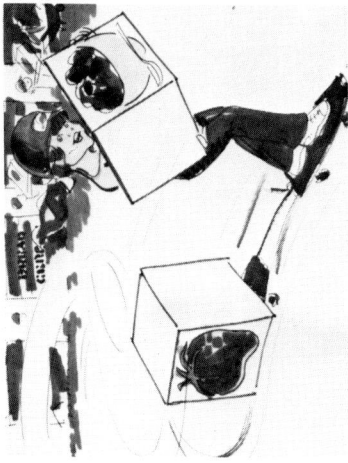

5. CU OF KID AND CORN FLAKES.
   KID: Make room for corn flakes from the bread and cereal group.

6. KIDS PILING BLOCKS TOGETHER.
   KID: Now that's a well-built breakfast.

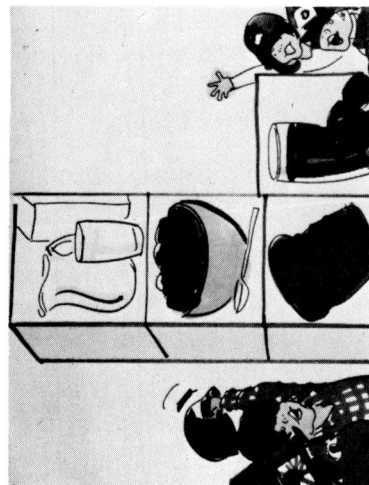

7. KIDS ADMIRING BLOCK BREAKFAST.
   KID: Yep! It's got the energy you need for an active day.
   KID: Build a better breakfast tomorrow.

8. SHOW 4 BREAKFASTS. SUPER: "KELLOGG'S."
   ANNCR: (VO) this better breakfast message is from Kellogg's.

FIGURE 14–5   Television storyboard (Courtesy Kellogg Co.)

TABLE 14-1 Terms commonly used in television scripts

Term	Definition
SFX	Sound effects
VO	Voice over
ANN	Announcer
Music up and out	A final blare of music
Music under	Background music that is under the dialogue
Music down and out	The music fades out
CU	Close-up shot
ECU	Extremely close up
Pan	To sweep the camera across the scene
LS	Long shot
MS	A medium distance shot
Dolly	To move the camera in and out of a scene
Cut	To move abruptly from one scene to another
Dissolve	To fade out one scene while fading in another
Optical	Any special visual effect such as dissolving a scene with a diamond shape, stopping motion in midflight, or dividing the screen into quarters
Super	To superimpose something—usually a word, phrase, or product name—over the picture

Don't let the desire to entertain get in the way of the message. This is the greatest danger in television writing. Television is such an outstanding entertainment medium that there is always the temptation to entertain rather than persuade. Entertainment is fine as long as it is used in support of the advertising message.

TELEVISION PRODUCTION

Television production begins with the client's approval of the storyboard and budget. During the process of production, a television commercial changes more than any other form of advertising. The television script and storyboard are essentially static, whereas the finished commercial is enhanced by casting, action, sets, optical devices, music, voices, and other sound effects. Although the script and storyboard provide direction and a constraint on what will be produced, an experienced, sensitive director can often strengthen a commercial immeasurably. On-the-spot modifications and changes are commonplace and often necessary. Many major advertising agencies insist that the television writer be present during production to make sure that such changes add to, and not detract from, the original concept of the commercial.

METHODS OF TELEVISION PRODUCTION

Television commercials may be delivered as live presentations or produced on film or videotape. The choice of production techniques depends largely on the nature of the commercial, budget, effects required, and producer's preferences.

Live commercials. Live commercials are usually delivered on camera by a station announcer or program personality. While live commercials were used extensively in the early days of television, they are rarely used today except on local news shows, talk shows such as the "Tonight Show," and audience participation shows where members of the studio audience compete for prizes or cash awards.

The advantages of live commercials are their spontaneity, the opportunity to capitalize on a program personality, and the ability to relate the product to topical subjects. Their disadvantages, however, are immense. There can be no retakes, editing, or corrections, and few special effects. Some stations will not accept live commercials because these stations do not have adequate production facilities, and the widespread use of spot television announcements in local markets makes them unfeasible.

Filmed commercials. About 80 percent of the commercial production of national advertisers is made on 35-millimeter film, similar to that used in commercial motion pictures; however, the use of 16-millimeter film is increasing.[17] Film is the most versatile and flexible production medium, although it is also the most expensive and time-consuming. It lends itself to complicated visual effects and trick photography, such as the invisible man sequence used by Haynes underwear or the miniature chuck wagon used in Purina's Chuck Wagon Dog Food commercials. Film is also easy to edit, so scenes can be shot at different locations and assembled for the final commercial.

Videotape. Both the video and sound portions of commercials can be recorded by videotape cameras on magnetic tape similar to that used on home tape recorders. Initially, it was thought that videotape would replace film as the primary production medium for television commercials because of its cost advantages over film, high quality of reproduction, and speed. Videotape, like the instant replays of professional football broadcasts, can be broadcast almost immediately after filming. However, practical reasons have limited its use in advertising. Film has greater versatility in editing and creating special visual effects. The development of new videotape equipment and production techniques is beginning to overcome the limitations of tape production, and a survey by Eastman Kodak indicates a substantial increase in videotape production, particularly among local and regional advertisers who do not have easy access to film production facilities.[18] For a variety of reasons, more advertising agencies are shooting on film and then transferring to videotape.

1 Higher fidelity sound can be obtained, since the original sound track is cut on magnetic tape and its transfer to film causes a slight loss in clarity.

---

[17]Arthur Bellaire, "Nat Eisenberg Tells Agencies: Videotape Commercials Merit More Consideration," *Advertising Age*, 5 May 1975.

[18]Hooper White, "Is Videotape An Art Form or Hardware Convention?" *Advertising Age*, 22 August 1977, 44–45.

2 It is possible to take a badly timed piece of film and electronically color-correct it on videotape in a matter of minutes; whereas the same color correction on film would take several days at an optical house.

3 When a network is supplied with film, the network transfers the film to videotape before it is broadcast, so the network should be provided with videotape in the first place.[19]

PREPARING FOR PRODUCTION

Regardless of the production method, thorough preplanning prior to the actual shooting of a commercial is essential. Production studios and shooting crews are paid according to the time they spend on the set or location. A cost of $20,000 to $30,000 for a day's shooting is not unusual. Therefore, to avoid costly delays the details of production should be worked out before actual shooting begins. Live commercials also require careful preplanning because there is only one chance to do the commercial right.

Selection of a production studio. Although many local and regional advertisers use television stations, national advertisers generally use production studios that specialize in commercial production. The studio should be selected early in the prepreparation stage because studio personnel play an important role in preproduction planning. Two primary considerations in the selection of a production studio are capability and cost. Some studios specialize in film and others in videotape. Some are uniquely equipped for shooting on location; others have elaborate studio facilities. Some specialize in animation; others specialize in live action. Select a production house that is adept in the required commercial techniques.

Since television production is expensive, a number of qualified production studios are usually asked to bid competitively. Bids are based on discussions of the storyboard, as well as other specifications provided by the advertiser or its advertising agency. These discussions not only provide comparative cost estimates, but often uncover opportunities for cost reductions or indicate that a particular studio is better qualified than others for achieving the desired result.

The selection of a recording studio for sound tracks follows the same procedures as those used in choosing a production studio. Since sound studios are less specialized than film or tape houses, the selection process is less complex.

Preproduction meetings. After a production house has been selected, preproduction meetings are scheduled to plan the actual shooting or recording sessions. Normally, these meetings include the agency producer, production house producer, director, and possibly the commercial writer or art director. Infrequently, the advertising manager or an agency account executive will attend.

Preproduction meetings are held to explain the concept behind the commercial, anticipate any special problems that may arise during the shooting sessions, and reach agreement as to how each scene is to be handled. These meetings also assign responsibility for

---

[19]Ibid., 44.

obtaining props, wardrobes, actors and actresses, selecting locations for scenes that cannot be shot in the studio, and making whatever other arrangements are necessary. Assembling props is a tedious chore, and a talent for detail is a prerequisite for those assigned this responsibility.

Casting. Casting for commercials is critical because the people selected must project the personality attributes envisioned in the commercial. In many cases, professional models are used; in other instances, professional actors or actresses are required because some models can't act. Occasionally, nonprofessionals are employed, particularly if the commercial requires testimonials from consumers. The agency producer usually serves as casting director, although he is often assisted by the production studio. Since professional models and actors belong to unions, most payments are standardized. When well-known actors or actresses are employed, a special fee is often negotiated.

Sound tracks. Sound tracks are often shot separately and then synchronized with the video portion of the commercial. When background music is required, a special score has to be prepared. It is not uncommon to shoot the video portion in one section of the country and record the sound track in another, especially if a particular musical group or announcer is desired.

SHOOTING THE COMMERCIAL

When shooting with actors, each sequence is shot separately and assembled during editing. In order to minimize set changes and actor's time, scenes are not shot sequentially. Individual scenes are rehearsed and shot several times from different camera angles and under different direction so that a good take is assured.

In the case of animation, the sound track is prepared first, and the action is designed around it. Artwork is then prepared and transferred to clear plastic sheets, called **cells,** for photographing. Finally, the video and audio portions are assembled and synchronized.

When actors have speaking parts, the sound is often recorded at the same time the picture is shot in order to insure that the audio and video portions are synchronized. In the case of **voiceover,** where the announcer is heard but not seen, and in animated commercials, the sound track is recorded separately and joined with the video during editing.

EDITING

Editing is the process of selecting, splicing, and synchronizing the video and audio portions of the commercial. Several thousand feet of film may be viewed in selecting the scenes that will be used in the final commercial. There are a number of sequential steps taken in the editing process. After the commercial has been shot, the film is sent to a laboratory for processing or developing. In the case of videotape, this step is unnecessary. The unedited film, called rushes, is viewed to make sure that the material on hand is adequate and no further shooting or retakes are necessary. The next step is to select scenes from the rushes, assemble them in sequential form, and synchronize them with a separate sound track. This process yields a **rough-cut,** or **interlock,** which is usually viewed by the agency account executive and the client. After the interlock has been approved, the film is sent to an optical house so that special visual effects, such as **wipes, dissolves, fades,** and **supers** can be added. Finally, the audio and video portions are assembled on a single film or tape referred to as an **answer print.** The answer print is corrected for color, quality, density, and synchronization of sound. The corrected answer print becomes the **master print** from which duplicates are made for distribution to the stations carrying the commercial.

The production of a television commercial is a complex operation, requiring the talents of many specialists and using highly sophisticated equipment. Normal production time runs from six weeks to two months, from the approval of the storyboard until prints are shipped to television stations for use.

SUMMARY

Broadcast deals with time; print advertising deals with space. Since the consumer has no opportunity to study and reflect on a commercial, the central idea must be presented simply, clearly, and memorably. Broadcast advertising also lends itself to a variety of special effects and attention getting devices that are not available to the print writer.

Radio commercials can be classified in many ways, such as humorous, jingle, narrative, dialogue, and straight delivery. No classification system can do justice to the variety of effects that can be created with sound, however. The primary reason for recognizing the various classifications of commercials is to emphasize the versatility of the medium.

Since time is the controlling factor, commercial length is a critical consideration. Normally, radio commercials run for 10, 20, 30, or 60 seconds.

Although there are no hard and fast rules for writing radio commercials, helpful guidelines include these admonitions: keep it simple; be specific; repeat basic ideas.

Radio commercials are usually prepared in the form of a script, although fact sheets are often used when well-known personalities are employed to deliver commercials. Radio commercials may be delivered live or prerecorded; each approach has its own strengths and limitations.

Television commercials are much more complex than radio commercials because they involve both sight and sound. The key to effective television commercials is demonstration, and the greatest danger in developing television commercials is to let the technique of presentation get in the way of the product story.

One useful approach to developing a television commercial is first to develop a print ad that condenses the selling message into its basic form: a picture and a headline. This print ad should then be used as the guide for the commercial.

Television has its own jargon, which is used in scripts and storyboards to describe how the commercial will be filmed. Regardless of the instructions written on the script or storyboard, final decisions on filming are the responsibility of the producer.

Certain guidelines can be helpful to the novice television writer. Basically, these guidelines emphasize the use of video, need for coordination between video and audio, and use of action.

Because of television's complexity, preproduction meetings are essential. The method of production (film versus videotape), selection of a production house, decisions on casting and sets, and determination of how various scenes will be shot must be made ahead of time in order to conserve both time and money. Television production proceeds through several well defined stages: the shooting of the film; assembling of the commercial; coordination of sight and sound, editing, and color corrections; and production of a master print.

REVIEW QUESTIONS

1   Identify and explain the four suggestions for being a good television writer.
2   Identify the major ways that broadcast writing differs from print writing.
3   Evaluate the use of rhyme in broadcast writing. What are its advantages and disadvantages?
4   What are the guidelines for writing effective radio commercials? Why are these only guidelines rather than rules?
5   Differentiate between live and prerecorded radio commercials. What are the advantages and disadvantages of each?
6   According to the text, what has been the consequences of rising costs and increased competition for television commercials?
7   What are the guidelines for writing an effective television commercial?
8   Differentiate among and evaluate the following forms of television production: (a) live; (b) filmed; and (c) videotape.
9   What are the reasons given for shooting in film and then transferring to videotape?
10 Identify and explain the major steps in television production.

DISCUSSION QUESTIONS

1   Television advertising has been criticized because of the proliferation of multiple-spotting. What is your reaction to this practice? Do you think it should be controlled? How would you defend it?
2   What is your reaction to the suggestion that, in developing a television commercial, one should first develop a magazine advertisement?
3   Translate a print ad for a current product into a radio commercial. Bring the print advertisement to class so that the radio commercial can be compared to it. What difficulties did you encounter in making the transition?

PROBLEM

Select a consumer magazine ad for a product that can be advertised on television.

1 Write a 30-second television script from it.
2 Write a 60-second television script from it.

Bring the advertisement to class so that it can be compared to your television scripts.

IV
Advertising Media— Strategy and Plans

The advertising portion of the marketing plan consists of copy and media. These two aspects of advertising are inseparable. Copy, no matter how well conceived and executed, has no business value until it is exposed to a target group of consumers and, without advertising copy, media is simply a public service. Most advertising agencies are haunted by the fears of missing a magazine closing date or failing to deliver television and radio commercials in time for a scheduled broadcast.

In this part of the book, we will deal with media strategy and the various media used to carry advertising messages to consumers. Chapter 15 deals with media strategy, major variables influencing media selection, sources of media data, media efficiency, and media costs. Because of budget constraints, all media selection is a compromise between reach, frequency, and continuity, and different theories of media use emphasize one or more of these variables at the expense of the others. In addition, the media used in advertising a particular product are influenced by the

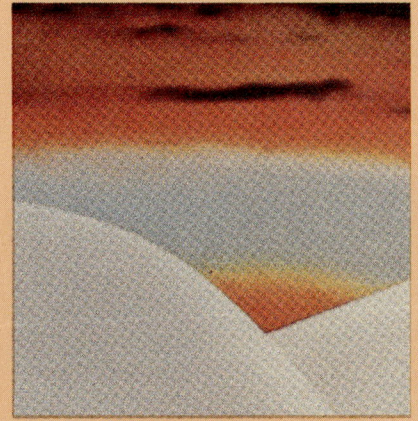

characteristics of the target market, the nature of the product, distribution channels, pricing, sales promotion activity, product life cycle, media flexibility, size of the appropriation, media availability, discounts, and editorial climate. The role of computers in media comparisons and selection is covered briefly, and the strengths and limitations of leading media models are identified. Measures of media efficiency are explained, and media costs and cost trends are described.

Chapter 16 is devoted to newspapers and magazines—two traditional media forms that are undergoing significant change. Topics include the importance of these media, the kinds of advertising for which they are used, their rate and discount structures, circulation, the ways they are sold, the merchandising programs they offer, and their strengths and weaknesses.

Chapter 17 examines broadcast media—television and radio. Broadcast media require different concepts and terminology from print media. With the advent of cable television, the basic structure of the industry is undergoing change, and the ultimate outcome for the broadcast industry is uncertain. The purpose of this chapter is to provide a basic understanding of broadcast media, the terminology it employs, its strengths and weaknesses, rate structure, and the ways it is purchased and used.

Chapter 18 is devoted to a little publicized but widely used group of media so diverse they defy classification. Media in this group include outdoor, transit, directories, direct, program, film, exhibit, specialty, and point-of-purchase advertising. On occasion these media may carry the entire burden of advertising for a product or service, however, they are used primarily to supplement the major media—television, radio, newspapers, and magazines. We will examine these media in terms of their most common forms, rate structure, and strengths and weaknesses.

15

Media and Media Strategy

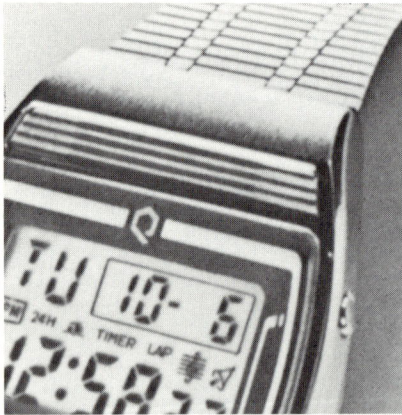

THREE STRATEGIES

WHY WANG USES TELEVISION

The Wang marketing story, like many in the computer industry, actually begins with IBM. In the fall of 1975, IBM introduced what was considered at the time a small business computer, recalls Wang Laboratories' director of corporate advertising and communications Harry Viens. Since 1972 Wang had been one of the few companies working in the small business computer area and, with about $75 million in sales, "we thought of it as our own area," says Viens.

IBM's introduction of small business computers, costing around $20,000, "presented both a problem and an opportunity," continues Viens. The problem: IBM, the computer giant with awesome marketing and sales resources, would be a tough competitor.

The opportunity: the IBM entry to the small business field gave legitimacy to the small business computer market, which had been generally ignored in favor of the mainframe computer market. "IBM immediately increased the market by at least one order of magnitude," estimates Viens. Wang management realized that IBM almost overnight "created a huge market for us," he recalls.

Wang would have to battle, however, for even a small slice of that market. IBM had immediate name recognition while Wang had literally next to none. In fact, in preliminary market research studies conducted for Wang, the company registered virtually no unaided recognition. Says Viens, "We fell within the statistical margin of error."[1]

Wang had to increase its name recognition among potential users of its products. A major print advertising campaign demonstrated that, given enough time, name recognition could be increased. Time was one commodity that Wang did not have. In the fast paced computer industry, failure to move quickly risks being left behind.

Market analysis revealed a predominantly male customer market of 23 million people, including data processing professionals, entrepreneurs, professional services, department managers, and busi-

[1]"Why Wang Is Sold On TV," *Marketing and Media Decisions* (December 1981): 62.

ness owners. Although the cost would be relatively high compared to what Wang had been spending, television could attract the attention of the customer market efficiently, particularly through network sports and current events–news programming.

Therefore, Wang changed its media strategy. Its first venture into television was a $1 million campaign that ran for three months during the professional football season. In 1981 the company's advertising expenditure had grown to $15 million, with the bulk invested in television. For fiscal 1976, company sales had grown to $96 million; in 1981 revenues exceeded $850 million.

KODAK'S EKTAPRINT COPIER

In contrast to Wang Laboratories, Kodak has used a completely different media strategy in advertising its Ektaprint copier. While competitors such as Xerox, Savin, and Canon have invested heavily in network television advertising, Kodak has used a highly selective media strategy, targeting its advertising in a select list of business publications.

Kodak has directed its marketing effort toward the high volume end of the copier business—government, law firms, and retail printing shops. With a budget only one-tenth the size of Xerox's, Kodak's Ektaprint copier has become one of the top three copiers in the high volume end of the business. [2]

LENOX CHINA

In the 1930s and 1940s, Lenox china had about 10 percent of the sales of fine china. Today, it holds a 50 percent share of the $80 million fine china market. Part of its success must be attributed to an advertising approach that has relied on consumer magazines to reach and persuade consumers.

Lenox's overall strategy of advertising to both the prebridal and postbridal market is unique. Using full color ads in every issue of *Seventeen*, Lenox introduces young women to its brand. Since

[2]For a more complete discussion of Kodak's strategy, see "Kodak's Copier Focuses on Business Publications," *Marketing and Media Decisions* (September 1981): 68.

young women are not interested in china, Lenox uses the concept of love to convey the importance of a top quality trade name in china and explain about bridal registry. The "Love leads to Lenox" teenage campaign has run in *Seventeen* since 1950. Its touch is light and playful; the boy says, "I'll get the license, you get the Lenox," as he sweeps the girl away.

Lenox advertises both its top selling Lenox china and Oxford bone china in bridal publications. However, that is not the extent of its media usage. According to the advertising manager: "We have a broad coverage of the bridal market, specifically targeting to the bride, with *Modern Bride, Bride's,* and *Better Homes and Gardens' Brides' Book*. We spell out what the bride who is looking for a premier china needs . . . Engaged girls are also reached through the pages of *Mademoiselle, Cosmopolitan,* and *Glamour*.[3] Lenox rounds out its magazine list with other women's service books and *Smithsonian, Architectural Digest, Town & Country,* and *Gourmet.*

All three exemplify media strategy as a part of the marketing program. Wang Laboratories used sports programming on television to acquire brand recognition quickly. Kodak obtained concentrated market coverage of its Ektaprint copier by enlisting select business publications; Lenox built its reputation and market share by directing its advertising to the prebridal and postbridal markets. Individual marketing strategies require quite different media strategies to deliver their advertising messages effectively and efficiently.

THEORIES OF MEDIA USE

No aspect of the advertising industry is free from disagreement and controversy. Media is no exception. Each medium has its advocates and detractors; disagreement exists among professionals about how media can be used most effectively and the one best approach. Yesterday's gamble is today's practice; today's practice is tomorrow's anachronism.

A number of theories of media use seek some compromise among the multiple demands of reach, frequency, and continuity; Few advertisers can afford all three.

Reach is defined as the unduplicated proportion of a defined audience that is exposed to an advertising message within four weeks, the traditional time period on which most media data is based.

Frequency refers to the number of times within a given four-week period that a particular audience or portion of that audience is exposed to the message. Frequency can be expressed in two ways: (a) *average frequency;* or (b) *frequency distribution*. If frequency is stated as an average of 4.0, the average member of the target market is exposed to the advertising message 4.0 times during the four-week period. Not all members of the target market will be exposed precisely this number of times, of course. Some will have more, and some will have fewer exposures. For example, the frequency distribution might look something like this:

---

[3]"Lenox's Spending Spree in Print," *Marketing and Media Decisions* (August 1981): 74.

0 − 1	exposures	10%
2 − 3	exposures	20%
4	exposures	40%
5 − 6	exposures	20%
6 +	exposures	10%

Average frequency is used for media planning purposes, and frequency distribution is used to measure the amount of variability around this average that is actually attained. Both are based on extremely gross estimates that imply a precision much greater than exists. Nonetheless, the concepts of average frequency and frequency distribution give a rough gauge for planning and evaluation purposes.

Continuity, as it is used in reference to media, refers to the continuous use of advertising over a specified period of time, usually for the duration of the one-year marketing plan. Thus, an advertiser whose advertising appeared every week for fifty-two weeks would be employing high continuity. Often, advertising will not be used throughout the year; instead, it will be concentrated during peak buying seasons. For example, the advertiser of suntan lotion usually concentrates advertising during the summer months when the product is in greatest demand. Continuity is sacrificed in order to gain reach and frequency during the peak buying period.

Most media plans end up as a compromise between reach, frequency, and continuity, with the nature of the compromise determined by the judgment of the media planner and based on an understanding of the competitive situation and the product's advertising needs.

What constitutes optimal frequency in an advertising schedule is a perennial concern in the industry. Robert H. Geis, vice-president and corporate media director of Wells, Rich, Green, Inc. notes:

> During my two decades in the business, we have collectively invested in more than $1 billion in media research. As a result, there are tons of data available to us. In order to process this information we have designed elaborate computer systems.
>
> But what does it all mean? Many of the numbers we are working with are unreliable, meaningless, or even erroneous. . . .
>
> We pride ourselves on having average audience figures for all major media vehicles, and reach curves that sort out duplication, and frequency distribution models that reveal potential exposure patterns. Unfortunately, much of this is suspect or based on mathematical formulae that produce, at best, "guesstimates". . . .
>
> We are not even close to getting answers on questions that I faced as a novice planner in the early '60s. Here are four such questions that focus on what should be of primary concern to us all—communication effectiveness:
>
> 1. How much frequency is enough?
> 2. Which is more effective—flighting or continuity?
> 3. What are the relative values of various television dayparts?[4]

---

[4]The term **television dayparts** refers to the time of day television is broadcast. Basically, there are three dayparts: (a) daytime television; (b) prime time—roughly between 7:00 P.M. to 10:00 P.M.; and (c) fringe time—immediately before and after prime time.

4. How can you weigh television apples with magazine oranges?

I realize that we have attempted to answer some of these over the years. Thus far, the research results are either inconclusive or proprietary. . . .

What concerns me even more than how little we know, is how much we think we know. All of the research data we have at our disposal leads to a false sense of security. We feel so secure that we base million-dollar decisions on shaky numbers.[5]

In 1979 the Association of National Advertisers published a review of major studies on the effects of frequency. Among the tentative conclusions drawn from this review are the following:

1. One exposure of an advertisement to a target consumer group within a purchase cycle has little or no effect in all but a minority of circumstances.[6]
2. Since one exposure is usually ineffective, the central goal of productive media planning should be to place emphasis on enhancing frequency rather than reach.
3. By and large, optimal exposure frequency appears to be at least three exposures within a purchase cycle.
4. . . . very large and well-known brands—and/or those with dominant market shares in their categories and dominant shares of category advertising weight—appear to differ markedly in response to frequency of exposure from smaller or more average brands.
5. Although there are general principles with respect to frequency of exposure and its relationship to advertising effectiveness, differential effects by brand are equally important.[7]

Frequency versus reach becomes even more complex for the advertiser who uses multiple media. Determining audience duplication between media is not a precise science, even though generalized formulas can be used.

Since advertising funds are always limited, media planners must use judgment as well as quantitative measures in order to reach an optimal decision on the particular media mix to employ and the relative weight that will be given to reach, frequency, and continuity. Broadly speaking, a number of theories or approaches may be used to seek a viable compromise among reach, frequency, and continuity. The most common are **wave theory, concentration theory,** and **reach theory.**

WAVE THEORY

Wave theory sacrifices continuity in order to achieve reach and frequency goals. In this approach, advertisers purchase time or space in various media for a relatively short period of time, perhaps four weeks, and move in and out of these media in waves. In other words,

---

[5]Robert H. Geis, "How Much We Know," *Advertising Age*, 22 June 1981, 58.

[6]A purchase cycle refers to the normal length of time between purchases. For example, if a consumer purchases a given product on the average of every two weeks, that product's purchase cycle is two weeks.

[7]Michael J. Naples, *Effective Frequency* (New York: *Association of National Advertisers*, 1979), 63–78.

an advertiser might purchase four weeks of television, take a four week hiatus, purchase another four weeks of advertising, take another four week hiatus, and so on until the end of the marketing period, which is generally one year. The assumption is that the effects of advertising will carry over from periods of heavy concentration to those in which no advertising appears.

CONCENTRATION THEORY

Concentration theory sacrifices reach in order to gain frequency and continuity. Under this approach, advertisers concentrate their advertising in a single medium or limited list of media. Adequate frequency and continuity are scheduled in one medium before another is added to the list. The number of media vehicles used depends upon the size of the budget.

REACH THEORY

Reach theory sacrifices frequency and continuity in order to gain reach. In this approach, advertising is scheduled in a wide range of media vehicles in order to reach the largest possible audience with little regard for frequency or continuity. **Scatter plans** are an example of this strategy. In a scatter plan, the advertiser contracts for a certain number of television commercials which are scattered across a number of programs or time periods. Maximum reach is achieved because many programs with different audience characteristics are used. However, frequency and continuity within a given program may be virtually nonexistent.

The best approach depends upon the product field being served and goals of the advertiser. If errors are committed, they arise from emphasizing reach at the expense of frequency and continuity. This is particularly true in the field of television where the high cost virtually precludes frequency and continuity for all except the largest advertisers.

THE ROLE OF MEDIA STRATEGY

The text in Chapter 4 pointed out that media strategy is subordinate to the marketing and advertising strategies. These strategies establish general media constraints such as: (a) the amount of money available; (b) the definition of the target group or groups of consumers; (c) the relative emphasis to be given to each target group when more than one exists; and (d) when advertising support is to be delivered. The basic function of media strategy is to show how media will be selected and used to meet these general objectives.

Generally, media strategy statements cover the following decision areas:

1 *Decisions concerning the general kinds of media, along with a rationale for these decisions* (use of local versus regional versus national media; use of print versus broadcast media; ways that two or more media will be combined to meet specific marketing and advertising objectives).

2 *Decisions concerning types of media within broad media classifications and the rationale for these decisions* (types of pro-

gramming within broadcast media—sports, drama, situation comedies, adventure, game shows, and so on; types of magazines, such as women's, men's, special interest, or general interest magazines).

3 *Decisions concerning space and time units and the reason for these decisions* (particular time or space units that will be used; way each medium selected will be used to meet the requirements of reach, frequency, cost efficiency, and other factors concerning media scheduling; ways that specific broadcast time periods or space positions will be used to achieve advertising objectives. For example, drive time, women's sections, or home furnishings sections).

4 *Decisions concerning the ways that other marketing factors will influence media timing* (Seasonality of sales; timing of media supported promotions; availability of copy).

Within the framework of such strategy statements, specific media may be selected and justified, schedules may be assembled, and costs estimated.

Obviously, a number of factors affect the development of a particular media strategy and the preparation of specific media plans.

FACTORS INFLUENCING MEDIA STRATEGY

Different media have inherent characteristics which recommend their use. For example, magazines provide high quality color reproduction and varied editorial climates. They permit leisurely perusal of the advertising message and can be used selectively to reach highly specialized audiences such as brides, sports car buffs, hunting enthusiasts, bridge players, new mothers, and an incredible array of other specialized consumer groups. Newspapers, generally thought of as a mass medium, can also be used selectively through position requests in the sports and financial sections or the women's pages. However, the outstanding strength of newspapers lies in their ability to localize advertising, provide intensive coverage of a particular city or suburb, and impart a sense of immediacy to the advertising. While providing some measure of selectivity through programming such as sports, soap operas, game shows, family programs, and children's programs, television derives its greatest strength from its unique combination of sight and sound and its ability to demonstrate product use. Because of its ubiquitous nature, radio not only provides audience selectivity through programming, but is unique in terms of its broadcast flexibility and its local nature. Other media, such as outdoor posters and transit advertising, also have characteristic strengths.

The task of media strategy and selection is matching the characteristics of individual media with the market requirements of the product. Many marketing considerations influence media strategy and the selection of particular media. In the following material, eleven such considerations are identified and discussed briefly. These are the target market, product characteristics, distribution channels, pricing policy and strategy, sales promotion activity, stages in the product life cycle, flexibility, size of the advertising appropriation, media availability, media discounts, and editorial climate.

THE TARGET MARKET

Few products are used by all people. Even products that enjoy universal use, such as clothing and furniture, are segmented in terms of style and price. An effective media program is one that concentrates on the target market with little waste circulation.

Geographic, demographic, psychographic, and behavioral variables can be used in segmenting markets. Media can often be found that will match many of these markets to an amazing degree. Sources of media data, such as W. R. Simmons and Associates, provide product usage data and media habits for a wide range of demographic characteristics. Through the use of such information, media can be selected to reach target markets with a minimum of waste circulation. Media efficiency in reaching target markets is not the only consideration in selecting media, however. Often, efficiency will be sacrificed for impact or the opportunity to demonstrate the product.

PRODUCT CHARACTERISTICS

Some media are better suited than others for expressing the unique attributes of particular products. For example, elegant furniture is best advertised in magazines where potential customers have an opportunity to study the furniture in natural settings and visualize it in their own homes. The nature of the product and the way in which the buying decision is made requires the use of magazines. In this particular instance, the desire for media efficiency does not have to be compromised in order to display the product properly because audience selectivity is a characteristic of magazines. In other instances, compromises have to be made. Automobiles are a case in point. Media efficiency in reaching the target markets for most new automobiles can best be served by using magazines. Although it involves substantial waste circulation, television is also widely used because it is an ideal medium for showing the performance characteristics of cars. Similarly, women's magazines are highly efficient in reaching the target market for dog food. Because magazines neither provide television's breadth of coverage nor offer the opportunity to show the dog's enthusiasm over mealtime, compromises have to be made. Morris the cat has become well-known as the television "spokesman" for 9-Lives cat food; however, this advertisement has a great deal of waste circulation because not all television-viewing families have cats.

DISTRIBUTION CHANNELS

The location, structure, and sales coverage of distribution channels may also have a major influence on media strategy.

Location.   While many brands have national distribution, others are regional or even local in their sales. Some may have spotty distribution. While they are sold from coast to coast, and from the Canadian to the Mexican border, distribution may be nonexistent or extremely thin in some major metropolitan areas. In all of these instances, the efficient use of media requires that advertising pressure be deployed only in those areas where the brand is available.

Brands that have truly national distribution may vary substantially in market share from one region of the country to another or among major metropolitan areas. In other cases, market potential for the product type will show marked regional differences. In such cases, a national advertising program in network television and magazines may be used to provide umbrella coverage for the total United States, with local media being employed to heavy up the schedule in selected metropolitan markets or regions where market share or market potential is substantially above average.

Distributor and retailer reactions to media.   Distributors and retailers often have personal preferences that influence media schedules. Some are vocal in their insistence on local media, which they believe is more effective than national vehicles. Others may prefer the prestige they believe national media lends to the brand. Distributor and retailer viewpoints must often be taken into consideration in formulating media plans. This is particularly true for products such as beer because the brand's success is heavily dependent on the quality and cooperation of local distributors.

Equalizing sales force coverage.   Disparities in sales force coverage may arise for a variety of reasons, ranging from rapid sales expansion that taxes the company's ability to provide sales support to regional differences in product potential that make it uneconomical to provide comparable sales coverage in all areas. In such instances, media weight is often expected to compensate for these differences by providing dealer and distributor contacts through regional trade publications in areas of weak sales coverage.

Distribution policies.   Companies follow a policy of intensive or selective distribution. Selective distribution is common in fields such as clothing, shoes, furniture, and some major appliances. Intensive distribution is characteristic of most grocery products, proprietary drug products, and competitively priced personal care items. Under a policy of selective distribution, dealer support through retail advertising and dealer promotions often carries much of the manufacturer's communication burden. In the case of intensive distribution, however, dealer support is minimal to nonexistent, and the manufacturer's advertising program must bear the responsibility of reaching and influencing consumers. Obviously, media strategy will be influenced by the manufacturer's distribution policies.

PRICING POLICY AND STRATEGY

Media strategy influences pricing strategy in a number of ways. First, pricing strategy is often a key consideration in product positioning. A brand that is premium priced, either for market segmentation or to impute quality to the brand within a given market segment, may require "prestige" media to support the basic product concept. Second, an economy or competitively priced brand may have limited contribution margins which reduce the funds available for advertising. Third, margins offered to distributors and dealers will often affect the amount of channel support that is given. Where channel margins are high, the resulting advertising and promotional support from distributors and dealers may influence the size of the manufacturer's media expenditures and the type of media. Thus, if distributors and dealers provide extensive local support, the manufacturer's expenditures may be confined to national media.

SALES PROMOTION ACTIVITY

For many product groups, sales promotion plays a major role in the marketing plan. It includes such activities as coupons, contests, sweepstakes, cents-off deals, self-liquidating premiums, display allowances, and trade deals (see Chapter 19). The effectiveness of a particular sales promotion often depends upon the amount of advertising support it receives as well as the type of media used. For example, a coupon promotion requires some method for distributing the coupons. Magazines, newspapers, and direct mail are often used for this purpose. A trade deal, while supported by sales force activity, also requires the use of trade publications for adequate coverage. Contests and sweepstakes require magazine advertising to spell out the prize structure and rules. Thus, media expenditures must be diverted from product advertising to provide adequate support for sales promotion activity, and the nature of the sales promotion will directly affect the type of media used.

STAGES IN THE PRODUCT LIFE CYCLE

During the introductory stage, broad coverage—using newspapers, magazines, television, and outdoor advertising—may be required in order to gain quick and widespread brand recognition. From an efficiency standpoint, such a widespread use of media is wasteful. Nonetheless, this kind of media coverage is often necessary if the brand is to gain distribution and obtain the initial trial that is necessary to launch it successfully.

In the maturity stage of the brand's life cycle, a different media strategy may be required. Audience selectivity becomes more important; media efficiency takes precedence; frequency of message may become more important than reach; and, in the case of food products, "service" advertising, which features recipes showing how to use the product in new and interesting ways, may demand primary reliance on magazines.

FLEXIBILITY

Media differ in the length of their commitments and closing dates. For example, the purchase of a television program on a weekly basis, affordable only by major advertisers, requires a year's commitment of funds. The purchase of a spot during the Super Bowl telecast must be concluded many months before "Super Sunday," and the scheduling of a television special just prior to Christmas may require a commitment in the preceding January or February. Similarly, magazine closing dates, particularly for unusual space units or cover positions, may require a commitment several months before the magazine appears on the newsstand.

In a volatile market, an advertiser may need greater scheduling flexibility than these commitments permit. In such instances, marketing strategy will call for flexibility in the commitment of funds, and media strategy must reflect this marketing requirement by specifying the use of media that have short closing dates and accept cancellations with minimum notice.

SIZE OF THE ADVERTISING APPROPRIATION

Advertising, particularly network television advertising, is expensive. In 1983 a 30-second commercial during the time slot of a prime time program ranged from $90,000 to $150,000; price increases of 15 to 20 percent a year are forecast for the future. The cost of a 30-second spot during the 1982 Super Bowl was as high as $345,000, although some early buyers purchased one for as little as $325,000. In 1983 the cost for the same spot during the Super Bowl was $400,000; the end is not in sight.

Many advertisers simply cannot afford network television, and despite attempts to reduce the cost of network television through the use of scatter plans, television is a medium that requires a substantial investment in advertising dollars. An adequate schedule in national magazines may also be beyond an advertiser's means; while spot television can be purchased in individual markets for a relatively small outlay, the aggregation of markets necessary to provide adequate national coverage may be completely beyond reason.

MEDIA AVAILABILITY

The desired media is not always available when and where it is needed. Although this is normally not a problem with magazine and newspaper advertising, it is often a major factor in network television and in local radio and television spot announcements in key markets. If a particular time slot has been sold, the radio or television station cannot create more time. Premium time slots are often not available in all markets in which the advertiser would like to have advertising appear.

MEDIA DISCOUNTS

Discounts, based on the size of the expenditure and the frequency of use, exist for virtually all media. These discounts are often complex and take one or more of the following forms:

1 Published, formal discounts based on volume, frequency, continuity, or some combination of these considerations.
2 Distressed media pricing in which the cost of a given media exposure is reduced because it remains unsold (primarily in broadcast media).
3 Special media plans where a combination of media exposures will be priced at a cost below the total cost of the separately priced

individual exposures (primarily in broadcast media, print, and newspapers; broadcast media has an infinite number of such plans).

4 Negotiated prices for media exposures (characteristic of network television; nonstandard space units in the print media field).

In computing media discounts, the time and space used by different brands of the same manufacturer is accumulated to qualify for discounts. Table 15–1 shows the average maximum discounts available to national advertisers, based on published rates.

For a major advertiser, the discounts can be significant. For a company such as Procter & Gamble, which spends over $600 million a year in advertising, the judicious use of media, as well as coordination of media among its various brands, can result in substantial savings. These savings can be used to extend media coverage, increase profits, or both. For this reason, large companies that use a number of advertising agencies for their different brands often appoint one or more as coordinating agencies to keep track of possible opportunities for media discounts through the coordination of media schedules. The magnitude of the savings may exert a profound effect on media planning.

EDITORIAL CLIMATE

Even among media that reach similar audiences, editorial climate may vary significantly. Some media are considered more reliable; others are considered more fun. Some are educational in nature; others prestigious. Shelter magazines such as *Better Homes and Gardens* catch readers who are thinking about home improvements as opposed to the news weeklies, which catch readers who are thinking about national or world events.

Media planners attempt to place their advertising in an editorial setting that attracts readers who will be particularly receptive to their advertising messages. Media, particularly magazines, often provide a great deal of audience research data which attempt to define the orientation of their readers.

TABLE 15–1   Discounts for selected media

Media	Average Maximum Discount (Percent)	Range of Maximum Discounts (Percent)
Network TV	10%	5–15%
Newspapers	18%	0–31%
Spot TV	20%	0–50%
Consumer magazines	32%	27–41%
Spot radio	36%	0–59%
Network radio	36%	23–53%

Source: Compiled from *Standard Rate and Data Service* and based on 50 major markets for local media and selected leading magazines.

A DAY IN THE LIFE OF A GROUP MEDIA DIRECTOR

Steve Phelps prepared himself for an advertising career at Northwestern University where he earned a masters degree in journalism. His first job in advertising was with the Leo Burnett agency in Chicago, learning media research. Within two years he advanced to the position of media supervisor on Kellogg, after having served a stint as a local broadcast buyer.

Steve moved from Leo Burnett to D'Arcy-MacManus & Masius as a media supervisor on the Ralston Purina account. Presently he is vice-president/group media director with responsibility for overseeing the planning, buying, and day-to-day activities on fourteen accounts including four Anheuser Busch brands.

8:30–9:00
Arrived at the office, glanced at *The Wall Street Journal,* and checked the mail to see if anything urgent had arisen. I always wonder if I'm going to start the day with a rush project that will result in changing my entire day's schedule. Today "appears" to be a normal, although full, day.

9:00–10:00
Reviewed major assignments in the group. Normally, we may have anywhere from 30 to 35 major assignments in the works, and I like to make sure they are on schedule. I hate surprises, particularly when they mean that we've missed a deadline. I have a good group of media professionals. They are doers; they have to be. But, they get busy with day-to-day activities, and sometimes this can result in a project getting sidetracked or delayed. We are currently preparing a recommendation regarding ad placement within a publication.

The recommendation is running slightly behind schedule, and I had to get it back on track. Deadlines are critical in media, and I feel the pressure when things get behind.

10:00–11:00
Worked on a presentation to be given to the client concerning the capabilities of our new network television computer system. Discussed various aspects of the project with our New York office, as well as the Media Information Research Department here in St. Louis. I'm pleased to see that the presentation is starting to jell.

11:00–12:00
Reviewed the status of the Anheuser Busch brand budgets in preparation for a client meeting this afternoon. Budget review is a continuing process in media. Although the associate media directors are actually responsible for the individual brand budgets, since we are agency of record for Anheuser Busch, it is my additional duty to

see to it that our brand budgets dovetail with those of other agencies who are assigned accounts.

12:00–1:30
Had lunch with a media representative from a national magazine who presented a media proposal for a multiple-page insert. I see a lot of proposals like this. Some are on target, and some aren't. Although innovative, this one wasn't quite ready for client review. I offered the publication a suggestion for improving the proposal which involved tying it more closely with sports, perhaps even keying the theme to a special event such as "the Derby."

1:30–2:00
Talked to the Outdoor Department regarding scheduled plans for the use of 8-sheet billboards in black communities. Also returned several phone calls that I had been too busy to answer that morning.

2:00–4:00
Met with the client to discuss year-end budget reconciliation. The media plan and the actual buys that are made have to continually be reconciled. Because there is a large amount of negotiation in the media buying process as well as the occasion to make opportunistic buys, this is a continual process that goes on until the end of the fiscal year.

4:00–5:00
Met with the media director to discuss reorganization of the A-B Corporate Media staff to better serve the needs of the Regional Account Executive field force. We have the basic structure in place, but now its a question of fine tuning and working out areas of responsibility.

5:00–6:00
The office formally closes at 4:45. But that's not when work stops. After 5:00 is a good time of the day to get the days work done without the interruption of telephone calls and "rep" visits. I reviewed the afternoon mail, noted phone calls that had to be returned the next morning, and worked on several on-going assignments.

6:00
Time to go home. It's been a busy day but I feel a good sense of accomplishment. I wonder what new assignments tomorrow will bring. I'm never quite sure. But, then, that's part of the excitement of the business.

Contributed by D'Arcy-MacManus & Masius, St. Louis.

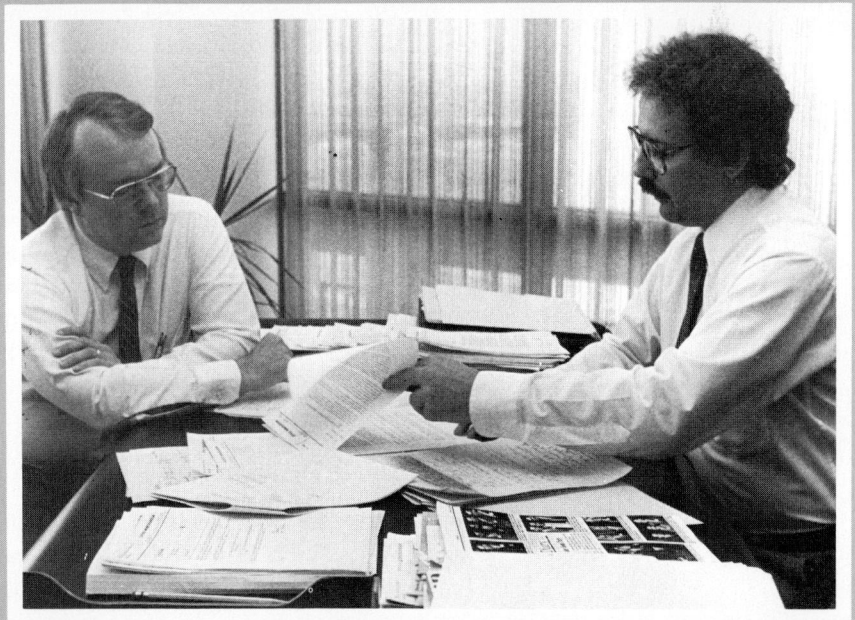

SOURCES OF MEDIA DATA

Media analysis and planning require a great deal of information on markets, media rates, advertising materials required by media, closing dates, circulation, audience duplication, and competitive expenditures. This information is available from sources ranging from the media themselves to a variety of subscription services that audit media claims and monitor advertising activity.

REPORTS BY MEDIA

The media themselves are a source of considerable information. They publish rate cards which provide information on rates, available advertising units, closing dates, mechanical requirements, circulation figures, and nonacceptable advertising. Media undertake special research studies on the demographic characteristics of their audiences, penetration of markets, product usage and brand preferences among members of their audiences, and other market related data. Although this information is often useful, it must be interpreted cautiously because media search out and present data that tends to put them in a favorable light.

REPORTS BY MEDIA ASSOCIATIONS

All major media have national media associations that publish material concerning the nature and merits of advertising in the media they represent. Leading associations include the Bureau of Advertising of the American Newspaper Publishers Association, Magazine Publishers Association, Radio Advertising Bureau, Television Bureau of Advertising, Outdoor Advertising, Inc., and Advertising Specialty Association.

STANDARD RATE AND DATA SERVICE (SRDS)

SRDS is the most widely used service for information on rates, circulation, mechanical requirements, issuance and closing dates, and other basic news on media. Published monthly, it is compiled from the rate cards of the various media and eliminates the need for advertising agencies to maintain a file of rate cards on each medium. SRDS issues separate volumes for magazines, newspapers, television, and radio.

AUDIT BUREAUS

A number of organizations impartially audit the claims of media. The Audit Bureau of Circulation (ABC) and Traffic Audit Bureau (TAB) check and verify the circulations of many newspapers, magazines, business publications, and outdoor advertising. In order to be audited, media have to comply with certain standard reporting practices. All advertising agencies of any stature subscribe to the audited reports.

INDEPENDENT RESEARCH SERVICES

Independent research organizations provide viewer data on broadcast media and readership information for print vehicles. Some services also contain marketing data on product use for a wide range of products. Others monitor advertising and publish data on competitive advertising expenditures. The table in Appendix 4 lists some of the major services, along with a brief description of the data provided and their method of pricing that information.

COMPARING MEDIA

After media strategy has been defined, the media planner's major task becomes one of matching media selection with strategic considerations. Since there are many possible media vehicles, the job is a monumental one that is compounded by conflicting claims and ambiguous research information. For example, in 1975 Time, Inc., brought suit against W. R. Simmons and Associates for allegedly underrepresenting *Time* magazine's total audience in their audience survey. Since Simmons's data is widely used by advertising agencies in making their media selections, Time, Inc., contended that such misrepresentation would severely depress its advertising revenues. At first, this controversy seemed to threaten the future of syndicated services, and the advertising trade press was in an uproar. However, the advertising industry's dependence on such data is so great that much of the industry rallied around efforts to devise validity studies for gathering audience data, and Time, Inc.'s lawsuit was dropped.[8]

In 1977 serious questions were raised by wide discrepancies between the consumer magazines' total audience figures developed by Simmons and Target Group Index. Subsequently, Simmons and Target Group Index were merged into Simmons Market Research Bureau (SMRB), but that failed to solve the problem.

Currently, the two major audience measuring services are SMRB and Magazine Research, Inc. (MRI). In 1979 a report comparing the two services found that MRI audience estimates ranged from 161 percent higher to 34 percent lower for the 104 magazines measured by both services.[9]

These differences arise, not because of chicanery or malfeasance, but simply because the task of developing valid data on magazine readership and program viewing for over 200 million U.S. consumers is an exceedingly difficult and costly one. Different sampling techniques, interviewing procedures, ways of asking questions, and methods of validating media exposure inevitably lead to discrepancies in the final results. Further, the harsh reality of the cost involved in gathering such data results in pragmatic compromises being made in sampling procedures and the collection and processing of the findings. These compromises, while both justifiable and necessary to keep survey costs within affordable limits, nonetheless increase the probability of error.

There is no solution to the problem as long as advertisers and advertising agencies insist on playing the numbers game. Clients demand that agencies justify their media recommendations by demonstrating the efficiency of their media buys. Advertising agencies pressure publishers for larger audience figures. Publishers respond

---

[8]"ARF Kills Proposal for Magazine Study, But Wants New Plan," *Advertising Age*, 19 January 1976, 1.

[9]"Does MRI Have the Answer?" *Marketing and Media Decisions* (November 1979): 66.

by emphasizing the size of their audiences. No one seems to care whether the audience figures are valid—only that they are large. The larger the audience, the happier the clients are with their advertising agencies. Thus, the game continues in a vicious circle.

MEDIA EFFICIENCY

Media efficiency is generally measured in terms of the cost-per-thousand exposures among members of a target audience.[10] Cost-per-thousand (CPM) is computed by multiplying the rate (cost of the advertising message) by 1000, and dividing by the number of people exposed to the message.

$$\text{CPM} = \frac{\text{rate} \times 1000}{\text{number exposed}}$$

A media program that costs $11.55 for 1000 exposures is obviously much more expensive than one that costs $9.50 for 1000 exposures. Let us assume that the target market for two media programs consists of women between the ages of 35 and 54, approximately 25 million people in the United States. Media strategy requires an average of 3.0 exposures against members of this audience during each four-week period for 52 weeks. The total number of exposures required is

Target audience	3.0 exposures each four weeks	13 four-week periods	Total exposures
25,000,000 ×	3.0 ×	13	= 975,000,000

At a cost of $11.55 CPM, the total cost of the media buy would be

$$\$11.55 \times 975,000 = \$11,261,250$$

At a cost of $9.50 CPM, the total cost would be

$$\$9.50 \times 975,000 = \$9,262,500.$$

This represents a difference of $1,998,750, a substantial savings for the lower cost-per-thousand campaign.

COMPARING EFFICIENCY IN MULTIMEDIA PROGRAMS

When a number of media combinations are being considered, thousands of comparisons must be made to arrive at the most efficient combination for a particular media schedule. Joseph St. Georges points up the magnitude of the problem with this commentary:

---

[10]Although cost-per-thousand is a standard measure of cost in the advertising industry and is used by magazines and broadcast media, other media may use a variation of this measure. For example, newspapers commonly use the milline rate, which is the cost per agate line for each million readers. Outdoor advertising sometimes uses **showings** for comparing costs. A 100 showing in a particular market is considered sufficient to expose virtually every mobile person in the market to the message in a 30-day period.

> As an example of the potential complexity of the media decision . . . in the simplest circumstances, a media buyer selecting 3 media from a group of 6 has 20 potential different choices. The same media buyer selecting 10 media from a group of 100, has 17,310,000,000,000 different alternatives available to him. If he could analyze 1 alternative per second, 24 hours a day, 7 days a week, he could cover all of his choices (in) one-half million years.[11]

COMPUTER MODELS IN MEDIA SELECTION

Computer technology came to the rescue of the media planner in the early 1960s. On October 1, 1962, *Advertising Age* announced: "Y&R, BBD&O unleash media computerization." Subsequently, BBDO ran full page newspaper and magazine advertisements claiming that their computerization system showed one BBDO client how to get $1.67 worth of effective advertising for every dollar in his budget. Other major advertising agencies accepted the challenge and began to investigate ways for using computers in media selection. Often, their investigations led them to dead ends. William Moran of Young & Rubicam (Y&R) said that his agency had spent two years trying a linear programming approach, finally abandoning it in favor of another alternative.[12]

Since computers burst into the media scene, several computer models have been developed as aids in media selection.

LINEAR PROGRAMMING

A linear programming model for selecting media is an **optimizing model.** This model attempts to select the one best alternative within the framework of strategic considerations such as the size of the advertising budget, minimum and maximum usage of specific media vehicles and classifications, and minimum exposure frequencies for target buyers. These constraints, along with information on media rates, audience size and characteristics, target market data, and the relative value of exposures in each medium versus value of exposures in other media, are fed into the computer. Out comes a recommendation indicating what specific media and size units will give maximum exposure.

However, five limitations of linear programming are that it: (a) assumes that repeat exposures have the same effect as the initial exposure, which may or may not be true; (b) cannot handle the problem of media discounts; (c) cannot handle the problem of audience duplication between media; (d) does not indicate when advertising should be scheduled; and (e) requires highly suspect or nonexistent quantitative data.

HIGH ASSAY MODEL

The high assay model, developed by Young & Rubicam, avoids many of the problems of linear programming by choosing media on a sequential basis rather than a simultaneous one. Using data similar

---

[11]Joseph St. Georges, "How Practical Is the Media Mode?" *Journal of Marketing* (July 1963): 31–32.

[12]William T. Moran, "Practical Media Decisions and the Computer," *Journal of Marketing* (July 1963): 26–30.

to that used in linear programming, the high assay model starts off by considering all of the media available during the first week of the schedule and selecting the single best buy. Then a second selection is made for the same week if the achieved rate of exposure is below the desired rate. When optimal exposure for the first week is achieved, the program proceeds to the second week and so on until the entire schedule is developed. The advantages of the high assay model are that it: (a) develops a schedule simultaneously with the selection of media; (b) handles the problem of audience duplication; (c) deals with media discounts; and (d) incorporates theoretically important variables such as brand-switching rates and multiple-exposure coefficients.[13] Its major limitation is that some of the data required is either suspect or nonexistent.

SIMULATION

Unlike linear programming and high assay models, simulation models don't attempt to find the best media plan. They estimate the exposure value of any given media plan submitted for analysis.[14] In simulation exercises, hypothetical buyers, along with their demographic characteristics, media habits, and program use patterns, are stored in the computer. Alternative media plans are fed into the computer, which develops an estimate of the exposures provided by each plan. The media planner then examines the results and determines how well each alternative meets the advertising needs of the product. Simulation has been criticized for three reasons. First, it does not include an overall "effectiveness" measure for each alternative; instead, it yields a multidimensional picture of reach and frequency for each plan. Second, simulation lacks a procedure for finding better media combinations. Third, the representativeness of the hypothetical population is suspect.

MEDIAC

One of the newer generation media models for computers is Media Evaluation Using Dynamic and Interactive Applications of Computers (MEDIAC).[15] Designed as a sophisticated mathematical model, this program incorporates important marketing considerations such as market segments, sales potentials, exposure probabilities, diminishing marginal response rates, forgetting, seasonality, and cost estimates. Hard data on many of these variables is simply not available. While this model overcomes many of the deficiencies of the earlier linear programming models, MEDIAC still assumes a linear cost structure for media that is not consistent with the complex discount practices existing in the field.[16]

Other computer models have been developed by other advertising agencies and concerned organizations. None are wholly satisfac-

---

[13]Philip Kotler, *Marketing Management,* 2nd ed. (Englewood Cliffs, New Jersey: Prentice-Hall, 1967), 689.

[14]*Simulatics Media-Mix: Technical Description* (New York: The Simulatics Corp., October, 1962).

[15]Philip Kotler, *Marketing Decision Making: A Model Building Approach* (New York: Holt, Rinehart and Winston, 1971), 460–64.

[16]Dorothy Cohen, *Advertising* (New York: John Wiley & Sons, Inc., 1972), 501.

tory. All must rely on ambiguous and inadequate quantitative data, as do media planners. An additional danger lies in the tendency to forget a computer's inadequacies and become enamored with the volume of pristine numbers that flash on the display screen or pour forth from the printer.

Used properly, however, computer models are a major asset in media selection. They do not and cannot replace the role of judgment and imagination in media planning, but they can process an unbelievable amount of data in a remarkably short period of time. They summarize and organize it into a usable form for the media professionals who, in the final analysis, make judgmental decisions on media selection and scheduling.

MEDIA COSTS AND PRICE TRENDS

Costs vary substantially between media and within the same medium for various target groups. For example, the CPM for reaching children with a 30-second television commercial on children's Saturday morning shows ranges between $2.75 and $3.75. By contrast, the CPM for reaching women between the ages of 25 and 54 with a 30-second prime time commercial ranges between $10.50 and $13.50, approximately four times as much.[17] Generally, as the target group becomes more selective, costs increase correspondingly.

In addition, inflation has driven media costs up substantially in recent years. Table 15–2 shows the CPM trend for selected media from 1978 to 1982, indexed on 1967. Since 1967, the CPM for newspapers has increased 184 percent (index 284). Network TV has increased by 177 percent (index 277), and spot TV has increased by 141 percent. The smallest increase since 1967 has been in spot radio which has shown a CPM increase of only 92 percent (index 192).

TABLE 15–2 Cost-per-thousand (CPM) trends for selected media (1967 = 100)

Media	1978	1979	1980	1981*	1982*
Newspapers	195	213	235	258	284
Magazines	145	158	173	185	196
Network TV	195	215	231	252	277
Spot TV	167	183	201	221	241
Network radio	147	161	178	197	213
Spot radio	140	149	164	179	192
Outdoor	187	202	222	242	261
Composite	179	195	212	234	254
National	173	189	207	226	245
Local	185	202	222	243	268

*Estimated

Source: Robert J. Coen, "Out, Out, Damned Inflation," p. S–2. Reprinted with permission from the November 9, 1981 issue of *Advertising Age*. Copyright © 1981 by Crain Communications, Inc.

[17]*Leo Burnett Media Costs & Coverage Guide: 1982* (Chicago: Leo Burnett USA, 1982). Since costs vary by season, the costs shown are for summer, 1982.

TABLE 15–3 Comparisons of expenditures in selected media, 1967–1980

Media	Expenditures (millions)		Percent Increase	Percentage of total expenditures	
	1967	1980		1967	1980
Newspapers	$ 4,910	$15,541	216%	29.1%	28.5%
Magazines	1,245	3,149	153	7.4	5.8
Farm publications	68	130	91	0.4	0.2
Network TV	1,455	5,130	252	8.6	9.4
Spot TV	1,454	6,236	329	8.6	11.4
Network radio	64	180	181	0.4	0.3
Spot radio	984	3,597	266	5.8	6.6
Direct mail	2,488	7,596	205	14.8	13.9
Business papers	707	1,674	136	4.2	3.1
Outdoor	191	600	214	1.1	1.1
Miscellaneous	3,304	10,767	226	19.6	19.7
Totals	$16,870	$54,600	224%	100.0%	100.0%
National Total	$10,210	$30,315	1.97	60.5%	55.5%
Local Total	$ 6,660	$24.285	2.65	39.5	44.5

Source: Reprinted with permission from the September 14, 1981 issue of *Advertising Age.* Copyright © 1981 by Crain Communications, Inc.

MEDIA USE

Advertising expenditures by media vary significantly. Table 15–3 shows a comparison of advertising expenditures in selected media for 1967 and 1980, as well as the split between national and local advertising. This table indicates that: (a) newspapers account for the largest expenditure, followed by direct mail; (b) the greatest growth during the period occurred in spot TV, followed by spot radio; and (c) approximately 56 percent of all advertising in 1980 was in national advertising, while approximately 44 percent was local.

SUMMARY

Media is surrounded by controversy. Each medium has its advocates and detractors. There is disagreement among professionals about how media can be used most effectively and little hard evidence that there is one best approach. Decisions regarding reach, frequency, and continuity pose the major problems in planning a media schedule. Most media plans end up as a compromise among the three, based on the media planner's understanding of the competitive situation and the product's advertising needs. Although media selection is replete with statistics and mathematical models, the numbers may be unreliable.

The basic decision areas covered by media strategy are those concerning: (a) the general kinds of media to be used; (b) specific types of media within broad media classifications; (c) space and time units; and (d) the way other marketing factors will influence media timing.

A number of factors influence media strategy; the media planner selects media that meet the requirements of these variables.

Media analysis and planning require a great deal of information on markets, media rates, circulation, audience duplication, and competitive patterns. The media themselves as well as a number of independent research organizations are the sources of this data. Using this information, the media planner is faced with the problem of comparing media that tends to overemphasize its quantitative aspects. Cost-per-thousand is the basic media concept used for determining media efficiency.

The job of evaluating alternative media combinations is herculean and can only be handled through the use of computers.

Although the cost-per-thousand for reaching various target groups varies widely, media costs have risen rapidly in the past decade. This rapid escalation is a matter of deep concern to advertisers and agencies because it not only increases the cost of advertising, but it often forces undesirable constraints on media planning.

REVIEW QUESTIONS

1 Differentiate among reach, frequency, and continuity.
2 According to the Association of National Advertisers, what are the tentative conclusions derived from its review of frequency research?
3 Identify the major decision areas in the media strategy statement.
4 How can media be used to equalize sales force coverage for a consumer product sold through retail outlets? What kinds of media would most likely be employed?
5 Why should research reports by media be interpreted cautiously?
6 What does SRDS stand for? What kinds of information does it provide? Why is it used?
7 Explain what is meant by the numbers game in media. Why is it a problem?
8 Explain what is meant by media efficiency. Given a media expenditure of $60,000 and an audience exposure of 12 million, what is the CPM?
9 Assume a target audience of 24 million consumers, to be reached on an average of 2.5 times each four-week period for 52 weeks. What would be the total cost of a media program that met the above requirements if its CPM were $4.75?
10 What are the primary advantages and disadvantages of computer models in media selection?

DISCUSSION QUESTIONS

1 Which media do you think would be most appropriate for advertising: (a) pocket computers; (b) wristwatches; (c) cold remedies; (d) cake mixes; or (e) carpeting? Why?
2 Do you believe that media discounts are fair to small advertisers? What justification do you see in offering media discounts?
3 After examining cost trends and media usage trends in Tables 15–2 and 15–3, which media do you think will show the greatest growth during the next ten years? Why?

PROBLEM

Circus Time protein spread is a soy-protein based spread that is manufactured in three flavors: chocolate, grape, and blackberry. Enriched with vitamins and protein based, Circus Time is a highly nutritious children's snack food that is spread on bread or crackers.

Company sales of the product during the past year were $30.5 million; the bulk of the $3.2 million advertising and sales promotion expenditure had been directed toward the 6 to 12 age group via weekend children's television programs.

Joan Weston, product manager for Circus Time protein spread, and Frank Claxton, advertising director for the company, were discussing the advertising and promotion plan for the forthcoming year.

"Joan," Frank said, "it seems to me that we should devote a significant part of our advertising budget to mothers this next year. The recent survey conducted by the research department indicates that mothers have doubts about the nutritional value of Circus Time. We know that our advertising on children's television programs is doing a good job in getting the kids to ask for the product, but mothers still have veto power, and their lack of acceptance is hurting our sales."

"I don't disagree with you," Joan said, "but I'm not sure we can afford to do everything that needs to be done. Our forecast next year is for $30.5 million, with an advertising and promotion budget of $2.5 million. The sales department wants $500,000 of that for a consumer coupon, which I also think we need."

"Is that forecast with or without the couponing effort?" Frank asked.

"Without," Joan answered.

"Based on our past couponing experience, plus an effort toward mothers and children, I suspect we could justify increasing the forecast by another million dollars," Frank suggested.

Joan thought for a minute, then said, "I think you're probably right; at least I'd be willing to recommend it. Frank, making the assumption that we can get the forecast revised, could you have someone rough some costs together to see what the program would look like? Let's plan on $500,000 for couponing and split the rest between women in the 25 to 49 age group who are full-time homemakers, and kids 6 to 12, with a heavier emphasis on kids than on mothers. I don't know the best split; it depends on how much reach and frequency we can get with each group."

After Joan left, Frank pulled out some of his media references and started putting some numbers together.

There are approximately 25 million children between the ages of 6 and 12, and the cost-per-thousand for reaching them on weekend television is $2.70. Ignoring duplication, it would cost $67,500 (25,000 × $2.70) to reach all of them once. Frank knew he couldn't afford to reach all of this age group with adequate frequency, but he could probably get adequate frequency on a part of this group, particularly if he used a wave approach.

Full-time homemakers between the ages of 25 and 49 were a different problem. He could use daytime radio, daytime television, or women's magazines. There are about 30 million women in this group. Cost-per-thousand for daytime television is about $7.60. For magazines, the cost-per-thousand is about $8.50 for a full page ad. Radio has a cost-per-thousand for this group of about $5.80.

Frank estimated that television production would cost about $40,000, and print production about $25,000. If he used radio, production costs would run about $5,000.

ASSIGNMENT

1 Prepare a recommendation for advertising Circus Time.
2 Show how available advertising funds will be split between children and mothers. Recommend the size audiences that will be reached and the average frequency that will be attained. Ignore the question of audience duplication.

16
Newspapers and Magazines

THE STATUS OF NEWSPAPERS

FALLING STARS

The 1980s have not been kind to newspapers. Television journalism, with its on-the-spot coverage and instant commentaries, has siphoned off readers and advertising revenues. High operating costs and declining profits have forced closings and mergers of some of the nation's largest and most prestigious dailies. In 1981 the *Washington Star* and *Philadelphia Bulletin* closed shop. In 1982 the *Cleveland Press* and *Buffalo Courier-Express* ceased publication; the *New York News,* once the nation's largest circulation newspaper, won a temporary reprieve when the pressmen's union agreed to the elimination of 1300 of the newspaper's 5000 jobs. The *Minneapolis Star* combined with the *Tribune* into a single paper. Dailies in Fort Lauderdale, Florida, Dayton and Springfield, Ohio, and Norfolk, Virginia, have undergone mergers, and more are in the offing.

It's really quite sad, and there is always the possibility that when a nation's citizenry stops reading, it will also stop thinking.

SUBURBAN MEDIA

With the decline of major daily newspapers, suburban media have grown at an explosive rate. Short on national news and long on local advertising and services, these media come in a variety of forms: (a) Free community newspapers, containing approximately a 30 percent ratio of news with a heavy emphasis on local coverage, are delivered free to all residents of a given geographical area. (b) Suburban newspapers, with news ratios as high as 40 percent, provide intensive coverage of the suburban community and may have either free or paid circulation. (c) Shoppers, generally tabloids, carry just advertising, sometimes leavened with canned features and local television listings. (d) Pennysavers, similar in style and format to shoppers, scatter classified advertising throughout the tabloid rather than placing it in a classified section.

The key to the success of suburban newspapers is local coverage in the areas of news, advertising, and classified ads for garage sales and personal items.

CONTINUING PROBLEMS AT ABC

Since the beginning of time, the Audit Bureau of Circulation (ABC) has represented stability in the publishing industry. ABC has kept the publishing field honest through semiannual audits of publishers' statements, validating circulation data by county, state, and regional classification and by issue. For years, election to the bureau's board of directors was predetermined, with little evidence of dissent or displeasure on the part of bureau members.

In 1977 a group of small circulation publications challenged the incumbent board, charging that even though the majority of ABC members were from small publishing concerns, the board was dominated by giants in the publishing field who ignored the interests of small publishers. The revolt failed, but trouble didn't go away.

In 1982 ABC was assailed for not remaining contemporary. An ABC audit takes one to one-and-a-half years to complete. These delays can lead to false claims.

> "Today more publishers are pushing their circulation as close to the top as they can," Mr. Green (president of the *New Yorker*) said. "Agencies put those numbers in their computers and multiply it by readers per copy. But what happens when the audit comes out two years later and you find some publishers have misstated? Who is going to do anything about it? Nobody. The decision was made two years ago and who wants to dredge up old decisions. That (practice) is institutionalized at the ABC."[1]

---

[1]Christy Marshall, " 'SA' Fight Blows Up at ABC," p. 87. Reprinted by permission from the February 15, 1982 issue of *Advertising Age*. Copyright © 1982 by Crain Communications, Inc.

Threatened by broadcast and cable television, beset by a readership decline, and characterized by special interest magazines and newspapers that emerge almost daily, the print field is one of the most turbulent and competitive in the advertising industry.

NEWSPAPER ADVERTISING

Newspapers hold the lion's share of total advertising revenues. In 1980 estimated newspaper advertising revenues were over $15.5 billion. The bulk came from local advertisers who accounted for $13,188 billion, or 85 percent of the total. Although national advertising in newspapers was only $2,353 billion, this substantial expenditure qualifies newspapers as a formidable national advertising medium.[2]

Daily and Sunday newspapers have a combined circulation of approximately 116.6 million (Table 16–1). Because many of these newspapers have morning and evening editions, the total circulation figures shown in Table 16–1 are for editions, not separate newspapers. Although these daily and Sunday newspapers account for the bulk of newspaper advertising, almost 10,000 semiweekly, weekly, biweekly, monthly, and bimonthly newspapers serve suburban communities, small towns, and rural areas. In addition to these general circulation newspapers, a multiplicity of small newspapers cater to various special groups, including foreign language, ethnic, religious, labor, professional, university, social, and special interest organizations. Thus, newspapers may not only be used as a mass medium, but also to reach highly specific target markets.

A number of newspapers also distribute Sunday supplements, often referred to as **Sunday magazines.** Some larger newspaper companies publish their own localized Sunday supplements; other supplements are nationally syndicated. For example, *Family Weekly* is distributed by 355 newspapers, *Parade* by 111, and *Sunday Magazine* by 56.

KINDS OF NEWSPAPER ADVERTISING

One classification system widely used to base newspaper advertising rates separates advertising into the categories of classified, retail, national, and reading notices.

TABLE 16–1 Circulation breakdown of daily and Sunday newspapers

Edition	Number of papers*	Circulation in 000's
Morning (AM)	408	30,552.3
Evening (PM)	1,352	30,878.4
Sunday	758	55,180.0
Total		116,610.7

*There are thirty newspapers classified as "all day newspapers." They are included in the "number of papers" column for both morning and evening editions. However, their circulations are counted only once in the circulation column.

Source: *Editor and Publisher Yearbook* (1982).

[2]Robert J. Coen, "Ad $ Outlook Brightens," *Advertising Age,* 14 September 1981, 48.

CLASSIFIED ADVERTISING

While classified advertising may be used by national or local advertisers, the bulk of the classified section of newspapers, referred to as **want ads,** are local in nature and placed by local firms or individuals. These ads are arranged by subject matter for the convenience of readers, and generally do not include headlines or illustrations. There is a form of classified advertising known as **classified display,** which uses different type sizes, white space to attract attention, and simple illustrations.

RETAIL ADVERTISING

As the name implies, retail advertising is placed by retail merchants and other local businesses. Normally, it is: (a) **sales promotion advertising,** based on price features, sales, or specials; and (b) **image advertising,** designed to position a retail store or business so that it appeals to a particular group of consumers. Retail advertising may be paid for entirely by the retailer or shared by a manufacturer. This latter form of advertising is referred to as **cooperative advertising;** it is run under the name of a local retailer in order to encourage retailer support and take advantage of local rates, which are usually lower than national advertising rates.

NATIONAL ADVERTISING

National advertising is used by manufacturers and producers to support their products. This advertising is part of the manufacturer's national advertising plan and is used to intensify coverage in a local area. National newspaper advertising is often used to introduce new products in test markets, assure widespread consumer recognition, and aid in gaining retail distribution.

READING NOTICES

Reading notices are advertisements that are designed to resemble editorial material, and they are charged at a higher rate than retail advertising. To prevent reading notices from being confused with news stories or editorial material, the word "advertisement" must appear at the top of the notice.

NEWSPAPER RATE STRUCTURE

The physical dimensions of newspaper pages vary in size, ranging from five to nine columns in width and from 300 to 315 lines in depth. The standard newspaper is eight columns wide and 300 lines deep, allowing 2400 lines to be printed on a page. Since the line measure in newspapers refers to agate lines and there are 14 agate lines to an inch, the standard newspaper is about 22 inches in depth. A tabloid newspaper, which generally appears only in major metropolitan areas, is five columns wide and 200 lines deep. This size is more convenient for people who use mass transportation systems and read the newspaper while commuting.

THE RATE CARD

Newspaper advertising rates vary according to classification and, sometimes, the volume of advertising purchased. Because newspaper rates are relatively stable, the prices are available on published rate cards.

The published rate card contains all of the information that an advertiser needs to contract for space in the newspaper including information on rates as well as copy and mechanical requirements. Figure 16–1 shows the American Association of Advertising Agencies' recommended rate card anatomy. A major feature of this card is that all information is given a standardized number and listed in a standardized sequence. If a newspaper has no information for a particular category, the number is skipped; this does not alter the remaining numbering sequence.

Figure 16–2 is an example of a newspaper listing. This is a listing for the *St. Louis Post-Dispatch* and *Globe-Democrat*, as it appears in *Standard Rate and Data Service*. To the uninitiated, rate cards appear hopelessly complex; however, experienced media buyers develop a facility for reading them and extracting relevant information quickly.

NEWSPAPER RATES

The major terms used to refer to newspaper rates are flat, open, discount, short, combination, position charges, color charges, and split runs.

Flat rate. When the line rate is fixed, regardless of the volume of advertising, it is designated as a flat rate.

Open rate. If a newspaper offers discounts, the open rate is the price charged advertisers who do not purchase a sufficient volume to qualify for a discount.

Discounts. Many newspapers have established discount levels for advertisers who use an unusual amount of advertising space. These discounts, while initially negotiated, become established, are published, and apply to any future advertisers offering a similar volume of linage. Discount practices vary significantly among newspapers. For example, while discounts on large purchases of retail advertising are commonplace, a number of newspapers offer no quantity discounts to national advertisers. In addition, a study of the discount structure for national advertisers in the top 50 United States markets revealed the pattern shown in Table 16–2.

The most blatant discrimination in media discounts occurs between types of advertisers. For example, as a generalization, large local advertisers such as major department stores often earn rates 50 percent below national advertisers.

Short rate. When newspapers offer volume discounts, the advertiser estimates the amount of space that will be used during the next 12-month period and contracts for that amount at the discount

Published Morning, Evening, Sunday   NAME OF NEWSPAPER   Rate Card Number
Publication Address   Issue Date
Telephone Number   Effective Date

1—PERSONNEL
   a. Name of publisher
   b. Name of advertising executives
      (Identify ownership first—parent and/or company.)

2—REPRESENTATIVES AND/OR BRANCH OFFICES
   a. Name of advertising representatives
   b. If there is no representative, please indicate contact, including WATS line number

3—COMMISSION AND CASH DISCOUNT
   a. Agency commission
   b. Cash discount/terms
      (State whether or not cash discount is allowed. Note all exceptions to agency commission and cash discount and key all exceptions.)

4—POLICY–ALL CLASSIFICATIONS
   a. Policy on rate protection and rate revision notice
   b. Regulations covering acceptance of advertising
   c. Policy regarding advertising which simulates editorial content

5—BLACK AND WHITE RATES
   a. Flat/open rates
   b. Combination rates—leeway of insertion dates
   c. All discounts—structure and application

5A—ZONE EDITIONS
   List *all* less-than-full circulation editions available, (except city and suburban), with circulation and rates. This is an area of particular concern to agencies.

6—GROUP COMBINATION RATES BLACK/WHITE AND COLOR

   Group combinations

7—COLOR RATES AND DATA
   a. Color availability—days of the week, leeway and number of colors
   b. Minimum size for ROP color advertisements
   c. Color rate—simple statement of structure
   d. Discount—applications to color rates
   e. Charge for nonstandard color

8—SPECIAL ROP UNITS
   To include Flexform, spacespots and other

9—SPLIT RUN
   Availabilities and rates

10—SPECIAL SERVICES
   a. Available research studies
   b. Other market information (i.e., route list)

11—SPECIAL DAYS/PAGES/FEATURES
   a. Position charge
   b. Best food day(s)
   c. Special pages or sections, e.g., garden, travel, etc.

12—ROP DEPTH REQUIREMENTS
   a. Minimum depth per column
   b. Line limit subject to full column charge

13—CONTRACT AND COPY REGULATIONS
   Regulations not stated elsewhere

14—CLOSING TIME
   a. All ROP including exceptions for color, special sections, etc.
   b. Indicate for material and order

15—MECHANICAL MEASUREMENTS
   a. Printing process
   b. Column widths
   c. Depth of columns in lines
   d. Number of columns to a page
   e. Number of lines to a page
   f. Number of lines charged to double truck and size in inches

16—SPECIAL CLASSIFICATION/RATES
   a. Full disclosure of classification rates
   b. Conditions to earn
   c. Exceptions to discount and commission policies

17—CLASSIFIED RATES
   a. Name of classified advertising manager and telephone number
   b. Classifications and rates including application of discount
   c. Mechanical specifications

18—CIRCULATION
   a. Year established
   b. Circulation verification (details in publisher's statement and audit report)
   c. If unaudited, basis for circulation claim
   d. Please indicate city and suburban circulation where applicable
   e. Single copy price

(Standard Form Rate Card recommended by the American Association of Advertising Agencies, Inc.).

FIGURE 16–1   American Association of Advertising Agencies' recommended anatomy of a rate card

POST-DISPATCH
GLOBE-DEMOCRAT
900 N. Tucker Blvd., St. Louis, MO 63101.
Phone 314-622-7000, TWX, 910-761-0479, Telecopier,
314-622-7132.

(ABC)

Media Code 1 126 7900 6.00   Mid 016878-000

Post-Dispatch—EVENING AND SUNDAY.
Globe-Democrat—MORNING AND WEEKEND.
(Evening edition not published on Jan. 1, Memorial Day,
July 4, Labor Day, Thanksgiving or Christmas. If holiday
falls on Sunday, no publication on Monday.)
Member: INAME; NAB, Inc.

1. PERSONNEL
V.P./Gen. Mgr.—Glenn A. Christopher.
Dir. of Marketing—James D. Cherry.
Advertising Director—Edward Newsome.
Gen. Adv. Manager—Gerry F. Anderson.
Retail Adv. Manager—Rex Sims.

2. REPRESENTATIVES and/or BRANCH OFFICES
Newhouse Newspapers Metro-Suburbia.
The Leonard Co.
Lenha Hawaii, Inc.

3. COMMISSION AND CASH DISCOUNT
15% to agencies 15th of month following previous
month's advertising; 2% cash discount—15th following
month.

4. POLICY-ALL CLASSIFICATIONS
30-day notice of any rate revision given to contract
holders.
Alcoholic beverage advertising accepted.
R.O.P. linage does not apply toward completing feature
section contract.

ADVERTISING RATES
Effective September 1, 1981.
Received July 20, 1981.

5. BLACK/WHITE RATES

	Per line			
	E & M or Wknd.	Sun. & M or Wknd.	E or M or Wknd.	Sun.
Open rate	4.40	5.10	2.75	3.65
Within 1 year:				
2,790 lines	4.22	4.90	2.64	3.50
5,580 lines	4.14	4.79	2.59	3.43
11,160 lines	4.05	4.69	2.53	3.36
16,740 lines	3.96	4.59	2.48	3.29
36,270 lines	3.92	4.54	2.45	3.25
72,540 lines	3.87	4.49	2.42	3.21
145,080 lines	3.78	4.39	2.37	3.14

Combination advertising shall consist of identical copy
without change except for timelines, to be run within a 7
day period.

STANDARD AD UNITS (See Front of Book)

SAU	M or E or Wknd.	M&E	Sun.	Sun. & M or Sun. & Wknd.	CLE
1	7,365.60	11,773.80	9,765.00	13,671.00	2790
2	6,237.00	9,979.20	8,278.20	11,566.80	2268
3	3,613.50	5,781.60	4,796.10	6,701.40	1314
4	6,820.00	10,912.00	9,052.00	12,648.00	2480
5	5,544.00	8,870.40	7,358.40	10,281.60	2016
6	4,818.00	7,708.80	6,394.80	8,935.20	1752
7	3,753.75	6,006.00	4,982.25	6,961.59	1365
8	1,867.25	2,987.60	2,478.35	3,462.90	679
9	5,115.00	8,184.00	6,789.00	9,486.00	1860
10	2,409.00	3,854.40	3,197.40	4,467.60	876
11	4,262.50	6,820.00	5,657.50	7,905.00	1550
12	2,681.25	4,290.00	3,558.75	4,972.50	975
13	2,007.50	3,212.00	2,664.50	3,723.00	730
14	1,003.75	1,606.00	1,332.25	1,861.50	365
15	2,557.50	4,092.00	3,394.50	4,743.00	930
16	1,608.75	2,574.00	2,135.25	2,983.50	585
17	1,204.50	1,927.20	1,598.70	2,233.80	438
18	800.25	1,280.40	1,062.15	1,484.10	291
19	602.25	963.60	799.35	1,116.90	219
20	404.25	646.80	536.55	749.70	147
21	266.75	426.80	354.05	494.70	97
22	200.75	321.20	266.45	372.30	73
23	134.75	215.60	178.85	249.90	49
24	77.00	123.20	102.20	142.80	28
25	38.50	61.60	51.10	71.40	14

APPLICATION OF DISCOUNTS
When both less-than-page units and full page units are
used during contract period, full page linage may be
combined with less-than-page linage to earn lowest contract rate. If bulk contract rate is greater than page contract rate, the former applies to full pages. If page rate is
greater, bulk contract rate will apply on less-than-page
units.
Rotogravure, Comic and TV Magazine linage can be
combined with b/w linage to determine earned contract
rate.
NEWSPLAN—Linage Equivalent.

Pages	% Disc.	E&M or E or M Wknd.	S&M or Wknd.	EorM or Wknd.	Sun.	Lines
6	10	3.96	4.59	2.48	3.29	16,740
13	11	3.92	4.54	2.45	3.25	36,270
26	12	3.87	4.49	2.42	3.21	72,540
52	14	3.78	4.39	2.37	3.14	145,080

See Newsplan Contract and Copy Regulations—items 1,
3, 5, 6, 7, 9, 10, 13, 14, 18, 19, 20, 21, 22, 24, 25, 26, 28,
29, 31.

7. COLOR RATES AND DATA
B/w 1c or 3c available daily and weekend. No leeway
required. Minimum 700 lines.
Use b/w line rate plus the following applicable costs:

	b/w 1 c	b/w 3 c
Eve., Morn. or Weekend	1,840.00	2,700.00
Sun., Morn. or Weekend	2,040.00	3,000.00
Eve. or Morn. or Weekend	1,150.00	1,680.00
Sunday	1,400.00	2,065.00

Standard red, yellow, blue and black colors used.
Special inks at advertiser's expense. Require: repro
proofs, 3 progressive proofs, 4 registration marks and b/
w repro proofs on each color. Running head and dateline
not required.
Closing Dates: B/w 1 c reservations and printing material
3 days before publication; b/w 2 c or 3 c material 3 days
before publication; b/w or 3 c reservations and printing
material 7 days before publication date.
Cancellation 1 week before closing date.

8. SPECIAL ROP UNITS
SPACE SPOTS
Minimum 50 lines, maximum 250 lines per spot. 13 consecutive weeks, minimum 6 spots per week, no other
contract.

Maximum (short rate to volume discount earned, if
curtailed). Insertion at publisher's option. 33-1/3% discount from open rate. Linage not applicable to other contract.

9. SPLIT RUN
Post or Globe:
.20 per line, extra (min. 200 lines), minimum 200.00.
11. SPECIAL DAYS/PAGES/FEATURES
Best Food Day: Wednesday.
Travel: Post Sunday, Globe Weekend.
12. R.O.P. DEPTH REQUIREMENTS
As many inches deep as columns wide. Minimum depth
for Travel, Resorts, Hotels and Steamships on Sunday
Travel Page, 7 lines. Regular minimums apply to daily and
Sunday R.O.P. Ads ordered for 280 lines or more deep,
on any page, charged full column—310 lines.
13. CONTRACT AND COPY REGULATIONS
See Contents page for location of regulations—items 1, 2,
4, 6, 10, 11, 12, 13, 14, 18, 19, 20, 22, 24, 25, 26, 30, 31,
32, 33, 34, 35, 39, 45.
14. CLOSING TIMES
Daily: Post 5:00 p.m. 2 days before publication; Globe
noon, 2 days before publication; Sunday, noon Friday. No
copy, corrections or cancellations accepted after
deadline.
15. MECHANICAL MEASUREMENTS
For complete, detailed production information, see
SRDS Print Media Production Data.
PRINTING PROCESS: Offset.
9/8-7/4—9 cols/ea 8 picas-7 pts/4 pts betw col.
Lines to: col. 310; page 2790; dbl. truck 5735.
16. SPECIAL CLASSIFICATIONS/RATES

GLOBE-DEMOCRAT
POLITICAL

M or E	2.59	Sunday	3.43
M & E	4.14	Sunday & M	4.79

RESORT AND TRAVEL
Rates apply to Resorts, Hotels, Tourism, Tour Agencies
and Transportation in Sunday and Weekend Resort and
Travel pages and/or sections.

	Comb.	Sun.	Wknd.
Open rate	5.10	3.65	2.75
6 insertions	4.54	3.25	2.45
13 insertions	4.49	3.21	2.42
26 insertions	4.39	3.14	2.37

17. CLASSIFIED RATES
For complete data refer to classified rate section.
18. COMICS
Globe-Democrat
POLICY—ALL CLASSIFICATIONS
When orders are placed through Puck-The Comic Week-
ly—see that listing.
Effective September 1, 1981.
Received July 20, 1981.
COLOR RATES AND DATA
Four colors:

1 page	6,000.00	1/3 page	2,800.00
2/3 page	4,500.00	1/6 page	2,000.00
1/2 page	3,600.00		

Daily Comic Page—B/W
Inside back cover: 30 lines x 4 columns or 60 lines x 4
columns.
Accepted at R.O.P. rate. Minimum 13 times in 13 weeks.

CLOSING TIMES
5th Friday preceding publication. Cancellations 6th
Monday preceding publication.
MECHANICAL MEASUREMENTS
Standard page size 12-3/4" wide x 19-3/4" deep.
For ad sizes see Puck—The Comic Weekly listing.
Colors available: ANPA/AAAA; Standard Color—black,
red, yellow, blue.
Send printing material to Greater Buffalo Press, 302 Grote
St., Buffalo, N. Y. 14207.

FIGURE 16–2   (Courtesy Standard Rate & Data Service, Inc.)

earned, subject to year-end adjustments. Let us assume that a newspaper has the following rate structure:

Open rate	$0.60 per line
5000 lines	0.55 per line
10,000 lines	0.50 per line
15,000 lines	0.40 per line

An advertiser estimates advertising space to be 10,000 lines and
contracts for this amount at $0.50 per line. During the year, each
advertisement is billed at the $0.50 rate. However, the advertiser

Post-Dispatch
POLICY—ALL CLASSIFICATIONS
When orders are placed through Metro Sunday Comics Group—see that listing.
Effective September 1, 1981.
Received July 20, 1981.
COLOR RATES AND DATA
Four colors:

1 page	8,500.00	1/3 page	4,000.00
2/3 page	6,300.00	1/6 page	2,800.00
1/2 page	5,100.00		

CONTRACT AND COPY REGULATIONS
Contract will be cancelled 60 days after date if no space has been used.
6 times 2%
CLOSING TIMES
5th Friday before publication.
Cancellation 6th Monday before closing date.
MECHANICAL MEASUREMENTS
PRINTING PROCESS: Photo Composition Direct Letterpress. (NAPP.)
Page size 12-3/4" wide x 19-3/4" deep.
For ad sizes see Metro Sunday Comics listing.
Colors available: 4-Color Process.

19. MAGAZINES

Globe-Democrat
Rotogravure Magazine
WEEKEND.
POLICY—ALL CLASSIFICATIONS
When orders are placed through Metropolitan Sunday Magazine Group—see that listing.
Linage placed through national group may be combined with R.O.P. linage to earn bulk and frequency discounts for R.O.P. linage.
Color premium, net.
Effective September 1, 1981.
Received July 20, 1981.

BLACK/WHITE RATES
MONOTONE

Center Spread	7,100.00	2/5 page	1,360.00
Full page	3,400.00	3/10 page	1,020.00
7/10 page	2,380.00	1/5 page	680.00
3/5 page	2,040.00	3/20 page	510.00
1/2 page	1,700.00	1/10 page	340.00
9/20 page	1,530.00	1/20 page	170.00

Back page 10% additional.
COLOR RATES AND DATA
Duotone or spot color:
1/5 page (minimum) extra, per insertion 275.00
Full color:
2/5 page (minimum) extra, per insertion 850.00
FREQUENCY DISCOUNTS
Monotone only; color premium net.
Within 1 year:

7 times	3%	52 times	15%
13 times	5%	78 times	17%
26 times	7%	104 times	20%
39 times	10%		

CLOSING TIMES
Reservations, cancellations, and color copy due: 6th Thursday preceding publication date. Monotone copy due and camera-ready color: 5th Tuesday preceding publication date. Monotone camera-ready: 5th Tuesday preceding publication date.
Confirming order and copy must be in Cleveland, Art Gravure Corp., by space closing dates. Copy coming through group must conform to group closing dates.

MECHANICAL MEASUREMENTS
PRINTING PROCESS: Rotary Letterpress.
Lines to: col. 157; page 785.
Trim size 10" wide x 11-1/4" deep. 5 cols. to page.
Colors available: GTA Standard; 3 and Key.
Send printing materials to Art Gravure Corp. of Ohio, 1845 Superior Ave., Cleveland, Ohio 44114.

Globe-Democrat
TV Digest
WEEKEND.
Effective September 1, 1981.
Received July 20, 1981.
BLACK/WHITE RATES
MONOTONE

Center spread	2,770.00	1/4 page	330.00
Full page	1,320.00	1/8 page	170.00
1/2 page	660.00	1/16 page	85.00

COLOR RATES AND DATA
Color available on back page and centerspread.
Spot color:
1/2 page (minimum) extra per insertion 175.00
Full Color:
Back of TV magazine only 680.00
SPLIT RUN
125.00 extra charge. Page unit only. Advertiser to furnish 2 pages of camera-ready material.
BLEED
25% extra.
CLOSING TIMES
Reservations, cancellations, monotone or spot color copy due for proofs: 3rd Thursday prior to publication date.
Copy due for no proof and camera ready copy: 2nd Monday preceding publication date.
Covers printed in gang run 4 weeks at a time.
MECHANICAL MEASUREMENTS
PRINTING PROCESS: Offset.
Full page 6-3/8" wide x 10" deep.
Lines per page: 450.
Colors available: back page and centerspread.
Send printing material to newspaper.
10% discount when same ad is published in Post-Dispatch and Globe-Democrat same weekend.

P D Roto Magazine
SUNDAY.
Effective September 1, 1981.
Received July 20, 1981.
BLACK/WHITE RATES
MONOTONE

Center spread	10,900.00	2/5 page	2,080.00
Full page	5,200.00	3/10 page	1,560.00
7/10 page	3,640.00	1/5 page	1,040.00
3/5 page	3,120.00	3/20 page	780.00
1/2 page	2,600.00	1/10 page	520.00
9/20 page	2,340.00	1/20 page	260.00

Back page 10% additional.
COLOR RATES AND DATA
Duotone or spot color, extra 450.00
Four color, extra 1,020.00
Standard black, yellow, red and blue inks. Special inks at advertiser's expense. Additional tones obtained through blends.
Colorgravure sizes accepted:

157x 5	157x 2	
157x 3-1/2	94 x5	
157x3	78 x5	
157 x 2-1/2		

DISCOUNTS (Within 1 year)
Discounts apply to Monotone, Duotone or Colorgravure, or combination of all three.

785 line unit or equivalent.	Discount
7	3%
13	5%
26	7%
39	10%
52	15%
78	17%
104	20%

Advertisers using both color comics and rotogravure may combine rotogravure 850-line units or equivalent space with insertions in comics during a contract year to earn discounts.

Minimum space requirements:

Monotone	42 lines
Duotone or spot color	170 lines
Four-color	340 lines

SPLIT RUN
Minimum size: 425 lines; extra charge Monotone 198.00; Color 396.00.
CLOSING TIMES
Color reservations, cancellations: Copy 5th Tuesday before publication to Louisville (Standard Gravure Corp.). Send copy requiring processing or typesetting to Post-Dispatch, St. Louis, Mo. Discount orders placed through Metro Sunday papers must adhere to their cancellation policy.
MECHANICAL MEASUREMENTS
PRINTING PROCESS: Rotary Letterpress.
Page size 10" x 11-1/4".
Colors available: 4 Colors; Intag.
Lines to: col. 157; page 785.

Post-Dispatch
Television Magazine
SUNDAY.
Effective September 1, 1981.
Received July 20, 1981.
BLACK/WHITE RATES
Inside pages b/w only:

Center Spread	3,100.00	1/4 page	370.00
Full page	1,480.00	1/8 page	185.00
1/2 page	740.00		

COLOR RATES AND DATA
Back page (4-color only) 2,800.00
SPECIAL CLASSIFICATION/RATES
Inside covers (1 page minimum) 1,950.00
Contract required to earn frequency discounts.
FREQUENCY DISCOUNTS

6 insertions, per year	2%
13 insertions, per year	4%
26 insertions, per year	7%
39 insertions, per year	10%
52 insertions, per year	15%

BLEED
20% extra; 1/2 page minimum.
CLOSING TIMES
Reservations, cancellations, monotone, or spot color copy due for proofs: 3rd Thursday prior to publication date. Copy due for no proof and camera ready copy: 2nd Monday preceding publication date. Post inside covers and color back cover: 7th Thursday preceding publication date.
Covers printed in gang run 4 weeks at a time.
MECHANICAL MEASUREMENTS
PRINTING PROCESS: Offset.
Page size 4-3/4" wide x 6-3/8" deep.
Colors available: Back page only.

20. CIRCULATION
Post Dispatch established: daily 1878, per copy .20; Sunday 1887, per copy .75.
Globe-Democrat established: 1852, per copy daily .20; Weekend .50.
Net Paid—A.B.C. 3-31-82 (Newspaper Form)
PRIMARY MARKET AREA CIRCULATION

	Total	Prim.Mkt.	Outside
MxSat	261,329	190,337	70,992
ExSat	238,099	210,213	27,886
M&E	499,428	400,550	98,878
SatE	153,036	137,402	15,634
Wknd	248,668	171,432	77,236
Sun	443,422	365,154	78,268
Wknd&Sun	692,090	536,586	155,504

Max-Min rate: MxSat Max 10.34, Min 8.91; ExSat Max 11.35, Min 9.78; M&E Max 8.66, Min 7.44; SatE Max 17.66. Min 15.22; Wknd NA; Sun Max 8.09, Min 6.96; Wknd&Sun NA.
For county-by-county and/or metropolitan area breakdowns, see SRDS Newspaper Circulation Analysis.

FIGURE 16–2 (continued)

runs only 6,000 lines during the contract period, thereby qualifying only for the 5,000 line rate of $0.55. At the end of the year, the following adjustment is made:

Charged:	6,000 lines @ $0.55	$3,300.00
Paid:	6,000 lines @ $0.50	−3,000.00
	Short rate due:	$ 300.00

Had the advertiser run 15,000 lines instead of the 10,000 contracted for, he would have qualified for the $0.40 rate and would have received a rebate at the end of the year.

TABLE 16–2 Maximum newspaper discounts in the top 50 United States markets

Percent maximum discount	Number of papers offering
0%	18
1–15%	14
16–20%	11
21–25%	7
26–30%	9
31–36%	4
Number of papers represented	63

Source: Compiled from *Standard Rate and Data Service*

Combination rate. Combination rates are discounts for advertising appearing in the morning and evening editions of the same newspaper, combining a weekday insertion with a Saturday or Sunday insertion, or advertising in more than one newspaper in a newspaper group. At one point, some newspaper policies forced advertisers to use the combination of insertions or newspapers. However, courts have ruled against this practice and such combinations are now optional.

Position charges. An advertiser may place his advertisements R.O.P. (run of paper). R.O.P. means that: (a) The newspaper editor can place the advertisement anyplace; the advertiser has no control over where the advertisement will appear. (b) The advertiser may specify a position on the page or within a particular section of the paper. Higher rates, depending upon the newspaper involved, and the nature of the preferred position, are generally charged for these preferred positions.

Color charges. Normally, newspaper advertising appears in black and white. Color advertising is available in many papers on an R.O.P. basis and can be used in any paper through the use of preprinted inserts. R.O.P. color does not provide dependable quality because of high-speed presses, porous paper stock, and problems of off register reproduction. Off register is a term used to describe a situation in which colors overlap and demarkations between colors are not clear. For this reason, R.O.P. color is used sparingly and chiefly for making ads distinctive with bold backgrounds, designs, or color headlines. When R.O.P. color is used, there is an extra charge, and newspapers usually have a minimum space requirement.

One use of four color in newspapers that has gained widespread popularity is known as HiFi color or SpectaColor pages. The advertiser preprints the advertisement on a better quality paper than is normally used by newspapers. The advertisement is printed on one side of huge rolls of paper and consists of a continuous, repetitive illustration or design so that regardless of where the paper is cut to form a newspaper page, the complete ad will appear. The advertiser supplies the preprinted rolls to the newspaper, which prints its own material on the blank side. Generally, the advertiser pays for the color preprints plus the black-and-white page rate. Another form of color that appears in newspapers consists of multipage, preprinted inserts, often tabloid size. The advertiser prints the entire insert and sends it to the newspaper where it is inserted after the newspaper has been printed. The charge for such inserts is negotiated, but once a newspaper has established a price, this price applies to other advertisers with similar requests.

Split runs. Many newspapers offer split runs at a slight extra charge. The simplest form of split run is when an advertiser prepares two ads of the same size, differing in headline, illustration, coupon value, or even product. The plate for one ad is put on one press, and the plate for the other ad is put on a different press. Both presses feed alternately into a common stacking of newspapers so that the two ads appear in alternate copies of the paper, which are distributed throughout the newspaper's distribution area. In more complex forms of split runs, some newspapers can take up to three different ads that can be distributed to discrete areas, e.g., one ad to the central city, another to one group of suburbs, and the third to another group of suburbs.

Advertisers use split runs for a variety of testing and advertising purposes. For example, an advertiser might prepare two different ads of the same size, each offering a free sample of the product in the body copy, to see which ad would produce the larger consumer response. The responses to each ad could be identified by having consumers enclose a copy of the ad with their responses or write to a different department of the company (Dept. A for one ad and Dept. B for the other). Different headlines or the relative effectiveness of two coupons of different face values could be tested the same way.

NEWSPAPER CIRCULATION

Circulation figures appear on newspaper rate cards and in the Standard Rate and Data Service (SRDS) newspaper catalog. Newspaper circulation is generally divided into three categories: city zone, retail trading zone, and all other. The all other category includes all qualified circulation not included in the city zone or retail trading zone. Sometimes circulation is shown only for the primary market (city zone and retail trading zone) and outside circulation. See the *St. Louis Post-Dispatch* and *Globe-Democrat* listing (Figure 16–2, pages 452 and 453) for an example of this practice.

Newspapers differ in the way they provide coverage in these three areas. Some newspapers in a multiple-newspaper metropolitan area provide better coverage of the city zone than they do of the retail trading zone, and vice versa. Still other newspapers may have unusual strength in the all other category, which generally consists of small towns and rural areas. For example, the *Phoenix Republic* provides fairly good coverage of Flagstaff, Arizona, a town 140 miles north of Phoenix with a population of 40,000. The *Des Moines Register* offers coverage of small towns throughout Iowa, and the *Kansas City Star* has substantial out of state coverage in Kansas and

Missouri. These circulation patterns are taken into consideration when national as well as local advertisers select newspapers.

Since newspapers differ in circulation and costs, a standardized basis for comparison, called **milline rate,** is used. Technically, the milline rate is the cost of reaching a million people with an agate line; it is computed on the following basis:

$$\frac{1,000,000 \times \text{agate line rate}}{\text{circulation}} = \text{milline rate}$$

Thus, if the agate line rate for a particular newspaper is $0.90, and the circulation of the newspaper is 520,000, the milline rate is:

$$\frac{1,000,000 \times \$0.90}{520,000} = \$1.73$$

The 1,000,000 figure was chosen for convenience. The line rate divided by the circulation for the above example would be .00000173; that number is too cumbersome to use.

Standard Rate and Data Service also provides computations of the maximil and minimil rates for newspapers that offer volume discounts. The **maximil rate** is the milline rate computed on the basis of the open rate. The **minimil rate** is a milline rate computed on the basis of the lowest rate available, i.e., the one qualifying for the greatest discount offered by the paper.

HOW NEWSPAPERS ARE SOLD

Newspapers have local salespeople who take orders for classified advertising and local representatives who call on retail advertisers. Often, these representatives, called **reps,** help small retailers and classified advertisers in preparing their advertising and make them aware of any special marketing services or information that the newspaper has to offer.

National advertising is generally handled by newspaper representatives' organizations which have offices in major advertising agency centers such as New York, Chicago, St. Louis, and Los Angeles. These rep organizations represent a number of independent newspapers and newspaper chains and are paid commissions by the individual newspapers on the advertising space they sell. Since newspaper rates are relatively firm and not subject to negotiation, the job of the newspaper rep is threefold: (a) to make sure that advertisers and advertising agencies are familiar with the strengths of the newspapers and the markets they represent; (b) to keep advertisers and agencies informed about any merchandising or marketing services offered by the newspapers; and (c) to perform a general public relations function.

MERCHANDISING AND MARKETING SERVICES

Newspapers provide a variety of merchandising and marketing services for current and potential advertisers. Merchandising aids provided to the smaller advertisers include the creation of promotional pieces, planning and budgeting of advertising, and creation of copy and rough layouts.

For national advertisers, newspapers may conduct trade surveys, provide route lists for retail sales people, give presentations to trade groups, and send promotional pieces to major retailers. Some of the larger newspapers conduct annual consumer surveys to determine brand preferences or purchases. The *Chicago Tribune* became renowned for a permanent consumer panel that it maintained to measure consumer purchases.

STRENGTHS AND WEAKNESSES OF NEWSPAPERS

STRENGTHS

The Bureau of Advertising of the American Newspaper Publishers Association promotes the use of newspaper advertising by disseminating marketing information. According to the bureau, newspapers' strengths include broad coverage, high reader interest, flexibility, low cost per exposure, and cooperative advertising.

Broad coverage. Newspapers are truly a mass medium. Sixty-eight percent of adults 21 years old and over read newspapers on an average weekday. Over a five weekday period, newspapers will reach a cumulative audience of 80 percent of all adults 18 years old and over; on the average, over 80 percent of all newspaper readers will be exposed to the page carrying the advertiser's message.

High reader interest. Among newspaper readers, interest in advertising is as high as it is for editorial material. Because of the preponderance of retail advertising, newspaper advertisements are women's most popular section of the paper, and second only to sports for men. Further, readership is constant throughout the year, and the news value of newspapers adds immediacy to the advertising.

Flexibility. Newspapers are flexible in a number of ways: (a) Space units ranging from one inch to multiple pages can be used. (b) Advertising can be scheduled any day of the week. (c) Closing dates are late, so ads may be prepared on extremely short notice. (4) Since newspapers are essentially a local medium, they provide a great deal of geographic flexibility, allowing the advertiser to pinpoint his advertising pressure in terms of his advertising needs.

Low cost per exposure. On a cost-per-thousand basis, newspapers are relatively inexpensive compared to other media.

Cooperative advertising. Newspapers are excellent vehicles for cooperative advertising and for dealer tie-ins.

WEAKNESSES

As one would expect, newspapers' greatest strengths are also their greatest weaknesses. Major shortcomings include high waste circulation, high cost for national coverage, shortness of message life, poor color reproduction, and competition from retail advertising.

High waste circulation. Because of their mass coverage, newspapers do not provide audience selectivity except on a geographic basis. Special interest newspapers are generally small circulation publications and only useful on a supplementary basis.

High cost for national coverage. While newspapers offer a relatively low cost-per-thousand for intensive coverage of a particular market, their high waste circulation makes them too expensive to use on a national basis. For example, the cost of a 1000 line ad in newspapers necessary to provide 60 percent metropolitan area coverage in the top 50 United States markets is more than $250,000.

Shortness of message life.   Nothing is older than yesterday's news. Newspapers are read hurriedly, and the life of a newspaper advertisement is short. Unlike magazines, newspapers are unlikely to be put aside and read later.

Poor color reproduction.   One of the greatest limitations of newspaper advertising is the general poor quality of its color reproduction and the inability to use fine artwork. Progress has been made, but improvements are still necessary.

Competition from retail advertising.   The volume of retail advertising in newspapers detracts from the readership of national ads. Further, poor position often reduces readership more.

Used properly, the newspaper is a powerful medium. Used improperly, it is a waste of company resources.

MAGAZINES

Magazines, like newspapers, are a major print medium. However, whereas newspapers are primarily local in nature, magazines are, essentially, national. Whereas newspapers excell in mass coverage, magazines are recognized for their audience selectivity. In a real sense, these two media complement one another.

Standard Rate and Data Service lists approximately 3600 business and professional publications and 1200 consumer and farm publications. The SRDS listing does not contain hundreds of small publications that are not audited or lead marginal existences. Although the survival rate is less than 10 percent, new magazines are founded every month.

Most of the existing magazines lie outside the mainstream of advertising. For example, Simmons Market Research Bureau (SMRB) measures only 140 magazines. In 1980 consumer magazine advertising revenues were over $3.1 billion, an increase of 7 percent over 1979.

TYPES OF MAGAZINES

Geographically, some magazines are classified as national, although their circulation patterns tend to parallel retail sales distribution rather than population. Others, such as *Sunset Magazine*, are regional in nature. *Sunset*, one of the most successful magazines in the industry, is edited primarily for residents of the Pacific states, including Alaska and Hawaii. Little more than 10 percent of its circulation of over 1.25 million is delivered outside of these states.

Sunday supplements, such as *Family Weekly* and *Parade*, are often considered magazines because their size, format, and color reproduction are more similar to magazines than newspapers.

Magazines may also be classified in terms of size: (a) pocket size, such as *Reader's Digest* or *TV Guide* (about 4 3/4″ × 6 1/2″); (b) standard size, such as *Time* or *Newsweek* (about 8″ × 11″); or (c) large size, such as *Better Homes & Gardens* (about 9″ × 12″). There are a variety of miscellaneous sizes as well. Magazines can also be classified by frequency of publication, including weeklies, biweeklies, monthlies, quarterlies, and annuals.

By far, the most frequent way of classifying magazines is by editorial content and audience appeal. Business and professional magazines are classified by *Standard Rate and Data Service* into 176 different classifications, ranging from advertising to woodworking. Farm publications are classified by SRDS according to subject matter: dairy and dairy breeds, diversified farming and farm home, farm education and vocations, field crops and soil management, livestock and breed, poultry, and so on. Consumer magazines are classified into 58 subclassifications, ranging from airline inflight at one end of the alphabet, to youth magazines at the other end. Magazines such as *Time* and *Newsweek* are classified as newsweeklies, and magazines such as *Reader's Digest* and *TV Guide* are considered general editorial magazines.

Even these classifications do not do justice to the variety of magazines that exist. For example, *Atlantic Monthly*, *New Yorker*, and *Grit* are all classified as general editorial magazines, yet their editorial orientations are quite different. *Atlantic Monthly* is a magazine for intellectuals; *New Yorker* has a sophisticated, urbane appeal; and *Grit* is clearly edited for the small town market.

KINDS OF MAGAZINE ADVERTISING

Generally, magazines are characterized by three kinds of advertising: display, display classified, and classified advertising. Different rates and minimum size requirements apply to these three kinds of advertising in the published rate schedules.

Display advertising, also referred to as product or general advertising, accounts for the bulk of magazine advertising revenues. This advertising is characterized by the use of attention-getting devices such as illustrations, typographical variations, and the use of white space, thereby standing in contrast to the closely set and uniform type size that is associated with classified advertising. The primary purposes of display advertising are to project a brand concept and influence consumer attitudes.

Display classified advertising appears in the classified section of the publication but uses simple illustrations, different type sizes, and limited white space for attention value. Much of the display classified advertising appearing in magazines is direct mail advertising since the products and services being offered are not available through retail outlets. Some magazines run the display classified and classified advertising in the same section; others do not. For example, *Popular Mechanics* has a special section for display classified advertising called "The Bargain Hunter."

Classified advertising, also referred to as nondisplay advertising, is usually segregated in the back pages of the publication and available to individuals and companies. Such advertising is usually charged by the word and has certain minimal requirements. For example, the *Psychology Today* rate card that went into effect in April, 1982, charged $6.65 per word, with a minimum requirement of 15 words.

MAGAZINE RATE STRUCTURE

Magazine advertising rates are well structured and, normally, not subject to negotiation. The published rate card and discount conditions are inviolate. Unusual space units are subject to negotiation, but once a price has been set for a particular unit, this price applies to other advertisers with similar requests. Price concessions occasionally occur in the rate charged for cover positions. The magazine must have a cover, and if no advertiser can be found that is willing to pay the normal premium, these positions will go at the published rate for standard pages.

Cosmopolitan
A Hearst Publication

(ABC)　　　　　MPA

Media Code 8 728 0200 4.00　　　　Mid 001238-000
Published monthly by Hearst Corp., 224 W. 57th St., New York, NY 10019. Phone 212-262-5700.
For Shipping Info., See Print Media Production Data.
PUBLISHER'S EDITORIAL PROFILE
COSMOPOLITAN is edited for young women, single or married, and concerns self-improvement, careers, clothes, beauty, travel, entertainment and the arts with special emphasis on the world outside the home. Editorial emphasis is on helping young women realize the very most of themselves. Rec'd 7/19/79.

1. PERSONNEL
Publisher—Louis E. Porterfield.
Editor—Helen Gurley Brown.
Advertising Director—William T. Hunt. 262-7417.
National Sales Manager—Glenn R. Gray, 262-6408.
Production—Jerry D'Elia 262-6960.

2. REPRESENTATIVES and/or BRANCH OFFICES
Chicago 60606—Christopher Schuba, Western Adv. Mgr., 1 N. Wacker Dr. Phone 312-984-5111.
Bloomfield Hills, (Detroit) 48013—Chris Meyers, 1780 Kensington. Phone 313-646-4386.
Los Angeles, San Francisco—Perkins, Stephens von der Lieth & Hayward.

3. COMMISSION AND CASH DISCOUNT
15% to agencies; 2% cash discount 24th of month preceding cover date. Bills rendered 10 days prior to cash discount date.
20% commission to schools, colleges and camps advertising.
Cash required with order unless credit has been established.

4. GENERAL RATE POLICY
Orders beyond 1 month at rates then prevailing.

ADVERTISING RATES
Rates effective January 1982 issue.
Rates received August 31, 1981.

5. BLACK/WHITE RATES
1 page (429 lines)	21,535.
2/3 page (286 lines)	15,070.
*Digest (275 lines (bleed)	14,925.
*Digest (182 lines (non-bleed)	12,970.
1/2 page (215 lines)	12,970.
1/3 page (143 lines)	8,090.
1/6 page (71 lines)	4,545.
Per line	70.

(*) All digest size units receive 1/2 page credit toward contract.
Minimum display space accepted at 35 agate lines.
DISCOUNTS
Based on cumulative number of pages used within a consecutive 12 month period.
6 pages	5%	42 pages	26%
12 pages	10%	48 pages	27%

18 pages	14%	54 pages	28%
24 pages	18%	60 pages	29%
30 pages	22-1/2%	72 pages	30%
36 pages	25%		

Regional and special units are not subject to cumulative discounts but may be counted on a pro rata basis towards earning such discounts for additional space that an advertiser may run.

5a. COMBINATION RATES
Additional discounts above volume ones can be earned by Cosmopolitan national display advertisers who qualify for the Hearst Magazines Corporate Buy. See listing for Hearst Magazines Corporate Buy under classification No. 22.

6. COLOR RATES
	2 color	4 color
1 page (429 lines)	25,770.	28,980.
2/3 (286 lines)	18,390.	21,715.
*Digest (bleed)	17,710.	21,670.
*Digest (non-bleed)	15,400.	18,845.
1/2 page (215 lines)	15,400.	18,845.
1/3 (143 lines)	10,555.	14,495.
1/6 page (71 lines)	7,880.	

(*) All digest size units receive 1/2 page credit toward contract.
Minimum display space accepted at 35 agate lines.

7. COVERS
2nd cover (4 color)	34,580
3rd cover (4 color)	30,430.
4th cover (4 color)	37,595.

8. INSERTS
Novel Display Space:
Gatefolds, dutchdoors, inserts—available.

9. BLEED
Black and white and 2-color (all units), extra	10%
Covers and 4-color units, extra	15%

10. SPECIAL POSITION
Orders specifying positions other than those known as designated positions not accepted.

11. CLASSIFIED AND READING NOTICES
DISPLAY CLASSIFICATIONS
MAIL ORDER (ROB)
BLACK AND WHITE RATES:
1 page	18,985.
2/3 page	13,295.
1/2 page	11,440.
1/3 page	7,130

COLOR RATES:
2 color
1 page	21,575.
2/3 page	15,400.
1/2 page	12,890.
1/3 page	8,835.

4 color
1 page	26,240.
2/3 page	19,660.
1/2 page	17,065.
1/3 page	13,120.

All other mail order units less than 1/3 page must run in the Shopper section or take general display rate
COSMOPOLITAN SHOPPER
Ads restricted to offerings of merchandise sold exclusively by mail order and which is not generally available through dealer or retail outlets.
BLACK AND WHITE RATES

	1 iss	3 iss	6 iss	9 iss	12 iss
35 lines	1,435.	1,410.	1,375.	1,335.	1,290
70-71 lines	2,905.	2,845.	2,785.	2,700.	2,615
142-143 lines	5,820.	5,700.	5,590.	5,415.	5,240.
214 lines	8,725.	8,555.	8,375.	8,115.	7,850.
286 lines	11,625.	11,395.	11,160.	10,810.	10,465.
429 lines	17,435.	17,085.	16,740.	16,215.	15,690.

In addition, horizontal halves (not vertical halves) will be accepted.
Continuity discounts are based upon the number of different issues used by 1 advertiser within a 12-month contract year.

SCHOOLS, COLLEGES, CAMPS AND HOME STUDY
SCHOOL DIRECTORY
BLACK AND WHITE RATES:

	1 iss	3 iss	6 iss	9 iss	12 iss
7 lines	295.	290.	285.	275.	265.
14 lines	600.	590.	575.	560.	540.
21 lines	870.	855.	835.	810.	785.
28 lines	1,165.	1,140.	1,120.	1,085.	1,050.
35 lines	1,445.	1,415.	1,385.	1,345.	1,300.
42 lines	1,745.	1,710.	1,675.	1,625.	1,570.
56 lines	2,320.	2,275.	2,225.	2,160.	2,090.
70-71 lines	2,905.	2,845.	2,785.	2,700.	2,615.
105 lines	4,360.	4,275.	4,185.	4,055.	3,925.
142-143 lines	5,820.	5,705.	5,590.	5,415.	5,240.
214 lines	8,725.	8,550.	8,375.	8,115.	7,855.
286 lines	11,630.	11,395.	11,160.	10,815.	10,465.
429 lines	17,435.	17,085.	16,740.	16,215.	15,690.

Space is accepted in 7 and 14 line units or multiples thereof.
Continuity discounts are based upon the number of different issues used by 1 advertiser within a 12-month contract year.

TRAVEL ADVERTISERS AND AGENCIES
BLACK AND WHITE RATES:

	1 ti	3 ti	6 ti	9 ti	12 ti
1 page	17,435.	17,085.	16,740.	16,215.	15,690.
2 columns	11,625.	11,395.	11,160.	10,810.	10,465.
1/2 page	8,725.	8,550.	8,375.	8,115.	7,855.
1 column	5,820.	5,705.	5,585.	5,415.	5,240.

COLOR RATES:
2 color
	1 ti	3 ti	6 ti	9 ti	12 ti
1 page	19,575.	19,185.	18,790.	18,205.	17,620.
2 columns	13,305.	13,040.	12,775.	12,375.	11,975.
1/2 page	9,710.	9,515.	9,320.	9,030.	8,740.
1 column	7,130.	6,985.	6,845.	6,630.	6,415.

4 color
	1 ti	3 ti	6 ti	9 ti	12 ti
1 page	23,465.	22,995.	22,525.	21,820.	21,120.
2 columns	16,740.	16,405.	16,070.	15,570.	15,065.
1/2 page	12,675.	12,420.	12,170.	11,790.	11,410.
1 column	10,410.	10,200.	9,995.	9,680.	9,370.

FIGURE 16-3　(Courtesy Standard Rate & Data Service, Inc.)

THE RATE CARD

Magazines are audited by the Audit Bureau of Circulation and circulation statements appear on the rate card. The structure of the magazine rate card is similar to that of newspapers and contains all of the information needed to schedule and prepare an advertisement. A sample *Standard Rate and Data Service* listing for *Cosmopolitan* is shown in Figure 16–3.

MAGAZINE RATES

Magazine rates are quoted in terms of pages, fractional pages, column inches, agate lines, and special units. Since discounts and premium charges are common in magazines, these pricing practices are examined in the following material.

Discounts. Some magazines operate under a **flat rate** policy where all advertising is charged at the same rate. However, most magazines offer a variety of discounts. The most common are volume and

---

13a. GEOGRAPHIC and/or DEMOGRAPHIC EDITIONS
Only full page units acceptable.
Advertisers buying 2 or more regions in same issue (combinations excepted) will earn 15% discount.
NORTHEAST, MID-ATLANTIC, SOUTH EDITION
BLACK AND WHITE RATES:
1 page .... 17,575.
COLOR RATES:
2 color:
1 page .... 19,525.
4 color:
1 page .... 24,435.
CIRCULATION:
Publisher states: "Effective with January, 1982 issue, rates based on a circulation average of 1,208,756."
NORTHEAST, MID-ATLANTIC
BLACK AND WHITE RATES:
1 page .... 12,260.
COLOR RATES:
2 color:
1 page .... 13,755.
4 color:
1 page .... 17,575.
CIRCULATION:
Publisher states: "Effective with January, 1982 issue, rates based on a circulation average of 814,251."

MID-ATLANTIC EDITION
BLACK AND WHITE RATES:
1 page .... 11,180.
COLOR RATES:
2 color:
1 page .... 12,540.
4 color:
1 page .... 14,530.
CIRCULATION:
Publisher states: "Effective with January, 1982 issue, rates based on a circulation average of 669,374."
CENTRAL EDITION
BLACK AND WHITE RATES:
1 page .... 11,180.
COLOR RATES:
2 color:
1 page .... 12,540.
4 color:
1 page .... 14,530.
CIRCULATION:
Publisher states: "Effective with January, 1982 issue, rates based on a circulation average of 534,402."

PACIFIC COAST EDITION
BLACK AND WHITE RATES:
1 page .... 11,180.
COLOR RATES:
2 color:
1 page .... 12,540.
4 color:
1 page .... 14,530.

CIRCULATION:
Publisher states: "Effective with January, 1982 issue, rates based on a circulation average of 512,621."

SOUTH EDITION
BLACK AND WHITE RATES:
1 page .... 5,740.
COLOR RATES:
2 color:
1 page .... 6,435.
4 color:
1 page .... 8,505.
CIRCULATION:
Publisher states: "Effective with January, 1982 issue, rates based on a circulation average of 394,505."
STATE OF CALIFORNIA EDITION
BLACK AND WHITE RATES:
1 page .... 10,555.
COLOR RATES:
2 color:
1 page .... 11,850.
4 color:
1 page .... 12,770.
CIRCULATION:
Publisher states: "Effective with January, 1982 issue, rates based on a circulation average of 380,986."
SOUTHWEST EDITION
BLACK AND WHITE RATES:
1 page .... 5,740.
COLOR RATES:
2 color:
1 page .... 6,435.
4 color:
1 page .... 8,505.
CIRCULATION:
Publisher states: "Effective with January, 1982 issue, rates based on a circulation average of 327,296."
NEW YORK STATE EDITION
BLACK AND WHITE RATES:
1 page .... 9,070.
COLOR RATES:
2 color:
1 page .... 10,180.
4 color:
1 page .... 11,390.
CIRCULATION:
Publisher states: "Effective with January, 1982 issue, rates based on a circulation average of 241,594."
MOUNTAIN EDITION
BLACK AND WHITE RATES:
1 page .... 5,740.
COLOR RATES:
2 color:
1 page .... 6,435.
4 color:
1 page .... 8,505.
CIRCULATION:
Publisher states: "Effective with January, 1982 issue, rates based on a circulation average of 167,441."

NORTHEAST EDITION
BLACK AND WHITE RATES:
1 page .... 5,740.
COLOR RATES:
2 color:
1 page .... 6,435.
4 color:
1 page .... 8,505.
CIRCULATION:
Publisher states: "Effective with January, 1982 issue, rates based on a circulation average of 144,877."

14. CONTRACT AND COPY REGULATIONS
See Contents page for location—items 2, 3, 8, 15, 16, 18, 19, 24, 25.
15. MECH. REQUIREMENTS
For complete, detailed production information, see SRDS Print Media Production Data.
Printing Process: Web Offset.
Trim size: 8 x 10-7/8; No./Cols. 3.
Binding method: Perfect.

DIMENSIONS-AD PAGE
1   7 x 10-3/16   (*)   4-3/8 x 6-1/2
2/3   4-5/8 x 10-3/16   1/3   2-1/4 x 10-3/16
1/2   7 x 5-1/16   1/3   4-5/8 x 5-1/16
1/2   3-7/16 x 10-3/16   Sprd 14-3/4 x 10-3/16
(*) Jr. page (digest).

16. ISSUE AND CLOSING DATES
Published monthly.
On sale 27th of month preceding cover date.
All advertising closes 25th of the 3rd month preceding cover date.
No space cancellation accepted after 5 days prior to closing date. No cancellations accepted on postcards or inserts after 60 days prior to closing date.
None may be considered executed unless acknowledged by publisher.

17. SPECIAL SERVICES
MCC Media Data Form registered 4/16/82.
A.B.C. Supplemental Data Report released January 1981 issue.

18. CIRCULATION
Established 1886. Single copy 1.75; per year 24.00.
Summary data—for detail see Publisher's Statement.
A.B.C. 6-30-82 (6 mos. aver.—Magazine Form)
Tot. Pd.   Non-Pd   (Subs)   (Single)
2,802,494   7,122   152,384   2,650,110
TERRITORIAL DISTRIBUTION 1/82—2,944,561
N.Eng.   Mid.Atl.   E.N.Cen.   W.N.Cen.   S.Atl.
161,927   477,826   432,768   169,116   412,564
E.S.Cen. W.S.Cen.   Mtn.St.   Pac.St.   Canada
122,366   294,136   178,891   477,133   184,202
Foreign   Other
19,758   13,874
Publisher states: "Effective with July, 1981 issue, rates based on annual circulation average of 2,250,000."

FIGURE 16–3 (continued)

frequency, although combination discounts exist for some magazine groups. **Frequency discounts** are based on the number of insertions used during a contract period, with the size of the discount depending on the number of insertions (note Section 5 of the *Cosmopolitan* listing in Figure 16–3). In addition, some publications offer discounts for the renewal of a schedule beyond one year. **Volume discounts** are offered according to the total space used during a contract period and are offered in addition to frequency discounts. As in the case of newspapers, the advertiser contracts for space based on an estimate of the amount and frequency of the planned advertising. Should less space be used, the advertiser is subject to the short rate. Should the advertiser use more space than contracted and fall into a higher discount bracket, the magazine will issue a rebate at the end of the year.

Combination rates are offered by publications that are under the same corporate ownership or sold as a group to reach a particular market. For example, Condé Nast Publications publishes *Mademoiselle, Vogue, Glamour,* and *House and Garden.* Special discounts are offered for running the same advertising in various combinations of these magazines.

Maximum discounts in magazines may run as high as 35 to 40 percent. Because of differences in the size of circulations and the page rates charged, the amount of money which must be spent in order to earn the maximum discount in different magazines may range from less than $200,000 to several million dollars.

Position charges. With the exception of cover positions, magazines do not normally charge a premium for preferred positions since advertising throughout the magazine receives about the same consumer exposure. The advertiser may request a preferred position; while some magazines will try to grant these requests, they do not guarantee to do so. For example, an advertiser running a horizontal half-page may prefer a top-of-page position; or an advertiser may prefer to be in the first third of the book. In the case of a departmentalized magazine such as *Better Homes and Gardens*, a food advertiser may prefer to appear in the food section, and a furniture advertiser may prefer to be in the home decoration section.

In the case of cover positions, often a premium is charged for the **2nd cover** (the back of the front cover) and the **4th cover** (the back of the magazine). The premium for 2nd covers is generally about 10 percent more than the four color page rate, and the 4th cover premium generally ranges from 15 to 25 percent above the four color page rate. In addition, many publications do not offer discounts on any of the cover positions.

Color. Color reproduction is available in almost all of the leading magazines, including business and farm publications. The premium charged for color varies greatly, however. The premium for two color pages may range from as low as 5 or 6 percent to as high as 20 or 25 percent over the black and white page rate. Four color may carry a premium ranging from 20 percent for the larger circulation magazines to 70 percent for some of the smaller circulation publications. The average premium for four color advertising is about 30 percent.

Bleed pages.   A bleed page is one in which printing runs to the edge, or "bleeds" off the page. The premium for bleed ads generally ranges from 10 to 30 percent, depending upon the publication.

Splits, halves, and sectional editions.   Some magazines offer split runs for a slight premium. In addition, some of the larger publications offer partial runs and special editions. *Playboy*, for example, will run an advertisement in every other issue at a premium of about 20 percent over its normal cost-per-thousand rate. Therefore, a four color page will cost about 20 percent more than half the cost of the same unit in the full edition. *Playboy* also offers and charges premium rates for five regional editions—eastern, central, western, southeastern, and southwestern. Some magazines, such as *Time*, even offer metropolitan editions for a limited number of major metropolitan areas.

Having reviewed some of the major rate practices of magazines, you should now examine the *Cosmopolitan* listing (Figure 16–3) more closely. Note the types of discounts allowed, treatment of position requests, and how covers are charged in comparison to four color rates, special rates, and regional editions.

Magazine rate cards can be exceedingly complex. For a major magazine, the *Cosmopolitan* rate card is a relatively simple one. Further, with all of the possible space units available, e.g., variations in the use of color, regional editions, metropolitan editions, split runs, volume discounts, and frequency discounts, a countless number of different contracts can be written for magazine space.

MAGAZINE CIRCULATION

In preparing a media plan, magazines are evaluated on a variety of bases: circulation, demographic characteristics of their audiences, cost, editorial content, and general tone. Since magazines differ in circulation size and page rates, the standardized basis for comparing costs is the cost-per-thousand (CPM) discussed in Chapter 15.

The page rate used in the numerator in the cost-per-thousand computation may be the cost of a black and white page or some other space unit, depending on the nature of the schedule and the preferences of the media analyst. Cost-per-thousand computations are usually designated as B/W cost-per-thousand, four color cost-per-thousand, and so on to indicate which base has been used.

The denominator of the cost-per-thousand equation may be based on the **average issue circulation** (delivered circulation), **guaranteed circulation, reader exposure,** or **target audience exposure.** Any of these may be used as long as the analyst indicates which he is using.

AVERAGE ISSUE CIRCULATION

Circulation for magazines will vary from issue to issue, depending on the number of copies sold on the newsstand and subscriptions that are in effect for a particular issue. Average issue circulation is determined by dividing the total number of copies distributed during the past January through December period by the number of issues published. These are the circulation figures audited by the Audit Bureau of Circulation.

GUARANTEED CIRCULATION

Magazine advertising rates are based on a guaranteed circulation that is somewhat less than the average issue circulation figure. If the magazine fails to meet its guaranteed circulation, the publisher gives a pro rata rebate to the advertiser. Thus, if the delivered circulation of a magazine fell 5 percent below the guaranteed circulation for the issues that an advertiser contracted, the publisher would rebate 5 percent of the cost at the end of the year.

READER EXPOSURE

Magazines are generally read by more than one person. Sometimes, two or more people in a magazine household will read the magazine; it may be given to a friend or relative after the immediate family has seen it. All of us have had the experience of reading a magazine in a doctor's waiting room, barber shop, or beauty parlor. **Primary readership** refers to those individuals who live in the household subscribing to the magazine. Readership by someone outside the subscribing household is referred to as **secondary** or **pass-along readership.** The **total exposure** of a magazine includes both its primary and secondary readers and is substantially greater than its delivered circulation. Total exposure is measured by audience measurement services such as SMRB.

Table 16–3 shows the delivered circulation, guaranteed circulation, and total exposure for *Newsweek* and *National Geographic*. Note that the total exposure for both magazines is substantially greater than their delivered circulations. In addition, the total exposure of *Newsweek* is over six times greater than its average circulation, whereas *National Geographic*'s total exposure is only about two and one-half times greater than its average circulation. This is a normal pattern; newsweeklies tend to enjoy a large secondary readership while *National Geographic* is a magazine that subscribers tend to save.

TABLE 16–3 Comparison of delivered circulation, guaranteed circulation, and total exposure for *Newsweek* and *National Geographic* (numbers in 000's)

Magazine	Average Issue (delivered) Circulation	Guaranteed Circulation	Total Exposure		
			Men	Women	Total
Newsweek	2,955.1	2,950.0	10,468.0	7,465.0	17,933.0
National Geographic	8,687.1	8,440.0	12,109.0	10,322.0	22,430.0

Source: Average and guaranteed circulation from April, 1982 issue of *Standard Rate and Data Service.*
Total exposure from SMRB.

TARGET AUDIENCE READERSHIP

Target audience readership or exposure refers to the number of people in the target audience that are exposed to the advertising. In dealing with magazine readership figures, target audiences are defined on the basis of demographic variables such as age, education, marital status, product usage, and so on. Target audience data is provided by services such as SMRB.

MARKETING AND MERCHANDISING SERVICES

Magazines often undertake readership and product usage studies of their audiences; sometimes they prepare basic marketing studies in fields that interest current or potential advertisers. The research departments of major magazines are often repositories of a great deal of marketing information in a variety of product fields, which they supply to advertisers and advertising agencies upon request.

Magazines do not supply creative help in preparing advertising, but most magazines have departments that will prepare or assist in the preparation of counter cards, folders, special letters to distributors and retailers, and similar merchandising aids. Few magazines offer these services without charge or a major purchase of advertising space. Some of the major magazines will have merchandising specialists in areas such as fashion, cosmetics, and department store selling, who are available to help present advertising plans to client sales meetings and meetings of distributor organizations.

STRENGTHS AND WEAKNESSES OF MAGAZINES

Magazines have a number of advantages as an advertising medium. Full realization of these advantages is dependent upon variables such as type of product, nature of the product's distribution, effectiveness of advertising copy, and competitive activity.

STRENGTHS

Some major advantages of magazines for advertising are high audience selectivity, high quality reproduction, long life and reader interest, audience characteristics, and high prestige.

High audience selectivity. With the exceptions of direct mail and those cases where the audience is restricted to local geographic areas, magazines are the most selective media for reaching target audiences. A vast number of special interest magazines are available for use; magazines can even be selected to appeal to a variety of temperaments.

High quality reproduction. Most magazines are printed on paper that is excellent for use in detailed, four color reproduction. This reproduction enables food advertisers to capture appetite appeal and permits fashion advertisers to portray style in an arresting manner. Further, through the use of unusual space units, interesting effects and high impact can be achieved.

Long life and reader interest. Magazine exposure life is longer than that of most other media. Magazine advertising can be perused and studied at leisure; after the primary reader is finished reading the magazine, its life is extended through pass-along readership. Some magazines, particularly in the home service and fashion fields, are purchased as much for their advertising as for their editorial content.

Audience characteristics. Magazine readers tend to rank above the national average in the areas of income and education. Because magazine circulation tends to follow retail sales rather than population, it parallels the nation's purchasing power.

High prestige. Magazines lend prestige to products that appear within their covers. Although a certain amount of prestige is attached to all national media, magazines are particularly strong in this respect because of the education and relative affluence of magazine readers.

WEAKNESSES

Against these strengths, magazines have limitations such as lack of market penetration, inflexibility, lack of message immediacy, and high cost.

Lack of penetration. Magazines are essentially a national medium and cannot be used to dominate local markets. Sunday supplements can be used for this purpose, but the selectivity of the medium is lost in the process.

Inflexibility. Magazines are relatively inflexible in two respects: (a) Although regional and metropolitan editions are available in some magazines, it is generally difficult to vary advertising pressure geographically with magazines. (b) Magazine closing dates are often two or three months prior to the date of issue, thus precluding moving quickly to take advantage of marketing opportunities.

Lack of message immediacy. Immediacy is not available in magazine advertising. Magazines are basically an image medium, designed to sell over the long term.

High cost. Production costs for magazines are relatively high, particularly for four color advertising. Even though the cost-per-thousand may be relatively low for a high circulation magazine, the page cost may be well beyond the reach of many small advertisers.

SUMMARY

This chapter describes the salient characteristics of the major print media—newspapers and magazines.

Based on advertising revenues, newspapers are the largest advertising medium. Local advertisers account for over 80 percent of newspaper advertising revenue. Although there are only about 1500 daily and Sunday newspapers, almost 10,000 semiweekly, biweekly, monthly, and bimonthly newspapers serve suburban communities, small towns, and rural areas. A variety of newspapers also serve ethnic and special interest groups.

Newspapers are characterized by several kinds of advertising: classified, retail, national, and reading notices. Various rates are charged for these different kinds of advertising, but the rates are relatively stable and distributed on published rate cards. Most newspapers offer volume discounts. The size of the discount depends upon the amount of space used, and local advertisers are given more favorable rates than national advertisers.

Newspaper circulation is audited by the Audit Bureau of Circulation, and circulation figures are shown on the newspaper rate card. Since newspapers differ both in line rate and size of circulation, the basic device for comparing newspaper costs is the milline rate. The milline rate is the cost of reaching one million people with an agate line of newspaper space.

Newspaper space is sold to local advertisers through local salespeople. National advertising is generally sold through newspaper representative organizations that have offices in major advertising centers. These organizations represent a number of independent newspapers and newspaper chains.

Although newspapers have a number of advertising values, their primary values are their ability to provide broad coverage and high readership. The primary weakness of newspapers is their high waste circulation.

Magazines, like newspapers, are a major print medium but, whereas newspapers are recognized for their mass coverage, magazines are known for their audience selectivity.

Standard Rate and Data Service lists about 3600 business and professional publications, 800 consumer magazines, and 400 farm journals. Magazines may be classified in several ways, but the most frequent is on the basis of editorial content and audience appeal. SRDS classifies magazines into 176 different groups, some appealing to highly specialized interests. These categories only partly describe the diversity that is available through magazines.

Magazines generally carry three kinds of advertising: display, display classified, and classified. These forms of advertising have different rate structures and minimum size requirements.

Like newspapers, magazine rate structures are relatively stable and made available through published rate cards. Magazines offer a variety of discounts based on the volume of space used and frequency of insertions. They also have premium charges for such things as cover position, color, bleed, and regional editions.

Cost-per-thousand is the basic device for comparing the costs of magazines. CPM comparisons may be made on the basis of guaranteed circulation, average issue circulation, or total readership. Target audience exposure refers to the number of people in the product's target audience that are exposed to its advertising. Target audiences are determined on the basis of demographic variables and based on data published by readership services such as SMRB.

The primary strengths of magazines lie in their audience selectivity, high quality of reproduction, long life, quality audiences, and high prestige. Their primary weaknesses are their lack of market penetration, relative inflexibility, lack of immediacy, and relatively high cost.

REVIEW QUESTIONS

1 Differentiate among (a) free community newspapers; (b) suburban newspapers; (c) shoppers; and (d) pennysavers.
2 Identify and describe the various kinds of newspaper advertising defined in the chapter.
3 Assume that a newspaper has the following rate structure:

Open rate	$1.10 per line
5000 lines	0.95 per line
10,000 lines	0.90 per line
15,000 lines	0.80 per line

An advertiser contracts for 10,000 lines and is billed at this rate. During the contract year, however, 15,000 lines are used. Show the computations for the year-end adjustment.
4 Explain what is meant by a split run and indicate why it might be used by an advertiser.
5 Explain, without formulas, what the milline rate reveals and how it differs from the magazine cost-per-thousand. Why don't newspapers, like magazines, use a cost-per-thousand measure?
6 Identify the major strengths and weaknesses of newspapers.
7 What are the ways that magazines are classified in the text? What is the most common way of classifying magazines?
8 Explain what is meant by volume, frequency, and combination discounts.
9 Differentiate among average issue circulation, guaranteed circulation, and reader exposure. If you were recommending a schedule in a magazine, which of these bases would you use to compute cost-per-thousand? Why?
10 What are the major strengths and weaknesses of magazines?

DISCUSSION QUESTIONS

1 Compare regular newspaper advertising with that appearing in magazines. How do they differ?
2 What do you think the future of magazine advertising is? Why?
3 Since a great deal of controversy exists over the accuracy of the total exposure measurement of magazines, do you think this measurement should be used? Why or why not? If it is not used, what would you use in its place? Why?

PROBLEM

Using the *Cosmopolitan* SRDS listing in Figure 16–3, answer the following questions:

1 What is the maximum discount available, assuming that you are using no other Hearst publications?
2 What is the difference in cost between black and white and color pages?
3 What is the premium for bleed pages?
4 What is the policy on pricing covers?
5 What is the printing process?
6 What are the closing dates?
7 What is the cost of 24 pages, four color bleed in a contract year?
8 Compute the cost of using 12 pages, four color in the Mid-Atlantic, and Central editions.

17
Television and Radio

FROM RADIO TO CABLE

THE GOLDEN AGE OF RADIO

When we think of the golden age of radio, we generally think of the 1930s and 1940s—before the emergence of television. Radio was in its heyday as an entertainment medium before television drove it out of the spotlight. Jack Benny, Bob Hope, and the Fitch Bandwagon were premier entertainment vehicles. American families gathered around the set to listen to the latest episodes of "I Love a Mystery," "The Big Story," and "Mr. Keene, Tracer of Lost Persons." Rather than engaging in nostalgia, let's look at the numbers and at the future.

In 1940 radio billings were $215 million. In 1980 they were $3.8 billion. Network radio has suffered, growing only $67 million during this period (from $113 million to $180 million), but spot and local radio grew from $102 million to a staggering $3,597 billion—a whopping $3,495 billion increase.

According to *Advertising Age:*

> There is some evidence that we are seeing the dawn of a modern Golden Days of network radio—witnessed by a rapid proliferation in the number of networks and available programs . . . the increased demand for program material has caught the ears of traditional radio packagers and syndicators, and has opened new fields for ad agencies and media reps.[1]

DO TELEVISION AUDIENCES REALLY WANT CULTURE?

Television's critics have often disapproved of the medium's lack of cultural programming. In an effort to salve this complaint, CBS Cable was launched in 1981 with appropriate fanfare. By programming

[1]Don Perlman, "These Are New Golden Days," p. S–1. Reprinted with permission from the June 29, 1981 issue of *Advertising Age.* Copyright © 1981 by Crain Communications, Inc.

sophisticated drama, ballet, modern dance, modern history, and symphonic music, CBS attempted to appeal to those affluent consumers who had grown tired of standard television fare. With losses estimated at $30 million in less than a year of operation, CBS announced that it was abandoning its ambitious and prestigious cable service. Advertising revenues attracted by its five million household audience offset no more than $60,000 of the $325,000 cost of a one hour show. According to *Time* magazine:

> Arts organizations in the U.S., which have looked to cable to help replace federal funds cut by the Reagan administration, were saddened by the announcement but not surprised. Marc Nathanson, president of the 100,000-subscriber Falcon Communications in California, noted: "We take frequent surveys, and I was always shocked to see that CBS Cable attracted only 2% of our viewers on a weekly basis."[2]

PREPARING FOR THE FUTURE

The rapid growth of cable television has caused advertising agencies to set up in-house cable think tanks to deal with this media form. Ira Tumpoursky, vice-president—group supervisor for cable at Young & Rubicam, observed: "The planning area is the pivotal area of any media department. That's where recommendations are made. Once we believed cable to be a viable medium, we had to bring it into the planning process."[3]

Other agencies are following suit, although cable billings are still small compared to regular broadcast television. In 1981 cable advertising was less than $100 million compared to regular television's $11 billion, but the market is expected to grow as cable systems reach larger audiences, advertisers are discouraged by the inflation of regular television prices, and consumers become more discouraged by standard television programming. Changes will not

---

[2]"The Cadillac Runs Out of Gas," *Time*, 27 September 1982, 65.
[3]"Agency Cable Specialists the New Media Mixers," *Marketing and Media Decisions* (March 1982): 60.

occur overnight, however. Cable television is a capital intensive business that requires large investments to establish. In addition, developing appealing programs demands creative talent as well as financial expenditure.

The future of cable television, while bright, is filled with many obstacles. Nonetheless, forward looking advertising agencies are planning ahead by developing specialists in this medium.

The broadcast media is a big, diverse, exciting, and explosive field. Most of today's population has grown up with television and is no longer amazed by its wonder. Some have known radio from its inception. Yet, most of us know very little about the broadcast industry and even less about it as an advertising medium. Let's examine these two facets of broadcasting more closely.

AN OVERVIEW OF BROADCAST MEDIA

Broadcast media differ from print in regard to their characteristics and the structure of the industry.

DIFFERENCES IN THE CHARACTERISTICS OF THE MEDIA

In one sense, broadcast and print media are different worlds. A magazine buyer in an advertising agency can move fairly easily to newspapers. However, without special training in broadcast, this buyer is not prepared to deal with broadcast problems, and vice versa. Some major differences between the two media are identified in the following material.

Broadcast is a "time" medium whereas print is a "space" medium. Consumers do not have the opportunity to study broadcast commercials the way they can study print ads. The commercial appears for a few seconds or a minute, and then it is gone. Print media can be examined for as long as the reader chooses.

Broadcast is basically an entertainment medium. People turn on their television and radio sets to seek entertainment programs or catch up on the news. They do not tune in to hear or view commercials. Advertising is often viewed as an unwelcome interruption. How different this is from a magazine that is often bought because of its advertising.

Since people differ in their interests and tastes, broadcasters attempt to appeal to different groups through their programming. For example, radio may have several stations in a market. Each is beamed at different target audiences through country and western, rock, pop, or classical music. Appealing to different audiences is more difficult in television because there is a limited number of channels. As a consequence, most television stations are directed toward a general audience, and special programs on each channel are used to appeal to different audience segments via children's programming, soap operas, game shows, sports, adventure, situation comedies, and so on.

The emergence of cable television may change this pattern, however. Prevailing speculation is that the proliferation of cable television systems will give rise to **narrowcasting**, i.e., specialized programming subscribed to by discriminating viewers who want a particular form of entertainment, be it news, drama, opera, educational programs, sports, and so on.

Unlike print, which is the private property of individual publishers, the airwaves are public domain. The Federal Communications Commission (FCC), which licenses radio and television stations, exerts some control over program content and advertising.

Broadcast is a glutton for entertainment and editorial material. In radio, this issue is met by programming an abundant supply of music. The problem is more pressing in television. Material has to be written and produced in an unending stream. Magazines, which are printed once a week or month, don't have this problem in the same degree. Although newspapers are printed daily, they have a world of events to write about and more news than editors care to print.

The never ending demand for new material is one of the major reasons much of television's programming is mediocre. There simply are not enough creative people to meet television's voracious appetite for good material. In addition, television production is expensive.

Broadcast time is perishable. Each day a certain amount of commercial time is available. If the time is not sold, it is irrecoverable. Demands are less pressing in print. The amount of editorial material appearing in a publication is adjusted in accordance with advertising revenues. This difference between print and broadcast media leads to different pricing and selling practices. Unlike magazines, where advertising readership is relatively uniform throughout the publication, broadcast has prime listening times. For radio, the largest audience is during the daytime hours; for television, it is during the evening.

There is a difference between print circulation and broadcast coverage. **Print circulation** is the number of copies of a publication that are distributed to consumers. **Broadcast coverage** refers to a station's or network's potential audience, and circulation is equated to exposure, i.e., the average number of listeners or viewers during a given time period.

THE STRUCTURE OF BROADCASTING

Traditionally, the basic unit of broadcasting has been the local station, which is privately owned but is licensed by the Federal Communications Commission. Some stations are affiliated with networks; others are not. A local station that has a network affiliation is referred to as an **affiliate.** One that does not is referred to as an **independent.**

A station gains network affiliation by signing a contract with one of the national networks. Under the terms of this contract, the local station agrees to sell the network a certain amount of programming time for about 30 percent of the station's normal time charges. The local station, particularly in television, benefits from this arrangement in two ways: (a) It receives professional programming that it could not afford to develop itself, and which attracts large

CHAPTER 17 | TELEVISION AND RADIO

audiences. (b) Because of these large audiences, the local station is able to sell time between network programs at a premium price. Figure 17–1 shows the basic structure of the broadcast industry.

CHANGING STRUCTURES

The traditional structure of broadcasting is changing, however. The two events that are influencing this change are cable television and superstations.

CABLE TV (CATV)

CATV stands for **community antenna television** and is popularly referred to as cable television. Initially, cable television was established to provide television coverage for isolated communities in remote areas where surroundings interfered with television reception. Subsequently, the concept of cable television has expanded to provide a diversity of programming throughout the United States. Today, approximately 4400 cable television systems serve about 27 percent of homes with television. By 1985 cable television is expected to serve 50 percent of the television sets in the United States.

The concept of cable television is also changing. Originally, it paid a copyright charge, picked up network and independent stations' broadcasts, and delivered them to homes that were wired for cable for a subscription fee. As cable systems grew in size and re-

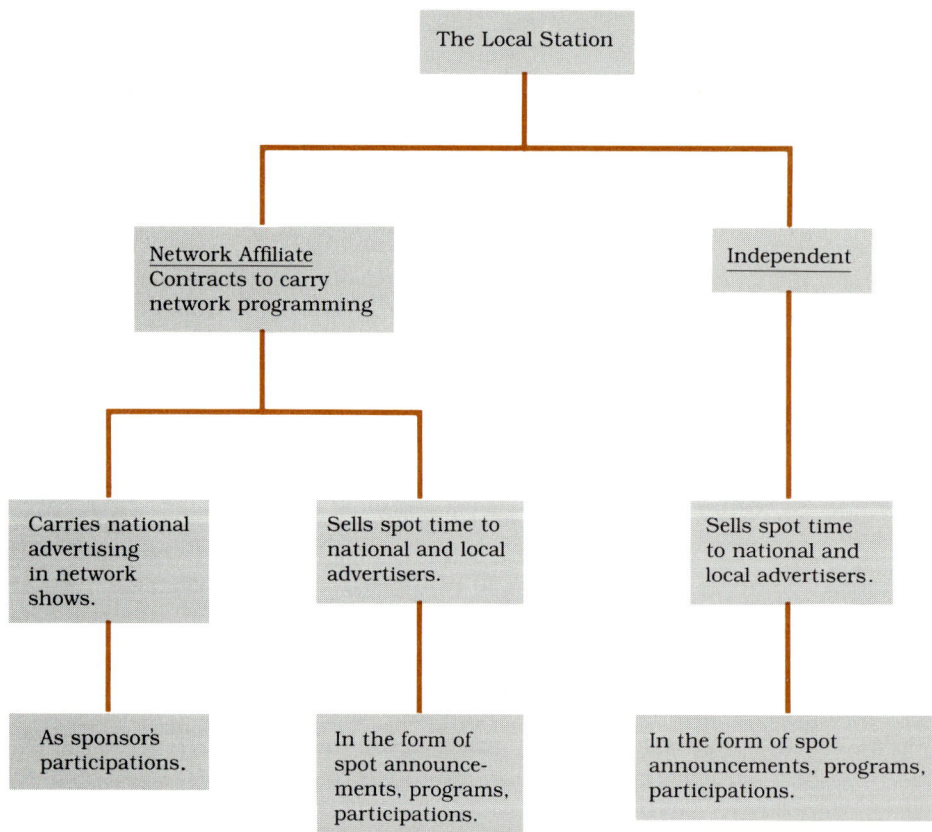

FIGURE 17–1 The traditional structure of the broadcast industry

sources, they acquired the rights to movies, television reruns, and sporting events which they transmitted to their subscribers. These offerings usually took the form of pay television—subscribers paid a special fee for programs without commercials. Other cable systems have specialized in narrowcasting, such as 24-hour news or cultural programming. With the advent of satellite transmission, a small number of cable systems offer as many as forty or fifty channels, but such systems are scarce.

The future of cable television is still an open question. Two problems keep advertisers from flocking to cable systems: (a) limited audiences; and (b) lack of adequate audience measuring techniques. Television industry experts think that advertisers will flock to cable when cable television is able to provide 30 percent coverage of United States homes. Although cable television appears to be emerging as a viable alternative to network programming, its growth rate is uncertain. Besides being a capital intensive industry, cable television involves considerable risk.

SUPERSTATIONS

Superstations send their signals to cable-equipped homes via satellite. The leading superstation in the United States is WTBS–TV in Atlanta. In July, 1982, ABC Radio Enterprises launched Superradio, a network program transmitted to licensed stations via satellite. These developments provide relatively inexpensive coverage of U.S. television and radio homes that may someday provide direct competition for the major broadcast networks.

TELEVISION

There are approximately 77.8 million television homes in the United States, providing 98 percent coverage of all U.S. homes. Eighty-five percent of the television homes, approximately 66.5 million, are equipped with color television sets. The 77.8 million television homes in the United States are served by over 1000 local television stations, three national television networks—American Broadcasting Company (ABC), CBS, Inc. (CBS), and National Broadcasting Company (NBC)—and 4400 CATV systems. Another 2000 CATV systems have been approved, but have not yet been constructed. Networks, local stations, and the CATV systems are all licensed by the FCC and must meet certain minimum operating and programming requirements in order to obtain and keep their licensed authority.

BASIC TELEVISION TERMS

A number of terms are used in connection with television planning and audience measurement, including **penetration, coverage, sets-in-use, share of audience,** and **rating.** Perhaps the easiest way to explain them is to borrow an example from Paul Roth's book, *How to Plan Media.*[4]

> *Penetration.* Start with a theoretical universe of 100 households. Ninety-eight of these 100 households own TV sets. TV *penetration* or *set ownership* is 98/100 = 98%.

---

[4]Paul Roth, *How to Plan Media* (Skokie, Illinois: Standard Rate and Data Service, Inc., 1969).

Coverage area. The TV signal of a theoretical network covers 80 TV households. The *coverage area,* therefore, is defined as 80 out of 98 TV households in the universe. This equals 80/98 = 82% *coverage.*

Sets-in-use. At 9–10 P.M., 60 TV households are watching TV. Thus, *sets-in-use* = 60 out of 98 households = 60/98 = 61% *sets-in-use.*

Rating. During the 9–10 P.M. period, 20 TV households are watching a particular program. The *rating* of this program is 20/98 = 20. A rating point, therefore, is one percent of all the households that have a TV set.

Share-of-audience. During this 9–10 P.M. period, 20 households are watching a particular program. However, 60 households are watching TV (sets-in-use). Therefore, that particular program's *share-of-audience* is 20/60 = 33%.

EVALUATING A TELEVISION COMMERCIAL

Television commercials are evaluated in terms of **reach, frequency,** and **weight.**

Reach. The reach of a commercial refers to the number of people or households exposed to it, generally in a four-week period.

Frequency. The frequency of the commercial refers to the number of times the average member of its audience, or the average household, is exposed to it within a four-week period.

Weight. The weight of a television schedule is measured in terms of **gross rating points.** Gross rating points are computed by multiplying the rating of the commercial by the number of times it is run. For example, suppose that a commercial appeared in a program four times in a four-week period with an average rating of 10. The gross rating points earned would be: $4 \times 10 = 40$.

Now, let's take a simplified example, using households, to see how a particular television schedule can be evaluated in terms of weight, reach, and frequency.

Since there are 77.8 million television homes in the United States, a weekly program with an average rating of 10 would reach 10 percent of the homes. This would be equal to 7,780,000 homes. In a four-week period, a 10 rating would accumulate (**cume**) 40 gross rating points ($4 \times 10 = 40$) and, theoretically, reach 31,120,000 households ($4 \times 7,780,000 = 31,120,000$). Thus, 40 gross rating points in a four-week period would generate 31,120,000 exposures for a commercial that appeared in the program once a week for four weeks.

However, not all of these exposures are new exposures. Some households will watch the program every week and thereby be exposed to the commercial four times. Other households will watch three weeks out of four, two weeks out of four, or only once. Thus, the 40 gross rating points represents a certain amount of duplication in the 31,120,000 exposures it provides.

Now, let's make some more assumptions about our theoretical program:

☐ Fifty percent of the total exposures were in households that saw the program four times.

□ Thirty percent of the total exposures were in homes that saw the program three times.

□ Fifteen percent of the total exposures were in homes that saw the program two times.

□ Five percent of the total exposures were in homes that saw the program one time.

With this information, net reach and average frequency can be computed (Table 17–1).

As you can see from Table 17–1, a weight of 40 gross rating points provides a total audience of 31,120,000 households, a net unduplicated reach of 10,892,000, and an average frequency of 2.86 exposures per household.

A commercial with a similar weight of 40 gross rating points but more, or less, duplication would deliver a different net reach and average frequency.

This simplified example has dealt with households and has not taken the composition of the audience within household into consideration. In order to do this, we need audience composition figures such as those provided by the audience measuring services. This information could provide comparable weight, reach, and frequency information for men, women, children, and even particular age groups. The essence of media planning is to develop an optimal balance between reach and frequency against some defined target audience, such as women between the ages of 18 and 39, or some other specified group.

TELEVISION COMMERCIAL TIME

Commercial rates for television time vary by time of day, with those time periods attracting the largest audiences commanding a higher price. The period of highest television viewing is referred to as **prime time.** On the East and West Coasts, prime time is between 7:30 and 11:00 P.M.. In the Midwest and Mountain states, it is 6:30 to 10:00 P.M. On network affiliated stations, the FCC permits two and one-half hours of prime time to be programmed by the networks and allows local stations to sell commercial time between the programs.

TABLE 17–1   Weight, reach, and frequency computations for theoretical program

Percent of Total Exposures	Number of Total Exposures		Number of Exposures per Household		Net Households Reached
50%	15,560,000	÷	4	=	3,890,000
30%	9,336,000	÷	3	=	3,112,000
15%	4,668,000	÷	2	=	2,334,000
5%	1,556,000	÷	1	=	1,556,000
100%	31,120,000				10,892,000

Weight: 40 gross rating points.
Net unduplicated homes reached: 10,892,000
Average frequency: $\dfrac{31,120,000}{10,892,000} = 2.86$

The hour or so adjacent to prime time is called **fringe time. Early fringe** precedes prime time and **late fringe** follows prime time. On the basis of cost, fringe time ranks second to prime time.

Local television stations often set up a variety of rate classifications based on the time of day the broadcast occurs. For a small station, the time classifications may be as simple as:

Class A—7:30 P.M. to 11:00 P.M.
Class B—All other times.

On the other hand, a key station in a major market may have an extremely complex rate structure. Figure 17–2 shows the SRDS listing for KPLR-TV, a major independent station in St. Louis. Note that KPLR has thirty-six time classifications for spot announcements, ranging in cost from $1,000 for a 30-second announcement to $10 for a 30-second announcement. Of course, few people will be awake during the time the $10 classification is aired.

KPLR-TV

ST. LOUIS
(Airdate April 28, 1959)

TELEREP

Subscriber to the NAB Television Code

Media Code 6 226 0500 4.00 **Mid 007563-000**

Koplar Communications, Inc., KPLR-TV
4935 Lindell Blvd., St. Louis, MO 63108. Phone 314-367-7211, Sales:, 314-367-9000. TWX 910-761-1093.

1. PERSONNEL
President—Edward J. Koplar.
Exec. Vice-Pres. & Gen'l Mgr.—Harold E. Protter.
Director of Sales—Michael A. Fisher.
General Sales Manager—Terence J. Brown.
Local Sales Manager—Harold Capron.
Traffic Manager—Jan Viner Pendleton.

2. REPRESENTATIVES
TeleRep.

3. FACILITIES
Video 316,000 w., audio 55,300 w. ch 11.
Antenna ht.: 1,007 ft. above average terrain.
Operating schedule: 24 hours daily. CST.

4. AGENCY COMMISSION
15% to recognized agencies on time charges; no cash discount.

5. GENERAL ADVERTISING See coded regulations
General: 1b, 2a, 3a, 3c, 3d, 4a, 5, 6a, 7b, 8.
Rate Protection: 10m, 11m, 12m, 13k, 14i.
Contracts: 20b, 21, 22c, 23, 25, 26, 27e, 31b, 32d, †34g.
Basic Rates: 40a, 41b, 41c, 41d, 42, 45a, 51, 52.
Comb.; Cont. Discounts. 60a, 60e, 62b.
Cancellation: 70a, 70b, 70i, 71, 72, 73a, 73d.
Prod. Services: 82, 83, 84, 85, 86, 87b, 87c.
(†) All toy, candy, fast food, soft drink and cereal advertising directed at children's audience and/or children's and adults audiences are considered non-competitive.
Multiple product spots receive no product protection.
Station reserves the right to cancel, advance the time of or interrupt or postpone the program or commercials of any advertiser without any liability against the station for talent engaged if it interferes with telecast of public necessity. In the event any telecasting period contracted for is not used, station reserves the right to provide a program at the expense of the advertisers and the advertisers agree to accept the substitute.
All spots sold at other than the fixed rate are preemptible. Priorities of preemptibility depend upon the price of the spot. What is stated in the SRDS is the station's best estimate at the time of submission as to which price, specifically corresponding to a specific class of time, will be subject to preemption with or without preemption.

Rotation Policy

Station does not guarantee an exact rotation either horizontally or vertically. Station does attempt an equitable rotation as possible. No credit or make-goods will be given for misinterpretation of this policy.

6. TIME RATES
No. 81-82A Eff 9/14/81—Rec'd 7/24/81.
Rev. Rec'd 8/17/82.

7. SPOT ANNOUNCEMENTS

Level	30 sec	Level	30 sec
1	1000	19	150
2	950	20	125
3	900	21	100
4	850	22	80
5	800	23	75
6	750	24	70
7	700	25	65
8	650	26	60
9	600	27	55
10	550	28	50
11	500	29	45
12	450	30	40
13	300	31	35
14	275	32	30
15	250	33	25
16	225	34	20
17	200	35	15
18	175	36	10

120 sec: 4 x 30 sec.
90 sec: 3 x 30 sec.
60 sec: 2 x 30 sec.
10 sec: 6 x 30 sec.
Break positions may be used as part of program commercial rotation at station's option.

8. PARTICIPATING PROGRAMS
Rec'd 8/17/82.
DAYTIME

	F
MON THRU FRI:	
Newswatch II—5:30-6 am	7
Space Coaster/Ranger/Bugs/Popeye/Heckle & Jeckle/Woody—6:30-9 am	9
All In The Family/Carol Burnett/Morning Movie—9 am-noon	20
PM:	
Muppets—noon-12:30	20
12:30 Movie—12:30-2:30	20
ROS—9 am-2:30 pm	20
Gilligan/Bugs/Woody/Scooby Doo/Tom & Jerry—2:30-5	6
Charlie's Angels—5-6	1
Little House On The Prairie—6-7	1
ROS—5-7	2
Prime Time Super Movie—7-9	1
Joker's Wild—9-9:30	11
ROS—7-9:30 Mon thru Sun	10
Newswatch—9:30-10	7
Soap—10-10:30	3
People's Court—10:30-11	5
The Big Movie—11 pm-1 am	17
Last Picture Show—1-4:30 am	30
Health Field—4:30-5 am	30
Continuous Weather—5-5:30 am	30
SAT:	
U. S. Farm Report—5:30-6 am	7
Newswatch III—6-6:30 am	7
Today's Black Woman—6:30-7 am	7
Big Blue Marble—7-7:30 am	4
Bugs Bunny—7:30-8 am	15
Tom & Jerry—8-8:30 am	15
Saturday Fun Time—8:30-10 am	15
Hardy Boys/Nancy Drew—10-11 am	15
Best Of Midnight Special—11 am-noon	15
PM:	
Movies—noon-5	10
Solid Gold—5-6	1
Hee Haw—6-7	1
Super Movie—7-9	1
Nashville Music—9-9:30	10
Newswatch—9:30-10	7
Benny Hill—10-10:30	5
The Big Movie—10:30-midnight	15
Last Picture Show—midnight-1 am	30
Best Of Midnight Special II—1-2 am	30
Laugh Trax—2-3 am	30
Rock Concert—3-4 am	30
Continuous Weather—4-5:30 am	30
SUN:	
Newswatch IV—5:30-6 am	4
Religion—6-8 am	4
Woody Woodpecker/Tom & Jerry/Tarzan—8-10 am	10
Saturday Night Live—10-11 am	10
Wrestling At The Chase—11 am-noon	4

	F
PM:	
Movies—noon-6	10
Super Movie—6-8:30	1
Glen Campbell—8:30-9	10
Newswatch—9-9:30	7
Think About Tomorrow—9:30-10	4
Religion—10-11	4
Phone Power—11-midnight	4
Missouri Football '82—midnight-1 am	7
Farber/Susskind/Religion—1-4 am	4
Newswatch V—4-4:30 am	7
Continuous Weather—4:30-5:30 am	30

120 sec: 4 x 30 sec.
90 sec: 3 x 30 sec.
60 sec: 2 x 30 sec.
10 sec: 6 x 30 sec.
R—Rotation. Program titles & times subject to change.
F—Fixed.
P—Preemptible.
IP—Immediately preemptible.

10. PROGRAM TIME RATES
Mon thru Fri 3:30-5:30 pm, 1 hr 1500
All program buys subject to an additional preemption fee.

11. SPECIAL FEATURES

COLOR
Schedules network color, Satellite color, film, slides, 1″ & 2″ tape and live.
Equipped with high and low band VTR.

13. CLOSING TIME
Commercial material must be in the station 72 hours before play date. Change in original commercial scheduling is accepted if received 72 hours prior to play dates. Verbal changes are accepted, but the station is not responsible for errors unless changes are received in writing.

FIGURE 17–2 (Courtesy Standard Rate & Data Service, Inc.)

COST OF TELEVISION TIME

The cost of television time varies widely, depending not only on the time of day but also the station's coverage area. Network time can be exceedingly expensive. For example, a 30-second commercial during a prime time network show can easily cost between $130,000 and $140,000. For many national advertisers, prime time television is unaffordable.

One consequence of the high cost of television advertising has been a reduction in the length of commercials. In the 1950s and early 1960s, most commercials were 60 seconds in length. Under the pressure of rising prices, however, Procter & Gamble pioneered the use of 30-second commercials, the dominant commercial length used today. However, 30-second commercials are often too short to permit the development of the advertising message. In the early 1980s, Procter & Gamble began using some 45-second commercials. Some stations do not accept commercials of this length, however. Table 17–2 shows the percent of commercials of various lengths that were used during the first half of 1980.

AVAILABILITY OF COMMERCIAL TIME

Prior to 1982, the *Television Code of the National Association of Broadcasters* limited the actual amount of television time available for advertising. A portion of the television code relating to nonprogram (commercial) material is reproduced below.

> In order that the time for non-program material and its placement shall best serve the viewer, the following standards are set forth in accordance with sound advertising practice.
> 1. Non-Program Material Definition: Non-program material, in both prime time and all other time, includes billboards, commercials, promotional announcements and all credits in excess of 30 seconds per program, except in feature films. In no event should credits exceed 40 seconds per program. The 40-second limitation on credits shall not apply, however, in any situation governed by a contract entered into before October 1, 1971. Public service announcements and promotional announcements for the same program are excluded from this definition.
> 2. Allowable Time for Non-Program Material.
>   a. In prime time on network affiliated stations, non-program material shall not exceed nine minutes in any 60-minute period.
>   b. In prime time on independent stations, non-program material shall not exceed 12 minutes in any 60-minute period. In the event that news programming is included within the three and

TABLE 17–2   Percent of commercials of various lengths

Commercial Length	Network	Nonnetwork
30-second	85.5%	84.2%
45-second	0.8	0.1
60-second	1.9	4.1
Other	11.8	11.6
Totals	100.0%	100.0%

Source: *Advertising Age Yearbook: 1981*, p. 281–2. Reprinted with permission from *Advertising Age Yearbook: 1981*. Copyright © 1981 by Crain Communications, Inc.

CHAPTER 17 | TELEVISION AND RADIO

one-half hour prime time period, not more than one 30-minute segment of news programming may be governed by time standards applicable to all other time. Prime time is a continuous period of not less than three and one-half consecutive hours per broadcast day as designated by the station between the hours of 6:00 P.M. and midnight.

    c. In all other time, non-program material shall not exceed 16 minutes in any 60-minute period.

    d. Children's Weekend Programming Time—Defined as that contiguous period of time between the hours of 7:00 AM and 2:00 PM on Saturday and Sunday. In programming designed primarily for children within this time period, non-program material shall not exceed 12 minutes in any 60-minute period.

3. Program Interruptions.

    a. Definition: A program interruption is any occurrence of non-programmed material within the main body of the program.

    b. In prime time, the number of program interruptions shall not exceed two within any 30-minute program, or four within any 60-minute program. Programs longer than 60 minutes shall be prorated at two interruptions per half-hour. The number of interruptions in 60-minute variety shows shall not exceed five.

    c. In all other time, the number of interruptions shall not exceed four within any 30-minute program period.

    d. In children's weekend time, as above defined in 2d, the number of program interruptions shall not exceed two within any 30-minute program or four within any 60-minute program.

    e. In both prime time and all other time, the following interruption standard shall apply within programs of 15 minutes or less in length:

      5-minute program—1 interruption;
      10-minute program—2 interruptions;
      15-minute program—2 interruptions.

    f. News, weather, sports and special events programs are exempt from the interruption standard because of the nature of such programs.

4. No more than four non-program material announcements shall be scheduled consecutively within programs, and no more than three non-program material announcements shall be scheduled consecutively during station breaks. The consecutive non-program material limitation shall not apply to a single sponsor who wishes to further reduce the number of interruptions in the program.[5]

In 1982 the Federal Trade Commission (FTC) challenged the television code, charging that limiting the amount of commercial time in programs was a restraint of trade. As a consequence, the code is no longer enforced by the National Association of Broadcasters. However, the networks and most major stations have indicated that they would continue to follow code guidelines.

OPTIONS IN TELEVISION ADVERTISING

Television advertisers have a number of options available when selecting the geographic areas to be covered by their advertising schedules. These options may be broadly described as network versus local buying.

[5]*The Television Code of the National Association of Broadcasters,* 17th ed., April, 1973 (Washington, D.C.: Code Authority, National Association of Broadcasters, 1973), 14–17.

PART IV | ADVERTISING MEDIA—STRATEGY AND PLANS

NETWORK SCHEDULING

Network scheduling may be either national or regional in nature. Normally, ABC, CBS, and NBC require the advertiser to contract for a minimum number of their affiliated stations. These stations provide national coverage, although some remote or isolated areas will not be reached by network stations. Under certain conditions, an advertiser can purchase only a portion of the network, referred to as a **network leg.** One network leg may cover the Mountain and Pacific states, Southeast region, or Eastern Seaboard. NFL football is often broadcast on a regional basis with various sections of the country receiving the games of those teams based in their region. NCAA basketball and other sports are often broadcast in a similar fashion. Regional networks cover certain portions of the country, such as the Northeast and Southeast. **Tailor-made** or **ad hoc networks** are formed when a group of stations join together for a special program. As soon as the program has been broadcast, the network passes out of existence. Additional regional options have been made available by cable television systems, similar to those of the individual cable systems.

To obtain the type of programming they want, advertisers put their own regional network together. In the 1960s, the Pet Milk Company produced a country music television program and then negotiated an arrangement with a line up of television stations in the southeastern region of the United States to carry the program in exchange for commercial time. Participating stations sold commercial time to local advertisers. Pet eventually abandoned the project because the program's production costs made it economically unfeasible.

LOCAL SCHEDULING

Local scheduling refers to those programs or commercials that originate with local television stations. An advertiser can build up regional or even national coverage through the use of local stations. Building national coverage in this way is usually undesirable because:

1 Buying is more complex because each local station must be contacted individually; a network purchase requires a single contract.
2 High cost rated local time is often unavailable when and where it is needed. The advertiser must run more commercials in order to achieve equivalent gross rating points, and reach and frequency estimates are more difficult to prepare and less accurate than those based on network programming.
3 Commercials purchased on a local basis often lose their effectiveness because of commercial clutter. They may be surrounded by other commercials, some for competing products.
4 A separate film or videotape must be sent to each participating station. Therefore, the flexibility offered by building national coverage through local purchases is often offset by higher costs.
5 Control, i.e., confirming the fact that the commercial ran when and where it was supposed to, is much more difficult through local stations than through the network.

As a consequence of these factors, most national advertisers that invest heavily in television use network schedules to provide basic national coverage and supplement their network schedule with local spot purchases in markets where additional coverage is needed.

METHODS OF BUYING TIME

Television advertisers can select from the **sponsorship, participations,** or **spot announcement** methods for buying time. Sponsorship and participations are available on a network and local market basis; spot announcements are available only from local stations.

Sponsorship. When an advertiser sponsors a program, the company assumes total financial responsibility for the production of the program as well as the advertising appearing within it. The advertiser may or may not control the content of the program. In the mid-1970s, the question of program control became a major issue in the advertising industry.[6] In their frenzied race for ratings, television networks resorted to excessive use of violence, sex, and nightclub humor that many viewers found offensive. Since viewers tend to blame the advertiser rather than the networks for these programs, advertisers live in constant fear of consumer boycotts. During the Vietnam War, a major package goods company cancelled the Smothers Brothers' television show from its schedule because the entertainers' protests against the war offended many viewers; these viewers wrote irate letters to the advertiser. General Motors withdrew its sponsorship of "Jesus of Nazareth" because of a storm raised by some fundamentalist religious groups. In the latter instance, General Motors lost approximately $6 million that it had invested in producing the program. Procter & Gamble picked up the broadcast after GM's cancellation and ended up with one of the best buys in television history.

Despite these contretemps, program sponsorship offers worthwhile values. First, the advertiser does have control over the type of program in which its commercials appear, such as sports, drama, adventure, situation comedies, or variety. Second, sponsorship offers the opportunity for extensive merchandising and collateral advertising, often employing the star of the program as a product spokesperson. Third, sponsorship offers the opportunity to run two and three minute commercials that develop the product's story fully. Unfortunately, the cost of television production is so high that few advertisers can afford the luxury of sponsorship, particularly in prime time. One alternative is multiple sponsorship, when two or more advertisers underwrite the production costs and share the commercial time. This approach is frequently used for sports events such as the World Series and prestigious, prime time programs.

Participations. About 90 percent of network commercial time is sold on a participating basis. Each of a number of advertisers pays for 30 seconds or 60 seconds of commercial time in one or more programs. An advertiser may participate in a particular program one time only or have multiple participations on a regular or irregular

---

[6]"Protests Mount Against More Advertiser Control of TV Content," *Advertising Age,* 14 November 1977, 1.

basis. In contrast to sponsorship, the participating advertiser does not assume financial responsibility for the production of the program. The network or the individual station underwrites programming costs and then prices commercial time within the program at a rate that will recover costs and provide a profit.

There are a number of advantages to using participations rather than sponsorship. First, since the advertiser may use any number of participating spots, the size of the television expenditure can be adjusted to the available budget. Second, using participating spots on a number of programs enables the advertiser to achieve greater reach while reducing frequency within the same number of gross rating points. Third, the advertiser's cost-per-thousand may be substantially reduced over the cost-per-thousand for sponsorship.

One disadvantage of participations is that the individual advertiser loses program identity and merchandising opportunities. Second, advertisers normally lose some control over the programs in which their commercials appear. All media planning and buying is a trade-off. One balances reach against frequency, weight against budget, impact against continuity, and control against flexibility.

Spot announcements.   Spot announcements are bought from local television stations and appear between programs rather than within them. There is little opportunity for an advertiser to identify a product with a show since the announcements are isolated from the shows themselves. Another disadvantage is that the break between programs is often filled with competing commercials, station identification, and promotional spots for upcoming programs. Since viewers expect several minutes of solid advertising, they often use the time in other ways.

BUYING TELEVISION TIME

Network time is sold by network representatives who negotiate directly with advertisers and advertising agencies. Local stations use local salespeople to contact local advertisers; national rep organizations operating on a commission basis represent a number of stations throughout the country, although one organization will normally represent no more than one station in a particular market.

NETWORK SELLING PRACTICES

Network selling can be divided into four periods, each with different pricing practices. These periods are: (a) early preseason; (b) late preseason; (c) beginning of the season; and (d) seasonal selling.

Early preseason.   Historically, the network season starts in September. Early in the preseason (six to eight months before the season starts), prices are established by the seller. Presumably, these prices are related to the seller's costs and projected profit needs; prices are relatively inflexible.

Negotiation is still a major factor because of the diversity of the buying needs that the seller faces. Buyers may: (a) have options on or control programs and seek desirable time segments; (b) have options on time segments and seek desirable programs; (c) seek a limited number of programs and time slots designed to reach well-defined audiences that will provide an appropriate commercial environment for their products; (d) seek a large number of programs and time segments and participate in a wide variety of programs with quite different audience characteristics.

Late preseason. This period is one to six months prior to the television season and the time when buyers' influence becomes apparent. Unit prices fluctuate widely because the seller is constantly aware of his unsold position versus the availability of buyers. Unit prices begin to give way to packages, wherein the cost of each element in the package is not defined. A number of time units, usually scattered among many shows, are offered at an arbitrary price.

Beginning of the season. At the beginning of the actual television season, pricing of unsold inventories is a reflection of the individual network's profit position, size of its unsold inventory, and availability of buyers. Packages of commercial time may be available at half the price they were offered at six months earlier. On the other hand, the buyer is in the position of evaluating and purchasing a limited number of opportunities that consist of shows with little prospect for large audiences.

Seasonal buying. After the season is under way, the size of the unsold inventory and availability of buyers continue to be the prime pricing determinants. The audience rating of each unsold show, or segment of a show, becomes a major factor in focusing buyer interest and results in further volatility in the market.

As a result of this buying and selling climate, the role of published discounts is minimized. This is particularly true since published discounts in network television apply only to time charges and are not applicable to program costs. Considering the importance of negotiation and renegotiation, it is almost impossible to determine whether two advertisers in the same network program at the same time are paying the same price, even though they both may be earning the same published discount. The variable is not the discount, but the sum of the base prices upon which discounts are taken. As a result, in evaluating network value one needs to look at the cost-per-thousand viewers paid, not the discount earned.

The following example illustrates the variations in pricing that often occur in network television. For an expenditure of $6,240,000:

☐ During the preseason, Company A buys a 30-second participation per week for 52 weeks at $120,000 per participation.
☐ After the season is underway, Company B opportunistically buys two 30-second participations per week for 45 weeks at $69,300 per participation.
☐ Company C opportunistically spends $1,500,000 and purchases twenty-four 30-second participations in a four-week period at $62,500 per participation.

This is not to say that the average ratings' audience per participation purchased by Company C will be similar in size to those purchased by Company A. It is quite possible that some of the twenty-four participations purchased by Company C were offered months earlier to Company A at almost double the price paid by

Company C. Therefore, published discounts for network television aren't all that important.

Generally, network television is a national medium, oriented to the national advertiser whose product has broad, national distribution and sales. In some instances, network television can be purchased on a regional basis through the use of network legs. The premium for such purchases is generally about 30 percent over national rates for the same coverage area.

LOCAL (SPOT) SELLING PRACTICES

The pricing policies and published discounts applying to advertising placed with local television stations depend on the station involved, its competitive market position, size of the market, and number of competitive stations.

Some factors present in network television buying and selling are present in spot television. However, the large inventories of available time on network affiliated stations are found outside of network time. On these stations, the supply of local time during and immediately adjacent to prime time is quite limited. Since the largest television audiences are available during prime time, it is common practice to price these time segments at premium, nondiscounted rates. The supply of local commercial time is greatest and the audience much smaller during the remainder of the broadcast day. These time segments are discounted to a substantial degree.

Stations without network affiliations have a sizable supply of commercial time, regardless of the time of day. The pricing policies of these stations are generally characterized by liberal discounts, flexible pricing, and negotiation.

The demand for spot television fluctuates widely from market to market and by time of the year. In periods of low demand, negotiation by buyer and seller may result in concessions in the requirements for discounts and, in some cases, price cutting. As in the case of newspapers, the rates charged national advertisers are generally higher than those charged local purchasers.

The volume of weekly activity determines discount levels in spot television. A company spending $1 million to run twelve announcements per week for four weeks may earn a 50 percent greater discount than another company spending $5 million to run six announcements for thirty-seven weeks. Additional discounts may be earned by accepting preemptable schedules, giving the station the right to preempt any particular spot at its discretion. Table 17–3 shows the number of stations in the top fifty markets offering maximum discounts at various levels. These discounts include both dollar volume and preemptability discounts.

STRENGTHS AND WEAKNESSES OF TELEVISION

Television is generally considered the most powerful of advertising media because of its unique combination of sight and sound, ability to deliver large audiences, and flexibility it offers for varying coverage on a market by market basis.

The advantages of television are:

☐ *Product demonstration.* To a much greater extent than other commercial media, television provides an opportunity for product demonstration.

TABLE 17–3 Television discount ranges in top fifty markets

Discount Range	Number of Stations
0 – 9%	3
10 – 19%	34
20 – 29%	34
30 – 39%	59
40 – 49%	33
50 –	25
Total stations	188

Source: Compiled from *Standard Rate and Data Service*.

☐ *Captive audience.* Unlike print media where advertising can be easily ignored, a person has to make a special effort to avoid being exposed to commercials during a television program one is viewing.

☐ *Wide coverage.* Because 98 percent of U.S. households have television sets, television provides penetration of 77.8 million homes. In the average week, television will be viewed by 70 percent of all adults and teenagers, and 80 percent of all children between the ages of 2 and 12. A popular program can reach 12 million households; a major event such as the Super Bowl will reach almost 35 million homes.

☐ *Flexibility.* Television is highly flexible in time of day and geographic coverage. Advertisers may use as many commercials as they can afford and buy a single market, national coverage, or anything in between. In addition, advertising weight can be adjusted by market in terms of the advertiser's needs.

On the negative side, television's two major limitations are:

☐ *Expense.* Television is expensive, from the standpoint of commercial production and cost of television time. The cost for a 30-second commercial during a popular prime time, network show may exceed $140,000. A 30-second spot in a major market such as Chicago may exceed $3,500. As a result, many advertisers cannot afford a significant television effort throughout their areas of distribution.

☐ *Lack of selectivity.* Although some selectivity is available in television, it is not really a selective medium. For example, although the average soap opera is thought of as a woman's program, it will reach an audience consisting of approximately 62 percent adult women over 18, and 38 percent men, teenagers, and children.

RADIO

Radio is the most ubiquitous of media. About 440 million radio sets, over five sets per household, are in use in the United States. This figure includes some 85 to 90 million car radios, as well as stationary and portable radios of every size, shape, and description. The radio audience is served by approximately 4600 AM stations, 4400 FM stations, and four national networks—the American Broadcasting Company,[7] Columbia Broadcasting System, Mutual Broadcasting System, and National Broadcasting Company. In addition, there are a number of regional networks. Some are highly specialized, such as the Country Music Network, Farm Directors Network, National Spanish Language Network, and the Ivy Network Corporation (college radio).

With the appearance of television, many people forecast the death of network radio. Radio was in critical trouble for some time, but it has survived and grown stronger since about 1961. The character of radio has changed substantially, however. Table 17–4 compares advertising expenditures in radio for 1950 and 1980. This ta-

[7]The American Broadcasting Company is segmented into four operating divisions: American Contemporary Network; American Entertainment Network; American FM Network; and American Information Radio Network. Each appeals to the particular programming formats of their affiliated stations.

TABLE 17–4 Comparison of radio advertising expenditures, 1950–1980

	Expenditures in Millions of Dollars		Percentage of Total Expenditures	
	1950	1980	1950	1980
Network radio	196	180	32.3%	4.8%
Spot	136	774	22.5	20.5
Local	273	2,823	45.2	74.7

Source: Reprinted with permission from the September 14, 1981 issue of *Advertising Age*. Copyright © 1981 by Crain Communications, Inc.

ble indicates that radio has become, primarily, a local and spot medium.

RADIO COVERAGE

Radio coverage varies from station to station depending on the station's power, its antenna system, soil conductivity, and the **Heaviside layer.** The Heaviside layer is an atmospheric condition consisting of a ceiling of electrical particles that bounces radio signals back to earth, particularly at night. Because of this phenomenon, night coverage for a radio station is generally greater than day coverage. In order to minimize interference between stations, the FCC may require a station to operate under a lower power output at night. The FCC also assigns station licenses on the basis of four classes of channels:

☐ *Class 1.* Clear channel stations are assigned 50,000 watts, receive almost exclusive use of a particular frequency, and serve a wide area free from interference.

☐ *Class 2.* These stations are clear channel during the day only and, because of the Heaviside effect, must go off the air at sunset so that they will not interfere with Class 1 stations.

☐ *Class 3.* Regional stations have a power range up to 5000 watts and may cover several markets. The actual coverage of a regional station will be limited by other, distant stations that share the same frequency.

☐ *Class 4.* Local stations, designed to serve a single community, fall in this class. Generally, they operate on 250 watts or less and have a receiving range of about 25 miles.

The actual coverage of a station is measured in terms of its **field intensity.** Using portable measuring equipment mounted in a car, signal strength is measured at various distances and in different directions. On the basis of these measurements, coverage maps are drawn showing primary and secondary coverage areas. A primary coverage area includes those areas in which the signal is consistently strong. The secondary coverage area is that area in which the signal is strong most of the time.

BUYING RADIO TIME

Radio is sold in the same way television is; like television, radio may be bought on a network, spot, or local basis. However, network pricing practices differ in some respects from local and spot practices.

CHAPTER 17 | TELEVISION AND RADIO

NETWORK RADIO SELLING PRACTICES

Pricing in network radio, as in the case of network television, is influenced by the same conditions attendant to any perishable, volatile commodity. Compared to network television, the total amount of time available for sale on network radio is relatively small, being restricted for the most part to network news shows and a few other news or sports features. Further, production and programming costs are quite low compared to television; therefore, the financial risks are substantially less and the networks have a much lower break-even point.

In periods when the market is soft, and especially when a large advertiser withdraws from the medium, network radio selling practices become fiercely competitive. Concessions in base price, as well as discount requirements, are common incentives for prospective advertisers. Because the medium does not have a programming season like network television, these concessions are not seasonally predictable. Instead, they are triggered by the individual network's profit position at any time. Since network radio is nationally oriented, the advertiser who desires to use it regionally generally pays a premium for this privilege. The size of the premium is determined by negotiation and heavily influenced by the network's inventory position.

Because of the importance of negotiation and wide variations in base prices, the actual price of a network radio buy may have little relation to published discounts, which range as high as 53 percent.

LOCAL AND SPOT RADIO

The pricing policies and practices in local and spot radio are more liberal than those generally found in spot television. Two factors attribute to this. First, on the average, there are four to five times as many radio stations per market as television stations. Thus, selling competition is more intense. Second, because there is less network programming in radio, the amount of commercial time for sale on network affiliated radio stations is about twice as great as that available on network affiliated television stations.

As in the case of television, local radio stations establish several time classifications based on audience size and price these time segments accordingly. Figure 17–3 is an example of a radio listing for station WAFB (FM) in Baton Rouge, Louisiana. Note the rate differences in Item 6 between time classifications and the discounts based on the number of spots per week.

Wide differences in the pricing practices of different radio stations in the same market are a common occurrence. Generally, three or four stations will attract 60 to 70 percent of the listeners in a major market. These stations adhere fairly rigidly to published prices and discounts. The other stations in the market compete for the scraps with liberal pricing and discount policies, an emphasis on negotiation, and frequent price concessions.

Weekly rather than annual volume is the most significant factor in earning discounts on spot and local radio. An examination of the 500-odd radio stations in the top fifty markets indicates that maximum discounts range from 0 to 60 percent.

STRENGTHS AND WEAKNESSES OF RADIO

Radio is an interesting medium and, since it is overshadowed in the broadcast field by television, its unique virtues are sometimes overlooked.

- ☐ *Low cost.* Time and production radio costs are relatively low; therefore, radio advertising is within the reach of most national or local advertisers. On a cost-per-thousand basis, radio is the most economical major commercial media for reaching consumers.
- ☐ *Selectivity.* Radio can be highly selective in reaching certain target markets. For example, farm radio with its reports on the weather, livestock, and grain markets zeros in on the farmer's interests. Teenagers can be reached efficiently with rock music stations, and there are dozens of stations that broadcast partly, or entirely, in a variety of foreign languages for various ethnic groups.
- ☐ *Flexibility.* Radio is highly flexible in geographic reach and time exposure. On the average day, radio will reach 75 percent of United States adults.
- ☐ *Useful supplementary medium.* Radio is an excellent supplementary medium that can be used to intensify coverage for relatively short periods of time at a minimum cost. Many advertisers use it only as a supplementary medium, but it can be used as a primary medium through intensive schedules.
- ☐ *Local personalities.* Some local radio personalities have loyal followers and are extremely effective in selling products.

On the negative side, the reach of individual programs is relatively small. Ratings of two and three are not uncommon. As a consequence, intensive programming is necessary to build reach. In addition, radio is an aural medium; it is relatively easy to tune out a radio commercial.

Baton Rouge

(7 AM; 4 FM)
East Baton Rouge Parish—Map Location D-4
See SRDS Consumer market map and data at beginning of the state.

WAFB (FM)
BATON ROUGE
1969

Katz Radio

RAB NRBA

Media Code 4 219 0775 9.00 **Mid 010700-000**
Guaranty Broadcasting Corp.
844 Government St., Baton Rouge, LA 70802. Phone 504-383-9999, TWX, 510-993-3406.
Mailing Address: Box 2671, Baton Rouge, LA 70821.

PROGRAMMING DESCRIPTION
WAFB (FM): Programmed to reach an adult 18-34 audience. MUSIC: adult contemporary. Contact Representative for further details. Rec'd 10/28/81.

1. PERSONNEL
Manager—Manuel R. Broussard.
Sales Manager—Mike Norwood.

2. REPRESENTATIVES
Katz Radio.

3. FACILITIES
ERP 100,000 w.; 98.1 mhz. Stereo.
Operating schedule: 24 hours daily. CST.
Antenna ht.: 1,550 ft. above average terrain.

4. AGENCY COMMISSION
15%.

5. GENERAL ADVERTISING See coded regulations
General: 1a, 2a, 3a, 4a, 4d, 5, 8.
Rate Protection: 15b.
Basic Rates: 20a, 21b, 28b, 29e.
Contracts: 40a, 41, 45, 46, 51c.
Comb.; Cont. Discounts: 60a, 60k.
Cancellation: 70b, 70e, 71a.
Prod. Services: 81.
Affiliated with CBS.
Member: The Louisiana Network.

TIME RATES
NATIONAL AND LOCAL RATES SAME
No. 17 Eff 6/1/81—Rec'd 6/22/82.
AAA—Mon thru Fri 5:30-10 am & 3-8 pm; Sat 9 am-5 pm.
AA—Mon thru Fri 10 am-3 pm; Sat 6-9 am & 5-8 pm; Sun 6 am-8 pm.
A—Mon thru Sun 8 pm-1 am.
BTA—Mon thru Sun 5-1 am, immediately preemptible.

6. SPOT ANNOUNCEMENTS

PER	1 min				30 sec/less			
WK:	6 ti	12 ti	18 ti	24 ti	6 ti	12 ti	18 ti	24 ti
AAA	25	24	23	22	22	21	20	19
AA	22	21	20	19	19	18	17	16
A	19	18	17	16	17	16	15	14
BTA	...	19	18	17	...	16	15	14

Fixed position, extra 5.00 per spot.

FIGURE 17–3 (Courtesy Standard Rate & Data Service, Inc.)

SUMMARY

Broadcast media differ from print media in the characteristics of the media themselves and the structures of the industries. Television and radio also differ in terms of their characteristics, the ways that they are used, and the selling practices that characterize their industries.

In discussing television, it is important to understand the relationships between weight, gross rating points, unduplicated reach, and frequency.

Television time can be bought on either a network or local basis, and there are advantages and disadvantages to each method of buying. In addition to these geographic options, advertisers may buy television on the basis of program sponsorship, participations, or spot announcements. Each of these approaches has strengths and weaknesses.

At one time, radio occupied the role that television does today. With the rapid growth of television, radio has become primarily a local and spot medium.

Like television, the basic unit of the radio industry is the individual station. Unlike television, however, local radio stations vary in terms of their power output. Four classes of stations are licensed by the Federal Communications Commission.

REVIEW QUESTIONS

1 Identify the major differences between print and broadcast media.
2 Describe the structure of the broadcast industry.
3 Explain the following terms: (a) penetration; (b) coverage area; (c) sets-in-use; (d) rating; and (e) share-of-audience.
4 Explain what is meant by the weight of a television schedule. How is weight related to reach and frequency?
5 Explain the major geographic options that an advertiser has in buying television time.
6 Distinguish among sponsorship, participations, and spots as ways of buying television advertising. Given no budget constraints, which would you prefer to use and why?
7 Briefly characterize the selling practices in network television in the: (a) early preseason; (b) late preseason; (c) beginning of the season; and (d) during the season.
8 Identify and distinguish among the four classes of radio stations licensed by the FCC.
9 How does the selling of time in spot radio differ from the selling of spot television? Why do these differences exist?
10 Why is it suggested that radio is an excellent supplementary medium rather than a basic medium for national advertisers?

DISCUSSION QUESTIONS

1 Television has been criticized by many for clutter, an excessive number of commercials. Do you think that the FCC should issue regulations designed to reduce the number of commercials? Why or why not?
2 Do you think cable television can cause regular television to become as fragmented as radio in terms of programming? If so, what would be the effects on: (a) television networks; (b) the cost of commercials; (c) the

television measurement services; (d) local television stations; (e) time buying?

3 As pointed out in the text, the high cost of television time precludes many smaller companies from using television. Do you think this is equitable? Why or why not? What do you think should be done about this situation?

PROBLEM

As advertising manager for a major food marketing company, you are negotiating with the networks for a package of participating spots in prime time shows. You are considering two offerings; both consist of participations on established shows.

Your cost for Package A, which will have estimated average ratings of 20, is $4,757,688 for a 30-second commercial, once a week for 52 weeks. Based on audience research, this package will provide the following exposure pattern:

☐ Forty-five percent of the total exposures will be one time in a four-week period.
☐ Twenty-five percent will be two times in a four-week period.
☐ Twenty percent will be three times in a four-week period.
☐ Ten percent will be four times in a four-week period.

Package B is expected to achieve an average rating of 23 and will cost $5,192,356 for a 30-second participation, once a week for 52 weeks. You expect the following pattern of exposure:

☐ Thirty-five percent of the total exposures will be one time during a four week period.
☐ Twenty-five percent will be two times.
☐ Twenty-five percent will be three times.
☐ Fifteen percent will be four times.

You want to achieve a net unduplicated reach over a four-week period of approximately 38 to 39 million households. In selecting a television vehicle, you are interested in the greatest unduplicated reach as long as the cost-per-thousand for unduplicated reach is not out of line.

ASSIGNMENT

Knowing that there are approximately 77.8 million television households in the United States, analyze the audiences of the two packages in terms of:

1 Four-week cume.
2 Net unduplicated reach in a four-week period.
3 Cost-per-thousand for total audience.
4 Cost-per-thousand for net unduplicated households.

On the basis of this information, answer the following questions:

1 How well do each of these vehicles accomplish your objectives?
2 Which do you recommend, if either, and why?

18
Other Media

FROM MINUSCULE BUDGETS TO SHOPPING MALLS

'THERE ARE NO TERMITES IN SPOKANE'

Western Insecticide, a small company in Spokane, was doing poorly. Overenthusiastic real estate salespeople were convincing home buyers that there were no termites in Spokane, a persuasive but inaccurate assessment. Western Insecticide had another problem—a minuscule $5,000 advertising budget to counter the "no termite" propaganda.

Corker-Sullivan, a local advertising agency, came up with an imaginative and effective use of Western's advertising funds. Corker-Sullivan rented a 48-foot-wide outdoor board in a secondary location in downtown Spokane. Emblazoned on the board under Western's logo were the words: "There are no termites in Spokane." A week after the board went up, the agency had a huge chunk cut out of the side of the board, as though a giant termite had taken a bite out. Every few days additional bites were taken until nothing was left but the Western logo. As a result, Western's business increased by 65 percent. People went out of their way to see the board; local authorities reported that the daily traffic count at the board's site increased from 28,000 to 32,000.[1]

RIDE AN AD TO WORK

Advertising has long been a source of funds that made a free and independent press possible in the United States. Television, newspapers, magazines, and radio, primary sources of free and unfettered expression, have always been largely supported by advertising. And now, advertising is being recognized for its role in supporting low cost public transportation.

[1]Ed Zotti, "Far from the Prosaic Crowd," *Advertising Age,* 13 July 1981, S–12.

The city of Seattle is starting a new mass transit system. One problem is how to finance the venture. If all goes according to plan, Seattle will pay for the system by ad revenues from car cards and fares. Official estimates are that $52,000 of the annual operating costs will be paid for by advertising.[2]

ADVERTISING AND SHOPPING MALLS

Shopping malls may become one of the leading out-of-home advertising vehicles of the 1980s. Studies have indicated that shopping malls attract nearly 80 percent of the adult residents of a market, 66 percent of whom are female and 44 percent between the ages of 18 and 34.

Since malls are intended to be architecturally pleasing, many mall operators have been reluctant to display advertising, fearing it would destroy the ambience of the mall setting. However, out-of-home advertising companies are designing mall advertising furniture that blends into the overall mall design. Using mirrors and various wood finishes, the new approach is expected to attract the interest of mall developers who, because of the high cost of mall construction and maintenance, are looking for extra sources of revenue.[3]

Billboards, car cards, and mall advertising are but three examples from a group of media that are sometimes called **minor, supplementary,** or **unmeasured media.** All of these terms are misnomers when one considers the diversity of the media involved and the scope of their activities. Direct mail, for example, is generally considered a minor medium, even though it is estimated to account for over $7.5 billion in advertising per year. While $7.5 billion is probably a low estimate, it is substantially larger than the expenditures in magazines, radio, or business papers.

[2]"Seattle Trolley Rides on Advertising," *Advertising Age*, 10 May 1982, 50.

[3]Anna Sobczynski, "A Scrapbook of Technology," *Advertising Age*, 13 July 1981, S—16.

Outdoor advertising, generally thought of as a supplementary medium, is sometimes used as a primary advertising effort by some national brands. Technically, outdoor advertising is a **measured medium,** but there is more uncertainty and dissatisfaction over its measurement than broadcast or print media. Thus, the advertising press periodically raises questions about the reliability of the audience projections for outdoor advertising.

The purpose of this chapter is to briefly examine some of the more widely recognized miscellaneous media, pointing up their salient characteristics, strengths, and weaknesses. Under appropriate conditions, all of them have value for a particular advertiser. None, however, have the stature and prestige of print and broadcast. The advertising media covered in the following material are: (a) outdoor; (b) transit; (c) directory; (d) direct; (e) program; (f) film; (g) exhibit; (h) specialty; and (i) point-of-purchase.

OUTDOOR ADVERTISING

Outdoor advertising is generally considered the dominant out-of-home medium. Not all advertising that appears outdoors is considered outdoor advertising, however. Only those signs or billboards that meet standards established by the Outdoor Advertising Association of America (OAAA) and are placed by recognized plant operators are so considered. Under OAAA definitions, most of the signs and posters seen along roads, on buildings, restaurants, or bars are not considered outdoor advertising in the technical sense. Approximately 5 percent of all outdoor signs are recognized by the organized outdoor advertising industry.[4] The organized industry, however, accounts for an estimated $600 million, about two-thirds placed by national advertisers.[5] Since there is no dependable data on outdoor signs not placed by the organized industry, and national advertisers generally contract only with recognized outdoor plants, this is the segment of outdoor advertising that will be discussed in the following material.

ORGANIZATION OF THE INDUSTRY

Outdoor advertising is a local medium, and the basic unit of the industry is the local plant operator. There are over 1000 recognized plant operators in the United States, covering 11,000 markets. Plant operators are independent business firms which own or lease sites for outdoor displays, erect the structures for the signs, and sell space to advertisers for a period of time ranging from one month to five years. Plant operators are also responsible for physically placing the advertising on the sign structure and for its maintenance. In major markets, several plant operators compete for sites which have high traffic counts, i.e., streets or intersections which carry heavy traffic.

OAAA is the trade association for the industry. A division of the OAAA, the Institute for Outdoor Advertising (IOA), serves as a mar-

---

[4]Report, *This Outdoor Advertising,* Institute of Outdoor Advertising, 1971.
[5]Robert J. Coen, "Ad $ Outlook Brightens," *Advertising Age,* 14 September 1981, 48.

keting and promotional arm for the industry. Its activities include the publication of *The Buyers' Guide to Outdoor Advertising*, a quarterly publication containing the rates and number of panels (billboards) per showing in all markets represented by association members.

Until 1977, the National Outdoor Advertising Bureau (NOAB), a service organization owned by a group of advertising agencies, performed a contracting function, at a commission of 3.66 percent, for major outdoor advertisers. NOAB also handled billing and paying, sent instructions to plant operators, and carried out field inspections to guarantee that instructions were being followed and outdoor posters were being properly maintained. To save money, agencies began assuming these services themselves; NOAB became unprofitable and closed shop.

FORMS OF OUTDOOR ADVERTISING

The major types of outdoor advertising used by national advertisers are **posters, painted bulletins,** and **spectaculars.** Posters are the most commonly used and are the mainstay of the industry. Painted bulletins are more costly and usually placed in better locations. Spectaculars are the largest, most expensive, and most dramatic of the outdoor forms. They may have moving parts, belch smoke, or employ other attention-getting devices. Spectaculars are usually reserved for locations where the traffic count warrants their cost.

Posters. Poster sizes are referred to in terms of **sheets.** The term originated when it took twenty-four of the largest sheets of paper that printing presses could hold to cover a sign 12 by 25 feet.[6] Even though the size of presses has changed, the term "24-sheet" is customarily used to refer to a standard sized poster. Today, posters are still mounted on 12 by 25 foot signs, but three sizes of posters are generally used:

1 *24-sheet posters.* (104″ × 234″) The rest of the board area is a margin of blank paper.
2 *30-sheet posters.* (115″ × 259″) Twenty-five percent more advertising space than 24-sheet, surrounded by a blank margin.
3 *Bleed posters.* Extends artwork to the edge of the frame. Bleed posters average 40 percent larger than 24-sheet.

In addition to these large-sized posters, there are also 6-sheet and 3-sheet posters, which are generally found in suburban shopping areas and on neighborhood store walls.

The most commonly used poster size is 30-sheet. This size is available in all major markets in the continental United States, except Alaska. Posters may be illuminated or regular (nonilluminated); in markets of over 100,000 population, about two-thirds of the posters are of the illuminated type. The percentage of illuminated posters drops to about 5 percent in markets under 10,000. Situated on

---

[6]When referring to the dimensions of large outdoor posters, the width is vertical and the length is horizontal.

CHAPTER 18 | OTHER MEDIA

primary and secondary arteries throughout a market, poster locations may be specified to conform to ethnic and demographic marketing areas. Figure 18–1 shows a typical 30-sheet poster for Swift's Premium Franks. Note the sparseness of copy. Since posters are often seen from a passing car, copy is generally restricted to package identification and/or brief copy point.

Painted bulletins.   The second major type of outdoor advertising is the painted bulletin. Instead of being printed on paper and mounted on a sign, painted bulletins are painted directly on movable steel panels which are then mounted on the sign structure. While the size of painted bulletins may vary, the most common size is 14 by 48 feet, substantially larger than a 30-sheet poster which is about 9.5 by 21.5 feet.

Painted bulletins are commonly illuminated and may include protrusions that extend beyond the top, bottom, or sides; they may also contain some form of animation. These bulletins may be mounted in a single location or rotated from one location to another on a monthly or bimonthly basis in order to increase coverage. Because of their cost, which may exceed $1,000 a month for a single bulletin, they are generally found only in high traffic areas. Figure 18–2 shows a painted bulletin for Montgomery Ward.

Spectaculars.   On the bases of size and construction, spectaculars are the most conspicuous outdoor signs. Since they are individually designed and constructed, there is no standard size; the cost of the space and construction are negotiated. Prices range from $25,000 to several hundred thousand dollars a year; the most elaborate may include flashing lights, animation, simulated waterfalls, simulated explosions, or virtually anything else that can be conceived. The best known single location for spectaculars is the Times Square area of New York City where the spectaculars on display are viewed by mil-

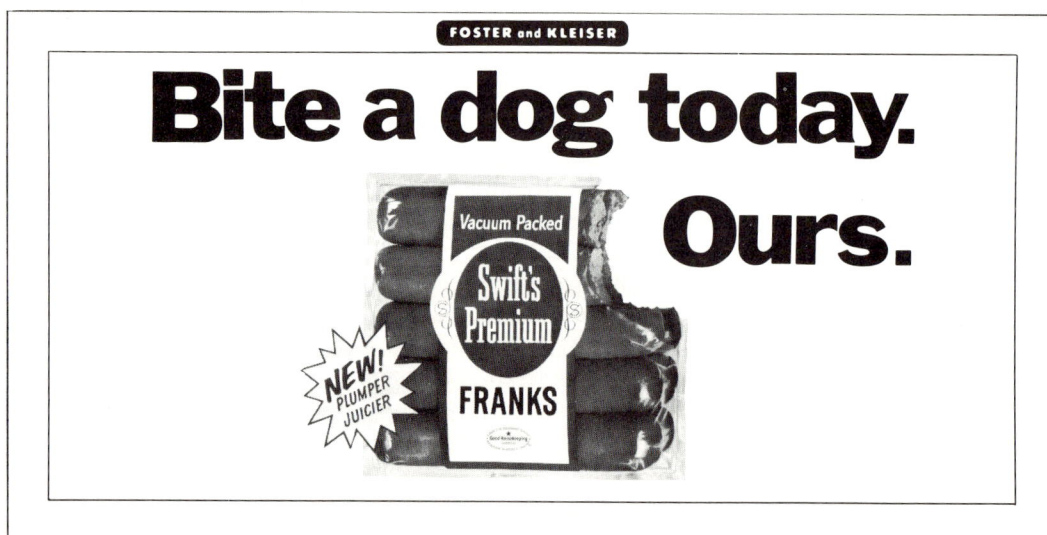

FIGURE 18–1   30-sheet poster (Courtesy Swift & Co. and Foster and Kleiser)

FIGURE 18–2   Painted bulletin (Courtesy Montgomery Ward & Co., Inc.)

lions of people each year. Figure 18–3 shows a spectacular for the Bulova Accutron.

OUTDOOR ADVERTISING SHOWINGS

Historically, outdoor advertising was measured in terms of **showings.** The base unit was a 100 showing; this designation did not

FIGURE 18–3   Bulova Accutron spectacular. The picture and numerals constantly change. (U.P.I. photo)

CHAPTER 18 | OTHER MEDIA

refer to the number of panels used. A 100 showing in a particular market consisted of whatever number of boards was necessary to reach approximately 90 percent of the adult population during a 28-day period, with an average frequency of a little over once a day. Therefore, a 100 showing in a small community might consist of a single panel, whereas a 100 showing in a large metropolitan area might require several hundred panels. A 50 showing, which consisted of about half as many panels, would normally reach about 85 percent of the adult population with an average frequency of once every other day. Since there is considerable duplication among people who drive a great deal, net reach will be significantly less than theoretical reach. However, no accurate estimates of net reach exist because the standard method of measurement is a traffic count, thereby making it impossible to estimate reach without including duplication.

In 1973 the OAAA replaced the term "showing" with **gross rating points.** A 100 gross rating points, the approximate equivalent of a 100 showing, theoretically provides a daily effective circulation equal to the population of the market. Both terms are currently in use, but gross rating points is becoming standard. In the following discussion, "showing" will be used for convenience; however, recognize that gross rating points could also be used without a substantial change of meaning.

Showings are normally sold in multiples of 25; advertisers may buy 25, 50, 75, 100, 125, and so on. Some outdoor plants offer only 50 and 100 showings. Others sell fractional showings, i.e., odd amounts of panels in quantities of less than a 25 showing. Generally, a 150 showing is considered sufficient to saturate a market.

BUYING OUTDOOR ADVERTISING

Posters are generally bought on the basis of a particular size showing, a certain proportion of which will be illuminated. The cost of a 100 showing will depend on the size of the market and number of panels required. The minimum length of a purchase is one month. Table 18–1 shows the costs and other relevant data for 100 and 50 showings or gross rating points for the top 100 metropolitan areas in the United States.

TABLE 18–1   Estimated outdoor poster costs for top 100 markets

	100 Gross Rating Points			50 Gross Rating Points		
Markets	Unilluminated Panels	Illuminated Panels	Monthly Cost	Unilluminated Panels	Illuminated Panels	Monthly Costs
Top 10	516	2,315	$ 873,487	263	1,163	$ 438,954
Top 20	885	3,227	1,218,349	449	1,619	613,350
Top 30	1,041	4,066	1,500,766	527	2,041	755,288
Top 40	1,292	4,663	1,700,727	652	2,340	855,268
Top 50	1,552	5,116	1,871,673	780	2,575	941,935
Top 100	2,407	6,373	2,319,594	1,221	3,221	1,173,751

Source: Institute of Outdoor Advertising, *Buyers' Guide to Outdoor Advertising* (January 1979).

Unlike posters, painted bulletins are bought separately on the basis of a traffic flow map showing the location of the sites in relation to the main arteries and traffic routes of the market. The cost of a particular bulletin will depend upon the amount of traffic exposed to it which, in turn, will depend upon its location and position. Table 18–2 shows the average cost per month per painted bulletin for various groups of the top 50 markets. Bulletins are generally purchased for 12 months.

Spectaculars are negotiated on an individual basis. Because of the costs of construction, they are generally contracted for three to five years, with an option for renewal.

OUTDOOR ADVERTISING CIRCULATION

Circulation in outdoor advertising refers to the number of people who may pass a given location and have a reasonable chance of seeing the advertising. By convention, this number is measured as half the pedestrians, half the automobiles, and one-fourth of the surface transportation passengers who pass the sign. The primary source for such data is the Traffic Audit Bureau, composed of members of the advertising industry. The Traffic Audit Bureau serves the same function as that of the audit bureau of circulation for print media; it audits and validates the circulation figures claimed by plant operators.

STRENGTHS AND WEAKNESSES OF OUTDOOR ADVERTISING

Although it can be tailored to reach ethnic and demographic groups through selective placement in major markets, outdoor advertising is a mass medium. As a local medium, it is geographically flexible and may also be used seasonally for periods as short as one month. On a cost-per-thousand basis, it is relatively inexpensive.

Outdoor advertising also has severe shortcomings. Limitations must be placed on the amount of copy that can be employed. Viewers are usually moving, either in moving vehicles or walking. For the most part, product identification and a short slogan is all that is functional. In addition, its audience figures are ambiguous, and meaningful duplication figures as well as circulation by age groups are nonexistent. While outdoor advertising may be used as either a

TABLE 18–2 Rotating painted bulletin costs within top 50 markets

Markets	Average Monthly Cost Per Bulletin
1–10	$1,934
11–20	1,540
21–30	1,284
31–40	1,200
41–50	1,007

Note: Costs shown are estimates for 1981 projected from earlier data developed by the *BBDO Audience Coverage and Cost Guide* (1976).

CHAPTER 18 | OTHER MEDIA

primary or supplementary medium, it is most often used in the latter fashion.

TRANSIT ADVERTISING

Transit advertising consists of paper posters placed inside or on transit vehicles, and in transit stations. While there are about 380 markets in the United States where transit advertising is available, only seven markets have extensive rapid transit systems and station platforms on which advertising can be displayed. These cities are Boston, Chicago, Cleveland, New York, Philadelphia, San Francisco, and Washington, D.C. Partly because of its limited availability, transit advertising only attracts expenditures of about $70 million a year. However, in the major markets where it is available, transit advertising is a healthy and growing medium. Under the impact of the energy crisis and the apparent need for more public transportation, the industry will probably continue to grow.

TYPES OF TRANSIT ADVERTISING

The most common types of transit advertising are **car cards, exterior displays,** and **station posters.**

Car cards. Car cards are used as interior displays in overhead racks and other locations in subway trains, buses, commuter trains, and other rapid transit systems. The standard car card size is 11 inches high, with widths of 28, 42, and 56 inches. "Square" cards, measuring 21 by 22 inches, are also used at the ends of rail transit vehicles, and miscellaneous sizes are available for special positions, such as over doors. An example of a car card is shown in Figure 18–4.

Exterior displays. Exterior displays are waterproof posters appearing on the outside of buses and other transit vehicles. There are a number of standardized sizes. The most popular has a height of 21 inches and a width of 44 to 88 inches. Figure 18–5 shows a number of such signs and the ways that they are most often displayed.

The Bus-O-Rama, an illuminated rooftop panel measuring about 22 by 145 inches, is available in some markets.

Station posters. Although smaller in size, station posters are similar to outdoor posters and are displayed on and in stations of subways, rapid transit systems, and suburban railroads. Although similar to outdoor posters, they are sold by the same firms selling car cards because of where they are located. The most common sizes for station posters are one-sheet (46″ by 30″) and two-sheet (46″ by 60″). Since waiting passengers have more time to read advertising copy than drivers of cars, station posters often carry more copy than the larger, outdoor posters.

Other forms of transit advertising. In addition to these common forms of transit advertising, there are also floor exhibits, diorama displays, and clock spectaculars located in train and airline terminals. Although on a smaller scale, these displays are usually custom

FIGURE 18–4   Car card

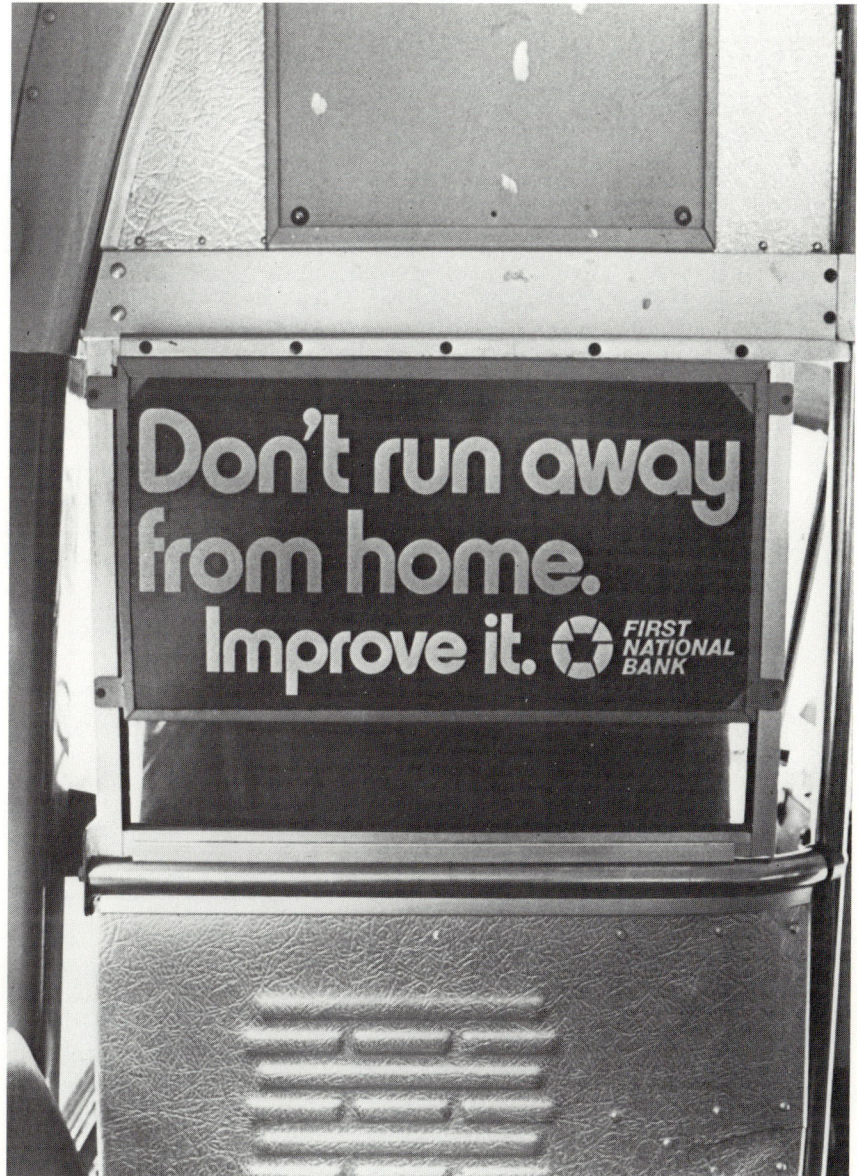

designed for advertisers and similar to outdoor advertising spectaculars.

Another form of transit advertising is the **merchandising bus.** Such buses are usually chartered by advertisers in connection with sales meetings and/or major promotional efforts. The outside of the bus is covered with advertising messages. The interior contains special displays and exhibits. Merchandising buses are sometimes placed in shopping center parking lots in order to take advantage of the high traffic flow.

BUYING TRANSIT ADVERTISING

Approximately 70 transit advertising companies serve 380 markets. These companies are referred to as operators and function in a man-

FIGURE 18–5 Exterior displays

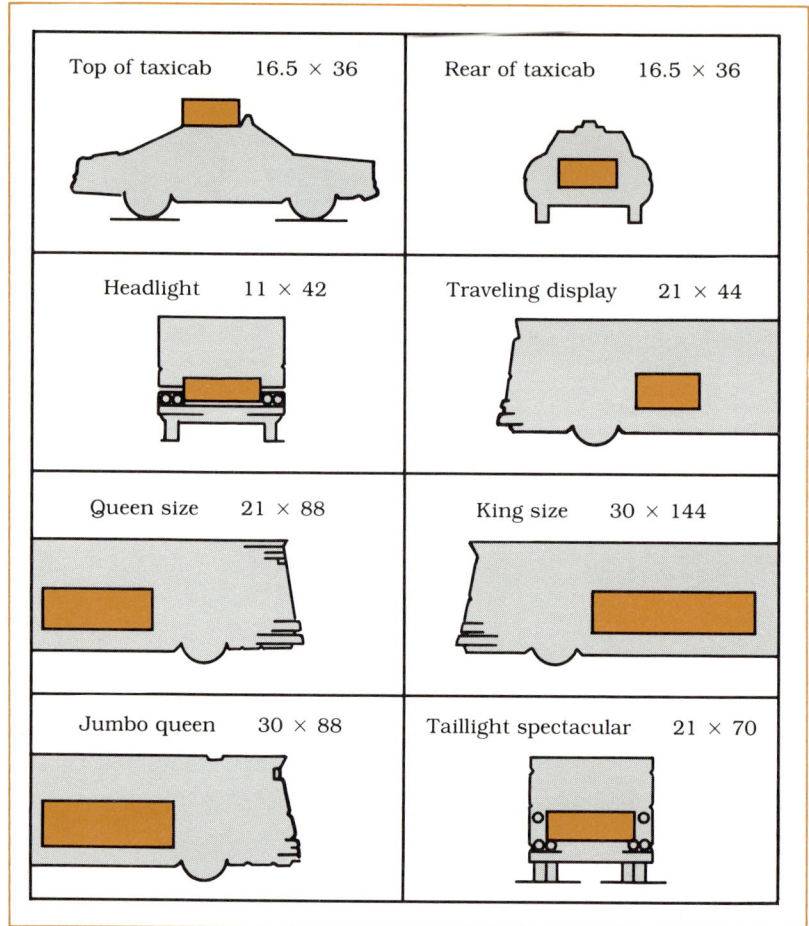

Top of taxicab 16.5 × 36	Rear of taxicab 16.5 × 36
Headlight 11 × 42	Traveling display 21 × 44
Queen size 21 × 88	King size 30 × 144
Jumbo queen 30 × 88	Taillight spectacular 21 × 70

ner similar to outdoor advertising plants. The Transit Advertising Association (TAA), the national association for the industry, establishes and maintains standards, and promotes the use of the medium. Mutual Transit Sales, a subsidiary of one of the major transit companies, represents many of the transit operators in selling transit space to national advertisers and advertising agencies.

Standard Rate and Data Service has discontinued publication of a transit advertising directory, presumably because lack of demand by agencies and advertisers made it unprofitable. However, Table 18–3 shows estimated advertising costs for transit advertising in various groups for the top 50 markets.

CIRCULATION OF TRANSIT ADVERTISING

The circulation for car cards is based on the number of fares that are collected. Transit operators submit sworn statements each year, reporting the average number of passengers carried each month. Attempts have been made to measure the exposure of exterior displays by using electronically controlled cameras to count the eyes exposed to the moving vehicle, but the value of this measure is highly questionable.

STRENGTHS AND WEAKNESSES OF TRANSIT ADVERTISING

Transit advertising is selective only in a geographic sense. Since approximately 70,000 vehicles carry transit advertising in densely populated areas, it has a potential for broad reach in these markets. Transit advertising also offers high frequency because transit riders repeat their trips frequently. Its cost-per-thousand is extremely low, with inside cards having a cost-per-thousand of less than twenty-five cents and external signs costing less than 10 cents per thousand viewers.[7]

On the negative side, transit advertising is limited to urban areas, and there is little validated information on its effectiveness. Essentially, it is a supplementary medium for national advertisers, although it may be used as the primary medium for local firms.

DIRECTORY ADVERTISING

Directories are a useful form of advertising for consumer product companies with limited distribution and industrial firms that market industrial supplies and equipment. Directory advertising may consist merely of the name of a firm or product, along with an address and/or telephone number; or it may consist of display advertising. There are an infinite number of local, regional, and national directories, ranging from industrial buying guides to the classified, yellow pages of the telephone book. From the standpoint of consumer use, the best known directory is the yellow pages.

YELLOW PAGE ADVERTISING

Most consumers have recourse to the yellow pages of the telephone directory at one time or another. Whether searching for a plumber

TABLE 18–3 Transit advertising costs in the top 50 markets

Basic Markets	100 Showing: Exterior bus space, 30-inch × 144-inch posters		Full Run: Interior bus space, 11-inch × 28-inch cards	
	Posters	Monthly Cost	Cards	Monthly Cost
1–10	3,670	$234,000	30,300*	$ 66,700
11–20	1,520	77,100	6,280	19,900
21–30	660	41,000	2,920	9,400
31–40	465	26,500	1,430	4,360
41–50	440	23,900	1,410	3,080
1–50	6,755	$402,500	42,340	$103,440

*Includes subway cards in New York City.

Note: 50 showing and half-run rates and allotments are approximately 65 percent of 100 showing. Exterior and/or interior space may not be available in all markets.

Source: Reprinted with permission from McCann-Erickson Worldwide and Campbell-Ewald Worldwide, members of the Interpublic Group of Companies. From *1979/1980 Media Planning and Buying Guide* (New York: McCann-Erickson Worldwide, 1979) and *1979/1980 Media Information Guide* (Warren, Mich.: Campbell-Ewald Worldwide, 1979).

[7]*Transit Advertising Rate and Data* (Skokie, Illinois: Standard Rate and Data Service, 1977).

or local outlet for a national brand, the admonition, "Let your fingers do the walking through the yellow pages," is a part of the national consciousness. Yellow pages often constitute local merchants' only advertising; but for national advertisers, the directory is a supplemental medium used to facilitate the location of products and/or to provide consumers with an address and telephone number, usually toll free, of a central or regional office that consumers can call for information or to register service complaints.

There are 6000 classified telephone directories in the United States; approximately 8000 companies use yellow page advertising as a part of their national advertising effort. Advertisers can buy listings or display space in up to 4000 markets through a single source, the National Yellow Page Service. The remaining 2000 directories must be bought locally.

The cost of directory advertising listings vary, depending upon the sizes of the ad and market selected. A one inch ad in the top 100 markets costs about $48,000; one-quarter of a column in these same markets costs about $82,000. Table 18–4 shows costs and other data for yellow page advertising in the top 100 markets.

The extent to which the yellow pages are used by adults, along with selected data about the users, is shown in Table 18–5.

OTHER DIRECTORIES

Aside from the yellow pages, the greatest use of directory advertising occurs in firms that manufacture products for the industrial market. Many of these industries are highly specialized, and a number are designed to meet their specific needs. For example, media advertise extensively in the *Standard Rate and Data Service* directories because they are the basic sources of media information used by advertising agencies. The *Thomas Register of American Manufacturers* is widely used by a variety of industrial manufacturers, as are more selective directories such as *Post's Paper Mill Directory*, the *Data Processing Yearbook*, and many others. The advertiser's primary concern when using directory advertising is whether the value of the directory in reaching a particular target audience is worth its cost. This determination is difficult to make because the published information on the advertising readership of most directories is limited.

TABLE 18–4 Yellow pages quick-cost reference for top 100 metropolitan markets (central city directories only)

Major Markets	Central City Directory	Directory Circulation (000)	Directory Area Persons (000)	Trade-mark ($)	Bold-face Listing ($)	Trade Name ($)	One-Inch Space ($)	Quarter Column ($)
1–10	25	18,384	28,299	11,798	2,113	2,587	7,804	17,069
1–25	47	34,348	48,252	21,622	3,865	4,839	15,009	34,097
1–50	84	49,802	66,566	34,550	6,311	8,005	24,228	55,153
1–75	126	60,203	78,434	47,192	8,834	10,999	33,126	75,036
1–100	160	67,810	86,376	56,499	10,801	13,492	48,170	81,806

Source: L. M. Berry and Company (March 1979 rates and data)

TABLE 18–5 Yellow pages adult consumer usage

		Percentage of Adults Using Per Year	Average References Per User	Followed By Action
All Adults (20+)		81	34	84
Sex	Men	81	37	83
	Women	82	33	86
Age	20–39	88	42	87
	40+	77	28	82
Household Income	Under $10,000	72	37	81
	$10,000–14,999	78	34	86
	$15,000+	90	33	86
Household Size	1 or 2 persons	76	32	82
	3 or 4 persons	85	38	87
	5 or more persons	86	34	84
Residential Mobility	Moved within two years	87	42	86
	Has not moved	79	32	84
Home Ownership	Own	82	33	85
	Rent	81	40	85

Source: An independent survey conducted by Chilton Research Services, 1976.

DIRECT ADVERTISING

Direct advertising is different from other media because there are no ready-made media vehicles that the advertiser may use. Instead, the advertiser must develop the entire advertising effort—the vehicle for reaching the desired audience, as well as the advertising copy itself.

TYPES OF DIRECT ADVERTISING

The Direct Marketing Association has suggested a threefold classification of direct advertising based on two criteria: (a) the way in which the advertising is delivered; and (b) the intent or purpose of the advertiser.

Direct mail.   Individual advertisements, either in display or letter form, are mailed directly to current or potential customers. The purpose of the advertisement may be to inform the customer of the availability of a product, deliver a coupon or an actual product sample, or pave the way for a salesperson's call at a later date. Used in this way, direct mail is a supplement to other media, part of a sales promotion program, or way of increasing the frequency of contact with selected customers.

Mail order.   Advertising sent through the mail, referred to as **mail order advertising,** is meant to persuade the recipient to order something by return mail. Widely used by hobby and other specialty manufacturers, mail order advertising may involve shipping catalogs featuring hundreds of items to selected customers. Unlike direct mail advertising, mail order is the ultimate selling tool of its users and is frequently their only contact with customers.

Unmailed, direct advertising. This form of direct advertising is not sent through the postal system; it is delivered directly to consumers either at home, in stores or shopping centers, or placed on parked cars. This advertising may consist of a handbill for a local merchant, but it is also frequently used as a device for distributing product samples that are clumsy to send through the mail.

Mail order advertising is a huge, specialized business. For purposes of this text, our primary concern is with direct mail and unmailed forms of direct advertising. Direct mail advertising is widely used by industrial marketers whose customers are restricted to a relatively small number of manufacturing concerns. Both forms of direct advertising are widely used by manufacturers of retail distributed products as a part of major sales promotion programs.

DIRECT MAIL LISTS

The key to successful direct mail advertising is the development of a list of prime prospects. Department stores often use their list of charge account customers for their mailings. In addition to lists of past customers, direct mail lists are available from a number of commercial sources. These lists range from quite general to highly specialized groups of people. An advertisement that was distributed to the occupant of every household, or every third household, in a particular market would represent a general, nonspecialized, method of distribution. A more specialized approach would be mailing the advertising only to upper income neighborhoods. A high degree of specialization can be attained by restricting distribution to special groups with predetermined characteristics, such as marketing professors, presidents of corporations, licensed optometrists, owners of late model sports cars, medical doctors, or builders.

Although it is an expensive and time consuming operation, advertisers often compile their own lists. More often, advertisers buy lists from firms that specialize in list compilation. In its directory *Direct Mail List Rates*, Standard Rate and Data Service offers an extensive description of the mailing lists that are available. This description includes: (a) the cost of the list; (b) the source of the list, to help the advertiser assess its quality; (c) how the list is maintained; (d) whether the list owner will permit the advertiser to test the list by mailing to a sample of the names it contains; and (e) other services offered by the list owner, including printing, stuffing, addressing, and mailing. Figure 18–6 shows a page of direct mail listings from the sports section of SRDS. Note both the sources and specificity of the lists.

DIRECT ADVERTISING COSTS

Direct advertising costs vary so greatly that few generalizations can be drawn; however, the components making up the costs can be identified.

☐ *Cost of the list.* Although it is impossible to generalize about the costs of compiling one's own list, purchased lists generally range from about $40 to $75 per thousand names.

Affluent Sports Minded Physicians

Media Code 3 602 0036 4.00   Mid 020952-000

1. PERSONNEL
  List Manager
  Global Lists, 3006 Holmes St., Kansas City, Mo. 64109.
    Phone 816-561-3561.
  All recognized brokers.
2. DESCRIPTION
  Physicians who have responded to a sports-oriented
  travel offer. Average income is 60,000.00.
  ZIP Coded in numerical sequence 100%.
  List is computerized.
  Selections available: 5 digit ZIP Code, 3 digit ZIP
  Code—sectional centers, state.

(D-B. D-C)

55,000

Affluent, Sports-Minded Professionals

. . . who have responded to a sports-oriented travel offer.

Avg. ann'l income: $60,000+ Test Order: 5M min.
Addressing: 4-up Ches. Sample required.
Total List: 55,000 Price: $35/M

Brad Moore

Global Lists

3006 Holmes St., Kansas City, Mo. 64109
800-821-6647/(816) 561-3561

4. QUANTITY AND RENTAL RATES
              Rec'd July, 1982.
                                Total   Price
                                Number   per/M
  Total list 55,000   35.00
5. COMMISSION, CREDIT POLICY
  Standard commission to all recognized brokers.

6. METHOD OF ADDRESSING
  4-up Cheshire. Pressure sensitive labels, 5.00/M extra.
  Magnetic tape available.
7. DELIVERY SCHEDULE
  5 days after acceptance of order.
8. RESTRICTIONS
  Sample required for prior approval.
9. TEST ARRANGEMENT
  Minimum 5,000.
10. LETTER SHOP SERVICES
  Complete lettershop services available.
11. MAINTENANCE
  Cleaned regularly.

All American Sports (Tennis)

Media Code 3 602 0051 3.00   Mid 020956-000

1. PERSONNEL
  Broker and/or Authorized Agent
  Names Unlimited, 183 Madison Ave., New York, N. Y.
    10016. Phone 212-752-5522.
2. DESCRIPTION
  Individuals and families inquired about or purchased
  tennis vacations, club memberships, also inquired about
  tennis camps, all exclusive of transportation. Camps
  primarily located on East Coast but some inquiries from
  Midwest and Calif.; median age 37; average income over
  25,000.00. Most are married and selections can be made
  for men and women.
  ZIP Coded in numerical sequence 100%.
  List is computerized.
3. LIST SOURCE
  Space ads in Tennis Magazine, New York Times, World
  Tennis and direct mail to tennis associations and club
  memberships.
4. QUANTITY AND RENTAL RATES
              Rec'd July, 1982.
                                      Total   Price
                                      Number per/M
  Respondents (1979-81) 127,000 *40.00
    (*) Competitors 50.00/M.
  Selections: 5 digit ZIP Code and sectional centers 5.00/M
  extra; state 2.50/M extra; keying 1.00/M extra.
6. METHOD OF ADDRESSING
  Computer; 4 or 5-up Cheshire tape; magnetic tape available.
8. RESTRICTIONS
  Minimum 5,000. Less than 5,000-50.00/M payment in
  advance.

FIGURE 18–6 Examples of direct mail listings (Courtesy Standard Rate & Data Service, Inc.)

☐ *Cost of the advertising material used.* Since the material delivered may range from a single page letter to a product sample, no generalizations can be made about material costs.

☐ *Mechanical costs for stuffing, addressing, and mailing.* While these costs will depend on the nature of the material being sent, the hourly rates are minimal because providing these services is not skilled work. There are commercial companies that will handle the mechanics of the mailing for a fee.

☐ *Cost of delivery.* Whether the material is mailed or delivered in some other way, the cost of delivery can be substantial.

All in all, mail advertising is relatively expensive. Whereas most major media cost somewhere around $5 to $15 per thousand, direct mail can easily cost $600 to $1,000 per thousand. As a consequence, it tends to be used selectively.

With the exception of coupons and samples, there is little published information on the effectiveness of direct advertising; therefore, most advertisers who use these methods extensively compile data from their own experiences. Nonetheless, evidence suggests that direct mail advertising material is well read. For example, the director of the United States Postal Services' Market Research Department has estimated that 80 percent of direct mail recipients read the material they receive. Actual readership, however, is strongly influenced by the nature of the recipient and the content of the mailing. An industrial advertiser sending current product information to a select list of customers probably approximates 100 percent readership. Lists tailored to special interest groups undoubtedly receive greater readership than material sent to more generalized audiences. The secret of success in direct advertising is linked closely with the quality of the list and attractiveness of the material delivered.

STRENGTHS AND WEAKNESSES OF DIRECT ADVERTISING

The Direct Marketing Association advances the following advantages of direct advertising.

1. It can be directed to specific individuals or markets with greater control than any other medium.
2. It can be made personal to the point of being absolutely confidential.
3. It is a single advertiser's individual message and is not in competition with other advertising and/or editorial material.
4. It does not have the limitations on space and format as do other mediums of advertising.
5. It permits greater flexibility in materials and processes of production than any other medium of advertising.
6. It provides a means for introducing novelty and realism into the interpretation of the advertiser's story.
7. It can be produced according to the needs of the advertiser's own immediate schedule.
8. It can be controlled for specific jobs of research, reaching small groups, testing ideas, appeals, reactions.
9. It can be dispatched for accurate and in some cases exact timing, both as to departure of the pieces as well as to their receipt.
10. It provides more thorough means for the reader to act or buy through action devices not possible of employment by other media.[8]

Offsetting these obvious advantages is the problem of cost. On a cost-per-thousand basis, direct advertising is high. While it offers a great deal of selectivity, it is unaffordable for most mass marketing. For this reason, advertisers of retail distributed products use

---

[8]"Advantages of Direct Advertising," *Direct Mail Manual* (New York: Direct Mail Advertising Association, Inc.), Manual file: 1201.

direct advertising sparingly and usually only in connection with major promotions.

PROGRAM ADVERTISING

Many advertisers reach target audiences through display advertisements scheduled in programs of public events, such as plays, concerts, opera, and sporting events. Although this medium is primarily used by local restaurants, cocktail lounges, and bars to suggest a place to go for dinner or a snack, it is also used to some extent by national advertisers of beer, distilled spirits, fashions, furnishings, and other products. By selecting programs carefully, the advertiser can often reach selected audiences. Symphonic concerts, plays, and opera, for example, attract upper income, better educated, and sophisticated consumers.

Program advertising is not a highly organized medium and often must be purchased on a catch-as-catch-can basis, particularly in the case of infrequent special events such as police circuses, ice follies, and traveling entertainment groups. In New York City, however, advertisers can reach most playgoers through *Playbill,* an established minimagazine tailored to the programs of the participating theaters. Similar opportunities exist in other metropolitan areas large enough to have an extensive theatrical season.

The cost-per-thousand for program advertising is usually high, and since the medium is not systematically measured, it is often difficult to verify circulation or find meaningful data on reach, frequency, and duplication.

FILM ADVERTISING

Films are used in a variety of ways by advertisers, ranging from minute movies shown in commercial theaters to sponsored films on television. Films are also used in sales presentations and by club groups to fill out the program time of their meetings. Whether films should be considered an expense of the advertising, sales, or public relations department depends on their use. A film used only for a sales presentation is clearly a sales expense. A film deliberately produced for public relations purposes is a public relations expense. Other uses are more ambiguous. If we adhere to a strict definition of advertising as paid media, it is probable that a large but unknown proportion of film usage falls outside of this definition.

Nonetheless, films are a form of communications widely used by major companies. An estimated 150,000 short films are in use. A ten-minute, animated Disney cartoon for children that dramatizes ways of preventing colds is sponsored by Kleenex tissues; the Kendell Company sponsors a film titled *Athletic Injuries—Their Prevention and Care;* and Elanco, a major manufacturer of veterinary medicines, has developed a film to help teach veterinarians appropriate pet-side manners.

One form of film usage that clearly falls in the realm of advertising is the **minute movie,** or theater commercial. These films, ranging in length from one to several minutes, are used in some 12,000 regular and drive-in theaters. To be acceptable to theatergoers, the longer films should be entertaining and noncommercial in the television sense, with the sponsor's product shown naturally, but unobtrusively. More recently, commercials similar to those shown on television have invaded cinemas throughout the country. These commercials are scheduled by organizations such as Screenvision and Cinemavision. Most theater owners welcome this use of commercials as a way of offsetting rising operating costs. However, the reaction of moviegoers is mixed. Many resent the commercials; however, most are becoming inured to them.

Costs for theater commercials depend upon audience figures provided by individual theaters. The cost is relatively high, running $15 or more per thousand. On the surface, it would appear to be a good medium for reaching teenagers and young adults because these groups make up the bulk of movie audiences. It should also provide relatively high frequency because avid movie fans go to movies often.

EXHIBIT ADVERTISING

Exhibit advertising, with some exceptions, is primarily an industrial medium. The exceptions include: (a) annual boating and sports shows in major cities; (b) world, state, and county fairs; and (c) special display sites such as Disneyland and Busch Gardens, a private amusement park operated by Anheuser Busch. However, by far the greatest use of exhibit advertising is in the industrial and trade fields.

Trade exhibits offer advertisers an opportunity to display and demonstrate their products for key buyers. Exhibits are particularly useful for highly technical products and bulky equipment that sales personnel cannot easily carry. They are also widely used for other products. For example, all of the major college textbook publishers have exhibition booths at the professional meetings of the American Marketing Association, Academy of Management, medical associations, chemical conventions, and so on. In fact, these exhibits often constitute one of the major promotional activities of publishers. Further, the conventions of retail, wholesale, and industrial associations usually have an exhibition hall where suppliers display their wares.

The major costs in exhibit advertising include: (a) space rental; (b) exhibit design and construction; (c) personnel to man the exhibit; and (d) miscellaneous expenses such as transportation, installation, and furniture. The total cost for a particular exhibit may be quite low or relatively high, depending upon the discretion of the advertiser. While circulation can be measured in terms of the number of people attending the show or stopping at the exhibit for information, it is often difficult to assess the value of the exhibit or project this data to future shows.

The primary values of exhibit advertising lie in: (a) its selectivity, because only interested prospects attend; (b) the opportunity for demonstration; and (c) the ability of salespeople to contact new customers, make appointments, and take orders. Often, manufacturers will time the introduction of new items and models to coincide with major trade shows. This is particularly true in the furniture and fashion fields.

The weaknesses of exhibit advertising are its expense and the difficulty in measuring its results. This latter point is also true of advertising in general, even where there is a plethora of statistics on reach, frequency, and duplication.

SPECIALTY ADVERTISING

Specialty advertising is a various assortment of advertising that accounts for approximately $2 billion a year in advertising revenues. It is basically a reminder medium, consisting of items from swizzle sticks to clocks, bearing the name of the advertiser and often a brief sales message. Specialty advertising items are usually given free to potential customers and anyone else who happens to be in the vicinity of their distribution. The only limitations placed on items used for specialty advertising are that they be affordable and have a printable surface.

The cost of advertising specialties depends on the item used and quantity purchased. Three types of organizations operate within the industry: **suppliers, distributors,** and **direct-selling houses.** Suppliers either manufacture, import, or convert items for sales through distributors. Distributors develop ideas for advertising specialties, locate suppliers who can produce them, and sell them to advertisers. Direct-selling houses combine these two operations into one organization. The trade association for the industry is the Specialty Advertising Association International (SAAI). Most major advertising agencies and many client organizations have someone on their staffs who has expert knowledge of and maintains active contacts with the various organizations that supply specialty items.

The primary advantage of specialty advertising is that it offers a relatively inexpensive form of reminder advertising that, because of the relatively permanent nature of the item used, has a long advertising life. For example, a calendar imprinted with the advertiser's name may be visibly displayed for a year in a buyer's office or home. Book matches, while having a much shorter life than calendars, offer a potential exposure every time a match is struck; ballpoint pens have a life of several weeks or months; and an expensive executive gift, such as a desk set, may occupy a central position on a customer's desk for several years.

On the negative side, specialty advertising seldom offers an opportunity to deliver a persuasive product story. As reminder advertising, it can be easily ignored. There is no measure of its effectiveness, and when specialty advertising is used as an executive gift, it often raises the question of bribery. For example, a gift of a $100 or $200 desk set is in questionable ethical taste, and many companies forbid their employees to accept such gifts.

POINT-OF-PURCHASE ADVERTISING

Most consumer products are sold through retail outlets. As a consequence, the last chance an advertiser has to influence consumers before the purchase is made is within the store itself. This influence may be exerted through a variety of on-premise devices, such as window signs, store banners, shelf-talkers, counter cards, end-aisle displays, gondolas, and permanent display racks.

FIGURE 18–7 (Courtesy L'eggs Products)

A point-of-purchase display is a broad term referring to any visual device, other than normal shelf stocking, used in a store to call attention to a particular product or group of products. An in-store display may or may not include a price inducement. It may range from a simple **shelf-talker** (a paper strip attached to the shelf calling attention to a brand) to elaborate gondolas (special displays of merchandise and advertising material occupying a position in the aisle of the store). The use of point-of-purchase material has grown dramatically in recent years; today, in-store displays represent an expenditure of almost $4 billion.

Separating point-of-purchase advertising from special product displays is difficult because much of this material's use is in connection with sales promotion activities. One important distinction that can be made, however, is between temporary and permanent in-store advertising material.

Temporary in-store advertising material is generally printed on paper or cardboard, keyed to a short-term consumer promotion (contest, price-off promotion, tie-in promotion with another product, and so on), and designed to be thrown away after the promotion has run its course. **Permanent in-store advertising** usually consists of a permanent display rack such as that used by L'eggs hosiery in grocery stores (Figure 18–7), a special display case for items such as pen and pencil sets, or display cards for small items. These display cards, identified by the advertiser's brand name, contain a dozen or more separate items that the consumer detaches when he makes his purchase. Permanent in-store material is often made of wood, plastic, glass, or metal and may contain back-lighted panels displaying product features.

Since point-of-purchase (p.o.p.) material is noncommissionable media, advertising agencies which design and supervise the production of such material generally do so on a fee or hourly basis, although they may also receive a negotiated commission for supervising the printing by outside production houses. In addition to advertising agencies, a number of point-of-purchase houses specialize in the development of in-store material.

In this chapter, we have touched on a few forms of miscellaneous media. Many others have not been mentioned; new ones are introduced everyday. Skywriting, baskart advertising (advertising on the push baskets in supermarkets), shopping bag advertising, and fluorescent signs over bars which identify brands are already used. Wherever there is space for advertising to appear and no law against it there, someone will eventually try to sell the space for advertising purposes.

SUMMARY

The chapter is devoted to a variety of miscellaneous media that are variously referred to as minor, secondary, supplementary, and unmeasured media. Because of the diversity of the media included in this group and the wide variations in the extent of their use, none of these terms is really an adequate description of the media involved.

Outdoor advertising is generally considered the dominant out-of-home medium. Although it is extensively used, only about 5 percent of all outdoor advertising is a part of the organized outdoor advertising industry. The basic unit in this industry is the plant operator who, on a city-by-city basis, is an independent business firm that owns or leases sites, constructs structures for signs, sells space, erects the advertising posters, and maintains the advertising after it is erected. There are several forms of outdoor advertising, each with its own advantages and disadvantages.

Transit advertising, which consists of paper posters placed inside or on transit vehicles and in transit stations, is available in some 380 markets, although only seven United States cities have extensive transit systems.

Other forms of advertising are directories, direct, program, films, exhibits, specialties, and point-of-purchase advertising.

Each of these forms has unique values which, under the appropriate conditions, may be useful to an advertiser; each also has shortcomings that limit its use. One of the major shortcomings of minor media is the lack of readership data and effectiveness of the various media included within the classification.

REVIEW QUESTIONS

1 Why are the terms minor, secondary, supplementary, and unmeasured media each inappropriate when applied to the media discussed in this chapter?
2 Identify and describe the major forms of outdoor advertising discussed in the text.
3 What are the major strengths and weaknesses of outdoor advertising?
4 Identify and describe the major forms of transit advertising.
5 Distinguish between the various forms of direct advertising. Which of these forms would a national advertiser of packaged goods most likely use?
6 What are the basic components making up the cost of direct mail advertising? Why is it difficult to make generalizations about the costs of such advertising?
7 What are the primary advantages of direct mail advertising?
8 What are the primary advantages and disadvantages of exhibit advertising?
9 What is meant by the term point-of-purchase advertising? Identify some common examples of this form of advertising.
10 What is the strategy behind using executive gifts as part of an advertising and promotion program? What are the ethical problems involved?

DISCUSSION QUESTIONS

1 Explain how direct mail advertising might be used by a: (a) local clothing store; (b) manufacturer of technical industrial machinery; and (c) marketer of packaged goods sold through grocery stores.
2 Can you think of forms of minor media other than those discussed in this chapter? What do you think their advantages and disadvantages would be?

CHAPTER 18 | OTHER MEDIA

3 Why do you think outdoor advertising is beginning to use gross rating points rather than showings as a way of describing their coverage? What advantages and disadvantages do you see in this trend?

PROBLEM

As a media buyer, you have been asked to estimate the costs for a 100 showing and a 50 showing for outdoor advertising in Chicago, St. Louis, Cleveland, Kansas City, and Cincinnati. In addition to estimating the total costs for these markets, indicate the closing date for a 12-month schedule beginning January 1. The client, a regional bottler of a line of soft drinks, is not sure whether this is the best medium for his product. What other media do you think should be considered? What are their advantages and disadvantages?

V

Sales Promotion— Strategies and Plans

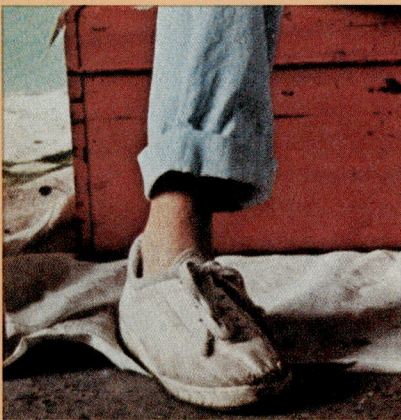

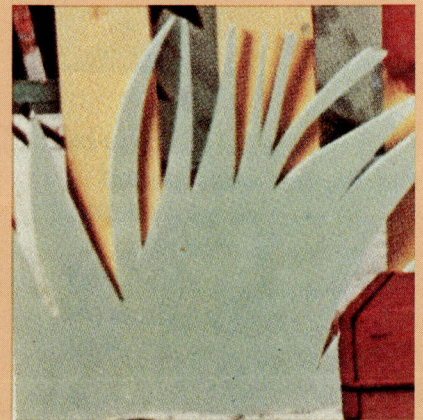

In Chapter 4, it was pointed out that the term "sales promotion" is used to designate those selling activities that fall outside the areas of major media advertising and publicity. Thus, sales promotion activities include temporary point-of-sale material keyed to particular promotions, sampling, coupons, price-off labels, store demonstrations, trade incentives of various sorts, and sales force incentive programs.

Some activities may not appear in the marketing plan. For example, incentives for the sales force are often an integral part of the sales compensation program, budgeted by the sales department, and detailed in the sales plan rather than marketing plan. Such incentives should always be coordinated with the objectives and strategies sections of the marketing plan.

Let us assume that marketing strategy calls for increasing distribution on a large package size from 30 percent to 65 percent. The sales promotion section of the marketing plan details a stocking allowance on all initial orders, as well as trade advertising and consumer coupons on the large package size. The sales plan, on the other hand, might set up a point system for sales force compensation which, in addition to giving points for meeting or exceeding quota, would give points for gaining distribution on the large package size. Sales force bonuses would be based on the total number of points earned, regardless of their source. This

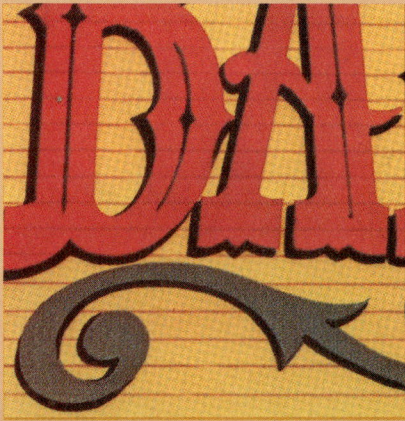

sales force incentive program would be budgeted in the sales plan, not in the marketing plan. In addition, the sales plan might specify that a certain percent of the sales force's time be devoted to "selling the promotion" two or three months prior to the coupon distribution. A well conceived and executed marketing program leaves little to chance because it coordinates all aspects of the company's activities.

As a practical matter, some of the advertising media we have referred to in Chapter 18 are

considered sales promotion media, not advertising media. Thus, specialty advertising, exhibits, and direct advertising are found in the sales promotion section of the marketing plan more often than the media section.

Finally, major media advertising is often used to support sales promotion activities. When this occurs, major media costs are generally charged to the advertising budget, while costs such as

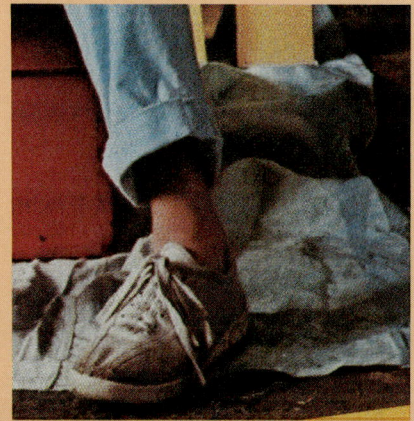

allowances, coupons, mailings, and point-of-purchase material are charged to the sales promotion budget. Individual advertisers may depart from this conventional practice and charge all, or part, of the major media support to the sales promotion budget.

In Chapter 19, we will examine the role of sales promotion and some of the major promotional devices. Whenever media enter into the discussion, they will be considered sales promotion rather than advertising expenditures.

19

The Role of Sales Promotion

COUPONS AND SWEEPSTAKES

$598 MILLION IN CONSUMER SAVINGS

According to *Advertising Age*, over 90 billion coupons are distributed each year at a cost of $1.05 billion to the advertiser; the estimated savings to consumers is $598 million.[1] The reason for widespread use of coupons is obvious—coupons increase sales. A study in Portland, Maine, indicated that sales increases from consumers redeeming coupons ranged from 4 to 174 percent. Further, coupons are an effective device for attracting nonusers of a product. In one study, redemption by nonusers ranged from a high of 65 percent of all redeemers for one brand to a low of 38 percent for another. In addition, nonusers who purchased a brand as a result of having a coupon were more apt to purchase the brand nine months later than nonusers who didn't redeem a coupon.[2]

$40 BILLION FOR SALES PROMOTION

Coupons are only a part of sales promotion activity. Total expenditures for sales promotion are $40 billion per year and still growing. The growth of sales promotion as a marketing tool may be related to the growth of the brand management system. According to Louis J. Haugh, a leading promotion expert:

> The growth of the brand manager system has had a profound and expansionary effect on the promotion category . . . A brand manager can often easily change a promotion tactic or sales distribution portion of his or her marketing strategy without major consequences.
> Another reason, of course, is that sales promotion is often a source of quick and easy short-term sales gains, although it may not contribute as much to the long-term health of the brand as

[1]Louis J. Haugh, "How Coupons Measure Up," p. 58. Reprinted with permission from the June 8, 1981 issue of *Advertising Age*. Copyright © 1981 by Crain Communications, Inc.
[2]Ibid., 58.

advertising, market research, business building tests, and other slower but surer marketing activities. Since brand managers often see brand management as a stepping stone to higher corporate positions, they may be tempted to opt for short-term gains and the immediate recognition that it brings.

But, whatever the cause, sales promotion is a big business in contemporary marketing. As sales promotion has grown, it has also become more sophisticated, and both client organizations and advertising agencies have developed cadres of sales promotion specialists to design and implement their sales promotion activities.[3]

TRENDS IN SALES PROMOTION

In an effort to discern sales promotion trends, Dancer Fitzgerald Sample, a major advertising agency, made a 12-month study of 5155 consumer promotions in six major markets. Their findings included:[4]

1 *A change in method of coupon distribution may be taking place.* Co-op coupon programs in newspapers and freestanding inserts are becoming more important in the total couponing picture. Sunday comics are also emerging as a couponing vehicle, and manufacturers seem to be using their packages more as a method of distributing coupons.

2 *Combination promotions are skyrocketing.* There is a growing tendency for manufacturers to use two or more devices in their promotions—a coupon and some other device, e.g., premiums combined with coupons, and refunds involving both cash and coupons.

3 *A switch from cash to coupons.* Traditionally, many manufacturers have offered cash refunds for proof of purchase, usually a

[3]Louis J. Haugh. "Sales Promotion Grows to $40 Billion Status." Reprinted with permission from the April 30, 1980 issue of *Advertising Age.* Copyright © 1980 by Crain Communications, Inc.

[4]Ed Meyer, "Sum of Year's Events Tipoff Coming Trends," *Advertising Age,* 4 May 1981, 66.

package label, mailed to the company by consumers. Today, over 50 percent of refund offers involve coupons instead of cash.

4 *A change in the design of sweepstakes promotions.* Travel was the first prize found most often in media-delivered sweepstakes, followed by cash, then automobiles. However, cash was the number one prize found in on-package sweepstakes; travel was second, and automobiles third. A substantial growth in package rub-off games is probably the main reason that cash is the number one prize offered on the package.

5 *The product package is becoming increasingly important as a promotion vehicle.* Package panels are being used more and more for promotional purposes. Because food stores are putting up less in-store material, manufacturers may be turning to their packages as an innovative way to attract attention to their products.

AN OVERVIEW OF SALES PROMOTION

Sales promotion includes so many diverse and unmeasured activities that it is not possible to estimate total expenditures accurately. Ninety billion coupons and over $2 billion in point-of-purchase material, contests, sweepstakes, cents-off label promotions, display allowances, advertising allowances, stocking allowances, in-store demonstrations, and premiums are part of the activities normally thought of as sales promotion. Many sales promotion activities are applicable to both consumer and industrial products. Some, such as retail displays, are more applicable to consumer items; others, such as exhibits, are primarily used for industrial, wholesale, and retail trade shows. In this chapter, we will direct our attention to sales promotions used in support of retail distributed consumer products. In doing so, recognize that many of the points made and some of the activities described are equally applicable to industrial products and products sold directly to consumers, bypassing retail channels. This restriction of our focus is necessary because the sales promotion field is so diverse that a complete description is beyond the scope of this text.

DEFINITION OF SALES PROMOTION

Most definitions of sales promotion, including the one given in this book, are negative definitions. That is, they define sales promotion is terms of what it is not: (a) It is not advertising, although advertising may be used in its support. (b) It is not publicity, although publicity is often a part of a sales promotion program. (c) It is not normal sales activity, although sales promotion is an indispensable tool of the sales force.

One way of gaining insight into the nature of sales promotion is to define some of its salient characteristics. **Sales promotion** is:

1 A relatively short-term activity.
2 Directed toward the sales force, distribution channels, or consumers, or some combination of these groups.
3 Used in order to stimulate some specific action.

Two key thoughts in this definition are that sales promotion is of short-term duration and designed to stimulate some specific action.

An analogy useful in distinguishing between advertising and sales promotion can be borrowed from the field of armaments:

> Advertising is like a shotgun.
> Sales promotion is like a rifle.

Advertising is a shotgun in that it scatters its charge against the broad objective of reaching target audiences with a message about the product. Normally, advertising is not expected to generate immediate action, but to disseminate information, persuade, influence attitudes, and contribute to sales. In fact, advertising that is designed to generate immediate action, such as advertising featuring a price reduction or sale, is referred to as *sales promotion advertising.*

By contrast, sales promotion is like a rifle because it zeroes in on a specific objective and is designed to provoke immediate action. The typical objectives of sales promotion are to sample consumers, induce trial, deplete inventories, increase distribution, gain retail support, and provoke the sales force to focus on a particular activity.

Sales promotion is more precise in its target objective and time span than advertising. Unless a particular sales promotion is aimed at a specific and relatively narrow objective, it will probably be ineffective. In fact, the major cause of failure among sales promotions is that they try to do so many things that they do nothing well.

Sales promotion is always a supplementary activity. It does not, and cannot, replace advertising. Without a solid advertising base to build product recognition and acceptance, promotions tend to fizzle. A brand that is well conceived and carefully positioned may decline in sales because of inadequate advertising support. If it does, an increase in advertising expenditures, supported by strong copy, can reverse the decline and lead to a continuing pattern of growth in market share. This growth can be accelerated by supplementing the advertising with periodic sales promotion activity.

The same brand, without an infusion of advertising, can seldom achieve a permanent reversal of a share decline by sales promotion alone. Instead, it only achieves temporary arrests on its journey to oblivion. This point has been demonstrated over and over again through studies of consumer products by companies such as A. C. Nielsen that measure product movement at the retail level. Figure 19–1 shows the typical share of market patterns for two situations. Example (a) demonstrates the effect of advertising and consumer promotion on a well positioned product. Example (b) demonstrates the typical effect of sales promotion alone. These two patterns show that sales promotion works best on products for which advertising is generating recognition and acceptance. A coupon on a well-known brand is an incentive to buy. The same coupon on an unknown brand is no bargain. To express it another way, the history of a successful brand is characterized by three phenomena:

1 Advertising, which creates value.
2 Sales promotion, which induces trial.
3 The product itself, which provides satisfaction.

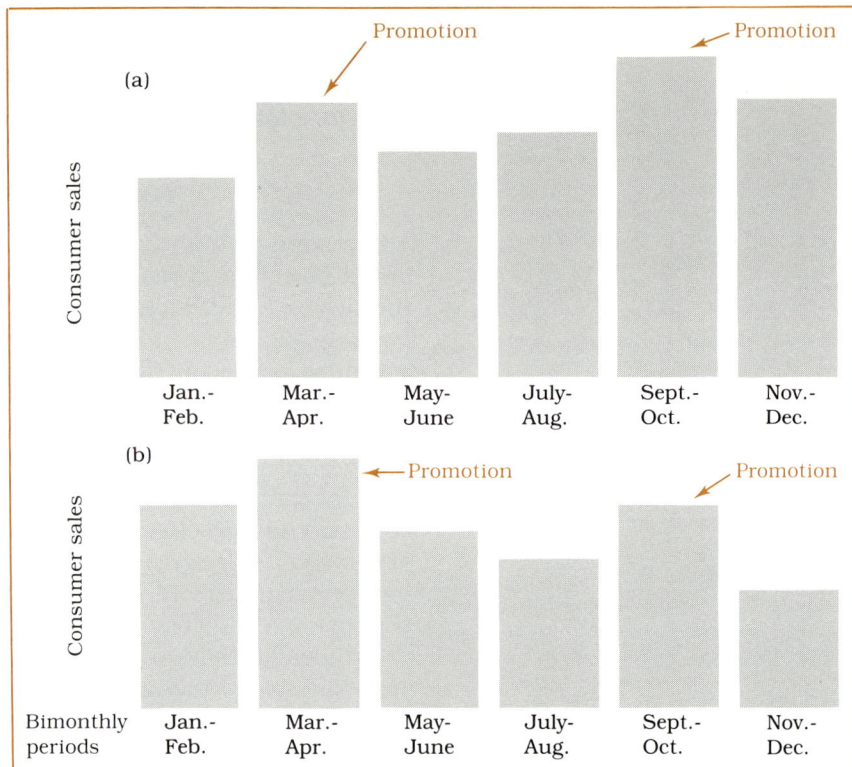

FIGURE 19–1 Typical sales pattern of (a) a brand supported by advertising and sales promotion, and (b) a brand supported by sales promotion alone.

The purpose of the foregoing example is not to discredit promotion as a marketing tool. In some fields and at certain periods of time, it is exceedingly important. In the marketing mix, sales promotion generally plays a larger role in fields marked by similar products than fields in which product differentiation is clear. It generally plays a larger role in the mature and decline stages of the product life cycle than in the introductory and growth stages; it plays a larger role in times of economic recession than in times of affluence.

TYPES OF SALES PROMOTION

One way of classifying sales promotion devices is in terms of their intended audiences. In the following material, we will examine typical sales promotion activities designed for the sales force, trade, and consumers. However, a combination of devices directed toward two or more of these groups is often used. For example, a stocking allowance to encourage retail distribution of a new brand or package size will be accompanied by a consumer coupon to stimulate consumer purchases, thereby consolidating the new distribution gained. Or, a consumer price-off label allowance may be coordinated with a display allowance to the trade in order to make the consumer offer more effective. The selection of a particular sales promotion technique, however, must always be made in terms of the specific problem to be solved.

SALES FORCE PROMOTIONS

Earlier, you learned that sales promotions directed to the sales force are often considered an integral part of the sales force compensation system, are charged to the sales budget, and do not appear in the marketing plan, per se. Since sales compensation is a complex and sometimes controversial subject, it will not be treated in detail in this book. Nonetheless, recognize that sales force activities must be coordinated with marketing objectives and strategies in order to obtain optimum results from the marketing program.

Many companies use some form of commission system—either straight commissions on sales or salary plus commissions—as a basic device for motivating sales people. When these compensation systems are standard practice, they are not considered sales promotion. However, a short-term sales force incentive in support of a particular marketing strategy, such as gaining distribution on a new product, increasing shelf facings, obtaining displays, or obtaining cooperative advertising support, is properly considered sales promotion. In these instances, a sales contest, awarding points to salespeople for their performance, may be used. For example, assume that the sales promotion section of the marketing plan calls for a major consumer contest, supported by media advertising and in-store product displays, with point-of-purchase material describing the contest, its prize structure, and method of entry. In order to assure sales support for the consumer promotion, a separate contest might be structured for the sales force with 100 points being awarded to individual salespeople for each in-store display of 50 or more cases of merchandise obtained—50 points for each 25-case display, 10 points for each 10-case display, and so on. Prizes would be awarded to the salespeople in each sales district or region that accumulated the most points.

If it is considered crucial to the success of a consumer or trade promotion, sales promotion directed to members of the sales force should not be neglected. In fact, it can be argued that the well conceived sales promotion should contain something for every level in the distribution chain in order to gain their cooperation in making the promotion a success.

PROMOTIONS TO THE TRADE

With the exception of the infinitesimal part of retail sales accounted for by company-owned stores and franchised distribution, the ultimate fate of the retail distributed product is in the hands of the retailer, who determines whether a particular brand will be stocked, where it will be stocked, how many shelf facings it will receive, and whether it will be given special displays, price features, and retail advertising support.

In-store treatment can have a profound effect on the sales of retail distributed brands. In the case of products requiring personal sales support, such as appliances, home furnishings, clothing, cameras, and hi-fi equipment, backing by retail sales personnel is critical. A retail salesperson only has to say, "Our customers have been extremely pleased with Brand X, but have had nothing but trouble with Brand Y," to relegate Brand Y to the black list of unwanted merchandise. The behavior of the retail salesperson need not be that blatant. By subtly directing the customer's attention to a particular brand, and extolling that brand's merits, the prospect's choice of brands may be swayed.

In the case of self-service grocery, drug, and variety stores, in-store treatment is a significant but less obvious factor in influencing sales. If a particular brand is not stocked or is temporarily out of stock, it cannot be bought; a substitute may be chosen. A. C. Nielsen, in a survey of 1173 grocery shoppers, found that 58 percent will accept a substitute brand if the one they want is not available.[5]

Aside from brand availability, in-store treatment may also spell the difference between success and failure. The introduction to the book *Display Ideas for Supermarkets* states:

> As any veteran of the food and grocery business knows, the so-called "self-service revolution" owes much of its success to the selling power of displays. For display almost single-handedly has assumed the function of countless sales clerks. Its historic mission has been to uphold the high-volume, low-unit profit principle of mass retailing— to cut operating costs, increase productivity, decrease prices for consumers. . . . The modern grocer builds his sales dramatically with the help of four merchandising tools—namely, special displays, promotional pricing, departmentalization, and storewide promotions.[6]

A variety of sources testify to the value of displays, feature pricing, and shelf position in generating sales.[7] In the face of heavy advertising competition, some authorities believe that in-store treatment may be the single most important variable in determining brand sales and market share.[8]

A number of devices are used to elicit retail cooperation. Although each may also have desirable side effects, most can be classified on the basis of their primary purpose. Thus, a sales promotion designed to obtain special displays may also result in price features or retail advertising support. Major purposes of retail promotions are to: (a) obtain distribution or increase inventories; (b) gain support of retail sales personnel; (c) gain special displays and/or price features; and (d) gain retailer advertising support. Often, these devices are used in combination with one another or consumer promotions. In any event, the sales promotion plan should specify the primary purpose of the device and what it is expected to accomplish.

GAINING DISTRIBUTION OR INCREASING INVENTORIES

There are two promotional devices used primarily to gain distribution or increase inventories. One, **stocking allowances,** clearly falls within the realm of sales promotion. The second, **consignment sell-**

[5]James O. Peckham, Sr., *The Wheel of Marketing* (Chicago: A. C. Nielsen Co., 1973), 10.

[6]M. Alexander, ed., *Display Ideas for Supermarkets* (New York: Progressive Grocer, 1958), 2–3.

[7]Ibid.; "The Dillon Study," *Progressive Grocer* (October 1960): D81; "Improving Sale Item Display: The Display and Merchandising Workshop," *Chain Store Age* (January 1965): 64; *Awareness, Decision, Purchases* (New York: Point-of-Purchase Advertising Institute, 1961), 14; *Drugstore Brand Switching and Impulse Buying* (New York: Point-of-Purchase Advertising Institute, 1963), 11; "Shelf Merchandising Strategy: A Key to Increased Sales," *Progressive Grocer* (March 1964): 126.

[8]H. S. Gorschman, "New Dimensions in Unhidden Persuasion," *Journal of the Academy of Marketing Science* (Fall 1973), 110–18.

ing, is borderline. In some fields, consignment selling is a standard operating procedure; in other fields, it is infrequently used thereby qualifying as a sales promotion technique.

Stocking allowances. Stocking allowances are the most frequently used sales promotion device to gain distribution. A retailer is given an allowance for each case on initial orders or all orders for a specified period of time, such as one month. The ethical justification is that a stocking allowance compensates the retailer for the expenses incurred in adding a new item to inventories. Practically speaking, it is a legal bribe that has become hallowed by use and thoroughly institutionalized as an acceptable and ethical practice. Using stocking allowances to increase the inventories of brands already stocked is called **loading.** Loading may be used by manufacturers to increase dealer inventories prior to a consumer deal that is expected to accelerate sales or prevent out of stock problems. Stocking allowances are widely used in package goods marketing, particularly in the food and drug fields.

Modifications of stocking allowances are often used. The most common is the "one free with . . . " offer, i.e., one package free for each six bought; for larger retailers, one case free with the purchase of six cases. This approach is widely used in drugstores, particularly for items that are carried only seasonally. Prior to the season it is customary to make a "one free with . . . " offer to encourage early ordering.

A second modification is leasing store space. This approach is used when trying to expand product distribution into nontraditional outlets. For example, a manufacturer of fancy chocolates might lease space in a supermarket for a display stand carrying its brand. This tactic relieves the supermarket of the risk of stocking a new product and guarantees an income from the venture. If the venture proves successful, fancy chocolates may ultimately be incorporated as a normal food store item, and the leasing arrangement will be terminated. Leased departments, an expansion of the lease idea, have been used in department stores, notably by Russell Stover candies.

Consignment selling. In consignment selling, the manufacturer retains ownership of the product while giving possession of it to retailers so that they can sell it to consumers. Thus, the manufacturer absorbs the full cost of carrying the inventory, and the dealer pays for the goods as they are sold. The Hanes Corporation used consignment selling to induce supermarkets and drugstores to handle its L'eggs brand of pantyhose.[9] A single display rack of L'eggs can generate $1,300 a year in profits to the retailer since stocking and inventory control are performed by the manufacturer. Consignment selling is also used as a standard selling practice for some big ticket items, particularly to industrial distributors. When it is used as a device to obtain new distribution, however, it may be considered as a sales promotion tactic.

---

[9]*Business Week,* 25 March 1972, 96–100.

GAINING SUPPORT OF RETAIL SALES PERSONNEL

Retail sales personnel have a minimal role in the selling of self-service products. However, in fields such as cars, appliances, furniture, carpeting, electronics, clothing, fabrics, and proprietary drugs, retail salespeople are extremely important in consummating the final sale. There are four broad sales promotion devices sometimes used to enlist retail sales personnel support: (a) **retail training;** (b) **contests;** (c) **push money;** and (d) **merchandising the advertising.**

Retail training. In this approach, sales seminars are held for retail salespeople. Technical information about the product is provided, as well as suggestions on how to approach customers, sell related items, close a sale, and so on. Since retail salespeople like to sell merchandise they are knowledgeable about and are often appreciative of the sales training, such efforts can pay off handsomely.

Contests. Contests designed for retail store owners and/or their employees are often used to gain retail support. Such contests may take a variety of forms. For example, the Frigidaire Division of General Motors undertook a major promotional effort to regain a major share of the appliance industry after a slump of several years. Prominent in its plans were dealer support programs, such as dealer incentives, volume rebates, sales literature, and even a minitheater for in-store movies. Among the dealer incentives were a series of minivacations for retail dealers and their spouses. It was estimated that about 100 people in each region (50 dealer couples) would be eligible for trips earned through points from Frigidaire's on-going "Sell 'n' Share" promotion. In addition to the minivacations, dealers could earn points redeemable in merchandise, including General Motors cars.[10] As part of a dealer incentive program in 1952, Admiral Corporation sent 50 dealers and their wives to witness the coronation of the Queen of England. The promotion was considered so successful in enlisting dealer support for Admiral's products that it became a key factor in the company's marketing program. During the past 20 years, over 20,000 dealers and their wives have traveled to virtually every major tourist attraction and world capital on the globe. Themes used to attract dealer attention and enlist their participation in the travel incentive program have included "London Getaway," "Rendezvous in Rome," "Holiday in Majorca," "Fiesta in Mexico," and "Tour de Paris."[11]

Push money. Push money (PM) involves paying retail salespeople commissions to "push" a particular brand. PMs are sometimes used in selling cosmetics, other personal care items, and proprietary medicines, as well as other products where consumer knowledge is weak and recommendations are welcome.

Merchandising the advertising. To "merchandise the advertising" is to sell the advertising and sales promotion program to channel

---

[10]S. Ayling, "Merchandising Helps Turn Frigidaire Around," *Promotion,* 29 April 1974, 22.

[11]R. Gransee, "Admiral Finds Travel Motivates, Builds Goodwill, and Has Glamour," *Promotion,* 4 March 1974, 2, Section 2, Business Meetings Selector.

intermediaries, particularly the retail trade, in order to generate enthusiasm and gain support. Annual sales meetings, scheduled by a manufacturer for its sales force, usually devote a significant portion of the meeting to outlining the advertising and promotion plans for the forthcoming year. At the conclusion of these meetings, salespeople are often provided with a summary of planned activities, called merchandising kits, to show to channel members in order to engender enthusiasm for the firm's advertising and promotion activities.

GAINING SPECIAL DISPLAYS AND/OR PRICE FEATURES

One of the most effective devices for influencing product movement, particularly in self-service stores, is the special display. The term **special display** refers to any visual device, other than normal shelf stocking, used in the store to call attention to a particular product or group of products. It may or may not include a price inducement; it may range from a simple shelf-talker to elaborate gondolas.

The effectiveness of special displays in selling merchandising is well supported by research. One study, carried out in Super Value stores over a period of 12 weeks, tested the effects of approximately 1500 separate displays. The study found that, on the average, an item given special display will sell five and one-half times as much as the one on the normal shelf position.[12] These findings have been confirmed by the Dillon study, which found that the average display boosted sales by 536 percent over normal shelf movement.[13] Still another study reports that 5 percent of all supermarket sales are the results of displays.[14] If this figure is projected to total grocery volume, it would indicate that over $4 billion worth of merchandise is sold from grocery displays each year.

However, products differ widely in terms of their responsiveness to special displays. The Super Value study found increases as high as 3453 percent for candy and as low as 36 percent for paper towels. Display effectiveness for a particular product will depend upon: (a) the product field; (b) the type and size of display used; (c) whether the display includes a price inducement; and (d) the type of point-of-purchase material used with the product display. For example, point-of-purchase material that is tied in with advertising is generally thought to be more effective than point-of-purchase material that is not.

There is no shortage of studies testifying to the effectiveness of special displays in selling merchandise. It is little wonder that sales promotions designed to obtain displays are a major preoccupation of consumer goods marketers.

The primary methods used in obtaining special displays of the product, particularly in self-service stores, are **display allowances, display cards** or **stands,** and **nonbranded promotions.**

Display allowances. A manufacturer using a display allowance offers retailers a payment, perhaps 25 cents or 50 cents a case, for

[12]Alexander, *Display Ideas for Supermarkets*, 35.

[13]"The Dillon Study," *Progressive Grocer* (October 1960): D81.

[14]"Improving Sale Item Display: The Display and Merchandising Workshop," *Chain Store Age* (January 1965): 64.

each case placed on special display. For simplicity in administration, display allowances are often based on fixed quantities, e.g., $2.50 for a 10-case display, $6.25 for a 25-case display, $12.50 for a 50-case display, $25 for a 100-case display. Manufacturers usually provide free point-of-purchase material for use on the display; this material may range from posters and banners to easily assembled structures made of metal or wood and cardboard. Display allowances and display structures are frequently used in conjunction with major consumer promotions, such as coupons and contests.

Display cards or stands. Another device for obtaining in-store displays is a brand identified display card or stand for stocking merchandise. A display card of key rings might take the form of a **counter card** that can be mounted near the cash register and have a number of key rings affixed to it; the customer would make a selection by removing a key ring from the card. The Kodak display stand (Figure 19–2) is an example of a display stand used in drugstores and grocery stores. Another example is the one used to display sunglasses.

Nonbranded promotions. Nonbranded promotions, sometimes called **storewide promotions,** consist of a wide variety of nonidentified promotional material offered by an advertiser to enable the retailers to decorate their stores. The material usually consists of window signs, store banners, display cards, shelf talkers, price stickers, and other decorative material with a theme, such as Thanksgiving, Christmas, Valentine's Day, back to school, or new store openings. Included with the nonbranded material will be brand identified point-of-purchase pieces of the advertiser offering the material. The basic philosophy underlying the use of nonbranded promotions is reciprocity. The advertiser provides the material free; as an expression of appreciation, the retailer gives special displays to the advertiser's brands.

GAINING ADVERTISING SUPPORT

Retail advertising support of a national brand appears to be an excellent way to extend national advertising dollars and localize a brand's advertising. Rates for retail advertising are significantly lower than national rates and the ad's cost is sometimes shared by the retailer; therefore, the advertiser receives more for each advertising dollar. Advertising that appears in the local media is identified with the store or stores carrying the brand. Two basic devices are used by national advertisers to gain retail advertising support: (a) **advertising allowances** and (b) **cooperative advertising.** Both of these devices are among the most widely used and severely abused forms of sales promotion.

Advertising allowances. An advertising allowance is similar to a display allowance in that the retail organization is given a case allowance for advertising purposes. Sometimes the allowance is offered on a continuing basis; in other instances, it is offered only on

FIGURE 19–2   (Courtesy Eastman Kodak Co.)

orders placed during a specified period of time. The retailer agrees to use the allowance for advertising and verifies this by sending the advertiser: (a) tear sheets of the retail advertising containing the advertiser's brand and (b) an apportioned cost statement indicating the amount spent.

Advertising allowances can be effective when the retailer accumulates the allowances so that significant space can be devoted to the brand and the sponsoring brand is given a price feature. However, the retailer usually gives the brand a column inch or less in a full page newspaper advertisement or a mention in a radio or television spot without a price feature. In newspaper ads, these casual mentions are referred to as **obituaries** by the advertising industry.

Particularly in the food and drug trade, advertising allowances are often more trouble than they are worth; at best, they represent a form of legal blackmail by retailers. Advertising allowances can be worthwhile only if: (a) they are carefully policed by the advertiser; (b) advertising materials of a minimum size are supplied with the requirement that the material be used to qualify for the allowance; and (c) a price feature is given or required.

The worst form of advertising allowance is the **continuing allowance.** Under this arrangement, the retailer's advertising support can easily become casual; if the allowance is withdrawn the advertiser runs the risk of offending the retail organization and losing distribution.

Cooperative advertising. Cooperative advertising is most generally used on big ticket items. Often, it represents the major advertising effort of the manufacturer. Used properly and carefully policed, cooperative advertising can be extremely effective; used carelessly, it is a waste of company resources.

Under a cooperative advertising agreement, the manufacturer agrees to pay a portion, usually 50 percent, of the advertising cost for its brand run in local media under the name of the cooperating retailer. The annual obligation of the manufacturer is specified (usually based on an estimate of sales that will be made through the retailer organization), and payment is made upon receipt of a tear sheet and a copy of the media's invoice. For example, a retailer runs a full page ad in the local newspaper on the manufacturer's brand; the cost of the advertisement is $1800 at local rates. Upon receipt of a tear sheet and copy of the invoice, the manufacturer rebates half of the total cost ($900) to the retailer in the form of a check or credit memorandum. The manufacturer usually provides the mats or other advertising material required by the medium.

The $7.5 billion spent on cooperative advertising is evidence of the fact that this arrangement has advantages for both the manufacturer and the retail store.[15] The manufacturer obtains local advertising that is identified with a local retailer, gains the advantage of local rates, is only obligated for half of the advertising space costs, and retains control over what is said in the advertisement. On the other hand, the retail organization obtains advertising at half its

[15]Renee Blakkan, "Partnership Perks Up Profits," *Advertising Age,* 17 August 1981, S–1.

normal cost, is provided with professionally prepared advertising copy, and is identified with a prestigious national brand.

Cooperative advertising also has disadvantages, however. Implementing and policing the program requires a great deal of paperwork. To assure their participation, retailers must be carefully supervised, and tear sheets must be checked to see that advertising is run according to specifications. When broadcast advertising is used, verification requires that station logs be checked or the actual broadcast monitored. Since these procedures are expensive, a more common practice is to obtain an affidavit from an executive of the broadcast station certifying that the commercial actually ran. Such affidavits are widely used but subject to error or fraud. A retailer may conspire with the media to submit an invoice that reflects a higher rate than was actually paid, or fail to follow up with in-store support in accordance with the cooperative agreement. Local newspapers and television are basically mass media and provide little selectivity for the advertiser, therefore, waste circulation becomes a problem.

Cooperative advertising does have value for the manufacturer who uses selective or exclusive distribution; it has less value for the brand that is widely distributed. When cooperative advertising is used for convenience products, such as detergents or other grocery store items, it is usually a device to give the retailer a price discount, with no expectation that the advertising will contribute any appreciable value.

Trade promotions may take a number of forms and involve more than one activity. The Maxwell House "Lucky Cup" sweepstakes (Figure 19–3) is an imaginative and effective use of trade promotion money.

CONSUMER PROMOTIONS

Consumer promotions are generally used for two primary purposes: (a) attract new customers; and (b) increase the purchases of existing customers. Inherent in these two purposes are two other functions that consumer promotions often serve. First, they create an aura of excitement around the brand, calling attention to it in fresh and unusual ways. Second, they may serve to deplete surplus inventories and stimulate retailers to reorder or order in larger than usual quantities. In the case of new product introductions, consumer promotions are widely used as a forcing device to get retailers to stock the product; if customers start demanding the product, retailers will be forced to stock it in order to maintain customer good will and patronage.

Consumer promotions are often used in conjunction with related trade promotions. For example, a consumer contest or coupon distribution will often be backed up by display material, display allowances, stocking allowances, or even cooperative advertising.

CONSUMER PROMOTIONS TO SAMPLE NEW CUSTOMERS

No attempt will be made to identify all of the consumer promotions or combinations of promotions that may be used to attract new customers. The type of promotion used is limited only by the budget

Objectives
1 Increase share of market for Maxwell House with take-out coffee accounts
2 Increase consumption of coffee
3 Demonstrate new uses for co-op money

Basic idea
1 Supply retailers with paper cups that have three rub-off squares. Instant winners receive free coffee or cash prizes ranging from $1 to $5,000.
2 The retailer provides the free coffee and Maxwell House provides the cash.
3 Hold a second chance drawing for unclaimed prize money.
4 Maxwell provides the cups at 16 cents each, but uses co-op money to discount cups for larger orders and for putting display material in stores.
5 Retailers are supplied with free p.o.p. material and advertising kits.

Budget
$175,000

Results
1 Gained new distribution
2 Volume up considerably
3 About 40 chains participated with all outlets; other chains tested promotion in some of their stores

and imagination of the marketer. Time-worn promotions are constantly being refurbished by the addition of new wrinkles. At the heart of most effective consumer promotions are five basic approaches: (a) coupons and price-off label offers; (b) sampling; (c) demonstrations; (d) premiums; and (e) contests and sweepstakes.

COUPONS AND PRICE-OFF OFFERS

One of the more popular devices for attracting new customers is coupons. If price-off label offers are added to the 90 billion coupons distributed annually in the United States, the number of consumer deals represented by these two devices defies imagination.

Basically, coupons differ in terms of face value, breadth of distribution, method of delivery, and method of redemption. When New Purina Dog Chow was test marketed in Little Rock, Arkansas, a coupon redeemable for a two-pound box of the product was mailed to every other household in the Little Rock metropolitan area.

Generally, a coupon should be for at least 10 to 15 percent of the normal product price to attract consumer attention; coupons offering less than 10 cents off the regular price are generally ignored. Table 19–1 shows the estimated costs for delivering 25 million coupons by a variety of delivery methods. The average face value of the coupons used in these calculations was 14 cents; 5 cents per coupon was paid to retailers for handling, and a one cent charge has been included for internal processing. No allowance was made for misredemption, although it was estimated at 20 percent. If misredemption is as high as the 33 percent that some recent industry sources contend, the effectiveness of the programs would be reduced even further. The cost per coupon redeemed ranges from a low of 23.3 cents to a high of 75.5 cents.

Another method of delivering coupons is the in-package coupon, redeemable on the next purchase. This method is not particularly effective in attracting new users because it provides little incentive value for the consumer who has doubts about making the first purchase. As a sales promotion device, this approach is more effective in generating additional purchases by current users. A variation of the in-package coupon, used by marketers who have multiple products, is **cross-couponing.** For example, a coupon in a package of Betty Crocker Hamburger Helper is redeemable on a box of Betty Crocker Cake Mix.

There are also variations in the way that coupons are redeemed. Normally, coupons are redeemable at the retailer's checkout

TABLE 19–1   Cost per coupon redeemed based upon redemption rates

Circulation Method	Cost Per 1000 Printing and Delivery	Average Redemption (Percent)	Distribution Cost (1)	Total Number of Redemptions (2)	Redemption Costs (3)	Total Program Costs	Cost Per Coupon Redeemed (cents)
Direct mail							
Co-op	$14	11.7%	$ 350,000	2,925,000	$585,000	$ 935,000	31.9¢
Solo	90	16.2 (e)	2,250,000	4,050,000	810,000	3,060,000	75.5
Magazine							
Solo	6	3.5	150,000	875,000	175,000	325,000	37
Page plus coupon	12	9.1	300,000	2,275,000	455,000	755,000	33.2
Newspaper							
600-line r.o.p.	3.75	2.4	93,750	600,000	120,000	213,750	35.6
1000-line r.o.p.	6.25	2.8 (e)	156,250	700,000	140,000	296,250	42.3
Co-op r.o.p.							
Coupon only	1	3	25,000	750,000	150,000	175,000	23.3
With copy	2	4.5 (e)	50,000	1,125,000	225,000	275,000	24.4
Supplements							
Solo	6	3.1	150,000	775,000	155,000	305,000	39.3
Free-standing inserts							
Coupon only	2.25	5.4	56,250	1,350,000	270,000	326,250	24.1
With copy	3.50	6.4 (e)	87,500	1,600,000	320,000	407,500	25.4

(1) Distribution cost based on circulation of 25,000,000; some programs have more, others less distribution.
(2) No allowance made for misredemption, estimated by some industry sources at 20 percent.
(3) Average cost based on 14 cents face value plus 5 cents handling charge and one cent internal handling charge.
(e) Estimated.
Note: Redemption rates based on A. C. Nielsen Co. figures where available or industry sources; distribution costs based on published rates and industry estimates.
Source: Reprinted with permission from the October 25, 1976 issue of *Advertising Age.* Copyright © 1976 by Crain Communications, Inc.

counter. An alternate method requires the consumer to mail the coupon along with a label from the product directly to the manufacturer. The manufacturer then rebates the face value of the coupon to the consumer. This technique may decrease misredemption, but it is an extremely weak promotional device because few consumers will bother to mail the coupon in unless its value is exceedingly high. If the coupon value is high enough to overcome consumer inertia, the cost of the couponing effort may become exorbitant, and imaginative methods of misredemption will be invented.

A price-off label is a substitute device for couponing that eliminates some of the handling problems and reduces, but does not eliminate, cheating. Price-off label offers are generally limited to a certain production quantity, such as a one-month supply at retail. The manufacturer either prints the price-off label offer: (a) directly on the package; or (b) on a removable **sleeve** or band that encircles the package. In either case, additional packaging costs are incurred. The merchandise is then sold to retailers at a reduced cost to maintain retailer margins. When the offer is printed on a removable sleeve or band, unscrupulous retailers may remove the band and sell the packages at the normal shelf price.

Price-off label offers are usually more expensive for the manufacturer than coupons because income is lost on the face value of all packages carrying the price reduction; the average coupon redemption generally runs less than 10 percent, depending on the face value of the coupon and its method of delivery. In addition, marketers are often reluctant to use a price-off label offer during a new product introduction because the retail value of the product has not yet been established. As a consequence, coupons are the preferred incentive for new product introductions.

Sampling. Consumer sampling is a direct device for reaching new customers. In this method, a sample of the product, usually a miniature package, is distributed to consumers at home, in retail stores, on shopping center parking lots, or in other high traffic locations. Sampling is expensive, and costs are dependent upon the size of the sample, number distributed, and method of distribution. Sampling can be a highly effective device if the product is discernibly superior in some relevant way to competitive brands. Because of the costs involved, sampling is generally restricted to new product introductions and major consumer promotions.

Demonstration. Demonstration is a form of sampling that is widely used for products ranging from food items to automobiles. Although product demonstrations may be made at the home or place of purchase, they are most frequently made at the latter because of the economy of having a central demonstration point. In the case of automobiles, a demonstration ride is a conventional selling technique. Most department stores will from time to time have in-store demonstrations of carpet sweepers, microwave ovens, sewing machines, and so on. Department stores and drugstores often have in-store demonstrators offering dabs of new fragrances to passersby. Food stores also have demonstrators handing out samples of food items.

Since they require payment of a salary to a demonstrator in each store and the cost of the product involved, demonstrations are expensive. For this reason, demonstrations are usually restricted to high volume outlets and peak shopping periods.

Premiums. Premiums of all kinds are used to attract new customers. In-pack, near-pack (the premium is stocked in the store near the product), mail-in, trading stamps, combination offers (buy one and get one free or at a reduced price), and premiums for opening a new bank account are only a few of the methods used as new customer incentives.

Many marketers think that premiums are often unimaginative and overused. Louis J. Haugh, a promotion authority, observes:

> Why so many banks and other financial institutions persist in turning their quarterly quest for new savings deposits into bug eye advertising featuring multiple premiums defies common sense.
>
> Some members of this financial community use such unimaginative advertising with its panoply of electronic appliances and other gimcracks that even the defense that such ads are successful in pulling in new savings and new accounts can hardly hold water.
>
> All too often, banks festoon their lobbies with displays of the products used in the premium offer, running the very real risk, it would seem, of confusing someone who may think he or she has walked into a department store rather than a bank.[16]

Despite abuses, premiums remain a major incentive, both for attracting new customers and rewarding loyal ones.

Contests and sweepstakes. Contests differ from sweepstakes because the consumer is required to do something that is judged, and prizes are awarded to the winners. Consumers may be asked to name a product, compose or complete a limerick, write an essay, think up a slogan, or guess a number, e.g., how many beans are in a jar. Participants may prepare something using the manufacturer's product and submit it for judging. An outstanding example of this approach is the Pillsbury Bake-Off that has been run annually since 1949. Heavily supported by advertising, the contest attracts approximately 250,000 women a year who submit their favorite recipe made by using Pillsbury flour. One hundred winners are flown to New York for the final judging at the Waldorf Astoria. This contest has provided some outstanding payoffs for Pillsbury. For example, Bundt Cake, a prepared cake mix that has earned Pillsbury several millions of dollars in profit since its introduction in the early 1970s, was the winning recipe in one of the bake-offs.

The attractiveness of a contest depends on the magnitude of the prize structure and complexity of the task. Some consumers avoid contests because the requirements are too great or rules too exacting. There are also professional contest entrants who sometimes make a sizable, but unknown, proportion of the entrants;

---

[16]Louis J. Haugh, "Banks Going Premium Crazy, But Promos Lack Imagination," *Advertising Age,* 19 December 1977, 44.

some consumers avoid contests because they believe that these professional contenders win most of the prizes.

Sweepstakes avoid the skill element of contests by awarding prizes on the basis of chance. Entrants' names are pooled, and the winners are selected at random. The number of people likely to enter a sweepstakes is much higher than contests because it requires less effort. On the negative side, it also requires less personal involvement.

Participation in a sweepstakes sometimes requires the consumer to purchase one unit of the sponsor's product and send the product's label with the entry. Lottery laws in some states prohibit this requirement because it involves a payment (purchase of the product); this payment is interpreted as gambling. To circumvent lottery laws, many sweepstakes either require no qualification for entry, permit entrants to submit a facsimile of the label, or allow them to print the brand name on the entry blank.

The success of a sweepstakes depends upon the prize structure, number of winners, and amount of advertising devoted to it. In its annual drive for magazine subscriptions, Publishers' Clearing House offers a $100,000 house as first prize, plus a vacation home, cars, and a galaxy of other prizes as consolation. On the other hand, Pepsi-Cola ran a sweepstakes in the mid-1970s which offered 65,000 prizes, ranging from $1 to $50 worth of groceries.

While the primary purpose of consumer promotions is to acquire new customers, few pay for themselves on this basis alone. Important collateral values include retaining existing customers, combatting competitive promotions, creating excitement around the brand, and stimulating the sales force and trade.

CONSUMER PROMOTIONS DESIGNED TO INCREASE PURCHASES OF CURRENT CUSTOMERS

While some of the sales promotion techniques used to gain new customers are also used to increase the purchases of existing patrons, these methods are usually modified when the latter objective is the primary purpose of the promotion. For example, the primary purpose of a blanket mailing of coupons or the use of magazine distribution is the acquisition of new customers. On the other hand, an in-pack coupon good on the next purchase is more appropriate for generating loyalty and repeat purchase by current customers. Similarly, a one-time premium offer may be effective for attracting new customers, while a continuing premium offer (a set of dishes or silverware, one piece with each purchase) is intended to retain the loyalty of existing buyers.

Some brands are known as **premium brands** because continuing premiums constitute their major promotional effort. Bonus, a Procter & Gamble detergent, contains a premium in every box (a dish towel, piece of dinnerware, or some other premium) and is positioned to appeal to those consumers for whom premiums are a primary motivation for purchase. Similarly, Raleigh cigarettes offers a coupon on every package; these coupons are saved and exchanged for a variety of merchandise, such as bridge tables, lawn chairs, small appliances, household furnishings, sports equipment, and personal items, selected from a premium catalog.

In addition to these devices, two other sales promotion techniques are commonly used to increase purchase among present customers: (a) two-for-one offers; and (b) multiple packs. In the two-for-one offer, two packages will be banded together and sold for the price of one, or at a substantial discount from the normal price. In multiple packs, products are sold in special packaged multiples, such as three, four, six, or so on, as well as in individual packages. Soft drinks, beer, fruit juices, and antacid tablets are examples of products that are sold in this way. A standard brewing industry sales promotion is the "Pick a pair of six-packs" promotion, widely used in the height of the beer drinking season. While these approaches may also attract new customers, their primary intent is for people who have already tried the brand and are familiar with it. Customers unfamiliar with the brand are less likely to commit themselves to multiple purchases on their first trial.

In the foregoing discussion, sales promotion methods have been classified in terms of their primary objective. Sales promotions are relatively short-term, limited objective marketing devices. The primary functions are to solve particular marketing problems, take advantage of specific opportunities, deplete inventories, encourage stocking, and so on; these tasks require activities above and beyond the normal advertising program. While sales promotions are an essential part of consumer marketing, using them too frequently dulls their effectiveness, diminishes their excitement, and depreciates the value of the brand in consumers' minds. Sales promotions are a supplementary marketing activity, not the major effort of most advertisers.

Each year, *Advertising Age* runs a feature on the best promotions of the year. Three of these promotions are summarized in Figures 19–4, 19–5, and 19–6. Note that the promotions often include a variety of techniques, directed at both consumers and the trade.

SUMMARY

Sales promotion is a big, diverse, and complex activity that comprises over 80 billion coupons, $2 billion in point-of-purchase materials, contests, sweepstakes, cents-off coupons, display allowances, stocking allowances, in-store demonstrations, and an untold number of premiums.

Sales promotion has three salient characteristics: (a) It is a relatively short-term activity. (b) It may be directed toward the sales force, distribution channels, consumers, or some combination of these groups. (c) It is used to stimulate some specific action. In this latter respect, it differs from advertising because it is designed to provoke some immediate action as opposed to disseminating information, persuading, and influencing attitudes. Sales promotion is a supplementary marketing activity and does not replace advertising.

Sales promotion directed to the sales force is designed to encourage some particular form of sales activity and is often used in conjunction with trade or consumer promotions.

Brands involved

Little Friskies, Fish Ahoy, and Chef's Blend

Objectives

1 Generate trial for all three brands of dry cat food

2 Increase volume

Basic idea

Run four separate promotions from June through November, varying the promotional offer in each promotion to span the broadest spectrum of cat owners.

1 In June: Offer an exclusive cat feeder free in the mail, with 12 proofs of purchase from any of the three brands. Support with ads carrying three coupons.

2 In August: Run a graduated refund, supported by coupon ads on all three brands.

3 In October: Offer a personalized calendar, with the cat's own photo, free for 12 proofs of purchase. The calendar also carries continuity coupons. Offer supported with package flags (notices on the package) and coupon ads.

4 In November: For Chef's Blend only, offer a self-liquidating premium (an au jus meat cutting board) and support it with coupon ads.

All four promotions to be supported with media advertising and in-store material.

Budget

$3,300,000 (June, $850,000; August, $1,000,000; October, $900,000; November, $550,000)

Results

1 Six-month volume increased by 8 percent over previous year.

2 Proofs of purchase for 5 million pounds of cat food received.

3 Gained 130 major new accounts.

Example of advertisement

FIGURE 19–4 Carnation multiple-brand promotion (Courtesy Carnation Co.)

FIGURE 19–5 Molson Golden Canadian Beer Treasure Hunt (Courtesy Martlet Importing Co.)

Objectives

1 Increase awareness among men 21 to 34
2 Increase distribution and sales in Chicago metropolitan area

Basic idea

1 Stage a treasure hunt for "gold" nuggets, worth $5,000 in Canadian gold coins, hidden in a public park.
2 Offer 50 additional prizes of Molson T-shirts and hats and a second chance sweepstakes for unclaimed prizes.
3 Provide a series of clues to the treasure's location over four weeks, with a treasure map, point-of-purchase displays, newspaper ads, radio commercials, and a public relations event involving Canadian Mounties delivering the final clues. Tie promotion in with sales force and retailer programs.

Budget

$115,000 (media, $45,000; sales promotion, $60,000; trade, $10,000)

Results

Distribution and sales doubled during and after the promotion.

Example of "treasure map" ad

Objective
Increase cookie sales during a normally depressed
sales period

Basic idea
1   Develop a new recipe for making ice cream
    cookies with Slice 'n Bake.
2   Offer the recipe and 15 cents off coupon in ads,
    and back it up with heavy television support.
3   Provide additional incentive with a $1 refund
    on ice cream at participating retailers.

Budget
$1,721,000 (media, $960,000; sales promotion,
$389,000; trade, $372,000)

Results
1   Sales up 65 percent over previous year
2   Share of market up 2.8 percent

Example of coupon advertisement

Sales promotions directed toward the channels of distribution
are designed to: (a) gain distribution or increase inventories;
(b) gain support of retail personnel; (c) obtain special displays
and/or price features; or (d) encourage retail advertising support.

Consumer promotions are usually used to: (a) sample new customers; and (b) increase purchases of existing customers.

Although sales promotion is an essential marketing activity, it
should not be relied upon so heavily that more basic marketing activities are neglected.

REVIEW QUESTIONS

1 Explain the distinction drawn between advertising and sales promotion.
2 Explain why the use of sales promotion has grown with the growth of the brand management system. What are the possible consequences of this trend for the health of individual brands?
3 Identify the basic groups that are the target of sales promotion. Are any of these groups more important than others? Why or why not?
4 Identify and explain the major sales promotion devices designed to gain distribution and increase inventories.
5 Explain what is meant by consignment selling. Under what condition may consignment selling be considered a sales promotion device?
6 Identify and explain the major sales promotion techniques designed to elicit support of retail sales personnel.
7 Identify and explain the major sales promotion devices used to gain displays and/or price features.
8 Evaluate the use of advertising allowances.
9 Explain what is meant by cooperative advertising and identify the major problems associated with it.
10 Identify and explain the various forms of sales promotion used to sample new customers.

DISCUSSION QUESTIONS

1 During the past two seasons, a major league baseball team has suffered a decline in game attendance. A decision has been made to employ sales promotion to increase attendance. Suggest how this problem might be approached and some sales promotion ideas that might be useful.
2 Visit a supermarket, drugstore, and department store. Make a list of all of the sales promotion devices that you are able to identify. What differences did you find?
3 A local bank has decided to use sales promotion to attract new customers and increase the use of the bank's services (savings accounts, checking accounts, safety deposit boxes, loans, and so on) among existing customers. How would you approach this problem? Consider the groups against which promotions should be directed and the types of promotions that would be appropriate.

PROBLEM

You are a member of the sales promotion department of an advertising agency. One of your clients is the maker of a brand of toothpaste that has recently experienced share losses because of flavor improvements by a leading competitor's product. Your client has recently completed a formula modification that, according to consumer tests, has significantly improved the flavor of your product. The sales promotion strategy for the forthcoming year states:

1 In view of the product flavor improvement, primary emphasis will be placed on a consumer coupon promotion, coupled with a display allowance.

2   A 15-cent consumer coupon will be used since company experience has shown this coupon value to be the most efficient in generating redemption.

3   It shall be a point of strategy to sample 2 million households with the improved product.

4   The coupon effort shall not cost more than 55 cents per sampled household, and it is a point of strategy to minimize duplication among coupon recipients.

5   The couponing effort will be supported by a display allowance to encourage in-store displays, with emphasis given to displays of 25 cases or more.

6   The promotion period will extend from September 1 through October 31 to avoid the decrease in effectiveness characteristic of summer promotions for dental care products and conflict with the Thanksgiving/Christmas holiday season.

You have been asked to recommend a specific sales promotion plan and prepare a budget for the sales promotion effort.

You have past figures on cost-per-thousand for printing and delivering various types of coupons, as well as the redemption rates for each method of coupon distribution. (Use the figures from Table 19–1 for these two variables).

You estimate that misredemption will be 20 percent; to sample 2 million households with the product, you will have to make an allowance for misredemption. Coupon costs will include a 15-cent coupon plus 5 cents for handling by retailers and one cent for internal handling.

In estimating display costs, you know there are 50,000 Class A stores. If you offer $25 for 25-case display, you estimate, on the basis of past experience, that 15 percent of these stores will cooperate. There are also 250,000 Class B stores. Here you estimate that an offer of $10 for a 10-case display will obtain cooperation from about 5 percent of these stores.

Prepare your recommendation and budget.

VI

Special Objectives— Strategies and Plans

The "special objectives and strategies" section of the marketing plan for an established product normally deals with such topics as product, packaging, pricing, and distribution. For a new product, these variables are an integral part of the marketing plan; for an established product, they exist as givens unless unanticipated developments in the marketplace require that they be reexamined.

In the plan of presentation followed in the text, these variables were moved forward in the discussion because they are so crucial to the basic marketing effort. Other variables, such as product publicity, market testing, and marketing research, have not yet been discussed as elements of the marketing plan because they are optional and are included in a given plan only under special circumstances. Chapter 20 will address these topics. In addition, a portion of the chapter will be devoted to corporate advertising.

Product publicity, a specialized form of public relations, is a controversial element in the marketing mix. Some marketers believe that it is an important part of a well-rounded marketing program. Others believe that it is a waste of resources. In our discussion of product publicity, we will recognize that it can be either, depending upon how it is planned and executed.

Market testing is often a part of the marketing plan because it is an economical way of testing new ideas before deciding whether major resources

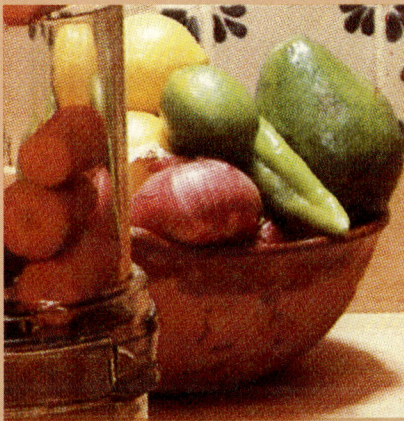

should be allocated to finance them.

Marketing research appears in the marketing plan in two ways: (a) a routine method for gathering information about the effectiveness of other marketing variables; or (b) a marketing objective itself, when marketing analysis identifies major gaps in available marketing information. In this latter instance, a particular marketing research program may become a key objective of the "special objectives and strategies" section of the marketing plan.

Normally, corporate advertising has no place in a product marketing plan. It is a separate communications effort designed to accomplish special corporate objectives and should be supported by a separate planning document, usually referred to as a "corporate advertising plan." Although widely used, much corporate advertising is ill-conceived and poorly executed, and could benefit from the systematic approach and rigorous thinking that characterizes the product marketing plan.

Since the corporate advertising plan has a great deal in common with a product marketing plan, a brief discussion will be devoted to adapting the structure of the product marketing plan to the needs of a corporate advertising program.

This section completes our basic discussion of the marketing plan and its role in developing effective advertising. In the final section of the text, we will turn our attention to some special topics in advertising.

20

Publicity, Research, and Corporate Advertising

OTHER OPTIONS

PUBLICITY

Press briefings are often an integral part of a product publicity program. The following example involves a copying machine manufacturer that didn't have an adequate advertising budget to introduce a new product. As a consequence, product publicity was an essential ingredient in establishing product identity in a highly competitive market.

The challenge: How to introduce most effectively a new table top copying machine, the first of its kind to make copies from bound books.

The action: Arrange an unveiling of the machine at the leading national trade show for business equipment in a 1980, futuristic setting. A special "desk of tomorrow" was built to house the copying machine and a variety of other 21st Century office gadgets.

Teaser announcements in the form of imitation passports were sent out to the appropriate press four weeks in advance of the briefing. The front cover of the latest issue of each of the key magazines was shown in the passport in place of the traditional passport holder's picture. The teaser asked the editors to be on the lookout for an important news announcement from the client. Enclosed with the passport to the client's world of copying was the editor's official press pass to the trade show.

Two weeks before the event, a complete press packet with background information, photographs, and releases were distributed in a "book." Made like a college annual, the book was hollow and the press materials were housed inside. Editors were reminded to see the product in operation the first day of the business equipment show. The briefing took place two hours before show opening with the editors as guests of the client for the entire show.

Results: An outstanding turnout. More than 50 editors attended. Special photography was provided for those wanting custom photos of the new product in the "Desk of Tomorrow." All major business and trade publications covering the industry ran major stories, most with photographs. The United Press ran a photo caption story that produced over 5,000 inquiries alone. The *New York Times* and major horizontal business magazines including *Business Week*, ran stories. *Wall Street Journal* ran a page one column on how the client used highly creative techniques to generate attention for its product introduction.[1]

A GOOD STEWARD

A major consumer products company, both emulated and feared by its competitors, owes at least a part of its success to its almost biblical emphasis on stewardship. Its product managers are thought of and sometimes referred to as stewards of the brands assigned to them; a good steward always sets part of his budget aside for learning more about his product and its responsiveness to changes in marketing strategy. Good stewardship often takes the form of market testing, and most marketing plans make provision for some sort of marketing test, such as a business building test to determine the effect of increased spending on market share; a media test to observe the effect of a media shift on consumer awareness; a promotion test to determine the appeal of a new premium; an advertising test to evaluate a new copy approach; a package test to assess the influence of a package change; or a pricing test to gain knowledge of the price elasticity of a brand. Not all of these tests appear in a single marketing plan. One is often sufficient. In the aggregate and over a period of time, however, a remarkable amount of market testing is done. Nor are large amounts of money spent on most tests because the tests are restricted to a few, limited geographic areas. Not all tests are successful; many fail. Because of inability to control all of the variables that affect test results, not all tests are valid. But it is this ceaseless probing, this constant search for marketing opportunities through testing that keeps the company aware of the strengths and limitations of its marketing programs and keeps com-

[1]James B. Strenski, "Tips for Better Press Briefings," *Public Relations Quarterly* (Fall 1976), 28.

petitors off balance. When a test succeeds, the findings are incorporated in the next year's marketing plan, and the scope of the test is expanded to a larger geographic area for verification. The concept of market testing is firmly entrenched in the company's marketing philosophy and made manifest in its marketing strategies.

CORPORATE ADVERTISING—A $1 BILLION QUESTION MARK

In 1970 total expenditures for corporate advertising approximated $150 million. Ten years later, these expenditures had grown to over $1 billion. Walter Margulies, a New York-based communications and design consultant, has summed up the growth of corporate advertising in the following way: "Clearly, corporate advertising is finally on its way. Precisely where it is on its way to—and how—is the troubling question."[2]

Corporate advertising is one of the more controversial areas of advertising, primarily because the reasons for it are not always clear. However, properly used, it may play an important role in company communications.

The foregoing examples of publicity and stewardship are typical of the optional activities that may be included in the other objectives and strategies section of the marketing plan. Whether they appear as a part of a marketing plan depends upon the marketing situation and the judgment of the marketing planner.

On the other hand, corporate advertising has no role in the product marketing plan. It is a separate form of advertising which has its own advertising plan—an adaptation of the product marketing plan. In this chapter, we will see how the product marketing plan can be adapted for corporate advertising.

PRODUCT PUBLICITY

Publicity is a somewhat ambiguous term that is used in a variety of ways. For example, Norman A. Hart, in a book titled *Industrial Publicity*, said:

> The term *publicity* here is used in an all-embracing sense of publicising anything for any purpose. It thus includes activities which contribute to selling and are known as sales promotion. . . .
> Under the heading *sales promotion* are included all the various 'channels of persuasion' such as advertising, direct mail, exhibitions, and so on.[3]

In contrast, Rolf Gompertz in *Promotion and Publicity Handbook for Broadcasters* has said:

> But whatever publicity is, it is *not* advertising and it is *not* promotion. It is important to make this distinction and to keep it in mind.
> Much confusion arises among the general public—not to mention among some clients—over this difference and the failure to

---

[2]Walter P. Margulies, "A Stepsister to Consumer," *Advertising Age*, 6 July 1981, S–2.

[3]Norman A. Hart, *Industrial Publicity* (New York: John Wiley & Sons, 1971), 3.

make that distinction. The difference between advertising and publicity is quite simple: advertising is *paid for* space (or air time), while publicity is *free* space (or air time).

> You can *control* what goes into an ad (or a commercial). You *cannot control* editorial content or editorial space. (You can influence it by the information you make available and the professional service you render, but you *cannot* control the way this information is used. You cannot even guarantee that it will be used.)[4]

This latter definition is the one that is generally accepted by the advertising industry and the one that is used in this text. In Chapter 4, publicity was defined:

> Publicity is a form of promotion. It differs from advertising because it is not paid for at standard rates, and the sponsor is not identified. Usually, publicity appears (unidentified as such) in the editorial or news columns of printed media or in the noncommercial portion of radio or television programs.[5]

Two key points are implied by this definition and made explicit in the quotation from Gompertz that precedes it: (a) Publicity is free. (b) The advertiser does not control it. Both of these points deserve further comment.

Even though media do not charge for it, publicity does involve cost. Plans have to be made and coordinated; personnel have to be assigned to the activity; press releases have to be prepared; and press conferences are often elaborately staged. Further, when a press conference is given in behalf of a product, product samples, as well as product literature, are often distributed to those attending. As a consequence, a budget must be established for a well organized publicity program, and the budget should be a part of the marketing plan because it does represent a cost for promoting the product.

The second point is that the advertiser has no control over the way that publicity will be used or whether it will be used at all. At best, the advertiser can try to influence what will be said by releasing favorable information. But sometimes even the best of publicity programs backfires. For example, as a part of a product publicity program, a series of press conferences are scheduled for newspaper writers in the cities where the product is being introduced. The press conferences are well staged and include a free dinner and brief presentation by company executives on the product and its values. A popular columnist of a major metropolitan newspaper writes a satirical column that ridicules the client company, its executives, and the product. As a result, client executives can become offended, talk about suing the newspaper, or simply prolong some uncomfortable meetings. Although this example does not represent a common occurrence, such things can happen. Normally, the worst outcome of a publicity program is that press releases are ignored and the effort is largely wasted.

In view of these limitations, many companies do not bother with publicity. They prefer to devote their efforts to advertising and

---

[4]Rolf Gompertz, *Promotion and Publicity Handbook for Broadcasters* (Blue Ridge Summit, Pennsylvania: Tab Books, 1977), 13.

[5]S. W. Dunn and A. M. Barban, *Advertising: Its Role in Modern Marketing* (Hinsdale, Illinois: The Dryden Press, 1974), 9.

sales promotion activities over which they have greater control. However, other companies use product publicity extensively, primarily for the following reasons:

☐ *Publicity is free.* The greatest value of product publicity derives from the fact that it is not paid for in the normal sense of payment. As a consequence, its appearance in media implies independent editorial validity of product claims. Generally, the public trusts media, and the product benefits from this trust.

☐ *Advertising is expensive.* Few clients could afford to pay for the media space and time that results from a successful product publicity campaign. In the competitive world of marketing, products need all of the support they can get.

☐ *There is a demand by media for information on products.* Newspapers and magazines provide this information as a service to readers, often in the form of a column devoted to consumer products. An advertiser should take advantage of this demand; there is the strong possibility that his competitor will.

THE BASIC INGREDIENT OF PUBLICITY

The basic ingredient of successful publicity is news. Publicity releases that are truly newsworthy have a high incidence of use. It is generally true that product publicity is more effective for a new product than for an established one. On the other hand, there are news opportunities for established products. The fact that a particular brand of reconstituted citrus drink is used by astronauts in their extraterrestrial perambulations because of its high nutritional content is news. The selection of a particular brand of trucks for construction work on the Alaskan pipeline because of its ruggedness and starting dependability is news. Preference for a particular brand of tires or sparkplugs by the winner of the Indianapolis 500 because of its performance under trying conditions is news. The manufacturers of outboard motors spend fortunes entering boats powered by their motors in national and international outboard races because the fact that the winning boat was powered by a Mercury or Evinrude motor is news.

The facts surrounding many established products contain elements of news. While news is only one of the techniques of advertising, it is the primary technique of product publicity.

STAFFING FOR PRODUCT PUBLICITY

Some companies maintain their own public relations departments that are responsible for product publicity and work closely with the marketing department. Product publicity is seldom a direct function of the marketing department. Similarly, a few advertising agencies have a public relations department staffed with experts to serve the publicity needs of their clients.

Often, advertisers and advertising agencies rely on specialized public relations agencies, which charge for their counsel and time on a fee basis, depending on the scope and duration of the services required.

Regardless of whether the advertiser has a publicity department or retains a public relations agency, a great deal of product publicity is poorly done. A survey reported in the *Public Relations Journal* concludes: "far too many new-product releases are targeted for the wrong publications, and a depressing number are poorly written, not clear, or do not contain enough information."[6] Among the findings of the survey were:

- ☐ 78.6 percent of the releases were for products not relevant to the publications to which they were sent.
- ☐ 39.3 percent of the releases were poorly written, not clear, or did not contain enough information.
- ☐ 32.1 percent of the releases contained too much puffery.
- ☐ 28.6 percent of the releases were old releases or for products that were not new.

Other complaints included "product not newsworthy," "poor photographs," "sloppy, illegible typing or printing," " 'Dum-dum' agency omitted client's name, address, and phone number."

PLANNING PRODUCT PUBLICITY

Not all product publicity releases are preplanned. Sometimes they arise spontaneously and erratically, depending on the environment. If an unanticipated opportunity for product publicity arises, the company will take advantage of it on an ad hoc basis.

Our primary concern is the systematic use of product publicity as a part of the marketing plan. When used in this way, references to product publicity will appear in various parts of the marketing plan.

Problems and opportunities. The problems and opportunities section of the marketing plan for a particular product might carry the following statement: "The development of a new circuitry and display mechanism for our model 3062 pocket computer, which extends the life of the battery from 30 to 2000 hours, appears to be a newsworthy technological advance that should be featured in our advertising and promotion during the forthcoming fiscal period."

Marketing strategy. The marketing strategy section of the plan might state: "Because of the newsworthiness of the extended battery life of model 3062, product publicity will be used to capitalize on this development. Particular attention should be devoted to: (a) retail buyers of pocket computers in major department stores; (b) technical journals; (c) product columns in newspapers and magazines; and (d) general news writers.

Objectives and strategy. An objectives and strategy section for product publicity would be prepared by appropriate specialists. This section would include:

---

[6]"Why New-Product Releases Don't Get Published," *Public Relations Journal* (June 1980): 43.

1   A brief statement of the purpose and rationale for publicity program.

2   An identification of the specific audiences to be reached.

3   A description of the publicity activities that will be undertaken and the timing of each.

4   A statement of how product publicity will be coordinated with the advertising and sales promotion programs.

5   An estimate of the costs of the publicity program.

6   A statement explaining how the effectiveness of the publicity program will be evaluated.

MARKET TESTING

Some form of market testing is often a part of the marketing plan. It can be argued that some form of market testing should *always* be a part of the marketing plan. No marketer ever knows all that could or should be known about his product and its responsiveness to a change in marketing variables. A thorough analysis of the marketing review section of the marketing plan will usually raise questions; the answers will remain obscure until they are subjected to investigation. Further, market tests can be used to explore the potential of a new premium or sales promotion device before risking national exposure and possible failure. The search for new premiums and promotions is an endless task. Almost anyone who has worked extensively in this area has had the experience of watching a promotion fail, or has ended up with a warehouse full of premiums that no one wanted and belatedly wished that a test had been run before committing funds for national exposure.

There are occasions where market testing is deemed too risky. A test may tip off competitors who will seize the idea and use it, thereby reaping its benefits. This is one of the prices of systematic marketing. The decision to test or not to test is a question of marketing judgment.

General Foods sat quietly by while Purina test marketed New Purina Dog Chow, built a multimillion dollar plant to produce the product, expanded the initial test into five markets and then ten markets, and eventually captured leadership in a market that General Foods' product, Gaines, probably should have owned. Their rationalization was that since the chunks in Purina Dog Chow were larger than in the Gaines product it wouldn't really be competitive.[7] Then, Purina sat back and watched General Foods develop Gaines•burgers and establish a new "moist" category in the dog food market that became a multimillion dollar bonanza.

In Chapter 8 we discussed how Betty Crocker and Pillsbury procrastinated while Nebraska Consolidated Mills, a small milling company, took the midwestern cake mix market for Duncan Hines Cake Mix, later purchased by Procter & Gamble. They continued to watch as Procter & Gamble introduced Duncan Hines into the eastern part of the country where it became a major brand.

[7]Milton P. Brown, Richard N. Cardoza, Scott M. Cunningham, Walter J. Salmon, and Ralph G. M. Sultan, *Problems in Marketing*, 4th ed. (New York: McGraw-Hill, 1968), 728.

The big three companies in the American automobile industry did not consider that Volkswagen and other imports would take over the small car market until profits began to plummet and federal legislation initiated by the energy crises compelled them to trim the size of their cars. These three companies also lagged in the development of front wheel drive automobiles while foreign imports were exploiting this feature and benefiting from it. Besides, the idea of front wheel drive has been a practical alternative for the past thirty years.

Large companies tend to become victims of their own inertia. They may see something happening in the marketplace, but all too often they decide to watch it and see what develops. When they finally arouse themselves to action, their activities are delayed by their commitment to what they are currently doing, cumbersome internal procedures, or a cautious and conservative management. There is a reluctance in many companies to "rock the boat."

Fear of competitive reaction is often overblown, and there are important values in making market tests a regular part of the marketing plan. Testing is one way a company prepares for the future. Undoubtedly, there are legitimate instances when prudent judgment will militate against testing. Such instances are relatively rare, however; failure to conduct a market test for fear of what competitors *might* do is probably a poor decision.

What to test, how extensively to test, and when to test are difficult marketing judgments. If one must err, it is generally better to err on the side of testing. A major purpose of systematic marketing is to reduce risks. That is precisely what market testing does.

If market testing is a part of the marketing plan, then the basis for it should be laid in the marketing review and the problems and opportunities sections of the plan. The marketing strategies section should identify the market test as a strategic decision, and the general structure of the test, along with estimated costs and the basis for evaluation, should appear in a testing objectives and strategies section.

Another important facet of testing is the follow-up evaluation of the test results. After a test is completed, someone in the company should prepare a written evaluation of the findings, distribute it to concerned executives, and place it in a permanent file. Evaluations should be made in written form so that valuable pieces of knowledge will not be lost. One of the most successful marketers of packaged goods in the United States turns the task of preparing written evaluations over to a junior executive. Company spokesmen say that this practice helps train young executives and generates a permanent file of company experience that can be called up for future reference. They believe this gives them an advantage over competitors who are not so thorough nor systematic in recording the results of their experiences, and, as a consequence, have little accumulated company experience to call on.

MARKETING RESEARCH

While the use of marketing research is often called for in the marketing plan, it seldom appears as a major objective or point of strategy in and of itself. Most frequently, marketing research appears as an adjunct to other objectives and strategies. For example, the section on copy strategy might contain the statement: "The effectiveness of the new copy in registering the 'high protein' theme will be measured by recall tests through the use of a 'dummy' magazine prior to its commercial use." Or, "The new copy will be evaluated by attitude tests prior to use to provide assurance that the 'high protein' theme is effective in improving consumer attitudes toward the product." The research itself would be described in a separate document. In the case of a market test for a new premium, the objectives and strategies section for the market test might contain the statement: "The new premium will be subjected to in-store testing in at least three markets. Research procedures for the test will be described in a separate document." The estimated budget for the research would then appear in the appropriate section of the marketing plan (copy section for the first example given and market testing section for the second) and a total for all research would be shown in the budget summary.

Occasionally, a major research expenditure will be isolated and referred to in the marketing objectives and marketing strategy sections of the marketing plan. In these instances, the research proposal itself will be given a special section. This normally occurs when a major research project is required to obtain data for future marketing purposes.

An article in *Business Week* points out that, over time, research questions often accumulate to the point that a major research endeavor is required to find the answers.[8] When this occurs, a major research project finds its way into the marketing plan.

Let us assume that a company manufacturing a food or drugstore item decides to subscribe to the A. C. Nielsen service at an annual cost of $70,000 to $100,000. This strategic decision would certainly appear in the marketing strategies section of the marketing plan, and a section on research objectives and strategies would be included to briefly describe the rationale behind this decision and define the kinds of information that would be obtained from the investment. If the company continued to purchase the A. C. Nielsen data in subsequent years, the only reference that would need to be made to it would be a budget item in the budget summary because the same strategy is being continued. Should a decision be made at a later date to discontinue the service, the marketing plan in which this decision becomes effective would acknowledge this strategy change in the marketing strategy section; a special marketing research section would be included to explain why the company's basic research strategy had been modified. In this way, the historic file of marketing plans would provide a complete record of the company's thinking and decisions in regard to the use of the A. C. Nielsen service.

When a research project is of such importance that it is described in a separate section of the marketing plan, this section should contain:

---

[8]"Why Business Is Spending Millions to Learn How Customers Behave," *Business Week*, 18 April 1964, 90ff.

1 The objectives of the research, along with its rationale;

2 A brief description of the information to be obtained, and an indication of how it will benefit future activities of the brand;

3 A summary description of the research methodology (If a more detailed description is desirable, it should be relegated to a separate, back-up document.); and

4 An estimate of the cost of the project, and a completion date.

CORPORATE ADVERTISING

A clear distinction needs to be made between brand or product advertising on the one hand, and corporate or institutional advertising on the other. The difference is one of primary focus.

☐ Brand or product advertising is advertising undertaken in support of the objectives of a particular brand. It influences consumer attitudes about the brand and increases the probability of brand purchase.

☐ Corporate or institutional advertising is advertising undertaken in support of the objectives of a company. It provides information and influences attitudes concerning the company itself. Favorable attitudes toward a company probably will help sales of the company's brands, but the focus of corporate advertising is on some aspect of the company itself, not on individual company brands.

Corporate advertising may be undertaken for a variety of reasons and directed toward a number of diverse publics. The purpose may be financial, political, recruitment, or public relations. A survey conducted by the Association of National Advertisers provides a summary of some general objectives of corporate advertising as viewed by the companies that use it. These objectives include the following six items:[9]

1 Enhance or maintain the company's reputation or goodwill among specific public or business audiences. Figure 20–1 shows an advertisement designed for this purpose by Prudential Insurance Company of America. The audience is real estate investors; the ad's purpose is to register Prudential's experience in financing and handling real estate properties.

2 Establish or maintain a level of awareness of the company's name and the nature of its business. Figure 20–2 by Allegheny Ludlum Steel Corporation is a direct and simple execution of this objective.

3 Provide a unified and supportive marketing approach for a combination of present and future products and services. Figure 20–3 by General Electric is an excellent example of an umbrella advertisement. Notice the corporate punch line just over the logo: "We Bring Good Things To Life."

---

[9]Harry L. Darling, *Current Company Objectives and Practices in the Use of Corporate Advertising* (New York: Association of National Advertisers, Inc., 1975), 6–7.

© 1982 The Prudential Insurance Company of America, Newark, N.J.

What we know about real estate could fill a portfolio.

In fact, it already has.

Prudential maintains the largest real estate portfolio of any company in the world—with over $22 billion in assets under management.

And with over 100 years in the industry, we offer a level of experience and expertise no one else can equal.

We handle a broad range of income-producing properties—from hotels and shopping centers to office and industrial complexes. And our innovative financing arrangements could lower your overall cost and help maximize your return on investment.

So before you invest in real estate, talk to Prudential. And put our experience in your portfolio.

Prudential

4 Educate the audience on subjects of importance to the company's future, such as profits, free enterprise, and economics. Figure 20–4 by United States Steel takes this approach by informing readers of the stifling effects of the United States tax structure on industry.

5 Establish the company's concern for environmental or social issues. Figures 20–5 and 20–6 are interesting examples of such advertising. In Figure 20–5, Bethlehem Steel Corporation addresses the problems of alcoholism and drug abuse and tells what the company is doing to help employees who have these problems. Mobil Corporation's ad (Figure 20–6) deals with conserving national resources—physical and human.

6 Bring about a change in audience attitudes toward the company or its products. The advertisement in Figure 20–7 is an attempt by Buick to allay consumer concerns about the quality of its automobiles. This concern has caused many consumers to purchase foreign-built cars because they believe the foreign

models are made better. This advertisement is simple, confident, and assertive.

The foregoing objectives sound impressive. Although corporate advertising can have value, too many corporate ads are poorly conceived, badly executed, and a waste of company resources. Too frequently, corporate advertising is meaningless because there is no objective need for it.

THE PROBLEM OF CORPORATE ADVERTISING

Advertising Age ran the following editorial on the problems that surround corporate advertising:

> There seems to be a widespread recognition that businesses need to use "corporate" ads to communicate their problems and views to the public. If only we knew how to do it.
>   There was a time when much "corporate advertising" was primarily an ego trip—an opportunity for management to reassure

FIGURE 20–2   (Courtesy Allegheny Ludlum Steel Corp.)

CHAPTER 20 | PUBLICITY, RESEARCH, AND CORPORATE ADVERTISING

GE HELPS YOU SAVE THE MOST VALUABLE THINGS IN YOUR KITCHEN: TIME, SPACE AND EFFORT.

GE, with over 80 years of kitchen experience, recognizes their value more than anyone else.

After all, we developed many innovations to make your kitchen more productive—from toaster ovens to self-starting coffeemakers.

Today we offer a full line of kitchen appliances designed to save you valuable time, space and effort.

WAKE UP TO FRESHLY BREWED COFFEE.

The GE Brew Starter™ drip coffeemaker saves you time when you need it most— in the morning.

You simply put in coffee and water and set the timer before going to bed. The Brew Starter drip coffeemaker will turn itself on so you can wake up to freshly brewed coffee.

And it keeps the coffee hot too. So your next cup is always ready.

BIG PERFORMANCE IN SMALL OVENS.

The versatile GE Toast-R-Oven™ broiler can

save a busy family time.

The Toast-R-Oven broiler will quickly bake, broil or toast small meals or snacks. It also makes reheating portions of meals easy and convenient.

And since the Toast-R-Oven broiler does much more than just toast your bread, it uses counter space efficiently.

OPEN UP MORE THAN BOTTLES AND CANS.

The GE Spacemaker™ can opener quickly and easily opens cans, bottles even plastic bags. And since it mounts under the cabinets, it opens up valuable counter space as well.

BLEND, CHOP, GRATE, MINCE, MIX, PUREE, ETC.

In just a few seconds, a GE Food Processor can help do some of your most tedious cooking chores.

One of our models even doubles as a blender to save you space as well.

MORE GE HELP.

GE can help you save time, space and effort

throughout your home.

You'll find the GE Home Library, four booklets about the home, filled with useful ideas and information.

To get your free copy, send your name, address and zip code to: GE Home Library, Box 4523, Monticello, MN 55365. Be sure to include 50¢ for postage and handling.

If you have any questions on any GE consumer product or service, call the GE Answer Center™ information service, toll-free, at 800-626-2000, 24 hours a day, 7 days a week.

And if something ever does go wrong with a GE appliance, our nationwide network of service centers staffed by factory-trained technicians is ready to help.

After all, designing quality products you can trust, with features and reliable performance you expect, is part of the GE commitment to help make your life a little easier.

WE BRING GOOD THINGS TO LIFE.

GENERAL ⊕ ELECTRIC

GE appliances help make your kitchen more productive.

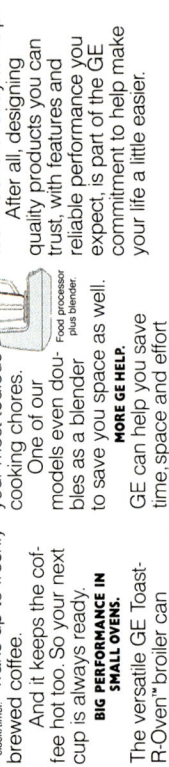

FIGURE 20–3 (Courtesy General Electric)

FIGURE 20–4 (Courtesy United States Steel Corp.)

"THE UNITED STATES NEEDS A MODERN TAX SYSTEM THAT WILL ENCOURAGE INVESTMENT AND CREATE JOBS"

W. Bruce Thomas,
Executive Vice President,
Accounting and Finance,
United States Steel

"American industry has become less competitive internationally because of our outdated tax laws. We must compete with one hand tied behind our back, because the nation's income tax laws do not recognize the existence of inflation; they _penalize investment_ rather than reward it.

"Most of us are now painfully aware of the impact of inflation on prices—and on interest costs. But not everyone is as fully aware that our _tax laws discourage investment_ in new industrial plant and equipment.

"Present United States tax laws require companies to stretch out deductions for their plant and equipment expenditures over a very long period—twelve years in the case of steel. In a period of substantial inflation, this long capital cost recovery results in _taxing "phantom profits"_ because the depreciation deductions are far less than the real cost of replacing the facilities.

"The United States lags behind other major industrial nations in the speed with which capital expenditures can be recovered. For example, in Canada the recovery period for steel producing facilities is about five times as fast as in the United States.

"As a result, since 1960 _the United States has ranked dead last_ among major industrial nations in the portion of gross national product devoted to plant and equipment spending. We've also ranked dead last in the rate of improvement in output per manhour. As a result, _not enough jobs have been created_, because there is a direct relationship between spending for plant and equipment and the creation of additional jobs.

"Reversing these alarming trends will require a change in the nation's tax laws to furnish American industry with a modern tax depreciation system that is competitive with the laws of other major industrial nations.

"_The need for this reform in our tax laws is critical_—and urgent—if our country is to have the new plant and equipment that will restore the strength of America's industrial base and provide the growth in meaningful jobs that American workers need and deserve.

"Quite clearly, the time to act is now!

"That's the way we see it.

"How do you see it?"

United States Steel
600 Grant Street, Pittsburgh, PA 15230

investors and peers, who were already true believers. It was also apparent that the message wasn't getting through to the outside world.

Interviews with the press do not necessarily solve the problem either. "Corporate advertising," used effectively, can help because it gets the message to the right audience in the words management wishes to use.

If this kind of communication is important, then it is also important that it be effective. Alexander Kroll, president of Young and Rubicam U.S.A., fears some corporate ads actually frighten people by projecting the image of business as "rugged, unstoppable, all powerful."

FIGURE 20–5 (Courtesy Bethlehem Steel Corp.)

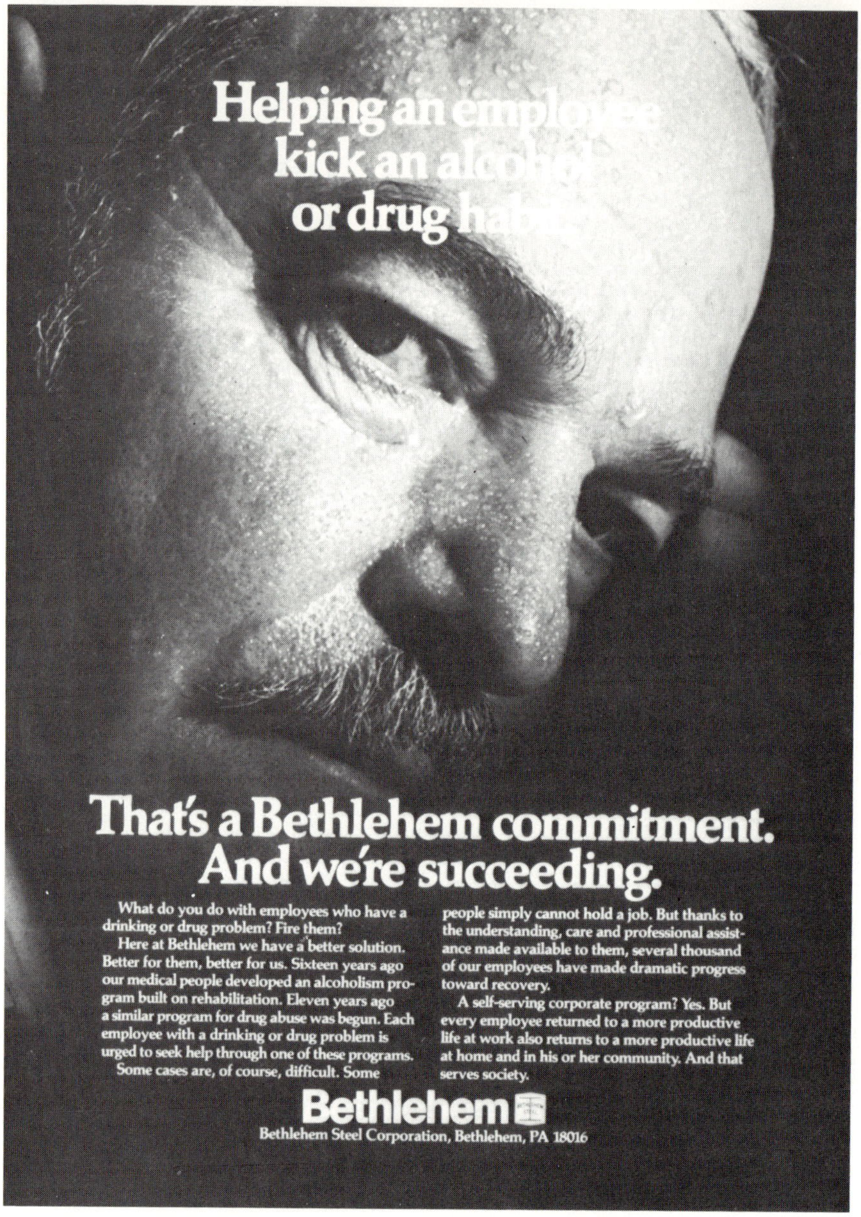

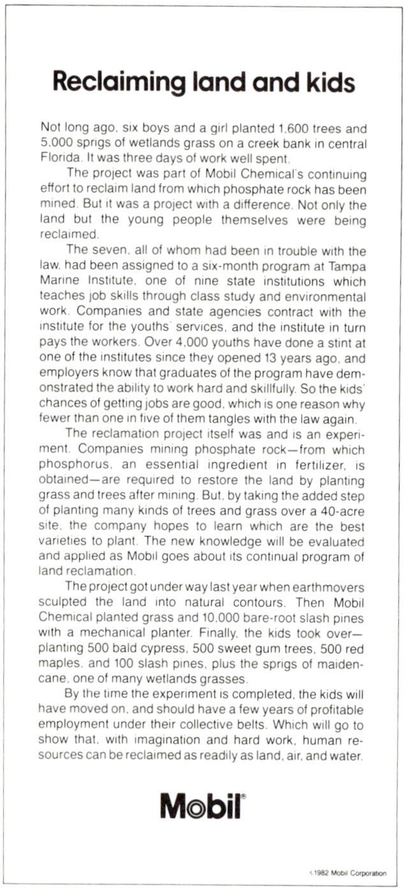

FIGURE 20–6 (Courtesy Mobil Corp.)

He praises companies like Gulf and ARCO, which deliberately use copy that leaves room for feedback and admits to "warts" on the corporate face.

At the Assn. of National Advertisers meeting a few days ago, Prof. Irving Kristol, who is among the distinguished economists writing regularly for the *Wall Street Journal,* embraced what appears to be the opposite view. He favors clear, candid, issue-oriented ads like those used by Mobil. Critics of those Mobil ads miss the point, he says. The ads aren't aimed at "who reads newspapers, but who writes them," and he says they are beginning to pay off. Prof. Kristol has his caveats. U.S. Steel's current campaign, "We're involved," seems to admit that before they ran the ads they weren't involved, he told ANA.

Backlash is the big danger. Frantic ads in newspapers, magazines and tv concerning a subsidy bill by maritime interests—management and labor working together—may actually have helped bring defeat by encouraging those who say the industry is already too heavily dependent on federal subsidies. Prof. Kristol deplores ads which plead poverty without providing really serious education. "It's bad for the system when major corporations go around whimpering and whining and apologizing all the time," he says.

In corporate advertising, as in other forms of advertising, there are geniuses and charlatans. We'd like to think Mr. Kroll and Prof. Kristol have provided clues which help to distinguish one from the other. But just as we think we can identify the "geniuses," a "charlatan" racks up a success. Which is one of the reasons the debate over what to say in corporate ads goes on . . . and on . . . and on.[10]

The problems are: (a) when one should use corporate advertising; and (b) what one should say. In today's complex economy, major economic and social issues arise that may have a profound effect

---

[10]"Which Corporate Ads Work?" p. 16. Reprinted with permission from the November 7, 1977 issue of *Advertising Age*. Copyright © 1977 by Crain Communications, Inc.

FIGURE 20–7   (Courtesy General Motors)

Today, the American car buyer is more demanding, critical, uncompromising and quality-conscious than ever.

We're looking forward to another very good year.

BUICK

Wouldn't you really rather have a Buick?

upon individual companies or industries, or on the basic concepts that underlie business in its entirety—concepts such as profit, risk, competition, growth, investment, supply, and demand. Far too often, these issues are raised by those with antibusiness sentiments, and the news coverage that these issues receive is one-sided. Faced with these situations, there is an understandable temptation to use corporate advertising to communicate corporate values and points of view. When companies understand what they want to say, why they want to say it, and that they must say it honestly, corporate advertising is a legitimate vehicle for expressing company beliefs.

To be effective, corporate advertising needs to be as thoroughly planned as any brand advertising campaign. It needs a communications plan, just as a brand needs a marketing plan.

THE CORPORATE ADVERTISING PLAN

The justification for a corporate advertising plan is rooted in the overall objectives and strategies of the corporation and will arise from the situation in which the corporation finds itself. As a consequence, the corporate advertising plan will differ in some respects from a product marketing plan. Its basic purposes are the same, however, namely to: (a) identify problems and opportunities; (b) specify objectives and strategies; (c) develop a specific program; and (d) provide for the program's evaluation.

Like a product marketing plan, the corporate advertising plan should be objective, reasoned, and systematic. Its persuasiveness should arise from its real strengths, such as knowledge, logic, incisiveness, and imagination, rather than the irresponsible enthusiasm of one-sided argument. The format for a corporate advertising plan is outlined in Figure 20–8.

In all other aspects (form, tone, appearance, etc.) the corporate advertising plan should follow the same guidelines that have been laid down for product marketing plans.

This procedure will not *guarantee* a successful corporate advertising program. However, it will enable the company to avoid the ill-considered and poorly thought through corporate advertising programs that have been major problems in the past.

SUMMARY

This chapter has dealt with subjects that are normally considered optional in the design of the marketing plan—product publicity, market testing, marketing research, and corporate advertising.

Product publicity differs from advertising in two major respects. Advertising is paid space or time, whereas publicity is free space or time; the advertiser has no control over publicity, although he may attempt to influence it through the information he releases and the services he performs. The secret of effective product publicity is news. For this reason, we normally associate publicity with new products, but many established products have newsworthy features.

Test marketing enables companies to gain information about proposed activities and reduce the risk of wasting company re-

1. **REVIEW OF ADVERTISING OPPORTUNITIES**

   This section is equivalent to the marketing review section of the product marketing plan and consists of a survey and summarization of all pertinent facts concerning the company, competition, and environment. Normally, this section will include such factors as:

   a. the strengths and weaknesses of the company and competition as they pertain to the need or reason for corporate advertising;

   b. a review of important developments or changes within the company, industry, environment, or audiences that the company wishes to influence through advertising;

   c. a review of any research data pertaining to the audience groups that the company wishes to reach with its advertising, particularly audience knowledge of and attitudes toward the company and its competition.

2. **PROBLEMS AND OPPORTUNITIES**

   This section highlights those key facts, assumptions, and conclusions drawn from the review section that help shape and direct the overall plan. It includes such things as:

   a. why corporate advertising should be undertaken;

   b. to whom it should be directed;

   c. how it can help the company achieve its objectives;

   d. identification of any special problems and/or opportunities.

3. **ADVERTISING OBJECTIVES**

   The advertising objectives section takes the place of the marketing objectives section of the product marketing plan. Here, corporate objectives must be clearly specified, and an advertising budget established.

4. **ADVERTISING STRATEGY**

   Same as the product marketing plan.

5. **COPY STRATEGY**

   Same as the product marketing plan.

6. **COPY PLAN**

   Same as the product marketing plan.

7. **MEDIA STRATEGY**

   Same as the product marketing plan.

8. **MEDIA PLAN**

   Same as the product marketing plan.

9. **EVALUATION STRATEGY AND PLAN**

   Every corporate advertising plan should contain a section on how the advertising program will be evaluated in terms of its accomplished objectives.

   This will involve a program of research that may include: (a) special consumer research among the intended audiences; (b) pertinent research among company sales and management personnel; and (c) use of commercial advertising research services such as Starch and Readex.

   Audience research designed to measure changes in the attitudes and beliefs of the target audience is particularly important for corporate advertising. Unlike a product plan, one does not have concrete sales results against which to compare the plan's accomplishments.

FIGURE 20–8 Format for corporate advertising plan

sources through the commission of major marketing blunders. Although some companies are reluctant to test market for fear that they will tip off competition concerning their future activities, these fears are probably exaggerated.

Marketing research normally appears in the marketing plan as an adjunct to other marketing activities. On some occasions, a major research project is required to gather information that will facilitate future marketing activities. When this occurs, marketing research becomes an object of marketing strategy, and a section of the marketing plan should be devoted to this subject.

Most corporate advertising is poorly conceived and executed and requires more careful planning than it is normally given. Although it has no place in the product marketing plan, corporate advertising can adapt the systematic approach of the product marketing plan for its own use.

REVIEW QUESTIONS

1 What are the primary characteristics that distinguish product publicity from product advertising?
2 What are the primary arguments of those who use product publicity as a regular part of their marketing programs?
3 Outline the information that should be covered in a product publicity plan.
4 Companies often avoid test marketing for fear that competition will learn about their future activities and take steps to counteract them. Discuss this dilemma.
5 Under what conditions does marketing research become an object of marketing strategy?
6 When marketing research is an object of marketing strategy rather than an adjunct to it, what topics should be dealt with under the marketing research section of the marketing plan?
7 How does corporate advertising differ from product advertising?
8 Identify the major objectives that companies seek when undertaking corporate advertising.
9 According to the text, why is a great deal of corporate advertising ineffective?
10 How does a corporate advertising plan differ from a product marketing plan?

DISCUSSION QUESTIONS

1 Select a familiar consumer product. Identify some newsworthy characteristic about this product and write a press release for it. To what type of publications should this news release be sent?
2 Corporate advertising is used for many purposes. To what audiences might corporate advertising be directed? What are the purposes for advertising to each of these publics?
3 Many corporations use corporate advertising to express their political and economic philosophies. Some people have criticized this practice as being a misuse of corporate resources. Others do not believe that corporate advertising should be tax deductible. What is your point of view on these two issues?

PROBLEM

You are the public relations counsel for a consumer products company that markets a number of personal care items through drug and food stores. Your client has recently developed a revolutionary new toothpaste that, with regular use, eliminates plaque (dark spots that form on teeth, particularly along the gum line). Extensive clinical tests have proven the product to be both safe and effective. These tests have been reviewed and approved by the American Dental Association which has agreed to let you use their endorsement of the product.

Because of the revolutionary nature of the product, its proven effectiveness, and highly favorable responses from consumer tests, the company has decided to forgo test marketing and introduce the product nationally. The national introduction has been planned one month after the national meeting of the American Dental Association.

Since the product is highly newsworthy and there are limited advertising and promotion funds, the company has decided that product publicity will play a major role in the product introduction.

The company is planning to set up a booth at the American Dental Association meeting to introduce the new product, along with the results of the clinical tests, to dentists attending the meeting. In addition, a film has been developed and will be shown in the booth. You have been asked to plan a press conference to be held on the first day of the meeting.

ASSIGNMENT

1 Identify the media audiences that you wish to reach.
2 Outline a program of publicity to insure the success of the press conference and obtain widespread media coverage.

VII
Special Topics in Advertising

The final section of the text deals with four special topics in advertising—industrial advertising, international advertising, advertising evaluation, and legal restrictions surrounding advertising.

Chapter 21, "Industrial and International Marketing," has been added to the text at the request of users of the first edition. There are a number of good texts on industrial

marketing, although most of them devote little attention to advertising. One reason for this is that advertising's role is less prominent. For many industrial products, advertising is a minor element in the marketing mix, with the major communication burden being carried by personal selling. Nonetheless, although its value varies greatly by product, advertising may have an important role in industrial marketing. Our discussion of industrial marketing will clarify

the unique characteristics and complexities of the field, and identify how advertising can be used most effectively.

The consciousness of international marketing opportunities has emerged relatively recently. In our discussion of multinational markets, we will examine the international marketing environment, the nature of international marketing decisions, and some of the pitfalls that trap the unwary.

Chapter 22 deals with an important but highly controversial topic—the measurement of advertising effectiveness. Few subjects have received so much attention with so little progress over the last thirty years. Copy research, the element of advertising research with which we will be concerned, is characterized by glowing promises, dismal disappointments, and violent disagreements. In this chapter, we will identify major issues, the problems that make copy research difficult, and discuss the research procedures that are most often used.

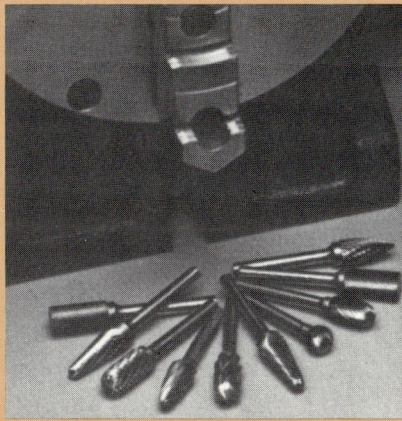

Chapter 23 discusses some of the legal restrictions surrounding advertising. The past two decades have witnessed a massive increase in legislation designed to curb business abuses and consumer criticisms of marketing practices and advertising. The subject of advertising regulation is not a simple one. Well-intended legislation often has unanticipated consequences, and the distinction between fair and fraudulent advertising claims is not always clear. In this chapter, we will identify the major regulatory agencies, the advertising industry's efforts at self-regulation, and discuss some of the major trends in regulatory interpretation that have emerged in the past twenty years.

21

Industrial and International Marketing

INDUSTRIAL MARKETING

MONSANTO—FROM COUPON TO BOTTOM LINE

Generating inquiries from qualified prospects is a prerequisite for successful industrial advertising. This point is demonstrated in the following case history from the Monsanto Company.

Therminol heat transfer fluids are used in many applications from chemical processing to offshore drilling, textile manufacturing to barge operations. The Monsanto product line consists of six fluids, each with a different operating temperature range. Key to our commercial strategy is focusing on the engineer early in the design phase of a new heat transfer system. Then we rapidly place Therminol engineering data in his hands.

Since there are tens of thousands of design engineers, in-depth or frequent contact by any sales force would be cost-prohibitive. Magazine advertising has been used consistently since the early '60s to identify design engineers and help our salesmen follow-up before competition could. Our latest product, Therminol VP–1 was launched in 1975 and received modest magazine advertising support from 1975 to 1978. Ads like Figure 1 [text Figure 21–1] ran frequently in chemical engineering journals.

The gross profit generated from a single coupon clipped from a Therminol VP–1 ad generated enough cash flow to pay for all the magazine advertising done for Therminol VP–1 . . . 12 times over. One coupon, followed up by the advertising department with literature, and later by the field with a personal call, led to a very large first sale and subsequent reorders. And heat transfer fluids are very competitive. If we hadn't gotten that order first, competition would have.

Was this an isolated case? We doubt it, since nearly 11,000 other engineers received product literature and design assistance as a result of our advertising department follow-up. This business has been on an enviable sales curve, not from advertising alone, but resulting from the teamwork of advertising doing the prospecting and salesmen doing the selling.[1]

This example points up three characteristics of much industrial advertising: (a) Advertising is used to search out prospective buyers who then must be contacted by the advertising department and sales personnel. (b) Individual sales are often large; in this instance, a single coupon resulted in sales that paid for the entire advertising campaign 12 times over. (c) The audience for industrial advertising is often highly specific; in this case, design engineers.

THE TWO BEST TRADE EXHIBITS IN 1981

Trade shows are of primary importance to industrial marketers. Xerox and Caterpillar demonstrate their use.

Xerox

Xerox Printing Systems division took first place honors as the most remembered exhibit of the year among smaller (100,000 sq. ft. or less) shows. Its display of IWP Syntopicon IX generated 52% recall among the show attendees.

Giltspur Exhibits/Rochester built the 1200 sq. ft. double deck exhibit. Ray Crouch designed it; Peggy Reed coordinated the project for Xerox.

A demonstration with live formal narration generated traffic to the exhibit. Sales people gave informal one-on-one demonstrations between the formal narrations. Next to the high interest in their products, the demonstrations were the key reason for the attendees remembering the Xerox exhibit.

Xerox says it created the overall design to accent its products and create an atmosphere for private business transactions via a

---

[1]"Monsanto Traces Ads from Coupon to Bottom Line," *Industrial Marketing* (April 1982): 57.

Why the switch from Dowtherm* A to Therminol® VP-1?

© Monsanto Company 1978

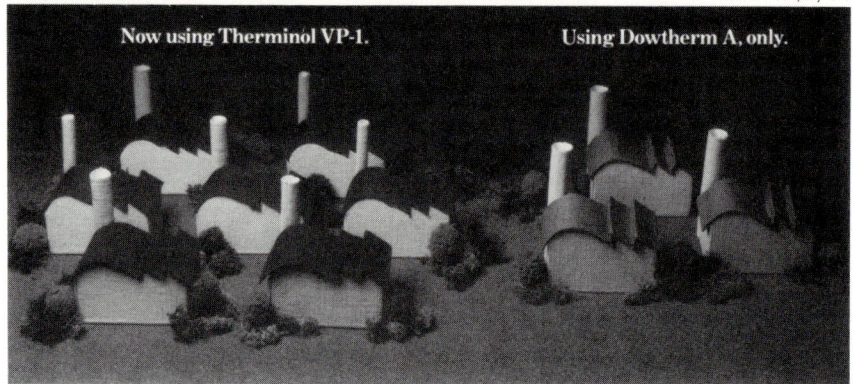

Now using Therminol VP-1. Using Dowtherm A, only.

Today, seven of the top ten synthetic fiber producers use Therminol® VP-1 heat transfer fluid. (In the tall oil industry, it's six out of eight.)

Two years ago, none of them did. (That's because we only introduced our vapor phase fluid in 1976.)

Curiously, Therminol VP-1 is virtually identical to Dowtherm A. In crystallizing point, boiling point, operating range, heat transfer and every important physical characteristic.

Why the switch? Many of these producers have been buying our liquid phase heat transfer fluids for years and they like our service. What's more, they like the way Therminol VP-1 performs.

Maybe it's time you took a look at our alternative to Dowtherm A. Our reports indicate people who've switched aren't sorry.

*Dowtherm is a trademark of Dow Chemical Co.

For more information on Therminol ® VP-1, mail coupon to: Dept. B1NB, Monsanto, 800 N. Lindbergh Blvd., St. Louis, Mo. 63166.

☐ Send free booklet "Chemical Facts of Life."

My application is _____

Name_____ Title _____

Company_____ Address _____

City & state_____ Zip_____

Monsanto

Without chemicals, life itself would be impossible.

conference area on the lower level. Both levels were used for product demonstrations.[2]

Caterpillar

Caterpillar ranked first among the large (more than 100,000 sq. ft.) shows with a 41,340 exhibit at CONEXPO '81. Designed by George P. Johnson and coordinated by L. B. Arvin of Caterpillar, the exhibit used the entire Astroarena, part of Houston's Astrodome complex where the show appeared.

---

[2]"Trade Shows," *Industrial Marketing* (April 1982): 62.

Spotlighting 16 individual pieces of construction equipment against a black-draped background provided a dramatic effect. The exhibit was basically a static display, with the emphasis put on one-on-one discussions between sales personnel and visitors.

Attendees, entering the Astroarena at a level above the exhibit could view the entire display. Visitors who wanted to talk to a sales representative or observe the equipment up close had to walk down the stairs to the arena floor. Based on personal observations that tended to keep the "lookers" off the equipment and away from sales people, boosting their efficiency.

Attendees said that interest in Caterpillar's products was the overwhelming reason for remembering the exhibit.[3]

Trade exhibits such as those used by Xerox and Caterpillar are expensive, often costing several thousands of dollars. However, the investment is cheap when a system or single piece of equipment sells for several hundred thousand dollars.

DIFFERENCES BETWEEN INDUSTRIAL AND CONSUMER MARKETS

In 1979 the consumption of goods and services by industrial and government markets approximated $1.7 trillion, a somewhat larger total than that spent by consumers. In addition to this size difference, industrial markets, referred to as **intermediate, business,** or **organizational markets,** differ from consumer markets in a variety of ways that directly affect marketing activities. Some of the more significant differences are in market concentration, personal consumption, purchasing decisions, reciprocity, buying criteria, and supply and delivery schedules.

Market concentration. Industrial markets are more concentrated than consumer markets in terms of the number of customers and geographic locations. A manufacturer of consumer products may have millions of potential customers. By contrast, the potential customers of an industrial producer may be numbered in the thousands, hundreds, or even less than a dozen. This difference implies:

1 Personal selling, rather than advertising, is often the primary form of marketing communication.
2 Each customer may become disproportionately important to the producing firm; therefore, personal relationships between the producer and buyer become more critical. For example, a producer of consumer products may offend or lose a customer with no apparent effect on sales. However, the loss of a single customer for an industrial producer may result in layoffs, production cutbacks, and financial loss.

Personal consumption. Instead of buying for personal consumption, industrial firms purchase goods and services for the production of other goods and services. One marketing implication of this characteristic is that price is usually more critical in the industrial purchase than in the consumer purchase.

---

[3]Ibid., 62.

CHAPTER 21 | INDUSTRIAL AND INTERNATIONAL MARKETING

Purchasing decisions. The complexity of a purchasing decision is greater because more people are involved in an industrial purchase than one by a consumer. Thus, the purchase of raw materials or equipment used in production may require the participation of personnel in corporate management, design, engineering, production, purchasing and, possibly, other departments. Each participant may have different criteria for the product or service being purchased. Therefore, the seller of industrial goods and services must determine which of the customer's personnel, often as many as four to six people, are involved in the purchase decision. In extreme cases, such as the purchase of a computer for an aerospace missile, forty people may be involved.

Reciprocity. Many industrial firms sell to one another. For example, about 30 percent of the sales in the chemical industry are intra-industry sales. Under reciprocity, firms buy from firms that buy from them.

Buying criteria. Many consumer purchases are highly subjective. Although some subjectivity exists in industrial purchases, objective criteria, defined by written purchase specifications, are a major factor.

Supply and delivery schedules. Since industrial firms often purchase in large quantities that are to be delivered at specific times, dependability of supply and scheduled delivery are often major considerations in making a purchase. For example, a manufacturer of light aircraft must order engines from an independent supplier three years ahead of its production year. Based on a sales forecast, a company might order 24,000 engines to be delivered at the rate of 2000 per month, three years hence. Failure of the supplier to meet this delivery schedule will result in production disruption and, possibly, financial disaster for the buyer.

TYPES OF INDUSTRIAL MARKETS

Industrial or business markets are really made up of three quite different markets, called **producer, reseller,** and **government markets.**

Producer markets. Producer markets often conjure up images of huge factories, billowing smokestacks, thousands of workers engaged in repetitive tasks, noisy machinery, assembly lines, and automation. Indeed, the term "manufacturing" is often used to refer to producer markets. In order to understand the size and diversity of producer markets, we need to expand our traditional stereotypes of industrial production. Producer markets not only include manufacturing firms, but also advertising agencies that produce advertising, banks that produce credit, insurance companies that produce protection against risks, and restaurants that produce meals. In short, producer markets are very diverse; however, a general definition is: The producer market is made up of all individuals and business firms that buy products and services used in the production of other products and services that, in turn, are sold, rented, or leased to individual consumers or other business firms.

The diversity of products and services purchased by producer markets is immense. Many classifications of products and services have been made, none of which is exhaustive. Table 21–1 shows one such classification. Note that producers use raw and manufactured materials that become a part of their products, as well as other items and services that facilitate the production process; these goods and services do not become a part of the finished product.

For the individual marketer, however, the aggregate of products purchased is not important. Rather, individual marketers are interested in those segments of the producer market that they sup-

TABLE 21–1 Goods and services classification for the producer market

Products that become a part of the finished product
☐ Raw materials
  Agricultural, forestry, and fishing products (examples: cotton, wool, grains, vegetables, fruits, livestock, wood, raw rubber, fish, seaweed)
  Extractive products (examples: mineral ores, crude oil, salt, silicates)
☐ Manufactured material
  Processed materials (examples: leather, yarn, finished lumber)
  Manufactured products (examples: synthetic fibers, steel, wire, cement, plastic resins)
  Fabricated parts (examples: motors, tires, fabricated metals, screws, fasteners, castings)
Production facilities, equipment, and processes
☐ Land and buildings
☐ Production equipment (examples: sanders, grinders, punch presses, drill presses)
☐ Accessory equipment (examples: forklift trucks, hand trucks, pallets)
☐ Processes (examples: patents and processes upon which royalties are paid such as Sanforizing and freeze-dry processes)
Maintenance equipment and supplies
☐ Equipment (examples: hand tools, machinery, paint brushes)
☐ Supplies (examples: screws, nails, paint, cleaning compounds, lubricants)
Office equipment and supplies
☐ Office equipment (examples: typewriters, adding machines, copiers, file cabinets)
☐ Office supplies (examples: paper, staples, paper clips, ledgers, envelopes, typewriter ribbons)
Facilitating products/services
☐ Financial (examples: banks, insurance companies, brokerage houses)
☐ Communication (examples: advertising agencies, printing companies, media)
☐ Transportation and warehousing (examples: trucking companies, airlines, trains, barge companies, public warehouses)
☐ Advisory services (examples: business consultants, tax consultants, production designers)

Source: From Kenneth E. Runyon, *The Practice of Marketing* (Columbus, Ohio: Charles E. Merrill Publishing Co.), 159.

ply or could supply. As a consequence, market analysis is as important in searching out producer markets as consumer markets.

The size of each market segment for individual industrial products varies widely. For example, the market for diamond saw blades or transistor bonding nozzles may be extremely limited, amounting to only a few hundred thousand dollars annually. By contrast, the market for processed steel products exceeds $18 billion.

Similarly, different industrial goods or services have varying numbers of suppliers; highly technical fields may have fewer than six suppliers, while hundreds compete for the existing business in other fields.

Producer markets tend to be much more highly concentrated than consumer markets. Producers cluster in areas close to their natural resources, where labor is readily available and transportation inexpensive. Seven states—New York, California, Pennsylvania, Illinois, Ohio, New Jersey, and Michigan—contain over 50 percent of the nation's manufacturing firms. Some industries, such as petroleum, electronics, and motion pictures, are even more concentrated along geographic lines. In addition, many major companies with geographically dispersed production facilities centralize their buying at the company headquarters.

Reseller markets. Generally, resellers are synonymous with retailers and wholesalers and are sometimes referred to as **middlemen** in the economic structure. Some resellers (retailers) sell directly to consumers; some (wholesalers) sell to other resellers; some (industrial distributors) sell to producers. Unlike producer firms, resellers do not modify or change the products that they purchase for resale. Rather, they simply operate as a conduit for transferring products from one group of participants in the economic system to another.

The reseller market may be defined as those firms that purchase products or services for the purpose of reselling, renting, or leasing them to individuals or other business firms. Thus, resellers have five functions in a marketing economy:

1 Bringing together a particular assortment of goods that are of value to a particular group of customers;
2 Locating these assortments at places more convenient for customers than those provided by producers;
3 Providing goods and services when they are wanted;
4 Providing customers with desired products in the desired quantities; and
5 Generally offering a variety of other marketing services, such as credit, delivery, sales help, alterations, and service.

The reseller market ranges from small, family owned and operated establishments to multibillion dollar firms such as Safeway and Sears, Roebuck and Company. The variety of products handled by the reseller market consists of virtually everything that can be bought and sold, from services to raw materials to manufactured products.

Government markets. Government markets consist of federal, state, and local governmental units that acquire goods and services in order to carry out their functions. Approximately 60 percent of these purchases are made by the federal government, with the remainder being made by subordinate governmental units at the state and local levels. In the aggregate, the federal government is the largest purchaser of goods and services in the United States economy. However, government purchases are not made by a single office; they are divided among hundreds of separate agencies and divisions, operating at both national and local levels.

Governments buy military equipment, space missiles, and milk for school lunch programs; they operate police forces, fire fighting services, schools, public utilities, research laboratories, commissaries, offices, hospitals, and liquor stores; they are involved in defense, education, social work, health delivery services, insurance, pension funds, construction, communications, transportation, environmental protection and development, recreation, housing, and urban renewal. Virtually all areas of economic activity include government as a producer, consumer, or reseller.

ANALYZING INDUSTRIAL MARKETS

In analyzing industrial markets, the marketer should always ask certain basic questions; the same questions should always be asked of consumer markets. While the questions are the same, the answers will vary depending on the product involved as well as the market.

- ☐ *What is the market?* What is its size? What are its trends? What is its competitive structure?
- ☐ *Where is the market?* Where is it concentrated geographically?
- ☐ *Who is the market?* Does the market spread across all industrial classifications, or is it concentrated in a relatively few classifications? Is the market dominated by a few firms in the relevant classifications, or are there many?
- ☐ *When is the market?* When are the products and services bought? Are there seasonal factors? What is the lead time for purchases?
- ☐ *How does the market buy?* How are buying decisions made? Who participates in the buying decisions? What factors influence purchase participation?
- ☐ *Why does the market buy?* What are the relevant buying motives of the market? Which ones are most important?
- ☐ *How can the market be reached most economically and effectively?* Is advertising an effective vehicle for reaching the market? Are trade shows important? What is the role of personal selling?

Each of these questions must be answered for every product that is being marketed. The marketing plan must be addressed to these questions; the marketing strategy must be based on the answers.

THE ROLE OF ADVERTISING IN INDUSTRIAL MARKETS

In markets that contain few customers, and where personal selling and on-site problem solving are the keys to generating product familiarity and sales, the role of advertising is relatively unimportant. However, in markets where there are many, geographically dispersed customers, advertising plays a major role in the marketing effort. Advertising is useful in industrial marketing when it performs one or more of the following functions:

1 *To reach key people who directly or indirectly influence the purchase of the product being sold.* Often this involves diverse groups, such as designers, engineers, production executives and plant foremen, plant maintenance personnel, controllers, corporate executives, purchasing departments, and others. Specific media are listed in *Standard Rate and Data Service* for reaching these groups. Some media are industry specific, i.e., they reach people in selected industries. Others are occupation specific, i.e., they are directed to particular occupations, cutting across industry lines. Figure 21–2 is an example of an occupation specific advertisement. Appearing in the *Journal of Marketing,* the advertisement is addressed to marketing personnel. Its purpose is to promote the company's expertise in mini-market testing.

2 *To create awareness and preference for the product or products being sold by identifying their relevant sales features.* Figure 21–3 shows an advertisement for Cushman Industries that appeared in *Industrial Distribution,* a well-known trade publication. Note that the body copy emphasizes: (a) the range of tools offered; (b) the products' reputation for quality; (c) the availability of technically trained sales representatives to help customers with their problems; and (d) a comprehensive distributor support program that includes distributor schools, seven stocking locations (implying prompt service), and a well developed catalog program. The ad signs off with an invitation to write or call Cushman for more information.

3 *To identify new customers by soliciting inquiries through coupon advertising.* The Monsanto example for Therminol heat transfer fluids (see Figure 21–1) is an example of this use of advertising. Another example is the Sony advertisement in Figure 21–4. Note that features of Sony products are identified in the body copy of the advertisement, while the coupon invites readers to either send for literature on the products or to request that a sales representative call upon them.

4 *To build the reputation of the company and its products in order to prepare the way for personal calls by company salespeople.* Although most trade advertising is directed to this purpose, the Nixdorf Computer advertisement (Figure 21–5) specifically addresses this purpose. Note that the headline qualifies the company by stating that they do business with thousands of the world's largest companies. The body copy explains that Nixdorf is one of the fastest growing computer companies in the busi-

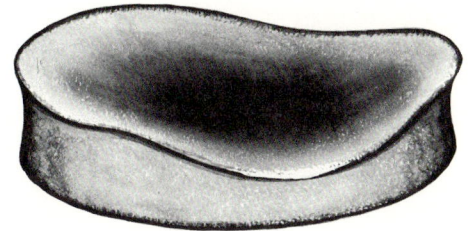

ness with experts both in hardware and software. It points out that the company has been in operation for 30 years, earned over a billion dollars in sales, installed over 100,000 systems worldwide, and established over 400 service centers. In short, the advertisement is designed to build the reputation of the company in the eyes of its intended audience. The importance of this role for industrial advertising is emphasized in a famous advertisement run by *Business Week.* The ad shows an old, cantankerous purchasing agent saying gruffly to a salesperson:

FIGURE 21–3 (Courtesy Cushman Industries)

"I don't know who you are.
I don't know your company.
I don't know your company's product.
I don't know what your company stands for.
I don't know your company's customers.
I don't know your company's record.
I don't know your company's reputation.
Now—what was it you wanted to sell me?"

The ad winds up with the following statement: "MORAL: Sales start before your salesman calls—with business publication advertising" (Figure 21–6).

Machines that understand people.

Presenting state-of-the-Sony dictation.

It took Sony to bring dictation machines into the 20th century. Now Sony brings them into the 21st.

Dictation without frustration.

Sony not only has the most complete state-of-the-art microdictation line in the business. Sony brings you more.

Sony brings you psychology with its technology. When machines get too complicated, or look too threatening, people don't want to use them. (The fact is, lots of new dictation equipment is being under-used for just that reason.)

That's why Sony dictation machines are simple to operate and easy to use. There's no point in having advanced technology if people are afraid to use it. So Sony engineers know they can put all the highly complicated technology on the inside as long as it's uncomplicated on the outside.

Sony: the future of desk-top and portable dictation.

If you want the world's smallest dictator/ transcriber, Sony has it.

BM-750. State-of-the-art micro dictator/transcriber.

BM-600 World's smallest desk top dictator/transcriber.

Three-digit liquid crystal display. Sony has it. "Executive Recall" memory for instant access to priority notations. Sony has it. Two tape speeds for twice as much dictation. Sony has it. The lightest full function microphone you've ever held. Sony has it. Automatic gain control, so your voice remains level no matter where you move. Sony has it. In fact, Sony has just about every new state-of-the-art advance. Period.

For a big choice, there's only one choice.

Right now Sony has the largest selection in microdictation. That means you'll find machines in every price range and for every need. All with up-to-the-minute technology. If you've been waiting for the right time to get into microdictation, it's now. **SONY.**

BM-520. Micro dictator.

For complete information on Sony dictation machines call **1-800-821-7700, Ex. .516.** at any hour, or mail this coupon to Sony Office Products, P.O. Box 1624, Trenton, N.J. 08650. *In Missouri call 1-800-892-7655 Ex. 516.

☐ Please send me literature. ☐ Please have a sales representative call.

NAME

POSITION

ORGANIZATION ____ (AREA CODE) PHONE

ADDRESS

CITY ____ STATE ____ ZIP

SONY OFFICE PRODUCTS
Machines that understand people.

INC2-81 D

© 1981 Sony Corporation of America Office Products Div. Sony is a trademark of Sony Corp.

---

5 *Motivate company distributors by demonstrating to them that you are helping them sell your product.* One purpose of all industrial advertising is to secure the support of distributor and sales organizations. It is customary for industrial advertisers to merchandise their advertising to sales and distribution networks. In other words, they emphasize their advertising support to their sales and distributor organizations by providing them with copies of the advertisements as well as a list of the media and dates on which the advertising will appear.

In addition to advertising, industrial advertisers have other, more powerful ways to communicate with potential customers, such

FIGURE 21–5 (Courtesy Nixdorf
Computer)

Thousands of the world's largest companies share this secret of success.

You're looking at a system built by Nixdorf Computer Corporation, the seventh largest computer manufacturer in the world, and used by thousands of the world's largest and most successful companies.

Who is Nixdorf?

In our thirtieth year of operation, we've grown to be a billion dollar company with over 100,000 systems installed worldwide. We have more than 15,000 employees and more than 400 service centers, 100 in North America alone. Through our network of sales, service and support organizations, · we continue to meet the hardware and software requirements of customers worldwide.

Nixdorf is one of the fastest growing computer companies in the world, due in large part to our industry orientation and our ability to provide total systems for the complete range of information processing applications. Our hardware is acknowledged as the most reliable and easiest to use. And our software expertise is second to none. In fact, Nixdorf is the leading supplier of IBM-compatible system software in the world.

The bottom line is that we understand the computing requirements of specific industries and we supply systems that consistently outclass the competition in speed, capacity and savings in meeting those needs.

At Nixdorf, we've made a name with the top names by being different. We listen to you, learn what you need and build your system to meet your specific requirements with the ability to expand as you grow. The result is a more efficient and productive operation. The proof is that 94% of our customers show how happy they are by coming back for more.

To share our secret, call Nixdorf Computer Corporation toll free (800) 225-4384 and ask for Dave Todd, Director of Industry Marketing, or contact the Nixdorf Sales Office in your city.

Nixdorf. We're on your side.

NIXDORF COMPUTER

as trade shows, personal salespeople, on-site demonstrations, and catalogs. Trade shows provide an economical way to show and demonstrate one's wares to a select group of potential buyers. Most major industries have annual trade shows that attract buyers from all over the country—furniture mart in Chicago, fashion mart in New York, frozen food show, premium show, industrial equipment shows, and many others. The annual premium show in New York attracts 25,000 to 30,000 buyers from advertising agencies and client organizations who are shopping for premiums to use as incentives for the coming year.

The industrial market is large, complex, and challenging. Buying practices vary by industry and different companies within the same industry. There are no simple solutions or gimmicks for tapping this market. As in all other areas of marketing, success in in-

"I don't know who you are.

I don't know your company.

I don't know your company's product.

I don't know what your company stands for.

I don't know your company's customers.

I don't know your company's record.

I don't know your company's reputation.

Now—what was it you wanted to sell me?"

MORAL: Sales start **before** your salesman calls—with **business** publication advertising.

McGRAW-HILL MAGAZINES
BUSINESS • PROFESSIONAL • TECHNICAL

dustrial marketing requires a systematic approach, thorough analysis, thoughtful use of marketing research, hard work, and a
willingness to adapt one's approach to market requirements.

INTERNATIONAL MARKETING

In our discussion on consumer behavior (see Chapter 6), we referred
to culture and the differences that exist among nations. These differences present unusual hazards for international marketing and
advertising. Literature is full of gaffes that have been made in international marketing. Consider the following:[4]

[4]Ann Helming, "Culture Shock," *Advertising Age*, 17 May 1982, M–8, 9.

□ A restaurant in Vienna advertised these key features on its bill of fare: "Children sandwiches" and "fried milk."

□ An Italian dressmaker proudly displayed a sign with the words: "Clothes suited for streetwalking."

□ A U.S. airline lost customers after advertising its rendezvous lounge on flights to Brazil. In Portuguese "rendezvous" means a place to have sex.

□ To African men, a commercial for a men's deodorant showing women chasing a male down a street meant the product would make them weaklings overrun by women.

All problems are not caused by language. When General Mills first began introducing its cereals in the United Kingdom, it misread the British attitude toward children. In its product introduction, General Mills used a typical American cereal package, showing a freckle-faced, red-haired, smiling boy saying, "Gee kids, it's great!" Unfortunately, the British family is not as child oriented as its American counterpart. The British contend that children should be seen and not heard. As a consequence, the British housewife rejected both the package and the product.[5] A water recreation company operating in Malaysia affixed a green corporate symbol to everything the company made. In Malaysia, however, green symbolizes the death and disease found in the jungle, and its use effectively sabotaged the company's promotional efforts.[6]

THE INTERNATIONAL MARKETING ENVIRONMENT

United States marketers contemplating foreign ventures should recognize that the marketing environment in foreign countries differs radically from that in the United States; they run the risk of failure if they do not. Three variables that influence international marketing are political climate, economy, and culture.

Political-legal variables. International marketers often find themselves adrift in a sea of political-legal considerations. For example, United States marketers are subject to three sets of laws when they enter foreign markets. First, there are the laws of the United States. These laws define the foreign countries with which one may trade, impose restrictive taxes on profits earned abroad, and may involve antitrust actions if a foreign subsidiary of a U.S. firm exports to the United States. Second, marketers must deal with the laws of the foreign countries in which they do business. Few countries are as economically free as the United States, and government bureaucracies can ensnare apparently simple transactions in mountains of red tape. Often, they prohibit marketing activities that are taken for granted in the United States. For example, Italy forbids the advertising of cigarettes; France prohibits door-to-door selling; and Australia requires justification for price increases. Tariffs may be levied either

---

[5]E. A. McCreary, *The Americanization of Europe* (Garden City, New York: Doubleday & Co., 1964), 120–30.

[6]Kevin Lynch, "Adplomacy Faux Pas Can Ruin Sales," *Advertising Age,* 15 January 1979, S–2ff.

on the physical quantity of goods sold or the value of shipments; quotas set limits on the amounts and types of goods that will be accepted; and in some countries, local facilities must be managed by nationals of the host country. One recurrent problem is transferring foreign profits back to the United States. When nations face shortages of foreign exchange, controls may be levied over the movement of capital in and out of the country. This may require the foreign investor to reinvest profits in the country of their origin, or they may take their profits in the form of locally produced goods which may be virtually worthless in the world market. In many countries, labor unions have strong government support and have exacted special concessions from business. Layoffs may be forbidden, profits may have to be shared, and innumerable special services may have to be provided. Third, international laws that cross national borders must be observed. The United Nations and the European Economic Community have established commissions to develop commercial codes applicable to all participating nations.

As a consequence, large multinational companies have established international legal departments to keep abreast of legal developments. Small companies which lack these facilities may unknowingly find themselves in conflict with domestic, foreign, or international legal restrictions.

Aside from the legal complexities that may plague the international marketer, government instability, particularly in undeveloped countries, is a constant threat. A friendly government may be overthrown by violent revolution or a peaceable coup d'etat. Production may be disrupted by nationwide strikes, transportation brought to a standstill, factories seized or destroyed, or corporate executives kidnapped or murdered. Expropriation of foreign investments by beleaguered governments is always another possibility.

This does not mean that foreign investments should not be made, or foreign trade avoided. However, foreign involvements should be undertaken cautiously and with a realistic analysis of the risks and problems.

Economic variables. The nations of the world vary widely in their economic purchasing power. Unfortunately, nations representing much of the world's population have very little economic clout. At the present time, as much as half of the world's population is economically unattractive to marketers. Per capita disposable income ranges from as high as $12,000 in Nauru to as low as $70 in Bhutan.[7] Table 21–2 shows the average per capita income for major geographic areas of the world in the mid-1970s. For North America, the average per capita income was in excess of $7,000. For Africa, it was only $430. Although the average per capita income for Asia was $1,560, it was less than $200 for some countries in this geographic area.

As a generalization, those countries with a low per capita income represent poor markets for manufactured goods, whereas those with high per capita incomes represent good markets for such products. This generalization is an oversimplification, however, be-

---

[7]*United Nations Statistical Yearbook,* 1978.

TABLE 21–2 Per capita income by geographic areas of the world

Geographic Area	Per capita Income	Population (in millions)	Percent of Population
North America	$7,150	240.2	6.0%
Oceania	5,190	21.9	0.5
Europe	4,950	478.1	12.0
Asia	1,560	2,485.9	62.2
Caribbean and Latin America	1,150	341.6	8.5
Africa	430	430.7	10.8
Total		3,998.4	100.0%

*Data does not include per capita income nor population from centrally planned economies.

Source: Compiled from Table 193 of the United Nations *1977 Statistical Yearbook* and the *Statistical Abstracts of the United States, 1978.*

cause the rate of economic development and governmental emphasis on consumer versus industrial goods influence the demand schedules for products. Further, wide variations in income distribution within individual countries mean that many countries must be analyzed on a region-by-region basis. Morocco is a case in point. With a per capita income of $540, strong agricultural and mineral base, and growing industrial community, Morocco has all of the earmarks of a developing country. Yet, illiteracy is high, its population growth exceeds that of its gross national product, and unemployment is widespread, while poverty and affluence exist side by side. Casablanca, Tangier, and other tourist centers are modern cities with department stores, attractive shops, and an abundance of consumer goods. Yet, in its small villages and countryside, Morocco is almost prebiblical in its economic development. It is a nation of contrasts; wooden plows are operated next to modern combines; and motorized forms of transportation share the roads with donkeys. Government currency restrictions also caution foreign investors who contemplate investing in the country.

Cultural variables. The major error U.S. marketers make is to assume that foreign countries hold the same values, use the same symbols, exhibit the same behavior, and operate under the same decision making processes as those in the United States. Usually, they do not.

Ethnocentrism, combined with the obvious cost advantages of using the same marketing or advertising strategies everywhere, leads to crucial marketing mistakes. Consider the following example:

Suppose that an American manufacturer had been selling his designer jeans coast to coast with the help of a catch jingle set to a disco beat. He decides teenagers in France would like his product as much as those in California or New York. So he gets ready to export. To save money, he hires a French major from a local university to translate the words of his jingle. The music, he feels, needs no translation.

In fact, he transfers his advertising campaign whole cloth to France; after all, it works in the States.

Should he settle back and wait for the francs to roll in? Or prepare to fall flat on his face?

Unfortunately, say international marketing experts, he'd better brace for a crash. In his attempt to go overseas, our marketer has made three errors, any of which could be fatal:

. . . He has hired a nonnative speaker to translate his message.

. . . He is assuming that a commercial that appeals to Americans will sell to the French.

. . . He has made no studies of the French market itself.

"It's wide-eyed and naive to believe that a straightforward translation" of any ad will work, says Jean-Claude Barre, director of corporate relations with All-Language Service, a New York company that translates everything from promotional brochures to medical treatises into 59 languages ranging from Afrikaans to Urdu.

Mr. Barre, who was born in France, points out the error of our hapless manufacturer's ways. "The disco beat marries itself well to English, because English is a concise tongue," he says. "It's not discursive like French or the other Romance languages; the accents and rhythm are different. To be effective, (this manufacturer) must rewrite his commercial entirely, and discard the English lyrics completely."[8]

Sociocultural differences are filled with traps for the unwary. Marketers who hope to avoid costly errors should familiarize themselves with the cultures in which they plan to market their products or services. Through marketing research or other knowledgeable sources, they should:

1 Ascertain the central values of the target cultural group.
2 Investigate the buying practices and decision patterns characteristic of the group.
3 Identify the marketing institutions and channels applicable to the product.
4 Familiarize themselves with the appropriate symbols for communicating with the target cultural groups.

Usually, this process requires the counsel of knowledgeable marketing consultants who are thoroughly familiar with marketing and business practices in the target country and employ experienced nationals to guide the company through the intricacies of their foreign involvement.

INTERNATIONAL MARKETING DECISIONS

Although the risks in international marketing are often great, the incentives are also attractive. U.S. exports exceed $120 billion; for companies such as Boeing and Union Carbide, exports account for over 40 percent of their total sales. Generally, those United States based companies that have been most successful in their interna-

---

[8]Helming, "Culture Shock," M–8.

tional enterprises tend to be in high technology and capital goods industries, as well as those, such as IBM, Xerox, and Texas Instruments, which provide a highly integrated package of production and marketing services that cannot be easily matched by local competitors or other multinationals. The least successful have tended to be those in low technology, leather goods, tires, agricultural chemicals, beverages, and highly competitive industries such as textiles and apparel.

Companies contemplating international marketing must decide how they will modify their existing products and marketing programs to capitalize on foreign markets. Some products have universal appeals while, in other cases, tastes vary across national borders. For example, Pepsi-Cola and Coca-Cola sell the same product in their domestic and international operations. Oil of Olay, a skin moisturizer, uses the same formula wherever it operates. On the other hand, Nestlé has found it necessary to blend many varieties of coffee to meet local taste preferences; the British prefer a different style of cake than that produced from American cake mixes; the voltage of office equipment has to be adapted to the electrical systems of the countries in which such products are marketed; and Exxon reformulates its gasoline to meet varied climatic conditions. How much products must be modified varies by product and country; no single product strategy applies in all cases.

Similarly, even though the product itself may not be changed, the marketing strategy often requires revision. Bicycles and mopeds are used mainly for recreation in the United States, but they are basic transportation in other countries. A food product used as an entrée in one country may be an appetizer in another.

Few assumptions can be made about the product, marketing strategy, or advertising. Rather, the marketer must be alert to the needs of the host country and be prepared to make adaptations that are necessary.

Selecting an advertising agency. The international advertiser has a number of alternatives in selecting an agency for international advertising. Most major United States agencies have international branches and have incorporated the term "international" in their agency title. Other, wholly American, advertising agencies have international affiliates they use when conducting international business. Many companies choose to use local agencies in the host country. All of these alternatives are viable under certain circumstances. The approach selected should depend on the company's needs and resources.

International advertising media. International advertisers have a choice of two types of media: (a) international media that cut across national borders; and (b) foreign media that are localized to particular countries.

Magazines, such as *Reader's Digest, Time,* and *Newsweek,* have international editions, edited and written in the languages of various countries. Many European media, as well as technical and scientific journals, are also international in scope. One problem with these media is that they often have highly selective audiences and are inadequate for providing mass coverage in most countries.

As a consequence, foreign media receive the bulk of the advertising budget for companies marketing consumer products in foreign countries. Unfortunately, the availability of media differ markedly from country to country, depending upon the stage of a country's economic development and its political and legal environment. For example, low literacy rates preclude the use of print media in many undeveloped countries. Television is not available in some countries; in other countries, radio and television stations are owned or controlled by the government, and advertising is either prohibited or restricted. Additional forms of available media are outdoor, direct mail, transit, and film shown in theaters.

Advertisers must adapt their advertising messages to the media available, often using different media or combinations of media in certain countries.

INTERNATIONAL ADVERTISEMENTS

Despite cultural differences, international advertisements look surprisingly like American advertisements. Figure 21–7 shows an unfamiliar ad for a familiar product–Nescafé.

Figure 21–8 simply indicates that, while it may no longer be appropriate to say that the sun never sets on the British empire, it is appropriate to say that the sun never sets on British scotch whiskey.

The Cellini after shave advertisement (Figure 21–9) reminds us that the basic motive for using an after shave lotion is the same in any language; a translation is unnecessary.

In any language, advertising is still advertising.

SUMMARY

Industrial markets differ from consumer markets in a variety of ways: (a) Industrial markets are more concentrated in terms of customers and geographic location. (b) Industrial firms do not buy for personal consumption. (c) Purchasing decisions are more complex. (d) Reciprocity is often a factor in industrial sales. (e) There is a greater dependence upon objective buying criteria. (f) Dependability of supply and delivery schedules are often major purchasing considerations.

Industrial markets consist of producer, reseller, and government markets. Each market segment is large, diverse, and complex. In analyzing industrial markets, the analyst should ask seven basic questions: (a) What is the market? (b) Where is the market? (c) Who is the market? (d) When is the market? (e) How does the market buy? (f) Why does the market buy? and (g) How can the market be reached most economically and effectively?

In some business markets, the role of advertising is relatively unimportant because these markets contain few customers; personal selling and on-site problem solving are the keys to marketing success. In markets where there are many customers, advertising plays a major role in the marketing effort. Advertising useful in in-

FIGURE 21–7 Translation: The taste of friendship. Anytime can be a good moment. Offer a steaming cup of Nescafé. It will be a quality moment. Friendly. Relaxed. Taste it very slowly. So you can appreciate, with satisfaction, its friendly aroma; taste the flavor of the better coffees. Nescafé. The familiar coffee. Nescafé pure coffee. The taste of the well made. (Courtesy Société des Produits Nestlé SA)

FIGURE 21–8 Translation: Big Ben. Big Bell's! In Great Britain, the number one Scotch whiskey. Bell's number one for your pleasure. (Courtesy Arthur Bell & Sons)

FIGURE 21–9 Translation: To seduce is an art. (Courtesy Faberge, Inc.)

dustrial marketing has one or more of the following functions: (a) reach key people who influence buying decisions; (b) create awareness and preference for products; (c) identify new customers; (d) build the reputation of the company and its products; and (e) motivate company distributors. In addition to advertising, industrial advertisers have other, more powerful ways of communicating with potential customers, such as trade shows, personal salespeople, on-site demonstrations, and catalogs.

United States marketers contemplating foreign ventures should recognize at the outset that the marketing environment in foreign countries often differs radically from that in the United States. Three major variables are: (a) political climate; (b) economy; and

(c) culture. Failure to recognize these differences often leads to costly errors and the waste of company resources.

Although the risks of international marketing are great, the incentives are also attractive. U.S. exports exceed $120 billion, and some companies have as much as 40 percent of their total sales in foreign markets. Companies contemplating international marketing must decide how they will modify their existing products and marketing programs to capitalize on foreign markets. Often adaptations must be made in the products, marketing strategy, and advertising.

International marketers have a number of alternatives in selecting an advertising agency for international marketing. Most major U.S. agencies have international branches; other, wholly American, agencies have international affiliates; one may also use local agencies in host countries.

International advertisers have a choice between two types of media: (a) international; and (b) foreign. Since international media often have highly selective audiences, they are inadequate for mass coverage in most countries. The availability of local media varies widely in foreign countries. As a consequence, advertisers must adapt their advertising messages to the media available.

REVIEW QUESTIONS

1 Identify and explain the major ways that industrial and consumer markets differ.
2 Distinguish among producer, reseller, and government markets.
3 What are the basic functions of resellers in a marketing economy?
4 What are the basic questions that should be asked when analyzing industrial markets?
5 What are the functions of advertising in industrial markets?
6 Identify and explain the three major variables that differ widely among nations.
7 Why must many countries be analyzed on a region-by-region basis?
8 What should marketers do to minimize marketing errors in foreign countries?
9 What alternatives do advertisers have in selecting an agency for advertising in a foreign country?
10 Describe the media situation in foreign countries.

DISCUSSION QUESTIONS

1 Using the *Reader's Guide to Business Periodicals*, find an article on international advertising. Prepare a brief summary of the article for presentation to class.
2 When marketing in foreign countries, some advertisers centralize control of their marketing and advertising activities. Others decentralize by leaving marketing and advertising decisions to foreign managers. What do you believe would be the advantages and disadvantages of each approach? Are there conditions when one approach or the other would be preferable?

3 Procter & Gamble is one of the most successful marketers of consumer goods in the United States. Yet, they are not a major factor in foreign markets. Why do you think this is so?

PROBLEM

Select a foreign country of your choice. Using library resources, develop basic economic and marketing information on this country. Be prepared to present your findings in class. What kind of difficulties did you experience in finding information?

22

Measuring Advertising Effectiveness

AWARDS AND TESTING

CLIO AWARDS

Each year, CLIO sponsors a film festival and gives awards to the best radio and television commercials submitted for judging. Reels of these commercials are prepared and available for rental from the CLIO Educational Division for use by schools and other interested groups. Awards are also given for several classifications of techniques: editing, optical effects, and graphics; animation design; cinematography; film direction; musical scores and jingles; and use of humor.

Presumably, those chosen are the brightest and best of national and international broadcast productions. Perhaps they are. Certainly, the CLIO reels contain many excellent commercials. The winners are selected by a panel of judges, but hard evidence of effectiveness in the marketplace is notably lacking when selections are made.

COPY TESTING—AN OLD UGLY SORE

Copy testing is a perennial problem in advertising. The field is rife with stories of commercials and ads that were highly successful in moving merchandise despite low test scores; others received high test scores but performed poorly at the cash register. Harry McMahan and Mack Kile, widely respected television commercial consultants, have charged: "There are commercials that aired despite low test scores and were winners at the cash register. Others scored high but failed to move merchandise."[1]

Regardless of whether the testing method is a measure of recall or one of attitude change, the same charges are applicable. Advertising testing has been in vogue for over 30 years, and there is little evidence that controversy surrounding measurement techniques has diminished.

[1]Harry McMahan and Mack Kile, "Testing Copy Research An Old, Nasty Sore," *Advertising Age*, 3 August 1981, 40.

VARIABLE RESULTS

On-air testing of television commercials, using recall scores as a measure of effectiveness, is a widely used method employed by major marketing research firms and some of the nation's leading advertisers. Yet, the following evidence suggests that the results of such tests may be meaningless.

Four years ago, a major copy testing experiment (called the Program Environment study) was undertaken by JWT (J. Walter Thompson, a major advertising agency) in tandem with six leading advertisers. The intent of the study was to determine whether commercials perform differently in a violent program context than in nonviolent programs.

The most startling finding of the study was the discovery that day-after-recall score for a commercial varies dramatically depending upon the specific program in which it is tested. For all six sponsors' commercials, we found that the same commercial can achieve radically different recall scores from different programs even when the programs are all of the same type . . . As a result of this study (as well as other independent research over the years), we confidently asserted that on-air testing as it is commonly practiced, provides highly unreliable recall scores because of the severely biasing effects of the program context.[2]

The three foregoing examples are evidence that the state of advertising evaluation hasn't changed very much since advertising became a national preoccupation. This is true despite the fact that some $54 billion a year is spent on advertising, volumes have been written on advertising evaluation, and untold research dollars have been applied to its measurement. Perhaps the current situation is best summed up by the following quotation:

Today, the money spent on advertising resembles tribute laid on the altar of some savage and arbitrary god.

[2]Sonia Yuspeh, "A Recall Debate," p. 47. Reprinted with permission from the July 13, 1981 issue of *Advertising Age*. Copyright © 1981 by Crain Communications, Inc.

If you don't advertise, you're dead. If you do, you still may be. The unknowable deity must be appeased. But it's costing too much. Advertisers are rebelling.

They can't stop advertising: they don't want to. But they want to know what they are getting for their money.

So the time of the researcher is at hand. Formulas, concepts, systems of measurement are being invoked. But the answers are confusing, often irrelevant. What should be measured—"exposure," "readership," "awareness," what else? And how? Through a box attached to the TV set, or a personal interview, or by measuring dilation and contraction of the pupils?

If the v-p of sales or marketing could measure anything he wanted, chances are he would say: Measure advertising's relationship to sales and profit. Tell me how much it costs.[3]

Corporate executives and marketing practitioners keep asking for an ultimate, absolute answer to the question of advertising. Perhaps the reason the answer is so elusive is that there is no absolute answer—only a relative one. As pointed out earlier, advertising does not stand alone. It is firmly embedded in a matrix of other marketing activities, influenced by the media in which it appears, mitigated or enhanced by what competitors are doing, and dependent on what often appears to be the whims of consumers. An advertising campaign that was an outstanding success one year may be a complete failure the next year because a major competitor markedly improved its product. A new advertising technique that commanded widespread attention when it was first used may quickly become obsolete and routine as it is copied by countless imitators trying to capitalize on its success. Indeed, the field of advertising is like quicksilver—constantly moving and changing, and hard to hold on to and examine. Certainly, there are some constants in the mix: honesty; clarity of expression; product concept that is appealing to consumers; and creative presentation that lifts the product above competition and gives it visibility. However, variables that influence the outcome of marketing programs include shifting consumer values and concerns, the state of the economy, the product itself, packaging, pricing, distribution, sales promotion, advertising weight, reach, frequency, and the activities of competitors. The effect of advertising on sales is obscure; thus, the answer to how much advertising should cost is elusive.

Despite the difficulties inherent in measuring the effects of advertising, pressure continues to mount to cast some light on its contribution to the marketing effort. This point is emphasized by the following quotation from a publication sponsored by the Association of National Advertisers.

The great debate over whether or not advertising can be measured has been going on as long as most advertising men can remember. Some claim it cannot be done, so why try. Others say that if as much time were spent in researching advertising as is wasted in debating whether or not it can be done, we would be twice as far as we are now. As is usually the case, semantic difficulties and emotional

---

[3]A. J. Vogl, "Advertising Research," *Sales Management*, 1 November 1963, 40. Reprinted with permission from *Sales Management, the Magazine of Marketing.*

involvement account for the 180-degree difference in opinion. Clarifying these differences is necessary to progress.

A big stumbling block is the word "measurement." Those who expect to find a formula which will accurately relate advertising efforts and short-term sales results will, with a few rare exceptions, be disappointed. But the answer to the question, "Can advertising be *evaluated*?" is unreservedly "Yes." Every business function *must* be evaluated in terms of the contribution it makes to the profit and growth of the enterprise, on the one hand, and the costs incurred, on the other hand. A business cannot survive without some means of appraising benefits in relation to costs.

The principle of placing dollars at risk in anticipation of a gain is fundamental in the American incentive enterprise system. Obviously this principle must apply to advertising as it does to every other function of the business. The evaluation of advertising effectiveness, both before it appears, and after it appears, is an inescapable business function. The only debatable question—and herein lies a time-worn controversy—is whether this process of evaluation is carried out objectively or subjectively, systematically or haphazardly.[4]

This quotation contains the key to the problem of advertising evaluation. Since advertising is going to be evaluated, the proper questions are whether the evaluation is to be carried out subjectively or objectively, systematically or haphazardly.

Complete objectivity cannot be attained in advertising evaluation; our evaluation tools are simply not that precise. However, insofar as is possible, objective criteria should enter into and be a part of the evaluation process. Further, we can be systematic rather than haphazard in our approach to advertising. To do so means that we begin our evaluation with the marketing plan, not with advertising.

EVALUATING THE MARKETING PLAN

Evaluating the effectiveness of a particular marketing plan is not difficult; either it achieves its objectives within its cost constraints or it does not. If the objectives call for the sale of 10,250,000 cases with a marketing expenditure of $6 million within a given fiscal year and sales approximate or exceed this level, the marketing plan was successful. If sales fall significantly below the expected level, the plan is a failure.

Difficulty lies in determining the specific contribution that each element of the plan makes to the marketing plan's success or failure. Let's take an example.

A cake mix manufacturer test marketed a new type of cake mix. The product concept called for a cake mix image rooted in early American traditions—a low, heavy, rich cake like grandmother used to make. All elements of the marketing plan were, quite properly, designed around this concept. However, in the process of execution, no one was really happy with the package design. The package design was not inappropriate; rather, the package design could be better. In the judgment of the marketing group, too much input from

---

[4]Russel H. Colley, ed., *Practical Guides and Modern Practices for Better Advertising Management: Evaluating Advertising Effectiveness*, VII (New York: Association of National Advertisers, Inc., 1959), 1.

too many individuals and committees had routinized the design and dulled its communication potential. Nonetheless, under the pressure of deadlines and concern about competitive activity in developing a similar product, a decision was made to go ahead with test marketing, but to revise the package before expanding nationally, should the test market be successful.

The test market was highly successful. Sales exceeded the expectations of the client and agency. Everyone was jubilant. However, now they had a problem. They were afraid to modify the package because they did not know how much the test market version of the package contributed to the product's success.

In the case of a marketing plan that fails to achieve its objectives, the problem is compounded. What element or elements failed to perform adequately? Were the objectives unrealistic? Did the problem lie in the product concept? The product itself? Pricing? Distribution? Advertising? Or in some other element of the marketing plan?

At this point, a major analysis must be undertaken. Each element of the marketing plan must be carefully scrutinized in order to assess its strengths and weaknesses. Sometimes, certain elements may be easily exculpated. For example, if the product performs adequately in well designed tests against leading competitive products, then the problem does not lie there. If high levels of distribution were achieved, then this variable can be eliminated. Each element must be investigated against some criterion of performance. Since the primary concern of this text is advertising, no attempt will be made to develop and discuss performance criteria for all elements of the marketing plan; however, note that developing performance criteria is often a difficult task and specific performance objectives must be set before meaningful evaluations can be made.

EVALUATING ADVERTISING

Advertising often represents the single largest expense item in the marketing budget. This is particularly true for proprietary drugs and personal care items where advertising and sales promotion may represent 40 percent of company sales for leading brands. For other consumer products, the advertising to sales ratio may be lower, but it still represents a significant sum. When the 100 leading advertisers spend almost $12 billion in advertising, advertising's effectiveness must be a major concern.

Strangely enough, advertising is probably as little understood by its users as by its detractors. Disagreement among advertising professionals regarding what constitutes good advertising is evidence of this fact. A company can run a brilliant campaign one year and follow it the next year with one that is mediocre or worse. Still, major company resources are allocated to advertising, and it is the responsibility of marketing and advertising management to see that such expenditures are made wisely.

Advertising research is the manager's primary instrument to provide some assurance that advertising monies are being used well. Few major companies will invest significant funds in a television or print campaign that has not been thoroughly tested. While advertising research techniques may not be infallible, they can be helpful.

Generally speaking, advertising research can be subdivided into three major areas: budget, audience, and copy. Each is a field of investigation in its own right.

1 **Budget research** is concerned with the amount of money allocated for advertising.
2 **Audience research** is concerned with advertising weight, reach, frequency, and efficiency, and the effectiveness of different media and combinations of media in reaching target audiences.
3 **Copy research** deals with what is said and how it is said in the employed media.

These three areas are interrelated and interdependent. For example, the effectiveness of what is said may depend upon the media used. Media effectiveness may be influenced by the available budget. For our purposes, we will isolate copy research and direct our attention to this aspect of advertising evaluation.

PROBLEMS IN COPY RESEARCH

Copy research is beset with problems of definition, measurement, and interpretation. Perhaps the most difficult problem in copy research is determining the objectives against which advertising should be measured. While the ultimate goal of advertising may be to increase sales, advertising may contribute to this goal in a variety of ways. On the one hand, the direct mail advertiser succeeds or fails depending upon whether advertising does or does not generate immediate sales. On the other, the president of a large life insurance company says:

> Advertising does not sell life insurance. Only agents can sell a policy. Advertising can simply make the prospect more interested in the idea of investing in insurance and more receptive to our agents than to the agents of our competitors.[5]

Most advertisers of consumer goods fall somewhere in between these two extremes. For the most part, the marketer who attempts to evaluate advertising in terms of its short-term effect on sales or share of market faces a formidable task. There are a number of reasons why sales and market share are misleading criteria of the effectiveness of a particular advertisement or advertising campaign.

☐ *Advertising does not work alone.* Advertising is part of a total marketing effort. A product that is poorly positioned, overpriced, inadequately distributed, badly packaged, or inferior to competition may suffer sales declines even though the advertising itself

---

[5]H. D. Wolfe, J. K. Brown, and G. C. Thompson, *Measuring Advertising Results,* Studies in Business Policy 102, The National Industrial Conference Board (1962), p. 7.

is well conceived and professionally executed. If sales are stagnant or declining, advertising may be the scapegoat even though some other part of the marketing mix is the real culprit.

☐ *Sales response does not always parallel advertising expenditure.* In response to advertising, sales may build slowly at first, and then accelerate. Thus, there is often a lag between the appearance of advertising and the sales response. The length of the lag itself may be a variable because of the product being advertised and the advertising appeals employed. A lag between advertising and sales response is expected with most products, but it may be particularly acute for big ticket items or items that are infrequently purchased.

☐ *Advertising may be subject to threshold effects.* Advertising response may be the result of an advertising campaign's cumulative effects as opposed to being a response to a single advertisement or commercial. A $500,000 campaign may have no apparent effect, whereas a $750,000 expenditure for the same product may break through the consumer's barrier of awareness and pay for itself many times over.

☐ *Advertisers may find it difficult to associate changes with a specific medium.* Sales response may result from the combination of media, or one medium generating the bulk of the sales response with the other contributing relatively little.

☐ *Uncontrollable variables may obscure the relationship between advertising and sales.* Competitive activity and other marketing variables may cause sales not to reflect advertising effectiveness. For example, let us assume that a tire advertiser ran a brilliant campaign for snow tires. If the winter in which the campaign runs is a mild one, sales will be down regardless.

Since short-term sales results may be neither a sensitive nor valid measure of advertising effectiveness, it seems obvious that we need turn to other bases for evaluation.

In Chapter 9, it was argued that the basic purpose of advertising is persuasive communication; any effect advertising has must be dependent upon what it communicates to consumers. Hierarchy of effects models are all communications models and, while they differ in minor details, they visualize the advertising tasks of provoking the sale and creating awareness, acceptance, preference and intention to buy. Provoking the sale is the only task that demands specific action from the consumer. The rest are purely communication measures; they communicate something to the consumer.

Action is the ideal measure of advertising effectiveness, but it is often too insensitive or contaminated by other marketing activities to be useful. As a consequence, most measures of advertising effectiveness must depend upon communication measures mentioned above. Even here, there is danger of contamination from other marketing activities. For example, awareness of a product may arise because a package is seen in a retail outlet, not because of advertising exposure. Nonetheless, measuring advertising in terms of its communication accomplishments is often the only practical way of assessing its contribution. The following discussion of copy research must be considered against this background.

COPY TESTING

For the advertising practitioner, copy testing may perform two basic functions: (a) measuring the effectiveness of an advertisement or advertising campaign in achieving some predetermined objectives; and (b) providing diagnostic material that can be used in developing or improving an advertising effort. The ideal copy test would be one that fulfilled both functions. No practical testing devices perform both functions equally well. Sales response, the ultimate goal of marketing effectiveness, generates no diagnostic information for improving advertising. Attitude and communications tests, often rich in diagnostic data, provide no real measure of sales response. The basic conflict is between quantitative and qualitative data. Advertising effectiveness is measured by numbers, while diagnostic data may not be amenable to quantitative forms. As a consequence, marketing managers normally employ both kinds of testing—qualitative or diagnostic testing to help the advertising staff develop advertisements, and effectiveness tests to measure the performance of the finished product.

Essentially, three stages of research can be used in developing advertising copy: (a) **preliminary,** where concepts may be tested and elements of the proposed advertisement or commercial assessed; (b) **pretesting,** where advertisements or commercials are tested in a rough or finished form; and (c) **posttesting,** where the results of an advertising campaign are evaluated for their effectiveness in achieving predetermined objectives.

PRELIMINARY STAGE

Preliminary testing often starts with concept testing wherein a product concept is exposed to consumers in order to determine its effectiveness in arousing interest. For example, in an attempt to develop a concept for a new brand of coffee, General Foods exposed consumers to a series of descriptive words, such as rich, full-bodied, full-flavored, and dark, to determine which word or which combination of words evoked the greatest interest.[6] A detergent advertiser might test such concepts as "a detergent that gets clothes whiter," or "a detergent that gets clothes cleaner," or " a detergent that makes colors brighter" to determine which concept elicits the most positive consumer response. A variety of research techniques may be used at this stage, such as simple expressions of preference, extended interviews, projective techniques, or physiological measures. The object of the research is to obtain a measure of the product concept's ability to arouse consumer interest.

Discrete elements of a final advertisement may also be tested in the preliminary stage. A model or celebrity may be tested to determine his or her appeal as a product spokesperson; the video portion

---

[6]M. P. Brown, R. N. Cardoza, S. M. Cunningham, W. J. Salmon, R. G. M. Sultan, *Problems in Marketing* (New York: McGraw-Hill, 1968), 7.

of a television commercial may be tested to see how well it tells the basic product story without the benefit of the audio portion; a headline or print illustration may be tested to ascertain its communication value; a particular demonstration of a product feature may be checked for its effectiveness in communicating the product benefit; or body copy may be tested for its clarity of expression.

In other words, various elements of an advertisement or commercial may be subjected to research to determine whether they should be included in the final production, or whether some alternative execution would be more effective.

When copy research is used in this way, it is used to develop an advertisement or commercial, not evaluate the overall effectiveness of the advertising communication against some defined objective.

PRETEST STAGE

In the pretesting stage, complete advertisements are tested to determine their effectiveness against some objective or objectives. Complete advertisements may be tested in a variety of forms, ranging from rough layouts to finished art for print advertisements, and from still photographs with superimposed audio to finished commercials for broadcast. Many pretests involve a potpourri of measures, including attention value, interest, comprehension of message, recall of the advertisement (in total, or specific points), and attitude change.

There is no simple way to catalog the types of tests used in the pretesting stage because flexible research designs permit combinations of a variety of measures in any given test. In addition, the tests may be structured in such a way that the advertisement or commercial simply serves as the focal point for extended interviews with individuals or groups. The test's structure depends wholly on the kinds of information sought.

In addition to obtaining measures of interest, attention value, and comprehension of the message, the pretesting stage often attempts to assess the overall effectiveness of the advertisement in terms of its ability to change attitudes or generate recall of key sales points. Note that attitude and recall tests are based on different theories of advertising effectiveness and generate quite different kinds of information.

Attitude tests.   The theory underlying the use of this test is to create a preference for the product being advertised, thereby changing the consumer's attitude toward the product. Such tests use some form of attitude scaling to compare brand preferences before and after exposure to the advertisement or commercial. An effective advertisement is one that increases consumer preference for the brand; the greater the increase in preference, the more effective the advertisement.

Recall tests.   Recall tests operate from a different philosophical base. Rooted in the psychological phenomenon of selective perception, recall tests hypothesize that consumers will remember those products and sales points that are psychologically important to them. High recall is equated with commercial excellence, although neither logic nor evidence provides assurance that what is psychologically relevant is necessarily positive. For example, a consumer exposed to an automotive advertisement may recall that the advertised product is powered by a 360 horsepower V-8 engine, not because he or she is charmed by having "360 horses" under the hood, but because the individual is grossly offended by what he or she perceives to be wasteful and irresponsible use of production facilities and fossil energy.

While attitude and recall tests are extensively used in estimating advertising effectiveness and are logically sound, neither is supported by unassailable evidence of experimental validity. Within recent years, attitude measures have gained in popularity, although in many cases the two measures are combined into a single test. The primary reason for combining the two measures is that: (a) attitude tests of effectiveness often provide insufficient diagnostic information for modifying the advertising approach; and (b) although recall techniques are a rich source of diagnostic data, they may be criticized because they do not distinguish between favorable and unfavorable recall.

Pretest procedures. Most advertising pretests are conducted with small, nonrepresentative samples of consumers, selected on a judgment or convenience basis. As a consequence, it is not possible to assess the sampling error involved, or make statistical judgments on the validity of the data. This is one of the reasons that pretest results often vary widely. Pretest sampling practices are usually defended on the basis that they are not intended to yield precise findings, but are only meant to provide general assurance that the advertising is appropriate. The legitimacy of this defense is questionable, however, since the results are often treated as though they are precise and valid. In an industry where personal judgment generally takes precedence over statistics, expediency is often the rule rather than the exception, and rationalization is frequently accepted as a substitute for wisdom.

Research techniques that may be used individually, or in combination, in pretesting advertisements are: (a) laboratory tests; (b) portfolio tests; (c) simulated media tests; and (d) limited media tests. Generally, these research approaches vary on the basis of the artificiality of the testing situation; laboratory tests are the most artificial, followed by portfolio, simulated media, and limited media tests, respectively.

Laboratory tests. Laboratory tests involve a laboratory setting and special equipment. The most commonly used instruments are: (a) pupillometers, designed to measure the change in the size of the pupil of the eye in response to a stimulus, as well as its pattern of fixation when exposed to a complex stimulus; (b) tachistoscopes, special projectors used to control the duration of a visual stimulus; and (c) psychogalvanometers, which measure the electrical conductivity of the skin and are central components of the battery of instruments that are collectively called a lie detector. These devices are most often used to assess interest and emotional response to advertisements, although they may be used simply as a point of departure for extended interviews or some other information gathering approach.

One interesting application of operant conditioning theory in a laboratory setting has resulted in a behavioral measure of commercial effectiveness. This application is based on the finding that reinforcement (reward) of a response will increase the probability that the response will be repeated. Many laboratory experiments with animals measure the strength of a reinforcing device by the number of responses that a subject will emit in order to receive the reinforcement. Associates for Research in Behavior (ARBOR) has developed equipment in which the brightness of a television commercial and clarity of the audio portion are controlled by the viewer by pumping foot pedals. The faster the viewer pumps, the clearer the picture. Interest in a commercial is gauged by how hard the subject is willing to work (frequency of emitted responses) to see and/or hear it.[7]

Since it is sometimes difficult to get subjects to come to a laboratory, a number of commercial research organizations have installed laboratories in motorized vans so that laboratories may be taken to the consumer. The van is driven to the parking lot of a shopping center, or some other consumer gathering place, and tests are conducted on the spot. The test sample in this case is a convenience sample, with all of its shortcomings.

Portfolio tests. Portfolio tests are usually used to pretest print advertisements; a modification of the approach has been adapted for television commercials. Normally, five to ten advertisements are assembled into a portfolio and given to the subject to peruse. One or more of the advertisements will be test advertisements, while the remainder will be controls. Advertisement position in the portfolio is usually controlled because position affects recall. After the subject has leafed through the portfolio and closes it, some intervening activity, such as a series of questions on the socioeconomic characteristics of the respondents, is undertaken to provide a diversion and induce the forgetting process. Then the subject is asked a series of recall questions about the portfolio material. Attitude information can also be gathered through questions on preferences, beliefs, and values about the product or brand and its attributes.

In the television version of the portfolio test, several commercials are presented via a portable projector that is brought into the home or is available in a van or laboratory.

Simulated media tests. In this approach, the researcher attempts to simulate a normal media situation without actually using commercial media. The two best known techniques in this classification are the proven name registration test for print media and the competitive preference measure for commercials.

In the proven name registration procedure, advertisements are added to a dummy magazine that also contains a normal quota of editorial material. Under the guise of obtaining consumer responses to a proposed new media venture, the magazine is placed in the

---

[7]P. E. Nathan and W. H. Wallace, "An Operant Behavioral Measure of TV Commercial Effectiveness," *Journal of Advertising Research* (December 1965): 13–20.

home and left for several days to give the subjects a chance to read it. Through a series of aided and unaided recall questions, interviewers determine which advertisements are remembered and what is remembered about them. The technique, originally devised by Gallup-Robinson, is a recall technique, and advertising effectiveness is measured by the percent of the sample that can prove they recall a particular advertisement by remembering something specific about it. Young & Rubicam developed its own testing service along these lines, using its own version of a dummy magazine.

The competitive preference approach was originally developed by Horace Schwerin, who invited subjects to a theater, ostensibly to preview the pilot show for a new television series. Today, commercials to be tested are embedded in the format of the show, as they are in a regular television program. Under the guise of giving away a year's supply of products in the product fields being tested, consumer preferences for specific brands are obtained before and after the program is shown and the commercials seen. An effective commercial is one that causes consumers to change their brand preferences after seeing the commercials. Obviously, the more people who change preference in the desired direction, the better the commercial. The competitive preference method, as opposed to the proven name registration technique is an attitude test, since it relies on brand preference rather than recall for its measure of effectiveness.

Limited media tests. The essential characteristic of all limited media tests is that a commercial or advertisement is tested under normal conditions in a limited geographic area before major funds are committed to it. Media tests can take a number of forms. A split-run copy test in a metropolitan newspaper is one form; a test market is another. In a split-run test, the criterion of effectiveness is usually the response to a hidden offer. In a test market, the criterion of effectiveness may range from measures of awareness to sales response as measured by store audits or consumer panels.

One form of media testing widely used for television commercials is a commercial that is scheduled during the late movie in a major metropolitan area; the next day telephone interviews are conducted to elicit recall information. Traditionally, this method has been used by Procter & Gamble as well as other major advertisers.

Another highly sophisticated form of television testing is offered by AdTel, a commercial research organization that maintains a dual cable system and two balanced consumer purchase diary panels in each of several markets. By virtue of the dual cable hook-up, AdTel can funnel different commercials into the homes of its two consumer panels in a given market. Commercial effectiveness can be evaluated either in terms of the sales response measured by the consumer diaries, or from follow-up interviews designed to obtain recall and/or attitude data.[8]

POSTTEST STAGE

Posttesting is an extension of limited media testing. Rather than actual testing, it is a final evaluation. Many research and marketing personnel make no distinction between testing and evaluation. How-

---

[8]AdTel advertisement, *Advertising Age*, 15 July 1974, 31–33.

CHAPTER 22 | MEASURING ADVERTISING EFFECTIVENESS

ever, from the standpoint of business performance accountability, the distinction is crucial. Testing is what is done *before* committing major company resources to a program. The purpose of testing is to provide empirical support for judgments, reduce risk, and eliminate or modify questionable material. Evaluation is made *after* company resources have been committed to a campaign. Its purpose is to determine if company objectives have been achieved. For the marketing or advertising manager, this is the moment of truth.

Both testing and evaluation are the responsibility of the marketing manager, although some companies hire an outside consultant to make a periodic audit of various marketing activities. The wise marketing manager will make program evaluations personally and make sure that these assessments are communicated to higher management along with recommendations for future improvements in areas where improvement may be needed.

Evaluation must be made against some predetermined objectives or criteria. Although many specific objectives can be set for advertising, the measurement of these objectives can usually be accommodated by three types of measurements: (a) **recall**; (b) **attitude**; and (c) **action.**

Measurements of recall. The purpose of recall tests is to find out what consumers can remember about the advertising. There is disagreement among researchers about how much aid subjects should be given in eliciting their recall of advertising. Thus, recall tests are often divided into two forms: **aided recall** or **recognition**; and **unaided recall.**

Aided recall (recognition). In the aided recall approach, respondents will be shown an advertisement and asked: (a) whether they remember seeing it; and (b) which portions of the advertisement they paid attention to. This method is employed by the Starch Inra Hooper Ad Readership Service and is commonly referred to as the Starch test because it was originated by Daniel Starch in 1923. Interviewers of the Starch organization operate throughout the United States. Each interviewer is provided with copies of the magazine to be tested. Each interviewer contacts 100 to 150 women and 100 to 150 men who claim that they have read the magazine being tested. The interviewers go through the magazine, page by page, with the respondents and ask them to indicate which ads they have read. For one-half page and larger advertisements, respondents are asked whether they saw the various elements of the advertisement—headline, illustration, body copy, and logo. Responses are recorded, by percentage of respondents, on three levels of readership: (a) noted—those who say they have seen the advertisement; (b) seen-associated—those who associated the advertisement with the advertiser or with the product's brand name; and (c) read most—those who report that they read half or more of the copy. An example of a Starched ad is shown in Figure 22–1.

The Starch organization claims that their service enables advertisers to determine whether their advertisements are read, how they compare in readership to competitive advertisements, and how the readership of individual ads compares with past advertising. Critics of the Starch method contend that the technique is too easy, and the aided recall method may give rise to false recall, thereby inflating readership scores.

Unaided recall. The unaided recall method, introduced by Gallup-Robinson, is more difficult than the Starch test because it requires respondents to recall advertisements and their content without having the advertisement in front of them. In the Gallup-Robinson technique, respondents are shown the front cover of the magazine being tested, and they must qualify by identifying the contents of at least one article that they read in the magazine. After respondents qualify themselves as readers of the issue in question, they are given the names of advertisers appearing in the issue and are required to qualify as having seen a particular advertisement by describing some part of it—headline, illustration, or general appearance. Then respondents are asked to recall everything they can about the advertisements they have seen.

Gallup-Robinson provides three measures of advertising effectiveness from this technique:

1 Proven name registration (percentage of respondents who demonstrate that they have seen the advertisement by describing some part without having it in front of them)
2 Idea communication (percentage of respondents who can recall the various sales points in the advertisement)
3 Favorable attitude score (percentage of respondents who express a favorable attitude toward the advertiser, message, or product)

Since the Gallup-Robinson test is much more difficult than the Starch test, many advertisers prefer it as a more valid measure of advertising readership.

Measurements of attitude. Attitude tests develop qualitatively different data than recall tests. Aided recall tests reflect exposure to advertisements. Unaided recall tests reflect consumer learning. Attitude tests reflect the effects of this exposure or learning on the learner's perceptual organization.

Presumably, a consumer who holds a more favorable attitude toward Brand A than Brand B will buy Brand A, provided no other overriding considerations influence the choice, such as lack of product availability or a large price differential in favor of Brand B. This chain of logic leads many advertisers to evaluate their advertising programs on the basis of their effectiveness in creating favorable attitudes, often expressed as measures of brand preference or intention to buy. In fact, attitude measures hold such a hallowed place in the minds of many marketing practitioners that few marketers attempt to evaluate advertising without including some attitude questions in the study design. Sometimes, the attitude scaling devices are simplistic; at other times, they utilize sophisticated psychological and mathematical designs.

Those who prefer attitude tests to recognition or recall tests generally do so for two reasons: (a) Psychologically, attitude tests are

STARCH
READERSHIP REPORT

Reader's Digest
Total of 39 1/2 Page or Larger Ads

January 1982
Men Readers

PAGE	SIZE & COLOR	ADVERTISER	RANK IN ISSUE BY NUMBER OF READERS	PERCENTAGES			READERSHIP INDEXES		
				NOTED	ASSOCIATED	READ MOST	NOTED	ASSOCIATED	READ MOST
		BLDG. EQUIP./FIXTURES/SYSTEMS							
35	H1/2P4B	HUNTER CEILING FAN/ ROBBINS & MYERS	18	42	30	13	131	103	217
		COMMERCIAL TRUCKS/LEASING							
183	1P4B	TOYOTA SR5 SPORT TRUCK	3	59	58	18	184	200	300
		COMMUNICATION/PUBLIC UTILITY							
203	1P	AT&T LONG LINES INTERNATIONAL	12	37	33	8	116	114	133
		COSMETICS/BEAUTY AIDS							
10	1P4B	LUBRIDERM LOTION DRY SKIN CARE	33	19	13	2	59	45	33
30	1P	OIL OF OLAY	38	17	7	2	53	24	33
170	1P4B	SOFT SENSE SKIN LOTION	35	16	12	3	50	41	50
219	1P4B	VASELINE DERMATOLOGY FORMULA LOTION & CREAM OFFER	37	13	10	2	41	34	33
		FIRE/CASUALTY INSURANCE							
12	1P2	AMERICAN INSURANCE ASSOCIATION G P	24	29	25	6	91	86	100
		FOOD BEVERAGES							
181	1P4B	MAXWELL HOUSE MASTER BLEND COFFEE	21	28	28	6	88	97	100
		FRUITS/VEGETABLES							
167	1P4B	VAN CAMP'S CANNED BEANS	26	24	23	4	75	79	67
		HOUSEHOLD FABRICS/FINISHES							
209	1P4B	SEARS CUSTOM DRAPERIES & BLINDS	29	23	18	3	72	62	50
		JEWELRY/WATCHES							
196	1P4B	DE BEERS DIAMONDS	29	32	18	5	100	62	83
		LIQUOR & WHISKEY							
45	1P4B	SEAGRAMS V.O. CANADIAN WHISKY	5	51	49	8-	159	169	133-
145	1P4B	SOUTHERN COMFORT	9	43	39	11	134	134	183
163	1PB	HOUSE OF SEAGRAM G P	15	37	32	15	116	110	250
199	1P4B	LORD CALVERT CANADIAN WHISKY	9	40	39	3-	125	134	50-

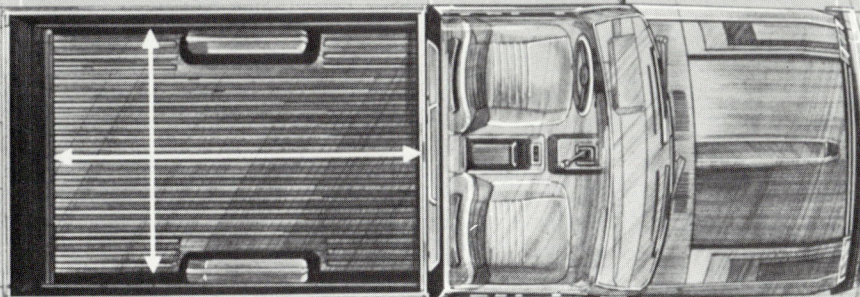

FIGURE 22–1   (a) Starch readership report. (b) Example of a Starched ad. (Courtesy Starch Inra Hooper, Inc., and Toyota Motor Sales, U.S.A., Inc.)

a step closer to purchase than mere recognition of advertising, or the ability to recollect product attributes or sales points. (b) Normally, attitude measurement represents the last point, with a reasonable degree of confidence, that advertising can be isolated from other variables in the marketing mix. Once the consumer gets to the purchase decision, it is usually difficult to separate advertising's contribution from that of in-store display material, sales clerk influence, packaging, pricing, or other marketing variables.

Nonetheless, attitudes are substitute measures for sales effectiveness. If it is at all possible, the marketing or advertising manager should seek hard evidence that advertising is, in fact, producing sales.

Measurements of action. Ultimately, product advertising is expected to produce sales. This is true whether the immediate goal of the advertising is to generate inquiries, produce sales leads to be followed up by salespeople, stimulate immediate sales response, increase store traffic, or instill consumer goodwill.

Sometimes sales response is easy to associate with an advertising message. Direct mail advertising succeeds or fails in direct proportion to the number of orders that result from its appearance. Advertising used by retail outlets features a sale on certain days for a specific item or group of items. A major consumer promotion run by a manufacturer features a coupon, price pack, or combination deal.

Direct sales results are more difficult to trace to display advertising, which is designed to inform consumers about a product or its attributes with the expectation that purchases will be made at some future date. Wolfe, Brown, and Thompson emphasize this point:

> Product qualities, selling effort, brand prestige, dealer loyalty, consumer inertia, product distribution, size and location of displays, discount policies, delivery and other seller services, transportation allowances, reciprocal buying—these and other factors consciously or unconsciously influence the buyer in making his purchase decisions. To isolate advertising from these factors is often difficult if not impossible to accomplish.[9]

Even where it is possible to relate advertising to sales, there is often the question of whether the sale that is made is a *new* sale or a substitute for a sale that would have been made anyway. This is particularly worrisome in the case of promotional advertising involving some sales incentive, such as a coupon or price-off label. Characteristically, consumer sales following a promotion period drop below the level of sales preceding the promotion, suggesting that the promotion itself appropriated sales from future periods. For the manufacturer of consumer goods, an increase in recorded sales may simply reflect a buildup of retailer inventories without creating a corresponding increase in purchases by the ultimate consumer. Such inventory buildups often signal a drop in future orders.

All of this means that careful record keeping, thoughtful analysis, and audits of consumer sales and channel inventories are nec-

---

[9]Wolfe, et al, *Measuring Advertising Results,* 159.

essary before reasonably sound conclusions can be drawn concerning advertising effects. The best results are often obtained by identifying a sample of consumers who have been exposed to a firm's advertising, and a sample which has not, and taking a measure of brand use from each group. Such measures can be made either through specially designed surveys or from the purchase-diary records of continuing consumer panels, such as those maintained by Audits and Surveys, Inc. Even in these instances, though, clear conclusions cannot be reached because of the secondary effects of advertising. For example, an individual may not have personally seen the advertising for a product but may have been influenced to buy the product by someone who has seen it.

SELECTING A TESTING PROCEDURE

Because of the number of specific research techniques and study designs, the alternatives for testing are almost limitless. In the face of this diversity, the key questions are: (a) whether to test; and (b) what to test.

TO TEST OR NOT TO TEST

Cornelius Dubois has suggested that, before choosing a testing method, a marketer should consider whether to use any method at all.

> Do not test everything—not by any means. One does not need numbers to reject an ad that is in bad taste or too strident, irrelevant, or tinged with the unethical. Some things are too small to test with the instruments available to us. Some are too big and basic to test; some are too nebulous to test, and some are so obvious that they do not require testing.
>
> Copy testing has both its real uses and its real imperfections. It can help us uncover the flaws and weaknesses that might spoil a good ad yet fail to reveal, in the test situation, the strength that a good ad will have in the marketplace.[10]

The rumor mills of advertising are full of horror stories about highly successful campaigns that succeeded because the advertiser ignored negative copy tests and ran the advertisement anyway. For example, it is widely rumored that: the Avis "We're Only No. 2" campaign bombed out in pretesting;[11] the Ajax "White Knight" was a pretest mediocrity; and "Charlie" would not have become a leading seller among perfumes had it been subjected to the obstacles of advertising research rather than owing its existence to the inspiration of Charles Revson.

Most major advertisers test advertisements and commercials that they plan to put substantial resources behind, even though they do not always abide by the test results. Sometimes advertisers will ignore negative research findings if, on the basis of creative judgment, they strongly believe the advertising should be used. Ultimately, the question of whether to test can only be resolved by the

---

[10]Cornelius Dubois, "Copy Testing," in *Handbook of Marketing Research*, R. Ferber, ed. (New York: McGraw-Hill, 1974), 4–132.

[11]Lois G. Ernst, "703 Reasons Why Creative People Don't Trust Research," *Advertising Age*, 10 February 1975, 35.

marketing or advertising manager based on such criteria as the magnitude of the expenditures involved, personal belief in the adequacy of the advertising in question, and willingness to take risks. All of these criteria are subjective and, despite the advances of decision theory, do not lend themselves to computerized solutions.

WHAT TO TEST

What to test is even more provocative than the question of whether to test at all because it leads to more alternatives and raises the basic question of what advertising is expected to accomplish.

In the earlier discussion of advertising testing, we recognized that advertising may be tested at various stages. At one extreme, we can test an advertising concept for its promise; at the other extreme, we can test a completed advertisement for its effectiveness against some predetermined objective. Advertising practitioners differ in their orientation toward testing in this regard. Arthur Pearson, who was director of marketing services for Clairol in the mid-1970s, believed that the principal role of copy testing is to decide whether to run a particular piece of advertising or not. On the other hand, Larry Light, senior vice-president and research director for a major advertising agency during the same period, argued less for win-lose tests of finished advertisements than for a "disciplined copy development system" that emphasizes the use of advertising research at the preproduction level of writing advertising strategies.[12] While both positions may have merit, the present sophistication of advertising research lends itself to the more tentative application inherent in the second approach than it does to the win-lose philosophy of the first.

If the advertising is expected to generate measurable sales increases, tests of awareness or recall are poor substitutes. On the other hand, if the advertising is intended to communicate a certain product attribute to consumers, recall tests may be appropriate.

Before marketing managers can possibly evaluate an advertisement or advertising campaign, they must set forth the advertising's specific objectives. If advertising objectives are not clearly spelled out, rational evaluation is impossible. If they are clearly spelled out, evaluation is only difficult.

Sometimes it may not be possible to isolate the effects of advertising from other marketing activities, particularly when the ultimate goal of advertising is to increase sales. Under such conditions, marketing and advertising managers may have to forsake the evaluation of advertising alone for an evaluation of the entire marketing program. Alternately, they may choose to evaluate the advertising on the basis of substitute goals, such as its ability to generate awareness or create favorable attitudes among an identifiable group of consumers. This is a matter of choice; different choices will be made by different managers.

However, advertising is such a major part of the marketing effort for consumer products and demands such a substantial share of company resources as an investment that effective marketing and advertising managers find it necessary to come to terms with some

---

[12]"Copy Testing Is Still a Nebulous Area," *Advertising Age*, 1 December 1975, 54.

form of advertising measurement that is acceptable both to them and their management. As the measurement program becomes more systematic, it becomes more adequate in helping to develop effective advertising.

SUMMARY

Evaluation is a key part of the marketing effort. It is not difficult to evaluate the success or failure of a marketing plan in its entirety, since the essential criterion is whether or not it achieves the projected sales goal within the constraints of available funds. What is difficult to ascertain is the extent to which individual elements of the marketing plan contribute to its success or failure. In the case of a plan that fails to achieve its objectives, the problem becomes one of determining where the problem lies.

There are three kinds of advertising research—budget, audience, and copy research. Although these three forms are closely interrelated, copy research is isolated for consideration in this chapter.

In most cases, short-term sales results are inadequate as a basis for evaluating advertising effectiveness. As a consequence, the most valid measure is one of communication value.

Copy testing has three stages of development: preliminary, pretest, and posttest. Qualitatively, posttesting differs from the other stages in that preliminary testing and pretesting are undertaken to develop advertising and reduce risk; posttesting occurs after advertising funds have been committed, and it serves as a final evaluation.

The actual testing procedures depend upon what the advertisement is supposed to do and the predilection of those authorizing the test.

Different copy testing philosophies exist within the advertising industry. For some, copy testing should be an integral part of copy development and be used to provide guidance and direction. For others, testing should be the final stage to determine whether a particular ad or commercial should be used. In view of the limitations surrounding copy testing methods, the first approach may be the wisest.

REVIEW QUESTIONS

1. How does one evaluate the effectiveness of a marketing plan? Why is it easier to evaluate the effectiveness of a marketing plan than to evaluate advertising effectiveness?
2. Identify and explain the three major areas of advertising research.
3. Identify the reasons that short-term sales or marketing share changes may be misleading measures of advertising effectiveness.
4. What are the two basic functions of copy testing? Why are different testing measures required for these two functions?
5. Explain what is meant by pretesting. Give examples.
6. What are the different philosophies underlying attitude and recall tests?

7 Explain what is meant by a simulated media test, and give examples of such tests.
8 How does posttesting differ from preliminary testing and pretesting? Why is this difference important?
9 Some research practitioners argue that aided recall questions are a better measure of advertising effectiveness than unaided questions. What is the basis for this argument?
10 Why is "what to test" such an important question in advertising research?

DISCUSSION QUESTIONS

1 What do you think are some of the reasons that advertising research is surrounded by controversy?
2 Select a magazine advertisement or a television commercial that you think is highly effective and one that you think is ineffective. How do they differ? How might you test them for effectiveness? Bring copies of the magazine ads and descriptions of the commercials to class.
3 In one of the examples at the beginning of the chapter, it is pointed out that on-air recall tests often yield variable results. One reason given was that the context of the programs biased results. Can you think of any other factors that might influence results?

PROBLEM

Using the *Reader's Guide to Business Periodicals,* locate a recent article on copy testing. Prepare a brief summary of the article to present to the class.

23

Legal Restrictions and Advertising

REGULATION AND ABUSE

THE TAMING OF THE FTC

The Federal Trade Commission (FTC) is the primary government agency that has jurisdiction over marketing and advertising practices. During the 1960s and early 1970s, the FTC flexed its muscles and directed an assault on a wide variety of marketing and advertising activities. In its enthusiasm, it succeeded in alienating many consumers, most businesses, and a good part of Congress.

After months of acrimonious debate, charge and counter charge, the FTC Improvements Act, derogatorily referred to by FTC commissioner Michael Pertschuk as a "businessman's relief act," was enacted.[1] A key provision of this act is the legislative veto. The legislative veto permits Congress, by a majority vote of both houses, to override administrative decisions of the FTC and other agencies, thereby limiting the FTC's power to interpret legislations in ways that go beyond the intention of Congress.

THE UNBELIEVABLE CASE OF SELF-REGULATION THAT WORKED

Until a few years ago, the failure of the advertising industry to assume the responsibility for self-regulation was both a scandal and an object of frustration. However, the formation of the National Advertising Review Council, under the auspices of the Council of Better Business Bureaus, has changed that. According to *Advertising Age*:

> With characteristic modesty, the advertising industry's national self-regulation program has just marked its tenth anniversary. The program was created at a time when a cresting wave of consumerism was pressing for an upgrading of advertising practices. A recently rejuvenated Federal Trade Commission was pounding the industry. It

---

[1]Michael Pertschuk, "The FTC Outcome: Battered But Alive," *Advertising Age*, 14 December 1981, 44.

became a matter of do it yourself or prepare for ever-expanding government intrusion that would inevitably endanger freedom of expression.

Even among the leaders of the industry who brought the program into being, there was considerable skepticism that it would achieve worthwhile results. But their misgivings were unwarranted. Operating openly, but quietly, the self-regulation program has faced up to difficult issues and sensitive competitive relationships. In any one month, it deals with the blue chips of advertising as well as the less lordly. There has not been a single instance of advertisers ultimately refusing to accept its verdicts, and only a handful of cases have been appealed beyond the National Advertising Division staff level of the Council of Better Business Bureaus to the hearing panels of the National Advertising Review Board.

It is difficult to quantify the benefits that the advertising self-regulation program has bestowed on the industry and the public. But so far as national advertising is concerned, the docket at the FTC is virtually bare—and not for lack of trying on the part of the commission. Instead of long, costly litigation, disputes over ad claims are negotiated within the self-regulation system for a pittance.

If there is any failure, it is a failure to publicly celebrate the achievement so the whole nation knows of this enlightened activity and this exemplary act of good citizenship on the part of the industry. At a time when President Reagan is calling on Americans to take greater responsibility for the policing of their society, the advertising industry national self-regulation program already in place should be an example for others to follow.

It should be especially encouraging to the American Advertising Federation, now reviving its plan to establish similar self-regulation programs at the local level.[2]

These two examples focus attention on the problem of regulation and abuses in the advertising industry. In the following pages, we will examine the need for advertising regulation, regulatory agencies that have emerged, and trends in advertising regulation.

---

[2]"A Decade of Self-regulation," p. 16. Reprinted with permission from the July 27, 1981 issue of *Advertising Age*. Copyright © 1981 by Crain Communications, Inc.

REASONS FOR ADVERTISING REGULATION

Advertising regulation is necessary and probably will continue to be. These are the reasons why:

1 There are differences of opinion over what constitutes deceptive advertising; the line between deception and truth is often unclear.

2 The sheer volume of advertising has become so vast it is inevitable that some portion of the industry will violate canons of honesty and good taste.

3 In large companies, top management often loses touch with some of its corporate activities; control of these activities is exercised by lower echelon managers whose personal ambitions often dull their critical judgment.

4 As product fields become more crowded and competitive, there is a temptation to use deceptive and exaggerated claims as an easy substitute for imagination and product innovation.

5 At a time when costs are being driven up by inflation and prices are being driven down by competition, the constant pressure for corporate profits leads to the substitution of shoddy material and a lowering of quality control standards.

6 The widespread consumer discontent with many of our institutions includes that of advertising.

Although many believe the government has been overzealous in its attacks on advertising, advertisers are far from blameless.

The Drug Research Corporation advertised Regimen tablets as being capable of bringing about large losses in body weight without the reduction of food intake. A federal court found the advertiser guilty of using false advertising, fake laboratory reports, and television models who resorted to drastic dieting rather than using Regimen as claimed.

Dr. Samuel Massengell packaged sulfanilamide in a liquid form and sold it as a patent medicine called Elixir Sulfanilamide. The product had not been properly tested for toxicity, and it ultimately caused 73 deaths in seven states before the Food and Drug Administration seized the remaining supplies.

Rapid Shave produced a television commercial that purported to show the shaving cream's moisturizing effects by applying it to sandpaper and then removing the sand with one stroke of a razor. Actually, sandpaper was not used in the demonstration; instead, loose sand was spread on plexiglas to simulate sandpaper.

Campbell's Soup placed marbles in the bottom of a bowl of soup used in a television demonstration. The marbles caused the vegetables to rise to the top of the bowl where they could be seen, giving the impression that the product contained more vegetables than it actually did. Campbell defended the use of the marbles, arguing that without them the vegetables sank to the bottom of the bowl, giving the impression that the bowl contained less vegetables than it actually did.

Profile bread advertising claimed that each slice contained fewer calories than competitive breads without bothering to point out that the slices were also thinner than the slices of competitive products. The FTC required the company to devote 25 percent of its advertising for a year to correct the erroneous low calorie impression that had been created.

Sears attracted consumers to its stores by advertising an attractive sewing machine for $58. According to an FTC complaint, salespeople disparaged the item by such statements as: "(1) the advertised sewing machines are noisy and are not guaranteed for as long a period of time as the firm's more expensive models; (2) certain of them will not sew straight stitch, zigzag stitch, or in reverse; (3) none of the advertised sewing machines is available for sale and, if ordered, there will be long delays in delivery."[3]

Many other examples can be cited. In some cases, advertising is the culprit; in some, other marketing practices have been singled out. In some cases, the intent to deceive is apparent; in others, it is moot. Advertisers have won some cases in courts; others have been won by the government. Marketers have contributed to the woes of the industry and must bear some fault for consumer distrust and government intervention into the marketing process.

Business became subject to special regulating legislation with the passage of the Sherman Antitrust Act in 1890. Subsequent legislation has extended government concern to the complete range of marketing activities—products, pricing, selling practices, sales promotion, and advertising. A number of government regulatory agencies have been established to monitor marketing practices, and special-interest consumer groups have been increasingly active in recent years. In 1962 President Kennedy enunciated certain consumer rights: (a) the right to safety; (b) the right to be informed; (c) the right to choose; and (d) the right to be heard. These rights had far-reaching implications for marketing and advertising. There has also been a persistent and controversial movement to establish a Department of Consumer Affairs at the cabinet level of the federal government.

As the most visible feature of marketing in the lives of most consumers, advertising often bears the brunt of consumer criticism and government activity. Legislation governing other marketing practices has not been neglected. Indeed, the Robinson-Patman Act of 1936, dealing with a wide range of competitive activities, is often a central concern of United States marketers. However, advertising is the part of marketing that most people see. For this reason, it is advertising's real and alleged sins that most often catch our attention. These sins give us conversational tidbits with which to regale our friends and neighbors. They serve as a focus for frustrations when the climax of an exciting television show is interrupted for a commercial announcement or when the product that is supposed to solve all of our problems doesn't live up to our expectations.

Over $54 billion a year is spent on advertising. It is a major vehicle for reaching consumers and persuading them to buy. Without the communication economies of advertising, mass marketing in a nation of over 230 million consumers is unthinkable. From

---

[3]In re Sears, Roebuck & Co., CCH 20,652 (July 1974) BNA ATRR no. 672 (July 16, 1974) A–20. Quoted material from *Journal of Marketing* (January 1975): 101.

the standpoint of the advertising practitioner, legislation and regulatory commissions are often seen as a major threat to advertising creativity.

Most major advertisers go to considerable lengths to avoid the use of poor taste and misrepresentation in advertising, but often their efforts are frustrated by fly-by-night operators and the public's willingness to believe the worst. This climate has caused the advertising industry, regulatory agencies, and legislative bodies to focus on the problem of advertising misrepresentation.

REGULATORY AGENCIES

A number of regulatory agencies monitor advertising. Some of these agencies are established by legislation; others are inspired by industry groups. The various agencies' effectiveness generally depends upon whether they have and use sanctions against offenders. For example, as a federal agency, the FTC has the weight of the federal government behind it and often seeks legal injunctions to enforce its rulings. On the other hand, many industry-organized regulatory groups are relatively weak. In the following material, a number of the better known regulatory agencies will be identified and briefly discussed.

FEDERAL REGULATORY AGENCIES

There are several federal regulatory agencies that have an impact on advertising and marketing. The Securities and Exchange Commission (SEC) has control over all advertising of public offerings of stocks and bonds. Except for certain legal exemptions relating to small offerings, advertising a security under SEC jurisdiction without having it registered is a criminal offense. The alcohol tax unit of the U.S. Treasury Department has jurisdiction over a number of practices relating to the sale and advertising of distilled spirits; these regulations include packaging, labeling, and advertising. The U.S. Postal Department has authority to stop the dissemination of obscene materials and delivery of mail (including magazines) from firms using the mails to defraud.

Three federal agencies with the most impact on advertising are the Federal Trade Commission, Federal Communications Commission, and the Food and Drug Administration.

The Federal Trade Commission (FTC). The FTC was initially established in 1914 to provide technical counsel to the courts in cases involving restraint of trade arising from the Sherman Antitrust Act of 1890 and investigate complaints related to this issue. Subsequent legislation strengthened and broadened the powers of the FTC, extending its jurisdiction into pricing, packaging, selling practices, sales promotion, and advertising. In addition to investigating complaints made by others, the FTC was given the authority to initiate actions in the public interest. Among its responsibilities is the policing of false advertising. False advertising is interpreted as advertising that misleads through untrue assertions, implication, or the omission of material facts. Obviously, such a broad definition of misleading advertising often calls for highly subjective judgments on the part of the FTC. The subjectivity of many of these judgments fuels the ongoing controversy over regulation in the advertising industry.

For example, in the Wonder Bread case the commission held that the advertising claim "Helps build strong bodies 12 ways" was misleading because it was not unique; other enriched breads could make the same claim. In this instance, the commission's ruling was reversed by the federal court system when challenged by the Continental Baking Company, the marketer of Wonder Bread. In the case of cranapple juice, the FTC charged that the advertising phrase "more food value" was misleading because, technically, food value means calories, a fact not recognized by most consumers. In this case, the offending company expiated its guilt by running corrective advertising designed to explain the meaning of food value and confess that it really means calories.

In carrying out its responsibilities, the commission undertakes an investigation of questionable practices, and if the situation warrants, issues a complaint against the offending advertiser. These complaints are often settled by negotiation. In some cases, a cease and desist order (an order to stop an unlawful practice) will be issued by the FTC and accepted by the advertiser. In other instances, the advertiser will enter into a consent decree (an agreement to stop the practice in question without agreeing to its illegality). If the advertiser wishes to contest the FTC's complaint, a hearing is held before a trial examiner who is a member of the commission's staff. The findings of the trial examiner are considered by the full commission, which rules upon them and issues orders for remedial action. The decision of the full commission can be appealed by the advertiser through the federal court system—Circuit Courts of Appeal and the Supreme Court.

The most common remedy resulting from FTC hearings is a cease and desist order prohibiting further use of the offending advertising. More recently, the FTC has turned to corrective advertising, requiring the offending company to devote a certain proportion of its advertising funds for a given period of time (for example, one year) to explaining to consumers that previous advertising may have been misleading. In rare cases, charges can be brought against individuals, and fines and jail terms can be imposed.

The Federal Communications Commission (FCC). In addition to the FTC, the FCC exerts control over broadcast advertising through its authority to license radio and television stations. The FCC has imposed a number of restrictions on products that may be advertised on broadcast media and on the content of advertising. Prior to the congressional ban on broadcast advertising by cigarette advertisers, the FCC required television stations to schedule antismoking advertising.

Although the FCC has the power to use its licensing authority to control program and advertising content, it has been reluctant to do so. The FCC has preferred to refer specific complaints and general concerns to agencies such as the FTC for investigation and action. Nonetheless, the FCC has disapproved, on moral and ethical grounds, advertising by physicians, clergy, those offering advice on marriage and family matters, lotteries, contraceptive devices, and hard liquor.[4] Although disapproval carries weight and encourages caution on the part of the station licensees, it does not necessarily prohibit an ad's use.

The Food and Drug Administration (FDA). Since the passage of the Pure Food and Drug Act and the Meat Inspection Act in 1906, the federal government has shown an increasing concern over labels and packaging. Today, the FDA regulates labels, packaging, and other materials that accompany the package for foods, drugs, therapeutic devices, and cosmetics. It is authorized to require warnings and cautions on labels, when appropriate, and has developed detailed rules regulating cents-off and other sales promotions utilizing the package label. With the passage of the "truth in packaging" bill in 1966, the authority of the FDA was broadened to include: (a) use of appropriate words to describe a particular package size, such as large, family, or giant; (b) size and location of type used to indicate the volume or weight of a package; (c) slack-fill (failure to fill the package); and (d) standardization of package sizes.

STATE AND LOCAL REGULATION

In addition to federal agencies, advertising is also regulated at the state and local level through a multiplicity of laws and enforcement agencies.

State regulation. All states, with the exceptions of Arkansas, Delaware, Mississippi, and New Mexico, have state laws designed to prevent fraudulent and dishonest advertising. Most state laws are based on a *Printers' Ink* model statute that was prepared in 1911 by this now defunct advertising trade publication. The original statutes were directed primarily toward print advertising but have been revised to include broadcast. In addition, many states have established consumer protection agencies.

State statutes are often poorly enforced because of lack of personnel; since many state statutes involve criminal rather than civil law, local authorities are often reluctant to enforce them and thereby brand violators as criminals. The problem is made more difficult because interpretations of what is misleading in a particular state may differ from those of other states and federal practices. Thus, an advertiser can comply with 49 states and the U.S. government, but offend the statutes of the fiftieth state. This is particularly true in product fields such as distilled spirits where local prohibition groups may have forced through highly restrictive legislation. Nonetheless, the existence of state statutes and the possibility that they will be

---

[4]Dorothy Cohen, *Advertising* (New York: John Wiley & Sons, 1972), 199.

enforced complicates the life of national advertisers and serves as a constraint on their activities.

Local regulation.   Below the state level, many counties and cities have also enacted laws governing advertising and marketing and, in some cases, have established consumer protection agencies to enforce them. Generally, such action is taken to offer protection against unfair and deceptive practices by local merchants since the federal government is primarily concerned with national and regional advertisers. Local regulation is more characteristic of large population centers, such as New York City, than of less populous areas. New York City has established a department of consumer affairs and enacted a consumer protection act that covers a wide range of deceptive selling and advertising practices. Over 50 cities and 20 counties have organized consumer protection agencies;[5] it is probable that this number will increase in the future.

SELF-REGULATION BY MEDIA

Advertising media have the prerogative of rejecting advertising that does not meet the standards of honesty and good taste that individual media have established for the conduct of their business. For example, *Good Housekeeping* follows a practice of testing all products scheduled for advertising in its pages. If the advertising claims are at variance with the tests, the advertising is not accepted. Brands that are accepted for advertising are entitled to use the *Good Housekeeping* "Seal of Approval" on their labels and in other advertising. *Reader's Digest* does not accept tobacco advertising, and *The New Yorker* refuses ads for feminine hygiene products. Since 1969, *Sunset* magazine has refused advertising for products containing dangerous insecticides, although prior to that time *Sunset* carried more insecticide advertising than any other nonfarm publication. Such decisions are at the discretion of the media, and it is generally recognized that as media become more financially secure, they also become more discriminating in terms of the advertising material they will accept.

Although standards may vary widely at the local level and the thoroughness of the screening process is suspect, network and individual stations in the broadcast industry also screen commercials for acceptability. The radio code and the television code of the National Association of Broadcasters serve as standards for the industry, and the major networks maintain a continuity department that screens all commercials before they are aired. Relatively strict network standards require that advertisers provide substantiation for claims made about their products.

Other groups, such as the Direct Marketing Association and the Outdoor Advertising Association, also have standards of ethical practices that members are expected to observe. However, supervision is weak; sanctions are limited; and conformance is largely determined by the ethics of the individual firm.

---

[5]"Consumers Battle At the Grass Roots," *Business Week,* 26 February 1972 86–88.

SELF-REGULATION BY AGENCIES AND ADVERTISERS

Both advertising agencies and advertiser organizations promulgate ethical standards of practice. Thus, the American Advertising Federation, American Association of Advertising Agencies, Association of National Advertisers, and a number of individual industry organizations have established codes of conduct to which individual members presumably subscribe. The creative code of the American Association of Advertising Agencies is shown in Figure 23–1 as an example of an industry code of advertising ethics.

As shown in the examples of deceptive advertising given earlier in the chapter, some members of the American Association of Advertising Agencies have not always been scrupulous in abiding by this code. Further, the code is essentially a statement of intent, and is not backed up by a policing mechanism for enforcement or meaningful sanctions for violators. Perhaps the most effective industry efforts to control deceptive and fraudulent advertising are those by the Better Business Bureau and the National Advertising Review Board.

Better Business Bureau. The Better Business Bureau concept grew out of a "truth in advertising" campaign developed by the American Advertising Federation in 1911. Today, over 240 bureaus operate at both the local and national level to protect consumers against deceptive advertising and selling practices. These bureaus, made up of advertisers, advertising agencies, and media, receive complaints, investigate questionable practices, and maintain files on violators; the files are open to the public. While the bureaus have no legal authority, they often work with local law enforcement officials in prosecuting perpetrators of fraud and misrepresentation. According to one source, bureaus handle over 2.5 million complaints annually and investigate over 40,000 advertisements for possible violation of truth and accuracy.[6]

National Advertising Review Board. Historically, the National Association of Better Business Bureaus directed some of its attention to national advertising, while local bureaus attended to complaints at the local level. In order to increase the effectiveness of the national organization, a reorganization was undertaken in the early 1970s, and the Council of Better Business Bureaus was formed. This new organization, along with the Association of National Advertisers, American Association of Advertising Agencies, and American Advertising Federation, set up a policy making group known as the National Advertising Review Council. Under the direction of this council, two regulatory divisions were established: (a) National Advertising Division (NAD), an investigatory body; and (b) National Advertising Review Board (NARB), an appeals body for NAD decisions. Both divisions are staffed by advertising professionals. Figure 23–2 diagrams the relationship between the NAD and NARB.

The authority of the NAD and NARB is severely limited. They cannot: (a) order an advertiser to stop running an ad; (b) levy

---

[6]Otto Klepner, *Advertising Procedures*, 6th ed. (Englewood Cliffs, New Jersey: Prentice-Hall, 1973), 687.

CREATIVE CODE

American Association of Advertising Agencies

The members of the American Association of Advertising Agencies recognize:

1. That advertising bears a dual responsibility in the American economic system and way of life.

To the public it is a primary way of knowing about the goods and services which are the products of American free enterprise, goods and services which can be freely chosen to suit the desires and needs of the individual. The public is entitled to expect that advertising will be reliable in content and honest in presentation.

To the advertiser it is a primary way of persuading people to buy his goods or services, within the framework of a highly competitive economic system. He is entitled to regard advertising as a dynamic means of building his business and his profits.

2. That advertising enjoys a particularly intimate relationship to the American family. It enters the home as an integral part of television and radio programs, to speak to the individual and often to the entire family. It shares the pages of favorite newspapers and magazines. It presents itself to travelers and to readers of the daily mails. In all these forms, it bears a special responsibility to respect the tastes and self-interest of the public.

3. That advertising is directed to sizable groups or to the public at large, which is made up of many interests and many tastes. As is the case with all public enterprises, ranging from sports to education and even to religion, it is almost impossible to speak without finding someone in disagreement. Nonetheless, advertising people recognize their obligation to operate within the traditional American limitations: to serve the interests of the majority and to respect the rights of the minority.

Therefore we, the members of the American Association of Advertising Agencies, in addition to supporting and obeying the laws and legal regulations pertaining to advertising, undertake to extend and broaden the application of high ethical standards. Specifically, we will not knowingly produce advertising which contains:

a. False or misleading statements or exaggerations, visual or verbal.

b. Testimonials which do not reflect the real choice of a competent witness.

c. Price claims which are misleading.

d. Comparisons which unfairly disparage a competitive product or service.

e. Claims insufficiently supported, or which distort the true meaning or practicable application of statements made by professional or scientific authority.

f. Statements, suggestions or pictures offensive to public decency.

We recognize that there are areas which are subject to honestly different interpretations and judgment. Taste is subjective and may even vary from time to time as well as from individual to individual. Frequency of seeing or hearing advertising messages will necessarily vary greatly from person to person.

However, we agree not to recommend to an advertiser and to discourage the use of advertising which is in poor or questionable taste or which is deliberately irritating through content, presentation or excessive repetition.

Clear and willful violations of this Code shall be referred to the Board of Directors of the American Association of Advertising Agencies for appropriate action, including possible annulment of membership as provided in Article IV, Section 5, of the Constitution and By-Laws.

Conscientious adherence to the letter and the spirit of this Code will strengthen advertising and the free enterprise system of which it is part. *Adopted April 26, 1962*

Endorsed by
Advertising Association of the West, Advertising Federation of America, Agricultural Publishers Association, Associated Business Publications, Association of Industrial Business Publications, Newspaper Advertising Executives Association, Radio Code Review Advertisers, Association of National Advertisers, Magazine Publishers Association, National Board (National Association of Broadcasters), Station Representatives Association, TV Code Review Board (NAB)

FIGURE 23–1 American Association of Advertising Agencies' creative code

NAD

NARB

START HERE

Complaint or question.

NARB chairman appoints panel.

NAD evaluates.

OR

Panel finds advertising not misleading. Dismisses.

NAD dismisses (Trivial, etc.).

Advertiser contacted. Substantiation requested.

OR

Advertiser asked to change or discontinue message.

NAD dismisses. Advertising substantiated.

OR

OR

Advertiser agrees. Panel dismisses.

(Note below)

Substantiation not acceptable. Advertiser asked to change or discontinue message.

Advertiser refuses. Matter referred to government for further action.

Advertiser agrees. NAB dismisses.

OR

Advertiser disagrees. Matter appealed to NAFB by NAD or advertiser.

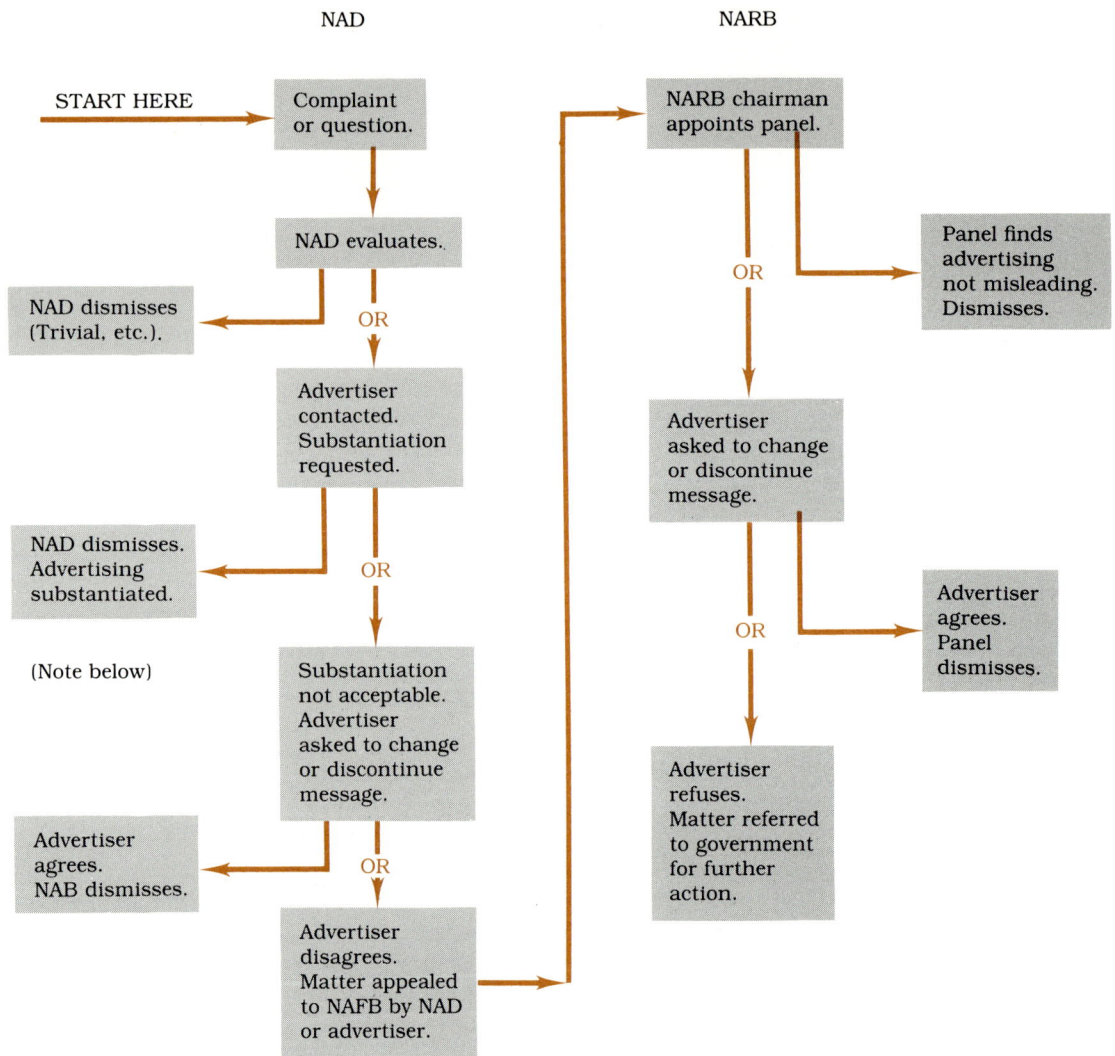

Note: If the original complaint originated outside the system, the outside complainant at this point can appeal to the chairman of NARB for a panel adjudication. Granting of such appeal is at the chairman's discretion.

FIGURE 23–2 Diagram of steps followed by NAD and NARB in dealing with complaints filed against an advertiser [Source: *The National Advertising Review Board: 1971–1975* (New York: National Advertising Review Board, 1975), 12.]

fines; (c) require corrective advertising; or (d) impose any other legal sanctions. However, they can: (a) bring the moral weight of the industry to bear on practices that are judged injurious to advertising; and (b) refer cases to the FTC when offenders do not cooperate. The value of the NARB is indicated by the following statement of an FTC official: "NARB helps relieve us (FTC) of much of the burden in the regulatory area."[7]

Until the advent of the NAD and NARB, attempts at self-regulation by the advertising industry had generally met with limited success.[8] The outstanding success of these two industry spon-

---

[7]*Advertising Age*, 6 June 1975, 66.

sored agencies, however, suggests that the advertising industry is finally maturing enough to assume responsibility for its own conduct.

TRENDS IN ADVERTISING REGULATION

Legislation regulating marketing and advertising is often stated in ambiguous terms giving administrative agencies such as the FTC the task of developing more precise guidelines and interpretations. Thus, the Supreme Court has observed that "precision of expression is not an outstanding characteristic of the Robinson-Patman Act"[9]; Lowell Mason, a former FTC commissioner, has said: "Nowhere is institutional whim more apparent and more deadly than in the choice of defendants the FTC sues under the Robinson-Patman Act."[10]

Similar charges might be made against Section 15 of the Wheeler-Lea Act, which defines false advertising in the following way:

> The term "false advertisement" means an advertisement, other than labeling, which is misleading in a material respect; and in determining whether any advertisement is misleading there shall be taken into account (among other things) not only representations made or suggested by statement, word, design, device, sound, or any combination thereof, but also the extent to which the advertisement fails to reveal facts material in the light of such representations or material with respect to consequences which may result from the use of the commodity to which the advertisement relates under the conditions prescribed in said advertisement or under conditions as are customary or usual.

Under this definition, false advertising is almost anything the FTC, FTC staff, complainants, or competitors decide is false advertising. As a consequence, the FTC has an extremely broad mandate in determining the truth or falsity of an ad. This fact is manifested by some of the charges that the agency has brought against advertisers. Further, under pressure from consumer groups and as a natural expansion of its functions, FTC interpretations of false and misleading advertising tend to become broader with the passage of time.

MATERIAL FALSITY vs. FALSE IMPRESSIONS

Initially, under the Wheeler-Lea Act, advertising had to contain a literal untruth to be held false. However, over time, judicial interpretations have extended the act to include the "creation of false impressions," even though individual statements may be literally true. For example, the commission contested a claim by Chevron gasoline that an ingredient, F-310, helps reduce pollution. The FTC

---

[8]Past failures of the advertising industry to regulate itself led some experts in the field to conclude that advertising would eventually become a regulated industry, very much like railroads, utilities, and banks. See E. B. Weiss, "51 New Advertising Marketing Regulations Offer Lively Future," *Advertising Age,* 25 October 1971.

[9]346 U.S. 6173 Supreme Court 1017.

[10]"Robinson-Patman Act: It Demands a Closer Look Now," *Printers' Ink,* 20 October 1961, 24.

argued that, while F-310 did indeed reduce pollution, the total amount of pollution reduction was not significant and, therefore, could not be claimed in the advertising.[11] Other examples of the trend are the Profile bread and cranapple cases mentioned earlier.

BURDEN OF PROOF

In cases of false and misleading advertising, there has been a trend to shift the burden of proof from the FTC to the advertiser. In effect, this changes the tradition-honored doctrine of innocent until proven guilty to guilty until proven innocent. In one instance, the FTC filed a complaint against Pfizer's Unburn, a burn remedy, demanding that Pfizer produce evidence to support its product claim rather than requiring the commission to produce evidence that the claims were false. Although this specific charge was dismissed by the full commission, the FTC ruled that it is unlawful for an advertiser to make a product claim unless there is a reasonable basis for it.[12]

In 1971 the FTC initiated an ad substantiation program requiring advertisers to submit, upon demand by the commission, data supporting past or current advertising. A number of advertisers in a variety of fields have been required to submit such information. Recently, as a consequence of this program, the FTC fined the STP Corporation $500,000 and required $200,000 in corrective advertising for violating an FTC consent order. The FTC charged that STP's advertising claim that its use would decrease oil consumption by 20 percent was based on faulty tests. A company spokesperson pointed out that: "Nowhere (in the FTC complaint) is there any challenge to the efficacy of the product. It's merely a question of some defective tests done years ago."[13]

LIMITS OF PUFFERY

Subjective claims such as "amazing," "unsurpassed," "beautiful," "better," and so on are referred to as **puffery.** Puffery has generally been considered beyond the scope of FTC authority because such statements represent personal opinions that cannot be measured by objective tests. One observer, however, has noted that the FTC has never fully accepted puffery as a legitimate advertising tool and has grown more intolerant of it in recent years.[14]

While puffery has not yet been banned, it has become an object of scrutiny by the FTC. The head of the FTC's Bureau of Consumer Protection has suggested that puffery is permissible when the: (a) claim is immaterial; (b) exaggeration is insubstantial; and (c) exaggeration is of a type that cannot be measured.[15]

[11]John Revett, "Standard Oil, FTC Face Off Over F-310," *Advertising Age,* 3 April 1972, 8ff.

[12]Stanley E. Cohen, "Enforcer Petofsky Explains FTC's New Get Tough Policy," *Advertising Age,* 18 January 1971, 14.

[13]"Corrective Ads For STP Publicize Settlement Costs to Business Execs," *Advertising Age,* 13 February 1978, 1ff.

[14]Ivan L. Preston, "Puffery in Advertising," *Advertising Age,* 14 February 1972, 39–40.

[15]Stanley E. Cohen, "TV Revolutionized FTC's Limits of Permissable Puffery," *Advertising Age,* 24 March 1971, 121.

FULL DISCLOSURE

There has been a spate of legislation in recent years requiring full disclosure. The philosophy behind this legislation is that the consumer must be given sufficient information about products in order to make an informed judgment. Under this reasoning, advertisers are expected not only to provide information of the positive attributes of their products, but also on the negative features when these features may constitute a health, safety, or economic hazard. For example, drug manufacturers are required to report on the side effects and contraindications of their products. For a number of years, cigarette manufacturers have had to include a health warning on their packages. The truth in lending law requires that the actual amounts and interest rates for installment loans and credit be publicized. Automobile manufacturers must include a suggested list price on new automobiles. Flammable fabrics must be clearly labeled as such, and a number of other legislative acts require a fuller disclosure of product information than has traditionally been offered in advertising and on labels.

Much of this legislation is clearly desirable. However, advertisers' concern for the future is that administrative agency interpretations of full disclosure will exceed good judgment. It has been suggested that a government that insists on protecting consumers from the consequences of their own folly will create a nation of fools. There is concern in some quarters that the federal government is well on its way to this consequence.

UNIQUE CLAIMS

Traditionally, advertising has thrived on unique claims. The unique selling proposition theory of advertising holds that marketing success depends upon the use of unique product claims, whether these claims are truly unique or simply preempted. The FTC has argued that uniqueness must be real in order to avoid being misleading. The landmark case in this area is the Wonder Bread example used earlier in which uniqueness is implied by the claim "Helps Build Strong Bodies 12 Ways." The FTC charged that since this same claim could be made by any producer of an enriched bread, Wonder Bread was guilty of deceptive advertising. FTC's challenge was not sustained by the courts.

EMOTIONAL CLAIMS

Much advertising is based on the social and psychological benefits that will accrue from using a product. Implications of beauty, confidence, social success, prestige, masculinity, femininity, and so on are the advertising bases of most personal care items as well as a variety of other highly visible products. Many believe that the FTC would like to broaden the concept of false advertising to include these implied psychological benefits, although no such complaints have been filed thus far.

NUTRITIONAL CLAIMS

Claims of nutritional benefits came under fire from the FTC in the mid-1970s; the cereal and confection industries bore the brunt of the attack. For example, the FTC forced Carnation Company to change its advertising for Instant Breakfast because the company was exaggerating the nutritional claims of its product. Cereal companies have been challenged for their nutritional claims; the FTC has contended that much of the nutritional value of ready-to-eat cereals comes from the milk that is poured over the cereal, not from the cereal itself. The FTC also cited: Milky Way candy advertising for emphasizing the milk content of the product; Hostess cupcakes for focusing on the iron and vitamin content of this delicacy; and Hi-C because of the product's name and its claim that Hi-C is the "sensible drink."

These are only a few of the nutritional cases initiated by the FTC. Advertisers who make nutritional claims should be well buttressed with nutritional and irrefutable facts supporting their copy.

CORRECTIVE ADVERTISING

One rapidly growing practice of the FTC is to require corrective advertising from companies who are unsuccessful in defending themselves against its charges. The commission felt that existing penalties were too light and insufficient to deter advertisers from making false and misleading statements. How far the doctrine of corrective advertising can be extended before it invokes a legislative rebuke under pressure from business interests is an open question. Certainly, the use of sanctions more severe than those provided by the original legislation is a bold extension of administrative authority.

COMPARATIVE ADS

The FTC has taken a strong position in favor of comparative advertising. This stand is of particular interest because comparative advertising is a highly controversial issue among advertisers and advertising agencies. Although comparative advertising has been used sporadically in the past, usually comparing the advertised product with Brand X, its modern day use emphasizes the naming of competitive brands in the comparison. Schick Flexamatic electric shaver ushered in the modern trend in 1972 with the claim that Schick was superior to Norelco, Ronson, and Remington.[16] Subsequently, comparative advertising has become rampant in other fields, notably foods, antiperspirants, automobiles, and analgesics.

Opponents argue that it creates confusion, publicizes competitive brand names, and more often than not, the consumer who remembers the comparison forgets which brand was best. The president of the Council of Better Business Bureaus has blasted comparative advertising "as damaging to ad credibility and a negative value in business conduct."[17]

Advertisers who approve of comparative advertising argue that it encourages a flow of facts and enables consumers to make in-

---

[16]"Weston: Comparative Ads Spur Flow of Facts," *Advertising Age,* 4 November 1977, 6.

[17]Ibid., 6.

formed judgments. There is little hard evidence to support either point of view. On balance, the little known brand probably benefits by comparing itself to a well-known competitor, gaining acceptance and stature from the association. On the other hand, its use by the leader in a field probably is more detrimental than helpful. Occasionally, comparative advertising does produce some amusing copy, as exemplified by the following Coca-Cola commercial run in response to Pepsi-Cola's comparative taste tests which demonstrate that consumers prefer Pepsi to Coke.

The Coke TV spot shows an interviewer with his back to the camera asking a respondent to "first try 'S', sir, then 'L'."

Respondent: "Come from a big city, don't you, boy?"

Interviewer: "Yes, I do."

Respondent: "Thought so. You got one of those skinny little big city mouths. Now look here. Let me tell you something. You can't tell nothing from no test like this. Give me that bottle of Coke. I'll show you how we drink them down here. We don't sit around in no fancy bar taking little bitty sips and wearing skinny britches and pointy lizard shoes. You can't come down here flim-flamming honest people. You got to watch what you do down here, boy."

Announcer: "There's more to Coke. Coke adds life."

ADVERTISING TO CHILDREN

During the 1970s, various consumer groups became agitated over advertising that was addressed to children. Their basic argument was that children are unable to distinguish between fact and fancy and between truth and exaggeration; therefore, they must be protected from the persuasiveness of commercials. They further argued that when parents refused children's requests for products seen in advertising, the child-parent relationship was injured. Opponents of this point of view generally respond that: (a) if parents don't want their children to see commercials, they should turn off the set; or (b) one of the time-honored functions of parents is to protect their own children by saying "no" occasionally.

Nonetheless, in 1978, the FTC's staff proposed major strictures on children's television ads. The proposed rule urged by FTC's Bureau of Consumer Protection would:

1 Ban all advertising from television shows seen by substantial audiences of children under 8 because they are too young to understand the selling intent of the message.

2 Ban advertising of sugary foods that pose a dental health risk from television shows seen by significant numbers of children between ages 8 and 11.

3 Allow continued television advertising of less hazardous sugared foods to the 8- to 11-year-old group, but only if individual food advertisers found "balancing" nutritional and/or health disclosures.[18]

---

[18]"Report by FTC's Staff Recommends Major Strictures On Children's TV Ads," p. 1ff. Reprinted with permission from the February 27, 1978 issue of *Advertising Age*. Copyright © 1978 by Crain Communications, Inc.

A curious question raised by these guidelines is: Will FTC commissioners sit in family living rooms to prevent children under 8 from watching inappropriate television commercials?

This may have occurred to the FTC staff; under pressure from the Congress, it concluded that enforcement of its standards was unfeasible and withdrew its recommendations.

MONOPOLY EFFECTS

A final regulatory trend to be noted is concern over the monopolistic effects of advertising. Despite substantial evidence to the contrary, the FTC continues to subscribe to the "barrier to entry" charge against advertising. One major target of the FTC is the cereal industry.

Specific charges were filed against the Kellogg Company, General Mills, General Foods, and The Quaker Oats Company. The charges in the FTC complaint against these companies were many and complex, but the essence of the advertising charges was that the ". . . practices of proliferating brands, differentiating similar products, and promoting trademarks through extensive advertising result in high barriers to entry into the RTE (ready-to-eat) cereal market."[19]

In 1980, after eight years of litigation, thousands of pages of testimony, and legal costs to the cereal companies in excess of $27 million, the charges against the cereal companies were dismissed by a federal judge.

THE FUTURE OF ADVERTISING LEGISLATION

Government regulation of advertising and marketing practices reached its peak in the late 1970s. Subsequently, the FTC has been less aggressive in its attacks on business. There are three possible reasons for a softening of the FTC stance.

1 The FTC Improvements Act of 1980, which restricted FTC powers and served as a warning against administrative excesses.
2 Public rebellion against government intervention in their lives and the election in 1980 of an administration dedicated to reducing the power of government.
3 The success of the NAD and NARB in intercepting and settling advertising malpractices before they reach the FTC.

The outlook for future advertising legislation will probably depend largely on how advertisers conduct themselves. If the industry continues to exhibit responsibility in self-regulation, further government intervention will probably be unnecessary. If the industry fails to exercise prudent restraint and falls back to abusive and deceptive practices, further government intervention is inevitable.

This is the challenge that faces the advertising industry and the young people who are preparing themselves for careers in marketing and advertising. Meet it well, and both you and your industry will prosper. Meet it poorly, and both will suffer.

---

[19]Nancy Gibes, "Kellogg Calls FTC Order Devastating," *Advertising Age*, 31 January 1972, 8.

SUMMARY

Misrepresentation and abuses are a perennial problem in the advertising industry. A number of reasons for this situation are: (a) differences of opinion about what constitutes deceptive practices; (b) the sheer volume of advertising, making it inevitable that some portions of the industry will violate canons of honesty and good taste; (c) in large companies, top management losing touch with some of its corporate activities; (d) a temptation to use deception and exaggerated claims as a substitute for imagination and product innovation; (e) constant pressure for corporate profits leading to the substitution of shoddy materials and a lowering of quality control standards; and (f) widespread consumer discontent with many of our institutions, including advertising.

While many think that the government has been overzealous in its attacks on advertising, advertisers are far from blameless and have sometimes invited government intervention.

Regulatory agencies at the federal level have been established to monitor advertising. The three most important are the Federal Trade Commission, Federal Communications Commission, and Food and Drug Administration. In addition to federal agencies, advertising is regulated at the state and local level. A number of industry agencies have also been established to promote self-regulation. The most important and effective of these is the National Advertising Review Council and its two regulatory divisions: (a) National Advertising Division (NAD), an investigatory body; and (b) National Advertising Review Board (NARB), an appeals body for NAD decisions.

Several trends characterize advertising regulation: (a) increased concern over false impressions as opposed to material falsity; (b) shifting the burden of proof to advertisers; (c) limiting the use of puffery; (d) full disclosure requirements; (e) validation of nutritional claims; (f) use of corrective advertising; (g) emphasis on comparative ads; and (h) concern over the monopolistic effects of advertising.

Government regulation of advertising reached its peak in the mid-1970s. Subsequently, the FTC has been less aggressive in its attacks on business because of: (a) restrictions imposed by the FTC Improvements Act of 1980; (b) public rebellion against government intervention and the 1980 election of an administration dedicated to reducing the power of government; and (c) the success of the NAD and NARB in intercepting and settling advertising disputes before they reach the FTC.

The future of advertising regulation will depend largely on how the advertising industry conducts itself. By exercising responsibility in self-regulation, the industry can limit government intervention. However, if the industry resorts to abusive and deceptive practices, government regulation is inevitable.

REVIEW QUESTIONS

1 Define legislative veto and explain its purpose.
2 According to the text, what are the reasons that regulation of advertising is necessary?
3 What types of regulatory agencies or groups attempt to monitor advertising? Which agencies or groups have the most influence and why?

4   What are the three federal regulatory agencies that have the major impact on advertising and marketing? What are the primary responsibilities of each?

5   Differentiate between a cease and desist order and a consent decree.

6   Who are the founders of the NAD and NARB? What is the relationship between these two divisions?

7   Discuss the area of material falsity versus false impression in advertising. What is the trend in this area by the FTC?

8   Evaluate the use of comparative advertising. What is the FTC's position on this practice?

9   According to the text, what are the reasons for the FTC becoming less aggressive?

10 What is the outlook for the future of advertising regulation? What does it depend upon?

DISCUSSION QUESTIONS

1   What is your opinion of the legislative veto? Do you believe it is desirable? Why or why not?

2   Do you think children should be protected more than adults from advertising? Why or why not? If so, how should they be protected?

3   What are the benefits and dangers of government regulation of advertising?

PROBLEM

Find an advertisement that you think is deceptive or untruthful and one that you think is truthful. Bring these advertisements to class for discussion.

APPENDICES

Appendix 1
A Sample Marketing Plan

The following marketing plan, devised to illustrate the way that a marketing plan should be written and its typical subject areas, is for Golden Grain Grits, a fictitious product.

Throughout the plan, references are made to exhibits that are not a part of the main body of the plan but represent detailed analyses from which data appearing in the plan itself have been abstracted and summarized. These detailed exhibits have not been reproduced in this appendix. They serve to emphasize the kinds of backup data available if the reader of a marketing plan wants a more detailed understanding of the data presented.

The plan is a summarization of relevant findings that have been developed from extensive analyses of all data that might have a bearing on marketing objectives and strategies.

MARKET REVIEW

The following section summarizes key trends and developments in the canned grits market during the past 12 months. Except as otherwise noted, data on retail distribution and sales is drawn from the A. C. Nielsen Food Index.

1. <u>Market Growth</u>

Total industry retail sales of canned grits products through grocery outlets reached 9.9 million cases during the year ending March 31, 1982, up 5.3 percent from the previous year. Based on the relatively uniform rate of growth during the past five years, it is estimated that the total market during fiscal 1982–83 will reach 10.4 million cases.

Fiscal	Industry Retail Sales (1000s Cases)	Increase vs. previous year
1978–79	8,523.4	5.0%
1979–80	8,975.1	5.3%
1980–81	9,396.9	4.7%
1981–82	9,894.9	5.3%
1982–83 (est.)	10,399.5	5.1%

2. <u>Regional Variations in Market Development</u>

Growth of the market continued to be uniform in all regions (Exhibit 1) with the result that two regions (S.E. and S.W.) continue to account for over 60 percent of all sales.

Regions	1000s Cases Fiscal 1981–82	% of Cases	% of Population	Consumer Index U.S. Average = 100
N.E.	791.6	8%	22%	36
S.W.	3,166.3	32	20	160
S.E.	2,968.5	30	18	167
N.C.	1,979.0	20	28	71
PAC.	989.5	10	12	83
U.S. TOTAL	9,894.9	100%	100%	100

3. Shipments

Golden Grain sales for fiscal 1981–82 are currently estimated at 2,632,000 cases. While this represents an increase of 29,000 cases over last year, it is almost 100,000 cases below our 1981–82 objective of 2,730,000 cases. Failure to meet the case objective is attributed primarily to two factors: (a) trade loading during the final quarter of last year which adversely affected first quarter sales; and (b) failure to achieve projected market share of 27.6 (estimated performance, 26.6 percent).

	Quarters				
	1st	2nd	3rd	4th	Total
Est. '81–'82 (1000s cs.)	695.0	663.0	681.0	691.0	2,730.0
Actual (1000s cs.)	645.0	651.5	660.0	675.5	2,632.0
Difference (1000s cs.)	−50.0	−11.5	−21.0	−15.5	−98.0

4. Competitive Shares

a. National. Examination of national share data for fiscal 1981–82 compared to last year reveals three significant points: (1) Golden Grain's market share has decreased over one share point; (2) Chef's Choice exhibited a significant increase in market share; and (3) the long-term share growth of the All Other group appears to have been arrested.

Brand Share—Total U.S.

	1979–80	1980–81	1981–82	1981–82 Percent Point Change
Golden Grain	27.2	27.7	26.6	−1.1
Chef's Choice	35.0	32.5	35.0	+2.5
Martin's	14.3	15.3	14.5	−0.8
All Other	23.5	24.5	24.0	−0.5
Total	100.0%	100.0%	100.0%	

*Based on 8 months Nielsen data.

b. Regional. Golden Grain's national share loss can be traced entirely to the Southeastern region where it experienced a share decline of 4.0 percentage points. This loss is the result of a sharp gain made by Chef's Choice at the expense of all brands.

Regional Share Comparisons for Golden Grain and Chef's Choice

	1981–82		Share Change vs. Previous Year	
Regions	Golden Grain	Chef's Choice	Golden Grain	Chef's Choice
N.E.	21.0%	32.5%	+0.2	—
S.W.	23.4	34.3	+0.5	−0.2
S.E.	30.2	38.1	−4.0	+5.3
N.C.	24.5	35.1	+0.9	+0.1
PAC.	28.7	37.6	+1.0	−0.4
Total	27.6%	35.0%	−1.2	+2.5

(See Exhibit 4 for detailed analysis of regional brand share trends for all brands.)

c. Chain vs. Independent. Golden Grain's market share continues to lag behind Chef's Choice in chain stores to a greater extent than it does in independent outlets. This difference in performance is attributable to two factors: (1) distribution weaknesses in chains compared to Chef's Choice; and (2) lower sales per store stocking than Chef's Choice in chains compared to independents.

	Chain Outlets		Indep. Outlets	
	Golden Grain	Chef's Choice	Golden Grain	Chef's Choice
Brand Share	24.0%	37.1%	29.0%	32.9%

A SAMPLE MARKETING PLAN

	Chain Outlets		Indep. Outlets	
	Golden Grain	Chef's Choice	Golden Grain	Chef's Choice
All Commodity Distribution	75%	85%	76%	78%
Sales Per Month Per Store Stocking	125	175	73	72

5. Distribution

   Regional examination of distribution for Golden Grain and competitive brands indicates: (a) no major changes during the past year; and (b) relatively uniform distribution by region. (See Exhibit 5 for detailed distribution analysis.)

6. Competitive Advertising and Promotion

   a. Expenditures. Both Chef's Choice and Martin's continue to outspend Golden Grain on a per case basis, and Chef's Choice consumer advertising remains the dominant force in the market. Significant competitive developments during the year have included:

      (1) Chef's Choice's return in September to the use of daytime network television and increased advertising and promotion activity in the Southeastern region directed primarily to blacks.

      (2) Martin's shift in media emphasis from national magazines to local spot television concentrated in the top 50 U.S. markets.

      Estimated competitive expenditures are summarized below in comparison to Golden Grain.

Estimated Direct Expenditures			
January-December 1980 ($1000s)			
	Media	Promotion	Total	Est. expenditures per case (retail)
---	---	---	---	---
Golden Grain	$1,520.0	$380.0	$1,900.0	$0.72
Chef's Choice	2,200.0	500.0	2,700.0	0.80
Martin's	1,000.0	400.0	1,400.0	1.04

   b. Copy Evaluation. Three measurements of Golden Grain's 1981–82 advertising were employed during the past year.

      (1) Theater tests of one of a pool of three commercials resulted in a competitive preference score of 14.8. This is significantly higher than our previous theater average (9.7) and the average of all competitive commercials tested (8.2).

      (2) Although portfolio tests of our current magazine campaign indicated that it was on a par with last year's effort, subsequent Starch ratings have shown that it is significantly below the current Chef's Choice campaign in terms of both noted and seen-associated scores.

   c. Promotional Activities. Promotion activity in the market continued to be characterized by periodic advertising allowances and intensive use of unbranded display material.

      The only significant developments were: (1) the appearance of price-packs employed by Martin's nationally during the fall (results not yet available); (2) the use by Chef's Choice of heavily advertised mystery shopper promotions in black areas of the Southeastern region.

7. Product Evaluation and Development

   a. Competitive Product Tests. A blind product test conducted by Golden Grain's Marketing Research Department in October indicated that Chef's Choice has improved its product texture and flavor.

      The present Chef's Choice product has apparently overcome disadvantages that it has had in these areas and is fully competitive with Golden Grain in terms of consumer preference.

   b. Product Research. R&D personnel have reported a temporary setback in their development of an improved product containing vitamin additives. Six-month storage tests of several alternative formulas are now being initiated in an attempt to improve product stability.

      Even if current storage tests are successful, manufacturing considerations will preclude introduction of an improved product before 1984.

8. Special Activities

   a. Product Usage. A special research study undertaken by the Clay Andrews Company reveals that: (1) black per capita consumption of grits is substantially greater than was previously estimated (almost double the consumption of white families); and (2) there has been a sharp increase in multiple unit purchases since the previous study in 1978.

% of Total Transactions	1978 Study	1981 Study
1 can	50%	36%
2 cans	35	32
3 or more cans	15	32
All transactions	100%	100%

% of Total Unit Volume (All Brands)		
1 can	27%	21%
2 cans	45	27
3 or more cans	28	52
Total Units	100%	100%

b. <u>Advertising Research.</u> An advertising penetration study conducted in September to establish a benchmark for advertising awareness revealed the following:

	Percentage of Housewives Using Grits	
Brand	Claimed Aware of Advertising	Recalled One or More Sales Points
Golden Grain	30.4%	15.3%
Chef's Choice	40.3	17.2
Martin's	15.0	3.1

CONCLUSIONS—PROBLEMS AND OPPORTUNITIES

Based on the foregoing marketing review, the brand group has drawn the following conclusions pertinent to 1982–83 advertising:

1. <u>Market Growth.</u> The continued strength of the grits market reaffirms our belief that the company should continue its aggressive advertising and promotion activity in order to achieve the long-range goal of brand leadership.
2. <u>Media Strategy.</u> Our 1981–82 media strategy involving national magazines and spot television in selected markets appears to have been successful in achieving effective message penetration.
3. <u>Advertising Copy.</u> The encouraging performance of our television commercials reaffirms our confidence in our copy strategy. However, the disappointing Starch performance of our print advertising indicates a need to strengthen the execution of the print effort.
4. <u>Black Market.</u> Two factors contribute to the conclusion that special emphasis should be given to the black market: (a) new research data showing high per capita consumption of grits by blacks; and (b) share gains by Chef's Choice in the Southeast region apparently achieved through stepped-up advertising and promotion activity directed to blacks.
5. <u>Chain Outlets.</u> There is a continued need to find effective devices for increasing our distribution and sales per store stocking in chain outlets.
6. <u>Rate of Expenditure.</u> The elimination of Golden Grain's product advantage resulting from Chef's Choice's recent product improvement increases the burden that will have to be borne by advertising and promotion and decreases our confidence that we can continue to make share gains if we continue to be outspent by competition on both a total and cost-per-case basis.
7. <u>Packaging.</u> Research findings that indicate an increase in multiple unit purchases by consumers suggest an opportunity for increasing our market share through the introduction of a multiple-pack or a larger package size.

GENERAL MARKETING OBJECTIVES

Proposed strategies and plans for fiscal 1982–83 are based on the following basic marketing objectives:

1. To attain the following case volume and market share, with a total expenditure of $2,580,000 for advertising and sales promotion:

	Est. Fiscal 1981–82	Actual Fiscal 1982–83	Proposed Change 1982–83 vs. 1981–82
Industry Sales (cases)	9,894,900	10,399,500	+5.1%

| | Est. Actual | Proposed | Change |
	Fiscal 1981–82	Fiscal 1982–83	1982–83 vs. 1981–82
Golden Grain Sales	2,632,000	2,870,000	+9.0%
Golden Grain Market Share	26.6%	27.6%	+1.0 points
Expenditures (adv./pro)	$1,900,000	$2,580,000	+36%
Expenditures per case	$.72	$0.90	+25%
Golden Grain Expenditures as % of Chef's Choice Estimated Expenditures	70%	90%*	

(Note: Sales and share figures may not correspond exactly due to inventory changes and minor errors in Nielsen volume estimates.)

*Assumes Chef's Choice will increase expenditures 5 percent, holding case rate constant and yielding a budget of approximately $2,830,000.

2. To develop and test market both a multiple unit package and a large package size in order to ascertain the relative effectiveness of these two approaches in increasing market share—with the long range objective of adding to the product line during fiscal 1983–84.

GENERAL MARKETING STRATEGY

Recommended activities designed to achieve the foregoing objectives are based on these major points of general marketing strategy:

1. Total planned expenditures for advertising and promotion during fiscal 1982–83 will be increased substantially versus this year in recognition of: (a) the competitive threat posed by Chef's Choice product improvement and dominant advertising weight; and (b) the objective of reversing Golden Grain's recent competitive setback by achieving volume and market share gains during 1982–83.

2. The augmented total marketing budget for 1982–83 will be allocated generally as follows:
   a. Five percent of the total budget (130,000) will be held in unallocated general reserve against the possibility that the volume objective cannot be met. A special recommendation for the disposition of this reserve will be submitted to management before November 1, 1982.
   b. An additional sum, not to exceed 5 percent of the total budget ($130,000), will be set aside to defray the costs of test marketing and researching consumer acceptance of the multiple-unit and larger packages.
   c. The remaining budget will be allocated between advertising and sales promotion in the ratio of approximately 80 percent/20 percent, implying that:
      (1) Primary emphasis will continue to be placed on consumer advertising as a basic selling technique designed to influence brand preference among current users as well as to contribute to further growth in the grits market.
      (2) Secondary emphasis will be given to sales promotion techniques capable of achieving temporary, periodic competitive advantages within the existing market.

3. Consistent with recent practice, total marketing support will be distributed to:
   a. Provide effective minimum sustaining advertising and promotion support in all areas of the country.
   b. Concentrate media weight in the Southeast and Southwest Sales regions, where per capita brand and total industry sales are heavily concentrated. In view of the heavy inroads made by Chef's Choice in the Southeast region, 1982–83 plans will place increased emphasis on this area.
   c. Concentrate promotion support insofar as practical: (1) against chain outlets; and (2) so as to capitalize seasonally on the October-March peak in consumer movement and the established trade pattern of "loading" during September.

4. In recognition of new information bearing on the importance and responsiveness of the black market, increased emphasis will be placed during 1982–83 on special supplementary advertising and promotion activities directed specifically to the black consumer.

5. In view of the apparent success of our current media and copy strategies, these basic strategies will be followed in 1982–83, with the recognition that:
   a. Increased advertising funds will permit both an increase in our broad national effort as well as a concentration of pressure in key markets.
   b. New print copy must be developed and tested to strengthen execution of the current copy strategy.

ADVERTISING OBJECTIVES

1. To direct advertising to housewives as the primary purchase group and place primary emphasis on:
   a. Current users of grits, estimated to be 25 percent of total U.S. households, heavily concentrated in the two Southern regions where breadth of usage reaches 50 percent of all families.
   b. Those socioeconomic groups that include the bulk of heavy users. That is, blacks; families in which the head of the household is under 40 years of age; larger, urban families; and families with average to slightly below average incomes.
2. To increase advertising penetration levels as shown below and as measured by a new penetration study to be conducted approximately January, 1983 (16 months after the previous study).

	Awareness Level	% Recalling One or More Sales Points
From (September, 1981)	30.4%	15.3%
To (January, 1983)	33.0%	16.5%

The objectives which appear above are based solely on judgment, since data is lacking that would provide a reliable basis for forecasting annual rates of change in advertising penetration.

3. To encourage retail grocery trade cooperation—especially within chain outlets—by communicating Golden Grain brand strength to dealer personnel in buying, merchandising, and store management roles.

ADVERTISING STRATEGY

Key strategic considerations governing the use of advertising:
1. Advertising support will be sustained throughout the year, but will:
   a. Be reduced during June-August in recognition of reduced retail sales and media efficiency.
   b. Provide peak support during two periods of major promotional activity (September-October and February-March).
2. Advertising expenditures in support of the two major promotions will not exceed $400,000 (20 percent of total media budget).
3. The basic copy unit for print advertising will be a full-color page. This conclusion reflects both:
   a. Media requirements for continuity and brand reach.
   b. Creative requirements for dominant space and appealing product-use illustrations.
4. Recognizing the need to achieve maximum consumer pressure in view of aggressive competitive activity, advertising production expense will be limited to a maximum of 3 percent of the total advertising budget through the reuse of existing television commercials and the production of not more than four new print ads.

COPY STRATEGY

1. Consumer Copy
   a. Golden Grain will be sold primarily on the basis of its superior creaminess and flavor.
   b. Copy presentation will identify the product with appealing Southern traditions and institutions (Detailed rationale for the foregoing conclusions is provided in Appendix 7).
   c. The mood of the copy will be dignified but friendly, emphasizing the gracious traditions that are associated with Southern living.
   d. Copy will recognize that grits are a staple food that may properly be served at any meal or on any occasion.
2. Trade Copy
   a. Golden Grain will be presented to the trade in terms of its high dollar volume and its superior opportunity for profits.
   b. This representation is possible because of Golden Grain's strong market position, its growing consumer franchise, its relatively high unit profit, and its responsiveness to display.
   c. The copy tone will be responsible, straightforward, and businesslike.
   d. Golden Grain Grits is a food staple which, because of its compatibility with a wide variety of foods, offers ample opportunity for tie-in promotions.

COPY PLAN

1. Television copy. TV copy, executed last year in the form of a pool of three 30-second commercials, is characterized chiefly by the following:
   a. Both creaminess and flavor claims are employed. Emphasis is given to the creaminess claim, which is supported by a video comparison of the particle sizes of Golden Grain (extra fine) and an unidentified "leading brand" (coarse).

A SAMPLE MARKETING PLAN

b. Important use is made of extreme close-up shots of the product in usage situations in association with appetizing Southern specialties such as ham, yams, and black-eyed peas.

c. The introduction and concluding 10-seconds of each commercial employ the grits jingle sung by an off-camera chorus.

d. Product usage situations include family dining occasions characterized by graciousness and family participation.

e. User families are depicted as younger families with children in the 6–12 age group.

f. All package close-ups open with a view of the product itself and pull back to reveal the entire front panel.

2. Consumer print copy. New print copy is currently under development. A revised print copy plan will be submitted on or about February 1, 1982.

3. Trade print copy. Trade print copy represents an extension of the 1981–82 campaign and is characterized by:

a. Pictorial emphasis on the product selling from mass display.

b. Statistics from the Dillon Study demonstrating the profit importance of grits.

c. The use of various headlines that dramatize the sales increases obtained by actual retailers when they displayed Golden Grain Grits.

MEDIA STRATEGY

Recommended media plans were developed within the framework of these basic points of media strategy:

1. National consumer magazines will be employed as the product's basic medium primarily on the basis of: (a) their national coverage; (b) their ability to concentrate messages among younger housewives; and (c) their unique strength as a vehicle for both the dissemination of recipes and the appetizing portrayal of the product itself.

2. Local spot television will be employed on a regional basis as an important supplementary medium designed to: (a) complement the coverage achieved with consumer magazines; and (b) permit the brand to apply increased media weight in sales regions where potential is greatest. Spot television is selected in preference to other local and regional media primarily on the basis of its cost efficiency, broad reach, ability to extend message reach into middle and lower middle income groups, and its strength as a fully dimensional copy vehicle.

3. Black radio will be employed in selected markets to provide selective, supplemental coverage of blacks in recognition that the basic consumer magazine program will not achieve broad reach among this high-potential group.

4. The relative emphasis to be placed on each of the three consumer media will be determined primarily on the following two points of strategy:

a. Total media expenditures per case of Golden Grain retail sales will be approximately the same in each region, except that additional weight will be applied in the Southeast region to counter Chef's Choice's aggressive effort there.

b. Total media expenditures per case will be relatively greater in markets that include substantial concentrations of black population.

5. Significant strategic conclusions regarding the use of each recommended medium include:

a. Consumer Magazines

(1) A minimum of six insertions will be run in each magazine used to insure adequate frequency of impressions and provide continuity of support throughout the year.

(2) Preferred position space (basic unit: one page, four colors) will be used where available at attractive rates to increase readership of each ad.

b. Spot Television

(1) Thirty-second daytime and late evening commercials will be purchased in order to reach housewives with the greatest possible efficiency.

(2) Spot television will be purchased in separate waves of support during the year in order to maintain competitively effective short-term levels of reach and frequency and to concentrate support during the peak months of consumer sales.

MEDIA PLAN

The principal features of the media plan (see budget summary) are:

1. The use of eight consumer magazines. Five of these publications have been employed during the past two years and are considered the primary coverage group (nine insertions each). True Story and Modern Romances have been added to the list this year to extend coverage of "blue-collar" housewives (see Exhibit 8 for analysis of magazine coverage by income and occupational subgroup). Ebony has also been added this year to increase coverage of blacks. The three new publications are scheduled to receive only six insertions each (all insertions are full-page, four color units).

2. The plan also provides for the use of spot television in 30 markets. The proposed market list (Exhibit 9) includes all major markets in the Southeast and Southwest regions. These 30 markets will provide coverage of an estimated 80 percent of all households in the Southeast and Southwest regions.

3. Each spot television market will receive 60 to 100 gross rating points weekly for a total of 26 weeks, which will be divided as follows into four waves of spot activity:

Wave No.	No. Weeks	Weekly GRP	Period
1	6	60	4/1-5/15
2	8	100	9/1-10/30
3	4	60	11/1-12/1
4	8	100	2/1-3/30

It is estimated that the proposed levels of spot television weight will develop reach and frequency as follows during each four-week period of activity:

	60 GRP	100 GRP
Reach (% TV homes covered)	40%	60%
Average Frequency	6.0	6.6

4. The plan also provides for 30 weeks of spot radio activity on 26 black stations in 21 markets (Exhibit 10 provides market list, estimated costs, and a brief rationale for the market selection). These 21 markets together provide coverage of an estimated 64 percent of total U.S. black population.

SALES PROMOTION STRATEGY

Within the broad framework of its role in providing strong, periodic sales stimulus, it is proposed that the specific objectives of Golden Grain's 1982–83 promotion program continue to be to stimulate product trial and repurchase by: (a) gaining trade support in the forms of in-store display and price features by retailers; and (b) communicating appealing new product usage ideas to consumers via both point-of-purchase materials and general consumer advertising integrated with the promotion effort.

Basic strategy for achieving these objectives will provide that:

1. Primary emphasis will continue to be placed on direct trade incentives in the form of merchandising allowances. This recommendation is in keeping with the generally favorable results achieved by similar promotions during the past two years.
2. Departing from recent practice, merchandising allowance support will take the form of contractual payments to retailers for in-store displays complying with substantial, but reasonable minimum quantities of product (that is, $5 payment for a 10-case display; $15 for a 25-case display). The specific purpose of this approach will be to stimulate cooperation on the part of chain and large independent outlets.
3. All major promotions involving merchandising allowances will be designed to capitalize on the special opportunities to tie in with other manufacturers in order to: (a) reduce investment requirements for point-of-purchase materials; (b) extend sales force coverage by utilizing personnel of the cooperating manufacturer; and (c) extend consumer advertising support.
4. Total basic national promotional weight will be concentrated in two tie-in merchandising allowance efforts during the year. These major efforts will be timed to capitalize on the seasonal peak in consumer movement and the established pattern of trade loading during September-October and February-March.
5. In recognition of the special opportunity for promoting the product among blacks in the Southeast region, a supplementary effort will be initiated regionally during the year on a trial basis. Strategy governing this effort will provide for:
   (a) Adoption of the proven "pay day" promotion format based on cash payments to black families who have the product on hand when called upon by a representative of the company.
   (b) The use of aggressive local media advertising to support this promotion. Local spot radio will be devoted entirely to this program during the promotion period.

SALES PROMOTION PLAN

The basic sales promotion plan (see budget summary) provides for:

1. Two major, tie-in promotions, one during September-October, and the other during February-March. (See Exhibit 12 for basis of allowance cost estimates.)
2. A regional (Southeast region) black promotion to be initiated in September (the earliest possible date for the availability of materials) and to continue throughout the fiscal year. (See Exhibit 13 for assumptions and estimated costs.)

SPECIAL ACTIVITIES—NEW PACKAGE TESTING

General marketing objectives and strategy provide that test marketing will be employed during 1982–83 to evaluate two new packaging concepts: (1) a larger size can; and (2) a multican package.

Basic points of strategy affecting the development and testing of these new packages are as follows:

1. The two package concepts will be developed and test marketed independently. Although it may subsequently prove desirable to gain market experience with both new packages in a single area, testing during the 1982–83 period will be con-

ducted independently to: (a) allow each project to progress at its own rate; and (b) limit the number of variables to be evaluated under controlled conditions.

2. Basic strategy provides that each package will be introduced in limited test areas representing 1–3 percent of total U.S. population for a period of at least six months. Further, the program(s) of introductory support for each new package will be developed on the basis of a national effort, which will then be translated to the test areas.

3. The basic technique for evaluating test market results will be the measurement of brand market share by means of retail store panel audits. Field checks and sales reports will be employed as secondary measurements of distribution, pricing, and trade attitude.

4. Study of various alternatives for executing the two packaging concepts leads to these conclusions:
   a. That the large-size can should be 16-ounces because:
      (1) A 16-ounce can will meet the needs of larger families (16 ounces will provide 5 to 7 servings).
      (2) A 16-ounce can could probably be priced to retail in the favorable 43¢ to 45¢ range and permit special promotional pricing of 39¢ with trade cooperation.
   b. The multican package should contain three 8-ounce cans banded together to retail at 59¢ versus an average of 63¢ for three 8-ounce cans purchased separately.

5. It will be a basic point of marketing strategy to limit the investment involved in introducing one or both of the new packages to not more than $70,000 during any one fiscal year and to conduct all special activities in behalf of the new packages on the basis of a one-year theoretical payout. This implies that new funds may be requested if a volume increase can be projected.

6. Basic strategy will also provide that national expansion will be executed in a series of two to four steps covering a period of not more than 18 months and not less than 9 months. A minimum of 9 months is recommended to insure adequate time for appraisal of results in the first expansion area.

7. Label design work for the new packages will proceed on the assumption that it is strategically sound to relate the new labels very closely to the existing label for the 8-ounce can. However, it will be an important objective in the final test plan to use marketing research to make sure that the recommended label designs are free from confusing elements.

Specific objectives and plans and estimated expenditures will be submitted separately (by June 15, 1982) when complete data is available regarding: (a) delivery schedules for the new packages; (b) costs and margins; and (c) consumer acceptance of the new packages in panel placement tests.

GOLDEN GRAIN:
SUMMARY OF PROPOSED ADVERTISING AND SALES PROMOTION
ADVERTISING

1. Consumer Magazines
   6–9 4-color pages in each of 8 magazines; total exposure of 84.5 million. Estimated net unduplicated coverage of 56% of U.S. households: $940,000

9 Pages 4C	6 Pages 4C
LH Journal	Ebony
Good Housekeeping	True Story
Redbook	Modern Romances
Family Circle	(Exhibit 11 provides detail)

2. Spot Television
   60–100 Gross Rating Points weekly for 26 weeks in 30 markets in the SE and SW regions (Exhibit 19).   710,000

3. Spot Radio
   15–20 60-second commercials weekly for 30 weeks on estimated 26 radio stations in 21 markets (Exhibit 10).   173,000

4. Production, Preparation, Use
Magazines:	Prepare 4-color pages	$15,000
TV:	Est. talent fees and misc.	8,000
Radio:	Production and est. talent fees for pool of 6 commercials	4,000
	Total Advertising	$1,850,000

1.	Major tie-in promotion based on 50¢/case display allowance; national magazine support.	200,000
2.	February-March: Repeat fall tie-in promotion.	200,000
3.	"Pay Day" black promotion—SE region	40,000
4.	Promotion materials	30,000
	Total Promotion	470,000

RESERVES

1.	For test marketing two new packages	130,000
2.	General reserves (5% of budget)	130,000
	Total Reserves	260,000
	Grand Total	$2,580,000

CALENDAR OF MARKETING ACTIVITIES

	A	M	J	J	A	S	O	N	D	J	F	M
Consumer Magazines: (Page 4-C Bleed)												
LHJ	X	X	X			X	X	X	X	X		X
GH	X	X	X			X	X	X	X		X	X
Redbook	X	X	X			X	X	X	X		X	X
FC	X	X	X			X	X	X	X		X	X
WD	X	X	X			X	X	X	X		X	X
Ebony	X	X				X		X		X		X
TS	X	X				X		X		X		X
MR	X	X				X		X		X		X
Spot Television GRP Weekly	60	60	-	-	-	100	100	60	-	-	100	100
Spot Radio 15-20 Spots—Wk.	X	X				X	X	X	X	X	X	X
Fall Tie-in Promotion						X	X					
Winter Tie-in Promotion											X	X
Black "Pay Day" Promotion (S.E. region only)						X	X	X	X	X	X	X

Appendix 2
Checklist of Facts on Product Marketing

The following checklist may be helpful in preparing the market review section of the marketing plan. It may also be helpful to creative groups as they seek out information about the products or services for which they are preparing advertising. Its purpose is to provide a relatively exhaustive list of questions that help identify the truly significant facts of the marketing situation.

The list contains questions that are not pertinent to *all* products. For example, questions on styles or models are not relevant to a food product. Nor are all of the questions relevant to the normal marketing plan. For example, questions on profitability, cost of goods, and so on may not be pertinent in a particular case. Nonetheless, these are relevant questions that must be dealt with at some point in the planning process. In addition, the list tends to overemphasize the importance of historical data as opposed to data that illuminates the current situation.

Basically, this list is intended to serve as a reminder of the wide range of factors that need to be considered in developing a successful marketing effort. As such, the list provides an example of the art of asking questions.[1]

---

[1]Reprinted with permission from the May 10, 1957 issue of *Advertising Age.* Copyright © 1957 by Crain Communications, Inc.

SECTION 1—The Size, Scope, and Share of Market

A. Sales History
   1. What is the sales history of all manufacturers of this product in dollars?
   2. In units?
   3. In percentage share of the market in dollars?
   4. In units?
   5. Same data on consumer purchases?
   6. How do geographical differences affect the share of the market held by various manufacturers?
   7. City size differences?
   8. Price differences?
   9. Seasonal differences?
   10. Racial differences?

B. Market Potential
   11. What is the trend in the sales history of the total market per 1000 population?
   12. What is the trend of the total market, as a percentage of the Gross National Product?
   13. What is the trend in use by consumers of related products?
   14. What is the trend in use by consumers of products which produce a need for this product?
   15. What is the trend in use by consumers of products which eliminate the need for this product?
   16. What statements have been made by responsible men in this field about the future potential for this product?
   17. What is the manufacturing potential of all principal manufacturers?
   18. What new manufacturers are expected to enter this field?
   19. How do geographical differences affect the market for this product?
   20. Seasonal differences?

C. Pricing History
   21. What is the pricing history of the most popular unit of sale charged by major manufacturers to their distribution channels?
   22. Charged by the distribution channels to the consumer?
   23. Same data on other units, manufacturers to distribution channels?

24. Distribution channels to consumers?
25. What are the reasons for the principal fluctuations in pricing?

SECTION II—Sales, Costs, and Gross Profits on Our Product

A. Sales
26. What is the sales history of our product in manufacturers' dollars by different sizes or models?
27. In units?
28. What is the history of introduction of the product and the sequence of marketing steps which led to its present distribution?
29. What is our sales history, in dollars by sales districts?
30. In units?
31. What is our sales history by sales districts, in units per 1000 population?

B. Cost History
32. What is the cost history of our product in total cost of goods delivered?
33. In selling expense?
34. In advertising expense?
35. In administrative expense?
36. In all other expense?

C. Gross Profit
37. What is the cost history of our product in total cost of goods delivered?
38. In selling expense?
39. In percentage of net sales?
40. What is known about the profits of other manufacturers in this field?

SECTION III—The Distribution Channels

A. Identification of Principal Channels
41. What is the sales history in dollars handled by each type of distribution channel for our product?
42. In units?
43. In dollars, for our competitors?
44. In units, for our competitors?
45. What distribution do we have in each type of outlet, by districts?

B. Buying Habits and Attitudes of Principal Channels
46. What is the attitude of the principal distribution channels toward these aspects of our product versus competitors?
47. Price?
48. Availability?
49. Credit?
50. Purchase deals?
51. Assortments?
52. Styling?

53. Packaging?
54. Turnover?
55. What are the purchase habits of our principal channels in terms of the time they buy our product?
56. The quantity?
57. The assortment?
58. What shelf frontage is given our product versus our competitors?
59. What are the inventories of our product currently held by each of our principal channels?
60. What is the out-of-stock situation in each channel?
61. What information is available on net profits enjoyed by each of our principal channels of distribution?
62. What variations exist in the volume handled by different channels because of geographical differences?
63. Population differences?
64. Differences of sizes or models?

C. Our Selling Policies and Practices
65. How do our sales practices differ from competitors on these points?
66. Percent of accounts covered?
67. Frequency of call?
68. Length of call?
69. Quality and training of [people]?
70. Method of selling?
71. How do our sales policies differ from our competitors on these points: Damaged goods?
72. Display allowances?
73. Advertising allowances?
74. PM's (Push money or promotion money)?
75. Fair trade?
76. Free samples?
77. Discounts to employees?
78. Retail clerk training?
79. What do the [people] in distribution channels like most about our sales policies and practices?
80. Dislike most?
81. Like most about our competitors?
82. Dislike most?

D. Pressure Promotions
83. What is the history of pressure promotions we have used with the distribution channels?
84. Which type of promotions have been most effective?
85. Which least effective?
86. What pressure promotions have our competitors used with the distribution channels?
87. How effective have their pressure promotions been?
88. What do the people in the distribution channel like or dislike about our pressure promotions?

89. About our competitors' pressure promotions?
90. Which type of distribution channel has been the most cooperative on pressure promotions?
91. Which the least?

E. Trade Advertising, Literature, and Exhibits
92. How does our strategy on trade advertising differ from our principal competitors'?
93. What have been the objectives of our trade advertising?
94. What evidence is available to show whether these objectives have been met?
95. What is the history of our trade advertising in dollars spent?
96. In media selection?
97. In copy theme?
98. In size of space?
99. In frequency?
100. As a percent of net sales?
101. What types of sales literature have we furnished the distribution channels?
102. What are the objectives of this literature?
103. What evidence is available that these objectives have been met?
104. Which types have been most effective?
105. Which least effective?
106. How does our strategy on sales literature differ from our competitors'?
107. What do the [people] in the distribution channels like and dislike about our sales literature?
108. Our competitors'?
109. What is the history of our trade exhibit and convention participation?
110. How does our strategy on participation in trade exhibits and conventions differ from our competitors'?
111. How effective has this strategy been?
112. What do the people in the distribution channels like and dislike about our participation in trade exhibits and conventions?

F. Point-of-Sale Display
113. What types of point-of-sale displays have we used in the last five years?
114. Which type was most effective?
115. Which least effective?
116. Which type is preferred by people in the distribution channels, and why?
117. Which of our competitors' point-of-sale displays have been effective?

SECTION IV—The Consumer or End User

A. Identification of Person Making Buying Decision
118. Who makes the buying decision of our product—classified by age?
119. Sex?
120. Income level?

121. Education?
122. Geographical locations?
123. Urban versus rural?
124. Race?
125. Religion?
126. Occupation?
127. Marital status?
128. Size of family?
129. Home ownership?
130. Car ownership?
131. TV ownership?

B. Consumer Attitudes
132. What is consumer attitude on our product versus our competitors' on these points: Quality?
133. Maintenance?
134. Price?
135. Availability?
136. Selection?
137. Styling?
138. Packaging?
139. Guarantee?
140. Ease of use?
141. Benefits of use?
142. Length of useful life?
143. What personality does our product have in the consumer's mind?
144. How many potential consumers are there for our product?
145. To what extent are potential consumers informed of our product?
146. How many potential consumers have tried our product?
147. How many have stopped using our product?
148. Why?
149. Same data on competitors' products?
150. How many have switched from our brand to a competitor's?
151. From a competitor's to our brand?
152. How many consumers now use our product?
153. What influenced them to try it?
154. What do they like most about it?
155. What least?
156. Same data on competitors?
157. How does folklore, tradition, social ritual and prejudice affect consumers' attitudes toward our product?

C. Consumer Purchase Habits
158. What are consumers' purchasing habits for our product, by season?
159. By months?
160. By weeks of the year?
161. By day of week?
162. By price level?
163. By type of outlet?
164. By frequency of purchase?
165. By method of purchase (case or credit)?

166. By full price versus discount?
167. By sizes or models?

D. Consumer Use Habits
168. What are the major uses for our product, in order of popularity?
169. Under what conditions is our product used?
170. How frequently?
171. By whom in the family?
172. Where is it kept?
173. What is average rate of consumption of a standard unit of our product?
174. What consumer differences affect this rate of consumption?
175. What personal characteristics identify our largest consumer?
176. How is our product misused?
177. What is the extent of misuse of the product?
178. What new uses does our product have other than those we promote?
179. To what extent are these other uses practiced?
180. How does the consumer judge when the useful life of our product has ended?

E. Our Advertising History
181. What is the history of our advertising expenditures in dollars?
182. Per unit?
183. As a percent of sales?
184. Per 1000 population?
185. By geographic region in relation to sales?
186. By sales districts in relation to sales?
187. By city size in relation to sales?
188. By media?
189. By seasons?
190. By months?
191. What is the history of competitive advertising expenditures in total dollars?
192. As a percent of estimated sales?
193. By geographic region?
194. By media?
195. How does competitive advertising differ from ours in timing?
196. In size of space?
197. In frequency?
198. What is the most important single impression to deliver with our advertising?
199. Second most important impression?
200. Third?
201. Fourth?
202. What is the copy strategy used on our product for the past five years?
203. What are the reasons for major changes?
204. What basic copy themes have been used on our product?
205. Why were they changed?
206. What copy strategy has been used by our competitors?

207. What research results are available on the effectiveness of our copy: Starch?
208. Nielsen?
209. Surveys?
210. Market tests?
211. Hidden offer tests?
212. Gallup-Robinson?
213. Other tests?
214. What media strategy have we used for the last five years and why?
215. What major changes have been made in media strategy and why?
216. What measurements are available on the effectiveness of the media we have used?
217. How has our budget percentage in each of the following media compared with our competitors: Newpapers?
218. Newpaper supplements?
219. Magazines?
220. Television?
221. Radio?
222. Business papers?
223. Outdoor?
224. Car cards?
225. Other media?
226. What trends are evident in media which might affect our advertising?
227. What has been the media strategy of our competitors for the last five years?

F. Publicity and Other Educational Influences
228. What devices have been used to influence consumers other than advertising and point-of-sale material: Publicity?
229. Donation of prizes?
230. Educational films?
231. Stockholder mailings?
232. Sampling?
233. House-to-house?
234. Leaflet throw-aways?
235. Dealer envelope stuffers?
236. Consumer parties?
237. What has been our strategy in the use of these devices over the last five years?
238. What are the reasons for changes, if any, in this strategy?
239. How has our strategy with these devices differed from our competitors?
240. What evidence is available on the effectiveness of these devices?

SECTION V—The Product

A. Story of the Product
241. When was the product developed?
242. By whom?
243. Why?
244. How was it developed?

CHECKLIST OF FACTS ON PRODUCT MARKETING

245. What improvements have been made in the product since it was introduced?
246. When was it introduced?
247. When were different sizes and models introduced?
248. Why?
249. Same data on competitive products?
250. How long has the current label been in use?
251. What are the reasons for the various elements on the label?
252. How long has the current package been in use?
253. What are the reasons for the various elements of package?

B. Comparison with Competition
254. What are the principal differences between our product and competitors?
255. What evidence is available on the quality and performance of our product versus competitors' from: Production Department?
256. Research Department?
257. Engineering?
258. Designers?
259. Quality control laboratory?
260. Independent testing organizations?

261. Consumer research groups?
262. Consumer surveys?
263. What is the product's outstanding advantage over competitive products?
264. What information is available on competitive plans to overcome this advantage?
265. What are the product's shortcomings in relation to competition?
266. What plans are being made to overcome them?

C. Product Research
267. What research is being conducted on our product to improve its quality?
268. Improve design?
269. Lower its price?
270. Make it easier to use?
271. Lengthen its useful life?
272. Make the label more attractive?
273. More useful?
274. Make the package more attractive?
275. More convenient?
276. Reusable?
277. Improve servicing of the product?
278. What information is available on areas of product research being explored by competitors?

Appendix 3
Media Cost and Coverage Data

The material in this appendix has been provided by the Leo Burnett U.S.A. advertising agency. It serves as a "quick source of basic audience and rate data, useful as a broad guide in the early stages of media planning. It is not intended as a device for making intermedia comparisons nor as a strict reference for estimating and budget preparation. In the latter case, rates and audience data must refer to the specific media units purchased and the rate and discount structure in effect at the time."[1]

[1]*Media Costs and Coverage 1983* (Chicago: Leo Burnett U.S.A.). Reprinted with permission from Leo Burnett U.S.A.

Basic Statistics

Population Estimates

Persons in TV Households - 1982/83 (Millions)

	House-holds	Women 18+	Women 18-49	Men 18+	Men 18-49	Teens 12-17	Children 2-11
Total	83.3	86.4	54.1	77.8	52.2	21.7	32.3
County Size							
A	34.6	35.9	22.9	32.3	21.9	8.7	12.6
B	24.9	25.9	16.4	23.0	15.8	6.5	9.8
C & D	23.8	24.6	14.8	22.5	14.5	6.5	9.9
Household Size							
1	18.8	11.5	3.1	7.2	4.6	0.2	0.0
2	26.5	26.8	11.3	24.4	10.3	0.8	1.0
3+	38.0	48.1	39.7	46.2	37.3	20.7	31.3
4+	23.3	30.9	27.0	30.2	25.9	17.4	26.1
Household Income							
Under $10M	18.9	17.3	7.3	10.0	5.1	3.0	5.8
$10M–$20M	21.1	20.7	12.2	17.6	10.9	4.4	8.0
$20M+	43.3	48.4	34.6	50.2	36.2	14.3	18.5
$30M+	25.4	29.9	21.5	31.8	22.8	9.3	10.2

Total Population - 1982 (Thousands)

Total U.S. Population	232,600
Total Males	113,276
Men 18+	79,597
Total Females	119,324
Women 18+	87,049
Total Households	84,966

Sources: A.C. Nielsen, TV Household Estimates as of January 1, 1983; U.S. Bureau of the Census, Population Estimates and Projections.

Advertising Expenditures—Total

National vs. Local (1960, 1970-1983)

	Total (Billions)	National (Billions)	Local (Billions)
1960	$11.9	$ 7.3	$ 4.6
1970	19.7	11.5	8.2
1971	20.8	11.9	8.9
1972	23.1	12.9	10.2
1973	25.1	13.8	11.3
1974	26.7	14.7	12.0
1975	28.3	15.4	12.9
1976	33.7	18.6	15.1
1977	38.1	21.0	17.1
1978	44.0	24.0	20.0
1979	49.5	27.1	22.4
1980	54.7	30.4	24.3
1981	63.1	34.4	28.7
1982	68.4	38.7	29.7
1983 (est.)	73.5	42.3	31.2

Sources: Television Factbook, 1981; Advertising Age, June 21, 1982 and December 1982 for 1982; Leo Burnett estimate for 1983.

Advertising Expenditures by Medium

	1982		
	Total (Millions)	National (Millions)	Local (Millions)
Cable TV	$ 254	$ 219	$ 35
Network TV	6,275	6,275	—
Spot TV	7,635	4,290	3,345
Radio	4,281	1,185	3,096
Magazines	3,745	3,745	—
Newspapers	17,666	2,975	14,691
Direct Mail	10,576	10,345	231
Other Media	17,997	9,670	8,327
Total	$68,429	$38,704	$29,725

Source: Advertising Age, December 1982.

Advertising Expenditures—Major Media(†)

Total U.S. vs. Top 100 Advertisers (1960, 1970-1983)

	Total (Billions)	Top 100 (Billions)	Top 100 % of Total
1960	$ 7.8	$ 1.7	22%
1970	13.0	3.4	26
1971	13.7	3.5	26
1972	15.2	3.7	24
1973	16.4	3.9	24
1974	17.5	4.2	24
1975	18.5	4.3	23
1976	22.3	5.4	24
1977	25.3	6.1	24
1978	29.3	7.0	24
1979	33.1	8.0	24
1980	36.3	8.4	23
1981	40.3	9.4	23
1982	44.5	10.2	23
1983 (est.)	48.6	11.1	23

(†)Direct mail and miscellaneous categories are excluded.

Sources: Total - Television Factbook, 1979; Advertising Age, January 5, 1981 for 1979 and 1980. Top 100 - Advertising Age, annual top 100 issues for 1981-1982; Leo Burnett estimate for 1983.

Top 100 Advertisers
(Expenditures in Six Major Media - 1981)

	Dollars (Millions)	% of Total	% Change '81 Vs. '80
Magazines	1581.5	19.1%	+4%
Newspaper Supplements	138.8	1.7	−6
Network Television	4311.3	52.0	−8
Spot Television	1878.2	22.7	−3
Network Radio	135.7	1.6	+7
Outdoor	241.4	2.9	+4
Total	8286.9	100%	+1%

Source: Leading National Advertisers, January-December 1981.

Media Cost Trends

Network Television - 1972 to 1982

	Avg. Cost/Commercial (:30)		CPM Homes	
	$000	Index	$	Index
Prime Time				
1972	30.5	100	2.32	100
1973	34.5	113	2.72	117
1974	39.0	128	2.93	126
1975	37.8	124	2.88	124
1976	49.4	162	3.49	150
1977	58.0	190	4.13	178
1978	62.6	205	4.41	190
1979	76.6	251	5.06	218
1980	74.3	244	4.94	213
1981	78.8	258	5.23	225
1982	84.9	278	5.65	244

	Avg. Cost/Commercial (:30)		CPM Homes	
	$000	Index	$	Index
Daytime				
1972	4.5	100	0.89	100
1973	4.6	102	0.93	104
1974	5.3	118	1.04	117
1975	6.2	138	1.35	152
1976	7.4	164	1.49	167
1977	9.0	200	1.96	220
1978	9.3	207	1.96	220
1979	10.7	238	2.14	240
1980	10.8	240	2.22	249
1981	11.4	253	2.35	264
1982	12.0	267	2.47	278

Source: A.C. Nielsen, NAC Cost Supplement, October 1982.

Spot Television - 1972 to 1982
Top 20 Markets

	Avg. Cost/Commercial (:30)		CPM Homes	
	$	Index	$	Index
Prime Time				
1972	$14,198	100	$3.32	100
1973	14,650	103	3.46	104
1974	17,078	120	3.50	105
1975	17,825	126	3.84	116
1976	22,516	159	4.86	146
1977	27,180	191	5.90	178
1978	30,330	214	6.42	193
1979	32,063	226	6.88	207
1980	37,371	263	7.35	221
1981	41,226	290	8.15	245
1982	41,568	293	8.69	262
Daytime				
1972	$ 1,861	100	$1.34	100
1973	1,701	91	1.24	93
1974	1,744	94	1.18	88
1975	1,647	86	1.36	101
1976	2,248	121	1.60	119
1977	3,024	162	2.17	162
1978	3,035	163	2.05	153
1979	3,344	180	2.12	158
1980	3,637	195	2.21	165
1981	4,159	223	2.63	196
1982	4,293	231	2.86	213

Source: TVB Spot Television Planning Guide, 1982/83.

Network Radio - 1972 to 1982

	Cost Per Adult Rating Point		CPM Adults	
	$	Index	$	Index
1972	1,538	100	1.10	100
1973	1,564	102	1.10	100
1974	1,576	102	1.09	99
1975	1,671	109	1.14	104
1976	2,105	137	1.39	126
1977	2,358	153	1.55	141
1978	2,558	166	1.64	149
1979	2,904	189	1.84	167
1980	3,186	207	2.00	182
1981	3,473	226	2.24	204
1982	3,820	248	2.46	224

Source: Media Decisions, August 1982.

Spot Radio - 1975 to 1982
Top 50 Markets

	Avg. Cost/Commercial (:60)		CPM Adults	
	$	Index	$	Index
Daytime				
1975	$2,448	100	$1.52	100
1976	2,652	108	1.68	110
1977	3,078	126	1.86	122
1978	3,460	141	2.20	145
1979	3,984	163	2.57	191
1980	4,100	167	2.90	191
1981	4,305	176	3.04	200
1982	4,736	193	3.28	216

Spot Radio - 1975 to 1982 (continued)

	Avg. Cost/Commercial (:60)		CPM Adults	
	$	Index	$	Index
Drive Time -Morning				
1975	$3,267	100	$1.51	100
1976	3,520	108	1.64	109
1977	4,039	124	1.87	124
1978	4,435	136	2.10	130
1979	5,071	155	2.43	161
1980	5,848	179	2.78	184
1981	6,140	189	2.91	193
1982	7,452	212	3.14	208

Sources: Katz Spot Radio Planning Guide for 1975 through 1981; Media Decisions for 1982.

Consumer Magazines - 1972 to 1982
Ten Selected Magazines

	Cost/Page 4 C		CPM-Circulation	
	$000	Index	$	Index
1972	$388.9	100	$4.43	100
1973	404.6	104	4.48	101
1974	425.6	109	4.75	107
1975	443.1	114	4.94	112
1976	452.2	116	4.91	111
1977	478.9	123	5.24	118
1978	539.9	139	5.90	133
1979	576.8	148	6.33	143
1980	625.4	161	6.97	157
1981	666.6	171	7.69	174
1982	719.9	185	8.31	188

Source: S.R.D.S., June of each year.

Daily Newspapers - 1972 to 1982

	Line Rate		Line Cost/MM Circ.	
	$	Index	$	Index
1972	$419.57	100	$ 6.71	100
1973	446.66	106	7.07	105
1974	508.08	121	8.21	122
1975	561.78	134	9.26	138
1976	620.30	148	10.17	152
1977	655.42	156	10.66	159
1978	714.29	170	11.61	173
1979	743.66	177	12.00	179
1980	802.00	191	12.89	192
1981	899.71	214	14.46	215
1982	990.00	236	15.76	235

Sources: Editor and Publisher Yearbook; Leo Burnett estimate for 1982.

Syndicated Supplements* - 1972 to 1982

	Cost/Page 4 C		CPM-Circulation	
	$	Index	$	Index
1972	$109,900	100	$4.12	100
1973	117,845	107	4.21	102
1974	136,600	124	4.68	114
1975	161,505	147	5.46	133
1976	161,295	147	5.45	132
1977	173,480	158	5.64	137
1978	194,870	177	6.05	147
1979	215,500	196	6.45	157
1980	235,095	214	6.98	169
1981	266,480	242	7.81	190
1982	321,100	292	9.28	225

* *Parade* and *Family Weekly* only.

Source: S.R.D.S., June of each year.

Outdoor - 1972 to 1982

	Cost/Month*		CPM
	$000	Index	Index
1972.	$2,070.8	100	100
1973.	2,215.9	107	105
1974.	2,357.9	114	105
1975.	2,602.1	126	114
1976.	2,943.4	142	118
1977.	2,964.9	143	125
1978.	3,273.1	158	139
1979.	3,608.9	174	148
1980.	3,969.8	192	162
1981.	4,354.9	210	178
1982.	4,877.5	235	199

*100 GRPs in all markets.

Source: Institute of Outdoor Advertising.

Number of Media Outlets—1982
Television

	Total	Commercial	Noncommercial
Stations (1) - Total	1,068	801	267
VHF	629	525	104
UHF	439	276	163

TV Homes (2) -	83,300,000
Color	89%
Multi-set	55%
Cable TV	32%

Radio

Stations (3) - Total	9,159
Commercial AM	4,668
Commercial FM	3,379
Noncommercial FM	1,112
Radio Homes (3)	84,300,000
Radio Sets (3) - Total	470,000,000
Home/Personal	347,000,000
Auto.	123,000,000

Newspapers (4)

	Number of Papers	Avg./Day Circulation (000)
Daily - Total	1,507	59,611
Morning	227	14,409
Evening..............	1,101	18,825
Morning & Evening	179	26,377
Sunday...........................	717	54,752

Magazines

Consumer/Farm (5)	1,558
Business (6)........................	2,675

Sources: (1) Broadcasting, January 3, 1983; (2) A.C. Nielsen; (3) R.A.B., Radio Facts, 1983; (4) S.R.D.S., Newspaper Circulation Analysis, 1982-83; (5) Magazine Publishers Association; (6) American Business Press.

Electronic Media

Network Television—1982–83 (†)

Prime Time
I. Unit Costs and Efficiencies

	Avg. 30-Second Commercial		
	Unit Cost	CPM Homes	Women 25-54	Men 25-54
Fall 1982	$81,950-104,300	$5.50-7.00	$13.00-15.50	$17.00-18.00
Winter 1983 ...	66,150- 88,200	4.50-6.00	11.00-13.50	12.80-14.50
Spring 1983....	76,050- 81,900	6.50-7.00	16.00-17.50	17.90-18.50
Summer 1983 ..	54,000- 70,200	5.00-6.50	13.50-16.00	15.70-16.25

II. Audience Delivery

		Delivery (MM)		
	HH Rtg.	Homes	Women	Men
Fall 1982	17.9	14.9	15.5	13.9
Winter 1983	17.7	14.7	15.2	13.8
Spring 1983.......................	14.1	11.7	12.1	11.0
Summer 1983	12.0	10.8	10.4	9.3

III. Audience Composition

	Men V/HVH*	Women V/HVH	Teens V/HVH	Children V/HVH	Total V/HVH
Regular Programs 7-11 p.m. ...	61	80	15	22	178
Feature Films	66	80	16	19	181
Situation Comedy.............	56	78	18	31	183
Suspense & Mystery Drama....	64	80	15	17	176
General Drama	53	86	12	18	169

*Viewers per 100 viewing households (HVH)

Daytime (M-F)
I. Unit Costs and Efficiencies

	Avg. 30-Second Commercial		
	Unit Cost	CPM Homes	CPM Women 25-54
Fall 1982	$11,600-15,950	$2.00-2.75	$5.50-6.40
Winter 1983................	10,980-13,730	1.80-2.25	4.50-5.50
Spring 1983	9,400-13,160	2.00-2.80	5.25-7.00
Summer 1983	7,950-14,840	1.50-2.80	4.50-6.75

II. Audience Delivery

		Delivery (MM)		
	HH Rtg.	Homes	Women	Men
Fall 1982	7.0	5.8	6.0	5.4
Winter 1983	7.3	6.1	6.3	5.7
Spring 1983......................	5.6	4.7	4.8	4.4
Summer 1983	6.4	5.3	5.5	5.0

III. Audience Composition

	Men V/HVH*	Women V/HVH	Teens V/HVH	Children V/HVH	Total V/HVH
M-F 10 a.m.-4:30 p.m.	25	85	12	14	136
Daytime Drama	23	90	11	10	134
Quiz & Aud. Participation......	30	79	11	17	137

*Viewers per 100 viewing households (HVH)

Early Evening News (M-F)
I.   Unit Costs and Efficiencies

	Avg. 30-Second Commercial		
	Unit Cost	CPM Homes	CPM Women 25+
Fall 1982	$36,400-39,200	$3.25-3.50	$11.75-12.50
Winter 1983...............	28,500-31,920	2.50-2.80	8.50- 9.25
Spring 1983	31,500-38,250	3.50-4.25	12.75-13.75
Summer 1983	24,900-35,280	3.00-4.25	11.75-12.50

II.   Audience Delivery

		Delivery (MM)		
	HH Rtg.	Homes	Women	Men
Fall 1982	13.4	11.2	11.6	10.4
Winter 1983	13.7	11.4	11.8	10.7
Spring 1983	10.8	9.0	9.3	8.4
Summer 1983	10.0	8.3	8.6	7.8

III. Audience Composition

	Men	Women	Teens	Children	Total
V/HVH.....................	61	76	6	9	152

Late Evening (M-F, 11:30 p.m. - 1:00 a.m.)
I.   Unit Costs and Efficiencies

	Avg. 30-Second Commercial		
	Unit Cost	CPM Homes	CPM Women 25-54
Fall 1982	$15,540-18,480	$3.70-4.40	$10.60-12.25
Winter 1983................	11,500-14,720	2.50-3.20	7.00- 8.00
Spring 1983	15,910-19,350	3.70-4.50	11.50-13.00
Summer 1983	12,710-18,860	3.10-4.60	11.25-12.50

II. Audience Delivery

		Delivery (MM)		
	HH Rtg.	Homes	Women	Men
Fall 1982	5.0	4.2	4.3	3.9
Winter 1983	5.5	4.6	4.7	4.3
Spring 1983.......................	5.2	4.3	4.5	4.0
Summer 1983	4.9	4.1	4.2	3.8

III. Audience Composition

	Men	Women	Teens	Children	Total
V/HVH.....................	53	65	11	2	131

Children's Shows (Saturday)
I.   Unit Costs and Efficiencies

	Avg. 30-Second Commercial		
	Unit Cost	CPM Homes	CPM Children 2-11
Fall 1982	$17,850-20,210	$4.15-4.70	$4.90-5.30
Winter 1983................	7,990- 8,930	1.70-1.90	2.00-2.20
Spring 1983	9,990-14,060	2.70-3.80	4.00-4.75
Summer 1983	9,450-11,500	2.70-3.00	3.35-4.25

II. Audience Delivery

		Delivery (MM)		
	HH Rtg.	Homes	Children 2-11	Children 6-11
Fall 1982	5.2	4.3	1.7	.9
Winter 1983	5.6	4.7	1.8	1.1
Spring 1983......................	4.4	3.7	1.4	.8
Summer 1983	4.3	3.5	1.4	.8

III. Audience Composition

	Men	Women	Teens	Children	Total
V/HVH	25	31	20	87	163

Specials (Prime Time, 1982)
I. Audience and Efficiencies

	Entertainment	Informational
Average Household Rating.............................	10.0-26.0	8.0-14.0
Households Reached (000).............................	8,330-21,658	6,664-11,662

Note: The household cost per thousand is usually 10% to 25% higher than the cost per thousand homes for long term prime time units for a given quarter.

II. Audience Composition

	Men	Women	Teens	Children	Total
Entertainment - V/HVH	67	79	15	18	179
Informational - V/HVH	66	78	12	14	170

Source: A.C. Nielsen, Network Television Specials, '80-81.

Sports
I. Audience and Efficiencies

	$20M+ Homes Index To U.S. Avg.	All Households Avg. Rating	All Households AA Rtg. Range	CPM Homes Per :30 1982/83
Football (1982)				
NFL Regular Season				
ABC Monday Night	131	22	20-24	$6.50-7.50
CBS - Sunday	128	18	13-22	$5.75-6.50
NBC - Sunday	125	13	10-18	$5.75-6.50
Playoffs	125	28	24-35	$4.75-5.50
Super Bowl	120	49	—	$8.25-8.50
College - Regular Season	121	12	10-15	$5.60-6.00
Bowl Games (Major)	122	16	9-24	$5.50-6.25
Golf (1983)				
Tournaments...........................	122	5	2- 7	$5.50-6.50
Baseball (1983)				
Regular Season - Evening	107	10	8-13	$5.75-6.50
Regular Season - Sat. Afternoon.........	114	6	5- 9	$4.50-5.50
Playoffs...............................	107	14	11-18	$4.40-4.70
World Series...........................	120	30	28-35	$6.50-7.00
Basketball (1983)				
NBA - Regular Season Weekend	125	6	5- 7	$3.50-4.50
Playoffs	132	9	7-11	$5.50-6.00
Championships	126	9	7-12	$6.25-6.75
NCAA - Regular Season................	132	7	5- 9	$4.00-5.00
Championships..................	136	20	18-22	$6.00-7.00
Bowling (1983)				
Pro Bowlers Tournament................	103	9	8-10	$3.00-3.50
Tennis (1983)				
Tournaments...........................	125	5	2- 7	$6.00-6.50
Multi-sport Series (1982/83)	108	8	3-11	$4.00-6.00

II. Audience Composition

	Viewers Per 100 Viewing Households					
	Total Men	Men 18-34	Men 18-49	Total Women	Total Non-Adults	Total Viewers
All Sports	83	31	50	52	25	159
Football						
ABC Monday Evening	92	39	62	44	23	156
CBS Sunday..................	95	38	63	51	26	172
NBC Sunday..................	92	32	57	48	28	168
College......................	79	26	43	40	21	140
Golf						
Tournaments..................	74	19	32	58	16	148
Baseball						
Reg. Season - Evening	92	34	52	52	35	179
Reg. Season - Sat. Afternoon.....	72	23	36	40	20	132
World Series..................	83	28	50	66	21	170
Basketball						
NBA*........................	87	42	62	43	24	154
College......................	82	31	48	44	32	158
Bowling						
Pro Bowlers Tournament	70	23	38	64	25	159

	Viewers Per 100 Viewing Households					
	Total Men	Men 18-34	Men 18-49	Total Women	Total Non-Adults	Total Viewers
Tennis						
Tournaments.................	63	21	39	59	21	142
Multi-sports Series	76	27	46	55	27	157

*Regular season games only.

Network TV Reach and Frequency
(4-Week Period—Households)

Averages for schedule in which the number of commercials is about twice the number of different programs. Evening estimates are for one or two network schedules; daytime estimates assume more than one network and show type.

	Evening		M-F Day	
GRP Levels	Reach	Frequency	Reach	Frequency
100..........	62	1.6	45	2.2
150..........	74	2.0	55	2.7
200..........	81	2.5	61	3.3
250..........	85	2.9	66	3.8
300..........	88	3.4	69	4.3

Source: Leo Burnett U.S.A., Reach and Frequency.

Spot Television

Costs Cumed by Top Market Groups

Markets	% U.S. TV HH	Prime Time Cost/Rtg. Point	Daytime Cost/Rtg. Point	Early Fringe Cost/Rtg. Point	Late News Cost/Rtg. Point	Late Fringe Cost/Rtg. Point
Top 10	31	$2,212	$ 676	$ 840	$1,711	$1,170
Top 20	44	3,243	1,003	1,322	2,533	1,763
Top 30	53	3,848	1,219	1,602	3,017	2,129
Top 40	61	4,329	1,372	1,826	3,318	2,360
Top 50	67	4,681	1,512	1,988	3,570	2,554
Top 60	72	4,978	1,602	2,112	3,790	2,734
Top 70	76	5,243	1,694	2,217	3,988	2,906
Top 80	80	5,458	1,766	2,309	4,152	3,049
Top 90	83	5,667	1,828	2,391	4,294	3,159
Top 100	86	5,853	1,894	2,465	4,422	3,267

Source: Media Market Guide, Fall 1982.

Television Viewing

Hours of TV Usage Per Week

	7-Day 24-Hr. Total	Mon.-Sun. 8:00- 11:00 p.m.	Mon.-Sun. 11:30 p.m.- 1:00 a.m.	Mon.-Fri. 10:00 a.m.- 4:30 p.m.	Mon.-Fri. 4:30- 7:30 p.m.
All Households........	49.12	13.10	2.79	8.48	7.35
Households $20M+ ...	48.86	13.57	2.98	7.41	7.16
Households $30M+ ...	47.84	13.38	3.07	7.02	7.05
Total Men	27.54	9.11	1.86	2.44	3.93
Men 18-49	25.28	8.42	1.95	2.11	3.27
Men $20M+ HH.....	25.07	8.61	1.81	1.82	3.42
Total Women..........	32.03	9.81	1.75	6.01	4.74
Women 18-49	28.84	8.97	1.75	5.36	3.92
Women $20M+ HH ..	27.55	9.16	1.62	4.36	3.42
Women Employed.....	27.04	9.45	1.73	3.12	3.78
Women with Children .	26.74	9.14	1.73	6.21	3.35
Teens 12-17..........	22.48	7.69	.72	2.02	4.31
Children 2-11	24.63	5.63	.20	3.61	5.18

Source: A.C. Nielsen, National Audience Demographics Report, November 1982.

Households Using Television
(% of U.S. TV Homes)

Monday-Friday	Jan.-Mar. 1982	Apr.-June 1982	July-Sept. 1982	Oct.-Dec. 1982	Jan.-Dec. Avg. Month
7:00-8:00 a.m. (ET)	14	13	10	13	13
8:00-10:00 a.m............	17	16	18	19	18
10:00-12:00 Noon.........	24	21	23	21	22
12:00 Noon-2:00 p.m.	30	26	28	27	28
2:00-4:00 p.m.............	32	27	28	30	29
4:00-6:00 p.m.............	42	45	34	39	38
6:00-7:00 p.m.............	58	47	45	54	51
Monday-Sunday					
7:00-8:00 p.m.............	63	51	47	60	55
8:00-9:00 p.m.............	66	56	51	64	60
9:00-10:00 p.m............	66	60	56	65	61
10:00-11:00 p.m.	61	56	54	59	58
11:00-12:00 Midnight	43	41	41	42	41
12:00 Midnight-1:00 a.m. .	26	25	25	25	25

Source: A.C. Nielsen, Households Using Television Summary Report, 1982.

Network Radio

Cost Per Minute
Wired Networks — **Usual Range***

	Usual Range*
ABC Contemporary	$4,000-5,500
ABC Direction...........................	1,800-2,500
ABC Entertainment......................	2,500-3,500
ABC FM	2,000-3,500
ABC Information	2,500-4,000
ABC Rock	2,000-3,500
ABC Talk..............................	1,000-1,500
CBS....................................	2,000-3,500
MBS	2,000-3,500
NBC	2,500-3,500
NBC Talk-Net..........................	1,000-1,500
RKO One...............................	2,500-3,500
RKO Two...............................	1,800-2,500
Sheridan Broadcasting Network..............	850- 950
Source.................................	2,500-3,500

*Costs based on an equal rotation basis of 12 announcements, Monday through Friday, 6:00 a.m. to 7:00 p.m.; 30-second costs are 50 percent of the 60-second rate on wired networks.

Non-wired Networks — **Usual Range***

	Usual Range*
Blair	$3,200-3,700
Eastman................................	2,500-3,000
Katz...................................	2,800-3,400
McGavren-Guild..........................	2,100-2,500
Torbet.................................	2,200-2,600

*Cost based on an equal rotation schedule of 12 announcements, Monday through Friday, 6:00 a.m. to 7:00 p.m. (top 50 markets only); 30-second costs are usually 80 percent of the 60-second rates on non-wired networks.

Audience and Efficiencies

	Usual Range
Avg. Adult Listener Rating....................	1.0-1.5
Average Adult Listeners (000)	1,600-2,400
-Wired Networks	
CPM Adults (Per Minute).....................	$1.25-2.25

Source: Leo Burnett estimates; RADAR, Fall 1982.

Spot Radio

Cost Per Metro Area Rating Point Summary

Markets	Men 18+	Men 18-34	Men 25-54	Women 18+	Women 18-34	Women 25-54	Teens 12-17
1-10	$1,139	$ 848	$1,064	$ 928	$ 747	$ 939	$ 470
11-20	1,706	1,311	1,580	1,428	1,211	1,439	733
21-30	2,151	1,657	2,011	1,806	1,541	1,804	948
31-40	2,464	1,935	2,293	2,081	1,772	2,073	1,118
41-50	2,733	2,150	2,564	2,323	1,972	2,309	1,272
51-60	2,937	2,323	2,769	2,510	2,125	2,488	1,380
61-70	3,137	2,492	2,954	2,676	2,283	2,652	1,522
71-80	3,261	2,601	3,083	2,781	2,378	2,753	1,614
81-90	3,379	2,688	3,191	2,884	2,461	2,853	1,685
91-100	3,489	2,799	3,308	2,981	2,553	2,948	1,773

Source: Media Market Guide, Fall 1982.

Radio Listening

Percent Listening During Average Quarter Hour
(Monday–Sunday)

Daypart	Men 18+	Men 18-49	Women 18+	Women 18-49	Teens 12-17
6 a.m.-10 a.m.	20%	23%	24%	23%	15%
10 a.m.-3 p.m.	22	24	22	23	12
3 p.m.-7 p.m.	19	22	18	19	20
7 p.m.-Midnight	11	14	9	10	17
Avg. 6 a.m.-Midnight..	18	21	18	18	16

Source: RADAR, Fall 1982.

Percent Listening by Location
(Monday–Sunday)

Daypart	In-home Men	In-home Women	In-home Teens	Out-of-home Men	Out-of-home Women	Out-of-home Teens
6 a.m.-10 a.m.	53%	77%	82%	47%	25%	19%
10 a.m.-3 p.m.	36	58	64	66	42	30
3 p.m.-7 p.m.	38	59	70	66	43	29
7 p.m.-Midnight.........	60	75	76	40	26	23
Avg. 6 a.m.-Midnight....	45	66	73	57	35	25

Potential Radio Audience

Monday-Sunday, 6 a.m. to Midnight

	Cumulative Audience Men	Cumulative Audience Women	Cumulative Audience Adults	Avg. Qtr. Hour Audience Men	Avg. Qtr. Hour Audience Women	Avg. Qtr. Hour Audience Adults
Total Radio						
Number (000)........	74,178	80,610	154,788	14,238	15,494	29,732
Population Percent	96	94	95	18	18	18
Network Radio						
Number (000)........	62,320	65,185	127,505	7,770	8,241	16,011
Population Percent	80	76	78	10	10	10

Source: RADAR, Fall 1982.

Cable Television

I.   NTI Sample: Cable Penetrations by Market Divisions

	Cable	Pay Cable
Total U.S..................................	38%	21%
County Size		
A..................................	23	17
B..................................	24	62
C & D	53	21

Non-Adults		
None	37	40
Any	18	25
Any of HOH		
Under 50	36	39
50+	24	18
HH Income		
LT $20M	33	42
$20M+	13	27

Source: NTI - Cable Status Report, July 1982.

II. Cable and Pay Cable Penetration

Year*	Number of Systems	Cable TV Homes MM	Cable TV Homes % U.S.	Pay Cable Homes MM	Pay Cable Homes % U.S.
1960	640	.7	1.0	—	—
1970	2,490	4.5	7.5	—	—
1975	3,560	9.2	13.2	—	—
1980	4,225	17.7	22.6	7.6	9.8
1981**	4,400	23.1	28.3	12.1	14.9
1982	4,782				
Feb		23.6	29.0	13.0	16.0
May		27.2	33.4	14.3	17.5
July		27.7	34.0	15.2	18.7
Nov		29.2	35.0	16.9	20.3

*November of each year.

**Change in Nielsen method for estimating cable homes.

Sources: A.C. Nielsen Company Cable Universe Estimates; Cable Status Report; and CableVision.

III. Satellite Fed Cable Services

Superstations

WTBS, WGN, WOR

Pay Cable

Bravo, Cinemax, EROS, Galavision, Home Box Office, Home Theater Network Plus, The Movie Channel, The Playboy Channel, Showtime

Basic Cable

News:	Cable News Network (CNN), CNN Headline News, Dow Jones Cable News, Financial News Network, Reuters News View, Satellite News Channel 1
Sports:	ESPN, USA Network
Women:	Daytime, Modern Satellite Network, USA Network, Satellite Program Network
Children:	Nickelodeon
Electronics:	Electronic Program Guide
Ethnic:	Black Entertainment Television, Spanish International Network
Culture:	Alpha Repertory Television Service, CBS Cable, Satellite Program Network
Music:	Music Television
Education:	ACSN: The Learning Channel
General Entertainment:	The Entertainment Channel, CBN Cable Network
Health:	Cable Health Network
Weather:	The Weather Channel
Religious:	Eternal Word Television Network, National Christian Network, National Jewish Television, PTL Television Network, Trinity Broadcasting Network
Public Affairs:	Cable Satellite Public Affairs Network

Source: CableVision.

IV. Top Ten Cable Interconnects

Interconnect	Number of Cable Systems	Number of Subscribers
Bay Area Cable	27	470,000
Cox Cable San Diego	3	330,500
Seattle	5	298,800
Connecticut	8	297,900
Buffalo	3	209,000
Boston	13	203,600
Centre Video	7	146,000
KUTV Intermountain	7	145,000
Orlando	4	135,000
Norfolk	3	131,600

Source: Cable Television Advertising Bureau.

V. Top 20 DMA Cable Markets

DMA	Cable Homes	Percent of TV Homes
New York	1,920,240	29.7%
Los Angeles/Palm Springs	1,025,400	23.8
San Francisco	885,680	44.1
Philadelphia	879,310	36.3
Pittsburgh	619,580	51.1
Boston/Manchester	529,340	27.1
Seattle/Tacoma	470,560	42.0
Houston	436,210	33.3
Cleveland/Akron	431,450	30.4
San Diego	416,660	57.5
Dallas/Ft. Worth	376,000	26.8
Hartford/New Haven	371,010	51.6
Atlanta	361,650	32.8
Chicago	354,290	11.9
Miami/Ft. Lauderdale	344,130	30.0
Buffalo	338,480	54.8
Tampa/St. Petersburg	320,650	29.9
Wilkes Barre/Scranton	299,090	62.8
Orlando/Dayton	286,910	46.0
Charleston/Huntington	278,090	55.5

Source: A.C. Nielsen Cable Universe Estimates, November 1982.

VI. Top 10 Cable Markets

Market	Cable Penetration (% U.S. TV Homes)
Santa Barbara, San Marino, San Luis Obispo	79.5%
Marquette, Michigan	74.3
San Angelo, Texas	72.7
Johnstown/Altoona	68.3
Wilkes Barre/Scranton	62.8
Syracuse	58.2
San Diego	57.5
Champaign/Springfield/Decatur	57.3
West Palm Beach/Ft. Pierce	55.7
Charleston/Huntington	55.5

Source: A.C. Nielsen Cable Universe Estimates, November 1982.

Print Media

Newspapers

Cost and Coverage Cumed
By Top Market Groups

Daily newspapers in each market are included on the basis of circulation rank, until the combined circulations exceed 50% coverage of the market.

Market	No. Homes (000)	Metro Circ. (000)	Open Line Rate-B/W	Cost Per Page B/W
Top 10	17,734	9,702	$145.99	$305,974
Top 20	24,861	15,672	202.91	440,333
Top 30	29,745	19,657	247.83	541,366
Top 40	33,210	22,880	276.60	612,611
Top 50	36,035	25,490	305.39	686,173
Top 60	38,425	27,939	327.69	738,472
Top 70	40,443	30,105	349.83	790,698
Top 80	42,240	31,843	367.86	833,523
Top 90	43,708	33,332	382.20	869,545
Top 100	44,991	34,752	398.14	906,708

Source: Circulation 82/83.

Newspaper Readership
(Average Weekday)

	Adults	Men	Women
Total	67%	69%	65%
Age			
18-24	59%	60%	57%
25-34	61	65	58
35-44	69	69	68
45-54	76	77	75
55-64	75	74	76
65 + ...	69	72	66
Education			
Graduated from College	78%	82%	73%
Attended College	71	72	70
Graduated from High School	69	70	69
Attended High School	61	62	59
Did Not Attend High School	51	52	50
Household Income			
$40,000 + ...	78%	80%	76%
$30,000 + ...	76	78	75
$25,000 + ...	75	77	73
$20-24,999	70	71	70
$15-19,999	67	69	66
$10-14,999	64	63	65
Less than $10,000	52	50	53

Source: Simmons Market Research Bureau, 1982.

Newspaper Reach (Adults—Avg. Market)

Total Daily GRPs	Reach by Type of Schedule - Five Weekdays		
	1 Paper	2 Papers Each Day	2 Papers (1 Per Day)
25	34	30	50
35	47	41	67
45	60	52	82

Total Daily GRPs	Reach by Type of Schedule - Five Weekdays		
	1 Paper	2 Papers Each Day	2 Papers (1 Per Day)
55	73	63	—
65	85	73	—
90	—	90	—

Sources: Leo Burnett estimates; Newspaper Advertising Bureau.

Newspaper Readers Per Copy

Age	Avg. Daily Paper		Sunday/ Avg. Weekend Paper	
	Men	Women	Men	Women
18-24	.18	.17	.21	.21
25-34	.26	.23	.30	.27
35-44	.19	.19	.21	.21
45-54	.18	.18	.19	.19
55-64	.16	.18	.17	.18
65 + ...	.16	.20	.16	.20
Total.............	1.13	1.14	1.24	1.26

Source: Simmons Market Research Bureau, 1982.

Newspaper Readership by Section

	Percent of Readers Opening Average Page	
	Men	Women
All Sections (Avg. Page).................	69%	65%
Business	17	13
Classified............................	17	16
Comics...............................	17	18
Editorial	18	19
Entertainment	17	22
Food or Cooking	9	23
General News	32	30
Home................................	9	18
Radio - Television.....................	14	17
Sports	27	10

Source: Simmons Market Research Bureau, 1982.

Selected Consumer Publications

Circulation and Rates

	Circulation Rate Base* (000)	1-Time Rate	
		4-Color Page	B/W Page
General Editorial			
American Legion	2,500	$15,788	$11,406
Atlantic	400	11,200	7,465
Changing Times...........	1,350	24,160	16,210
Ebony	1,400	23,856	17,658
Games	600	10,200	7,130
Grit.....................	678	8,910	7,020
Harper's Magazine	140	4,320	2,830
Health	850	11,085	7,920
Life.....................	1,300	32,640	28,015
National Enquirer	5,069	29,800	23,650
National Geographic	8,400	97,970	75,360
Natural History	460	10,725	7,150

	Circulation Rate Base* (000)	1-Time Rate 4-Color Page	B/W Page
New York Magazine	400	15,980	10,150
The New Yorker	480	17,650	11,100
Outside	197	8,700	5,800
People	2,425	42,950	33,300
Psychology Today	850	20,470	14,180
Reader's Digest	17,750	103,600	86,200
Rolling Stone	775	19,190	12,870
Scientific American	550	27,000	18,000
Smithsonian	1,850	33,350	22,235
Travel/Holiday	780	10,950	7,995
Travel & Leisure	925	20,940	15,560
Us	1,100	16,830	13,035
Yankee	875	10,785	8,085
Entertainment Guides			
Playbill	1,370	$28,167	$18,775
TV Guide	17,000	77,400	65,600
News and Business			
Barron's	259	NA	$ 9,464
Black Enterprise	250	$10,270	8,035
Business Week	845	35,140	23,120
Dun's Business Month	285	12,800	9,465
Forbes	700	25,090	16,520
Fortune	670	33,040	21,740
Harvard Business Review	225	7,170	5,220
Jet	700	9,590	6,072
Money	1,000	30,010	19,180
Nation's Business	750	23,750	16,380
Newsweek	2,950	63,850	40,930
Time	4,500	94,420	60,525
U.S. News & World Report	2,050	45,910	29,090
Venture	200	8,850	5,900
Wall Street Journal	2,003	NA	62,853
Women's			
Bon Appetit	1,300	$20,660	$14,465
Cosmopolitan	2,350	32,170	23,905
Cuisine	750	16,510	11,555
Essence	700	13,000	8,670
Family Circle - January	6,900	60,000	49,800
Feb.-May	7,500	61,050	52,325
June-Sept.	7,000	58,950	50,500
Oct.-Dec.	8,000	67,350	57,725
Good Housekeeping	5,000	63,820	50,860
Gourmet	650	13,600	8,000
Ladies' Home Journal	5,000	48,000	39,000
McCall's	6,200	59,830	48,670
Ms.	450	9,800	7,300
New Woman	1,300	14,812	11,110
Parents	1,675	31,680	24,750
Playgirl	750	7,220	5,415
Redbook	3,800	42,675	32,270
Savvy	258	7,900	5,300
Self	950	17,900	12,000
Woman's Day - January	6,800	63,850	53,320
Feb.-May	7,000	65,730	54,890
June-Sept.	6,800	63,850	53,320
Oct.-Dec.	7,200	67,600	56,450
Working Mother	400	8,540	6,420
Working Woman	550	13,100	9,500

	Circulation Rate Base* (000)	1-Time Rate 4-Color Page	B/W Page
Home Service			
Better Homes & Gardens	8,000	$78,985	$65,300
Country Living	750	15,915	11,625
House Beautiful	800	21,750	14,880
House & Garden	550	16,575	12,100
Metropolitan Home	700	15,450	10,770
Southern Living	2,050	33,800	23,980
Sunset	1,250	23,609	16,963
Romance & Movies			
MacFadden Women's Group	2,475	$28,785	$22,140
True Story	1,475	16,880	12,965
Fashion & Bride			
Bride's	394	$15,450	$12,420
Glamour	1,900	28,370	20,100
Harper's Bazaar	650	17,980	12,430
Mademoiselle	1,000	18,720	12,850
Modern Bride	377	15,540	12,430
Vogue	950	20,000	14,000
Baby Care			
American Baby	1,000	$25,080	$18,135
Baby Talk	900	18,012	13,349
Expecting	1,050	22,250	15,335
Youth			
Boy's Life			
Co-ed	1,475	$14,590	$10,450
Scholastic Magazines	800	8,900	6,000
Group	2,450	22,265	16,200
Seventeen	1,500	20,900	14,450
Teen	1,000	13,455	8,970
Men's			
Esquire	650	$19,300	$12,900
National Lampoon	450	9,500	6,450
Oui	575	8,602	5,470
Penthouse	4,000	36,960	24,925
Playboy	5,000	53,925	38,510
Sports & Automotive			
Car & Driver	725	$25,340	$16,455
Car Craft	400	10,240	6,400
Field & Stream	2,000	36,460	24,235
Golf Digest	1,025	28,755	19,170
Golf Magazine	725	21,010	14,000
Guns & Ammo	475	10,070	6,295
Hot Rod	800	20,400	12,750
Motor Trend	750	23,705	14,815
Motorcyclist	225	7,400	4,625
Outdoor Life	1,500	25,890	17,840
Road & Track	675	21,720	13,825
Ski	410	15,140	11,025
Sport	900	18,800	12,900
Sports Afield	500	14,100	9,850
Sports Illustrated	2,325	60,195	38,585
Tennis	460	13,770	9,180
World Tennis	375	11,425	7,630
Ziff-Davis Network	3,555	71,600	45,705
Boating	175	7,020	4,545
Car & Driver	725	22,240	14,730
Cycle	460	14,285	9,460

MEDIA COST AND COVERAGE DATA

	Circulation Rate Base* (000)	1-Time Rate 4-Color Page	1-Time Rate B/W Page
Flying	360	13,005	8,555
Popular Photography	865	29,025	20,895
Skiing	430	14,510	9,610
Stereo Review	540	16,305	13,465
Mechanics/Science			
Discover	850	$23,800	$16,405
Mechanix Illustrated	1,600	24,815	17,500
Omni	825	18,350	12,230
Popular Mechanics	1,600	29,625	20,863
Popular Science	1,800	29,235	20,610
Science Digest	525	13,230	9,925
Science 83	700	16,909	11,836
Farm			
Capper's Weekly	413	$ 5,000	$ 4,100
Farm Journal	1,000	34,750	24,650
Progressive Farmer	650	19,990	14,180
Successful Farming	680	23,510	16,440

Source: S.R.D.S., December 1982, or publisher's announcement if more current.

Audience and Efficiencies
I. General Interest

	Average Audience (000) Men 18+	Men 18-49	Women 18+	Women 18-49	CPM Page 4 C (Adults)
General Editorial					
Ebony	2,972	2,447	3,879	3,109	$ 3.48
Life	4,865	3,635	4,537	3,441	3.47
National Enquirer	5,852	4,380	9,771	6,361	1.91
National Geographic	10,861	7,059	9,705	5,863	4.76
New York Magazine	570	357	627	457	13.35
New Yorker	1,228	856	1,116	785	7.53
People	7,443	6,528	11,960	9,696	2.21
Psychology Today	1,190	1,105	1,705	1,436	7.07
Reader's Digest	16,528	9,545	22,538	12,312	2.65
Scientific American	1,404	1,055	479	397	14.34
Smithsonian	2,263	1,448	2,256	1,366	7.38
Entertainment Guides					
TV Guide	16,702	12,948	19,631	13,804	2.13
News & Business					
Barron's	635	313	239	153	10.83
Business Week	3,139	2,381	1,034	748	8.42
Forbes	1,603	1,100	519	278	11.82
Fortune	1,903	1,501	763	543	12.39
Money	2,214	1,629	1,433	950	8.23
Newsweek	9,927	7,424	6,418	4,318	3.91
Time	11,806	8,942	8,894	6,117	4.56
U.S. News & World Report	5,885	3,929	3,374	2,001	4.96
Wall St. Journal	4,253	2,865	2,038	1,309	9.99

II. Male Orientation

	Avg. Audience (000) Men 18+	Men 18-49	CPM-Page 4 C Men 18+	Men 18-49
Sports & Automotive				
Car & Driver	2,359	2,205	$10.74	$11.49
Field & Stream	6,391	4,633	5.70	7.87
Golf Digest	1,463	751	19.65	38.29
Golf Magazine	1,379	877	15.24	15.96
Road & Track	2,419	2,204	8.98	9.85
Sport	3,167	2,721	5.94	6.91
Sports Afield	2,974	2,301	4.74	6.13
Sports Illustrated	10,668	8,795	5.64	6.84
World Tennis	306	251	37.34	45.52
Ziff-Davis Network	9,618	8,305	7.44	8.62
Men's				
Esquire	1,537	1,064	12.56	18.14
Penthouse	5,399	4,894	6.85	7.55
Playboy	9,109	7,982	5.92	6.76

	Avg. Audience (000) Men 18+	Men 18-49	CPM-Page 4 C Men 18+	Men 18-49
Mechanics/Science				
Discover	1,077	905	22.10	26.30
Mechanix Illustrated	3,932	2,875	6.31	8.63
Omni	1,772	1,647	10.36	11.14
Popular Mechanics	5,194	3,697	5.70	8.01
Popular Science	3,870	2,711	7.55	10.78
Science Digest	783	582	16.90	22.73
Science 83	827	636	20.45	26.59

III. Female Orientation

	Avg. Audience (000) Women 18+	Women 18-49	CPM-Page 4 C Women 18+	Women 18-49
Women's & Home Service				
Better Homes & Gardens	16,226	9,979	$ 4.87	$ 7.92
Cosmopolitan	8,036	7,085	4.00	4.54
Country Living	1,328	983	11.98	16.19
Family Circle	15,673	9,962	3.94	6.20
Good Housekeeping	15,203	9,994	4.20	6.39
House Beautiful	3,526	2,119	6.17	10.26
Ladies' Home Journal	12,390	7,755	3.87	6.19
McCall's	13,359	8,587	4.48	6.97
Metropolitan Home	737	579	20.96	26.68
Ms.	1,162	972	8.43	10.08
Parents	3,117	2,884	10.16	10.98
Redbook	7,590	5,470	5.62	7.80
Woman's Day	14,827	9,513	4.40	6.86
Working Mother	806	722	10.60	11.83
Working Woman	1,009	863	12.98	15.18
Fashion				
Glamour	5,376	4,884	5.28	5.81
Mademoiselle	3,407	2,975	5.49	6.29
Vogue	4,262	3,493	4.69	5.73

Sources: Audience - SMRB 1982 or Leo Burnett estimate if starred (*).
Costs - S.R.D.S. December 1982, or publisher's announcement if more current. (CPM's are based on the one-time, 4-color rate with the exception of Wall Street Journal, Barron's and the National Enquirer for which B/W costs were used.)

Magazine Reach

Average reach and frequency for schedules of approximately three insertion per magazine.

Type	Demo. Group	GRP Levels (3+ Magazines) 100	200	300	Magazine Reach of Magazine Type 4 Mos.	1 Year
Mass-News-	Men	44	64	74	84	88
Class-Supp	Women	44	64	74	84	88
Home Service-	Women	42	64	74	87	90
Women's	Women 18-49	42	64	74	87	90

Source: Simmons Market Research Bureau, 1982.

Magazine Networks

Magazine networks offer the opportunity of buying full-page ads in combinations of magazines in specific markets. Preprinted ads are bound into magazines such as Newsweek, Time, Sports Illustrated, U.S. News & World Report and a number of others, to be delivered to selected locations. While the CPMs are higher than for full-run advertising, they are below those charged for market-by-market purchases in individual magazines. Media Networks Inc. offers the following six magazine networks. In addition, four military networks are available.

Network	Magazines Available	No. of Markets
City News Urban	Newsweek, Sports Illustrated, Time	5
Business	Business Week, Dun's Review, Money, Nation's Business, Newsweek,	26

Network	Magazines Available	No. of Markets
	Sports Illustrated, Time, U.S. News & World Report	
Executive	Business Week, Dun's Review, Nation's Business, U.S. News & World Report	4
Suburban	Newsweek, Sports Illustrated, Time, U.S. News & World Report	32
Women's Home	Better Homes & Gardens, House & Garden, House Beautiful, Metropolitan Home	20
News Network	Newsweek, Sports Illustrated, Time, U.S. News & World Report	101

Source: S.R.D.S., December 1982.

Supplements

Circulation and Rates

	Average Circulation (000)	1-Time Rate 4-Color Page	1-Time Rate B/W Page
Family Weekly .... (362 Newspapers)	12,444	$115,125	$100,875
Parade .... (136 Newspapers)	22,163	$205,975	$167,835
Sunday .... (57 Newspapers)	22,069	$243,174	$199,238

Source: S.R.D.S., December 1982.

Audience and Efficiencies

	Men 18+	Men 18-49	Women 18+	Women 18-49	CPM Page 4 C (Adults)
Family Weekly ..	12,157	8,022	13,363	7,958	4.51
Parade..........	20,456	13,490	23,116	14,210	4.73
Sunday	23,027	14,983	24,355	15,123	5.13

Sources: Audience - SMRB, 1982.
Costs - S.R.D.S., December 1982.

Comics

Circulation and Rates

	Average Circulation (000)	1-Time 4-Color 1/2-Page Rate
Metro Sunday Comics		
Basic Network................ (70 Newspapers)	22,342	$153,350
Total Network................ (95 Newspapers)	23,986	$166,027

	Average Circulation (000)	1-Time 4-Color 1/2-Page Rate
Puck - The Comic Weekly		
National Network .... (67 Newspapers)	13,324	$104,111
American Network .... (74 Newspapers)	4,599	$ 36,078
Both Networks .... (141 Newspapers)	17,923	$140,189

Source: S.R.D.S. Newspapers, December 1982.

Readers Per Copy

Men	Women	Teens	Children	Total
0.6	0.6	0.35	0.36	1.91

Source: Leo Burnett, A Look At Newspaper Comic Sections.

Out-of-Home Media

Outdoor

Data for Top 100 Core Markets

	100 GRPs			50 GRPs		
Markets	Unilluminated Panels	Illuminated Panels	Monthly Cost	Unilluminated Panels	Illuminated Panels	Monthly Cost
Top 10	440	2,360	$ 970,174	220	1,180	$ 485,087
Top 20	764	3,836	1,533,878	382	1,918	766,939
Top 30	902	4,640	1,826,832	451	2,320	913,146
Top 40	1,168	5,224	2,049,246	584	2,612	1,024,623
Top 50	1,496	5,696	2,255,010	748	2,848	1,127,505
Top 100	2,332	6,844	2,697,948	1,166	3,422	1,348,974

Source: Institute of Outdoor Advertising.

Note: In addition to standard posting, painted display bulletins may be purchased in most major markets. These are known as "rotaries" because they usually are moved from site to site on a 60-day cycle. Painted bulletins typically measure 14' x 48' as compared with 12' x 25' for standard posters.

Transit

Commuter Advertising

Interior displays may be purchased in bus and subway vehicles. Their standard size is 11" x 28". Exterior bus posters, commonly 30" x 144", and train platform displays are also available. Rates vary depending on poster size, number of markets and number of displays per market.

Terminal Advertising

Various types of displays are available at rail, bus and airport terminals. Rear-lighted transparencies (dioramas) and posters are the most common forms. Costs vary depending on terminal traffic and type of display.

Appendix 4
Table of Some Syndicated Media Research Services

Services and Description	Method of Pricing
Arbitron TV Market Report. Estimates audience among households and sex/age categories by time period, station and program; three to eight times a year for 210 markets.	According to agency billings
Arbitron Day-Part Summary. Estimates market-by-market audiences by station within day-parts; 210 markets; three times yearly.	Either part of TV package or bought separately
Arbitron TV Markets & Rankings Guide. Annually offers TV market definitions and rankings by size, audience, station revenue, plus consumer expenditures.	Either as part of TV package or bought separately
Arbitron TV Ethnic Reports. Estimates audience among black or Spanish metropolitan households exclusively; four to 15 markets; two or three times a year.	Priced separately
Arbitron Radio Market Reports. Surveys 160 markets; 60 two times a year; 90 markets one time a year, two markets three times a year, eight markets four times. Day parts and demographics in all markets covered.	Based on agency billings
Arbitron Nationwide Radio Audience Estimates. Uses 880,000 diaries once a year to compile a national network report for both line and nonline networks; estimate by station or network.	Part of radio package*
Nielsen TV Index Basic Service. Reports biweekly on household rating nationally; options offered for fast weekly household report, including SIA dailies.	Based on agency billings
NTI Analysis Service. NTI ratings with persons data, including NTI/NAC (audience demographics) and market section audience (MSA); also 11 optional reports, supplements about persons, costs, household and persons rankings, brand cumes, cpms, cume audiences, etc.	Part of NTI package
Nielsen Station Index. Offers a four-week, viewers-in-profile report, with options for daily and weekly reports in New York, Chicago, L.A.; two-week reports in four to 10 markets, network programs by Dominant Market Area (DMA), syndicated programs, DMA trends by season, DMA-CATV audience distribution.	Based on agency billings
Pulse Radio Service. Measures local radio audiences in 150 markets.	Based on agency radio billings
Pulse Local Qualitative Radio Service. Measures income, educational levels, family size in approximately 50 markets.	Flat rate
Pulse Special Radio Service. Measures approximately 100 smaller markets.	Depends on the market size of desired report

*Radio package also includes overview of all markets surveyed in either spring or fall sweep; small market reports; trading area reports; regional, state, sport, network reports, ADI information; 15 black and two Spanish markets diary surveys issued in fall.

Services and Description	Method of Pricing
Pulse Ethnic Radio Service. Measures black and Spanish audiences.	Included in radio package or sold on special order
Pulse Syndicated Newspaper Service. Measures about 150 markets in alternate years.	Based on market size
BAR Network TV and Radio Service. Monitors three networks full time. Reports activity/estimated expenditures by brand, parent company, product class. Publishes weekly, with monthly, quarterly cumulative summaries.	Scaled to agency total broadcast billings
BAR National Spot TV Service. Monitors N.Y., L.A., full time, 73 other top markets one week per month. Reports activity, estimated expenditures by brand, market, parent company, product class. Publishes monthly market reports, with monthly, quarterly cumulative summaries.	Scaled to agency total TV billings
LNA Magazine Analysis Service. Monthly analysis of PIB member publications; pages, dollar revenue; includes product category.	Scaled to agency domestic billings
LNA Regional Advertising Service. Monthly analysis of regional advertising activity and dollars in selected PIB publications.	Scaled to domestic billings
LNA Multi-Media Reports Service. Three types: quarterly revenue reports; magazines, newspaper supps, network TV, spot TV, network radio, outdoor. (BAR furnishes broadcast data.)	Scaled to agency domestic billings
LNA Outdoor Advertising Expenditures. Expenditures of national outdoor advertisers in markets of over 100,000 population; quarterly.	Scaled to agency domestic billings
W. R. Simmons Study of Selective Markets. Measures 1976-77 magazine reading, radio listening, TV viewing, newspaper and supplement reading audiences; household and/or product consumption rates, brand usage of over 500 categories of package goods, durable goods and services and basic demographic characteristics.	Scaled to agency domestic billings
W. R. Simmons Local Multi-Media/Marketing Studies. Sample of 5000 adults, 1000 clusters; first personal interview: yesterday's newspaper reading, magazine reading, radio listening, shopping/marketing behavior, with week's personal diary left behind. Second interview TV diary retrieved, other media observations. All projected to total ADI. Field work: January-March 1977.	Scaled to agency domestic billings
Media Records Blue Book. Contains general and automotive linage and dollar expenditures taken from newspaper reports of over 200 daily and Sunday newspapers in 70 cities.	By subscription fee annually, $1500; special sections at own fees

Services and Description	Method of Pricing
Media Records Green Book. Offers much the same format as Blue Book; national investments in 61 Media Records measured cities covering 191 daily and Sunday publications; shows expenditures only in dollars.**	Also by annual subscription; 10% discount to buyers of both services
Media Records Local All-Media Syndication Studies. Figures on getting into the local measurement field in spring of 1977 with O'Brien and Sherwood doing the field research. Aiming at Detroit, Philadelphia, Chicago, St. Louis.	Not determined
Starch Inra Hooper Ad Readership Service. Measures performance of about 1000 issues of 90 consumer, general, business, trade newspaper publications. Also offers Profiles of Magazines Subscribers at $2,000 minimum; standardized surveys by mail of magazine subscribers.	$140 per report
Trendex TV/Radio Coincidentals. Measures viewing or listening activity at time of phone call; minimum sample size per day, 1000 calls.	Depends on number of calls
Media Statistics. Measures 280 small radio markets. Although basically for station groups, reports are available to agencies. Same owner, Jim Seiler, provides alternate service to Arbitron in big markets. Measures every two weeks and delivers on third week. Expanding from top 10 markets in 1977.	$5 per station report
Sigma 3 Local Multi-Media/Marketing Studies. A Bill Simmons operation, which started off with a study of the New York market. Charter supporters: New York Post, *Newsday*, Bergen *Record* and 13 radio and TV stations. Aiming at Philadelphia market next.	Flat rate per report to agencies
Scarborough Report (Scarborough Research Corp.). Initial local multimedia/marketing study: Washington market. Based on random sample of 3000 adult respondents. Besides media/product usage, measures frequency of shopping and where. Charter subscriber: *Washington Post*.	Available on subscription basis to agencies
The Source Reports (Dimensions Unlimited, Inc.). Surveys twice a year in L.A., San Francisco, Chicago markets re. consumer radio and newspaper usage and marketing habits (food stores, department stores, fast food patronage, movies, airlines). Original supporter: *Los Angeles Times*. Will measure New York market this spring. Places weekly diary after prequestioning of respondent.	$25 per market report for agencies
St. Louis Shoppers Quarterly Survey. Lee Creative Marketing conducts annual survey among 1000 randomly selected housewives in St. Louis metropolitan area, newspaper readership by day of week, radio, TV habits by day, hour, grocery, drugstore, hardware store shopping habits, plus awareness of selected TV commercials and demographic information.	Priced on annual or quarterly basis, or information desired

**Gray Book contains summary data report from Green Book with 125 classifications and subclassifications; top 100 newspaper advertisers.

Notes: *Erdos & Morgan's EM/CPM* surveys are not included in the above since they are custom-originated (they are underwritten individually by 19 magazines) and the reports are free to the top 100 agencies ($25 to others). However, the 19 magazines agreed to standardized questions for the basic demographics.

Belden Market Studies are not included because they are not a syndicated service.

Source: *Media Decisions*, February, 1977.

GLOSSARY

AAAA (4A's) American Association of Advertising Agencies. A national organization of leading advertising agencies.

AAF American Advertising Federation. A national association of advertisers, advertising agencies, media, and allied businesses organized to promote and defend effective advertising.

ABC Audit Bureau of Circulation. An organization sponsored by publishers, agencies, and advertisers to audit and validate circulation figures of magazines and newspapers.

ABP American Business Press. An organization of trade, industrial, and business papers formed by the merger of the Associated Business Publications and the National Business Publications groups.

account An advertiser. Used to refer to a client of an advertising agency.

account executive/supervisor A member of an advertising agency who is responsible for liaison with one or more accounts. Responsible for the supervision of marketing and advertising work done by the agency.

account service The department in an advertising agency to which account executives and account supervisors belong.

adjacency A broadcast time period immediately preceding or following a scheduled program.

advertising Any paid form of nonpersonal presentation and promotion of ideas, goods, and services by an identified sponsor.

advertising agency A business organization rendering advertising services to clients.

advertising specialty A form of advertising. Products bearing the name of an advertiser and given as gifts to prospective customers.

affiliate A broadcast station that enters into an agreement to carry programs provided by a network.

agate line A unit of measure of print advertising space, one column wide (regardless of column width) and one-fourteenth of an inch deep.

aided recall A research technique used to measure the communications effectiveness of advertising in which the respondent is given aid in the form of an advertisement, brand name, or some other device to facilitate recall.

all commodity distribution A measure of retail distribution expressed as a percentage of total retail sales of a particular outlet type. For example, 30 percent all commodity distribution in food stores means that a product has distribution in food stores accounting for 30 percent of all food store sales.

alternate sponsorship Sponsorship in which two or more sponsors assume responsibility for a program and share commercial time.

AM Amplitude modulation. A method of transmitting radio signals by varying the amplitude or size of the electromagnetic wave as opposed to varying its frequency. *See* FM (frequency modulation).

AMA American Marketing Association. A professional association of academic and business people devoted to furthering the development of marketing.

ANA Association of National Advertisers. A national association of advertisers dominated by larger manufacturers.

animation Giving movement to static objects for attention value or effect. Used in filmed cartoons and point-of-purchase displays or outdoor boards by adding moving parts.

ARB American Research Bureau. A broadcast rating service for television and radio. Uses both a viewer diary method and an electronic recording and tabulating system known as Arbitron.

Arbitron *See* ARB.

ARBOR Association for Research in Behavior. An independent research organization that measures commercials and conducts other marketing research.

audience The total number of people who are able to receive an advertising message delivered by a medium or combination of media.

audio Sound portion of a television commercial or program. *See* video.

availability A broadcast time period that has not been sold and is therefore available for purchase.

average frequency The number of times the average member of an audience is exposed to an advertising message within a given period of time, usually four weeks.

average issue circulation The average delivered circulation for all issues of a publication. Obtained by dividing the total annual circulation by the number of issues.

bait advertising An unethical practice in which a product is advertised at a highly attractive price in order to lure customers to the retail outlet where they find it difficult or impossible to buy the product at the advertised price.

BBB Better Business Bureau. Local organizations supported by advertisers, advertising agencies, media, and other businesses to discourage false and misleading advertising and marketing practices.

billboard (a) The television presentation of the name of the sponsor at the beginning and close of a program. (b) A popular name for an outdoor sign.

billing The amount of money charged to clients by advertising agencies, including media costs, production costs, and service fees.

bleed Printing to the edge of the page, leaving no margin.

block type A general typeface also known as sans serif. Characterized by vertical strokes of uniform thickness and the absence of cross strokes (serifs) at the bottom and top of the characters.

body copy The text of an ad, excluding headline, subheads, illustration, and logotype.

B of A Bureau of Advertising, American Publishers Association. Promotes the use of newspapers as an advertising medium.

boldface Type in which the strokes are heavier than other designs of the same type family.

boutique A limited service type of advertising agency that usually performs only a creative service for a fee.

BPA Business Publications Audit of Circulation. An organization that audits business publications, primarily controlled circulation publications.

brand A name, term, sign, symbol, or design, or a combination of them, that is intended to identify the goods or services of one seller or a group of sellers and differentiate them from those of competitors.

brand image The picture or likeness of the brand that exists in consumers' minds.

brand share The share of market held by a brand.

broker A manufacturer's agent who receives commissions for sales to channel members. Does not normally take title to merchandise sold.

campaign An advertising effort on behalf of a particular product or service that extends for a specified period of time.

caps A term used in typography. Refers to capital or uppercase letters in contrast to small or lowercase letters.

caption Explanatory text accompanying an illustration.

CATV Community Antenna Television System. A system for extending television coverage through the use of coaxial cable to subscribers in remote areas. Popularly known as cable TV.

center spread A single sheet of paper that forms the two facing pages in the center of a publication or brochure.

chain break An interruption in network broadcasting to permit local station identification. Also a commercial broadcast during this interruption.

channel The frequency in the broadcast spectrum assigned to a station for its transmission.

circulation The number of copies of a publication distributed. In broadcast, it is the average number of listeners or viewers during a particular time period.

city zone That portion of a newspaper's coverage area that includes the corporate city plus adjacent areas that have the characteristics of the city.

classified advertising Advertising arranged according to the product or service advertised. The advertisements are limited in size and use of illustrations.

class magazines A term used to refer to magazines that reach upper socio-income groups.

clear-channel station A radio station with interference-free broadcasting rights on a particular frequency, and with broadcasting power up to 50,000 watts. Also referred to as Class A stations.

client An advertiser with whom agencies and/or media do business.

closing date The date by which advertising materials must be delivered to a medium in order to appear at a particular time.

coaxial cable A special cable used to transmit telephone, telegraph, and television signals.

collateral material An advertising term used to refer to noncommissionable media used in connection with an advertising campaign.

color separation Used in connection with four-color advertising. In the printing process, the advertisement is decomposed into its primary color components.

column inch A unit of publication space, one column wide and one inch deep.

combination rate A discounted rate for advertising in two or more publications under the same ownership.

company forecast An aggregate forecast for all products sold by a company.

comparison advertising Advertising that compares two or more brands in terms of one or more product attributes. Also referred to as comparative advertising.

composing stick A small, adjustable metal box used in assembling type in hand composition.

composition Setting type and/or assembling it with engravings.

comprehensive A layout, accurate in terms of size, color, and location of elements, to show how the final ad will appear.

conspicuous consumption A term coined by the economist Thorstein Veblen that refers to the purchase of goods and services to enhance social prestige.

consumer orientation A key element in the marketing concept in which goods and services are designed in terms of consumers' interests.

continuity Repetition of the same basic theme. Continuity in media refers to the regularity with which advertising for a particular product appears in a particular medium throughout the marketing period.

continuous tone A screened photographic image that contains gradations of color or black and white.

cooperative advertising Retail advertising in which the cost is shared by the retailer and a national advertiser.

copy Broadly speaking, any material to be included in an advertisement. In a narrow sense, it refers to verbal material only.

copy plan A part of the marketing plan that consists of a summary statement of the essential elements to be included in an advertisement or commercial. The copy plan is usually written after a prototype ad or commercial has been developed and serves as a guide for other advertisements or commercials in the same campaign.

copyright A legal term referring to protection granted an individual or company against reprinting—use of an original production without express consent.

copy strategy A part of the marketing plan consisting of summary statements about how a product or service will be presented in advertising.

copy testing Measuring the effectiveness of an advertisement or an element of an advertisement against some predetermined objective.

corporate advertising Advertising designed to communicate corporate values as opposed to advertising done in support of a particular product or service.

corrective advertising A punitive sanction employed by the FTC in which advertisers are required to run advertising specifically designed to correct false or misleading impressions created by previous advertising.

cost-per-thousand The cost to an advertiser for delivering an advertising message to a thousand viewers, readers, or listeners. It is used as a basis for comparing the efficiency of alternative media.

cost plus A system for compensating advertising agencies for work done based on internal costs, out-of-pocket expenditures plus an agreed upon percentage of these costs to cover overhead and profit.

counter card Point-of-purchase material designed for display on a counter or near the cash register of a retail outlet.

cover The front of a publication is referred to as the first cover; the inside of the front page is the second cover; the inside of the back page is the third cover; and the back page is the fourth cover. Extra rates are often charged for cover positions.

coverage The percent of households or individuals exposed to a specific advertising medium in a designated area.

CU Close-up. A term used in television production.

cume   The total audience reached by a succession of advertising messages within a defined period.

cursive type   A general group of typefaces that resemble handwriting. Also referred to as script.

cylinder press   A printing press with a rotating cylinder under which a flat bed containing type or plates slides back and forth.

dagmar   A model for measuring the communication effectiveness of advertising. Conceptualizes the effects of advertising as four steps: awareness, comprehension, conviction, and action.

dayparts   A general term referring to the different segments of the television broadcast day. For example, daytime television, prime time (roughly between 7:30 P.M. and 10:30 P.M.) and fringe time (immediately before and after prime time) are each dayparts.

deal   Any of a variety of price incentives used to move merchandise. Examples are a cents-off-label or two for the price of one.

dealer   A retailer.

dealer tie-in   A national advertiser's promotion in which dealers participate.

delayed broadcast   A repeat broadcast of a program by tape or film. Routinely used by networks to compensate for time zone differences between the East and West Coasts.

design   The organization of the elements in a print advertisement.

direct lithography   A form of lithographic printing in which the printing plates are in direct contact with the printing surface. It is distinguished from offset lithography in which the plate image is transferred to an intermediate surface (blanket) for printing. *See* lithography.

directory advertising   Advertising in published directories, such as the Yellow Pages or other business and industrial directories of firms.

display advertising   Print advertising using illustrations, typography, colors, and design to attract attention, in contrast to classified advertising.

dissolve   A technique used in television production for changing scenes. One scene is brought into sharp focus as the previous scene fades out.

dolly   To move a camera in or out of scenes to gain a different camera angle or perspective.

down-and-under   A direction given in radio and television production to reduce the sound level of music or other sound effects so that it will not interfere with the dialogue to follow.

drive time   The peak period for radio listenership when people are driving to and from work. Normally, 7:00 A.M. to 10:00 A.M. and 3:00 P.M. to 7:00 P.M.

duplication   Multiple exposure of the same people to an advertising message.

economic profit   That profit above the profit required to meet the basic objectives of a firm. The concept of economic profit is often used in marketing budgeting.

ECU   Extreme close-up. A very close camera shot to show maximum detail.

electrotype   A duplicate of another plate made by the electrotype process.

em   A typographical measure based on the square of a body of any given typeface, and derived from the letter M which is as wide as it is high. By convention, the term usually refers to the 12-point em, which is equal to 1/16 of an inch.

en Half the width of an em.

engraving An original printing plate. Also a process for reproducing a design for printing by etching metal plates.

fact sheet A page of product selling features used by broadcast personalities and announcers in ad-libbing a live commercial.

fade A broadcast direction. To "fade in" is to gradually increase the intensity of sound or image. To "fade out" is to gradually decrease the intensity.

family of type A single design of a typeface in a range of sizes and variations, such as Caslon Bold, Caslon Bold Italic, Caslon Old Style.

FCC Federal Communications Commission. The Federal authority authorized to license radio and television stations and to assign frequencies.

FDA Food and Drug Administration. The Federal agency authorized to enforce Food, Drug, and Cosmetic legislation. Also regulates packaging, labeling, and advertising in these industries.

fee systems A method of compensating advertising agencies in which the client pays the agency an agreed-upon fee for its work.

field intensity The measurement of the coverage area of a broadcast station in terms of its signal strength. Field intensity contour maps indicate station coverage patterns.

finished layout A layout made to look as much like the finished ad as possible. Used primarily in sales presentations of the advertising campaign.

flat bed A printing press for letterpress printing containing a flat metal bed on which forms of type are locked for printing.

flat rate A uniform charge of space or time with no discounts for volume or frequency.

flight In broadcast, the concentration of commercials in a relatively short time period.

FM Frequency modulation. A method of modulating tone in broadcast by frequency of waves rather than amplitude. More limited coverage than AM, but less affected by static.

font A complete assortment of type characters of one style and size.

format The size, shape, style, and appearance of a book or publication. In broadcast, the structure of a program.

four-color process A photoengraving process for reproducing color illustrations by a set of plates—one for each of the primary colors and one for black.

frequency The number of times an advertising message is delivered within a specified period of time.

frequency discount A discount in advertising rates based on the number of ads or commercials used within a specified period of time.

fringe time The hours directly before and after prime time. Also may be specified as early fringe or late fringe.

FTC Federal Trade Commission. A federal agency concerned with the regulation of monopolies, unfair methods of competition, and fraudulent and misleading advertising.

full service agency An advertising agency offering a wide range of marketing and advertising services.

Gallup-Robinson A research organization, best known for its copy testing services.

general advertising National or nonlocal advertising in newspapers.

generic product (a) The essential benefit a consumer expects to get from a product. For example, the woman buying lipstick is not buying a set of chemicals and physical attributes; she is buying beauty. (b) Descriptive of an entire group or class of products (for example, aspirin or cake mix).

gestalt   A German word meaning pattern or configuration. It refers to the overall impression created by a stimulus (for example, an advertisement). Also a school of psychology known for its work in perception.

GNP   Gross National Product. The aggregate value of all goods and services produced by a country.

Gothic   A term sometimes used to refer to block type.

gravure   A printing process that transfers images to paper from ink in depressions in the plate, as opposed to letterpress which prints from raised surfaces. Also known as intaglio.

guaranteed circulation   A minimum circulation level guaranteed by magazines. If circulation drops below this level, the advertiser receives a prorata rebate.

gutter   The two inside margins of facing pages in a newspaper or magazine.

half run   In transit advertising, a half run is a car card placed in every other car of the transit system. Also referred to as a half showing.

half showing   *See* half run.

halftone   A photoengraving plate produced by photographing through a glass screen that breaks up the subject into small dots of varying size and thus makes possible the printing of gradation of shades or tones.

hand composition   Type set by hand as opposed to machine composition.

head-on position   An outdoor advertising location directly facing traffic, as opposed to an angled or parallel position.

heaviside layer   A layer of ions that encircles the earth. At night it bounces AM transmissions back to earth, extending the range of AM stations. It does not affect FM transmissions, however.

hi-fi color   A device used to obtain high fidelity color reproduction in newspaper advertising. An ad, consisting of a continuous design, is preprinted on one side of a roll of paper, leaving the other side blank for the newspaper's use. Since the ad is continuous, the roll may be cut at any point to form newspaper pages without damaging the effect of the advertisement.

high-assay models   A computer model used in media selection that selects media sequentially.

house agency   An advertising agency controlled by a single advertiser. Also referred to as an in-house agency.

house organ   A company magazine issued regularly for its employees, dealers, prospects, and other groups.

ID   Identification announcement. A broadcast term for a brief commercial between programs. The announcement is usually 8 seconds, thus allowing only enough time for the identification of the product.

impact   The degree to which an advertising message or medium affects the audience exposed to it.

insert   (a) A special page or pages preprinted by the advertiser and forwarded to a publisher who binds it in the publication. (b) A coupon or advertising message inserted in a package, often referred to as a package insert.

insertion order   Instructions from an advertiser or advertising agency authorizing a publisher to print an advertisement of a specified size on a given date at an agreed price.

institutional advertising   *See* corporate advertising.

intaglio   *See* gravure.

intensive distribution Widespread distribution of a consumer product in which many retail outlets are used, as opposed to selective distribution where few retail outlets are used.

island display A store display centered in the aisle or other open area.

island position A newspaper advertisement surrounded by editorial matter.

jingle Words set to music and used in a commercial.

judgment sampling A research sample selected on the basis of judgment as opposed to a random or probability sample. Widely used in advertising research.

justify type Arranging type so that the letters are evenly spaced, and the lines are the same length.

keyline A layout in which all elements are keyed to their exact position and size, including type specification. Used as a blueprint in producing a final ad.

kinescope Film of a live commercial or program made by photographing the television tube image.

king-size poster An outside transit display placed on the side of a vehicle. Size: 30″ × 144.″

Lanham Act The Federal Trademark Act of 1946, which governs the registration of trademarks and other identifying symbols used in interstate commerce.

layout (a) The process of laying out the elements of an advertisement. (b) The results of this process which show where the various elements of the ad will be placed.

leading Pronounced "ledding." The insertion of metal strips or leads between lines or type to increase readability and improve appearance.

letterpress A method of printing in which the image is transferred to the paper from a raised surface.

linage Any amount of advertising space measured in agate lines.

line cut (plate) A photoengraving made without the use of a screen and which produces only solid lines or masses without intermediate shades or tones.

line drawing A drawing made with a brush or pen with whatever shading that exists produced by variations in the size and spacing of the lines.

linotype A machine that sets type mechanically, casting the type one line at a time.

lip sync. In television, the synchronization of a speaker's lip movements with a separately recorded audio track.

lithography The process of printing from a flat surface on which the ink is retained by a greasy deposit. There are two forms of lithography: (a) direct lithography in which the plate prints directly on the receiving surface; and (b) offset lithography in which the printing plate image is transferred to an intermediate surface (blanket), which does the actual printing.

live program The broadcasting of a message without prerecording it.

local advertising Advertising that is placed by a local business, as opposed to a national or regional firm.

log In broadcasting, a detailed record of every program and commercial aired by the station, kept chronologically and required by law.

logotype (logo) A trademark or trade name expressed in the form of distinctive lettering or design and used to identify the advertiser.

loss leader A product offered at cost or below cost to attract store traffic.

Ludlow A typesetting process that is a combination of hand setting and machine casting.

machine composition Setting type mechanically or by machine as opposed to hand setting.

mail order advertising Advertising designed to produce orders by mail without the use of retail outlet.

make good The repeating of an advertisement by a publisher or station without payment in compensation for an ad or commercial that was omitted or which did not meet reasonable standards of reproduction.

margin The difference between the selling price and the cost of goods sold for a business firm.

market A generic definition is a group of people with purchasing power who are willing to spend in order to meet their needs.

marketing The performance of business activities that directs the flow of goods and services from producer to consumer or user.

marketing concept An approach to marketing that embodies three concepts: (a) consumer orientation; (b) internal organization of the firm in the service of the consumer; and (c) profit.

marketing mix The manipulation of marketing variables—product, package, price, distribution, channels, personal selling, advertising, and sales promotion—into a suitable marketing program for the firm.

marketing plan A written document that serves as a blueprint for the marketing program.

market profile A demographic and psychographic description of the target market for a product.

market review A part of the marketing plan that reviews the current marketing situation and lays the basis for future planning.

market segmentation A marketing strategy in which the total market for a product is divided into homogeneous subsets, so that each subset may be addressed in the most appropriate manner.

market share A brand's share of the market, expressed as a percentage.

market skimming A pricing strategy for a new product in which a relatively high price is charged in order to recover investment quickly.

markup The difference between the selling price of a product and its cost. May be expressed in terms of a percentage, or in terms of dollars and cents.

mass communication The delivery of a large number of identical messages simultaneously.

master print In television, the final, approved print of a commercial from which duplicates are made for distribution to stations.

matrix (mat) A mold of paper pulp, plastic, or similar substance made from type or plates. Molten lead poured in this mold forms a replica of the original plate known as a stereotype.

maximil rate A newspaper's milline rate based on its highest rate.

mechanical An assembly of pictures and proofs of type pasted in a desired arrangement, to be photographed by a camera and made into a printing plate.

media Vehicles that carry advertising messages, such as radio, television, magazine, newspapers.

MEDIAC A computer model used for the selection of media. Characterized by the ability to handle a variety of variables.

media plan A part of the marketing plan that details the media that will be employed in a marketing program.

Media Records, Inc. An organization that compiles and sells on a subscription basis records of the space used by advertisers.

media strategy A part of the marketing plan that specifies how media will be used to accomplish marketing objectives.

merchandising (a) Traditionally applied to retailing, the selection, pricing, and display of merchandise. (b) In advertising, a synonym for sales promotion.

merchandising the advertising The promotion of consumer advertising to the sales force and distribution channels.

milline rate A basic unit of comparison for newspaper costs. Computed by dividing the agate line rate by the circulation and multiplying by one million.

minimil A newspaper's milline rate computed on the basis of its lowest rate.

modular advertising agency A full-service agency that sells its services on a piecemeal basis. Sometimes called an a la carte agency.

monotype A machine method of composing type in which individual letters are separately molded and automatically assembled into lines.

motivation research An umbrella term applying to a variety of research techniques, mostly borrowed from the social sciences, that attempt to ascertain why consumers purchase the products they do.

MRCA A marketing research firm that gathers consumer purchase information through a mail diary and sells the results to advertisers on a subscription basis.

NAB National Association of Broadcasters. An organization of radio and television stations and networks.

NAD National Advertising Division of the Council of Better Business Bureaus. Investigates complaints of false and misleading advertising by national advertisers as part of the industry's self-regulation procedure. Refers disagreements to the NARB for adjudication.

NARB National Advertising Review Board of the Council of Better Business Bureaus. The final arbiter of complaints investigated by the NAD. If unable to resolve differences with advertisers, NARB may refer the complaints to the FTC.

narrative commercial A type of radio commercial, tells a story using a narrative format.

narrowcasting A broadcast term referring to a programming format designed to appeal to a relatively small, special interest group rather than to a mass audience. For example, cultural programming, news-programming, etc.

network In broadcasting, a group of stations affiliated by contract and usually interconnected for the simultaneous broadcasting of programs.

Nielsen Food and Drug Index A national research organization that audits consumer purchases through panels of food and drug stores and sells the results to advertisers on a subscription basis.

Nielsen Ratings Provides audience ratings for television in individual markets (Nielsen Station Index, NSI) and for network programming through the Nielsen Television Index (NTI).

NOAB National Outdoor Advertising Bureau. A cooperative organization for placement and inspection of outdoor advertising owned and used by advertising agencies. Disbanded in 1977.

noted (noting) *See* Starch.

OAAA Outdoor Advertising Association of America. An association of plant operators having standard outdoor advertising facilities.

off camera In television, action or sound outside camera range and not visible to the audience.

off mike   In broadcasting, sound away from microphone. In contrast to "on mike."

offset   A lithographic printing process in which the image from the plate is transferred to an intermediate surface (blanket), which does the actual printing.

one-time rate   The rate paid by an advertiser who does not use enough space to qualify for a discount.

open rate   In print, the highest advertising rate from which all discounts are computed.

ornamental type   A class of typeface characterized by embellishments or decorative forms. Difficult to read and used to create special effects.

outdoor advertising   Signs placed along highways that meet the standards established by OAAA.

overprinting   Printing headline or body copy over the illustration. A controversial practice in advertising.

package insert   *See* insert.

page proof   A proof of an ad in page form as it will finally appear.

painted bulletin   An outdoor advertising sign that is painted on movable panels, in contrast to one printed on paper.

pan   In television, to move the camera across a scene.

participation   A commercial within a program as opposed to one scheduled between programs.

pass-along readership   Readership of publications by individuals who are not members of the purchasing family.

paste-up   A layout in which all elements are combined in their proper places for reproduction as a single engraving.

penetration   The extent to which an advertisement reaches a particular audience. Usually expressed as a percent of the total audience.

penetration pricing   A pricing strategy in which prices are set relatively low in order to expand the market and to obtain a major share.

personality commercial   A commercial that gains its strength from the use of a well-known personality.

photocomposition   A method of setting type by a photographic process. Also referred to as cold type.

photoengraving   A relief printing plate made by a photochemical process. Also the process itself.

pica   A unit of measurement for type and printed materials. Six picas equal one inch.

picture-headline format   A format for print advertising utilizing a dominant illustration on the upper portion of the page with a headline under it.

plant operator   In outdoor advertising, the businessperson who leases, erects, maintains, and sells space on outdoor signs.

plate   The metal or plastic from which impressions are made by any of the various printing operations.

platen   The part of a printing press that holds the paper and presses it against the plate or type.

point   A unit of vertical type measurement. Equal to 1/72 of an inch.

P.O.P.   Point-of-purchase advertising. Any displays or advertising materials used in a retail store.

positioning   *See* product position.

poster   An advertising message printed on large sheets of paper and pasted on panels.

preemption   In broadcast, the appropriation of time from a scheduled program or commercial in order to broadcast another program or commercial.

preferred position   Any advertising position within a publication for which the advertiser must pay a premium price.

preprint   A reproduction of an advertisement prior to publication.

press run   The number of copies printed for a particular job.

primary colors   In printing, red, yellow, and blue.

primary demand   Demand for a type of product without regard for a particular demand.

prime time   A continuous period of time of not less than three hours per broadcast day as designated by the station. Usually, 7:00 P.M. to 11:00 P.M., E.S.T., and 6:00 P.M. to 10:00 P.M., C.S.T.

private label (brand)   Goods produced for exclusive labeling by distributors or retailers. Sometimes referred to as distributor brands as opposed to producer brands.

probability sampling   A statistical method of sampling in which every unit in the universe has an equal and known probability of being selected.

producer   In broadcast, the person responsible for producing a program or commercial.

product concept   A description of a product in terms of its physical and psychological attributes. The product concept serves as a basis for developing the product itself, as well as the product package, name, pricing, advertising, and so on.

product differentiation   A marketing strategy in which a product is differentiated from competitive products either through minor product modifications, appeals, or a combination of these two approaches.

production department   The department responsible for the production of advertisements and commercials.

product-life cycle   A concept that suggests that the life of a product can be divided into stages: introductory; growth; maturity; and decline. Each stage requires a different marketing approach.

product manager   The individual in the client organization who is charged with the responsibility for marketing a particular product.

product position   The location of a product in a product space. This position determines how the product will be presented to consumers in terms of its physical and psychological attributes.

product space   An abstract space bounded by relevant product attributes. Used as a logical device for defining a product in terms of consumers' needs.

progressive proofs   A set of engraver's proofs used in four-color advertising. These proofs show each color plate separately and in combination.

projective techniques   Research techniques used in motivational research. Based on the tendency of individuals to perceive the environment in terms of personal need-value systems.

psychographics   A way of classifying consumers based on their activities and interests.

publicity   A story or information about a product or company published or broadcast as editorial material and without cost to the company.

publisher's statement   A statement of circulation issued by a publisher.

puffery   Exaggeration of a product's attributes in advertising. As long as this exaggeration is in qualitative areas where it is a matter of opinion, puffery is not illegal.

Pulse   A research organization that reports on radio and television audiences as well as conducting other marketing research studies.

queen-size poster   An outside transit advertising display piece placed on the sides of vehicles. Size: 30″ × 88″. *See* king-size poster.

quota sampling   A method of sampling in which respondents are chosen to fill demographic quotas. For example, a certain number in each age, occupation, and income group. Inferior to a probability sample in terms of representativeness of the total population.

RAB   Radio Advertising Bureau. An organization of radio representatives, stations, and networks to promote radio as an advertising medium.

RADAR   A market research organization that has done extensive research on radio audiences.

random sampling   A form of probability sampling in which each member of the universe has an equal and known chance of being selected.

rate card   A card issued by an advertising medium listing its rates, mechanical requirements, and other information needed by an advertiser.

rating point   (a) In television, one percent of all television households in a defined geographic area. (b) In radio, one percent of all households in a defined geographic area.

reach   The number of different households or members of a target market exposed to one or more advertising messages during a specified period of time, usually four weeks.

readership   The number of people exposed to a specific advertisement, publication, or editorial in a given publication.

reading notices   Newspaper advertisements set in editorial style and identified by the word "advertising." Charged at higher rates than other advertising.

read most   *See* Starch.

recall tests   A method of testing advertising in which respondents are given clues (such as the product category) to aid their recall of specific advertisements or products.

recognition test   A test of advertising in which respondents are shown an advertisement and asked whether they have seen it and, if so, how much of it they read. This is the method used by the Starch readership studies.

reference group (person)   A group or individual with whom an individual wants to be associated and whose beliefs, attitudes, values, and behaviors the person will seek to emulate.

rep   Representative. A designation given to a salesperson of media or other suppliers.

reprint   A copy of an advertisement or editorial after it has been published.

repro proof   Reproduction proof. A proof of type used for photographic reproduction by the various printing processes.

retail advertising   Advertising designed to attract people to a retail outlet to purchase merchandise.

retail trading zone   An area surrounding a central city whose residents patronize stores in the central city.

retouching   Correcting or improving photographs or other artwork prior to photoengraving.

reverse type   Using white type on a dark background as opposed to black type on a white background. Research indicates that it tends to reduce readership.

Robinson-Patman Act   Amended the Clayton Act in 1936. Deals with unlawful competition, price discrimination, brokerage allowances, and promotional practices.

ROI   Return on investment. A financial measure used by business to evaluate investment opportunities.

roman type   A general type group distinguished by a variation in the weight of the strokes and the inclusion of serifs.

rotary press   A method of printing employing only cylinders. Used in high-speed newspaper presses.

rotation plan   In outdoor advertising, painted bulletins are rotated from one location to another at regular intervals, usually on a monthly basis.

rotogravure   *See* gravure.

rough   The first step in developing layouts. Also referred to as a rough layout.

run of paper (ROP)   Any location in the publication convenient to publisher, in contrast to preferred position.

rushes   In television, the first, uncorrected, and unedited film obtained in shooting commercials.

SAG   Screen Actors Guild.

sales promotion   Any supplemental sales activity, excluding personal selling, advertising, and publicity. Includes such things as displays, coupons, contests, sweepstakes, price-off-label.

sales promotion advertising   (a) Advertising in support of sales promotion activity. (b) Advertising products at reduced prices to attract customers.

sans serif   A typeface that has no cross strokes or serifs at the top and bottom of characters.

saturation campaign   A media pattern of intensive frequency over a relatively short period of time.

schedule   A listing of proposed advertisements and/or commercials by media, with dates, amount of space or time, specific publications and/or stations, etc.

screening   (a) A special viewing of a program or commercial for advertisers, agencies, or other special groups. (b) A method of printing. *See* silk screen.

script   In television, a description of the video along with the accompanying audio, used in the preparation of a storyboard, or in lieu of it. In radio, the audio portion, along with a description of the effects to be created.

script type   *See* cursive type.

secondary coverage   The geographic area in which the reception of a radio station is fair, but subject to variation.

selective demand   Demand for a particular brand of a product, in contrast to primary demand, which is demand for the general product type.

selective distribution   A distribution strategy in which distribution is restricted to a relatively small number of retail outlets in order to gain more control over the conditions of sale. *See* intensive distribution.

self-mailer   A direct mail piece that can be mailed without a wrapper or envelope.

serifs   The short cross strokes at the tops and bottoms of type characters.

serigraphy   *See* silk screen.

sets in use   In television, refers to the percent of total television households in a defined geographic area with their sets turned on at a specific time.

set solid   Lines of type set without leading.

SFX   Sound effects. A direction used in television and radio scripts.

share of audience   In broadcasting, the percentage of homes with sets in use turned to a particular program.

short rate The higher rate an advertiser must pay for failing to use the amount of space or time specified in the contract.

shoulder That part of a unit of type that extends above and below the type character, and which does not print.

signature (a) The advertiser's name in an advertisement. (b) A musical passage that identifies a radio or television program, or a commercial. (c) A single sheet of paper folded and ready for stitching for a book, usually four pages or a multiple of four pages.

silk screen A printing process operating on a stencil principle in which a stenciled design is applied to a screen of silk or other material, and ink is forced through the mesh of the screen to the paper beneath it. Also known as serigraphy.

simulation Used in computerized media selection. A process for introducing media data into a computer for the purpose of imitating the effects of a media schedule.

simulcast A program broadcast simultaneously over radio and television, or over AM and FM radio.

slug (a) A unit of type. (b) A notation placed on copy to identify it temporarily, and not to be reproduced in final printing.

specialty *See* advertising specialty.

spectacolor A sophisticated form of hi-fi color in which newspaper advertising is preprinted with registration points to fit the newspaper page so that a continuous design is not necessary.

spectacular (a) A large outdoor sign, electrified and usually animated. (b) In broadcasting, a special, irregularly scheduled program, usually an hour or more in length.

split run The use of two or more advertisements of the same size in alternate copies of a newspaper or magazine. Often used for testing purposes, or to feature different products in regional issues of a magazine.

sponsor An advertiser who pays for talent and time for a radio or television broadcast. Unlike a participation, the sponsor assumes financial responsibility for the production of the program.

spot announcement (SPOT) (a) A broad term used for a radio or television commercial. (b) Technically, a commercial bought from an independent station. In order to distinguish the different kinds of spot, the terms local spot, participating spot, or national spot are sometimes used.

spread Two facing pages in a publication. Also called a double-truck.

square serif A form of typeface that embodies features of both roman and block type. Like roman, it has serifs; like block, the strokes are of uniform thickness.

SRDS Standard Rate and Data Service. An organization that publishes current information on advertising rates, mechanical requirements, closing dates, and other related information for a variety of media.

Starch A research organization that conducts studies of magazine readership using a recognition technique. Starch provides three measures of readership: (a) noted—the percent of respondents who claim they saw the ad in the publication being studied; (b) seen-associated—the percent of respondents who claim that they associated the advertisement with the advertiser; (c) read most—the percentage of respondents who read half or more of the copy.

station break Designated time between network programs, or within programs set aside for local station identification.

station rep An individual or organization who sells time on local stations.

stereotype A duplicate printing plate cast from a matrix.

stop motion   A photographic technique for animating inanimate objects.

storyboard   A series of drawings used to represent the action in a television commercial. Used for getting advertiser approval, for obtaining estimates on production costs, and as a blueprint for production.

super (superimposition)   In television, the imposition of one image over another, usually used for names, slogans, or key sales points.

supplement   A special feature section in a magazine format distributed in newspapers, usually on Sunday. Also referred to as Sunday supplement or Sunday magazine.

Survey of Buying Power   An annual publication of *Sales Management* magazine that contains population, income, and retail data broken down by region, state, county, and metropolitan county areas. It is a basic market reference, sometimes referred to as the bible of marketing.

TAA   Transit Advertising Association. An organization of firms selling transit advertising.

TAB   Traffic Audit Bureau. A firm that provides uniform, objective data on outdoor advertising circulation.

tabloid   A newspaper, about half the page size of standard newspapers.

tape   In broadcasting, audiotape or videotape used to record programs or commercials.

target market   A population group believed to hold the greatest sales opportunity for a product and against whom marketing efforts are directed.

tear sheet   A page containing an advertisement, removed from a publication and sent to an advertiser for checking purposes.

theme   The central idea of an advertisement, program, or sales promotion.

thirty sheet   Designation for a size of outdoor poster. Contains about 25 percent more advertising space than a 24-sheet poster.

thumbnail   A rough layout in miniature form.

time buyer   An advertising agency employee who is responsible for buying broadcast time.

trade advertising   Advertising directed to the channels of distribution.

trade character   An animated cartoon or character used to identify an advertiser or product, such as Reddy Kilowat or Speedy Alka-Seltzer.

trademark   Any symbol or word used to identify the maker or origin of a product.

trade name   The name under which a firm does business.

traffic department   The department in an advertising agency that schedules work through the agency and makes sure that the work is completed on schedule.

transit advertising   A form of out-of-home media appearing in and on transit vehicles and in transit stations.

Trendex   A research organization engaged in marketing and audience research for various media.

type family   A group of typefaces of the same basic design, but varying in the weight of strokes, width of characters, and so on.

type groups   Broad groups of type with similar characteristics. *See* bold, roman, cursive, and ornamental.

UHF   Ultra High Frequency. Television channels 14 to 83, operating on frequencies from 470 Mc to 890 Mc.

unaided recall   A research technique in which respondents answer questions without any memory aids.

UPC   Universal Product Code. A computerized system for identifying and pricing products for use in checkout counters.

uppercase   Capital letters.

VHF   Very High Frequency. Television channels 2 through 13.

video   The visual portion of a television program or commercial.

videotape   An electronic unit that simultaneously records audio and video on the same tape and permits immediate playback.

visualization   The process of picturing in the mind what an advertisement will look like.

VO   Voice over. In television, the use of narration without the narrator appearing on the screen.

waste circulation   That part of the circulation of a medium that does not reach logical prospects for a product, or circulation in areas in which the product does not have distribution.

weight of type   The relative blackness of a typeface.

Wheeler-Lee Act   An amendment to the Federal Trade Commission Act intended to protect consumers against unfair trade practices and false and deceptive advertising. Enacted in 1938.

WIPE   In television, a rapid transition technique for replacing one scene with another.

zinc etching   A photoengraving in zinc.

zoom   A television term used to describe the effect of having the subject suddenly grow larger (zoom in) or smaller (zoom out).

NAME INDEX

Ennis, B. M., 251n.
Ernst, Lois G., 609n.
Evans, W. A., quoted, 18–19

F

Fiedler, John A., 117
Fields, W. C., 243
Fiore, Q., 272
Fisher, Kenneth G., 162
Forkan, James, 161n.
Foster, Gail, 68–69
French, Elbrun Rochford, 354n.
Freud, Sigmund, theory of, 169
Fryburger, Vernon, 23n., 72n.

G

Gabor, Andre, 218, 219
Gallup, George, 341
Garfield, M. S., 62n.
Garner, James, 161
Geis, Robert H., quoted, 425–26
Getchell, J. Sterling, 157, 308
    advertisement by, 119–20
Gibes, Nancy, 630n.
Glatzer, Robert, 115n., 281n.,
    283n.
    quoted, 2, 30–31, 281
Godfrey, Arthur, 403
Gompertz, Rolf, quoted, 546–47
Gonsior, M. H., 218
Gordon, Richard L., 236n.
Gorschman, H. S., 524n.
Granger, C. W. J., 218, 219
Gransee, R., 526n.
Gravitt, Cynthy, testimonial by,
    355–56
Green, Paula, 297
Gribbin, George, 146, 297
Gross, E. J., 135n.
Gubar, George, 163n.

H

Hall, Edward T., 160
Hart, Norman A., 546
Hartley, Mariette, 161
Hatwick, Melvin S., 168, 274
Haugh, Louis J., 518n.
    quoted, 518–19, 534
Helming, Ann, 579n., 583n.
Hendon, Donald Wayne, 343n.,
    362n.

Herold, Donald, 354
Higgins, Denis, 284n.
Hobbs, Whit, 330
Holton, Richard, H., 238n.
    quoted, 239
Hopkins, Claude, 300–301
Hustead, Ted and Dorothy, 258

J

Jackson, Michael, statement by,
    301–2
Joyce, Timothy, 287
Joyce, Walter, creativity techniques
    by, 315–17

K

Kelley, Eugene E., 226n.
Kelly, Maurice, 286
Kennedy, John E., advertising
    defined by, 21–22
Kennedy, John F., 84, 617
Kile, Corwin Mack, 161n., 592
Kingman, Merle, 33n.
Kirkpatrick, C. A., list by, 349–50
Klepner, Otto, 622n.
Kotler, Philip, 6n., 10, 215–16,
    440n.
Kratky, Warren, 20
Kristol, Irving, 558–59
Kroll, Alexander, 557–58
Krugman, Herbert E., 272
    quoted, 272–73

L

Landers, Bob, 403
Lasker, Alfred, 21
Lavidge, R. L., 251
Lazer, William, 226n.
Leavitt, Harold J., 218
Levitt, Theodore, 87
Levy, Sidney J., 6n.
Light, Larry, 610
Lindzey, Gardner, 270n., 271n.
Littlefield, James E., list by,
    349–50
Loomis, Carol J., 182n.
Lynch, Kevin, 580n.

M

Maas, Jane, 363, 364
Maloney, John C., 285–86

Margulies, Walter P., 206, 546
Marschutz, Elmer, 192
Marshall, Christy, 447n.
Maslow, Abraham, theory of, 153,
    155–56
Mason, Lowell, 625
Massengell, Samuel, 616
Mayer, Martin, 279, 280n., 282n.,
    284n., 308n.
    value-added theory, 22–23
McCreary, E. A., 580n.
McGuire, William J., 270, 271,
    272n.
McLuhan, M., 272
McMahan, Harry Wayne, 161n.,
    592
McNeal, James U., quoted, 265–66
Mertes, John E., 240n.
Meyer, Ed, 519n.
Miller, A., 242n.
Miracle, Gordon E., 226n.
Moran, William T., 439
Morgens, Howard M., quoted,
    182–83, 187
Morin, Bernard A., 187n.
Morris, R. T., 218
Morrison, Ann M., 85n.
Mortimer, Charles, quoted, 46–47

N

Naples, Michael J., 426n.
Nathan, P. E., 602n.
Nathanson, Marc, 471
Natheson, Don, 399
Nevin, Bruce, 19
Newman, J. W., 127n., 170n.
Norman, Norman B., 280, 308
Norris, Hanley, 399
Norris, James S., 298n., 410n.
Norris, Vincent, 23n.

O

O'Brien, Neil, 411
O'Connor, John J., 58n.
O'Connor, William J., 201
Ogilvy, David, 62, 278–79, 280,
    363
    quoted, 58, 279–80, 287, 308,
        328, 334, 341, 364–65
Ostrow, Joseph, 408

P

Packard, Vance, 171
Paepcke, Walter, 342
Palda, Kristian S., 252
Payne, Stanley L., 135
Pearce, M., 242
Pearson, Arthur, 610
Peckham, J. O., 45–46, 524n.
Perlman, Don, 470n.
Pertschuk, Michael, 614
Phelps, Steve, 434–35
Phillips, William, 62
Piconke, Leon, 172
Pirsig, Robert M., 26
Pliskin, Robert, quoted, 343, 348–49
Preston, Ivan L., 626n.

R

Raissman, Robert, 31n., 35n.
Reeves, Rosser, 279, 295n., 308, 368
quoted, 3, 20, 279
U.S.P. criteria by, 277
Reiling, Lynn G., 183n.
Revett, John, 626n.
Revson, Charles, 609
Rickles, Don, 403
Ries, Al, 26
Robertson, Thomas, 273n.
Robinson, Claude, 299
Rockwell, Norman, 342
Roman, Kenneth, 363, 364
Rosebrook, Jack, 297
Ross, Wallace A., 403
Roth, Paul, definitions by, 475–76
Rubicam, Raymond, 330
Rubin, D. M., 268n.
Rugg, D., 135n.

S

Sachsman, D. B., 268n.
St. Georges, Joseph, quoted, 439

Salmon, Walter J., 550n., 599n.
Sandage, C. H., 23n., 72n.
Sandman, P. M., 268n.
Scheuing, Eberhard E., 188
Schoner, B., 135n.
Schramm, Wilber, 269
Schwab, Victor O., list by, 274–75
Schwerin, Horace, 603
Scripps, Charles E., 314
Seiden, Hank, 408
Sherif, Carolyn W., 219
Sherman, Margot, 331–32
Sloan, Alfred P., 10n., 87
Smith, G. H., 142
Smith, W. R., 9n.
Sobczynski, Anna, 493n.
Stanley, Thomas B., 343n.
Starch, Daniel, 345, 604
Steiner, G. A., 160, 251
Stone, Jack R., 159–60
Strenski, James B., 545n.
Sultan, Ralph G. M., 550n., 599n.
Swan, John E., 187
Sweeney, Kevin, 401

T

Telser, Lester G., 240
Thomajan, Zareh Garabed, 323–24
Thompson, G. C., 251n., 597n., 608
Tocqueville, Alexis de, 241
Toffler, Alvin, 159
Treasure, John, 287
Trout, Jack, 26
Tull, D. S., 218
Tumpoursky, Ira, 471
Twedt, Dick Warren, 128n.
Tyler, William D., 61, 401n.

U

Uhl, K. P., 135n.

V

Vanderwicken, Peter, 87n., 172n.
Veblen, Thorstein, 159
Viens, Harry, 422
Vogl, A. J., 594n.

W

Wainwright, Charles A., 396, 399n.
Waldo, C. N., 13n.
Wallace, W. H., 602n.
Wanamaker, John, 236
Warner, Daniel S., 183n., 298n.
Wassen, Chester, 219
Watkins, Julian Lewis, 146n., 147n., 148n., 163n., 330n.
quoted, 148–49
Webster, Frederick E., Jr., 243
Weiner, Bernard, 157n.
Weiss, E. B., 625n.
Weiss, Edward, 317
Wells, William D., 163n., 170n.
West, Herbert, 92n.
Westfall, R., 135n.
White, Hooper, 414n.
White, Irving S., 19, 170, 187n.
Winer, Leon, 87
Winter, Willis L., Jr., 183n.
Wolfe, H. D., 251n., 597n., 608
Wright, John S., 183n., 240n., 298n.

Y

Young, James Webb, quoted, 325–26
Yuspeh, Sonia, 593n.

Z

Zeigler, Sherilyn K., 183n.
Zeltner, Herb, 60n., 73n.
Zielske, H. A., 165
Zotti, Ed, 492n.

SUBJECT INDEX

Cadillac advertisement, 148–49
California Avocado Advisory Board advertisement, 265
Campbell-Mithun, Inc. (advertising agency), 31–32
Campbell's Soup advertisements, 173, 175, 616
Car cards, 500, 501
Carnation brand promotion, 537
Cars. *See* Automobiles
Cascade dishwashing detergent advertisement, 339
Casting for commercials, 416
Catalog selling, 228
Caterpillar company exhibit, 568–69
CATV (cable television), 470–72, 474–75
  data, 656–57
CBS cable service, 470–71
Celebrity spokespersons, 161–62, 403
  testimonials, 355
Central needs
  behavioral expression, influences on, 158
  versus peripheral needs, 156–57
Cereal companies versus FTC, 236, 630
Channels of communication, 267
  influence of, 267–68, 270, 272
  multiple, 273
Channels of distribution. *See* Distribution
Children
  advertising to, strictures on, 629–30
  role of, in purchase decisions, 163, 164
Chivas Regal advertisement, 259, 261
Chocolates, fancy, distribution of, 227, 525
Chrysler automobiles
  Airflow, 184–85
  New Yorker, 304
Cigarettes
  Marlboro Lights campaign, 13, 15
  product space for, 15
  segmentation of market, 11–12, 13
Circulation
  magazines, 463–65
    table, 658–60
  newspapers, 448, 455–56

outdoor advertising, 499
transit advertising, 502
Class, social, 160–61
Classified advertising, 249
  examples, 251
  magazines, 460
    display classified, 459
  newspapers, 449
Clients, advertising. *See* Advertisers
CLIO awards, 592
Coca-Cola commercial, 629
Cognitive theory, meaning in, 167–68
Cold remedy advertising, 124–25
Cold type composition, 384–85
Colgate toothpaste advertisement, 278
Collateral services, 24
Color, use of, 264, 343–48
  in magazines, 462–63
  in newspapers, 454–55
  printing process, 389–92
Color separations, 389
Combination rates
  magazines, 462
  newspapers, 454
Come 'N Get It dog food advertisement, 244–45, 246
Comics, 661
Command headlines, 336
Commercials
  theater, 509–10
  See also Broadcast advertising
Commission system of agency compensation, 71–73
  negotiated commissions, 74
Commodities, advertising of, 302–3
Communications, 258–73
  dimensions, examples of, 258–60
  marketing
    budget. *See* Budget, communications
    See also Promotion
  multiple channels, 273
  nature of, 261–64
    connotative meaning, 262–63
    contextual meaning, 263–64
    denotative meaning, 262
    structural meaning, 263
  nonverbal, 264–66
  process, 266–70
    essential conditions, 269–70
    interference with, 269

model of, 266–69
research variables, 270–73
  channel, 270, 272
  chart of, 270
  message, 270, 271–72
  receiver, 270, 272–73
  source, 270–71
Community antenna (cable) television, 470–72, 474–75
  data, 656–57
Company-owned stores, 228
Comparative advertising, 628–29
Competition
  advertising's effect on, 236, 240–41, 630
  monopolistic, 217
  pure, 216–17
Competitive accounts, agency practice concerning, 61
Competitive position, analysis of
  by admaker, 302
  in market review, 93
Competitive preference measure, 603
Comprehensive proofs, 350
Computer models in media selection, 439–41
  high assay model, 439–40
  linear programming, 439
  MEDIAC, 440
  simulation, 440
Computers, small business, market for, 422–23
Concentration theory of media use, 427
Concept testing, 599
Conflicts in marketing, 25–26
Connotative meaning, 262–63
Conrail advertisement, 358
Consignment selling, 524–25
Consumer behavior, 146–81
  analysis
    dimensions, 120–21
    in market review, 93–94
  classic appeals to, 146–50
  intrapersonal variables influencing, 164–78
    attitudes, 172–73
    learning, 164–68
    perception, 173–78
    personality, 168–71
    self-concept, 171–72
  motivation, 121, 151–58
    admaker's analysis of, 308
    definition, 151–52
    generalizations about, 157–58

Consumer behavior, *continued*
    issues relating to, 154–57
    problems relating to, 151
    stages of transformation,
        152–54
  as problem solving, 150
  question areas for admaker,
    304–8, 648–49
    brand influence, 305, 307
    method of purchase, 307–8
    reason for purchase, 308
    user, 304–5
    use situation, 305–7
  research, 127–30
    analytical, 129–30, 140–43,
        169
    distributive, 127–29
    morphological, 129
    primary versus secondary,
        130–34
  social variables influencing,
    159–63
    class, 160–61
    culture, 159–60
    family, 163
    reference groups and persons,
        161–63
Consumer benefit. *See* Benefit,
  consumer
Consumer expectations, 186–87
Consumer goods, kinds of, 226
Consumer markets versus
  industrial markets, 569–570
Consumer orientation in
  marketing concept, 8, 9
Consumer promotions. *See* Sales
  promotion: consumer
Consumer satisfaction, 186–88
Contac advertisement, 292, 293
Contests
  for consumers, 534–35
  retail support through, 526
Contextual meaning, 263–64
Contiguity, principle of, 166
Continuity in media use, 425
Contribution to profit, 44
Controlled experiments, 131–32
Convenience
  as packaging function, 202–3
  as packaging strategy, 205
Convenience goods, 226
Convenience sample, 139
Cooperative advertising, 529–30
Coordinated product manager
  system, 40
Copy, body. *See* Body copy

Copy plan, 103–4
  in sample plan, 641–42
Copy research
  problems, 597–98
  See also Copy testing
Copy strategy, 102–3, 296–97
  in sample plan, 641
Copy testing, 592, 599–611
  functions, 599
  on-air, 593
  posttest stage, 603–609
    attitude tests, 605, 608
    recall tests, 604–5, 606–7
    sales response, 608–9
  preliminary stage, 599–600
  pretest stage, 600–603
    attitude and recall tests,
        600–601, 603
    laboratory tests, 601–2
    limited media tests, 603
    portfolio tests, 602
    simulated media tests, 602–3
    validity issue, 601
  questions, key
    what to test, 610
    whether to test, 609–10
Copywriters, 65
  consumers, keeping in touch
    with, 276
  coordination with art directors,
    297–98
Corker-Sullivan (advertising
  agency), outdoor board by, 492
Corporate advertising, 247–49,
  543, 546, 553–60
  examples, 249, 250, 553–59
  focus, 247–48, 553
  objectives, 248–49, 553–54
  plan, 560, 561
  problem, 555, 557–60
Corrective advertising, 619, 628
Cosmopolitan magazine, rate card
  for, 460–61
Cost-per-thousand (CPM)
  measurement, 438
  for magazines, 463
  trends, 441
Cost-plus systems of agency
  compensation, 74, 75–76
Coupon advertising, industrial,
  568, 574, 577
Coupons, consumer, 518, 531–33
  placement, 364–65
  trends, 519–20
Cranapple juice, FTC case of, 619
Creative boutiques, 70–71

Creative services of agency, 64–65
Creativity, marketing, 24–25
  agency decline in, 61–62
Creativity in advertising
  preparation,
    292–320
  case history, 310–13
  coordination of talents, 297–98
  copy strategy, 296–97
  examples, 292–94
  facts, search for, 298–309, 314,
    646–50
    advertising history of brand
        and competitors, 309, 314,
        649
    consumer, 304–8, 648–49
    marketing situation, 308–9
    product, 299–303, 649–50
  pitfalls, 317–18
  process, 314–17
    execution of idea, 325–26
    style, 297
Crest toothpaste, 85
Cultural differences, problem of,
  159–60, 582–83
Culture shock, 159
Cursive type, 379
Cushman Industries
  advertisement, 574, 576

D

DAGMAR model, 251
Dancer Fitzgerald Sample
  (advertising agency), findings
  by, 519–20
D'Arcy-MacManus & Masius
  (advertising agency), employees
  of
  account supervisor, 68–69
  group media director, 434–35
  marketing research supervisor,
    136–37
Dealer incentives, 526
Dealer listing advertisements,
  228–29
Deception in advertising, question
  of, 242–43
Decision patterns, consumer, 128,
  129
  family, 121, 163, 305, 307
Decline stage of product life cycle,
  191
Delivered (average issue)
  circulation, magazine, 463–64

Image, brand. *See* Brand image
Image advertising
    as product advertising, 244
       example, 245
    as theory of advertising, 278–80
Image building for consumer
    products, 171
Imputed attributes of product, 13
Income, per capita, by geographic
    areas of world, 581, 582
Incubation stage of creative
    process, 315
Independent distribution, 227–28
Independent Packing Company,
    St. Louis, Mo., 212
Indirect versus direct headlines,
    332–33
Industrial markets, 566–79
    advertising's role in, 574–77
    analyzing, 573
    consumer markets, differences
       from, 569–70
    Monsanto approach, 566–67,
       568
    trade shows, use of, 510,
       567–69, 578
    types, 570–73
       government, 573
       producer, 570–72
       reseller, 572
Information
    advertising as, 21
    advertising's provision of, 239
Ingestion stage of creative process,
    315
Ingredients, product, 300
Inherent drama advertising, 284
In-house agencies, 34, 70
In-package coupons, 532
Inserts, newspaper, preprinted,
    455
Inspiration stage of creative
    process, 315
Institute for Outdoor Advertising
    (IOA), 494–95
Institutional advertising. *See*
    Corporate advertising
In-store advertising, 511–12
Instrumental (peripheral) versus
    central needs, 156–57
Instrumental versus expressive
    performance, 187, 300
Intaglio (gravure), 386
    in method comparison, 388
    production process for, 376

Intended and transmitted
    messages, 267
Intensive distribution, 226–27
Intention to buy, 254
Intermediate markets. *See*
    Industrial markets
Internal need states, 152–53
    number/nature of, 154–56,
       274–76
Internal organization of company,
    8–9
    advertising agencies, 76–78
    See also Advertisers:
       organization
International marketing, 579–85
    advertisements
       examples, 585, 586–88
       problems, 579–80, 582–83
    agency for, 584
    media for, 584–85
    modifications for, 584
    successes, 583–84
    variables influencing, 580–83
       cultural, 159–60, 582–83
       economic, 581–82
       political-legal, 580–81
Interpublic Group of Companies,
    The, 62
Interviews
    extended, 142–43
    personal versus telephone, 133
Intrapersonal variables. *See*
    Psychological variables
Introduction stage of product life
    cycle, 191
Inventory increases, sales
    promotions for, 524–25
Investment
    recovery, payout plan for, 49
    return on, 47–48
Involvement of message receiver,
    272–73
Ivory Liquid advertisement, 371
Ivory Soap package changes, 207,
    209

J

Jack Daniel's whiskey
    advertisements, 259–60, 262,
       346–47
    bottle shape, 200
    facts used in advertising,
       298–99, 300

Jingle/rhyme commercials, 400
    radio, 401
Joy Manufacturing Company
    advertisement, 332, 333
Judgment sample, 139
J. Walter Thompson (advertising
    agency), 32

K

Kal-Kan and Gravy Train
    advertisements,
       comparison of, 122–24
    Kellogg Company advertisement,
       layout
       stages of 373–75
Kentucky Tourism commercial,
    401
Keylines (working layouts), 373–74
Kingsford Charcoal Briquets
    package, 202, 203
KitchenAid advertisement, 369,
    370
Kodak products
    display stand for, 528
    Ektaprint copier, media strategy
       for, 423
KPLR–TV, rate structure of, 478

L

Laboratory tests in copy pretesting,
    601–2
Lavidge-Steiner model, 251
Layout
    definition, 365
    stages, 372–74
       finished layout, 373, 375
       rough layout, 372, 374
       thumbnail sketches, 350, 372,
         373
       working layout, 373–74
Lead pricing, 222
Learning theory, 164–68
    contiguity, 166
    meaning, 167–68
    reinforcement, 167
    repetition, 165–66
Leasing of store space, 525
Legal restrictions
    international marketing, 580–81
    packaging, 207–8, 620
    trademarks, 194, 196–97
       conflicts arising from, 195–96

Marketing research and analysis,
continued
analytical, 129–30, 140–43,
169
distributive, 127–29
morphological, 129
criticisms, 116–17
definition, 127
departments, 67, 127
tasks, 128
examples, 114–16
judgment, areas of
objectives, 134–35
questionnaire design, 135
sampling, 138–40
primary, 130–33, 596–98
experiments, 131–32
observation, 130–31
See also Copy testing;
Surveys
secondary, 133–34
primary research versus, 130
supervisor, day in life of,
136–37
Marketing review, 92–95
in sample plan, 636–39
Marketing strategy, 97–99
in sample plan, 640
Market position (share of market)
influence of, on advertising,
118–20, 308–9
sales promotion, role of, 521,
522
and share of advertising, 45–46,
125–26
Market review, 92–95
in sample plan, 636–39
Market segmentation, 9, 10–13
cigarette market, 11–12, 13
definition, 10
and media strategy, 429
personality as basis, 168
by price, 10–11, 221–22
product attributes and, 13
product space, concept of,
13–16
segment characteristics required,
12
Market share. *See* Market position
Market skimming, 219–20
Market testing, 545–46, 550–51
Marlboro Lights (cigarettes),
advertising campaign for, 13,
15
Mary Kay Cosmetics advertisement,
364

Mass communications, 20
See also Advertising;
Communications
Materialism, advertising and,
241–42
Material strategy for packaging,
203, 205
Maturity stage of product life cycle,
191
Maximil/minimil rates, 456
Maxwell House "Lucky Cup"
sweepstakes, 531
Maybelline advertisement, 372
Meaning
connotative, 262–63
contextual, 263–64
denotative, 262
in learning theory, 167–68
structural, 263
Mechanical production. *See*
Production, print
Mechanicals (working layouts),
373–74
Media
agency commissions from, 71–73
negotiated commissions, 74
agency services, 66–67
broadcast structure of
industry, 473–75. *See also*
Broadcast advertising
as channels of communication,
267
influence of, 267–68, 270,
272
multiple, 273
comparison, 437–38
characteristic strengths, 428
with competition, 123–25
cost-per-thousand (CPM)
measurement, 438, 441
in multimedia programs,
438–39
computer models for selecting,
439–41
high assay model, 439–40
linear programming, 439
MEDIAC, 440
simulation, 440
coordination, multiple agency
use and, 35–36
cost trends, 441–42, 652–53
data
sources, 436–37, 662–64
summary, 651–61
for international advertising,
584–85

magnitude, 5–6
market segments, reaching, 12
print. *See* Print advertising
self-regulation, 621
National Association of
Broadcasters, 479–80, 621
strategy. *See* Media strategy
theories of use, 424–27
concentration theory, 427
demands, conflicting, 424–25
frequency, optimal, 425–26
reach theory, 427
wave theory, 426–27
See also Minor media.
Media associations, 72*n.*, 436
MEDIAC (Media Evaluation Using
Dynamic and Interactive
Applications of Computer),
440
Media director, group, day in life
of, 434–35
Media plan, 106
in sample plan, 642–43
Media strategy, 104–6
case examples, 422–24
decision areas, 104–5, 427–28
factors influencing, 428–33
appropriation size, 432
availability of media, 432
discounts, media, 432–33
distribution channels, 429–30
editorial climate, 433
flexibility, 431–32
pricing policy, 430–31
product characteristics, 429
product life cycle, stages in,
431
sales promotion activity, 431
target market, 429
in sample plan, 642
Media tests
limited, 603
simulated, 602–3
Merchandising
of advertising, 526–27
print media, services of, 456–57,
465
versus sales promotion, 90
Merchandising buses, 501
Message in mass communications
intended, 267
received, 267–68
transmitted, 267
variables, 270, 271–72
Michelob beer, distribution of,
223–24

N

Target marketing. *See* Market segmentation
Task method of budget determination, 46–47
Tasteless advertising, 243, 287–88
Ted Bates Advertising, 62, 295
  Unique Selling Proposition, 277–78
Telephone directory, yellow pages of, 503–5
Telephone interviews, 133
Television Code of National Association of Broadcasters, 479–80
Television commercials, 408–17, 475–86
  audience measurement, terminology of, 475–76
  cable market, 470–72, 474–75
    data, 656–57
  cost, 432, 478–79, 652
    data on medium, 652, 653–57
  evaluation, 476–77
    testing, 593, 603
  geographic scheduling, network versus local, 481–82
  guidelines for writing, 410–11, 413
  length, 479
  methods of buying time
    participations, 482–83
    sponsorship, 482
    spot announcements, 483
  and poor program quality, charge of, 243–44
  pricing practices
    local, 485, 486
    network, 483–85
  production, 413–17
    agency producers, 66
    editing, 416–17
    filmed, 414
    live, 414
    preparation, 415–16
    shooting, 416
    videotape, 414–15
  scripts/storyboards, 410
    examples, 411, 412
  terminology, 413
  star presenters, 161–62
  strengths and weaknesses of medium, 485–86
  time availability, 479–80
  time periods, 477–78
Temporary versus permanent in-store advertising, 512

Testimonial copy, 355–56
Testimonial headlines, 336
Testing
  copy. *See* Copy testing
  versus evaluation, 603–4
  market, 545–46, 550–51
  package, 206–7
    sample plan, 643–44
Theater commercials, 509–10
Theory of advertising. *See* Advertising: theories
Therminol heat transfer fluids, 566
Thompson, J. Walter, agency, 32
Three-dimensional product space, 16
Thumbnail sketches, 350, 372, 373
Time, Inc., lawsuit by, 437
Time magazine, quoted, 258–59, 471
Townhouse Instant Mashed Potatoes package, 201, 202
Trade advertising, 245–47, 248
Trade exhibits, 510, 578
  examples, 544, 567–69
Trademark
  definition of, 194
  legal requirements, 194, 196–97
  conflicts arising from, 195–96
Trade name, defined, 193
Trade promotions. *See* Sales promotions: trade
Traffic department, agency, 66
Trait theories of personality, 170
Transit advertising, 493, 500–503, 661
  buying, 501–2, 503
  circulation, 502
  strengths/weaknesses, 503
  types, 500–501
    car cards, 500, 501
    exterior displays, 500, 502
    merchandising buses, 501
    station posters, 500
Transmitted message, 267
Travelers Insurance Company advertisement, 353–54
Triumph Spitfire advertisement, 166
True Story magazine versus *New Yorker*, 160–61
Two-dimensional product space, 14, 16
Two-factor theory of consumer satisfaction, 187
Type, 377–85

faces, 377–79
  block, 378–79
  ornamental, 379
  roman, 377–78
  script, 379
families, 379
  Helvetica, variations in, 380
measurement, 379–81, 382
setting, 383–85
  hand setting, 383–84
  machine setting, 384–85
space between lines, 381
specifying, 383
Typefaces, 377–79
Typesetting, 383–85
Typography. *See* Type

U

Unaided recall, 605
Unique product claims, 627
Unique Selling Proposition (U.S.P.), 277–78
United States Steel Corporation advertisement, 557
Universal Product Code and Symbols (UPC), 202–3, 204
Unmeasured media. *See* Minor media
Unstructured (extended) interviews, 142–43

V

Value-added theory of advertising, 22–23
Van Cleef & Arpels advertisement, 322, 324
Vandermint liqueur advertisement, 178, 179
Variable expenses, 42–43
Videotape, use of, 414–15
Virginia Slims cigarettes, 12
Visualization, defined, 365
Visual techniques, projective, 141
Volkswagen (automobile), 2, 3–5
  print advertising, 322, 323

W

WAFB (FM radio station), rate listing for, 489
Wall Drug Store, Wall, S. Dak., 258–59

5. A